A Tribute

Floyd County Veterans

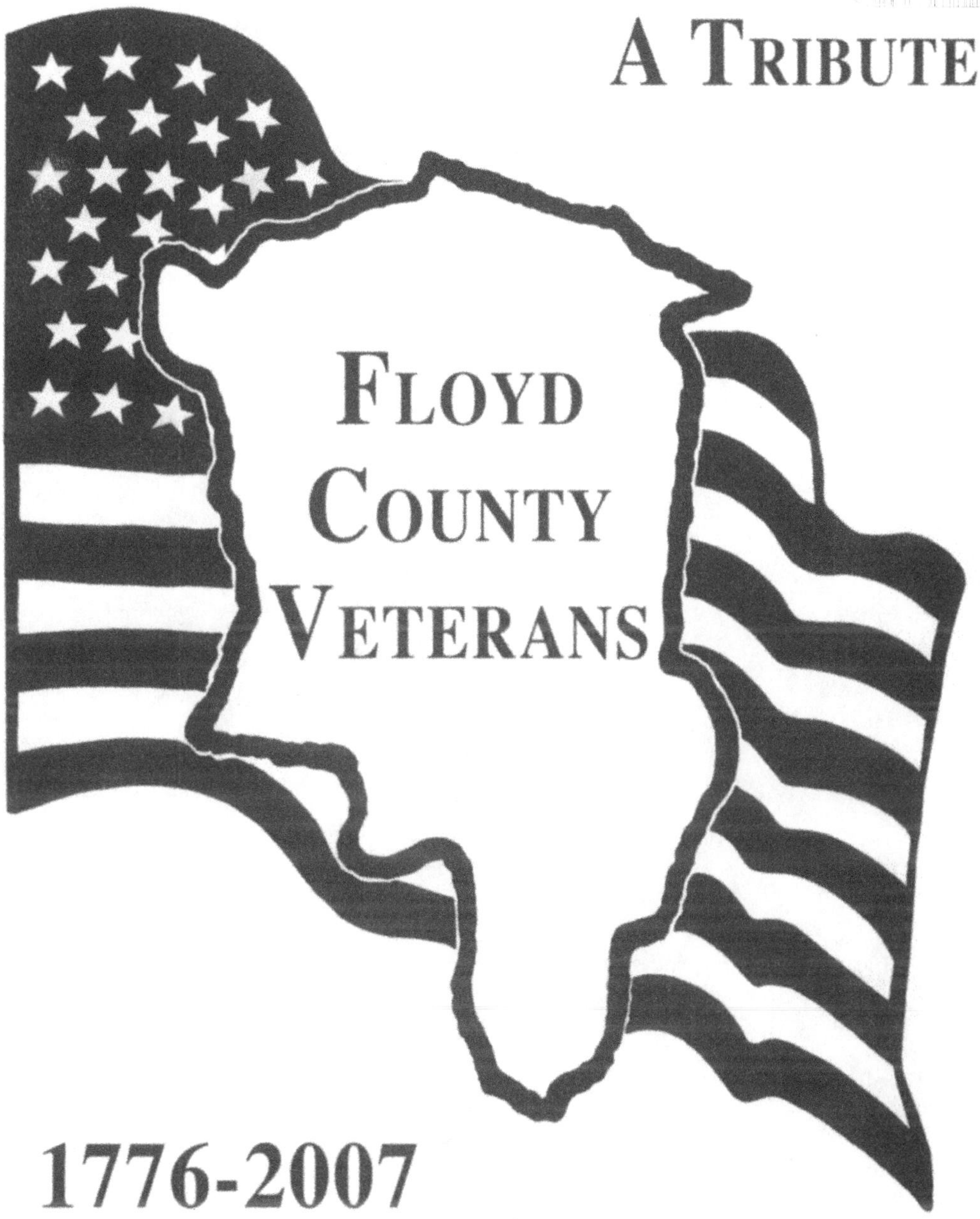

1776-2007

Turner®
Publishing Company
Nashville, Tennessee • Paducah, Kentucky

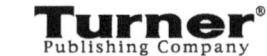

Turner Publishing Company
200 4th Avenue North • Suite 950
Nashville, Tennessee 37219
(615) 255-2665
412 Broadway • P.O. Box 3101
Paducah, Kentucky 42002-3101
(270) 443-0121
www.turnerpublishing.com

Copyright © 2007 Floyd County Historical Society
All rights reserved.
Publishing Rights: Turner Publishing Company

This book or any part thereof may not be reproduced or transmitted in any form or by any means, electronic or mechanical, including photocopying, recording, or by any information storage and retrieval system, without permission in writing from the authors and the publisher.

Library of Congress Control Number: 2006932084
ISBN 978-1-63026-969-2
Printed in the United States of America.

0 9 8 7 6 5 4 3 2 1

Table of Contents

Introduction 4
Poem 5
Revolutionary War Soldiers 6
Veterans of the War of 1812 8
Mexican War Veterans...Big Sandy Valley 9
High on a Mountain 10
The Nelson Boys 14
Johnson Family 15
Rice Family 16
Raymond R. Goble Story 17
Freedom Isn't Free 19
Land of the Morning Calm 21
Floyd County Veterans' Biographies 23
    Revoluntionary War 23
    Civil War 23
    Spanish American War 33
    World War I 33
    World War II 37
    Korean War 89
    Vietnam War 105
    Desert Storm/Gulf War 119
    Iraqi Freedom 120
    Unknown 122
Floyd County, Veterans Discharges 124
Sponsors 148
Index 158

INTRODUCTION

Officers of the Floyd County Historical Society are (from left): Jim Spencer, Sam Hatcher, Bertha Daniels and NavaJo Austin.

This project was the result of a desire by the Floyd County Historical and Genealogical Society to pay tribute to our Nation's Veterans, especially those associated with Floyd County. The Society chose to honor all veterans regardless of when and where they served or if in peacetime or wartime. This project covers veterans from the Revolutionary War to present day.

We would like to thank all Veterans and their families for supplying information and pictures. We would also like to thank the community for its continued show of respect and dedication to our veterans.

Our committee - Jim Spencer, Debi Manuel, Jean Burke, Sam Hatcher and NavaJo Austin - worked many hours in compiling this information. As with any worthwhile project, the amount of information can be overwhelming and we have made a tremendous effort to eliminate possible errors. We sincerely apologize if anything has escaped our attention.

With sincere thanks to our Veterans, we hope that we have given some insight to what our men and women have done for our community and our country.

The Floyd County Historical and Genealogical Society

POEM

Submitted by Sina Rice

My soul is bruised, my heart is tight,
Three sons I've sent to join the fight
For freedom;
Three strong men, in prime of health,
Reared on love and a country's wealth
Of Freedom.

Proud of their heritage, willing to give
Their lives in trinity for all to live
In Freedom;
War is cruel, it demands the best
Of all we have and puts to test
Our Freedom.

But sons will follow mine of three
To sing "My Country Tis of Thee,
Sweet Land of Opportunity"
And freedom!

Revolutionary War Soldiers

According to records compiled and published in *"The Big Sandy Valley"* W.R. Jillson, 1923, 1970, Appendix A. pp 141-143 and in *Pioneer Families of Eastern and Southeastern Kentucky*, William C. Kozee, 1973, pp 245-253, the following Revolutionary War Soldiers settled in the original Floyd County:

Floyd County

Auxier, Samuel, Private, Virginia Line
Bouney, Joseph, Private, Virginia Line
Brown, Thomas C., Cornet, Virginia Line
Brown, William
Caines, Richard, Private, Virginia Line
Cameron, James, Corporal, Virginia Line
Connelly, Henry, Captain, Virginia Line
Castle, Basil
Cassady, Thomas
Conley, David
Dorton, Edward, Private, Virginia Line
Davis, Zachariah
Fairchild, Abuid, Private, North Carolina Line
Ferguson, William, Private, Pennsylvania Line
Fitzpatrick, John
Fitzgerald, William
Flannery, James
Flatwood, Isaac
Fraley, James, Private, Virginia Militia
Graham, John, Virginia Continental Line
Hamilton Thomas
Hall, Anthony, Private, North Carolina Line
Hall, John
Harris, James, Private, Virginia Militia
Harris, Samuel
Haney, William
Hitchcock, Joshua, Private, North Carolina Line
Hopkins, Garner, Private, New York Line
Herrell, Reuben, Private, Virginia Line
Jacobs, William, Private, Virginia Line
Jones, Gabriel, Private, North Carolina Line
Jones, Ambrose, Private, Virginia Line
Justice, Simeon, Drummer, North Carolina Line
Justice, John
Kelly, John
Lovelady, Thomas, Private, Virginia Line
Matthews, Reuben
Moore, John, Private, North Carolina Line
Mullins, John, Private, Virginia Line
Murray, Thomas, Private, Pennsylvania Line
Nolen, William, Private, South Carolina Line
Patrick, James Sr., Private, Virginia Line
Pitts (or Pytts), Jonathan, Private, North Carolina Line
Porter, James, Private, Virginia Line
Porter, John W., Private, Virginia Line
Preston, Moses, Private, Virginia Line
Preston, Nathan, Private, Virginia Line
Morgan, David, Private, Virginia Line
Pitts, Mexico
Slone, Cudbeth, Private, Maryland Line
Smith John III, Private, Virginia Line
Sullivan, Petter, Private, Virginia Line
Thacker, Reuben, Private, Virginia Line
Wadkins, Benedict, Private, North Carolina Line
Wells, Richard, Sergeant, Virginia and North Carolina Line
Williams Phillip
Regem, Samuel
Young, Alexander, Private, South Carolina Line
Stratton, Solomon, Virginia Line (Clark's Illinois Regiment)

Breathitt County

Bowling, Jesse
Bush, Drury
Turner, Roger

Clay County

Baker, Bowling, Private, North Carolina Line
Benge, David, Private, North Carolina Line
Burge David Sr., Private, Virginia Line
Burns, William, Private, Virginia Line
Bowling, Jesse, Private, North Carolina Line
Chandler, John, Private, North Carolina Line
Garland, John
Lewis, Messenger, Private, New York Line
Martin, Azariah, Private, Virginia Line
Phillips, John, Private, South Carolina Line
Ratcliffe, Harper, Private, Virginia Line
Seabourn, Thomas, Private, Virginia Continental Line
Stapleton, Thomas, Private, North Carolina Line
Wood, Samuel, Private, South Carolina Continental åLine

Johnson County

Auxier, Simon
Clark, Samuel
Davis, Joseph
Flannery, John
Francis, Thomas
Larkin, Priestley
Van Hase (Van Hoose), John Private, Virginia Line (Clark's Illinos Regt.)
Walker, George R.

Lawrence County

Atkinson, David, Private, Virginia Line
Atkin, David, Private, Virginia Line
Bates, William, Private, Virginia Line
Brown, William, Private, Virginia Line
Burgess, William, Private, Virginia Line
Blumer, Gilbert, Private, New York Line
Castle, Basil, Private, Virginia Line
Cox, William, Private, Virginia Line
Childers, Abner, Private, Virginia Line
Crum, Adam, Private, Virginia Line
Davis, Joseph, Private, Virginia Line
Hensley, Joseph, Private, Virginia Line
Hardwick, George, Private, Virginia Line
Kitchen, James, Virginia Continental Line
Lee, Samuel, Private, Virginia Line
Lesley, John, Private, Virginia Line (Clark's Illinois Regiment)
Lyon, William, Private, North Carolina Line
Marcum, ___, Private, Virginia Militia
Marshall, John, Private, Virginia Militia
Mills, Richard, Private, Virginia Militia
Norton, James, Private, Virginia Militia
Patrick, James, Private, Virginia Militia
Perkins, George, Private, North Carolina Militia
Pratt, James, Private, Virginia Line
Sexton, John, Private, North Carolina Line
Ward, James, Private, Virginia Line
Wooten, Silas, Private, Virginia Line

MORGAN COUNTY

Barker, George, Private, Virginia Line
Blevins, James, Private, Virginia Line
Butler, John, Private, Virginia Line
Cooke, William, Private, South Carolina Line
Cooper, John, Private, Pennsylvania Militia
Day, John, Private, Virginia Line
Ellington, David, Private, Virginia Line
Hamilton, Thomas, Private, Virginia Line
Hamilton, Benjamin, Private, Virginia Line
Howrton, William, Private, Virginia Line
Johnson, Jacov, Private, South Carolina Line
Jone, Ambrose,
Keeton, Isaac, Private, North Carolina Line
Kelly, Samuel, Private, North Carolina Line
Kulby, John
Lewis, Thomas, Private, Virginia Line
McGuire, John, Private, Virginia Line
Mckinzie, Issac, Private, Virginia Militia
Montgomery, Alexander, Private, Virginia Line
Prewitt, John
Ratliff, Reuben, Private, Virginia Militia,
Smothers, John, Private, Virginia Line
Stevenson, Levi
Stevens, Gilbert, Private, Virginia Line
Swanson, Levi, Private, Virginia Militia
Wages, Benjamin, Private, Virginia Line
Walsh, William, Private, North Carolinia Line
Williams, Phillip, Private, Virginia Line

William Pelfrey Jr., Paymaster General in Revolutionary War. Moved from Henry County to Montgomery County, Virginia, married Nancy Hannah Crabtree in Henry County in 1785, came to Floyd County, Kentucky between 1800 and 1810, had 6 sons and 2 daughters. Authority: Sandy Valley Heritage Vol. 25, No. 3, pg 21.

PERRY COUNTY

Burns, Andres, Private, Virginia Line
Bush, Dewey, Private, Virginia Line
Caudill, James
Combs, John, Private, Virginia Line
Croft, Archelos, Private, North Carolina Line
Cordill, James, Private, North Carolina Line
Cordill Stephen, Private, North Carolina Line
Cornett, William
Ellis, Charles, Private, Massachusetts Line
Hurst, Hy, Private, Virginia Militia
Hagins, William, Private, No9rth Carolina Line
Harwell, Andrew, Private, North Carolina Line
Howard, James, Private, Virginia Line
Howard, Thomas, Private, Virginia Line
Justice, John, Private, South Carolina Line
Justice, Richard, Private, South Carolina Line
Justice, Simon, Private, South Carolina Line
Kelly, John, Private, North Carolina Line
May, David, Private, Virginia Line
Mullins, Joshua, Private, Virginia Line
McGeorge, Daniel, Private, South Carolina Line
Osborne, Ephraim, Private, Virginia Line
Patrick, Ezekiel, Private, North Carolina Line
Pigman, Leonard, Private, North Carolina Line
Polly, Edmunds, Private, Virginia Line
Stidham, Samuel, Private, North Carolina Line
Turner, Rovert, Private, North Carolina Line
Wadkins, Thomas, Private, North Carolina Line
Williams, William, Private, North Carolina Line
Wooten, Silas P., Private, Virginia Line

PIKE COUNTY

Atkinson (Adkinston), John, Trumpeter, Virginia Line
Blankenship, William, Private, Virginia Militia
Childers, Pleasant, Private, North Carolina Line
Collins, Meresith
Dailey, Dennis, Private, Virginia Line
Ford, Joseph, Private, North Carolina Line
Jackson, James, Private, North Carolina Line
Johnson, John
Mims, Robert
Maynard, James
May, John
Potter, Abram
Stepp, Moses, Private, South Carolina Line
Stewart, Thomas
Trout (Trant), Christian, Private, Maryland Line

FLOYD AND JOHNSON COUNTIES

(Addendum) Kozee submits, though without definite establishment that the following Revolutionary War Soldiers settled in this area:
Auxier, Micheal
Barnett, Jesse
Evans, John
Fitzpatrick, Solomon
Holt, William
Howe, Samuel
Janes, Stephen
Johnson, John
Kelly, Jesse R.
King, Oliver
Kirk, James
Ramey, John
Ward Sr., Isaac
Ward, James
Wheeler, Stephen
Wiley, Thomas
Wooten, Silas P.
Service units for these men are unknown.

The following information is found in *"The Stepp/Stapp Families Of America,* Henry P. Scalfin collaboration with Rudolph B. Stepp privately printed September 1974, page 207.

"Moses Stepp, Orange County, Virginia native and resident in Pike County, Kentucky, when he died was a soldier, Indian fighter, hunter explorer and backwoods settler of five states. He became a legend long before he succumbed to great age, so old his descendants said that when he died he had attained the age of 110 years. If his headstone dates are true on his grave beside the road on the Pigeon Roost Fork of Wolf Creek in the present Martin County, Kentucky, he was the oldest man to ever live in Kentucky.

He joined the Revolutionary forces when he was a mere youth. Fought Indians and Tories, helping to hang many of the latter. Moses Stepp filed a deposition with the Floyd County Court April 23, 1855 in which he states he was 112 years old - as to the death date of Moses, although the headstone had the date of 1855, records on the General Services Administration, Washington D.C., attest to the date of December 13, 1856."

In *"Kentucky's Last Frontier,"* Henry P. Scalf, 1966, page 111 we learn that "Peter Sullivan a Revolutionary War Soldier of the

Continental Line had settled near the present Ivel in 1816. He died in Wayne County, West Virginia, June 19, 1840.

According to the Map used by Kozee, Eastern and Southeastern Kentucky consisted of Knox, Clay, Floyd and Greenup counties and soldiers shown here for the War of 1812 and Revolutionary Officers and Soldiers shown separately would be included in these counties would include settlers in all of these counties as well as Floyd County.

There follows a list of Revolutionary War officers and soldiers whose descendants settled in Eastern or Southeastern Kentucky:
Burek, William, Private, Lee's (Virginia) Legion
Bragg, Thomas, Captain, Virginia Line
Brown, George, Newman Virginia Line
Bryson, John, Captain, Pennsylvania Line
Castner, Jacob, North Carolina Forces
Chandler, Thomas, Private, North Carolina Line
Culbertson, Joseph, Virginia Force
Connelly, Thomas, First Regiment, South Carolina Line
Dupuy, James Jr., Captain, Virginia Militia
Elliott, Richard, Colonel, Virginia Line
Fuqua, Peter, Virginia Line
Fugua, Moses, Captain, Virginia Line
Gilbert, Samuel, Private, Virginia Line
Grayson, William, Colonel 8th Virginia Regiment Continental Line
Harvie, John, Colonel, Virginia Forces,
Hager, John Sr., South Carolina Line
Hampton, Dr. Cary Henry, (surgeon) Colonel (?) Virginia Line
Hord, Thomas, Captain Virginia Line
Hord, John, Captain, Lee's (Virginia) Light Dragoons
Hord, Richard, Captain, Virginia Continental Line
Kilgore, Charles T., Virginia Forces
Leftwich, William, Colonel, Virginia Line
Means, John, Co, South Caroline Line (?)
Meek, Moses, Private, South Carolina Light Dragoons
McCarty, Richard, Captain, Virginia (Augusta Co) Militia
Nevile, George, Cornet, Virginia Continental Line
Poage, John, Ensign, Virginia (Augusta Co) Militia
Poage, George, Colonel, Virginia (Boutecourt Co.) Militia
Poage, George, Captain Virginia (Augusta Co) Militia
Poage, Robert, Lieutenant Virginia (Rockbridge Co) Militia
Poage, William, Tate's Company, Augusta County Virginia Militia
Price, Thomas, Private, Virginia Militia
Ramsey, Joel, Virginia Continental Line
Robinson, James, Virginia Line
Salyers, Benjamin Jr., Virginia Continental Line
Stafford, Thomas, Pennsylvania Line
Salyer, Zacheriah, Virginia Continental Line
Smallwood, Samuel, Captain, Maryland Militia
Strothers, Robert, Virginia Forces,
Waring, Thomas, Lieutenant and Captain Maryland Forces,
Witten, Thomas Sr., Virginia Line
Witten, Thomas Jr., Virginia Line
Witten, James, Virginia Line
Wells, George, Pulaski Legion
Wells, James, General (?) Maryland Continental Line (?)

Additional information on Revolutionary War Veterans in Floyd County has been obtained from *"The Big Sany Valley,"* William Ely, pub. 1887, Central Methodist, Catlettsburg, KY. As shown on following pages:
Moses Prestons, page 72,
Jerry Burns, page 115
Joseph Bevins, page 237
The Burchetts, page 224

Ely furnished more detail on Simon Auxier, page 104. The father of Simon Auxier came to Pennsylvania from the Rhein area in 1755, married a Hollander and had five sons: "Simon, the oldest, served seven years during the Revolutionary War. He was under Washington at the Battle of Trenton; he was with the troops sent from Virginia to aid General Greene in the South; he was at the Battle of Guilford Court-House (Now Greensboro); and he was at Yorktown when Cornwallis surrendered. Samuel, the grandfather of Major John R. Auxier, volunteered when fifteen years old, and served the last three years of the War; the other boys were too young to make soldiers."

Veterans Of The War Of 1812

There follows the remarks of W.R. Jillson on the above, pp 137-8;

"Is it any wonder then, that in the years that were to follow, when the Nation's honor was at stake in 1812 and 1814 that the Big Sandy gave with a prodigal hand of its sons to assist in the winning of these struggles so important in the life and continental expansion of the new nation? Young men from the backwoods of the Big Sandy were strapped in the rigging of Commodore Perry's ships off Put-in-Bay, Lake Erie, September 10, 1813, possible and closed the campaign in the northwest (n. l0). Men and boys from the Big Sandy were again with Andrew Jackson at New Orleans, leveling their trusty long-barreled squirrel rifles on the massed British regulars, and so won that great though needless victory for American arms. Trained from boyhood to the rifle and a sparing use of ammunition in their native hills, is it any wonder they everywhere distinguished themselves for bravery and accuracy of fire, until it was said that "no bullet from the gun of a Kentucky mountaineer failed to find its mark.

(n.20): The Battle of the Thames. B.H. Young.

Kozee, op cit. pp 252-3 furnishes a list of commissioned and non-commissioned officers from Eastern and Southeastern Kentucky, which would have included all of the original Floyd County, except for the small part apportioned in 1806 to Clay County, and it was considered proper to include them in this book. They are shown as per unit, as Second Regiment, Kentucky Militia, except those shown as recruited in Lewis and Greenup counties.

Roll of Field and Staff:
Lieutenant Colonel William Jennings

Majors:
First Major: John Faulkner
Second Major; Joseph Eve
Surgeon, William Craig
Surgeon's Mate, David Nelson
Paymaster, Jonathan Desert (Dysart)
Second Paymaster, Henry Beaty
Adjutant, Samuel Lapsley
Quartermaster Sergeant, James Morrison
Sergeant Major, Barney Young
Adjutant, Thomas McGilton

Captain Daniel Garrard's Company:
Captain, Daniel Garrard
Lieutenant, Daniel Cockrells
Ensign, William Cunningham

Sergeants:
Thomas Murphy
James Love
Benjamin Blythe

Horatio Bruce
John Alien
Lincoln Ames
David Fee

Corporals:
Daniel Sibert
John Cane
William Simpson
John Everidge

Musicians:
Valentine Percifield
Samuel Eldridge

Pogue's Regiment, Kentucky Militia
Field and Staff Officers:
Lieutenant Colonel Robert Pogue

Majors:
First Major William Reed
Second Major David Hart
Surgeon Ardemus D. Roberts
Surgeon's Mate Thomas Doniphan
Adjutant Benjamin Norris
Quartermaster Benedict Bacon
Quartermaster Sergeant John Huddlesgon
Sergeant Major Walter Lacey
Drum Major John Wire
Fife Major Joab Houghton

Captain Thompson Ward's Company:
Captain Thompson Ward
Lieutenant George Benaugh
Ensign Benedict Bacon

Sergeants:
James Ward
Thomas Wilson
Jacob Kouns
John Gholson

Corporals:
Samuel D. Fishback
Charles Jackson
Charles Crayfast
James Gibson

Poage's Regiment Kentucky Volunteers:
Colonel John Poage

Majors:
Aaron Stratton
Jeremiah Morton

Adjutant John E. McDowell
Quartermaster Samuel L. Crawford
Paymaster John Hockaday
Surgeon Anderson Donaphan
Surgeon's Mate Thomas Nelson
Quartermaster Sergeant Edward Brooks
Sergeant Major William Triplett

Captain Moses Demmit's Company:
Captain Moses Demmitt

First Lieutenant Thomas Hord
Ensign Joseph Thorn

Kentucky Mounted Volunteer Militia
Captain Johnston Dysarts Company:
Captain Johnston Dysart
Lieutenant Charles C. Carson
Ensign Joseph Henderson

Sergeants:
James Wilson
Jacob Frederick
Isaiah Ham
Samuel Vance

Corporals:
John Bustle
John Evans
George Watkins
Isaac Dillard

MEXICAN WAR VETERANS WHO WERE RESIDENTS OF THE BIG SANDY VALLEY

As shown in *"The Big Sandy Valley"* by W.R. Jillson, pp 143; 153.

Floyd County had been partially divided at the times of the Veterans shown would have been from other counties as well as Floyd County such as Perry (1820), Pike (1821), Morgan (1822), Breathitt (1839), Letcher (1842), and Johnson (1843), The Mexican War was in 1847.

John W. Keller, enrolled 3rd Sergeant, mustered in April 12, 1847 at Prestonsburg, mustered out August 5, 1848, at Newport.

Robert Brown, enrolled private, mustered in April 12, 1847 at Prestonsburg, mustered out August 5, 1848 at Newport.

Charles Foster, enrolled private, mustered in April 28, 1847 at Louisa mustered out August 5, 1848 at Newport.

Elihu Hawkins enrolled private, mustered in April 15, 1847 at Prestonsburg mustered out August 5, 1848 at Newport.

Thomas D. Hart enrolled private, mustered in April 19, 1847 at Prestonsburg, mustered out August 5, 1848 at Newport.

W.J. Whitley enrolled private, mustered in April 12, 1847, at Prestonsburg, mustered out August 5, 1848 at Newport.

John N. Brown, enrolled private, mustered in April 28, 1847 at Louisa, died July 26, 1848, near mouth of Salt River in Ohio River.

The above information was taken from the Muster Roll of Company "E" 16th Regiment, U.S. Infantry, Co. I. John W. Tibbett's called into the service of the United States for the Mexican War, being one of the battalion of four companies organized in Kentucky, and officered by the President of the United States, Act of Congress, February 11, 1847, pp 258-261 of Report of the Adjutant General of the State of Kentucky. Mexican War Veterans, pp 158-160. Frankforr, 1889.

Besides the seven soldiers named, there is good reason to believe there were other Big Sandians in the Mexican War. Due to the fact that their enlistment took place at points along the Ohio River, like Newport and elsewhere it is impossible to trace them in the official records, either at Frankfort or Washington.

Footnotes 3 and 4 page 153.

High On A Mountain
A Memorial Service For Henry Clay Hubbard
by Karen Marcum

I wonder what the thoughts were of 16-year-old Henry Clay Hubbard when he left his mountain home at the mouth of Mutton Fork on Bull Creek on September 13, 1862. It's certain that he never imagined he would die in a prison of war camp and that his remains would not be brought home for 139 years.

He and his brother, William Hubbard Jr., enlisted together in Prestonsburg on September 13, 1862 in Company A 10th KY Calvary Regiment of the Confederate Army. Henry Clay was a sergeant when he was wounded in his left leg and captured during the battle at Mount Sterling, KY on June 10, 1864.

He was sent to a hospital in Lexington, KY and from there to Camp Morton in Indianapolis where he died of spinal meningitis on February 27, 1865 just before the war ended.

On July 9, 2004, many descendants of his eleven brothers and sisters gathered high on what is left of the mountain top cemetery at the Forks of Bull Creek to give his remains a long awaited memorial service. Even though there's not many left in this area with the last name of Hubbard, there's many descendants as his siblings married into most of the families on Bull Creek.

Atlas Hall and Terry Music of the Sons of the Confederacy set his stone, told the sad story of his death, and gave a black powder salute. Several members of the Disabled American Veterans were on the mountain as well. Roger Nelson, a gg-nephew of Henry Clay Hubbard, told me to contact this group as we were looking for a bugle player. When I called and explained that the soldier had been dead for 139 years, I was told by the DAV that they didn't care how long he had been dead as all soldiers deserved a proper burial. They read a beautiful poem, did a 21 gun salute, and had their chaplain say a prayer. Their musician played a hauntingly beautiful song. Tom Nelson, another gg-nephew, gave a prayer thanking God for a family reunited. Gary Hubbard of Medina, OH, who descends through two of Henry Clay's siblngs, thanked everyone for coming and told how happy we all were to be on the mountain top that day. The ceremony ended with the singing of the old hymn, *Amazing Grace*. It is truly amazing that Henry Clay's remains now rest in his family cemetery.

When my husband patted down the earth over the box containing the soil from Henry Clay's prior grave in Indianapolis and said, "Welcome home, old soldier," I thought about a young boy who galloped off to fight in a war and who never came home again. Tears flowed down my cheeks as I thought about how his family must have grieved all those years ago. His brother, William, was captured in Blue Springs, TN, but returned from the war to marry Sarah Hammons and to raise a large family at Sugar Loaf.

There was a peacefulness during Henry Clay's Memorial Service that isn't often felt in this world. A gentle breeze blew across the mountain top. We thought that it was wonderful to have the remains of his earthly body buried between his father, William Hubbard Sr., and his brother, Marshall Hubbard. The property for the cemetery was donated many, many years ago by Marshall Hubbard as a community cemetery according to a great-nephew attending the ceremony, Paul Marsillett.

The credit for this occasion goes to Kathy Hubbard Hanlon of Texas as she located the remains of Henry Clay and did the paperwork to obtain the tombstone. She and her husband, Jim, traveled to Indianapolis to obtain the soil from his grave which had been moved to the Crown Hill Cemetery in Indianapolis.

The Civil War spilt families asunder as to had ours and almost everyone else's in this valley and across the nation. After Henry Clay's memorial service, we all felt that we had done a deed that needed to be done. After all, no one would want a family member to be left for 139 years in a grave provided by a prison. It was wonderful for the descendants of the siblings of Henry Clay to gather from various states across the nation for the ceremony. High on the mountain top, we met family for the first time and felt a kinship with them.

John Hensley and Charlie Chaplin, Jan. 10, 1919, WWI.

A story that depicts a tragedy of war is that of the Bolling family. Walter Karr Bolling came home from WW I, but died in 1934 before he could witness the plight of his sons. On December 7, 1941, Walter Karr Bolling, Jr., died at Pearl Harbor and on February 16, 1951, his brother Thomas E. bolling died in the Korean War.

World War II B-24. Cpl. Calvin E. Daugherty-nose-Marietta, OK; Cpl. Wallace D. Cummings-ball-Pawnee, OK; Cpl. George T. Flanigan -waist-Mapleton, ME; Cpl. Melville D. Hart-radio-Texas; Sgt. Neil J. Trotta-tail-Brooklyn, NY; Staff Sgt. Arthur W. Haywood-engineer-Wayland, KY; Lt. Guy R. Peterson-navigator-Chicago, IL; Robert L. Smith-bombardier-Illinois; Lt. Williams L. Sheppard-co-pilot-Illinois; Lt. Crawford-pilot-Colorado (not pictured).

During World War II Mrs. Lillian Keenon enlisted the men of Prestonsburg to help make surgical dressings for the American Red Cross. Most of those in the photo were members of the Kiwanis Club. Mrs. Keenon is shown at upper left, and Ella Noel White, executive secretary of Floyd Red Cross Chapter, is at rear right. Others in photo are from left: First row: Sam Isbell, Town Hall, Dr. Marvin Ransdell, Dr. O.G. Pennington; 2nd row: Ishmael Triplett, N.M. "Bud" White, Richard Spurlock, the Rev. W.B. Garriott; 3rd row: Edward P. Hill, Woodrow Burchett, Claude Caudill; 4th row: Ballard Herald, C.H. Smith, Charles Chumley, Bob Francis, Fred A. Martin.

The women also took a night at rolling bandages. Mrs. Lillian Kennon Chairman and her inspectors Muriel Kelly, Mrs. John Hale, Phyllis Hale (Rainer), Jean Herald (Burke) Mary Lou Layne. Others not all identified – known is Virginia Shivel, Virginia Smith, Grace Ford, Anna Hale, Francis Bolling (Gold Star Mother-Walter K. Bolling on the Arizona at Pearl Harbor), Rebecca Dingus, Mrs. Goble, Della Herald, Mrs. Hopson, Mrs. Elliott, Myrtie McGuire, Grace Goble, Mrs. Hobson.

U.S. Naval Training Station Company 1517 SPl/c A Company Commander, Nov. 5, 1943, U.S. Naval Training Station, Great Lakes, IL. Among them are Fred Harris, Palmer Patton, Newt Watkins, Edgar Hale and Edsel Glen Spradlin.

These pictures were displayed in the Veterans Show Case window of Edward Jones Investments - Sam Blankenship, Investment Broker, Court Street, Prestonsburg who is a two tour Vietnam Vet - are of following service people. Left is Ruby Bradley, POW nurse who was the most decorated woman at World War II. She is buried at Arlington National Cemetery. Lower left is Eugene "Sonny" Schutchfield who was killed in the Battle of the Bulge. Thomas Bolling who was killed in Korea. He was a brother of Walter Karr Bolling. Top center is Walter Karr Bolling who was killed at Pearl Harbor. Lower Center is Lawton E. Clark, Airforce - shot down over Germany. Upper right is Henry Lewis Holbrook who was killed in Italy. Lower right is Bob Spurlock who returned to his home in West Prestonsburg and worked for Kentucky West Virginia Gas Company.

Sam Blankenship celebrates the Floyd County Veterans by displaying war memorabilia in his office windows. For the entire month of July, war items such as pictures, medals, newspaper clippings, parachutes, battle flags and more are exhibited. People from all over the county and all branches of the military bring in their memorabilia. With the help of Jean Burke and Carolyn Meade, items keep coming in. The photos displayed along with the medals is of the distinguished Kentucky Veteran John Wallen who served in WWII. John served on four continents during the war. On the wall are uniforms belonging to Charlie Collins and Ballard C. Hearld. Note the "Rosie the Riveter" poster.

This photo of Orville Thomas Scutchfield, who served in WWII, was taken in 1943. Orville is on the right. He was killed while aboard the USS O'Brien off the coast of France on June 25, 1944. His body was not returned home until January 1949. (Photo courtesy of Elizabeth Barnett of Prestonsburg.)

Hi Mom I'm Home. Ballard C. Herald Jr. returned home to West Prestonsburg after being overseas for 23 months serving in the U.S. Navy during WWII. He volunteered in January 1942 and was discharged in December 1945.

This is a picture of the war memorial erected in the town of Wheelwright, KY by Inland Steel Corp. to honor the young men of the town who served their country in the military. My grandparents, A.L. and Victoria Hall, have four sons in this picture. The young man on the end holding the rifle is A.L. "Scooter" Hall Jr. and the one on the other end is William F. "Bill" Hall, the one holding the Post No. 223 flag is Clifford C. Hall and the one in the Navy uniform holding the rifle is Belmer Hall. These four all served in WWII and Clifford Hall served in Korea. They had seven sons, one of which died in infancy. Of the six that grew to adulthood, all six served in the military, the four mentioned above, plus Ivan E. Hall who retired from the U.S. Air Force and Edwin H. Hall, who served in the U.S. Army. As you can see, this is a family with a long history of military service. Submitted by Brenda England Youmans, Minnie, KY.

HMS Mauretania — Length: 772 feet; Beam: 89.6 feet. It was built at Burkenhead, England; launched July 28, 1938; completed May 31, 1939; made maiden voyage June 17, 1939 from Liverpool, England to New York, NY. Outfitted as a troopship, Sydney, Australia in Spring 1940 and served as troopship, 1940-45. Information furnished by Dr. Eric R. Craine, son of 1st Lt. Eugene R. Craine, Battery A, 464th AAA (AW) Bn. Photograph made at San Francisco Bay, January or February 1943.

The Nelson Boys

The Nelson Boys were a patriotic family to say the least. Ted, Sam and Will, served in the U.S. Military during WWII.

Ted Nelson with unknown soldiers. Ted is at the bottom of steps.

Sam Nelson is 5th from the left in the 2nd row.

Ted Nelson is in the back row, 6th from left.

Will Nelson (2nd from left) pictured with friends.

Johnson Family

The Tab Johnson family is patriotic to say the least. Tab's grandfather served in the Civil War. All of Tab's sons and stepsons served in the U.S. Military: Garfield, Jack, Decker and Grover all served in WWII. Jessie served with the U.S. Marine Corps in Korea and was injured on a hill called "Old Baldy." Kenneth served with the U.S. Army in Vietnam. They all received an Honorable Discharge and by the Grace of God returned home. Larry. Willie, Barry (Larry's son), Elmer Ray (Grover's son), Grover and Lloyd (Greenburry's son), all served in the U.S. Military.

Garfield Johnson family. Standing: Garfield, Jack, James Albert "Tab," Nervy, Velva, Alpha, Almeda and Grover. Kneeling: Lloyd, Jesse, Willie (in uniform), John Epp "Decker" and Kenneth. This picture was taken at Greenburry's funeral in 1953.

The Johnson family reunion, August 7, 2004. Kenneth, Jack (standing) and Garfield (sitting). These brothers had not seen each other in 24 years. They are the last remaining children of Tab Johnson.

Garfield Johnson and brothers Jack, Kenneth, Jesse, Decker, Grover. All served in the Armed Forces, This picture was taken August 25, 1966.

"Two old Soldiers," Decker Johnson, ex-Marine, age 84, and brother Garfield, ex-Army, age 74. Both served in WWII.

Rice Family

East Point, Little Paint Creek, Floyd County, Kentucky has well represented their county in time of war.

Raleigh Rice had six sons: Russell, U.S. Navy; Zellard, U.S. Army, lost in action Dec. 31, 1944, Belgium Bulge; Gordon retired from the U.S. Army with 22 years of service, 15 of which was on foreign soil; Claude, Navy; Montie, U.S. Army and Jackie David, U.S. Army. Kenneth Gordon Rice, son of Gordon Rice, served in the Vietnam Conflict.

Jud Rice had four sons: Sam K., two and a half years in Italy, North Africa, Sicily, Corisca Island; Thomas J., three and a half years in WWII; John D., WWII North Africa, Sicily, Italy and France. John was wounded in the invasion of Marsa, France; Roy served in the Korean War Conflict.

John Rice, C.P.L.; Luther J. Rice, 435th Sq. 479th Fighter Group.

Funeral Service for Samuel Zellard Rice. Kentucky, PFC, 134th Inf., 35th Div., WWII, was born Dec. 13, 1921. Deceased in action Dec. 31, 1944 in the Belgium Bulge. The funeral was held at his parents home Dec. 13, 1946. The small pictures in frames are Zellard and his only child Clara Evelyn Rice. The house is now the home of Jack and Phyllis Rice. Jack is the brother of Zellard.

Raleigh Rice Family in 1946. Front row: Emma Leah Bullock, born May 1932, died 2003; Montie Delno Rice, born July 23, 1938; Jackie David Rice, born April 4, 1941. Back row: James Russell Rice, born Nov. 14, 1919; Claude Douglas Rice, born Aug. 11, 1927, died Aug. 31, 1964; Francis Gordon Rice, born Aug. 19, 1924, died Oct. 15, 1990; Dialphia R. Rice, born Oct. 23, 1900, died Dec. 11, 1977, married Raleigh Rice on Feb. 11, 1919. Raleigh was born May 11, 1901, died May 7, 1999. All that are deceased at this time are buried in the Robinson Cemetery on Little Paint Creek, Floyd County, KY. This picture was taken in the home of Raleigh and Dialphia on the day of the funeral of their son Samuel Zellard Rice, who was killed in action during WWII.

Raymond R. Goble Story
Submitted by his daughter, Linda Bradley

Never thought I would be on a ship in the middle of the ocean, but here I am, on the *Queen Mary!* I'm on my way to England. I'm heading to war and I'm not looking forward to any of this. I thought being in the Three C's was something great and it taught me a lot of things that helped me through basic training. I had been traveling the states building hotels, parks and whatever they wanted us to do. I guess being a 15-year-old kid, I wasn't doing too bad. When the war broke out I went into the Local Board 8 in Trilla, Utah to sign up. When I got there, they told me to go back home, that my draft papers were in the mail. I was stationed in the desert in California for basic training. Never thought it got that hot on the face of the earth. I hate my Sergeant! He has to be the meanest man on the face of this earth. After basic training was over, they sent us to Louisiana (Camp Polk) and then up to Massachusetts (Camp Edwards). Going through Ashland, Kentucky was hard, being so close to home.

Here I sit aboard this great ship waiting and hoping this will end before I get there. We're on our way to France now. Wish I was on my way home. They gave me a 50 caliber and a 30 caliber machine gun and told me to shoot down the buzz bombs. If I had to guess, I'd say we shot down over 500 of these things. I also have a Ml rifle. Hoping I never had to use it. Nothing could have prepared me for the horrible sights that I've seen.

We're marching through France now on our way to Belgium. When we arrived at Omaha Beach the forces had already taken control. Smart men, they had big poles sticking out of the bank and made them look like big gun barrels. The German's wasn't coming anywhere near them. We're walking everyday until we can't walk anymore. Every now and then they'll let us rest for a few days before we have to go on. We're pushing the Germans back on our way through. It's to the point I could put together these big guns with my eyes closed. Each time we have to use them, we have to put them together and then take them apart when we move on.

Can't believe I'm stuck in this hospital bed when the rest of my buddies are still out there fighting. Looking at the men lying around me makes me feel blessed that all I have is a broken foot. The officers came around today and told me that they were going to give me a Purple Heart and I told them to tear that piece of paper up and I didn't want it. All these men going home with no legs and arms and all I have is a scratch. They can just rip that paper up! Everyone should know that the 125th Anti-Aircraft are one amazing group of men. After a bomb went off and buried me in my fox hole, they had me dug out so fast I couldn't believe it. It was a run for our lives at that point. I just wish this war was over and I could go home, but as long as it is going on I will be here. They moved me up to the 3rd Army Division right before this happened.

1st Army machine gunman in the Battle of the Bulge is not where I want to be. This winter is horrible and for three days I thought I was going to freeze to death. Some of the men did. When we can go out at night, we're killing rabbits to eat and trade. I found this farmer with a bunch of potatoes and we're trading some of the rabbits and some coffee, sugar and marmalade for some of his potatoes and steak. We use the potatoes like bread to hold our food together. I'm cold, hungry and tired now and I've seen things that I will never talk about as long as I live. If people knew what I've done and how mean I've had to be, they would never talk to me. The only good thing I can say at this point is that I have a new gun on wheels. No more loading and unloading the pieces in the back of the jeep. We're just pulling it now.

Germany surrendered. Everyone gets to go home now. Everyone but me. I'm on my way back to France. I'm going into training and becoming a Military Policeman. We'll be guarding the prison in Marine, France. They tell me that we'll be staying in hotels and palaces.

I'm on American soil again! The trip back here was a lot worse that the one over. I thought the General Howell was going to sink. I've never heard such popping and cracking in all my life. We came into New York and I got to see the Statue of Liberty. We're heading to Indiana next and that's where I'm going to be discharged. I have to admit that my boot camp Sergeant was the best man that I've every known. He saved my life and I thank him.

Today I got to say farewell to Indiana, the Army, and all my friends that I've made on this journey.

After standing in line, for what seemed like forever, waiting on my discharge papers, the time finally came. The sergeant told me to go over to the next room and get my medal. I just looked at him, smiled and told him I had the only thing I wanted and that I was going home. I just hope and pray that this never happens again.

Raymond Ross Goble was born June 29, 1924 at Alphoretta, Kentucky. His father passed away when he was 11 years old. He joined the Three C's and left home at the age of 15. One day after his 18th birthday he went to enlist with the U.S. Army. From July 1942 to January 21, 1945, he served his country. He doesn't like to talk about the war and it was hard for me to hear some of things that he went through. I'm just thankful that he's here and that he was willing to put his life on line to give us this great country that we have today.

Thanks Dad!

Photo taken at Sherman's in San Diego. Ermal Scutchfield is second from left.

The Japanese Flag
John W. Burke Sr. of Prestonsburg is shown at his home standing next to a Japanese flag.

The story of this flag is quite remarkable. This Japanese flag with veterans' signatures was found in a gun shop by Paul Dolle from Rogers, AR. The names written on the flag were all men with B Company of the 130th Infantry which included Mr. Burke. Dolle began to search for those whose names were on it and was successful in finding only one - John Burke.

In a letter written to Mr. Burke, Mr. Dolle states, "I prefer for you to have it, but could not accept any money for it after hearing the price you and Company B have already paid. Thank you for serving our country." Mr. Dolle had the flag framed and presented it to John.

Floyd County Boys. *These young men are Floyd Countians who graduated from Prestonsburg High School together, joined the military together and came home together. Upon their return they had this picture taken in Prestonsburg at Strahan's Photography Studio. From left to right they are: Joe Merritt, James Ed Alley, Carl Crum, Robert "Itch" Branham and John W. Burke.*

FREEDOM ISN'T FREE
by Karen Nelson Marcum

Sixty years ago search crews were searching for a PBY2 that had gone down into the ocean. The aircraft was leaking fuel. Twenty-year-old Clarence Wallen was the co-pilot. His family still misses him and knows from first-hand experience that freedom isn't free.

Lee and Lula Wills Wallen of Floyd County, KY watched all five of their sons go off to defend their country.

All five joined the United States Navy. Clarence, Curtis, and Richard were in WWII; Woodrow and Sam were in the Korean War.

The boys and their little sister, Mary Louise, grew up surrounded by love and laughter. Clarence was the first to go to war on June 23, 1941. His family received the telegram telling them that he was missing on Oct. 3, 1943, and their lives were forever changed. His mother couldn't believe that he was gone. She thought that he was on an island somewhere and would be rescued. In later years, she made the long journey to the ocean where he'd gone missing to drop flowers into the water and to bid her beloved son farewell.

This Wallen family has maintained a close and loving relationship even though they are scattered across the nation. Their heart strings keep them returning to Floyd County for long visits. One of the brothers laughingly remarked during this year's Labor Day visit that they still joked and aggravated each other as they had while they were young with one noticeable difference - the teasing now didn't result in a fight.

At this year's reunion they had their missing brothers picture in a place of honor. Even after 60 years, he is still missed. His last letters home lets the love he felt for them shine through the years. He ended his letter to his little sister with the words, "With a love that will last forever."

Last Letter To His Sister

My Dear Sister,

Honey, I am awful glad you had a good time, but you must study hard to make up for the week you missed.

Baby, you don't know how much I would like to see you now and how much I wanted to see you Christmas, but I couldn't. Yes, honey, I will spend next Christmas with you if possible, and I think it will be. Mary, you are my only sister, and I love you so much. I want you to always do as Mom and Dad want you to do and obey your teacher too.

Mary, how do you like your new sister? I am sure you like her though. You always did. Honey, you will be a fine girl like her one of these days. So, obey Mom and Dad and always remember I love you and Woodrow, Sam and Richard so much. And, honey, if you all ever want or need anything in school or out, let me know.

So long for this time. Be good and God Bless you. I love you and the boys and Mom and Dad so much. All of you be good.

Love that will last forever
Clarence - your brother

Last Letter To His Family

Hello Everyone,

This leaves me all right, and I hope it finds you all the same. Mom, you talk about cold weather. There's sure cold weather down here also, but this weather is so changeable. Next, it may be hot. It changes always. Boy, I sure would like to see a big snow right now.

Yes, Mom, Scott and Mollie sure is swell. I like them both an awful lot.

Mom, I hope Curtis don't have to go to the army, but I am awful glad they are happy, but I knew they would. They both are sweet and kind. Mom, she is a fine sister-in-law, but he deserved a good wife because he is such a kind and honest boy. They have all my best wishes. I love them both.

Mom, we will win this war and then I can come home for a while anyway. I know I will be as well as ever when it is over.

Mom, tell Dad to be careful and everyone hello and to be good.

So long for this time,
Love,
Clarence

116th Army Ground Force Band, Delta Base Section. Don Childers is first on left in third row. Taken in 1944, WWII.

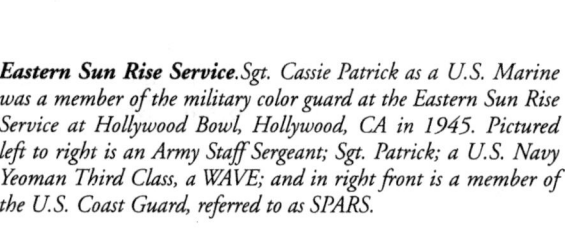

Eastern Sun Rise Service. Sgt. Cassie Patrick as a U.S. Marine was a member of the military color guard at the Eastern Sun Rise Service at Hollywood Bowl, Hollywood, CA in 1945. Pictured left to right is an Army Staff Sergeant; Sgt. Patrick; a U.S. Navy Yeoman Third Class, a WAVE; and in right front is a member of the U.S. Coast Guard, referred to as SPARS.

Battery B, 38th Field Artillery Battalion, Fort Lewis, WA, 1950. Photo by Billy D. Wallen.

Jim Hyden and a few of his soldiers kneeling beside the hole where Saddam was captured Dec. 13, 2003. He was captured by the 1st Bde. Combat Team, 4th Inf. Div.

Land of the Morning Calm
by Janice Shepherd

The following article was printed in the Floyd County Times in November 1994.

All around him his comrades were falling victim to enemy fire, but Lloyd Daniels stayed at his post and kept returning the enemy's fire during one of the bloodiest battles of the Korean War - the Battle of Pork Chop Hill.

Chinese forces bombarded United Nations troops on Pork Chop Hill. "Pork Chop was a shambles with many of the bunkers aflame and many dead and wounded," Walter G. Germes quoted from military reports in his book, *U. W. Army In the Korean War - Truce Tent and Fighting Front.*

Over 300 troops in the 7th Division of the forces were reported dead, wounded or missing in action. Chinese casualties were thought to be between 600-800 men.

Daniels, an Airborne Ranger, was one of 12 survivors of the battle. Some of the wounded left the hill in Daniels' arms as he tried to carry them to safety, his daughter NavaJo Austin recalled.

"Dad always said he was one of the few who came off Pork Chop Hill," she said. "He always worried about hurting somebody. He always said he hoped he never killed somebody."

His son Todd recalled seeing a picture his father had that showed dead bodies, stacked one on top of the other.

"When one soldier would die, he would fall on top of the other one. They'd have to climb over the dead soldiers to get to the wounded soldiers," he said.

NavaJo said her father told her he had been wounded and had received a bayonet wound in his foot.

Daniels mainly kept his war experiences to himself. "Pork Chop Hill was one he didn't talk about much," son Dennis said.

"He'd just shiver sometimes," Daniels' wife Joyce explained. "He had nightmares. He'd wake up in a cold sweat, but as the years went on that was better."

During one battle and after many troops had been killed, Daniels' group was relieved by another company. As Daniels' company made its way down the hill, the other company left their post and was soon on Daniels' heels. Exhausted and mad, Daniels' company had to turn around and retake the hill the fleeing soldiers had abandoned, Dennis said his father had often recalled.

Dennis also remembered about a battle when Daniels' unit was being charged by the Chinese and didn't have the right weapons.

"They had to take a 50 caliber machine gun and set the firing rate to the lowest mode to use it for snipers," he said.

Lloyd Daniels was also part of the Red Raiders unit. The unit would go behind enemy lines to kidnap enemy officers, Dennis said.

"Their point man was a Navajo Indian. Dad talked once about when they went out and found a sleeping bag beside the trail.

'The rest of the unit went out looking for the enemy, except the guide. They couldn't find any and when they got back, he already had him one.

"Dad said you never knew the Indian scout was there unless he wanted you to," Daniels said.

Lloyd Daniels sang lullabies in the Japanese language to his children when they were babies but, as his sons grew up, he occasionally told them about Korea and the conditions the soldiers had to face during war-time. Soldiers had to carry water from the creek in their helmets. They bathed from their helmets, then poured the water out. They'd go back to the creek to get more water and make coffee in the same helmets from which they had just bathed, son Todd Daniels said.

"The soldiers would wash their socks, roll them up and then put them under their armpits to dry." Joyce Daniels explained.

Todd Daniels recalled a story his dad told about the lack of hot food available for the soldiers.

"They hadn't eaten a hot meal in days when a Korean family asked them to eat with them. They told the family it was good and asked what it was they were eating. The Koreans kept saying 'Sopolary, Sopsolary,' and pointed outside," Todd said, with a chuckle almost escaping from him as he told the story.

"It was a dog running by," he said. "They had eaten a dog."

Lloyd Daniels entered the Army on August 2, 1951. The Korean War had been underway for almost one year. When he signed up, he lied about his age. He was too young to enlist. During his training as a paratrooper, Jerry Lewis and Dean Martin were filming the movie, *Jumping Jack,* at the base he was stationed. Daniels was one of the paratroopers in the movie's background.

By the time he was sent overseas, he was 18. He spent his 19th and 20th birthday in Korea. He spent one year, 11 months and five days in foreign service to his country. He was awarded the United Nations Service Medal, the Korean Service Medal, two Bronze Stars for the major battles in which in had fought, the National Defense Service Medal and the Good Conduct Medal.

Daniels was offered a Purple Heart, daughter NavaJo said, but he would not accept it.

Daniels was appointed acting platoon sergeant major on the field of battle when his command officer was killed. He could not become master sergeant because the government had frozen the ranks, Dennis explained.

At the end of his service, Daniels was a drill sergeant at Fort Knox. When President Eisenhower paid a visit to the base, Daniels was asked to be part of the President's Honor Guard. He declined.

"He was a Democrat back then and didn't know it," Joyce Daniels said about her husband. "He didn't like Eisenhower."

Todd compared his dad's feelings about Korea with the Gulf War.

"He didn't approve of us going in but he felt like we should have finished the job once we were there."

After two tours of duty, Daniels left military service on August 1, 1954, and came home to Floyd County. He and his family became residents of Lancer Bottom in Prestonsburg, and Daniels became a neon tube bender (sign maker). He worked in that capacity until around 1962 when he fell two stories after he was shocked by an electric current. He crushed three vertebrae and his spinal cord was lacerated,

"Doctors said he would never walk again," Daniels' wife said. But Daniels' fighting spirit saw him through the ordeal. Even though he couldn't walk, his wife and mom carried him to his truck and Daniels drove himself to Dewey Lake for a fishing trip. At the lake, someone would help him out of the truck and into his boat.

Daniels' survival instinct helped him to walk again and to get on with his life. Through it all, he kept his sense of humor.

His son recalled an incident that kept his family and the neighborhood chuckling. Daniels cut out a design for big feet. He then strapped the big feet to his son's feet and had his sons walk around the riverbank near his home and around the neighborhood leaving an impression that a "Bigfoot" had been in the area.

He also created a ghost for his children, grandchildren and neighborhood kids to love. When the wind would blow open a door, Daniels would tell his children that was a ghost named Fennymore. He made the ghost such a lovable creature that the neighborhood children even began leaving gifts for Fennymore.

Another ordeal was ahead for Daniels that would test his seemingly endless sense of humor. About three years ago, after many years of smoking cigarettes and being exposed to asbestos through his work with neon, his lungs deteriorated. He also often wondered if his exposure to the DDT the military had sprayed on the wooded areas of Korea and the soldiers underneath the foliage had affected him, his son said.

Daniels had to go on oxygen. The doctors gave him about six months to live. Then his wife saw a program on television about lung transplants. She contacted Sabrina Little, a former Floyd Countian who is the primary nurse for lung transplant patients at UK, and asked her about the program,

In 1993, Lloyd Daniels became the 13th patient to undergo a lung transplant at the University of Kentucky Medical Center.

Daniels spent most of the time in the hospital's cardio thoracic unit. He was out of the hospital in about 30 days. On June 2, 1994, he came home and stayed until September 7 when he returned to his doctor for a checkup.

While he was in the doctor's office, he went into respiratory arrest and had to be put on life support. He was put in the hospital again and stayed there for about 15 days.

His doctors felt he was doing well, but he needed physical therapy that wasn't available locally, Daniels' wife said, so he was put in Darby Square, a rehabilitation facility.

Daniels became ill and had to be sent back to the hospital. Last week on Tuesday, November 1st, Daniels died at the University of Kentucky Medical Center. His family stressed that Daniels did not die from the lung transplant, but from pre-renal failure.

Daniels' family praised the University of Kentucky's transplant program and plan to get involved in promoting organ donation. Once Joyce Daniels gets her life back in order, she said, she may write a book about the gift of life Daniels was given when he received the donated lung.

Daniels left a gift to children in Floyd County that changed many of their lives. On behalf of his grandson Jerry and the other Floyd County children who are handicaped, Daniels got a multi-handicapped unit started in the area.

When Jerry was three, Daniels approached the Kiwannis Club and asked for their help in establishing the unit. Businessman Huck Francis and the Kiwannis helped sponsor the unit that was started by Mountain Comprehensive Care at the Methodist Church building in Prestonsburg.

Floyd County Veterans Biographies
These biographies are placed into their respective sections according to the era in which they fell.

Revoluntionary War

JOSEPH DAVIDSON, born in Virginia around 1758 or 1759. He was the son of John G. Davidson and Martha Draper Davidson. He married Matilda Patton June 14 or 18, 1789 and they had six sons and four daughters.

As a soldier in the Revolutionary War, he moved from Tazewell County, VA, to Floyd County, KY on an unknown date. He applied for pension for service in the Revolutionary War. He died about 1850. His will was probated in Mercer County, VA.

JOHN FITZPATRICK, Revolutionary War Soldier, is buried in the Langley/Fitzpatrick Cemetery on the Old Middle Creek Road.

Photo submitted by Karen Nelson Marcum.

ANTHONY HALL, born in 1752. An old family Bible stated that he was born in Scotland. He died on Dec. 14, 1846 in Letcher County, KY. He enlisted in Halifax County, VA in 1777. He served one year under Capt. Bowyer in the 7th Virginia Regiment and was Honorably Discharged in Tazwell County, NC.

Around June 10, 1778, he enlisted again at Tazewell County, NC in a company under the command of Capt. Donohue in the 2nd North Carolina Regiment. Col. Litte was his Commander. He was taken a Prisoner Of War during the Siege of Charlestown, SC by the British. He was paroled afterwards.

His certificate of pension was issued on Dec. 14, 1825.

He married Ruth Butler on Dec. 23, 1794 in Halifax County, VA at the home of her father, George Butler. They applied for a license in Caswell County, NC. They had eight children. After the war, they came to Knox County, KY and are listed on the 1810 Tax Lists. By 1816, he and Ruth were living in Floyd County. He is buried at Deane, Letcher County, KY. His grave has a Revolutionary War Marker

DAVID MORGAN, born March 12, 1753 in Pittsylvania County, VA in a section that later became Patrick and then Henry County, VA, where he settled until moving to Floyd County, KY, 1799-1803; in Floyd County he was always known as Col. Morgan; he served as a Private and on the payroll in Capt. Edward Garland's Company of the 14th Virginia Regiment of Foot, under Col. Charles Lewis, enlisting in the unit on Dec. 17, 1776 until March 8, 1977 and again from April 29 to May 30, 1777, receiving a bounty of 200 acres for services in War of the Revolution.

He married Anne Poteet 1780/81 in Virginia and had two children, William and Mary. In October 1813 he and his son were killed by Edward Osborn, probably a tenant, on a farm he owned on the big Sandy River below the mouth of Ivy Creek.

Civil War

WILLIAM AKERS, Private, born 1835, died 1917, lived in Floyd County, KY. He was in Company A, 39th Infantry of the Civil War. He was the son of Thomas Blackburn Akers, born 1803, died 1888, and Keziah Meade.

He married Elizabeth Louise "Vicy" Baldridge, born 1851, died 1910, daughter of William Baldridge Jr. and Nancy E. Gilespie. He is buried on the Musick and Akers Cemetery on the Conley Fork of Abbott Creek, Floyd County, KY. He was the great-great- grandfather of Joe Skeens. His line goes back into the Valentine Akers line who lived on Mud Creek. That is Karen Nelson Marcum's family line.

William Akers' stone was set by Joe Skeens about 25 years ago. *Submitted by Karen Nelson Marcum.*

ANDREW JACKSON "GENERAL JACK" ALLEN, born Aug. 4, 1843, son of Samuel Allen and Sarah Ann Osborne. He served in Company F, 39th Kentucky Infantry, U.S. Volunteers in the Civil War. Andrew Jackson Allen as a teenager volunteered in the Union Army at the outset of the Civil War and fought valiantly for four years because, as he would later tell his children, "I just didn't like human slavery."

Allen was a name frequently recorded among English Immigrants to the New World during the American colonial period. After the war for Independence, those Allens who moved into Eastern Kentucky generally crossed the Appalachian Highlands from Virginia and North Carolina. Such was the case of the Andrew Jackson Allen Family who ultimately came into possession of land on Salt Lick Creek in Floyd County.

Andrew married Polly Patton on Aug. 15, 1879 in Floyd County, KY. She was born on Oct. 14, 1860. Polly's ancestors had, following the American Revolution, migrated south from Eastern Pennsylvania through the Shenandoah Valley into Eastern Kentucky. At least two of her direct ancestors were authentic Revolutionary heroes. Robert Morris, a Philadelphia merchant, was a signer of the Declaration of Independence and another was General Morgan, called "Hero of Saratoga."

Andrew Jackson and Polly Allen were the parents of nine children. Andrew died on March 23, 1919 and Polly died on Feb. 28, 1951. At the time of their death they still resided on Salt Lick Creek and are buried in the Allen Cemetery there.

Today, grandchildren, great-grandchildren and great-great-grandchildren appreciate and discuss their rich Allen heritage. *Submitted by a granddaughter, Eloise Allen Hall.*

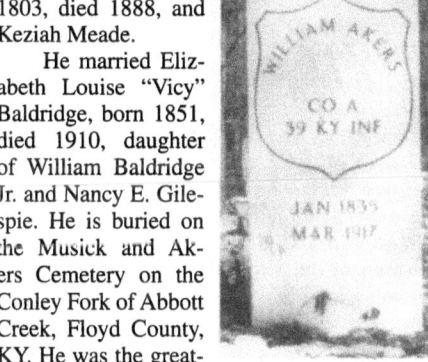

Andrew Jackson "General Jack" Allen and wife Polly (Patton) Allen

GEORGE JACKSON ALLEN, 1st Lieutenant, born in 1818 on Little Middle Creek, Right Beaver Creek, Floyd County, KY, the son of George Jackson Allen Sr. and Cynthia Patton. He enlisted in the Union Army in Company F, 39th Kentucky Volunteers on Nov. 6, 1862.

George Jackson Allen Jr.

The 39th Kentucky Infantry was raised by Col. John Dils from the counties along the Big Sandy River, and organized in camp at Peach Orchard, when it was mustered into service Feb. 16, 1863. Before it was mustered into service it began a series of fights and skirmishes with the enemy in that section which continued during almost its entire term of service.

The 39th saw action in Floyd, Pike, Carter, Magoffin, Johnson, Montgomery, Harrison and Lawrence counties in Kentucky, and in Southwest Virginia and Eastern Tennessee. Oral history says that George J. Allen captured Van Buren Bates of the 5th Kentucky Infantry in Pike County, KY. Van Buren Bates was known as the "Kentucky Giant" because of his height.

George resigned his commission on Nov. 14, 1865 and he returned to his farm on Right Beaver Creek, Floyd County, KY. Prior to the war George married Susannah Gearheart, daughter of Joseph Gearheart and Sarah Martin, who died as the War Between the States was beginning. They were the parents of Sarah "Sadie" Allen, Louise Allen, Cynthia Allen and Amanda Allen. After the war George married Nancy Jane Rice in Paintsville, KY. They had the following children: Lucy Allen, Martin Rice Allen, Amanda Allen, Katherine Allen, Susannah Allen, Florence Allen and Elizabeth Allen. After Nancy died George married Ellen Spradlin. George died on Dec. 15, 1900 in Paintsville, Johnson County, KY and is buried in the Old Town Cemetery there.

THOMAS H. AMBURGEY/BURGA, Civil War, son of Alfred and Mary Haggins Amburgey/Burga. He was born Sept. 9, 1844 and died June 6, 1927, Floyd County, KY.

Thomas H. Amburgey/Burga and wife Nancy.

He was in the Confederate Arms. Company A, 13th Kentucky Cavalry, Private, enlisted Sept. 2, 1862 Whitesburg, KY.

Thomas Amburgey was a highly respected citizen of this county, and was well known. During the War Between the States, he served as a Confederate solider. For the greater part of his life he was engaged in farming, and had lived about 45 years at his home on Johns Creek, Floyd County, KY. He died June 6, 1927, buried on Johns Creek, and later moved to Relocation Auxier Cemetery, Floyd County, KY.

He married Nancy L. Wheatley on Oct. 12, 1865 and died 1927, buried at the Relocation Auxier Cemetery. He had seven children. He is the grandfather of Bill Burga and great-grandfather of Bill Jr., Ollie Jr. and Thomas D. Burga.

JACOB "JAKE" BRYANT, born May 2, 1840, died July 4, 1920, buried Newman Cemetery, Hi Hat, KY. He is a Civil War Veteran, Private, 13th Kentucky Cavalry, Company E, CSA, Col. Ben Caudill's Camp (a new stone was set Jan. 24, 2000 by Faron Sparkman in charge of Confederate Markers).

He married Ellender Roberts and children in 1870 Floyd County, KY census are as follows: Cindy (Sidney) (male), 10; John, 8; Abner (A.B.), 5; Nancy, 3; David, 1.

Abner (A.B.) Bryant, born Jan. 5, 1865, died Nov. 23, 1946, buried Newman Cemetery, Hi Hat, KY, married (1st) Rilda (Surilda) Caudill, daughter of Preston Caudill who also served in 13th Kentucky Cavalry. Rilda Caudill died sometime between February 1890 and October 1891. Unsure of place of burial. Children from this marriage: Salisbury Bryant, born July 2, 1885, died June 15, 1969; Ransom Bryant, born May 13, 1889, died Jan. 4, 1951; Lawrence Bryant, born Feb. 17, 1890, died June 4, 1962.

Abner (A.B.) Bryant married (2nd) Lindy Bryant. Ransom Bryant married Nancy Johnson. Daughter Nellie Bryant married Charlie Johnson in 1942, Pike County, KY. Son Jimmy Johnson was born 1943 Floyd County, KY.

DRURY LEWIS BURCHETT, was the son of Benjamin and Nancy Lewis Burchett. He enlisted in the Union Army on Aug. 6, 1853 at Louisa, KY. He served with the Union forces until Sept. 15, 1865. He became disabled due to being a blacksmith and while he was shoeing a mule he was kicked in the back. Lewis passed away June 9, 1882 at 56 years of age.

DRURY BURCHETT JR., son of Drury Lewis, served in the Kentucky Confederate Cavalry, Company F 10. He was a Prisoner Of War in Tennessee. He was paroled on April 28, 1865, the same day as his uncle George W. Burchett.

GEORGE W. BURCHETT, was the son of Benjamin and Nancy Lewis Burchett. He was born circa 1834 and died in 1870 at 36 years of age. He lived on Ivy Creek in Floyd County, KY and was married to Marry Hunt on Oct. 14, 1855. George W. was in Company F, 10th Reg. Kentucky Confederate Cavalry in the Civil War. He was a Prisoner Of War in Tennessee and was paroled April 28, 1865.

JOHN T. BURCHETT, son of Armstead and Elizabeth Butler Burchett, was born 1830 in Floyd County, KY. In April 1860 he moved to Whites Creek in Boyd County, KY. In October 1861 he enlisted in Company H, 14th Regiment Volunteers with the Union States Army. After the war he returned to Floyd County in November 1865. His wife was Patsy Mullins. Then later he married Catherine Lewis. They had four children.

RICHARD LANDRUM BURCHETT, son of Thomas and Millie Maynard Burchett, was born circa 1842. He enlisted in the Union Army, 39th Kentucky Infantry Oct. 11, 1862. He was discharged with the rank of Sergeant in April 1864. After the war, he lived in Mason County, IL for 10 years. He married Harriett Van Bibber. He applied for his pension in 1895 and began to draw his check of $28 each month thereafter.

THOMAS KAGER BURCHETT, son of Armstead Burchett, was born Feb. 1, 1840 in Floyd County, KY. He enlisted Oct. 28, 1861 in the 5th Reg. Kentucky Infantry R. Confederate States Army. Also, records show that Thomas R. was a Private in Troop A, 10th Reg. Kentucky Cavalry. He was captured in Cynthiana, KY June 14, 1864 and released or exchanged at Point Lee Kurt 1864. He married Feb. 19, 1865.

THOMAS CALHOUN, born in Perry County in 1821 to David Calhoun, II and Eda Ayers. He married Virginia Jane Musick, the daughter of Elijah Musick and Nancy Combs in Letcher County, KY on Dec. 24, 1948.

He served the Confederacy in Company A, 13th Kentucky Cavalry. He moved to Floyd County with his family and settled on Water Gap Road on Bull Creek, KY. Thomas is the ancestor of the Floyd County Calhouns. He is buried in the Campbell-Calhoun Cemetery on the right side of the hill at the mouth of Campbell Branch on Water Gap Road.

Their children were Rachel, Mary, Martha, Hiram "Hite," William, John "John Cat," Thomas Benton "Dode," Sarah Ann "Sallie," Lovana "Duck," Minerva and Samuel "Sam."

He is the ancestor of Seth and Noah Marcum of Bull Creek, KY. *Submitted by Karen Nelson Marcum.*

ANDREW JACKSON "JACK" CAUDILL, Private, born in 1844 at present day Melvin, Floyd County, KY, the son of Alfred Caudill and Drucilla Hammond. He enlisted in the Union Army in Company K, 39th Kentucky Volunteers on Nov. 6, 1862 and was mustered into service on Feb. 16, 1863.

After he was discharged he married Louisa Jane McCown on Feb. 17, 1866, daughter of William "Billy" McCown and Jemima Osborne. They were the parents of Martha Caudill, William Albert Caudill, Millard Caudill, James Jackson Caudill, Mary Caudill, Wilburn Caudill and Ida Caudill. On Feb. 26, 1913 Louisa Jane (McCown) Caudill died. Andrew Jackson then married Mary Ratliff. They were the parents of Johnny D. Caudill, Jane Caudill, Andy Caudill and Orbie.

Andrew Jackson Caudill

Jack Caudill, as he was called, died Oct. 18, 1922 on Tim Henson Hollow, Beaver, Floyd County, KY and oral history says he is buried in the Elliott-Reynolds Cemetery there. His granddaughter, Chloie (Caudill) Howell was with him when he died. This biography is respectfully submitted by two great-great-grandchildren: Jim Spencer, Martin, KY and Danny Tackett, Melvin, KY.

ALEXANDER CLARK was a Private in Company E of the 5th Kentucky Infantry of the CSA. He was born Sept. 14, 1839 and died Oct. 5, 1904. He was the son of Samuel Clark Sr. and Margaret Hayes who moved from Virginia to the area that is now the Dewey Dam area and purchased 10,000 acres.

He was the father of Minerva Nelson, daughter of Emmarita Nelson. His daughter Minerva, born in 1865 and died in 1950, married John Wallen. John was the son of Shelby Wallen (another CSA soldier) and Susannah Hale of Bull Creek.

Alexander married Elizabeth Peary and had four more children: John B., James, Rosa and Polly.

He in buried at Auxier, KY in the Auxier relocation cemetery. *Submitted by Karen Nelson Marcum.*

JOSEPH D. COOLEY, Sergeant Major, Company E, 5th Kentucky Confederate Infantry. Also served in the 10th Kentucky Cavalry. He enlisted Dec. 30, 1862 at Prestonsburg. Born in Virginia in 1837, son of Judge Davis and Eliza Jane Cooley.

He was a member of General John Hunt Morgan's "Last Kentucky Raid" and fought at the Battle of Cynthiana, June 12, 1864. Being Outspoken for the Confederate cause, the Cooley family and others fled Prestonsburg during Gen. James A. Garfield's occupational following the Battle of Middle Creek in January 1862. At the close of the war, he practiced law in Prestonsburg.

JAMES CRAGER, son of Michael Crager Jr. and Elizabeth Miller, was born in 1825 and died in 1910. James Crager married Louise Sexton in Letcher County, KY June 6, 1848. Their children: Ambross, born 1850; William H., born 1852; Rebecca, born 1853; Joseph, born 1858; Caroline, born 1868.

James Crager married Elizabeth Patton July 10, 1873 in Floyd County. Their children were George W. and Samuel P. (twins) born 1881, and James, born 1883.

James Crager, Private, enlisted Oct. 14, 1862 in Floyd County, KY in the 13th Kentucky Cavalry, Company F.

Private James Crager

The above Confederate monument was dedicated on July 1, 2006 at the "Old Herald Cemetery" on Cow Creek, Floyd County, KY.

GREENVILLE ROBERT DAVIDSON, born Dec. 8, 1842, the son of Samuel Patton Davidson Sr. and Judith Morgan Lackey. He served in the Fifth Kentucky Infantry, CSA in the Battles of Ivy Mountain and Middle Creek and after this unit was dissolved, he served in the 10th Kentucky Cavalry CSA, joining it as 2nd Lieutenant or Ensign on Sept. 23, 1862, Company A at Prestonsburg, KY; he was "Brevet Captain" after January 1865.

He was captured Dec. 20, 1862 and exchanged before June 30, 1863.

Greenville R. Davidson

He was hospitalized at White Sulphur Springs from March 28, 1864 until April 10, 1864. He would have served in two major campaigns in Northeastern Tennessee in 1863. In 1864 his unit served with Gen. John Hunt Morgan in the "Last Kentucky Raid," a disaster, but rallied to help defeat Union forces under Burbridge at Saltville, VA.

Following the war he married Laura Cooley on Nov. 17 1867 and had a family of one son and five daughters. In 1866 he was elected Colonel of State Militia; he served as Deputy Sheriff and Deputy Clerk in Floyd County and became Floyd County Clerk in September 1878 and served as County Clerk until his death on Nov. 20, 1907.

CHARLES WESLEY DINGUS, born Oct. 29, 1843, Scott County, VA and died Sept. 21, 1889, Alphoretta, Floyd County, KY. He married Oct. 26, 1865 in Floyd County, KY, to Nancy Jane Flanery, who was born in 1840, Floyd County, KY, and died 1906 at Hite, Floyd County, KY. Nancy Jane was the daughter of Isaac Flanery and Caroline Halbert, daughter of John Halbert and Elizabeth Farrow Booker. Charles also served as a Private in Company G, 32 Kentuck Infantry, Civil War 1862-63. He and Nancy Jane had eight children.

DAVID CROCKETT DINGUS, born Oct. 10, 1837 and died Aug. 13, 1864 of typhus fever at Montgomery County, Mt. Sterling, KY, while serving in Civil War, Company F, 39 Inf. He married Victoria J. Halbert, daughter of John Halbert and Elizabeth Booker, They had two children.

JAMES HENDERSON DINGUS was born on Sept. 21, 1833, in Scott County, VA, and died on April 4, 1902, at Alphoretta in Floyd County, KY. James married on May 6, 1855, in Floyd County to Sarah Belieu Halbert, daughter of John Halbert and Elizabeth Farrow Booker. Elizabeth was born on Oct. 1, 1834, and died on Nov. 27, 1919. James was a Corporal in the Civil War for the Union Army, Company F, 39th Kentucky Mounted Infantry. James and Sarah had 10 children, all born at the Forks of Beaver Creek at Alphoretta (Dinwood), KY.

SAMUEL P. DINGUS, born Aug. 21, 1835, Scott County, VA (will proved 1892), married March 8, 1860, Floyd County, KY to Frances Artie Flanery who was born 1843 in Floyd County, KY. She was the daughter of Isaac Flanery and Caroline Halbert, daughter of John Halbert and Elizabeth Farrow Booker. They had four children.

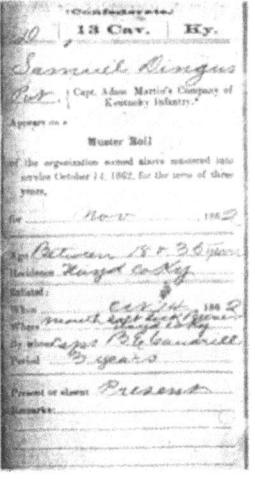

LARRY FLANERY was the son of Isaac and Carolina Halbert Flanery. He served in the Civil War.

ANDY "A.J. or UNCLE ANDY" FRAZIER, who almost three-quarters of a century ago carried General Lee's message ordering the famous charge at Gettysburg of General Pickett, is dead.

At the age of 96, "Uncle Andy" died peacefully at his home. He was thought to be Floyd County's oldest man and one of the last surviving veterans of the Confederacy in the county.

He died without learning the identity of the other courier who, with him, left General Lee's Headquarters at Gettysburg in July 1863 to carry the orders for Pickett's famous charge. "There were two of us, in case one got killed, and we both got through safely. I'd like to know who that other man was," he often said.

SAMUEL P. GARRETT, Private, born July 21, 1841, died Dec. 27, 1907, is buried on the Forks of Bull Creek Cemetery, Floyd County, KY. He was in Company E, 5th Kentucky Infantry CSA. He married Jane Scutchfield in June 1861 in Floyd County, KY. They had the following children: Millard, Bertah, Burnard, Seymore, Samuel P. Jr., Angeline, Charity and John P. Garrett.

ROBERT GEORGE, born in Floyd County, KY, June 12, 1830. He married Eliza Robinson in 1852, and they have a family of eight sons and daughters, born in the order named: Samuel G., Alexander M., Arminta A., Elizabeth, Thomas J., Macy J., William J. and Ara. The parents of both Mr. and Mrs. George are deceased.

When the war broke out in 1861 Robert enlisted at Louisa, December 10th of that year in Company K, 14th Kentucky Volunteer Infantry, 3rd Bde., 2nd Div., 23rd A.C., and with his command participated in numerous engagements, including Cracker's Neck, Paintsville, Puncheon or Half Mount, Middle Creek, KY, Dalton, Kingston, Altoona, New Hope Church, Peach Tree Creek, GA and many others. He served about six weeks on detailed duty as a guide to scouts and was discharged at Louisa, KY, Jan. 31, 1865. He had one brother, James II, who served in the same command and was killed before Atlanta, Aug. 11, 1864. Mrs. George had three brothers in the Army, John O., Thomas J. and Henry Robinson. Mr. George is a member of Auxier Post No. 73, GAR, is engaged in farming and lumbering, and his post office address is East Point, Johnson County, KY.

He is the great-grandfather of William H., Roger D., Jimmy D., O. David and Franklin Ray George. *From: Presidents, Soldiers, Statesmen, Vol. II by H.H. Hardesty, published in New York, Toledo, and Chicago, 1892 (from Floyd County, KY version).*

ISSAC GOBLE, 1st Lieutenant, was a veteran of the Civil War. He was also a medical doctor. He married Frances Emaline Hannah

who was the daughter of Samuel James Hannah and Frances Amelia Auxier.

Frances Amelia Auxier is a descendant of Revolutionary War soldier Samuel Auxier who is buried at Block House Bottom. Dr. Goble is buried at the mouth of Hyden Branch on RT 302 in Johnson County, KY. *Submitted by Karen Nelson Marcum, also a descendant of Samuel Auxier.*

WILLIAM KENAS GOODMAN, a Civil War soldier, is buried at the Forks of Bull Creek Cemetery. He was a Union Soldier of Company F, 39th Infantry, but there are four CSA soldier's buried there as well: William Hignite, Henry Clay Hubbard, Samuel P. Garrett and Henry Marshall.

There may have been more soldiers buried in unmarked graves as the four-lane highway took a large portion of the cemetery and many graves were relocated.

William Kenas Goodman was the son of Enoch Goodman and Susannah Hale, daughter of John and Sarah Mosley Hale). He was born in Hawkins County, TN May 10, 1834, but his family moved to Bull Creek in Floyd County, KY. He married Mary Wallen and they had the following children: Lourana, Susan, Emaline, Jefferson, Rueben Ann, Hiram Kenas, John B., Elizabeth, William and Catherine. *Submitted by Karen Nelson Marcum and Kathy Hubbard Hanlon.*

JOSEPH GRAY, 5th Sergeant, born Feb. 20, 1832 and died June 15, 1908. He served with Company E, 5th Kentucky Infantry in the Civil War. *Submitted by Karen N. Marcum.*

JEREMIAH HACKWORTH, Private, Company I of the 14th Kentucky Infantry. He was inducted at Louisa, KY, on Dec. 10, 1861 and discharged at Louisa, KY, on Jan. 31, 1865. He was military scout and served in the campaigns at Ivy Mountain, Middle Creek, Puncheon Creek, KY and all of Atlanta, GA campaigns. He was sick during the war and spent considerable time in the hospital.

Born on May 2, 1840 in Floyd County, KY and was the son of Thomas and Lucretia Spradlin Hackworth. On May 5, 1866 he married Clarinda Conley. He died in Magoffin County, KY on Nov. 26, 1881, he was 41. He was buried in Doe Miller Cemetery, Magoffin County, KY.

JESSIE HACKWORTH, Private, Company F & D of the 14th Kentucky Infantry. He was inducted at Louisa, KY on Aug. 30, 1863 and discharged at Louisville, KY on Sept. 15, 1865. He served in the following campaigns: Ivy Mountain, Middle Creek, Puncheon Creek, KY and all of Atlanta, GA campaigns. He was born on May 2, 1840 in Floyd County, KY and was the son of Thomas and Lucretia Spradlin Hackworth. He was brother to Jeremiah Hackworth who served in the 14th Kentucky also.

OWEN HALL, Private, born Dec. 2, 1833 on Mud Creek, Floyd County, KY, the son of Jarvey Hall and Elizabeth Elliott. He enlisted in the Union Army in Company B, 39th Kentucky Volunteers on Nov. 6, 1862. The 39th Kentucky Infantry was raised by Col. John Dils from the counties along the Big Sandy River, and organized in camp at Peach Orchard, Lawrence County, KY, when it was mustered into service on Feb. 16, 1863.

Although the 39th did not participate in any of the Civil War's major battles, it saw much service in combating the numerous guerrilla bands, as well as regular Confederate forces in Floyd, Pike, Carter, Magoffin, Johnson, Montgomery, Harrison and Lawrence counties in Kentucky, and in Southwest Virginia and Eastern Tennessee.

After he was discharged on Sept. 15, 1865, he returned to his home and farm on Frasures Creek on Left Beaver Creek, Floyd County, KY. Prior to the war Owen married Judith Stumbo, daughter of Frederick Stambaugh and Nancy Thornsberry. They were the parents of

Mary E. Hall, Marinda Jane Hall, William Preston Hall, Melvina Hall, Catherine Hall, John A. Hall, Greenbury Hall, James Emory "Polk" Hall, Floyd Hall, Beldory "Belle" Hall and Willard Scott Hall. Owen died on Jan. 3, 1913 on Frasures Creek, McDowell, KY and is buried in the Greenbury Hall Cemetery.

W.J. "BOLEN BILL" HALL,

Captain, was typical of the mountain patriarchs of the feud torn days of the 1880s who refused to become involved in clan differences and remained neutral to become a mainstay of society. His steadfast support of the law and the influence of his strong personality prevented the reign of anarchy in a region.

He was born May 11, 1826, a son of William J. "Gunsmith Billy" Hall, and was reared to manhood at Deane, KY, on Rockhouse Creek, now Letcher County. He married Florence Jones, July 14, 1850 at the mouth of Jones Fork, near the present Lackey. The marriage was solemnized by a mountain minister under the spreading branches of a giant sycamore. His eldest son, Marion Hall, became the first Knott County superintendent of schools.

Building a home on Upper Right Beaver Creek, then Floyd, now Knott County, he began the acquisition of land of which he was possessed of over 3,000 acres late in life. While engaged primarily in farming at first, he turned to storekeeping. His wagon trains were almost continually on the road bringing goods from London, Whitehorse and Prestonsburg.

During the Civil War he served as Captain of Company E, 13th Cavalry Regiment, CSA and was noted for his insistence that his troops refrain from foraging. While in the service guerrillas overran his section and he reminisced in later years that his wife buried food in the garden and sowed lettuce beds over it to cover the hiding place.

Following the Civil War he attempted to bring peace between the feudists of the area as he was a relative of both sides. He was serving as Floyd County Assessor when Knott County was formed. He died July 28, 1912, a respected leader of a wide section.

WILLIAM RILEY HALL JR.

was born on the Long Fork of Shelby, Pike County, KY, on March 13, 1824, a son of William Riley Hall Sr. and Nancy Higgins, who migrated to Kentucky from their homes in the state of North Carolina. He passed away on Feb. 24, 1911, on Little Paint Creek, near Prestonsburg, Floyd County, KY.

On May 27, 1842, in Pike County, KY, he married Lucinda "Sinda" Cook, a daughter of James Cook and Rebecca Hannah Tackett, by the Rev. William "Billy" Tackett, grandfather of the bride.

He enlisted in the service of the Confederate States Army on March 24, 1863, as a member of Company C, 10th Kentucky Cavalry, under the command of Capt. Anderson Moore. The Commander of the 10th Kentucky Cavalry was Col. George R. Diamond. His unit served in Eastern Kentucky and Southwest Virginia, and at the Battle of Saltville, VA, came under direct fire from Union units composed of former slaves. The 10th Kentucky Cavalry was mustered out of active service in April and May 1865, following the surrender of Confederate General Robert E. Lee.

ROBERT M. HAYWOOD,

Private, Company E, 5th Kentucky Infantry, CSA, born 1837, died about 1895, was the son of Lewis Haywood and Elizabeth Higgins.

Joe Skeens and his friends set the CSA stone on the Langley/Fitzpatrick Cemetery on the Old Middle Creek Rd.

Robert and Sarah (Baldridge) Haywood. (Courtesy of Joe Skeens)

He married Sarah Jane Baldridge, born about 1828, the daughter of Robert Baldridge, born 1814, and Elenore Hicks, daughter of Charley Hicks and Rebecca Gibson. *Submitted by Karen Nelson Marcum.*

JAMES H. HEREFORD JR.,

10th Mounted Kentucky Confederate Infantry, born in 1841, son of Dr. James H. and Meriba Ratliff Hereford. He enlisted in the Confederate Army in May 1861 at Prestonsburg.

He served under Colonel Andrew Jackson May and was captured at the Battle of Ivy Mountain in 1861. He was paroled in Pikeville, KY and returned to Prestonsburg and rejoined his unit. The 10th Kentucky participated in battles and skirmishes through out Eastern Kentucky, Western Virginia and East Tennessee.

After the war, James married Mary Florence May, daughter of Samuel May. They had six children: Burr, George, James III, Josephine, Sam and Thomas. He practiced law in Prestonsburg. He died in 1898 and is buried beside his wife in the Hereford cemetery at Cliff, KY.

Following the war, he wrote several publications protesting the policies of the Federal Government toward the former Confederate and border states. *Submitted by David R. Hereford.*

JOHN WESLEY HEROLD,

2nd Lieutenant, son of James Herold and Elizabeth Woods, was born 1833 and died 1887. He is buried on the "Old Herald Cemetery" alongside his second wife, Charity Hackworth, who died 1921. John Wesley Herold's first wife was Arimenta Burchett who died in 1855. They had one son, Joseph M. Herold, who married Mahala C. May.

The children of James Wesley and Charity Hackworth were James Nick Herold, a Methodist minister, who married Nancy May; Mary A. Herold, who married James L. Clark; twins, Ella Herold who married William Clark and Emma Herold who married Reuben Taylor.

John Wesley, a Floyd County school teacher, enlisted Oct. 28, 1861 in the 5th Regiment, Kentucky Mounted Infantry, Company E, Confederate States Army at Prestonsburg along with his brother William Oney Herold and brother-in-law, David Y. Kendrick.

The above Confederate monuments were dedicated on July 1, 2006 at the "Old Herald Cemetery" on Cow Creek, Floyd County, KY.

WILLIAM ONEY HEROLD,

Private, son of James Herold and Elizabeth Woods, was born 1842 and died 1878. He married Margaret Stanley in 1867. Their children: Alonzo Herold; Leottie Herold married Drewy "Flem" Burchett (children, Amma and Ollie); James T. "Jim Tom" Herold married Levatie Nesbitt (children: Mintie, Sophia, Laura Belle and Lonnie); Burris W. Herold married Fannie Williamson

(children: Taylor, Lovata Helen and Silivia); William O. Herold married Octavia Nesbitt (children: Bassil, William, Flossie, Bob and Ackman "A.J."

William Oney Herold enlisted Oct. 28,

1861 in the 5th Regiment Kentucky Mounted Infantry, Company E, Confederate States Army at Prestonsburg, KY, along with his brother, John Wesley Herold and brother-in-law, David Y. Kendrick.

The above Confederate monuments were dedicated on July 1, 2006 at the "Old Herald Cemetery" on Cow Creek, Floyd County, KY.

WILLIAM HIGNITE, Private, is buried on the Forks of Bull Creek Cemetery along with three other CSA soldiers and one Union soldier. William was born between 1818-22 in Knox County, KY to Moses and Phoebe Hammons Hignite. (Phoebe descends from Peter Hammons, a Revolutionary War soldier).

He married Margaret Stewart, and they lived in Floyd County, KY with the following children: Thomas Jefferson, Levi, Rosana, Joseph, Mariah, William Perry, and Greenbery Hignite.

He was in Company E, 5th Kentucky Mounted Infantry. He enlisted Oct. 26, 1861 and is listed as Distinguished Service in the Confederacy. He served Kentucky in Unit Number 1899. He mustered out Company E, Infantry Regiment Kentucky on Oct. 20, 1862.

He is the ancestor of Seth and Noah Marcum of Bull Creek, KY. *Submitted by Karen Nelson Marcum and Kathy Hubbard Hanlon.*

HENRY CLAY HUBBARD, Sergeant, served with Company A, 10th Kentucky Cavalry in Civil War. He is buried at Forks of Bull Creek Cemetery.

The re-enactment ceremony represented both Confederate and Union soldiers.

WILLIAM M. HUBBARD JR., a Floyd County resident, was a soldier during the Civil War, in Diamond's 10th Kentucky Cavalry (The Yankee Chasers), Company A. William was born in Clay County, KY in the year 1841, a son of William M. Hubbard Sr. and Frances "Fanny" Jackson. William was married on March 18, 1866, at Prestonsburg, to Sarah "Sallie" Hammons, a daughter of James and Stacy Broughton Hammons.

Seated in front, l-r: William Hubbard, Sarah "Sallie" Hammons Hubbard, grandson Mallory Hubbard, daughter-in-law, Lula Kendrick Hubbard holding Clyde Hubbard (infant). William's two children are standing in back, Mary Alice Hubbard Burchett and Rev. Malcom Hubbard.

Burial site of William Hubbard Jr. at Sugar Loaf. (Photo by Karen Nelson Marcum.)

William enlisted to serve in the Confederate Army on Sept. 13, 1862 at Prestonsburg. His brother, Henry Clay Hubbard, had enlisted on Sept. 10, 1862. Both brothers served in Company A, of Diamond's Yankee Chasers, under Colonels George R. Diamond, Andrew J. May, Edwin Trimble, and Major William R. Lee. Diamond's 10 Kentucky Cavalry took part in a fight at Blue Springs on Aug. 23, 1864, with Confederate General John H. Morgan's old brigade under Colonel Giltner. The Confederates fought for the next several months until on Sept. 4, 1864, at Greeneville, General John Hunt Morgan, CSA, was surprised and killed.

The battles during this time were bloody and a great number of Confederate casualties occurred. William was shot in the right arm, and taken as a POW, in a battle at Blue Springs, Greene County, TN on Aug. 24, 1864. His name appears on the roll of prisoners at Knoxville, TN on Sept. 4, 1864. William was sent to Chattanooga, TN on Sept. 13, 1864 and transferred to Rough and Ready, Georgia sometime between Sept. 19-22, 1864, by order of Maj. Gen. W.T. Sherman, Commander, Military Division, where William was to be exchanged for Union soldiers.

Per official records, William was exchanged for Union soldiers; however, per William's pension application, he remarks that he escaped and was never exchanged. William's statement is supported as an Oath of Allegiance to the United States was never signed by William and he continued to serve with his regiment. He was present with his regiment in Christianburg, VA, until Lee's surrender in 1865. William returned to Prestonsburg when his regiment disbanded at Appomatox in April 1865. He remained in Prestonsburg for the remainder of his life.

William and Sarah were the parents of six children: Robert Lee (died young), Julia B. (married William Green Burchett), Rev. Malcom Hubbard (married Lula Kendrick), Mary Alice (married Floyd W Burchett), Minnie M. (married Joseph Anson Hinchman) and Elizabeth (married Albert O. Burchett). William died Nov. 1, 1924 in Floyd County, KY and is buried in the Hubbard-Burchett Family Cemetery on Rt. 1428, across from Goble Lumber Co., three miles south of Prestonsburg, KY.

JAMES L. JERVIS, 5th Sergeant, in the 13th Kentucky Cavalry, Company E for the CSA. He was born Dec. 13, 1821 and died Feb. 28, 1904. He is buried on the Jervis Cemetery in the German Bridge area off RT 194. *Submitted by Karen N. Marcum.*

WILLIAM JUSTICE, Private, born 1828, was in Company C of the 39th Kentucky Infantry in the Civil War. He married Mary Ann Blackburn, born 1818, died 1898, who was the daughter of Hudson Blackburn and Mary Ann Romans. He is buried at the mouth of Buffalo Creek of Johns Creek on the Wheatfield Cemetery. *Submitted by Karen N. Marcum.*

DAVID Y. KENDRICK, Private, son of George and Edith Kendrick, born 1821 Tazewell, VA, died and buried in the "Old Herald Cemetery." He married Sophia Herald, daughter of James and Elizabeth Herald.

Their children: Dr. James Wesley Kendrick married Margaret Bannon, six children, married second, Ruthie Heizer, had two children; Dr. George Tivis

Kendrick married Dicie May, 11 children; Robert "Bob" Kendrick married Nancy Lockheart, seven children; Anna Kendrick married W.H. Vest, seven children; Molly Kendrick married George McGuire, seven children; Liz Kendrick married Benjamin Burgy; William Kendrick married Parthena Sturgill; Theodosia "Dosh" Kendrick married Melvin Morrison, nine children then Hiram Taylor, one son; Malcolm Kendrick married Claudia Vaughn, five children.

David Y. Kendrick, Private, enlisted Oct. 28, 1861 in the 5th Regiment, Kentucky Mounted Infantry, Company E, Confederate States Army at Prestonsburg, KY.

The Confederate Monument was dedicated July 1, 2006, on the "Old Herald Cemetery" Cow Creek, Floyd County.

JAMES LAFERTY, was born 1840 in Grundy, VA to William Laferty and Malinda Combs.

He was a Sergeant in Company A of the 10th Kentucky Cavalry of the CSA. He returned to Bull Creek in Floyd County and married Sarah Ann Bingham who was born in 1846 in Knott County to Joshua Grier Bingham and Mariah Hammons as her family was on their way to Floyd County from Stinking Creek in Harlan County. James Laferty lived out his life on Bull Creek where he was a minister.

His grave has been relocated from Bull Creek to the Richmond Cemetery in Prestonsburg, KY. *Submitted by Karen N. Marcum.*

HENRY MARSHALL, Private, is buried on the forks of Bull Creek Cemetery, Floyd County, KY.

He enlisted in the Confederacy Oct. 28, 1861 and is listed as Distinguished Service.

He served Kentucky in Unit Number 1899. He enlisted in Company E, 5th Infantry Regiment, Kentucky. *Submitted by Karen Nelson Marcum and Kathy Hubbard Hanlon.*

ADAM MARTIN, Captain, son of John and Anna Gearheart Martin, was born in 1838 at Wayland, KY. He joined the Confederate Army in October of 1862 and recruited a company of men to form a Cavalry Unit at Salt Lick on Right Beaver Creek in Floyd County.

He was Commissioned Captain of the company, whose base of operations included Eastern Kentucky, Southwest Virginia, and Eastern Tennessee. Capt. Martin commanded his Unit, designated Company F 13th Kentucky Cavalry, until the fall of 1864 when he was listed as Missing in Action during Gen. John Hunt Morgan's last Kentucky raid. It was said that he was wounded in this raid and was not able to return to his unit before the war ended.

Adam Martin married Emaline Martin in 1865 and had four children: James, Julie, Zella and Leck. After Emaline's death, he married Anna Harris and had one daughter, Artie. Capt. Ad, as he was known after the war, ran a large General Store at Wayland until his death in 1905. He is buried in the John Martin Cemetery at Wayland, KY.

JAMES MARTIN, Company F., 13th Kentucky Cavalry, Confederate States of America, born Jan. 12, 1844, Drift, Floyd, KY, was the son of Simpson Martin, born March 1820, and Elizabeth Turner, born March 4, 1814, Patrick County, VA. James married Rosimond Frazier, born July 9, 1845, Big Mud Creek, Floyd, KY on Jan. 25, 1869, Floyd County, KY. James and Rosimond "Rose" were the parents of Evan, born 1869; Creed, born 1871; Judy, born 1872; Annie, born 1874; Kenas Frazier, born 1876; Noah, born 1877; Samuel, born 1879; Elizabeth, born 1881; Frances, born 1883; Sarah, born 1886; and Floyd, born 1888.

James, or Uncle Jim as he was known, died Dec. 1, 1927 at Minnie, KY, of pneumonia after a six weeks illness. He was 83 years old and one of Floyd County's most prominent citizens. He was living with his son, Kenas "K.F." where he had been confined to his room with an infected foot.

Though Jim, a prominent farmer, lived modestly, he was at the time of his death, the possessor of a considerable fortune, which was gathered by dint of hard work and business acumen. His death marked the passing of one of the county's most quaint and best-known characters. *Submitted by Mary Rose Martin.*

DAVID MAY, Captain, Company D, 10th Kentucky Confederate Cavalry. Enlisted Jan. 1, 1863 in Pike County. Born Feb. 13, 1828, son of Thomas and Dorcas Patton May. He served with Gen. John Hunt Morgan and was killed at the Battle of Cynthiana, June 12, 1864. He is buried in the Battle Grove Cemetery, Cynthiana, KY. A merchant and Kentucky State Representative, he was expelled for "Rebel Sympathies" on Aug. 29, 1862.

SOLOMON MAY, Company D, 10th Kentucky Confederate Cavalry, enlisted June 1, 1863 at Camp Bowen, VA. Also served in the 4th Virginia State Line. Born in 1844 in Prestonsburg, son of Samuel and Mary Osborne May. He served with Gen. John Hunt Morgan and was killed at the Battle of Mt. Sterling, June 9, 1864. Family members say his body must have been buried in Mt. Sterling as it was never brought back to Prestonsburg.

WILLIAM MCGUIRE, a Union soldier, was the son of Issac and Delilah Moore McGuire of the Right Fork of Bull Creek. He was with Company F, 39th Infantry Regiment, Kentucky.

He came through the Forks of Bull Creek with a troop of Union soldiers and saw John Wallen. John was a young boy and had been sent to get supplies. The soldiers took John's supplies. John later told that one of the soldiers asked him what his name was. John said that he looked up and all he saw was a long pair of boots and a big horse. John told the soldier that he was John Wallen. The soldier told him that he was Will McGuire and lived down the road from him. Will made the other soldiers return little John Wallen's supplies and sent him on home.

William McGuire was wounded June 12, 1864 at Cynthiana, KY and died of wounds on June 15, 1864. His father heard that he was dead and went to Cynthiana along with his friend Parmer Scutchfield to bring back William's body. William must have already been buried when they reached Cynthia as they returned without his body. *Submitted by Karen Nelson Marcum and Clara Lucille Garrett.*

THOMAS MCCULAH MUSIC, Civil War, Company A, 39th Regiment Kentucky Infantry, was born in Wise County, VA in 1824 and died March 9, 1883. Russell, Zellard, Gordon, Claude, Emma Leah, Montie and Jackie David Rice are and were proud to be the great-grandchildren of Thomas McCulah Music.

ABRAHAM MUSICK, Private, for the CSA in Company K, 13th Kentucky Cavalry. He was born in 1815 and died in 1893. He is buried at the Auxier Relocation Cemetery in Auxier, KY. His family originally came from Russell County, VA. The wife of Thomas Calhoun, another CSA veteran, was Virginia Jane Musick and was part of this same Musick family. *Submitted by Karen Nelson Marcum.*

GEORGE WASHINGTON MUSICK, Private, Company A, 39th Regiment Kentucky Infantry, Civil War. He mustered in at Peach Orchard, KY, Oct. 11, 1862 for three years of service. On Feb. 28, 1863 he was absent for pay due to being a Prisoner Of War. Once he was paroled he continued with his service until he mustered out in Louisville, KY on Sept. 15, 1865.

With a soldier's pay of $42.78 and a bounty pay of $75.00 he returned to Floyd County. He was born 1810 in Washington, VA. He first married Nancy Hawks, then married Rachel K. Minix. He is buried on Left Fork of Little Paint Creek.

JACOB NELSON, Private, 39th Kentucky Volunteer Infantry, son of George and Nancy Tussey Nelson was born Dec. 25, 1840 in Hancock County, TN. He married Barbara Ellen Wadkins Feb. 5, 1860 at Middle Creek, Floyd County, KY. She was the daughter of Benedict Wadkins Jr. and Elizabeth Poe.

Jacob enlisted for the Civil War at Peach Orchard, Lawrence County, KY Nov. 13, 1862, assigned to the 39th Kentucky Infantry. Soldier mustered out Sept. 15, 1865 at Louisville, KY. Jacob lost most of his eyesight in the war.

Jacob Nelson died Jan. 23, 1916 at Nonchalanta, Greenup County, KY. He along with his wife Barbara, parents George and Nancy Tussey Nelson are buried at Shells Fork (Lawhorn) Cemetery, R#2 Greenup County, KY. *Information from Minnie Nelson Anderson and submitted by Karen Nelson Marcum.*

MATHIAS "MACK" OSBORNE, Private, a Civil War veteran having served in Company F, 22nd North Carolina Infantry, CSA.

CSA stone was set by Joe Skeens and friends.

Mathias Osborne and wife Kate Price are on horses at the rear of wagon. McDonald Osborne in the wagon is the son of Greenville Osborne and Julia Haywood who are standing beside the wagon. Sarah Jane Baldridge Haywood is holding her grandchild. Robert M. Haywood in on the horse beside the wagon. (Photo courtesy of Joe Skeens.)

He was born Nov. 24, 1836, died Jan. 19, 1914 and buried at the Langley/Fitzpatrick Cemetery on the Old Middle Creek Rd. *Submitted by Karen Nelson Marcum.*

AMOS REED, Private, born Sept. 6, 1831 in Floyd County, VA, the son of Humphrey Reed and Nancy Elizabeth Reed. He enlisted in Company E, 64th Virginia Infantry and the 21st Battalion, Virginia Infantry.

Amos married Permelia "Milley" Chafin, born Sept. 4, 1830, on May 2, 1854 in Floyd County, VA. They were the parents of Sylvester "Sigler" Reed, Charles Dillard Reed, Calihill Texas "Teck" Reed, Amos Lee Reed, Rosencrantz Reed and Albert Douglas Reed. Permelia died in about 1870 in Floyd County, VA. Amos then married Virginia Jane (Ross) Duncan, born Jan. 1, 1841, a widow, on April 18, 1871 in Floyd County, VA before migrating to Floyd County, KY. They were the parents of Andrew J. Reed, Doctor B. Reed, Woodson Reed, Jack Humphrey Reed, and Joseph Reed. Virginia Jane Ross was first married to a Duncan and they had one son who migrated with them to Hueysville, Floyd County, KY, his name was Samuel Henry Duncan.

Amos died on Sept. 30, 1918 and Virginia died on Dec. 26, 1921. They are buried at Hueysville, KY.

SAMUEL S.K. RICE, Civil War, Company I, 14 Kentucky Infantry, was born May 17, 1825 and died March 17, 1880.

His gravesite is located on "K" Fork Upper Twin Branch of Jenny's Creek, Johnson County, KY

Russel Rice in 1983 at the gravesite of his great-grandfather, Samuel S.K. Rice.

BENJAMIN F. RICHMOND, 2nd Lieutenant, Company B, 10th Kentucky Confederate Cavalry, commissioned May 1, 1863 at Big Stone Gap, VA. Born in 1841 the son of William Richmond Prestonsburg. At the end of the war he was associated with his brother Issac in the mercantile business.

ARCHIBALD SCALF, son of Britton and Tabitha Couch Scalf, was born Dec. 19, 1832. He enlisted Oct. 26, 1861 Company E, 5th Kentucky Infantry at Prestonsburg, KY for 12 months. They mustered out of Hazel Green, KY on Oct. 20, 1862. He re-enlisted in Company A, 5th Kentucky Mounted Infantry.

He was captured in Floyd County on July 8, 1865 and was transferred to Camp Chase, OH on July 20, 1862. He was later transferred to Camp Douglas, IL on Aug. 24, 1863 then released on May 15, 1865. Archibald received Kentucky Confederate Pension #1179. He married Sarah Ann Sellards on Sept. 19, 1852 in Floyd County. He passed away Oct. 22, 1922 he and Sarah are buried at the Government Relocation Cemetery at Auxier, KY.

HEZEKIAH SCALF, son of Britton Scalf and Tabitha Couch Scalf, was born on Jan. 30, 1841. He enlisted in Company E, 5th Kentucky Infantry at Prestonsburg, KY for 12 months on Oct. 26, 1861. Mustered out on Oct. 20, 1892. Kentucky Confederate Pension #4266. Buried at Scalf Cemetery, on Buffalo Creek Endicott, KY.

JONATHAN SKEANS, served with the Company H, Kentucky 14 Infantry during the Civil War.

JOSEPH SKEENS, Private, born 1803, died June 6, 1862 lived in Floyd County, KY. He was in Company K, 14th Kentucky Infantry of the Civil War and was the son of Jonathan Rees Skeens and Elizabeth Sergent.

He married Juliana Rasnake, born 1814, died 1858, daughter of Jacob Rasnake Jr. and Judith Finney. He was the ggg-grandfather of Joe R. Skeens of Prestonsburg, KY and is buried on the Langley/ Fitzpatrick Cemetery on the Old Middle Creek Rd, RT 114. *Info from Joe R. Skeens and submitted by Karen N. Marcum.*

His stone was set by Joe R. Skeens.

PRESTON TOLIVER SPENCER, 1st Sergeant, was born on June 17, 1846 in Patrick County, VA. He was the son of Martin Simpson

Spencer and Mary Tuggle. He enlisted in Company I, 5th Battalion, Virginia Reserves CSA on June 17, 1864 at the age of 18. He served until the end of the war. His company was involved in protecting the railroads and got caught up in the Siege of Petersburg.

Preston Toliver Spencer (From the collection of Jim Spencer.)

In 1867 he left his home in Virginia and moved to Floyd County, KY. On Jan. 1, 1874 he married Nancy Turner, daughter of John Burk(e) Turner and Mary Ann Martin. They had 11 children: Mary, Martha, Martin, Melvina, Sallie, Alexander Lackey, Emma "Emily," John Stout, Julia Anna "Cula," Robert Lee and Rosha Spencer.

He was a farmer and for a period of time a contract mail carrier. His passion was his church. He was Clerk of the Old Beaver Regular Baptist Church at Minnie, KY for 50 years. His son A.L. Spencer was Clerk of the Bethel Old Regular Baptist Church for 49 years. On Oct. 9, 1935 he stepped into the path a car while he was walking to the Post Office at Drift, KY and was killed. He was 89 years old.

MATTHEW TACKETT, Private, CSA, born March 14, 1840, son of William "Bucky" Tackett and Sarah (Rebecca) Caudill. He enlisted in September 1862 and served with Company E, 10th Regiment Kentucky Infantry under Archidas Hammonds and Colonial Ben Caudill. Matthew was at home when the Civil War ended, he returned to Louisa where he was discharged. He was paroled just before the war ended in Letcher County and took the Oath of Allegiance in order to have his citizenship restored.

Matthew married Lucinda Johnson on Dec. 10, 1860 at the house of his dad in Pike County. It was witnessed by Lucinda's dad Harvey and Mathew's brother Enoch. After Mathew returned to his home in Burk Branch (now Tackett Hollow), he continued farming. Mathew and Lucinda raised 12 children in a two-story log house on this farm.

The nearest Post Office was at Rail; this place is now known as Weeksbury. In the 1890s Mathew patented several tracts of land. He later sold his land grants to J.C.C. Mayo. Matthew passed away April 1, 1929, he was 89 years old and was buried on the point above his home at Melvin, KY.

HIRAM TAYLOR, Private, son of William and Nancy Taylor, was born in October 1844. Hiram enlisted in the Confederate States Army, Company A, 34th Battalion, Virginia Calvary on Dec. 11, 1861 at the Forks of Middle Creek (now the National Battlefield of Middle Creek) at age 17 years.

He served under Brigadier General Humphrey Marshall and Colonel Vincent Witcher. The 34th Battalion disbanded in Bristol, TN in April 1865. Hiram surrendered at Louisa, KY in May 1865.

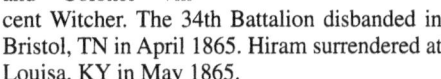

Hiram married Clarinda Clark in 1865. They had one son Reuben Taylor. Clarinda died in 1908. Hiram married Dosh Kendrick Morrison, a widow. They had one son, Alvin Taylor, whose living children are Emma Lou Martin, Patty Greer, Judy Childers and Butch Taylor.

Uncle High died Nov. 11, 1926 at home in Woods, Floyd County. His Confederate monument was dedicated April 26, 2003 by the Lt. Col. Vincent Witcher Camp of Grundy, VA at the Clark Cemetery on Buffalo Creek.

JOHN JEFFERSON VAUGHAN, Private, 10th Kentucky Cavalry, CSA, at the age of 20, joined the 3rd Kentucky Cavalry, which was incorporated into the 10th Kentucky Confederate Cavalry. John was the son of Patrick and Susannah Hatfield Vaughan, natives of Virginia and early settlers in Floyd County, KY. John was raised on the family homestead located along the banks of the Big Sandy River on State Route 321 below Spradlin Branch about two miles from Prestonsburg.

John Jefferson Vaughn and Cynthia Alice Hill Vaughn, wife of John J. Vaughn.

While visiting his future wife, Cynthia Alice Hill, who lived near John's parents, he was taken prisoner by Union authorities and charged with being a "Confederate Officer." He was sent to Camp Chase, a Confederate POW-processing camp located in Columbus, OH. From Camp Chase, John was transferred to the newly constructed Johnson Island POW camp built to house Confederate officers. The camp was located in Lake Erie about a mile off shore from Sandusky, OH.

As the war progressed the Johnson Island compound became more crowded and John and a number of other prisoners were transferred to Point Lookout POW Camp at Point Lookout, MD. The camp was located south of Washington, D.C. near the Chesapeake Bay. While at Point Lookout, John was again slated to be transferred to Camp Delaware POW Camp that was located on an Island in the Delaware River. Before this transfer was made, John was released under the terms of a Presidential proclamation and was allowed to return home.

John's journey home from the Point Lookout POW Camp led him through Louisa, KY. It was while visiting relatives and awaiting a ride by boat up Big Sandy River that he was taken into custody by Union Army personnel. The Union Army Provost Marshall at Louisa felt John's release papers were not "genuine and ordered John be held in confinement until written verification was received from the Adjutant of the Point Lookout POW Camp that John's papers were "genuine." After several days, Captain Watterman received a letter from Capt. J.D. Powers, Adjutant at Point Lookout that John's release papers were official. John was then released from confinement and continued his journey home.

Soon after returning home John married Cynthia Hill. Cynthia was from Johnson County and the daughter of James William Hill and Mahala George Hill. John and Cynthia remained on the Patrick Vaughan Homestead and had eight children. John died Oct. 30, 1902. After John's death, Cynthia moved to Oklahoma to live with her son Patrick. Cynthia died while visiting relatives in Prestonsburg. John and Cynthia are buried in the Vaughan Cemetery on the Vaughan homestead on Route 321 about two miles North of Prestonsburg.

SHELBY WALLEN, Private, was born in Hawkins County, TN in 1832. He was the son of John Wallen and Mary Neal. He moved to the Right Fork of Bull Creek, Floyd County, KY and was married on Nov. 1, 1851 to Susannah Hale, daughter of James Hale and Jane Sanders. He fought in the Civil War.

His gggggggg-grandsons, Seth and Noah Marcum located his grave and are standing by his stone.

A veteran of the Vietnam War, Joe Skeens and his friend, just set a new stone for Shelby. I can't even imagine how they got the new Veteran's Stone to Shelby Wallen's Cemetery as it is a long distance up a hollow and then up a hill.

Shelby had the following children: James B. Wallen married Amanda Baldridge, Jasper Wallen married Sarah Flint, Newton Perry Wallen married Caroline McFarland and then Nancy Jane Smith, John Wallen married Minerva Nelson (d/o Emmarita Nelson and Alexander Clark), William Wallen, Martin Wallen married Martha Dollarhide, Mary Jane "Mollie" Wallen married William Hall, Shelby "Banks" Wallen married Rebecca Belle Gearheart, Susan "Dollie" Eallen married Hiram Goodman, Joseph Wallen married Mary Belle Calhoun (d/o Hiram Calhoun).

JOHN FONTAINE "FOUNT" WARRICK/WARRIX,

Private, served in Company D, 13 Kentucky Cavalry, CSA, in the Civil War. He was born in May between 1830-32 in Virginia. He moved to Pike County with his second wife and children. The first wife died, and he later married Lucille "Lucy" Anderson, daughter of John Ruben Anderson and Lucy Burks from Scott County, VA. The Andersons had moved to Pike County, KY as well and lived close to the Warrix family.

John Fontaine and Lucille (Anderson) Warrick/Warrix.

John married Lucy in Letcher County, KY in 1863. She already had a 4-year-old son, Solomon Mullins (son of Sherrod Mullins, a Union soldier). John Warrix was in the Confederate Army.

After the war was over, the Warrix's moved to the Right Fork of Bull Creek where a hollow is now named for him. He and Lucy raised the children they had prior to their marriage as well as several of their own. He is buried in the McGuire Cemetery on the Right Fork of Bull Creek and his Civil War monument is in the Wallen Cemetery on the Right Fork of Bull Creek as that is where one of his descendants asked that it be put. *Submitted by Karen Nelson Marcum.*

John Warrix (Photo courtesy of Clara Lucille Garrett).

AMBROSE WHITE,

born March 17, 1837 in Ash County, North Carolina. He was a soldier, physician and faithful Christian.

Ambrose was drafted into the service of the Confederate Army against his will. when he got an opportunity, he deserted, and voluntarily joined the Union Army at Knoxville, TN. He was elected fifer of his regiment He kept the fife as long as he lived and played at many gatherings. In February, 1865, he entered the hospital at Knoxville with the measles. After a long illness and not able for duty, he served as a nurse. He began to study medicine under the assistance of the Army physicians.

He married Joanna Pauline Goforth of Wilkes County, North Carolina on October 20, 1866. They had nine children, one boy and eight girls. They were members of the Stony Fork Church in Wilkes County, NC and later of Samaria Church. Brother Ambrose served as a deacon and clergy of this church for several years. Pauline died June 17, 1917 and Ambrose died Oct. 20, 1929 in Floyd County, KY.

HIRAM WILLS,

Corporal, born March 22, 1822 in Grayson County, VA, was the son of William "Joe" Wills and Sarah Combs. He married Catherine Massey, the daughter of William Massey and Martha "Mattie" Lafferty on March 30, 1854 in what is now Raleigh County, WV.

Hiram Wills and Catherine Massey Wills.

Hiram served in the Union Army as a Corporal in the 7th West Virginia Cavalry. He mustered out on Aug. 1, 1865 after fighting in some major battles.

He moved his family to Water Gap, KY on Bull Creek after the war and is the ancestor of the Wills family in Floyd County. Hiram died Jan. 27, 1891 and is buried at the Wills Cemetery on the Water Gap Road.

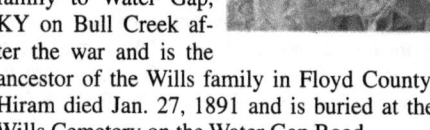

His children were Henrietta, William "Bill" Andrew (married Louemma Honaker), Andrew J., Eliza, Martha Jane (married John S. Baisden and then Andrew Jackson Wright), Ruhama (married Ben Craft), and Henry J. (married Bertie Pigman).

Following is a letter he wrote his wife during the war. It was sent to me by Dr. Bryan Griffith, a descendant through Martha Wills and Andrew Jackson Wright. Verbatim:

Martinsburg
Beckley County, WV
January 11, 1864

Dear Wife
I take the present opportunity to let you know that I am yet alive and in tolerable health, hoping that when this comes to hand it will find you and the children in good health. I have been thinking for a long time to get to come home, but it seems like that I cannot get to come home any more. But now we have got into winter quarters, I think that I will have a chance to get home some time this winter. But if I do not, why it will not be very long till my time will be out and I will try to stand it until I can home to stay. I think very hard of our commander for not giving us a chance to get home, but I think that our commander has but damned little respect for housewives and children. They want us to enlist again and I think that there will be a good many that will reenlist, and if they do, my judgment is that the rest will be discharged against warm weather, and I shall not reenlist, you may be well assured of that. You did not want me to volunteer, but I would do it any how and now I will do as I please. Again, I will not reenlist, but I suppose that the good Union boys in our country will take our place. That will look nice and it will show that they love the Union.

There is lots of fun in being a soldier. We have a pretty hard time once in a while, but it does not last long, and then comes the fun again and sometimes we have to fight like hell and when we whip them it is so nice to see the damned things take to their heels and run. It is like any other business-you may work hard or easy at it, and a soldier gets used to it and then they like the fun. We have been on a (unreadable, but appears to say "big trip") away over into Dixie and have destroyed all their western supplies. Now just let the damned Jeff Davis Club see if they think that there is no hell for rogues.

Do not fret yourself about me. I will take care of myself. Take care of yourself and the children a little longer, and all will be right. Tell Joseph and anybody else to write to me. I cannot get a letter from anybody, and I want to hear from you so bad. I think very hard of my relation for not writing.

I will close at the present.

Yours and Love,
Hiram Wills, to Catherine Massey

Hiram is the ancestor of Seth and Noah Marcum of Bull Creek, KY. *Submitted by Karen Nelson Marcum.*

JAMES WRIGHT, born Jan. 6, 1842 and died in 1930. He served with Company D, 13 Kentucky Cavalry, 4 Corps Confederate CSA.

He married Seattie Baldrige and they had five sons: William, Malcom, James, Henry and George, and six daughters: Melvina, Thersea, Sally, Nancy, Mary Ann and Susie.

Robert Perry giving a short speech at the Ivy Mountain Monument dedition on 10 November 2001. The lady to the right is Adrian Stransky.

Spanish American War

JACK "BOOMER" SALISBURY, son of William "Bud" and Mary Flutz Salisbury. He served in the Spanish American War. After the war he moved west.

SAMUEL L. SPRADLIN, was a veteran of the Spanish American War 1898. He earned his teaching certificate in 1892 and worked as a Floyd County schoolteacher during the 1890s. He was a member of the Prestonsburg City Council and also served as the 25th Master of the Zebulon Lodge in 1905. He is buried in the Porter Cemetery next to his wife Lida Davidson Spradlin. He was the son of Samuel Spradlin of Middle Creek.

Example of Spanish American War Campaign Service Medal (Navy).

World War I

WILLIAM G. AFRICA, Corporal, born in Jellico, TN about 1890. He enlisted in the U.S. Army Sept. 20, 1917 and served in Co. D, 309th Engrs. Cpl. Africa was discharged July 18, 1919. He received the Bronze Victory Medal.

He was a very active and dependable member of Floyd Post 129, American Legion. William is deceased, leaving children and grandchildren.

JOHN B. "FLOYD" AKERS, born April 24, 1890, at Dana, KY. He was a son of David and Alice Woods Akers and had three brothers and three sisters: Joshua (died in infancy), Charlie, Farley, Zella Hall, Nancy Sellards and Lillie Scalf Hamilton.

John B. was already married to the former Rhoda Williams and living at Banner when he enlisted in the U.S. Army in 1917. He served as a bugler during World War I.

After an Honorable Discharge, he moved to Ashland, KY, where he was employed by Armco Steel. He had one step-daughter, five grandchildren and a number of nieces and nephews who adored him.

His hobby was fishing and he lived to the age of 89.

CHESTER ALLEN, Private First Class, born on June 3, 1896, son of Andrew Jackson (General Jack) Allen and Polly Patton. After being drafted into the U.S. Army, WWI, he was stationed in Germany and France. He saw overseas duty from May 16, 1918 to April 20, 1919. During this time he was involved in many significant battles.

His mental acuity was remarkable until his death at age 93 and he often discussed battles and incidents that occurred during the war. One of his most vivid memories was Nov. 11, 1918, Armistice Day. As Mr. Allen recalled, on this date he was in a fox hole in France, the sky was ablaze, a volley of shells had gone over his head since midnight and at the agreed time, 11:00 a.m., there was a dead silence for miles around and it was as if the world stood still. This "One moment of Silence" in the eleventh month, eleventh day and eleventh hour of the year 1918 made an indelible imprint on the mind of this 22-year-old soldier. During the rest of his lifetime, on this date and exact hour, he would remind family members of this time in history.

Mr. Allen married the former Maxie Lee Cooley, a Floyd County School teacher, on May 27, 1931. They had two daughters, Eloise Allen Hall and Ruth Allen Daniels. He passed away Sept. 11, 1989 and is interred in the Cooley Cemetery at Eastern Kentucky.

JOSEPH H. ALLEN, M.D., 1888-1977, son of Thomas and Susan Stephens Allen. Served in WWI Medical Corps as a 1st Lieutenant. He married Bertha May on Nov. 11, 1910. He helped establish the first four-year high school in Maytown. He served 33 years as a member of the Floyd County Board of Education. J.H. Allen Central High School bears his name. He and his son, Dr. Claude Allen, owned Beaver Valley Hospital in Martin at one time.

ERNEST BALDRIDGE SR., born Sept. 12, 1895 in Prestonsburg, Floyd County, KY, the 7th child of Zachariah Taylor Baldridge and Mary Jane "Jennie" Spears. He was a miner at the Allegheny Coal Company before being drafted into the Army on March 18, 1918. He saw no military action during his tour. He was discharged shortly thereafter for medical disability.

Ernest first married Fanny Hall in December 1918; she contracted influenza in early 1919 and died that October in Pike County, KY. Fanny was pregnant with their first child, who was born shortly before Fanny's death and died a week later.

Ernest's second marriage was to Hazel Risner, youngest daughter of Lark and Rhoda Patrick Risner, in 1921. Hazel Risner was born in 1905 in Magoffin County, KY. By 1930, Ernest and Hazel were living in Prestonsburg, KY. Ernest died Jan. 22, 1982 in Ashland, Boyd County, KY. Hazel died in 1998 in Rock Island, IL where she resided with her youngest son and family. They are buried at Rosehill Burial Park in Ashland, KY.

Ernest and Hazel were parents of three children: 1) Ernest Baldridge Jr. who married first, Olive G. Music and second, Mary P. Patchen; 2) Elizabeth Janet Baldridge married James E. Nelson; 3) Jack Taylor Baldridge married Ellen E. Johnson.

ARTHUR BRADBURY, Private, was born April 17, 1898. He enlisted in the British Army in 1917 and was stationed in Ireland. His date of discharge is unknown; however, he was a Private.

Arthur and his wife Gurtrude had two sons, Raymond and John. His civilian employment included Superintendent with the Illinois Mine Rescue Station. He was also employed as Safety Director for the Inland Steel Company Mines at Wheelwright for 27 years He is now deceased.

TURNER BRANHAM, born in Floyd County in November 1891 to Andrew and Amanda Garrett Branham. He served in the Army during World War I for two years.

He married Janey Garrett and they had three children: Edith and Ruby (now deceased) and John Andrew, a Navy veteran of World War II.

Turner was a coal miner for 35 years. He and Janey were members of Community United Methodist Church. He passed away on his birthday in November 1968. Turner and Janey are buried at Mayo Cemetery in Prestonsburg.

TAYLOR PADGETT CALHOUN, born in June 1897 in Floyd County, KY to Hiram and Mary Belle Calhoun. He was a school teacher before joining the U.S. Navy in World War I. He also served in World War II.

I wouldn't have known about Taylor Calhoun's military service if my cousin, Clara Lucille Derossett Garrett, hadn't told me about it. She said that her Uncle John Warrix joined the U.S. Navy since he was so impressed with his former teacher Taylor Calhoun's military record. I received the following information from Taylor's granddaughter, Garland Bigley:

"Taylor Calhoun served during both World War I and II. He is buried in Worcester, MA. Early in World War II he invented some crucial parts for British aerial torpedoes for Winston Churchill. In World War I, he was Officer in Charge of Construction of the Norfolk Naval Supply Depot (in Portsmouth, VA).

"He lived in Norfolk in an area then called Edgewater. He married Grace V. Berry. Their daughter, Claire Lucille Calhoun, was born in 1919. Claire Lucille Calhoun also served during World War II. She was a Drill Instructor at Hunter College where she trained WAVE recruits. She later worked as a civilian for the Army in Yokohama, Japan during the Korean War at or near the end of the conflict." She is the mother of Garland Bigley who gave me this information. *Submitted by Karen Nelson Marcum.*

JOHN BASCOM CLARK, Sergeant Major, entered the U.S. Army on Jan. 11, 1918 and was discharged Feb. 11, 1919. He was in the 309th Ammo Train, 84th Inf. Div., Stenographer 3rd Inf. Bn. and the 159 Depot Brigade.

John married Vertner Francis, and they had two children, William Francis Clark and Jane Hamilton Clark. John was admitted to the BAR and practiced law in Prestonsburg, KY. He served as Master Commissioner in the Floyd Circuit Court.

MALCOLM COLLINS, Private, served in the U.S. Army with Co. E, 101st Engrs. He enlisted June 9, 1917 and served with Champagine Defensive and Miami Offensive. He was discharged May 6, 1919. Malcolm, born April 28, 1899, died in February 1972, was buried in the Shepherd Cemetery at Dwale, KY. *Submitted by Karen N. Marcum.*

ANDREW JACKSON DAVIDSON II, born April 2, 1883 to John Preston Martin Davidson and Judith Mayo Martin Davidson of Banner, KY. He lived with his aunt and uncle, Sam and Laura Davidson, as an elder brother to their 10 children.

He graduated from East or Eastern Kentucky Normal College, Louisa, KY, in 1904 as one of the first five graduates, and taught school at Johns Creek in Floyd County.

About 1905 he entered medical school and graduated from the University of Louisville in 1909 as a member of one of the largest medical classes at the time. He first practiced medicine in Jefferson County, KY.

In 1918 he served as 1st Lieutenant in the U.S. Army Medical Corps at Camp Zachary, Taylor, Louisville, KY.

On Sept. 11, 1915, he married Jessica Cornelia Correll at Louisville. They had two sons, Marshall and Andrew Jackson III, both of whom served in World II.

The couple also had one granddaughter, Deborah Davidson Hicks, a teacher with the Floyd County School System, and two great-granddaughters, Greta Davidson Hicks and Jessica Davidson Hicks, the first a graduate and the latter a senior at Transylvania University. Following a separation, Andrew married Virgie McCombs.

In 1919, he was admitted to medical practice in Tampa, FL and later practiced in Topeka, KS. He returned to Kentucky with his family in 1924 with medical practices in Louisville, Auxier, Winchester, Nicholasville and in Prestonsburg from 1932 until his death on July 17, 1960. He practiced medicine for 51 years. Doctor Davidson's principle interests were obstetrics and psycho-neurology. He was noted as a diagnostician in the Big Sandy Valley.

JAMES MORGAN DAVIDSON, served with the U.S. Navy during World War I.

FAIR DAVIS, son of Joseph Vincent and Nancy Beverly Davis, and brother to Minnie Hall, served in the U.S. Army during World War I.

VERLIN DECKER, Private, born in Wilton, KY in 1895 and enlisted in the service May 27, 1918. Assigned to Co. D, 141 MG BN; his foreign service was from Aug. 6, 1918 to Jan. 1, 1919. He was discharged Jan. 21, 1919. Verlin Decker is deceased.

JAMES HARVEY DELONG, Private, served in the U.S. Army during World War I. He entered service in May 1918 and was stationed at Camp Beauregard, LA.

He was born in 1883, son of R.C. DeLong and Missouri Wells DeLong of Edgar, KY. James married Eva Setser DeLong in 1918, daughter of W.J. and Mary Burchfield Setser of Edgar, KY. They all lived at the mouth of Dicks Creek until the Dewey Lake was built. He moved his family to Lawrence County, KY.

James DeLong in 1957.

James enjoyed working with bees and horse trading. James and Eva are the parents of: Gladie, Marvin, Earnest, James Edward, Arland, Alton, Thelma Grace and Elmer.

They lived at Adams, KY until their death. Eva died Jan. 29, 1956 and James on July 3, 1959. They are buried in Wells Relocation Cemetery, Auxier, KY. *Submitted by Arland DeLong.*

WILLIAM THOMAS EPLING, born Dec. 15, 1895, enlisted in the U.S. Army during World War I. He was married to Nellie Jones Epling and they had 10 children. Cleveland Epling, Villy Epling, Goldie Adkins, Alice Epling, Paul Epling, Gladys Dale, Elsie Adkins, Eva Mae Keatings, John Ed Epling and Ruth Ellen Howell.

William and Nellie had several grandchildren, great-grandchildren and great-great-grandchildren.

He worked in the mines as a foreman for several years before becoming a self-employed owner of a grocery store and later he had a used car dealership. He loved gardening and hunting. William passed away on June 13, 1988.

JOHN SHERMAN FANNIN, son of John Nelson Fannin and Sarah Easton, was born Jan. 26, 1888 and died March 21, 1965. He served in the U.S. Army's 5th Div., 6th Inf. Regt. during the Pancho Villa raids and World War I.

Pancho Villa retaliated by raiding U.S border towns, most notably Columbus, New Mexico. On the U.S. side of the border, after two U.S. Army "punitive expeditions" into Mexico in 1916 and 1919 failed to route Villa, the Mexican Government accepted his surrender and retired Villa on a General's salary to Canutillo, Durango. In 1923 he was assassinated while returning from bank business in Parral, Chihuahua.

Sherman Fannin also served in the following Army units in World War I and could have served in the following battles with 5th Inf. Div. 10th Inf. Bde. and 6th Inf. Regt. - Anould sector, Vosges, France (14 June-16 July 1918); St. Die sector, Vosges, France (17 July-23 August 1918); St. Mihiel offensive, France (12-16 September 1918); Meuse-Argonne offensive, France (12-22 October 1918); and Meuse-Argonne offensive, France (27 October-11 November 1918)

WILLIE RAYMOND FLANERY, was born Oct. 20, 1918 to William Isaac "Bill" and Flora (Stephens) Flanery.

CASH HACKWORTH, served in the Army. He had brown hair, ruddy complexion and was 5 feet 6 inches. He was discharged from service on Jan. 29, 1919.

He was born in 1895 in Floyd County, KY and was the son of Thomas and Anna L. Stone Hackworth. He was farmer. On March 24, 1921 he first married Rutha Spradlin, then on April 20, 1922 he married Pearl Adams.

He died in Arizona at the home of his daughter Juanita in June 1984 at age 89. He is buried in Preston Cemetery, Ada, OH, Section 3, Row 20.

HARRISON HACKWORTH, Private, with the 27th Co., 7th Inf. He was inducted at Floyd County, KY on May 27, 1918 and discharged at Camp Zachary Taylor, KY on June 3, 1918. He was born on Feb. 14, 1885 in Floyd County, KY and was the son of Jefferson and Sarah Prater Hackworth.

On Nov. 10, 1921 he married Millie Williams at Bonanza, Floyd County, KY. He was a United Baptist minister and on July 10, 1917 became a member at Chestnut Grove Church in Floyd County, KY. He died in Floyd County, KY at age 86.

OWEN HALL, a World War I Naval veteran, who served on the USS *Arizona*, was born Dec. 7, 1895, in Floyd County, KY to Robert and Henrietta Jane Hopkins Hall. Owen was murdered in Ashland, Kentucky on April 22, 1921 and is buried in the Greenberry Hall Cemetery, Frazier's Creek near McDowell, KY.

JOBE HAYWOOD, was born 1895 in Dock, KY. He enlisted in the service July 22, 1918, was assigned to Btry. C, 45th TAC, Camp Zachary Taylor. He was discharged Jan. 27, 1919.

ELI JOHNSON, was drafted into the U.S. Army during World War I. He was the son of Francis Marion ("B") and Eliza Hicks Johnson. Eli was assigned to Co. I, 46th Inf. Div. in France. He was wounded Nov. 10, 1918 in the Battle of the Argonne Forest, one day before the fighting stopped and the Armistice was signed. He died Feb. 2, 1919 at the age of 26 as a result of wounds he had received in battle. He was interred in an American Military Cemetery in France, however, his family had his remains brought back for burial in the Johnson Cemetery on the Caney Fork of Middle Creek in the fall of 1919.

RAYMOND D. LANGLEY, son of Wm. Langley and Florence "Belle" Bingham, was born June 30, 1897 at Spurlock, Middle Creek, Floyd County, KY. He married Mary Castello. He died in Bellefonte (Ashland), KY. He served in World War I.

SAMUEL LEEK (LEAKE), served in the U.S. Army during World War I. He was stationed in New York and while there preparations were being made for him to be shipped to France. When the war ended, he was discharged.

Samuel was the son of Marion McDonald Leake and Rhoda Shell. He and his wife Martha Moler Leake had 10 children. He and Martha lived in Warsaw, IN. Samuel has since passed away.

ELDER K. LEWIS, was born on Oct. 11, 1893 at Woods (present day Banner), KY, the son of Jefferson and Lucressia Pricie Endicott Lewis. He enlisted in the US Army on Feb. 18, 1918. During World War I, he participated in The Aisne-Marne Counter Offensive, The Oise-Aisne Offensive and The Meuse-Argonne Offensive (aka The Big Show). Elder

credited his helmet with saving his life during this battle. He was Honorably Discharged as a Private on July 17, 1919 from Fort Zachary Taylor. When he returned from the Army, he married Jessie Dillon and returned to work as a farmer. Into this marriage was born Josephine, Katheryn, Mary, James, Fred, Chester, Birkey, Bobby Gene and Glen. Jessie passed away Oct. 7, 1937. Elder later married Ida Lewis and Forrest and Generieve were born. Elder passed away on July 26, 1972.

BILL CODY MARTIN, entered the service during WWI and served with the Seabees. He was discharged on Oct. 29, 1945. Bill attended McDowell High School.

JACK MCGUIRE, was born March 22, 1892 on the Right Fork of Bull Creek and was the son of George and Artie McGuire.

He was a school teacher before going to World War I. He died June 19, 1963 and is buried in the McGuire Cemetery on the Right Fork of Bull Creek. *Submitted by Karen Nelson Marcum and Clara Lucille Garrett.*

MELVIN J. AND HENRY I. MEADOR, were brothers from West Prestonsburg, KY, who served in World War I. Little is known of Henry's birth, service, etc.

Melvin was born at Dock, KY in 1894 and died at West Prestonsburg in August 1936. He entered the service May 2, 1917 at Louisville, KY, serving AEC Oct. 6, 1918 to Dec. 22, 1918 in France. Melvin attained the rank of Sergeant and was awarded the Victory Medal.

Mack E. Meador, one of the Meador brothers.

After discharge on Jan. 8, 1919, Melvin worked as miner, homesteader in Oregon and Game Warden in Floyd County, KY. He enjoyed the outdoors. He died in August 1936, West Prestonsburg. *Submitted by son, Douglas M. Meador.*

JOE WHEELER "SMOKEY" MEADOWS, WWI, US Army, was born May 6, 1895 Floyd County, KY. He died April 1, 1982 and is buried on the Right Fork of Bull Creek on the Meadows Cemetery on the right

side of the road at an angle across from his old home place. *Submitted by Karen Nelson Marcum.*

HILAND NELSON, 1902-1980, served in World War I. He had five sons who all served in the U.S. Military: Sam, Will, Ted, Jack and Grady.

BENNY DOCK PORTER, born Feb. 12, 1903 and joined the U.S. Navy during World War I. The family does not have a lot of information on his time in the military, but he was out to sea on July 3, 1923, because this is when my mother was born and it took several days for him to find out.

I'm not sure what rank he held, on the brass plate on his tombstone it says Fl KY Navy. He was married to Rethia Younce Porter and had 2 children and had two children and four grandchildren.

One memory I have is him telling of crossing the International Date Line and receiving papers to document the event. While home on leave, he had an accident causing him to lose his leg and ending his Naval career. He then became a grocery store owner until his death on Dec. 22, 1959. *Submitted by his granddaughter, Freda Campbell.*

ERNEST REYNOLDS, Private, born 1890, son of William Jay Reynolds and Minerva Sizemore, was a veteran of World War I. He enlisted 1918 in Kentucky Company, Cl Pioneer Infantry.

Ernest married Catherine Shepherd and together they had six children: Oscar "Doc," Everett, Ernestine "Judy," Roger "Bud," Clara and Andrew Jackson "Jack." He also has another daughter, Bettie Lee.

Ernest worked many years in the coal mine as a foreman. He lived his entire life in Floyd County and died at his home in Water Gap in 1963. He is buried in the Reynolds. Sizemore Cemetery in Water Gap, KY. *Submitted by Renee Kyle and Karen Nelson Marcum.*

GARNER & GEORGE ROBERTS, were brothers who served in the military. Garner served in the U.S. Navy in World War I.

George was born in 1900 in Linwood, KY. He enlisted in the 158th Depot Brigade and was discharged Nov. 15, 1918 with the rank of Private.

George was married to Lack Davidson and had one child Laura Virginia and one granddaughter Judy Collins.

BEVERLY "BEB" SCALF, son of John B. Scalf and Belle Collinsworth Scalf, was born Aug. 10, 1892. He was killed during World War I at the Battle of Chateau Thierry, France on Oct. 3, 1918. Beb was buried with Military Honors at the Scalf Cemetery on Buffalo Creek, Endicott, KY.

LEE SPENCER, Private, born on June 21, 1895 at present day Drift, KY, son of Preston Toliver Spencer and Nancy Turner. He enlisted in the Army on May 1, 1918 at Fort Thomas, KY. He was last assigned to Co. B, 52nd Infantry.

Lee spent from Aug. 31, 1918 to Oct. 10, 1918 stationed in the Vosges Mountains in Alsace overlooking the Rhine in Central Europe; Nov. 1-10, 1918 in the Meuse-Argonne Offensive, which was the greatest American battle of World War I; and in the Army of Occupation in Germany from May 1-26, 1919.

He was discharged on June 20, 1919 at Camp Zachary Taylor, Louisville, KY.

On March 16, 1920 he married Nannie Daniels, daughter of Lee Daniels and Exer Ward, at Drift, KY. They had seven sons and five daughter.

CAGER SPRADLIN, Private, with the 84th Division National Army, He had light brown eyes, brown hair and was 6'10". He was discharged on Nov. 1, 1917 He was born in 1893 in Floyd County, KY, the son of John Wesley and Lydia (Prater) Spradlin. He was a farmer. On Dec. 24, 1917 he married Ducie Hackworth and they moved to Tekonsha, MI.

LEE STUMBO, Private First Class, born in July 1893 at McDowell, KY, the son of Greenville Stumbo and Hannah E. Stewart. He enlisted in the U.S. Army on May 27, 1918. He served in Headquarters Company, 5th Inf. Div. All of his service was in the continental U.S.

He was discharged on Feb. 21, 1919. After the war he worked as a coal miner. Lee married Annie Mae Hall on Oct. 24, 1924 at Orkney, KY. They had seven children: Walter Lincoln, Willie Kit, Charles Edward, Eleanor Kathleen, Mary Madeline and Betty Rae; 20 grandchildren and 11 great-grandchildren. Lee died on June 7, 1975 at McDowell, KY.

STARLIN SWEENEY, Private First Class, was born in Floyd County, KY and enlisted into the U.S. Army, Infantry Division during World War I. He was discharged in 1916 with the rank of Private First Class.

Mr. Sweeney, a patriotic man, received a letter from President John F. Kennedy thanking him for his part in defending his Country.

He was an employee for the city of Prestonsburg for most of his years and worked two jobs to raise the nine children he and his wife Mary Goodman Sweeney, had together. The eldest of which is Stella Sweeney, mother of Anna B. Nichols.

Starlin Sweeney died in February 1963 at the age of 68. He was the grandfather of Kathy Nichols Frasure, Jimmy Nichols and Angie Nichols. He had two great grandchildren, Trent and Kassidy Frasure.

NEWBERRY TACKETT, son of David and Bell Dora Tackett of McDowell, KY, served in the U.S. Army in World War I. He is now deceased.

FRANK VAUGHAN, son of William J. and Lillie Mae Osborne Vaughan of Prestonsburg, was wounded in battle in France during World War I.

Frank is seated on the left with two of his

military friends.

JOHN WARIX, of the Right Fork of Bull Creek joined the U.S. Navy during World War I. He was born in September 1899, the son of Solomon Anderson Mullins. Warix was the name of Sol's step-father, John Fontaine Warix, so several of Sol's family members used the Warix name.

Solomon's real father was Sherrod Mullins of Pike County, who fought for the Union. Solomon's mother, Lucille Anderson, later married John Fontaine Warix who fought for the Confederacy.

John's mother was Caroline McGuire, the

daughter of Issac McGuire and Delilah Moore of the Right Fork of Bull Creek.

John decided to join the U.S. Navy due to the fact that his former teacher, Taylor Calhoun, had joined.

John married Clara Gearheart and they lived on Bull Creek and later in Prestonsburg. *Submitted by Karen Nelson Marcum and Clara Lucille Garrett.*

World War II

GARLAND WHITFIELD ADAMS, born March 6, 1916 in Floyd County, KY, the son of William Cleveland Adams II and Angie Lou Johnson Adams. Garland saw action in the U.S. Army during World War II.

He married Alice Neeley. Garland worked in the aircraft industry after the war. He died Aug. 15, 1998 in Hebron, OH.

GEORGE EVERETT ADKINS, born Sept. 6, 1922 in Elkhorn City, KY to Wyatt and Mae Dixon Adkins. He attended Tram Grade School and Betsy Lane High School where he was a straight A student. He enlisted in the U.S. Navy in 1942 after serving in the Civil

Conservation Corps. He served as a Coxswain during the Pacific Conflict of World War II where he was awarded eight Battle Stars. Everett was discharged from duty in Great Lakes, IL on Jan. 28, 1946.

After returning to the States, he married Goldia Ann Epling on May 22, 1946. He began his career as a dental technician in Prestonsburg, KY. He became the father of John, his only child, in 1957 and later a grandfather to Breanne and Brooke.

After moving to Chillicothe, OH in 1960, he continued his dental career. In 1980, he became the owner of Adkins Dental Laboratory where he worked with his son. He retired in 1991 after 45 years as a technician.

Everett was an avid fisherman and spent

many hours listening to or watching the Kentucky Wildcats play basketball. Following an extended illness, Everett passed away on Aug. 20, 1996 in Mount Carmel Medical Center, Columbus, OH.

DAVID R. "SOCKER" AKERS,
born April 16, 1916 at Dana, KY. He enlisted in the U.S. Army in June 1942 at Fort Thomas, KY and served 43 months. He was a rifle marksman. He participated in the Battle of Ryukyas. David was discharged from the Army in January 1946 at Camp Atterbury, IN. Headquarters and Service Co., 1903rd Engrs. Avn. Bn.

Decorations included American Theater, Asiatic-Pacific Theater w/Bronze Star Medal, Good Conduct and WWII Victory Medal.

David was married to Goldie B. Brown and the father of two children, Joseph E. Akers and Nancy M. Lytle. Grandchildren are Joseph C. Akers, Lisa A. Shores and Dalton D. Reed and great-grandchild is Kelli S. Akers.

Returning to civilian life he was employed as a clerical worker for Island Creek Coal Co. He was a graduate of Betsy Layne High School and Alice Lloyd College. He was a member of AMVETS, John W. Hall Masonic Lodge 950 and DAV.

David was a very friendly and outgoing person. He had many friends, never saw a stranger. His interest was genealogy and traveling. David passed away Oct. 24, 2001.

ELDER AKERS,
of Louisa, KY received his medals 49 years after he was in WWII. He was proud that he was able to serve his country and happy that he stayed around long enough to get the medals. Gen. Douglas MacArthur kept his pledge to return to the Philippines in 1944. Elder was one of the U.S. Infantrymen who waded ashore before the General to help drive out the Japanese.

Elder saw action in Luzon and New Guinea before helping to launch the invasion on Leyte, October 20th. He and 10 other machine gunners of the Army's 34th Inf. Div. were given the mission to protect the left flank of the battalion which had dug in for the night.

He married his sweetheart, Sylvia, and they had four children, 10 grandchildren and 20 great-grandchildren. Elder worked as a construction worker at a power plant. He attended Little Salem Church as a devout Baptist. He passed away Sept. 23, 1993.

LEROY AKERS,
Private First Class, born Nov. 12, 1924 at Prestonsburg, KY, the son of Noah Akers and Lydia Thompson. After Lydia died Noah married Fannie Mitchell. Leroy enlisted in the U.S. Army on July 29, 1943 at Huntington, WV. He served with the 398th Inf. Regt. in the 100th Inf. Div. He was variously stationed at Camp Shelby, MS; Fort Sill, OK; Fort Lewis, WA, and Fort Meade, MD while in the United States.

His service overseas was in the Rhineland and Central Europe. His MOS was Special Vehicle Operator. He was discharged Aug. 1, 1946. His decorations include the Combat Infantry Badge, Good Conduct Medal, EAME Theater Ribbon, WWII Victory Ribbon and Army Occupation Medal.

Leroy was Magistrate in District 3 in Floyd County. He was also a U.S. Postal Service Contractor and was employed by Sandy Valley Explosive Company.

Leroy is currently married to Betty Stumbo. He has two children, Gerri Gail (Akers) Adkins, a daughter of Leroy and his first wife, and Greg Akers a son of Leroy and Betty (Stumbo) Akers. He has two grandchildren, Matthew Adkins and Allison Leann Akers. He also has one great-grandchild, Annabelle Adkins.

TRUMAN AKERS,
born Jan. 12, 1927 to Andy Akers and Wyona Hopkins Akers, was one of 14 children. He volunteered for the U.S. Army and served from March 1945 to November 1946 as a rifleman. He was awarded a Victory Medal, Asiatic-Pacific Theater Ribbon and an Army of Occupation Medal for his service in Japan.

After returning to the States and being Honorably Discharged, Truman married Charlos Fern Johnson on July 25, 1951. They had two sons and four grandchildren. He was employed by Inland Steel and later Island Creek Coal Company. Truman retired after 38 years as a coal miner.

He was a member of the UMWA, Wheelwright Freewill Baptist Church and the Wheelwright Masonic Lodge. Truman died on March 21, 2005 at Central Baptist Hospital in Lexington after a brief illness.

WILBURN L. AKERS,
born Sept. 1, 1926 to Ida (Hamilton) and Webster (Parsons) Akers and enlisted in the Army in November 1945 at Fort Riley, KS. He was stationed in Germany for almost a year and enjoyed his time there as a motor pool Sergeant. He received the Army of Occupation Medal.

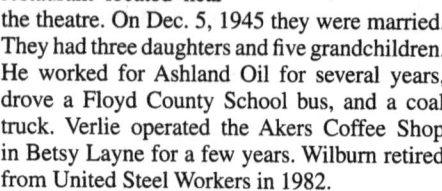

He met his wife Verlie (Walker) Akers at Betsy Layne, KY where she operated a restaurant located near the theatre. On Dec. 5, 1945 they were married. They had three daughters and five grandchildren. He worked for Ashland Oil for several years, drove a Floyd County School bus, and a coal truck. Verlie operated the Akers Coffee Shop in Betsy Layne for a few years. Wilburn retired from United Steel Workers in 1982.

Wilburn and Verlie loved their Country and proudly flew the American Flag at their Tolar's Creek home. Wilburn died in April 1995 of pancreatic cancer. Verlie died in April 1998 of heart disease.

CARL WALKER ALLEN,
born May 29, 1920 in Pyramid, KY. Assigned to 397th Antiaircraft Battalion and served in Normandy, Northern France, Rhineland and Central Europe.

His memorable experience was after his landing boat was sunk during the Normandy Beach invasion, he swam ashore and fought with an infantry unit; after hospitalization in Paris he re-joined his artillery unit and participated in the Battle of the Bulge.

His awards include the American Theater Ribbon, Good Conduct Medal, WWII Victory Medal and EAME Theater Ribbon w/5 Bronze Battle Stars. He was discharged Dec. 2, 1945 with the rank Tech 5.

As a civilian he was employed as Floyd County Deputy County Court Clerk, 1946-99; was Supervisor of Maintenance, Middleton, OH; and retired from Board of Education in 1981. His first wife Aileen Hall Allen died in 1950. He married second Bethel Moore Allen. He had three daughters: Susie Hall Allen (deceased), Diana Allen, Debra A. Reedy, and one son Kenneth D. Allen. Carl passed away at his residence in Hunterville, NC Sept. 28, 2002.

CASSIE PATRICK ALLEN,
Sergeant, was born in Burning Fork, KY and enlisted in the U.S. Marine Corps in February 1943. Assignments include U.S. Naval Training School, The Bronx, NY (Hunter College) 3rd Regt.; USMC Officer Procurement Officer, Los Angeles; USMC Southern California District

Headquarters Station, Los Angeles, CA; temporary duty, Dept. of the Pacific, USMC Public Information Training, San Francisco, CA.

Her memorable experience was being a spectator at Los Angeles WWII Victory Parade headed by Gen. George Patton Jr. and Gen. Jimmy Doolittle in 1945; also memorable was attending the American Legion Parade in Miami led by Gen. and Mrs. Douglas MacArthur in about 1950/51.

Cassie was discharged in October 1945 as Recruiting Sergeant. Her awards include the American Defense Service Medal and WWII Victory Medal.

She attended University of KY, 1946 and University of Miami, 1950-53. Civilian employment as Deputy Floyd County Court Clerk, 1946-49. Currently she volunteers at American Red Cross, is member and volunteer of Marine Corps League and Eastern Kentucky Detachment.

Cassie has two children, David Patrick and Patricia Allen, and grandchildren: David Patrick II, Whittney Dawn Allen, Catherine Danielle Huffman and Emily Ruth Huffman.

CLARENCE EDWARD ALLEN, born July 4, 1925 at Hueysville, KY, son of Wayne Dameron Allen and Mallie Belle Craft. He was drafted into the Navy on Sept. 30, 1943 during his first semester as a high school senior. He served with various Naval dispensaries, hospitals, schools and shore commands, mine sweepers, destroyers, aircraft carriers, and submarines.

Most of his duties were on a ship or station as the medical department representative directly responsible for all personnel assigned to the particular units. Allen was also assigned to duty in Tokyo during the occupation of Japan with the commander of Naval Forces Far East.

Although he suffered during his training and saw the horrors of WWII, Allen decided to stay in the Navy. "The rest of the wars were fearsome - WWII, Korea and Vietnam." He announced his retirement on Jan. 1, 1976, assigned to a submarine force in Norfolk, VA. He attained the rank of HMCM (SS) USN (Rct.) E-9 Masterchief Hospital Corpsman.

He married Sophie Bertha Motyl in Norfolk City, VA. Their children are Glenn Allen and Bruce Allen. Clarence died Dec. 6, 1997 at Chesapeake City, VA. He was cremated and his ashes buried at sea.

JAMES E. ALLEN, Buck Sergeant, with the 176th Army Engineers. He was born Jan. 17, 1919, one of 11 children born to Melvin V. and Lula Gayheart Allen.

After Maytown H.S. graduation, he worked for Kentucky, West Virginia until going into service March 12, 1941. He took basic training at Fort Leonard Wood, served in Alaska for 32 months, was moved to Okinawa for the planned invasion of Japan. He received an Honorable Discharge in December 1946.

James married Violet Coburn in December 1941. They have two sons, three grandsons and seven great-grandchildren. James started J.E. Allen Drilling and Construction Co. in 1947 which he has now turned over to his sons and grandsons. After spending over 20 years wintering in South Texas, he and Violet spend most of their time at home enjoying church activities, their many friends and grandchildren.

James feels that he has been blessed and still enjoys life. Past his mid-80s, he takes no medication, "gins around" is his company's mail carrier and "bosses the boys."

JARVIS ALLEN, Tech Sergeant, was born in Pyramid, KY and enlisted in the service May 14, 1942. Assigned to Sqdn. T 325th AAF Base Unit CCTS (HB) AC; Air Mechanics School, Keesler Field, MI; Lockheed AM School, Hollywood, CA; Air Corps Gunnery School, Wendover Fld., UT, U.S. Army Air Base, 8th AF, Bovingdon, England and participated in bombing mission, Aug. 17, 1943, Schweinfurt, Germany.

On five prior missions he crashed on English Beach; ditched in English Channel; bailed out over Patarages, Belgium returning from raid on ball bearing plant on Aug. 17, 1943 and evaded capture by Germans with the help of the French underground. He made his way to Portugal after four months of assistance in hiding and traveling. Later, stationed at Avon Park, FL as an aircraft instructor.

Discharged (disabled) on Oct. 18, 1944 with rank Tech Sergeant. He received three Air Medals, Purple Heat and OLCs, American Theater Ribbon, WWII Victory Medal, EAME Medal and Good Conduct Medal.

He was school teacher prior to WWII; County Court Clerk of Floyd County, KY, 1946-50; Attorney-at-Law, 1952 to retirement; Chief Counsel, Kentucky Dept. of Highways for 10 years.

His children are David P. Allen, Patricia Allen and Philip Edward Allen. Jarvis passed away Feb. 28, 1990.

JEWEL DAY ALLEN, born in Pyramid, KY and enlisted May 28, 1943. His stations include USNTS, Great Lakes, IL; Naval Ammunition Depot, Balboa, Canal Zone; Com. Ser. FN 7th FLT R/S Navy 3149, USS *Whitney* (ADA-4), Canal Zone and South Pacific area.

His memorable experience was being supervisor of Naval painting crew and as soon as the crew finished painting the USS *Whitney*, they had to start all over again because of salt rust on the ship.

Discharged March 14, 1946 as Painter 2/c USNR, his awards include WWII Victory Medal, American Campaign Medal and Asiatic-Pacific Campaign Medal.

Civilian employment was with C&O RR Co., Russell Co., Curtis Wright. His wife is deceased. Children are Shawn Allen and Debbie Allen.

VOLNEY D. ALLEN, BM1/c, son of Wayne D. Allen and Mallie Craft Allen, was born Feb. 27, 1923, in Hueysville, KY. He enlisted in the Navy on Dec. 13, 1940. The majority of Volney's service time was spent aboard the light cruiser, the USS *Richmond*. The ship took part in the Battle of Komandorski and remained in the Aleutians through the end of the war.

Volney was discharged on March 15, 1946, as a Boatswain Mate 1st Class. He is proud that seven from his family served in the military. Four, including himself, served during WWII.

After his return to Kentucky, Volney married Joyce Allen on June 15, 1946. Their son Volney Brent Allen was born Nov. 11, 1949. They have two grandsons.

Volney has worked a variety of jobs. He did pipefitting in the ice caps of Greenland and worked on towboats on the Mississippi River. For the past 25 years he has worked in Kentucky as a Master Plumber for the Floyd County Schools. Volney has a quick wit, and is a great storyteller (some of which are true!)

WILLIAM HARRISON AMBURGEY JR., born July 23, 1923 to William H. and Ada Francis Amburgey at Blackey, Letcher County, KY. His family moved to Estill, Floyd County, KY in 1940, William H. Amburgey Jr. attended Wayland High School in Floyd County.

William entered the U.S. Army on March 25, 1943 and was sent to Buckley

Fields, CO and assigned to the Army Air Corps. He succumbed to a serious illness while there and was hospitalized. He remained there until discharged on Oct. 30, 1943 after serving seven months and six days.

He returned to Estill, KY to be with his family. He met and married Miss Danese Fannin on April 1, 1944. They established their household in Estill. On Dec. 31, 1950, he converted to the Christian faith, and was subsequently ordained as a minister in the Free Will Baptist Church on Sept. 25, 1954.

As the result of complications from the service connected illness, William underwent experimental open heart surgery to replace his aortic valve on March 9, 1966 at an area Veterans Administration Hospital.

On Jan. 6, 1981, William finally succumbed to sequel of his early illness, and is buried in Richmond Cemetery, Prestonsburg, Floyd County, KY.

MARION ANDERSON, Sergeant, born Oct. 20, 1920 at McDowell, KY, son of Melvin Cox Anderson and Mary Jane Sizemore. He enlisted in the Air Force in May 1942 at Prestonsburg, KY. He attended Aerial Gunnery School in Las Vegas, NV, then transferred to Barksdale Field in Shreveport, LA; he was a Tail Gunner in a B-26 airplane;

On March 27, 1943 his plane caught fire and bounced across the Red River and he and crew were killed. His plane crashed the Saturday before the Monday Anderson was scheduled to go to England. He was 22 years old. His parents accepted a Presidential Citation on his behalf. Marion was buried in the Anderson Cemetery, McDowell, KY.

P.D. ARROWOOD, attended Maytown High School, then served in WWII.

DELMONT GREY BAILEY, Private First Class, born on May 16, 1923 at Ashland, KY, son of Wardie Lee Bailey and Mary Bessie Salyers. He entered into service in the Army of the United States on April 16, 1943 at Fort Thomas, KY. He spent the entirety of his service in Iceland. He served in the 448th Military Police Service Company.

He was discharged on Jan. 19, 1946 at the Separation Center at Camp Atterbury, IN. He received the carbine and Thompson sub machine gun marksmanship awards. The decorations and citations he received were EAME Theater Ribbon, Good Conduct Ribbon, and Victory Medal.

He married Nancy Vivian Spencer on June 20, 1946 at Paintsville, KY, daughter of Alexander Lackey Spencer and Katherine Turner. They had one son, Alec Grey Bailey, and two grandchildren, Ashley Grey Bailey and Alec Spencer Bailey, deceased. Delmont died Nov. 28, 1959 at Pineville, KY as a result of being hit in the head by fly rock while blasting for a gas well site near Pineville. He was employed by United Fuel Gas Company. He is buried in the Spencer Cemetery, Eastern, Floyd County, KY. His wife currently resides with Alec G. Bailey at Prestonsburg, KY.

SIDNEY E. BAILEY, born Sept. 23, 1923 at Hueysville, KY, son of Fred and Rebecca Bailey. He enlisted on April 1, 1943 at Prestonsburg, KY. He served with the 3119th Signal Service Battalion in New Hebrides, Philippines and in Japan. Bailey served overseas for 25 months. During that time, he was once sent into Japanese Emperor Hirohito's throne room. There he helped to re-establish telephone communications between the U.S. Government and Japan.

He was discharged from the Army Jan. 21, 1946 at Fort Knox, KY. Sidney married Marcella R. Bailey. Their children are James C. "Jim" Bailey and Sidney J. Bailey-Bamer.

Sidney died on Friday, April 30, 1993 at Martin, KY. He is buried in the Bailey Cemetery in Floyd County, KY.

ERNEST "ERNIE" BALDRIDGE JR., born April 4, 1922 in Prestonsburg, Floyd County, KY to Ernest Baldridge Sr. and Hazel Risner Baldridge. Ernie first married Olive G. Music, daughter of Samuel K. Music and Nora Bell Davis, in February 1940. They moved to Columbus, OH and both worked for the Curtis-Wright Corp. assembling planes for the war. Their daughter, Betty, was born in 1941.

In December 1944, Ernie was inducted into the U.S. Army out of Fort Hayes, Columbus, OH; he received specialized training at several Army bases across the U.S. and was discharged from service in February 1946 due to family hardship, he served in no wartime military action.

Ernie and Olive divorced and Ernie then married Mary P. Patchen, daughter of Nicholas Patchen and Mary Repasky, in June 1946. Ernie and Pat have two children, James G. Baldridge and Teri L. Baldridge. They currently reside in Florida (2006).

WILLIAM L. BALDRIDGE, Staff Sergeant, born June 1, 1921 in Floyd County, KY. He was drafted June 5, 1942 with basic training at Keesler Field, MS. At St. Petersburg, FL he was attached to Basic Training Center Headquarters as Supply Sergeant for 13 months. Transferred to Miami Beach, FL for 18 months as Supply Supervisor.

Received orders of deployment for overseas duty and in Spring of 1944 was in Naples and Bari, Italy. He participated in action in Po Valley, Italy and Polesti Oil Refinery in Romania. His memorable experience was V-E Day.

Returned to the States and discharged Nov. 14, 1945 as Staff Sergeant. His awards include the EAME Theater, Victory Medal, American Theater and Good Conduct. William's father was a WWI veteran.

William and his wife Betsy have two children, Sandra and Carolyn. Worked 26 years in state employment service, school teacher for seven years and five years in insurance sales. He is now retired.

DONALD B. BALL, born April 24, 1927 in Prestonsburg, KY, and enlisted in the U.S. Army Battery C 605th Field Artillery Battery Jan. 20, 1943. In WWII he served in Italy, North Apennines, Po Valley, Blood Group A. Don had three brothers who served in all divisions of the Armed Forces during WWII. He received

the Good Conduct Medal, EAME Campaign Medal, two Bronze Stars and Infantry Citation. He was discharged Dec. 3, 1945.

He owned Ball's Cafe in Prestonsburg and retired from Hardees in Lexington. He married Fannie Wallen and they had children, James and Donna, and four grandchildren and six grandchildren.

STEVE BERGER, Private First Class, was born Aug. 15, 1915 in Tipperary, PA to parents, Ida Keri and Johannes Berger. He was drafted into the Army on July 15, 1941. He was working in WV at the time. He entered the Army at Fort Hayes in Ohio and was later shipped for further training in the northeast before being deployed to Europe where he was placed

as a machine gunner with Btry. B, 495th AAA Gun Inf.

While honorably serving his country in Algeria-French Morocco, Sicily, Rome-Arno, Rhineland, Central Europe and Southern France, he received the EAME Theater Ribbon w/6 Bronze Stars and the Good Conduct Medal. He was discharged from Camp Atterbury, IN Sept. 25, 1945.

Returned to Melvin to live and where he married Mable Bryant on Dec. 31, 1945. They were parents of seven sons and had eight grandchildren. Steve worked in the mines for Inland Steel as a cutting machine operator and was a member of the UMWA local Union 5899 at Wheelwright until his retirement in 1977. He spent his retirement being a parent and a fisherman until his death on Oct. 31, 1984. He has been and will continue to be missed by all who knew him.

CURTIS BLACKBURN, born Sept. 30, 1915 to Oliver and Octavia Blackburn of Fishtrap, KY. He volunteered and enlisted in the U.S. Marine Corps June 9, 1943 at Charleston, WV. He was Drill Sergeant in the 2nd Div., 2nd Bn. while at Paris Island, SC. He served in the Asiatic-Pacific area and participated in action against the enemy in Okinawa.

He went to Japan serving in the peace keeping in Nagasaki after the atomic bomb had exploded. He was Honorably Discharged with a service of excellent character on March 29, 1946.

He married Hope Slone and had two children, Lance and Vicki Lynn, and four grandchildren. He was an ironworker until he retired in 1978. He has resided at Stanville, KY for the last 44 years. His favorite activities are playing rook and attending church.

LLOYD RONALD BLACKBURN, Corporal, son of Joe and Sola Osborne Blackburn, was born May 8, 1925 in Lackey, KY. He enlisted in the U.S. Marine Corps in Charleston, WV on Aug.13, 1943 at the age of 18 and was assigned to active duty as a member of the Marines Headquarters Company, First Marine Division, First Battalion - the oldest and most decorated division-sized unit in the U.S. Marine Corps.

Lloyd completed his "boot" training in San Diego and won a Rifle Sharpshooter's Medal while there. He was then transferred to Mare Island, CA where he served for one year. From Mare Island, Lloyd was shipped to Pavuvu Island in the Russell Islands and then to Guadalcanal where he received special military qualifications as a mortar crewman.

Lloyd participated in action at Okinawa, Ryukyu Islands from April 1 to June 21, 1945. On June 15, 1945, he was injured in Okinawa when rounds where fired on his battalion. Lloyd also participated in the occupation of China from Oct. 10, 1945 to Feb. 16, 1946.

He was discharged from the U.S. Marine Corps at Camp Lejeune, NC on March 21, 1946 receiving the Purple Heart, Honorable Service Button, American Campaign and Asiatic-Pacific Campaign Medals, China Service Medal, WWII Medal and a Good Conduct Medal.

When returning home to Little Paint, he married Loretta Burchett, daughter of Lonnie and Myrtle Baldridge Burchett, on Nov. 27, 1946. They have four daughters: LaDonna, Sheryl, Connie and Beverly; 10 grandchildren and nine great-grandchildren. Lloyd owned and operated the Four Sisters Meat Wholesale for 30 years until retiring in 1987. On his 80th birthday, Lloyd's family surprised him with a U.S. Marines theme party to honor his time spent in service.

ODIS DONALD BLANKENSHIP, Nov. 22, 1924 to Aug. 29, 1953. Odis was a rifle marksmen, inducted into Co. E of the 361st Inf. on July 29, 1943 at Fort Thomas, KY. He was awarded an EAME Medal w/2 Bronze Battle Stars, Purple Heart w/OLC, Victory Medal, American Theatre of Operations Medal and a Combat Infantry Badge. He was wounded in action in July 1944 and again in October 1944 in European Theatre.

He worked as a clerk with the Stevens Elkhorn Coal Company and died as the result of a firearm accident in Stevens Branch, KY.

He was the son of Beverly and Bertha Blankenship of Betsy Layne, KY. Odis was married to Pauline Click and they did not have any children. He is survived by his siblings: Helen Kendrick of Melvin, KY; Betty and Marvin Blankenship, of Michigan; and Jewell Sturgil (deceased).

PAUL BOGGS, served in U.S. Army during WWII. He married Gertrude Salisbury, daughter of Mae and Link Salisbury, and sister to Blaine, Wayne, Bert, Jay, Dessie (Rowe) and Cassie (Hall) Salisbury. Paul passed away in 1972 and Gertrude currently resides in Huntington, WV.

BOYD BOLEN, born in Garrett, KY, the son of Enoch and Sara Wallen Bolen. He had one brother Lloyd, and both brothers served in the U.S. Army. Boyd and wife Pansy have a son Mervin and daughter Susie.

LLOYD BOLEN, Private, son of Enoch and Sara Wallen Bolen of Garrett, KY, was born April 18, 1921. He was a Private in the United States military with Heavy Machine Gunnery 605 with Organization Co. B, 90th Operation. He was deployed Dec. 22, 1941. Lloyd was married to Myrtle Bolen and they had four sons: Danny Lee, Jimmy Darrell, Kenneth Ray and Timothy Douglas. His brother Boyd Bolen also served in the military.

WALTER KARR BOLLING, son of Walter and Frances Odell Bolling, who lost two sons in two wars. Their son, Walter Karr Bolling, was lost at Pearl Harbor while aboard the USS *Arizona*. His body was never recovered but there is a memorial stone for him on the Old Middle Creek Road past West Prestonsburg. The stone is next to his mother's. His brother, Thomas Edward Boiling, was killed in action in Korea. His stone is on the other side of his mother's. *Submitted by Karen Nelson Marcum.*

MONROE BOOTH, born on Oct. 1, 1922 in Whitehouse, KY and enlisted in the U.S. Army in 1941. He served with Co. A, 149th Inf. in Southern Philippines, Luzon and New Guinea. He received the Asiatic-Pacific Theater Ribbon w/3 Bronze Stars, American Theater Ribbon, American Defense Service Medal, Philippine Liberation Ribbon w/2 Bronze Stars, Good Conduct Ribbon and WWII Victory. Monroe also received the Combat Infantryman Badge and Expert Rifle Badge. The last 13 months of service, Monroe was squad leader with many responsibilities. Then at the end of WWII he was Honorably Discharged in November 1945.

In 1946 he married Evelene Stapleton from Whitehouse, KY. They had two children, Joyce and Jack. Monroe worked in the coal mines and was hurt by a rock fall in 1950. He was paralyzed from the waist down, but he loved people and made the best of each day.

The family moved to Lancer in Floyd County about 1952. Many children and neighbors enjoyed Monroe. He always had time for conversation or time to work on a child's bike.

Monroe and Evelene have four grandchildren and six great-grandchildren. He was an avid fisherman and enjoyed gardening. He passed away in September 1992.

KESSIE BOYD, served in WWII.

ORBIE BOYD, born Dec. 11, 1925 at Betsy Layne, KY, the son of Palmer and Goldie Conn Boyd. He had four brothers and three of them also served in the military.

He enlisted in the U.S. Army Jan. 26, 1944, and served in the 42nd Inf. Div. in the European Theater. His unit was sent to the battle front in France where he was captured by German Forces Jan. 9, 1945. While being held prisoner for four months, his weight went from 150 to 95 pounds, and his feet were severely frostbitten. He was liberated by British Forces and Honorably Discharged Nov. 16, 1945.

Orbie married Doris Gilliam in 1946 and they reside in Betsy Layne. They had two sons who died in infancy. He is retired from CSX Railway where he was employed as a mechanic for 26 years. He has served as a deacon in the Baptist Church and is presently active in Chapter 169 of the DAV in Betsy Layne.

THOMAS BOYD, born Oct. 27, 1925 in Glo, KY, and enlisted in the U.S. Navy May 9, 1944 and was stationed at USNTC Great Lakes, IL and the Asiatic-Pacific. He was discharged Jan. 30, 1946 and received the Asiatic-Pacific Medal w/star.

BALLARD FRANKLIN BRANHAM JR., born April 5, 1928, to Ballard and Mable Conners Branham. Mr. Branham died in January 1938.

Ballard Jr. and four sisters were transported to the Masonic Home outside of Louisville, KY where he remained until he completed 10th grade. He returned to Prestonsburg and graduated from Prestonsburg High School, lettering in both basketball and baseball. Between his junior and senior years, he signed to play with the Pittsburgh Pirates and played on their farm team, Salisburg Pirates in North Carolina.

He joined the Air Force and served one enlistment. After discharge he lived in Michigan, went to college, and taught on the secondary level. Later he went into construction. At the time of his death Aug. 30, 1986, he was Superintendent of a large Jewish cemetery outside of Detroit, MI.

ESTILL "ECK" BRANHAM, Sergeant, born Dec. 27, 1913, Prestonsburg and enlisted in the U.S. Army March 30, 1943. He was stationed at Wakeman General Hospital and Camp Atterbury, IN.

One of his military duties was to escort German prisoners to various military bases and was surprised by how polite they were. Sgt. Branham was discharged Nov. 16, 1945. His awards include the American Theater Ribbon, Good Conduct Medal and WWII Victory Medal.

After service he was high school teacher and coach. He married Hazel Keene (deceased) and Carol Ann Long (deceased). Eck died June 2, 2004 at Bowling Green, KY. He had a lifelong interest in sports, was a scout for the Cincinnati Reds, supported his alma mater Western KY University and provided an endowment for deserving students. Though many attended services for Eck in Bowling Green there was one young man who drove several miles to Prestonsburg to express personally his gratitude to Eck's family.

FRANK BRANHAM, Sergeant, born April 20, 1912, Prestonsburg, KY and enlisted Sept. 24, 1943, serving in the U.S. Army Infantry with Cannon Co., 118th Inf. Regt. in Northern France and Rhineland.

Discharged Jan. 2, 1946, he was awarded the EAME Ribbon w/2 Bronze Service Stars, WWII Victory Medal, Good Conduct Medal and Expert Infantry Badge.

After discharge he was employed by KY/WV Gas Company. He married Gertrude Hyden Leslie and has one son, four grandchildren, six great-grandchildren, one step daughter and three step children. Frank passed away March 20, 1994. His hobby was collecting ball caps and he had close to 200 at his death.

JAY BRANHAM, born Feb. 12, 1917 in Water Gap, Floyd County, KY, son of Polk and Nancy Branham. Jay married Callie Simmons and had one son, Paul Henry of Greeley, CO.

Jay died from wounds he received during the invasion of Italy on April 13, 1944. His body was brought back from a wartime grave, overseas, to Floyd County, KY in August 1948. He is buried in the Dwale Cemetery.

Jay's brothers and sisters include Dick, Joe, John, Ernest, Dee, Turner, Mary Ann, Margaret, Stella, Susie and Little Medley.

JOHN ANDREW BRANHAM, born in December 1920 to Turner and Janey Branham. He was a graduate of Prestonsburg High School in 1940.

John enlisted in the Navy in April 1942 serving in Alaska, New Zealand and Pacific Islands. He was discharged in 1948. His father, Turner Branham, was a two year veteran of the U.S. Army WWI.

John married Mary Coats in 1948 and resided in Mississippi where he worked for the Corp of Engineers. After his retirement, they returned to Prestonsburg in 1984. They were members of Community United Methodist Church. Mary passed away in June 1998 and John lives at May's Branch, Prestonsburg, KY.

ROBERT CLAYTON "ITCH" BRANHAM, Corporal, born July 3, 1924 in Prestonsburg, KY. His mother was Fanny Branham (a well known cook at Prestonsburg Elementary - she was famous for her chili and rolls). He graduated from Prestonsburg High School and joined the Marines. He enlisted on Aug. 10, 1942 with HQ SQD 9, 9th MAW FMF. He was awarded the Marksman Badge. He was discharged Jan. 30, 1946.

Robert was married to Francis of Betsy Layne and they had one daughter Judy. Itch operated and then owned Arrowood Hardware. He was a member of the Community Methodist Church and is buried at Mayo Cemetery.

THOMAS EDWARD BRANHAM, born Sept. 2, 1927 in Dwale, KY, son of John and Peg Branham. He enlisted in the U.S. Navy Aug. 14, 1945 and served aboard the USS *General A.E. Anderson* in Asiatic-Pacific, Japan, Guam and Hawaii.

After his discharge Sept. 1, 1948, he worked for Dow Chemical. Thomas

and his wife Mildred had four children: Sandy Goble, Tommie Sue Campbell, Janie Allen and John Robert (deceased). Thomas died Jan. 1, 2004. He was a member of the Prestonsburg First United Methodist Church.

WILLIAM "BILL" BRANHAM JR., born Feb. 27, 1924 at Water Gap, Floyd County, KY on Wills Branch, the son of William "Willie" Branham who was the son of John C. Branham and Lou Lafferty. His father was killed at Bull Creek on Sept. 2, 1923. He was shot off a horse as he was on his way to the church house to get his daughter and wife.

His mother was Darcus Wills, daughter of Richard Wills and Mary Bingham of Water Gap. His mother later married John E. "Monk" Lafferty. He and his half-brother, Joseph Lafferty, served in the U.S. Navy in WWII.

He married Kathleen Weber and is the father of three children: Sharon, Theodore and Patricia. He lives in Columbus, OH. *Submitted by Karen N. Marcum.*

DOUGLAS LLOYD BROWN, Tech 5, born Jan. 17, 1925, the son of George D. Brown and Molly Berry Brown. He attended Louisa High School. He enlisted in the Army on Aug. 5, 1943 and served in WWII. He was a member of the Battery D, 142nd Anti-Aircraft Artillery Gun Battalion.

His battles and campaigns included Ardennes, Rhineland and Central Europe.

He received the American Theater Ribbon, EAME Theater Ribbon w/3 Bronze Stars, Good Conduct Ribbon and Victory Medal. He was discharged March 14, 1946.

He married Mable Holbrook on Jan. 17, 1947, and had two son, Kenneth and Wayne; three granddaughters, two grandsons; and four great-grandchildren. Lloyd was a partner with his brothers as owners of Brown Foodservice Co., Inc. He was an avid golfer. Douglas passed away Aug. 22, 2003.

CLYDE BURTON BURCHETT, born Aug. 17, 1921 in Prestonsburg, KY, was the son of Tom and Rebecca Burchett. He enlisted in the U.S. Navy in December 1943 as an Ensign Mate 2nd Class. He was with the Amphibious Forces during WWII. He completed basic training in Great Lakes, MI. He was stationed in Fort Pierce, FL for 18 months aboard the USS *Sarita* until he was discharged Dec. 12, 1945.

His brothers also served in the military: Wade served in the USAF, Glen in the 24th Inf. in WWII, Andrew was an Airman 1st Class during Korean War and Kenneth was in the Army Reserve for six years. The father, Tom W. Burchett, served overseas in WWI.

Clyde married Eileen E. Wolf of Pittsburgh, PA and they had three sons: Randall, Thomas and Dr. Blake Burchett, and eight grandchildren. Clyde returned to Prestonsburg and operated Clyde Burchett Jewelry Store for 35 years.

BILL BURGA, Sergeant, born Oct. 9, 1923 Prestonsburg, Floyd County, KY, the son of Thomas Monroe and Polly Clark Burga. He served from Dec. 15, 1942 to Aug. 25, 1945 and was assigned to Co. B, 142nd Inf. Regt. His training was in Texas, then he was sent to Louisiana, to North Africa to France. While serving in France, he was wounded during combat on Sept. 17, 1944.

Award of Silver Star reads in part, "He was leading his squad across a clearing in the woods when an enemy soldier suddenly opened fire with a machine pistol. He swiftly dispersed his squad, located the soldier concealed in the underbrush and killed him with his first shot. As the advance continued, the squad was subject to heavy fire from enemy rifleman and snipers. Sergeant Burga skillfully placed his men in advantageous positions and directed their fire on the hostile force. He killed two of the enemy, and under his daring leadership, his squad killed nine more, completely routing the hostile group and eliminating a threat to the security of the company's flank."—Captain Dewey Mann.

He was awarded the Silver Star, Bronze Medal and the Purple Heart w/cluster.

He married first Alta and had two sons and one daughter. He married second Estelle, who already had eight children. He has five grandchildren, three great-grandchildren, 20 step-grandchildren, 28 step-great-grandchildren and three step-great-great-grandchildren. His brother, Thomas M. Burga Jr., also served in WWII. He worked in the coal mines for 35 years.

OLLIE BURGA JR., U.S. Army, was born Jan. 14, 1925, Floyd County, KY and died Oct 15, 1984 in Michigan. He was the son of Ollie Burga and Mary Lee Music Burga, the great grandson of Thomas H. Amburey/Burga, and had a sister Shirley. He served in WWII.

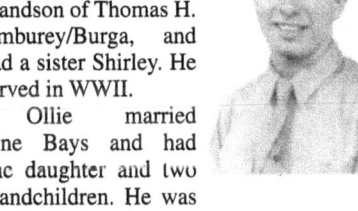

Ollie married June Bays and had one daughter and two grandchildren. He was a retired painter.

DR. FRANCIS E. BURGESS, born May 11, 1914 to Malcolm and Victoria Elam Burgess. He enlisted in the U.S. Navy in 1943 and was on the destroyer USS *Lindsey,* where he served as medical officer. The ship was attacked by a squadron of Japanese Kamikaze Fighter while engaged in the United States invasion of Iwo Jima and Okinawa. The Lindsey was literally cut into by the Kamikazes. Dr. Burgess was gravely injured, eventually losing his right lung due to his wounds. Dr. Burgess resigned his Naval commission in 1946 and returned to his Private practice. Dr. Burgess retired early from his medical practice and returned to his farm to write and reflect.

HERN D. BURKE, Tech Sergeant, born Sept. 1, 1913 at Bonanza to Robert and Louvada Burke. He enlisted in the Army Cavalry on Sept. 24; 1943 at Fort Thomas, KY. He served with the 16th Div., Co. F, 23rd Cavalry Reconnaissance Squad, and the First Field Artillery Observation Battalion in Fort Sill, OK.

Tech Sgt. Hern D. Burke of Prestonsburg, KY, WWII, in his jeep inspecting the streets of Germany after the bombing.

He was a tank mechanic and trained at Fort Knox with the Armored Division. He served in Central Europe, France, Germany and Czechoslovakia. After his re-enlistment, he returned to Germany. He was also a platoon leader with Co. B Battalion in Fort Sill, OK and was military escort with Graves Regular Division in Fort Worth, TX.

He was awarded the American Theater Ribbon, European Army Theater Ribbon w/Bronze Star, Good Conduct and Victory medals, and the WWII Commendation Medal. He was discharged from the military April 1949 at Camp Atterbury, IN.

During his second enlistment, he learned photography which upon discharge he turned into a profession as owner of Burke Photography Studio and partner with his brothers, Joe and John Burke, as co-owner of Fountain Korner Drug in Prestonsburg.

He was a Charter Member of Community United Methodist Church, Prestonsburg, KY, Floyd County Rescue Squad, and Kentucky Colonel.

He passed away April 28, 1983 and is buried at Davidson Memorial Gardens, Ivel, KY. He is survived by his wife Jean Herald Burke, his daughter Delia Burke Ormerod, both of Prestonsburg, and his granddaughter, Angela Kristen Ormerod of Lexington, KY.

JOE E. BURKE, Tech 3, born Jan 15, 1921, the son of R.A. and Louvada May Burke. He graduated from Prestonsburg High School in 1941 and enlisted in the Army on Oct. 5, 1942, and served in WWII. He was a member of the 583rd Signal Depot Company, and later one of his missions was to string telephone lines between battlefields. His battles and campaigns included Northern France, Ardennes Rhineland and Central Europe. Although he was never wounded, he did receive frostbite in the bitter cold winter.

He received the EAME Theater Ribbon w/4 Brass Stars, Good Conduct Medal and WWII Victory Medal. He was discharged on Jan. 22, 1946. He married Leslie Comstock on June 13, 1947, and had three daughters: Jeanne, Vicki and Kaye, three granddaughters, one grandson and one great-grandson. Joe was a partner with his brothers as owners of Korner Drug Store, "The Meeting Place of Prestonsburg" for over 40 years. He was a member of Community United Methodist Church and an avid golfer. He passed away Nov. 1, 1995 and is buried at Davidson Memorial Gardens.

JOHN W. BURKE, born Oct. 31, 1924 to Robert Alexander and Louvada May Burke. John was inducted into the U.S. Army April 9, 1943, at Fort Thomas, KY.

Shipped overseas on May 25, 1944 from Vancouver, WA on the SS *Cape Douglas* and landed on New Guinea at Finschhafen (Port Moresby Bay) on June 22, 1944.

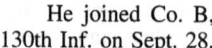

He joined Co. B, 130th Inf. on Sept. 28, 1944 and celebrated his 20th birthday in New Guinea. John left New Guinea on Dec. 19, 1944 for Morotai, Netherlands East Indies and spent Christmas in a fox hole on Morotai. First combat was on Dec. 30, 1944. They landed Philippine Island, Luzon, Jan. 10, 1945.

John was wounded Feb. 15, 1945 during the invasion of Baguio by a grenade explosion. He was transported by native stretcher bearers off the mountain to a Jeep then by ambulance to a field hospital and later flown to New Guinea for surgical treatment. He returned to Luzon April 3, 1945. On V-Day May 5, 1945, they landed Wakayama, Japan Sept. 25, 1945 then to Kyoto, Japan.

Discharged Jan. 18, 1946 receiving the Purple Heart and several Battle Stars.

After returning home John married Helen May on July 8, 1947. John was a partner with his brothers Hern and Joe as owners of Korner Drug Store for over 40 years. John and Helen have one son John W. Burke Jr. who married Debra Hyden in 1971. John and Helen have three grandchildren and two great-grandchildren.

John, Helen, and family are active members of Community United Methodist Church. John's beloved wife Helen passed away April 15, 2001. John is a Kentucky Colonel, member F&A Masons, Shriners, VFW and DAV.

ORVILLE BURKE, born April 8, 1926, son of Grant and Aggie Burke of Weeksbury, KY. He was inducted into the U.S. Army in 1944 at Camp Atterbury IN, and served four months in basic training.

He served with the 63rd Inf. Div. in the European Theatre of Operations for six months and barbered for nine months cutting hair of military personnel in an infantry company in the United States.

He received the Victory Medal, American Theater Service Medal, Army of Occupation Medal (Germany), EAME Medal and Good Conduct Medal.

Orville married Helen Sue Johnson on June 29, 1950. They had three children and six grandchildren.

He was a self-employed barber for 53 years until he died of a massive heart attack after working the shop the day before. He was an avid jokester, and always had the men in the barber shop laughing. He passed away May 21, 2004.

AURURN CALHOUN, was killed in WWII while following General Patton down the Rhine. He was the son of Charles Calhoun and Ella Hunt. His grandfather was Hiram Calhoun, and his great-grandfather was Civil War soldier Thomas Calhoun.

The family was told that he had drowned in the river and wasn't found, but the following information was located from the WWII and Korean Veterans Interred Overseas Record:
Name: Aururn Calhoun
Inducted From: Kentucky
Rank: Staff Sergeant
Combat Organization: 317th Inf. 80th Div.
Death Date: Feb. 21, 1945
Monument: Luxembourg
Last Known Status: Buried
U.S. Awards: Purple Heart and Bronze Star Medal
Submitted by Kathy Hubbard Hanlon and Karen Nelson Marcum.

CHESTER CALHOUN, son of Tom and Birdie Calhoun, was a veteran of WWII and was born in Floyd County, KY. He married Alberta Wills, born Feb. 26, 1927, who is the daughter of James Hiram Wills and Josie Deanna Jarrell. Alberta's brother, Ollie Wills, also fought in WWII. *Information from Helena Nelson and submitted by Karen Nelson Marcum.*

MARVIN CALHOUN, was a WWII veteran. He was born Sept. 26, 1922 in Floyd County, KY, the son of Job Calhoun and Mazel "Mae" Wallen. He was a member of the DVA Chapter 18 of Auxier, KY.

He married Delilah Miller and had one son, John Randall, who is married to Judy Nelson Calhoun.

His brother, Job Calhoun Jr., was also a WWII veteran, who went to Indiana to live.

Marvin and Job Jr. were descendants of the following Civil War Veterans, all of whom are buried on Bull Creek: Thomas Calhoun, William Hignite and Shelby Wallen. *Info and photo from Minerva Calhoun, niece of Marvin and Job Jr. and submitted by Karen Nelson Marcum.*

RAY CALHOUN, born Feb. 2, 1921 to Joe and Rosie Warrix Calhoun. He was the oldest of seven children. Ray served his country in WWII. He enlisted in the U.S. Army Sept. 15, 1942 and was stationed at Fort Thomas, KY; Camp Robinson, AR, and Camp Pickett, VA.

He also served 38 months in India, North Africa, Burma and China. He was with the 43rd Mobile Medical Hospital. He was awarded three Bronze Stars and the Good Conduct Medal. He was discharged Nov. 8, 1945.

Roy married Roselee on Oct. 5, 1946 and they had four children, eight grandchildren and seven great-grandchildren.

SHIRLEY MARTHA BENTON CALLIHAN, Second Lieutenant, born Dec. 5, 1919 in Tyler, MN, daughter of Howard and Hannah Hanson Benton. She enlisted in the Army Nurse Corps March 10, 1942. She was stationed at Enid, OK where she met William R. Callihan and married him on Dec. 31, 1942.

She was transferred to Harlingen, TX. She received the Good Conduct Medal, and was discharged from the service Oct. 1, 1944.

She moved to Prestonsburg, KY in 1945 with her husband and one daughter, Mary Jo. Later, she had another daughter, Ann Benton, and a son, William Robert Callihan. She also has three grandchildren, four stepgrandchildren, one great-grandchild and one step-great-great-grandchild.

Her civilian employment was a nurse at the Prestonsburg General Hospital, Dr. George P. Archer's medical office, and The Floyd County Health Department. She retired Dec. 1, 1984.

Shirley is a member of the First United Methodist Church in Prestonsburg where she is also a member of the sewing circle, and the Methodist Women. She is a charter member of Chapter G, PEO in Prestonsburg. She likes to read and watch her grandchildren mature.

WILLIAM "BILL" ROBERT CALLIHAN, born Dec. 31, 1919, in Prestonsburg, KY, son of William R. and Gertrude Nelson Callihan. He enlisted in the Army Air Force on June 5, 1942. He was in the 813 AAFB when he became a Sergeant. He was stationed at Enid, OK as a medical/surgical technician. While stationed at Enid, he married Shirley Martha Benton on Dec. 31, 1942. Later he was transferred to Fort Thomas in Kentucky and his first daughter, Mary Jo, was born.

He then was transferred to Robinsfield, GA, then to Sedalia AAFB in Warrensburg, MO and finally to Wright Patterson AFB when he was discharged in Nov. 30, 1945.

The awards that were presented to him during his time in the service were American Theater Ribbon, Good Conduct Medal, WWII Victory Medal and the Sharp Shooter Carbine Medal.

Bill and Shirley began residing in Prestonsburg in 1945 and had another daughter, Ann Benton, and a son, William Robert. He also has three grandchildren, four step grandchildren, one great-grandchild and one step great-great-grandchild. He was part owner of Carter and Callihan Funeral Home where he was a funeral director and embalmer. He is retired now.

Bill is a charter member of the Floyd County Rescue Squad. He is also a member of the American Legion. He always loves to talk to people he sees on the streets or in the stores. He also enjoys watching his grandchildren mature. He is a member of the First United Methodist Church in Prestonsburg.

CLAYTON CARROL, son of Marvin and Winnie Carrol of Dinwood. He served in the U.S. Army during WWII.

EARL CASTLE, Private First Class, born April 28, 1925 and enlisted in the Marines in 1943, serving with 4th Division in Maui, HI, Saipan, Tinian and Iwo Jima.

His memorable experience was standing on left of airport in Iwo Jima after running the telephone cable to the 5th Marine Division who were located north of them and a buddy called and pointed to Mt. Suribachi where the Marines were raising the flag over Iwo Jima.

He was discharged Nov. 24, 1945, his awards include the Presidential Unit Citation Ribbon and Asiatic-Pacific Theater Ribbon.

Earl, the son of Gar and Molly (Sparks) Castle, was the youngest of six sons. Earl was married to the late Myrene Hershberger. He has two children, two grandsons and one great-grandchild. Worked as a watchmaker and jeweler and is now retired.

DAMON CHAFFINS, born Nov. 6, 1925 at Rock Fork, son of Dave Chaffins and Minta Inmon. He served in the U.S. Army in Liverpool England, Germany and Central Europe. He also served as Sergeant at Camp Kilmer, NJ.

He received the Purple Heart after suffering frostbitten feet. He also earned the EAME Theater Ribbon w/3 Bronze Stars. He was discharged Nov. 28, 1945.

Married first to Myrtle Coburn and second to Jan McKinney. He was the father of Vonda, Chester, Dave Jr., Lori, Jeremy and John. As a civilian he was a mines foreman. Damon died Sept. 10, 2003 at Prestonsburg, KY and is buried in the Henry Tackett Cemetery at Melvin, KY.

DON C. CHILDERS JR., born Nov. 23, 1922 at Auxier, Floyd County, KY to Don C. and Bess Bingham Childers. Attended public and vocational schools in Prestonsburg, worked the summer of 1942 at G.L. Martin Aircraft in Maryland where he was a skin mechanic on nose section of the B-26 bomber. Don enlisted in the Army Nov. 30, 1942 in Huntington, WV and was sworn in Dec. 3, 1942 at Fort Thomas, KY. Childers did his training at Camp Wheeler, GA in radio communication. After training in March 1943, he was sent to Camp Shenango, PA, to Camp Kilmer, NJ to New York.

Overseas from New York to Casablanca, Morocco, then by train (40x8) to Bone, Algeria, where he joined the (Iowa National Guard) 34th, (Red Bull) Div., 168th Inf. Regt. Antitank Co. as radio operator.

Memorable experience was helping carry the wounded down a long steep hill to the aid station at Mount Cassino in the winter of 1943/44.

During combat in Africa most of the 168th Reg. Band was captured. Don was transferred to the Reg. Band, then on to Bizerte and Tunis in Tunisia on, to Oran, Algeria. In September 1943, the 34th, Div. landed at Salerno, Italy, and fought north to Mt. Cassino. Returned to Naples to prepare for a move to Anzio. While in Naples the Army combined two Reg. Bands, the 133 & 135 for a Division Band and the 168th was changed to 116th Army Ground Force Band and sent to Ajaccio Corsica "HQ Northern Base Section."

While in Corsica the 116th formed a 17 piece dance band named the Corsicans," they played music of the '30s and '40s. Don was chosen to sing and front the band in Corsica and Southern France. When the band landed in Marseilles in September 1944, the 116th was stationed in Caserne Beauvau, Av. De Toulon in Marseilles.

The Dance Band played all along the southern coast of France from Nice to Biarritz on the Atlantic Coast where they played for the opening of the Army University there in 1945. In December 1944, T/4 Childers met his wife to be, a 19-year-old French schoolgirl Suzanne Figuiere. After a lot of red tape they were married Dec. 22, 1945. The Army gave Don a seven day pass and a Jeep for a honeymoon at the Hotel Negresco in Nice on the Riviera. Don and Suzanne's children are Jerry F., Orlando, FL; Terry L., Ashland, KY; Denise A. McGill, Ashland, KY; Daniel P. Argelite, Greenup County, KY; and Carol S. Pennington, Ashland, KY. There are 12 grandchildren and two great-grandchildren.

In March 1946, Childers sailed from Le Havre, France for New York and was discharged March 26, 1946 at Atterbury, IN. He served in the Army Reserves unassigned from March 26, 1946 to discharge March 26, 1949. His medals include the Good Conduct, Rifle, MKM, EAME Theater Ribbon w/4 Bronze Stars, Combat Infantry Badge, Bronze Star, WWII Victory Medal and Army Reserve Ribbon.

Don worked for the C&O Railroad as Yard Brakeman in Ashland Yard until retiring Nov. 26, 1984.

EDFORD L. CLARK, Tech 5, born Dec. 1, 1922, son of R.B. and Nora A. Clark of Amba, KY. He enlisted in the U.S. Army on March 12, 1943 and completed basic training at Camp Butner, NC in the 7th Div. He was graded a Tech 5 Truck Driver Heavy (Btry. A, 309th Field Artillery Battalion, Lightning Division) for 25 months and served in France, Belgium and Germany for 15 months with the 78th Div. He "handled a 155mm Howitzer over rough roads and under perilous conditions."

He served in Ardennes, Rhineland and

Central Europe. Medals received were EAME Theater Ribbon w/3 Bronze Stars, American Theater Ribbon, Good Conduct Medal and WWII Victory Medal. He received an Honorable Discharge at Camp Atterbury, IN on Jan. 25, 1946. He had four brothers: Cecil, Carmel, R.B. Jr. and Bernard Clark, who were also in the service at the same time.

He returned to the States and married Mary Margaret Hyden on Aug. 2, 1947. He later enrolled at the University of Louisville and then went on to Pharmacy School at Idaho State College in Pocatello, ID. He worked as a pharmacist in Prestonsburg, Pikeville and finally in Martin, KY where he owned and operated Martin Drug for 30 plus years. He retired in 1989. He and Mary have two children and two grandchildren. He has spent his retirement doing woodwork, refinishing and repairing antiques and caring for a multitude of animals in and around his home.

JAMES M. CLARK JR., born in November 1922 at Honaker, KY, Floyd County, joined the U.S. Army in 1942 during WWII. James specialty was as lineman telephone and telegraph and rifle marksman. He spent over one year of his service in Alaska.

James received the American Theatre Medal, Good Conduct Medal, Victory Medal and Meritorious Service Unit Plaque. He was discharged in March 1946 with rank of T-5 grade.

He married Helen Branham of Prestonsburg. He is buried in Richmond Cemetery, Prestonsburg, KY.

LAWTON E. CLARK, USAAF 8th AF, son of William C. Clark and Ruth Ann Scalf Clark, was born on Oct. 12, 1919 at Gulnare, KY. Lawton made his home at Martin with his sister and brother-in-law, Gaynell Clark May and Ollie P. May. Lawton was a graduate of Prestonsburg High School.

Lt. Clark served in the U.S. Air Corps at Duxford, England with the 78th Fighter Group's 85th Fighter Sqdn., the "Duxford

Eagles," known for the black and white checkerboards painted on the nose of their Republic P-47 Thunderbolts. He arrived in June 1944, just in time for D-Day. His unit both escorted bombers deep into Germany and attacked ground targets in France and Germany. He had flown 40 missions by September 1944. He was killed in action on Sept. 10, 1944 while strafing marshalling yards near Heilbronn, Germany. At the time he was in P-47D WZ-E *Thoroughbred,* a good choice of name for a Kentuckian. The 84th FS lost another three pilots on that mission.

Clark received both the Purple Heart and the Good Conduct Medals. *Submitted by Jean Watson, Lawton's niece, and Marena Nelson, his great-niece.*

RUTHERFORD BURCHARD CLARK JR., Staff Sergeant, better known as Jr. Clark or R.B. Clark, was born at Amba, KY near Harold, KY on May 27, 1921. He was one of five sons of Nora Clark and Rutherford Clark Sr. who served in the military. He was inducted Jan. 20, 1943 in the 3704th AAFBU, Sqdn. E. MOS was airplane armorer-gunner. His qualification was marksman, carbine and pistol. Battles included Air Offensive over Europe.

He had 275 combat hours and completed 30+ missions. His decorations include Presidential Unit Citation, Air Medal w/3 OLCs, Distinguished Flying Cross, Good Conduct Medal, ETO Ribbon, two Bronze Stars, Carbine Pistol Pin, 8th AF Patch, EAME Campaign, WWII Medal, Efficiency Honor Fidelity and Wings. Jr. was injured over Brunswick, Germany on March 29, 1944 when an exploding 20mm cannon shell from a German fighter while under attack wounded Jr. during a bomb run. He was hospitalized for three months. Seven months after being injured, he received the Purple Heart.

His civilian occupation was aircraft assembler. He was a member of Chapter 134 Pikeville, KY, DAV. He carried, loaded and shot over graves during military funerals. He walked many times to grave sites to honor other veterans. Jr. received his education, opened his own business and preached 38 years in the Church of Christ in Floyd County, KY, prior to his stroke, which disabled him at age 74. He was cared for at home for 8-1/2 years until he needed 24 hour nursing and is now being cared for at Parkview Nursing Home, Virgie, KY.

He married Thelma Newsom and was blessed with three children: Brent Gilford (md. Karen DeRossett), Gwen Evelyn (md. Clyde Tackett) and Jennifer Ann (md. Jerry Keith Coleman. His four grandchildren are Brent Austin and Kelly Nicole Clark; Brooke MaShay Tackett and Madison Clark Coleman. *Submitted by Gwen Tackett.*

JOBIE CLICK SR., served in the U.S. Army in WWII. He married Rhonda Salisbury.

EUGENE CLINE, SM3/c, enlisted in the U.S. Navy on Dec. 14, 1942 he served two tours of duty in the Pacific Theater. His first tour was during WWII aboard the destroyer USS *Cotton* (DD-669). While in the Philippines he was transferred back to the States for a new assignment.

He reported to Seattle, WA to await the completion of the attack transport ship USS *Menifee* then under construction. He was the only Kentucky sailor assigned to the ship. In January 1945 he was in Guadalcanal preparing for the Okinawa Campaign. Although the resistance on Okinawa was light, he experienced one brief but scary moment. It happened at daybreak. The men were scrambling to get to their stations when he heard the roar of an aircraft engine overhead. Suddenly he saw a Kamikaze plane just off the starboard side hit the water.

By late October Eugene had accumulated enough points to be eligible for release from duty. On Nov. 17, 1945 he received an Honorable Discharge at Great Lakes Naval Training Station.

He married Jacquline Hancock on Dec. 18, 1947. Civilian employment was in the mining industry and as an instructor at Mayo Technical College. He is now retired.

VADIS CLINE, son of Exera and Kinley Cline, was born May 31, 1921, Johns Creek. He served in the U.S. Army during WWII.

Vadis married Cora Spears and they had two children, Connie and Scott. On Oct. 25, 1996 he died from stomach cancer.

EMMA-ALICE COLLINS, Y2/c, born Aug. 2, 1918 at Prestonsburg, KY. She was the daughter of Mr. and Mrs. Mont Collins of Prestonsburg, KY. She and her brother, Stanley, were graduates of Prestonsburg High School in 1936. Emma was the first Floyd County woman to join the WAVE.

She enlisted as AS on Jan. 15, 1943 at NOP, Richmond, VA and served on active duty from Jan. 15, 1943 to Oct. 24, 1945 at NOP, Richmond, VA; NTS (Yeoman) Stillwater, Oklahoma; NTS, San

Diego, CA; and RSTADCEN, Camp Elliott, San Diego, CA.

She was Honorably Discharged from USNTADCEN, Camp Elliott, San Diego, CA on Oct. 24, 1945. Her discharge rating was Yeoman Second Class, USNR.

BERT THOMAS COMBS, born Aug. 13, 1911, Manchester, KY, and was one of seven children born to Stephen and Martha Jones Combs. His father was a farmer and his mother a school teacher.

Graduated from the University of Kentucky in 1937 with a degree in law. He enlisted in the U.S. Army's Officers Candidate program, became a Captain and was Chief Investigator/Prosecutor, War Crimes Branch, Army Forces in the Pacific, July 1945-February 1946.

Discharged in May 1946, his awards include Legion of Merit, OLC, Bronze Star Medal and Medal of Freedom. He was discharged in May 1946 with the rank Captain.

Gov. Bert T. Combs on the capital steps, Frankfort, KY with a neighbor from Prestonsburg, 1960.

As a civilian he was a lawyer, judge of the old Court of Appeals, Governor of Kentucky, Judge, Sixth Circuit Court of Appeals and senior partner, Wyatt, Tarrant & Combs. He married Mabel Hall in 1942 and they had two children, Lois Ann and Thomas George. Married at time of death to Sara Walter Combs. He passed away Dec. 3, 1991.

CLEON KILMER COMBS, of Prestonsburg, KY, enlisted in the U.S. military services on June 10, 1942. He was with the 2nd Ind. headquartered at Camp Wolters, TX. He was discharged on July 9, 1943.

He went on to graduate Law School at the University of Kentucky in 1946. Mr. Combs was admitted to the Bar and practiced law in Prestonsburg and Lexington, KY. He passed away Sept. 28, 2001 in Lexington, KY.

He and his wife Jane had four children: Michael, Cecia, William and Catherine.

JOHN C. LEROY COMBS, was born March 6, 1910. He enlisted April 18, 1942 in the U.S. Army and served with the 14th JR Regulation Group stationed at Camp Gruber, OK and the European Theater. He was aboard ship in the Mediterranean when it was torpedoed. He had the choice of two lifeboats, and the one he chose made it back to safety, the other one didn't. He was awarded the EAME Ribbon and was discharged Oct. 21, 1945. John was an attorney in Prestonsburg through 1953, then he entered the Immigration Service. He was married and had several sons before he passed away.

PAUL C. COMBS, born March 15, 1919 in Prestonsburg, KY. He enlisted May 25, 1943, was Army Technician 4th Grade, Chief Clerk, 195th General Hospital. Stationed at Camp Atterbury, IN and Rhineland.

Discharged Feb. 14, 1946, his awards include EAME w/star, Bronze Star, American Theater, Good Conduct, Expert w/rifle, and Victory Medal.

He practiced law for 40 years in Prestonsburg, KY and retired to Lexington, KY. Married and has one son and one daughter.

GROVER G.B. CONLEY, Staff Sergeant, was born May 15, 1918 on Bucks Branch of Martin to Kelly and Hattie Crisp Conley. He graduated from Martin High School and attended Alice Lloyd College. He served with 1st Armored Division in WWII with tours of Italy and Northern Africa. He married Edna Ramey and they had four daughters: Brenda, Deanna, Leona and Gail, 19 grandchildren and eight great-grandchildren. He passed away March 16, 2006.

HOLLIE CONLEY, born Jan. 14, 1921 at Lackey, KY, son on Willis Conley and Mimia Coburn. He entered the U.S. Naval Air Force in May 1942 in St. Louis, MO as a Seaman First Class. He underwent preflight training in Iowa City, IA and flight training at Lambert Field, St. Louis, MO. He received aerial gunnery training in Pensacola and Jacksonville, FL. He spent 14 months in the U.S. Naval Air Station in Barbers Point, Hawaii. He was an instructor in aerial gunnery in Dam Neck, VA. Hollie was awarded the Overseas Medal.

He married Minnie Martin on May 26, 1943 at Prestonsburg, KY. Minnie died on June 22, 2004 at Lexington, KY. They are the parents of Melaine Ann Warfield, Mimia Judelle Conley, Danise White, and Hollie Martin Conley.

DEWEY CONN, is the son of Caldonia Stumbo Conn and Melvin Conn, formerly of Printer, KY and now of Martin, KY. Dewey is one of six brothers, five of whom volunteered for service during WWII, proudly served, and returned home after combat. SSgt. Dewey

Conn was a member of the U.S. Army Air Forces 8th Air Force, 448th Bomb Group, 714th Bomb Squadron stationed in Seething, England. Dewey served as waist gunner and flight mechanic on a B-24 liberator bomber.

During his 5th mission supporting the D-Day invasion, Dewey and the rest of his crew were shot down near Hamburg, Germany. Parachuting through the flak, he landed unconscious on the cobblestone streets and awakened to hostile civilians and German SS soldiers. Taken captive by the Germans, Dewey spent the next 11 months as Prisoner of War in Stalag-Luft IV. Of these 11 months 87 days were spent on the Black Death March as German captors tried to evade approaching Allied forces, marching prisoners over 500 miles on foot. Marching through the winter of '45, the POWs fought hunger, disease and the elements, sleeping on the cold ground of enemy territory. British forces rescued Dewey on May 2, 1945, one day before his 23rd birthday. During his ordeal, Dewey's weight had dropped from 178 to 130 pounds.

Dewey returned to Martin as a decorated Purple Heart Veteran. He spent his career as a dryer operator at a coal preparation plant for Inland Steel in Price, KY and in 1946 married Margarette Wohlford and welcomed daughter Gwendolyn in '47.

In 2004, Dewey realized a dream as a founding member of the WWII Memorial Campaign, attending the memorial dedication ceremonies in Washington, D.C with his family, including son-in-law Tom Williams and granddaughter Robyn Williams.

Dewey proudly flies the flag daily, and he knows that as long as he can see our flag, he will never go hungry again.

FED ROE CONN, Fed was born March 12, 1921 at Dana, KY. He was the son of James Conn and Lona Clark Conn. He had three sisters and seven brothers.

Fed entered the Air Force Jan. 20, 1943 and received training at Fort Thomas, KY, St. Petersburg, FL, Pocatello, ID, Salt Lake City, UT and Tonapah, NV. Fed went to India in November 1944, where he served in the China-Burma-India (CBI) Theater. They flew supplies into China for the war effort. He was discharged from Camp Atterbury, IN on Feb. 2, 1946 with the rank of Sergeant.

Fed married his high school sweetheart Eulavene Boyd on Jan. 19, 1946. They had two sons, Ronald Conn and Gary Conn; one daughter Donna Conn Williams; seven grandchildren and four great-grandchildren.

He was an electrician in the Betsy Layne

area where he lived with his family. He also served as a deacon of his church and was a devout Christian. Fed passed away July 22, 1999.

JAMES PAUL CONNORS, born May 1, 1924 at Betsy Layne, KY. He enlisted in the U.S. Navy on March 22, 1942 as an Apprentice Seaman, Merchant Marines. He was stationed in Louisville, KY, and the Great Lakes, IL Naval Training Station. He was in North Africa at Arzoo Invasion when the USS *Maragorda* was torpedoed and sank in the North Atlantic on July 3, 1942. The ship was disabled and burning while he was on watch service. 50% of the Merchant Marines and civilians lost their lives that day.

He was commended with the Asiatic-Pacific Theatre Victory Medal, Meritorious Service, Philippine Liberation Medal and Philippine Republic Presidential Unit Citation Badge. He was discharged on Jan. 1, 1946 with the rank of Seaman 1st Class.

His civilian employment was in the mining industry. He married Oma Connors and they have two children and two grandchildren. James is retired and living in Auxier. He is active in the DAV Veterans Chapter 18.

PRINTIS "PEE WEE" CONNORS, born Jan. 6, 1927. He enlisted Dec. 5, 1945 and served in the U.S. Army Field Artillery Battalion at Camp Campbell, KY and Fort Ord, CA. His MOS was gun crewman, light artillery. Discharged Nov. 6, 1946 with the rank of Corporal. He is now a retired minister.

DORLEN B. COOLEY, Tech 5, born Aug. 10, 1926 at Hueysville, KY. He was the son of Oakley "Oak" Cooley and Rosetta Osborne, He entered into active service in the Army on March 6, 1945 at Huntington, WV. He left for France on Nov. 17, 1945 and returned to the States in September 1946. He was attached to HQ CO 1st Bn., 30th Inf. Regt. He was a message center clerk.

Dorlen was discharged Oct. 21, 1946 at Separation Center, Fort George G. Meade, MD. His decorations and citations include WWII Victory Ribbon and Army Occupation Medal (Germany).

Dorlen married Velva Prater daughter of John Wess Prater and Hattie Allen on Oct. 6, 1945 at Garrett, KY. They did not have any children of their own but took care of Dorlen's nephew, Harold Vernon Cooley, until he died on June 12, 2004. Dorlen and Velva live on Prater Fork, Hueysville, KY.

JOE H. COOLEY, Tech 4, born Jan. 5, 1909 at Northern (Floyd County), KY, son of Harry C. Cooley and Amanda Turner. He was inducted in November 1943 and entered into active service on Dec. 11, 1943 at Huntington, WV. He left for the European Theater on Aug. 3, 1944 and returned to the States on Feb. 2, 1946. He was attached to the 3927th Ord BAM Co (ER) 143rd Ord. His occupational specialty was automotive mechanic. He participated in battles and campaigns in Ardennes, Rhineland and Central Europe.

He was discharged Feb. 7, 1946 at Separation Center, Camp Atterbury, IN. His decorations and citations include the EAME Theater Ribbon w/3 Bronze Stars. Good Conduct Medal and Victory Medal World War II.

Joe married Mary Mildred Stumbo on Dec. 1, 1934 at Goody, KY. They are the parents of Joe Hartman Cooley Jr. and Jennifer Meek Martin. Joe died May 15, 1958 at Prestonsburg, KY. His widow resides at Prestonsburg, KY.

SAVAGE W. COOLEY, Staff Sergeant, born Feb. 8, 1911 at Northern (Floyd County), KY, son of Harry C. Cooley and Amanda Turner. He enlisted on Feb. 18, 1942 at Fort Thomas, KY in the Army Air Force. He spent all his time in the United States. He was attached to the 2418th AAF Base Unit. His occupational specialty was airplane maintenance.

He was discharged Nov. 29, 1945 at Separation Base, Patterson Field, OH. His decorations and citations include American Theater Ribbon, Good Conduct Medal, and WWII Victory Medal.

Savage married Harriet Allen, daughter of James Hawley Allen and Bertha May on Jan. 8, 1953 at Williamson, WV. They divorced and did not have any children. Savage died on Sept. 7, 1963 at Lexington, KY.

WILLIAM R. COOLEY, was a son of Harry and Nora Cooley of Prestonsburg, KY. He entered the Army in 1941, and was part of what was called The European Theatre. He was in Germany in 1943. According to his writing, he was a medic and discharged just shortly before the war was over.

He joined his brother, Otis, in the grocery business. Cooley Grocery was then changed to Cooley Brothers Grocery. He married Minerva Holbrook and they lived in "Black Bottom" in Prestonsburg until their deaths.

Minerva was a school teacher and librarian. They had no children. He was a cheerful person and friendly to all who came in contact with him.

Bill was a member of Community United Methodist Church, Prestonsburg, and buried at Holbrook Family Cemetery, Middle Creek Road.

JAMES WOODROW CRAGER, Private First Class, born Dec. 5, 1918 at Auxier, KY. He was the son of James S. and Anna Burkett Crager. He was the father of two sons when he volunteered for the U.S. Army on Nov. 5, 1942.

He served for two years, 11 months and 11 days in Co. A, 77th Armd. Medical Bn. He was known as Medic Aidman #657. He left for overseas Dec. 12, 1943 and participated in battles and campaigns in Normandy, Northern France, Ardennes, Rhineland and Central Europe.

He returned to the States Oct. 2, 1945. His awards include the EAME Theater Ribbon w/5 Bronze Stars and a Good Conduct Medal.

Woodrow was married to Marietta Bingham. They had four children: Bobby, Buford, Brenda and Barbara, and seven grandchildren. He worked as a coal miner and as a painter/dry waller. He passed away Sept. 29, 1971 at age 52.

DELZIE CRAWFORD, Coxswain, born June 6, 1927, son of Sam and Rachael (Johnson) Crawford. He falsified his age and enlisted in the U.S. Navy at age 16. He trained at USNTS Great Lakes, IL and was also stationed at PHIB. TRA BASE SOLOMONS, MD. He served on the USS LST 658 in Co. "E" 6th Med. Bn. 6th Mar. Div.

He participated in the American Theatre in the Asiatic-Pacific and the Philippine Liberation. Delzie was discharged Feb. 7, 1946. His decorations included the Amphibious Force Insignia, the American Area Service Ribbon, Asiatic-Pacific Area Ribbon w/4 Bronze Stars, and the Philippine Liberation Ribbon w/Bronze Star.

Delzie returned to the job that had been held for him as a coal miner for Inland Steel Coal Corp. He was employed as a miner for almost 43 years. He was a proud UMWA member throughout his employment and served as President of Local Union 5899 for many years. He married Virginia Newsome July 2, 1947. They had four daughters, two of whom preceded him in death, and one grandson.

He was an avid sports fan, loved country music and most of all his home and family. He developed Alzheimer's disease shortly before his retirement in June 1986. He passed away Feb. 25, 1995 from complications associated with the disease.

ORVEL CURNUTTE, born Feb. 4, 1915 in Auxier, KY. He enlisted in the service June 11, 1940, served with the 149th Armd. Signal Co. as an auto mechanic. He saw action in Ardennes, Rhineland and Central Europe. Discharged Oct. 17, 1945 with the rank Private. Awards include EAME Theater Ribbon w/3 Bronze Stars and American Defense Service Medal.

ANDREW JACKSON DAVIDSON III, born in March 1922, the son of Jessica Corneilia Correll and Andrew Jackson Davidson II. He attended Millersburg Military Institute, Millersburg, KY in 1939 and Centre College in Danville, KY in 1947. Jack served in the U.S. Naval Hospital Corps from 1943-46, most of the time as a Corpsman attached to the U.S. Marine Corps stationed at Great Lakes Training Center, Camp Lejeune, NC, Camp Pendleton, CA and the Pacific area.

He was with the 5th Marine Division in the invasion of Iwo Jima from March-April 1945. He served with the Fleet Marine Force in the Caribbean and elsewhere. He served in the Mediterranean Sea from Morocco to the Greek Archipelago, sailed along the ports of Northern Europe and other areas of the Atlantic. Following discharge in 1946, he completed college and re-enlisted in the Navy for several years.

After discharge from the service at the end of his career, he served in the Floyd County Health Department in the education field and was instrumental in organizing the Floyd County Mental Health and Mental Retardation Board. He later transferred to the State of Kentucky Department of Health until his death in September 1978. He was survived by a brother Marshall and a niece Deborah Davidson Hicks, a teacher in Floyd County and two grandnieces, Greta Davidson Hicks and Jessica Davidson Hicks, who attended Transylvania University.

MARSHALL DAVIDSON, born July 4, 1917 at Norton Infirmary L, Louisville, KY. He attended school in Kansas, KY, Pennsylvania and North Carolina. He graduated from Millersburg Military Institute, Millersburg, KY and from Davidson College in 1939. He attended Law School at the University of Kentucky from 1940-42 and 1946-47, was admitted to the Bar Feb. 23, 1947 and graduated with LLB Degree in June 1947.

Marshall entered the Army Jan. 11, 1942 and was discharged Jan. 8, 1946. He enlisted in the Reserve and on July 2, 1948 was commissioned as 1st Lieutenant, Judge Advocate General's Department Reserve. He served in Regimental Headquarters Battery of the 602nd Coast Artillery Regiment AA Semi-Mobile Unit first in the Meteorological Section. He was later placed in charge of the newly formed Classification Section for the Regiment with the rank of Technician. Subsequently he was assigned to the Army Specialized Training Program in French Language, history and culture at Rutgers University, New Brunswick, NJ. Later he again served in the meteorological section in DivArty HQ 104th Inf. Div. at Camp Carson, CO.

He was transferred overseas with the 106th Inf. Div. Golden Lions in the Anti-Tank Platoon of HQ Co. 2nd Bn., 424th Inf. of the 2nd "Indian Head" Div. on the Belgian Frontier in December 1944 on a ridge overlooking the "Dragon Teeth" of the Siegfried Line, a few days before the Von Rundstedt Offensive in the Ardennes Region, a campaign known as "The Bulge."

Marshall qualified as a Marksman with M-l, Sharpshooter with the carbine and expert 57mm Anti-Tank Gun. He was awarded the Combat Badge w/Bronze Star.

Marshall practiced law in Prestonsburg, KY from September 1947 until retirement in 1993. He served as Referee for the Board of Claims with the Commonwealth of Kentucky from May 1948 until January 1957. He also served as Master Commissioner of the Floyd County Circuit Court.

Marshall married Roberta Wells on June 12, 1954 and they had one daughter Deborah Louise who married Derek Hicks. She is a school teacher with the Floyd County School System. Deborah along with daughters, Jessica and Greta, attended Transylvania University. Marshal has been a member of the Methodist Church since September 1924. He is the son of Dr. Andrew Jackson Davidson II and Jessica Cornelian Correll Davidson.

FLOYD DAVIS, born May 16, 1916, the son of Alka and Arrena Davis. He enlisted Oct. 17, 1940, was shipped to Fort Thomas, KY, and later to Battle Creek, MI, assigned to the Fifth Army, Co. C, 10th Inf.

In 1941 he shipped to Iceland and in late 1943 or early 1944 to Tidworth, England. Shortly after D-Day, he landed at St. Mere Eglise, Normandy. He saw action in France, Luxembourg, Germany, Czechoslovakia and Austria as a Technical Sergeant and Platoon Leader. He was wounded twice, Sept. 10, 1944 and Christmas Day, 1944. He was demobilized May 25, 1945.

His awards include the European Theater Ribbon w/3 Bronze Stars, American Defense Service Medal, Bronze Star, Lapel Button for no days lost under AW 107, two Purple Hearts w/OLC and Combat Infantryman Badge.

Floyd married Edna Castle in 1947, and has two children, four grandchildren, and six great-grandchildren. He was employed by Princess Elkhorn Mining until disabled in 1973. He lives with Edna on his farm at David, KY.

JAMES EDWARD DELONG, Private First Class, born at Dewey, KY June 1, 1926, son of James Harvey and Eva (Setser) DeLong of Edgar, KY. He served in the U.S. Army during WWII, entering at Fort Dix, NJ June 26, 1945.

Discharged Jan. 17, 1947. His assignment was in the European Theater with Pattons Army. His military occupational specialty was Radio Repairman 648 and Rifle. Decorations include Army of Occupation Medal and WWII Victory Medal.

James married Columbine Harmon of Louisa, KY in 1951. They had two sons, Larry and Michael. He was a construction worker in Columbus, OH, and died in 2003. *Submitted by Arland DeLong.*

FRANK DEROSSETT SR., Staff Sergeant, son of John and Anna DeRossett. He enlisted in the U.S. Army in July 1940, completed training at Fort Knox, KY with the 1st Armd. Div., later serving with the 6th Armd. Div. in Camp Chaffee, AR.

He later served 18 months in France, England, Belgium, Germany and Luxembourg, participating in the Battle of Normandy and the Battle of the Bulge. His outfit helped to liberate the prisoners at Buchenwald Prison Camp. Being the highest pointman in his company, he was sent home three days after the war ended.

Discharged from service at Camp Atterbury, IN in 1945. His decorations include the Bronze Star, Combat Medal w/4 stars, Victory Medal, American Defense Service Medal, Good Conduct Medal, Campaign Medal and the Victory Medal.

Married to Dordena Williams, they have three children, four grandchildren and two great-grandchildren. Frank served as Floyd Circuit Clerk for 30 years, retiring in 1995. He now enjoys gardening, hunting and working in his church.

JACK DeROSSETT, born Oct. 29, 1910, son of Jeff DeRossett and Julie Sizemore, served in the U.S. Coast Guard.

He was married to Angeline Bensey, died Jan. 16, 1997 and buried in Alex DeRossett Cemetery at Right Fork of Bull Creek.

JOE DEROSSETT, Private First Class, entered the U.S. Army April 8, 1944 at Fort Thomas, KY. He served in the 789th Field Arty. Bn. With the MOS of Gun Crewman, Heavy Artillery 845.

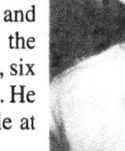

He served one year, nine months and 12 days and in the Asiatic-Pacific area, six months and 25 days. He participated in battle at Luzon.

Discharged Jan. 19, 1946, at Fort Knox, KY. His awards include the Philippine Liberation Ribbon, American Theater Ribbon, WWII Victory Medal, Asiatic-Pacific Theater Ribbon w/Bronze Star and Good Conduct Medal.

Z.S. DICKERSON JR., born Nov. 21, 1919, Prestonsburg, KY, son of Z.S. and Bertha Alley Dickerson, graduated from Prestonsburg High School and Eastern Kentucky State Teachers College. He was commissioned Second Lieutenant, and assigned to 316th Field Arty. Bn., 35th Inf. Div., a part of the Third Army under the command of Gen. George S. Patton Jr. The Division landed on Omaha Beach July 5th (29 days after D-Day).

The Division fought almost continuously for 10 months at the capture of St. Lo, the breakthrough at the Mortain Peninsula, through France west and south of Paris, at Nancy and Metz, at the Battle of the Bulge, and through Belgium and Germany to the Elbe River where it was halted to await Russian forces. Dickerson was awarded five Battle Stars and promoted to Captain.

The Division sailed from England on the *"Queen Mary"* September 5th, the second full division to return to New York. Its entry to the port was heralded by an array of fireboats and bands, best-known orchestras and entertainers. Plans for the Division to be deployed to the Pacific were cancelled following Japan's surrender. Dickerson was discharged in October 1945.

Dickerson enrolled at the University of Kentucky where he earned degrees of Master of Science and Doctor of Education. He taught and was Chairman of the Department of Business and Business Education, Florence State Teachers College, Florence, AL. In 1958 he joined the faculty of James Madison University, Harrisonburg, VA, as Chairman of the Department of Business Education and Administration and later was named Associate Dean of the College of Education. Service to professional organizations included President of the Southern Business Education Association, of the National Association of Business Teacher Education, and of the National Business Education Association. He retired in 1986.

Married to Mildred Gortney of Harrodsburg, KY June 26, 1943. Children are Richard Evans Dickerson, Staunton, VA and Margaret Dickerson Foster, Greensboro, NC. Following retirement, the Dickersons lived in Naples, FL. In 2000 they returned to Harrisonburg where they live in a retirement community.

BLANCHE E. DINGUS, born July 4, 1917 Alphoretta, KY, daughter of William and Flora Reynolds Dingus. She enlisted in the Women's Army Corps on Aug. 25, 1943. After short basic training in Georgia, she was stationed at Newport News, VA where she worked in the Intelligence Office.

She was assigned to filing 201's for troops that were transferring overseas and clearing soldiers for specific duties. While there, she was promoted to Corporal. After reviewing her college transcript she was sent to Physical Therapy School where she completed training to be a physical therapist. After school she was assigned to Walter Reed Medical Center in Washington, D.C. Other assignments included Moore General Hospital and Olive General Hospital in Augusta, GA.

Blanche was awarded the WAC Service Medal and Good Conduct Medal. She was separated from the military service by Honorable Discharge on Jan. 9, 1945 at Moore General Hospital, Swannanoa, NC. As Second Lieutenant, Physical Therapist she served in active federal service in the Army of the United States from Jan. 10, 1945 to March 27, 1946. Given at Separation Center, Fort Bragg, North Carolina on the 27th day of March 1946.

Before entering the Army and after returning home, Blanche was a teacher in the Floyd County School System. In 1953 she began working as Floyd County School Food Service Director and shortly before retirement in 1986 was an instructional supervisor. Blanche passed away March 7, 2002 at Highlands Regional Medical Center.

CHARLES P. DINGUS, T-5, born May 6, 1915, son of William Dingus and Flora Mae Reynolds Dingus of Hite, KY. He enlisted in the U.S. Army on Aug. 24, 1942 at Fort Thomas, KY. He was stationed at Fort Banks, MA and North Camp Hood, TX. He was in combat missions at Rhineland, Germany and Central Europe.

He received the American Theater Ribbon, EAME Ribbon w/2 Bronze Stars, Good Conduct Medal and a Victory Medal before being discharged on Feb. 28, 1946.

Philip married Virginia Campbell and they had three children. Virginia passed away in 1970. At the present Philip is married to Clista Sue Ratliff. He received a BS and MA Degrees at Western Kentucky University in Bowling Green, KY. He was employed by the Floyd County Board of Education for 45 years as a teacher, principal and attendance officer.

Philip is retired, but works in the family history library at the Church of Jesus Christ of Latter Day Saints, Martin, KY. He just celebrated his 90th birthday with family and friends.

TOM GRAHAM DINGUS, born July 19, 1920 in Prestonsburg, KY, served with the U.S. Army Infantry, 3rd Army Yankee Division as a Sergeant with the Military Police.

His tours include Southern U.S., France, Germany, Luxembourg, Austria, Czechoslovakia, the Rhineland, and Central Europe with particular distinction for his division's role in the Battle of the Bulge. He lost a lot of good friends in that battle and he recalled when his battalion toured cemeteries with General Patton's granddaughter as the tour guide.

Civilian employment found him as an insurance agent and investor, owning nursing homes and hotels. He married Gwendolyn Strugill on Valentines Day of 1941. They have three children, six grandchildren, and two great-grandchildren. He enjoys traveling and cruises.

WILLIAM JAMES DINGUS, born Oct. 3, 1914 in Prestonsburg, KY, and while serving in the Signal Corps he delivered messages to Gen. MacArthur.

During his time in the service he was in New Guinea, Southern Philippines and Luzon. One of his most memorable experiences was when his ship was torpedoed in shark infested waters, but they made it to shore.

William was awarded the Asiatic-Pacific Theatre Ribbon w/3 Bronze Stars, Philippine Liberation Ribbon w/2 Bronze Stars, Good Conduct Ribbon, WWII Victory Medal and Meritorious Unit Award.

After being discharged on March 7, 1946 he became the owner of a cable television system. William married Opal Wright. He enjoyed fishing and passed away in December 1994.

LLOYD R. "ED" EDWARDS, born April 25, 1926 in Estill, KY. He enlisted Aug. 15, 1944 at Huntington, WV, was sent to Camp Atterbury, IN for boot camp, then to Camp Hood, TX for 19 weeks. Because there was a big push in Europe and replacements were needed, his paratrooper class was canceled and he was shipped overseas as an infantry replacement.

Assigned first to the 10th Mtn. Div., a mule shipping outfit, then to the 51st Signal Corps as motor pool dispatcher. His outfit went all the way up to Northern Italy, through Rome, Pisa and Milan to Lake Garda. When the war was over, he returned to the States and was discharged Aug. 14, 1946 with the rank of Sergeant. He was awarded eight stars.

As a civilian he worked for Equitable Gas Co. and now does volunteer work with Shrine Hospitals. First wife Vera V. Conry is deceased. Currently married to Bobbie Jean Shepherd and lives in Prestonsburg, KY. He has a son Robert and two grandchildren, Marian and Marcus Edwards. *Submitted by his sister-in-law, Margaret Edwards.*

RALPH HOWARD ELKINS, Private First Class, born Feb. 22, 1925 in Pike County, KY, son of Ulis Elkins and Amy Branham. He enlisted in 1943 at Prestonsburg, KY in the U.S. Army and served with Co. I, 39th Inf. 9th Div.

Elkins fought across the Hürtgen Forrest, during the Battle of the Bulge at the Rhine River crossing at Remagen Bridge, and the meeting of the Russians on Elbe River at Dessau.

He sustained chest and face wounds on Aug. 6, 1944, during the Battle of Normandy when his company was hit with a German mortar shell. He was discharged in October 1945 at Camp Atterbury, IN. His awards were the Purple Heart, Bronze Star and the Ruptured Duck.

Ralph lives at Allen, KY. He married Palma Moore and their children are Debra Lynn Adkins and Cathy Ann Campbell.

WILEY ELLIOT, served during WWII in Europe and died for his country. After the end of the war his body was returned and buried at Martin, KY. Wiley attended Martin High School.

ROBERT V. ENGLAND, entered the Army on Jan. 10. 1942 at Fort Thomas, KY. He was a member of the 7th Ftr. Sqdn., 49th Ftr. Group and like a lot of other young men, was sent overseas immediately upon enlistment. He was put on a transport ship right after his enlistment with very little training and always said he learned how to take care of his weapon and how to shoot it on board the ship as they were going overseas, and how to take care of himself in combat by the seat of his pants.

One of his jobs was to set the timers on the bombs that were to be loaded onto the planes. He served in the Pacific Theatre during WWII in the East Indies, Southern Philippines (he was with MacArthur when he went back to the Philippines), Papua, New Guinea, and other places.

One war story that he told was about a fellow soldier who had his tent set up in the same place for two or three nights in a row. Each night the Japanese would come over and strafe the soldiers and drop their bombs, and each morning his tent and the area around it would be untouched. After about three nights of this he decided to change the location of his tent because he told them he felt like his luck was running out and he should move his tent. That night, once again the Japanese made their run and all hell broke loose. The next morning, when they looked, the place where their friends' tent had been before was untouched but where he had moved too, they only found one boot. That was the night Robert got his leg hurt and had to walk on it for three days to a medic station to get it taken care of. He had broken a bone in his lower leg and by the time he got aid for it, it had set up infection.

After he returned to the States, he was stationed at Eglin AFB near Pensacola, FL. He married Mabel E. Hall of Wheelwright, KY on April 28, 1945 and they moved to Milton, FL until his discharge in August 1945. His decorations include the Asiatic-Pacific Campaign Medal w/4 Bronze Service Stars, Distinguished Unit Badge w/2 OLCs, Good Conduct Medal and WWII Victory Medal. He had achieved the rank of Staff Sergeant upon his Honorable Discharge Aug. 31, 1945.

He returned to Wheelwright where he returned to his job as a coal miner with Inland Steel. Robert and Mable raised three children Bob, Danny and Brenda. He passed away Aug. 25, 1998.

Submitted by his daughter Brenda England Youmans, who would like to take this opportunity to thank all the brave men and women who wear the uniforms of our country and put their lives on the line each and every day so that we may continue to live this way of life. Please remember the next time you see a veteran to say thank you to them because without them who knows what kind of country we would be living in. REMEMBER - FREEDOM ISN'T FREE - THANK A VET.

TOMMY JAMES FAIRCHILD, born March 23, 1924 in Floyd County, KY, the son of Eli and Alta Fairchild. He was a Private with the 12th and 4th Inf. Divs. He was with an anti-aircraft detachment and died at age 20 in France on June 11, 1944. He is buried in the Hackworth Family Cemetery, Bonanza, KY, Floyd County.

GLENN EVERETT FANNIN, son of Joseph Thomas Fannin and Olive Margaret Rice Fannin, served in the U.S. Army during WWII. He entered service July 11, 1942 and was sent to Camp Robinson near Little Rock, AR for basic training. He left Camp Robinson in October 1942, was sent to Camp Claiborne, LA for additional training as a combat engineer.

Glenn went aboard the MSS *Jean DeWitt,* a troop transport ship, and departed the United States for a 14 day voyage across the Atlantic Ocean. He landed in England in June 1943 and served overseas for 29 months in the European Theater of Operations (France.) He was in the Normandy invasion and came ashore across the beach on "D-Day+2 (June 8, 1944). He also fought in the famed Battle of the Bulge, and was involved in combat in the Rhineland. He was awarded three Battle Stars, Unit Citation, Bayonet and Sharpshooters Medal, and a Good Conduct Medal. He was discharged in July 1945.

He returned to Glo, KY after the war and worked in the coal mines until the early 1950s. Then left Kentucky and worked for Kaiser Aluminum at their plant in Newark, OH until he retired in the early 1980s.

Glen married Zelda Kitchen of Lawrence County, KY and they had three children. He succumbed to a myriad of illnesses on April 19,

1999 at his home in Fairfield Beach, OH and is buried with his wife Zelda in the Lutheran Reformed Cemetery located in Thornville, OH.

RANDALL FANNIN, was the son of John Sherman Fannin and Lula May Derefield of Glo, Floyd County, KY. PFC Randall Fannin served in the 34th Div., 168th Inf. Regt. during the Italy Campaign that began on Jan. 22, 1944 with the American and British troops landing on Anzio Beach and ended with the capture of Rome on June 4, 1944.

Randall was killed in action (KIA) on May 20, 1944 and is buried at the Fannin Family Cemetery in Lawrence County, KY.

RAYMOND (WRAY) FANNIN, born Feb. 10, 1927, Martin County, KY, the son of John B. and Minnie Fields Fannin. He grew up in Lawrence County, KY at Louisa and enlisted April 25, 1945 in the U.S. Army at Huntington, WV.

Military locations were in Japan and Germany with military responsibilities of warehouseman, managing and keeping records of monthly inventory and preparing requisitions for ETO throughout Germany. Assigned as PFC, Btry. A, 751st Arty. Bn.

His medals include Army Occupation Medal and WWII Victory Medal. He was discharged May 5, 1947 at Fort Dix, NJ.

After discharge he worked for Columbia Gas and Transmission. Married first to Betty Griffith and second, Opal Branham. He had one child Glenna Raye Fannin and one grandchild Terry Wayne Cesco. He was a member of the Community Methodist Church and died Jan. 7, 1993.

WILLIS HERSHELL FANNIN, born Sept. 14, 1921 and served from 1942-44. He was sent home after his brother Randall was killed in action. He was the only living heir of Sherman and Lula Fannin. Willis died Feb. 1, 2001 and is buried beside Randall in the Fannin Cemetery, Lawrence County, KY.

JAMES FRANKLIN FERRELL, born March 26, 1924 at Laynesville, KY, son of Grover C. Ferrell and Louise Howell. He enlisted on July 21, 1943 at Prestonsburg, KY as a Quartermaster Third Class in the U.S. Navy and served with the heavy cruiser, San Francisco,

California CA-38. Ferrell's first operation was the Gilbert Islands. The carrier *Independence* was hit by a Japanese torpedo on Oct. 11, 1943. From there his unit hit all of the important ones - all the way to Okinawa.

Ferrell was discharged Dec. 13, 1945 at Great Lakes, IL, with the rank of Quartermaster Third Class. His most enduring memory of the war was watching the *Yorktown* firing all of its anti-aircraft guns at a Japanese plane that was directly in between them, killing and wounding several of our crew.

He married Olga Helen Hunter. Their children are Charlotte Collins, Russell Ferrell, Randy Ferrell and Ricky Ferrell.

CLAUDE BURNS FIELDS, served in the U.S. Navy during WWII. He married Ruble Wills Fields of Floyd County, KY, and they had three children: Lois, Sylvia and Doreta. Claude and Ruble were married 65 years when they were both tragically killed in a train accident in Titusville, FL in 2005.

RICHARD C. "DICK" FITZPATRICK, born Aug. 6, 1919 on Middle Creek, the son of Henry Clay Fitzpatrick and Alma Harmon Fitzpatrick. He enlisted in the Army in 1942 and completed basic training at Fort Blanding, FL. He obtained the rank of Staff Sergeant.

Dick saw quite a bit of action in the European Theater and ultimately was killed in the Battle of the Bulge. He was awarded several medals, including the Bronze Star. He was also awarded at least one Purple Heart, but only one has now been located by his family.

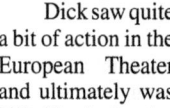

Dick was initially buried in a military cemetery in Belgium and was re-interred at the Happy Hollow Cemetery overlooking Middle Creek Bottom. He was survived by his young wife Opal and two children, Garnett Ann, age 4, and Dicky, age 10 months. It is ironic that on what would have been Dick's 26th birthday, WWII essentially came to an end with the dropping of the first atomic bomb on Japan.

CHARLES E. FLANERY SR., Private First Class, served during WWII with the Army Air Corps. He was with the 31st Bomb Squadron. Charles was the son of William and Clarinda (Johnson) Flanery. Charles had two brothers, Roy and William Raymond, who also

served in the Armed Forces. Charles married Audrey Lennemann and they had six children. Charles was born on June 27, 1921 and passed away on Oct. 19, 2002.

DAVE M. FLANERY, Sergeant T-4, was born Jan. 21, 1920 at Wayland, KY to James Melvin and Minnie Flanery. He enlisted in the U.S. Army on July 16, 1942 with the 227th AAA S/L Battalion. He served in Australia, New Guinea, Philippines, and Holland.

Camp Crowder, March 21, 1943.

National Prayer Clinic, Oct. 15, 1998, Grundy, VA.

He received the Good Conduct Medal, Philippine Liberation w/Bronze Star, Asiatic-Pacific Ribbon w/2 Bronze Stars and the WWII Victory Medal. He was discharged Jan. 4, 1946 with the rank of Sergeant T-4.

Dave was self-employed as a TV and electronic repairman. For the last 31 years and present, he is a minister with the Church of Christ.

HENRY EUGENE FLANERY, Corporal, born Jan. 20, 1925 in Martin, son of Henry H. and Rhea L. Flanery. He enlisted July 29, 1943 in Charleston, WV as a Private in the U.S. Marine Corps, Third Marine Air Wing, VMF-324. He served in Central Pacific area from Aug. 31, 1944 to Sept. 24, 1945.

His most enduring memory was leaving San Diego and returning to San Francisco. He was discharged April 23, 1946 in Cherry Point, NC with the rank of Corporal.

Henry and wife Margaret had two children, Kathryn F. Henry and Rhea Ann Flanery. Henry lived in Murray, KY and passed away July 24, 1999 in Calloway County, KY.

LOWELL FLANERY, son of Amos and Birdie Parrot Flanery of Bucks Branch, Martin, KY, served in the U.S. Air Force after WWII.

ROY LINDSAY FLANERY, Private First Class, born Oct. 10, 1915 and died April 12, 1948. He was son of William Isaac "Bill" Flanery of Martin.

According to his discharge papers, he served in Normandy, Northern France, Rhineland, Central Europe and Ardennes. He was decorated with the EAME Theatre Ribbon w/5 Bronze Stars, American Defense Service Medal and four Good Conduct.

Roy is said to have been easy-going, likeable and intelligent. Roy is buried in the Martin Cemetery (behind the depot). He never married and had no children. He was an Elder in the Church of Jesus Christ of Latter-Day Saints.

He was this sender's great-uncle.

WILLIAM RAYMOND FLANERY, son of William Flora (Stephens) Flanery, served with the Army Air Corps during WWII. He was the brother of Charley and Ray Flanery who also served during WWII.

ARNOLD FOUTS, born Oct. 20, 1921 at Kingdom Come, KY. He enlisted in the U.S. Army 4025th Signal Service Group Detachment 1 On July 7, 1942. He was a radio repairman. Campaigns included New Guinea, the Philippines and Luzon.

He received the Asiatic-Pacific Theater Ribbon w/3 Bronze Stars, Philippine Liberation Ribbon w/2 Bronze Stars, Good Conduct Medal, WWII Victory Medal and the American Theater Ribbon, He was discharged Jan. 20, 1946.

HAROLD FRALEY, served during WWII. He was married to Sidney Lou Flanery.

BILL FRANCIS JR. Corporal, son of Bill and Julia Yerrace Francis Sr., served in Army 13th Armd. Div. in the European Theater during World War II.

NELLO FRANCIS, born Jan. 25, 1920, in Garrett, KY. He is one of 11 sons and two daughters born to Julia and Bill Francis Sr. He is also one of four brothers to serve in WWII at the same time. He began his service with the U.S. Navy May 9, 1944.

Arriving via train at Great Lakes Training Center for basics, then to Camp Bradford, VA for amphibious training, then to the Fargo Building, Boston, MA. From Boston he shipped to San Diego via Panama Canal to Hawaii and Philippines as a 1st Class Seaman aboard LST-940 in the Pacific, American and Asiatic Theaters.

He received two Bronze Stars and ribbons for invasions of Okinawa and Iwo Jima and Philippines Liberation Victory Medal.

Some of his most memorable moments include crossing the Equator, the initiation ceremony, the International Time Zone and his most special memory was a surprise visit from two of his brothers while in the Pacific.

He was Honorably Discharged on his 26th birthday in 1946. He returned to Kentucky to his wife, Gladys Bellamy Francis whom he married in 1938. They have two children, James "Frankie" and Susan, three grandchildren and four great-grandchildren.

Nello was co-owner and operator of Kentucky Theater and Francis Water in Garrett. He retired as supervisor of EKCEP in Prestonsburg. Today he resides in Garrett with his wife. He still keeps in touch with shipmates and spends his spare time golfing.

TRULY FRANCIS, Sergeant USMC, son of Bill and Julia Yerrace Francis Sr., served in the South Pacific during World War II.

WINCHESTER FRANCIS, Fireman First Class, SVV6, served in the Philippine Campaign during World War II.

ELMER RUSSELL FRASURE, born on March 30, 1915 in Floyd County, KY. He was the son of Robert Elmer and Clara Stanley Frasure. He married Gladys Mae Shepherd Aug. 31, 1932. Elmer joined the Navy in 1944. The ship he was serving on sunk and he was in the water for some time before being rescued.

Elmer died on Oct. 24, 1950 and is buried in the Stanley Cemetery on the left fork of Abbott Creek.

HERSHEL DOUGLAS FRASURE, born Jan. 20, 1922 on the Left Fork of Abbott. He was the son of Robert E. and Clara Stanley

Frasure. He attended Lee's College before he joined the Navy. He graduated from the Navy Service Schools at Great Lakes, IL.

Hershel was serving on the USS *Lexington* and died while serving his Country. He was killed on May 8, 1942 during the Battle of the Coral Sea off the east coast of Australia. Hershel was buried at sea.

SCOTT GEORGE FRASURE, born Jan. 29, 1924 on the Left Fork of Abbott in Floyd County, KY. He was the son of Robert E. and Clara Stanley Frasure.

Scott went into the Navy during the summer of 1941 and was later released on a medical discharge.

Scott George Frasure, about 1941.

He married Ruth Neeley on Oct. 10, 1942. Scott worked various jobs, but retired from Hope Mining Co. June 22, 1984. He died Oct. 29, 2001 and is buried in the Frasure Cemetery at Bonanza Gap.

CHALMER FRAZIER, after Pearl Harbor was attacked in 1941, Chalmer H. Frazier tried to enlist in the military, but because of imperfect eyesight, he was rejected. Instead, he left his young wife, Kathryn, and a much loved teaching-coaching job in Floyd County to attend Radar School in St. Louis and New York.

Graduating Class, May 1943 at Boca Raton Field. Chalmer Frazier is on right in back row.

He was one of a very few non-military men to receive the training and was assigned in 1943 to an air force base near Boca Raton, FL to become an instructor of this rather new development to help in World War II. Kathryn joined him there and their first daughter, Kay Anne, was born in Ft. Lauderdale.

They returned to Floyd County in 1945 where Chalmer and Kathryn resumed their positions in the Floyd County Schools as well involvement in civic organizations. They became the parents of two more children, Elizabeth Lynne and William Chalmer.

PAUL FUGITT, of Martin, KY enlisted in the U.S. Navy on Aug. 8, 1943 at Local Board #45 Prestonsburg, KY. He served two terms. He was stationed in the Great Lakes area.

He attended Dinwood Elementary and Martin High School and lived at Dinwood in Martin, KY. He currently lives in East-Liverpool, OH.

CAMDEN GARRETT, Technician 4, born Aug. 16, 1920 and enlisted in the U.S. Army April 18, 1942. He served as a Technician 4th Grade, Co. C, 18th Tank Battalion and Co. C, 48th Tank Battalion in Northern France, Central Europe, Rhineland, Ardennes and Northern Europe. He was at the crossing of Bridge over Rhine in March of 1945.

He received the EAME Ribbon w/5 Bronze Stars, Good Conduct Medal and the Purple Heart. He was discharged Sept. 12, 1945 with the rank of Technician Grade A, 1st Class Gunner.

He married Ruby Conn and worked as a pipeline maintainer superintendent for the Columbia Gas Company. His brother, Douglas Garrett, also served in WWII.

DOUGLAS GARRETT, Staff Sergeant, born Oct. 10, 1926 in Floyd County, KY, the son of Seymour and Helen Calhoun Garrett. He served as a Staff Sergeant in the U.S. Army in World War II.

He married Clara Lucille Derossett, daughter of Alex and Loma Warrix Derossett. They lived on the Right Fork of Bull Creek. He died Sept. 27, 2004. Worked for Columbia Gas Co. 44 years and retired as supervisor.

Douglas and Clara Lucille Garrett.

He was one of three brothers who served in World War II. Doug's brother Cam lived through the war, but their brother Joe Wheeler was killed in action in 1944 in Germany.

JOE W. GARRETT, Staff Sergeant, son of Seymour and Helen Calhoun Garrett, was killed Aug. 2, 1944 in Germany. He is buried at Brittany American Cemetery, St. James (Manche) France, Plot I, Row 16, Grave 10. He received the Purple Heart.

Joe served in U.S. Army, 110th Inf. Regt., 28th Inf. Div. He was a brother of Douglas and Cam Garrett, who also served their Country.

EDWARD GEARHART, Private, U.S. Army, born Feb. 6, 1922 and died March 16, 1984. He is buried on the Right Fork of Bull Creek, Gearheart Cemetery. *Submitted by Karen Nelson Marcum.*

REX GEARHEART, Tech 5, born Oct. 28, 1915 and enlisted in the U.S. Army in September 1942. Served with Co. F, 106th Cav. Recon Sqdn. Stationed at Fort Thomas, KY, Normandy, Northern France, Rhineland and Central Europe. His military occupation was light tank crewman (gunner).

Discharged Oct. 28, 1945 at Camp Atterbury, IN. His awards include the EAME Theater Ribbon w/4 Bronze Stars, American Theater Ribbon and Good Conduct Ribbon.

Worked as a coal miner, auto mechanic and gunsmith. Married in December 1941 to Alice Allen who passed away in August 1994. Rex Gearheart passed away July 30, 2001. Children are Judith Reed, Rexford O. Gearheart, Jane Gross and Wesley Gearhart. Grandchildren are Lisa Barker, Tanya Elliot, Bryan Hall, James Gearheart and Onette Hanshoe.

JOSEPH GIBSON JR., born 1926 in Wayland, KY, the son of Joseph and Margaret Turner Gibson. With the outbreak of World War II he enlisted in the Navy at age 16. While he was aboard the USS *Steel* the Navy discovered he was underage and discharged him. He went back to school in Wayland, but his heart was still in the Navy.

As soon as he turned 18 he returned to the Navy where he spent 20 years. He was an Ordnanceman and served aboard many different ships. He was aboard a destroyer, the USS *Sigsbee,* when it was hit by a Japanese Kamikaze plane. The whole rear of the ship was destroyed. Twenty six of his shipmates were killed and 78 were wounded. Joseph received shrapnel wounds in his leg. He served aboard many aircraft carriers: *Midway, Roosevelt, Saratoga, Forestal, Enterprise* and the *Bon Homme Richard.*

He received many medals including the Purple Heart, National Defense Service Medal, WWII Victory, Asiatic-Pacific Campaign, American Campaign, Korean Conflict WWII Occupational, Lebanon Medal and Armed Forces Expeditionary Medal.

He retired from the Navy at age 38 and went to work for International Harvester in Fort Wayne, IN. In 1948 he met and married Shirley Sorensen. They live in Lafayette, TN and have five children.

LEROY GIBSON, Coxswain, enlisted into the U.S. Navy Dec. 5, 1942. He received military training at Great Lakes Naval Station 1-11. He was a Gunner 20mm. He received the Asiatic-Pacific Award w/6 stars, Philippine Liberation w/2 stars, WWII Victory Medal and the Good Conduct Medal. He was discharged Feb. 6, 1946. Leroy married Bonnie Gardner on Dec. 24, 1947. His civilian employment was with gas and water, East KY Gas Company, Prestonsburg, KY. He retired at 74 years old, Leroy is now 80 years old and enjoying retirement.

MILLARD GIBSON, Private First Class, born May 20, 1914, at Harold, KY, the son of George and Mary Clark Gibson. He enlisted in the U.S. Army on July 31, 1941. He was an Ammunition Handler 901 with Headquarters Company 1st Battalion 63rd and obtained a Combat Infantryman Badge. He served in New Guinea Luzon and was discharged on Nov. 2, 1945 serving four years, three months and three days.

His decoration and citations include the American Defense Ribbon, American Theater Ribbon, Asiatic-Pacific Theater Ribbon w/2 Bronze Stars, Good Conduct Medal and Bronze Arrowhead.

Before and after military service, Gibson was a coal miner. He worked in many mines in Floyd County, especially at Martin, and the Grundy, VA area. He was a member of the United Mine Workers of America. During World War II, Gibson's twin and only brother, Lillard, worked in the coal mine.

Gibson married Irene Hall Gibson of Floyd

County in June 1951. They became lifelong residents of Betsy Layne where they reared two daughters, Georgia Rose Gibson Burton and Mary Elizabeth Gibson Korreck. They had one granddaughter, Sarah Elaine Burton. Gibson was a member of the Betsy Layne Senior Citizens, Disabled American Veterans 169, and Betsy Layne Church of Christ. He was a humble man with few needs or wants. Growing up poor his family ate a lot of gravy. As an adult he would not eat gravy. He always said, "Eat the best and leave the rest." He was especially proud of his military service. Gibson passed away at the age of 81 on March 30, 1996.

RAY GIBSON SR., Seaman First Class, born a twin in September 1919 in Wayland, KY. Enlisted Nov. 15, 1943, U.S. Navy Armed Guard and took his basic training at Great Lakes Naval Center, IL. Served on the Liberty Ship SS *Amerigo Vespucci* and participated in Leyte Landing Oct. 29, 1944.

Memorable experiences include receiving the Neptunus Rex for crossing the Equator; flying in a B-25 to deliver mail and his seat was the tail-gunner's spot; The day he traded shifts and the ship was attacked by one plane that was returning to its base and the sailor he changed with was wounded. Besides the memories his souvenirs were seashells, Philippine money, a carved Gila monster, and a Marine's knife. He also traded a flying fish for a Japanese bayonet.

His awards include the America Campaign Medal, Asiatic-Pacific Campaign Medal w/star, WWII Victory Medal, Philippine Liberation Ribbon w/2 stars, EAME Campaign Medal and the SS *Amerigo Vespucci* received a Battle Star for the Leyte Landing.

After serving on the SS *Amerigo Vespucci*, he was stationed at Annapolis, MD Naval Base working as the duty Boatswain. He was discharged Dec. 23, 1945 as Seaman First Class.

Married Hessie Mae Corder on Oct. 1, 1938. During their 59 years of marriage, they had six children, 10 grandchildren and nine great-grandchildren. From 1938-54, they lived in Wayland and from 1954 they lived in Eastlake, OH. Ray retired from Bargar Metal Co., Cleveland, OH. He passed away July 3, 1998.

ROY GIBSON, Sergeant, was born a twin in Wayland, KY on Sept. 27, 1919 to Margaret and Joseph Gibson. He enlisted in the Army on Jan. 11, 1942 at Fort Thomas, KY. Roy was primarily assigned to the 20th Medical Corps, 3rd Army in World War II and was in the following battles and campaigns: Normandy, Northern France, Rhineland and Air Offensive Europe. Roy was one of a few U.S. Army Medical personnel loaned to the British Army. Roy's twin brother Ray and his younger brother Joseph (both in the U.S. Navy) served in World War II during the same time as Roy.

His medals include the Victory Medal, American Theater Ribbon, Middle Eastern Theater Ribbon w/4 Bronze Battle Stars, three Overseas Service Bars, one Service Stripe and the Good Conduct Medal. Roy was discharged at Fort Sheridan, IL on Nov. 7, 1945.

He returned to Wayland, KY where he met and later married Opal Gibson. They were married for 58 years, had four children, six grandchildren and two great-grandchildren. After owning a restaurant and a Firestone Store, Roy returned to college on the GI Bill and received an engineering degree in October 1954. Roy moved his family to Carbondale, IL and began what would be a 32-year career with the Illinois Department of Transportation.

Roy was an avid golfer, fisherman, and gentleman farmer. He passed away on Sept. 17, 2004, at the age of 84.

DONALD H. GOBLE, Sergeant, was born on Dec. 26, 1927 in Prestonsburg, KY. His parents were Hillard Goble and Chloe Branham Goble. On June 14, 1946, he enlisted into the U.S. Air Force and was stationed at Lackland AFB, San Antonio, TX. He was discharged from the Air Force on Feb. 25, 1947.

He was drafted into the U.S. Army on March 6, 1951 and stationed at Fort Jackson, SC, where he was discharged with the rank of Sergeant on March 6, 1953.

Donald and Maxine Newman were married on Aug. 22, 1953. They have three children: Donald Eugene, Ronald Earl and Pamela Sue. They have one beautiful granddaughter, Katherine Goble.

After his military career, he became a Kentucky State Policeman and retired after 27 years on the police force. Donald and Maxine live on St. Rt. 321 (Auxier Road) just outside of Prestonsburg, KY. Donald and Maxine are members of Community Methodist Church, Burke Ave., Prestonsburg, KY. Don was Sunday School Superintendent for three years and Maxine was secretary of administrative board.

FRANK GOBLE, Private First Class, born Oct. 8, 1918 at Lancer, KY, son of Vannie and Net Goble. He enlisted Jan. 30, 1942 at Fort Thomas, KY and entered the U.S. Army as a Medical Technician and served with the Anti-Aircraft Battalion Medical Detachment. His job was to identify bodies. He served in Normandy, Northern France, Ardennes, Rhineland and Central Europe.

He was discharged on Dec. 1, 1945 at Fort Knox, KY. He received a Distinguished Unit Badge, EAME Theater Ribbon w/5 Bronze Service Stars, American Theater Ribbon, Good Conduct Medal, and WWII Victory Medal.

Frank had four sons: Michael Van, Wendell C., Rodney and Dickie M. Goble; and two daughters, Judy Taylor and Leshia Fitch. Frank died Oct. 26, 2000.

JAMES E. GOBLE, PHM3/c, U.S. Navy, born Nov. 15, 1925 to Paris and Effie Hager Goble at Auxier, KY. He attended Auxier schools and graduated from Auxier High School in 1942. He was sworn into the Navy Dec. 27, 1943 at the Great Lakes Training Center. He finished boot camp at Great Lakes and Navy Medical Corps School in San Diego, CA. He then was placed on the staff at USN Hospital Long Beach, CA a short period of time.

He was transferred to San Bruno, CA for amphibious training and shipped out of San Francisco, CA in May 1944. He arrived off the island of Saipan in the Southwest Pacific and went ashore behind the invasion force in June. He helped set up and was on the staff of a U.S. Military Government hospital for 16 plus months.

Returned to the States as a patient and stayed in Navy hospitals for the next seven months. He was finally discharged April 16, 1946.

James married Fannie Hall Sept. 1, 1951, daughter of Florence and Riley Hall, Allen, KY. Four children, eight grandchildren and five great-grandchildren were the result of this union. Fannie passed away May 28, 2005. James enjoyed his 80th birthday Nov. 15, 2005.

JOHN GOBLE, Private First Class, born March 23, 1917 in Woods, KY, son of Elige Goble and Pearlie Kendrick. He entered the service on Aug. 18, 1942 and was a heavy machine gunner with the 3rd Army's 35th Division.

He was in five major battles in Normandy, Northern France, Rhineland, Central Europe and Ardennes. The battles that he remembers most are the Battle of St. Lowe and the Battle of the Bulge.

He was discharged from the Army Aug. 1, 1945 at Camp Atterbury, IN. His awards include the EAME Theater Ribbon w/5 Bronze Stars, Good Conduct Ribbon, Purple Heart, Expert

Rifleman and Expert Thompson's Submachine Gun.

Married to Molly Goble, they have children George H. Goble, Don D. Goble, Henry L. Goble and Alberta Wright.

RAYMOND ROSS GOBLE, born on June 29, 1924 at Alphoretta, KY, son of Abe Goble and Bessie Music. He entered the U.S. Army on June 30, 1943 at Fort Thomas, KY and was stationed in the desert in California for his basic training. Following that, he was sent to Camp Polk, LA, then to Camp Edward, MA, where he was shipped to France.

Assigned to the BTR D 125th AAA Gun Bn., he participated in battles and campaigns in Ardennes, Rhineland and Central Europe and fought in the Battle of the Bulge. He served his Country for two years, seven months and 13 days.

Discharged with honors from Camp Atterbury, IN, his decorations include the Good Conduct Medal, American Campaign Medal, EAME Campaign Medal w/3 Bronze Service Stars, WWII Victory Medal, Army of Occupation Medal w/Germany Clasp and Honorable Service Lapel Button WWII. Raymond was injured in battle and offered the Purple Heart Medal, which he declined. He felt his injury was nothing in comparison to the injuries others received in battle. One of his fondest memories was when he sparred with the great boxing legend, Rocky Marciano.

Raymond presently lives in Hippo, KY with his second wife Gertrude (Reed) Goble, daughter of Goble Reed and Rebecca Hughes. They were married Dec. 15, 1951 at Martin, KY. His first wife Violet Little whom he married on June 27, 1943 at Paintsville, KY was a victim of tuberculosis on June 1, 1950. Raymond fathered 11 children: Raymond Curtis, Gary Dean (deceased), Charlotte Raye Cook, Rowland Ross, Ralph, Donna Jean Spencer, Carl Junior (deceased), Jimmy Darrell, Linda Lou Bradley, Ollie James and Tammy Lynn Goble (deceased). He is blessed with numerous grandchildren and great-grandchildren whom love him very much.

VIRGIL GOBLE, Private First Class, born March 29, 1922 at Endicott, KY and enlisted on Oct. 1, 1942 in the Army and entered into active service on Dec. 4, 1942 at Lexington, KY. He left for the European Theater on Oct. 21, 1943 and returned to the States Feb. 21, 1946. He was attached to Co. B, 574th Signal Air Battalion. He was a Military Policeman.

He was discharged Feb. 27, 1946 at Separation Center, Camp Atterbury, IN. His decorations and citations include EAME Theater Ribbon, Good Conduct Medal and WWII Victory Medal.

He married Hazel while stationed in England. They had one son and one daughter. He died on July 1, 2004 and is buried in the Davidson Memorial Gardens, Ivel, KY.

GEORGE GOODMAN, Private First Class, was born Jan. 12, 1922, the son of Johnny and Jennie Wright Goodman. George was in the 149th Infantry and was killed in Germany during WWII. He is buried in the Shepherd Cemetery at Dwale, KY along with his brother Oscar Goodman.

OSCAR GOODMAN, Private First Class, was born Dec. 9, 1919 and his brother George was born Jan. 12, 1922, Floyd County, KY. They were the sons of Johnny Goodman and Jennie Wright. George was killed in Germany in WWII. The two Goodman brothers, George and Oscar, are buried in the Shepherd Cemetery at Dwale, KY. Their brother and sisters were Myrtle, Dave, Johnny, Banner, Sue, Eula Mae and Sandy (the only one still living).

Their sister, Myrtle, married Henry Robinson and they had two sons who were in Vietnam. Ellis Robinson was there from May 1965 to June 1966 with the 173rd Paratroopers and Lloyd Robinson went to Vietnam in 1969 with 101st Special Forces. Lloyd was wounded but survived. He had one daughter, Tara. Myrtle's brother-in-law, Russell Robinson, son of Lee and Lucy Elliott Robinson, was killed in WWII. *Information from Ellis Robinson and Peggy Robinson Howard and submitted by Karen Nelson Marcum.*

CHARLES W. GRAY, Corporal, born Jan. 20, 1927 at Sloan, KY. He enlisted and entered into active service in the Army on Dec. 6, 1945 at Camp Pickett, VA. He was in Co. D 8th Repl. Bn. 2nd Regt. He was a truck driver in the Infantry Army. He received the Army of Occupation Medal and WWII Victory Medal. He spent two months and 25 days in the United States, and nine months and 28 days in foreign service. He was Honorably Discharged on Dec. 28, 1946 at Separation Center, Fort Dix, NJ.

ED GREER, Corporal, was a native of Pike County, but married a Floyd County girl, Sonia Belle Flanery. They settled in Martin (on old Post Office Street) and had two children, Larry Greer and Darryl Craig Greer. Ed was born July 28, 1907 at Myra, KY and passed away in his sleep Feb. 9, 1971. He was a quiet, unassuming individual and was respected by everyone in the family and community.

He served under Gen. George Patton and commented that everyone who served under the famous General "hated his guts," but would do absolutely anything for the man. This writer recalls as a child playing with a couple of helmets that Ed still had in his possession in the early 1960s.

Ed served in Northern France, Rhineland, Central Europe and Ardennes. He received the EAME Theater Ribbon w/4 Bronze Stars and the Good Conduct Ribbon. He was a Corporal in the 974th Engr. Maint. Co.

ISHMAEL GREER, Private First Class, with the 1308th Engr. Co. A, was inducted at Huntington, WV on March 12, 1943. He was discharged at the Separation Center, Camp Atterbury, IN on Nov. 9, 1945. He was a Quarryman in the service.

He served in Northern France, Ardennes and Rhineland. His decorations include the American Theater Ribbon, EAME Theater Ribbon w/3 Bronze Stars, Asiatic-Pacific Theater Ribbon and Good Conduct Medal.

He was born Dec. 22, 1917 in Bonanza, Floyd County, KY, the son of Oscar and Laura Dotson Greer. On Oct. 3, 1940 when he was 22, he married Grace Hackworth, daughter of William Sanford Hackworth and Bell (Belle) Click in Prestonsburg Floyd County, KY. He was a miner. Ishmael died at his residence in Bonanza on April 28, 2004, age 86, and was buried at Mayo Cemetery, Prestonsburg, Floyd County, KY. He was a charter member of the Bonanza Freewill Baptist Church.

E.P. "PETE" GRIGSBY SR., born March 19, 1912, Lotts Creek in Perry County, was one of six children of Luke Pryor and Eliza Mae (Combs) Grigsby. He served for a short time in the U.S. Navy during WWII, enlisting in August 1943, but was released early as a "hardship case" because he was needed at home. His wife, Marena (Hayes) Grigsby, was pregnant with twins and trying to run the family businesses and also care for their other four children.

Pete was mayor of Martin for four terms during the 1950s, 60s and 70s; was on the town's city council for several terms; and ran

Federated Store Inc. in Martin for about 40 years until the mid-80s. He built the Catalina Motel in Lexington and ran it for about 35 years, selling it in the mid-90s. He was in the wholesale candy business at one time and at his death was still running the E.P. Grigsby Store in Martin, a variety store he began in 1934. He also owned commercial and residential rental property in Floyd County and townhouses in Lexington. He is survived by six sons, two daughters, 36 grandchildren and 39 great-grandchildren.

ALBERT HACKWORTH, born Sept. 29, 1920 in Floyd County KY, the son of Andrew Jackson and Maggie Elizabeth (Shell) Hackworth.

On Jan. 7, 1946 he married Edna Mae Hannah. He retired from the carpentry profession. He died at his home in Van Lear, Johnson County, KY, age 80, and was buried in Highland Memorial Cemetery Staffordsville in Johnson County, KY.

CHARLES HACKWORTH JR., Private First Class, was born March 9, 1919 in Brainard, Floyd County, KY, the son of Charles and Lula (Dotson) Hackworth. He was inducted at Huntington, WV on Oct. 8, 1942 and served with the 92nd Medical Battalion, Co. C. He was a hospital orderly and served in Northern France, Rhineland, Centeral Europe and Ardennes.

Charles was discharged at the Separation Center, Camp Atterbury, IN on Nov. 17, 1945. He received the EAME Theater Ribbon w/4 Bronze Stars, American Theater Ribbon, Good Conduct Ribbon and Victory Medal.

On Oct. 28, 1941 he married Mable Owens.

EARL HACKWORTH, Tech Sergeant, born Nov. 10, 1922, Bonanza, KY. He was inducted in Army at Fort Thomas, KY March 5, 1943. Basic training was in Little Rock, AR. For one year he was First Scout then upgraded to Platoon Sergeant, Americal Division Infantry.

He served in the Pacific Theater for 26-1/2 months and saw lots of action on Solomon Islands, Boganville, Philippines, Negro Islands and Japan.

Returned to the States Nov. 5, 1945 and discharged Nov. 9, 1945. His awards include the Combat Infantryman Badge, Good Conduct Badge, Asiatic-Pacific Campaign Ribbon, Purple Heart, Bronze Star, Oak Leaf Cluster, WWII Victory Medal and Honorable Service Button.

Returned to Little Rock, AR to his wife Bureeda (Brown) and a job waiting for him at Lima Locomotive, Lima, OH, where he worked 37-1/2 years, retiring in 1980. He keeps busy on a farm he bought in 1954. He had four children (one deceased), 12 grandchildren and three great-grandchildren.

EARNEST HACKWORTH, Tech 5, Americal Division, 164th Inf., was born to Greely and Lizzie Hackworth on Nov. 10, 1922 in Prestonsburg, KY. Earnest was drafted into the U.S. Army in March 1943. He completed basic training at Camp Robinson, AR, then sent to Fort Ord, CA.

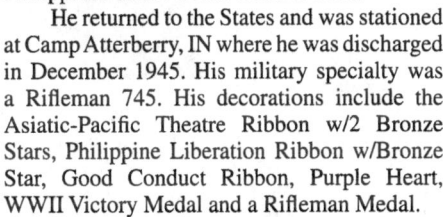

He was shipped to the Fiji Islands; served one year at Bougainville, where he was injured; sent to the Philippines where he served as a cook.

He returned to the States and was stationed at Camp Atterberry, IN where he was discharged in December 1945. His military specialty was a Rifleman 745. His decorations include the Asiatic-Pacific Theatre Ribbon w/2 Bronze Stars, Philippine Liberation Ribbon w/Bronze Star, Good Conduct Ribbon, Purple Heart, WWII Victory Medal and a Rifleman Medal.

Earnest married Susan Harmon on Feb. 5, 1946 and they live in Ada, OH. They have two daughters and four grandchildren.

JERRY HACKWORTH, Tech 5, was born Dec. 12, 1913 to Sanford Hackworth of Bonanza, KY. He enlisted into the U.S. Army Aug. 11, 1943. He was a Tech 5 with the CAC 834th. He had basic training at Fort Thomas, KY and served in Japan.

He was discharged at the end of WWII. His awards include the Bronze Star and Asiatic-Pacific Theater Ribbon.

Jerry's civilian employment was as a coal miner and custodian for the school system. He had four brothers and four sisters (all deceased). He and his wife Alta had three boys and three girls (including a set of twins), 15 grandchildren and 13 great-grandchildren. He passed away in September 2003.

MAYNARD HACKWORTH, Motor Machinist Mate 3/c, with the U.S. Navy. He was inducted Jan. 9, 1944 at Huntington, WV and discharged at Great Lakes, IL. He served in the South Pacific from March 1944 to December 1945 with Fleet Air Wing Two. He served on vessels and stations: USTS, Great Lakes, IL; Hedron FAW #2 and USNRS, Huntington, WV. He received points, Asiatic-Pacific and Victory Medal. On July 27, 1940 he married Rushie Wright, daughter of Fred Wright and Zora Williams, in Bonanza, Floyd County, KY. He died at the age of 74 at Lima Memorial Hospital, Lima, OH.

THOMAS DEWEY HACKWORTH, Private, with the 1560th Service Command Unit, Prisoner of War Camp. He was inducted at Huntington, WV on Aug. 13, 1943 and discharged at the Wakeman General Hospital, Camp Atterbury, IN Dec. 13, 1945. He was a Prisoner Of War guard and was a qualified rifle marksman and carbine marksman.

He served in the Rhineland Campaign and received the EAME Theater Ribbon w/ star, American Theater Ribbon, Purple Heart and WWII Victory Medal. He was wounded in action at Germany, Dec. 2, 1944.

He was born June 5, 1925, the son of James "Jim" M. Hackworth and Mary Ann Workman. He married Edith Harmon. He was killed in an auto accident in Wooster, OH. They were delivering church furniture from Warsaw, IN when a train hit their company truck. He was buried in Whitker/Hackworth Family Cemetery, Abbott Creek, Floyd County, KY.

THURMAN HACKWORTH, Private, born Nov. 5, 1916 in Brainard, Floyd County, KY, the son of Charles and Lula (Dotson) Hackworth. He served with the Special Training Battery, Anti-Aircraft Replacement Training Bn. He was inducted at Fort Thomas, KY Jan. 11, 1942 and was discharged at Fort Sam Houston on May 2, 1942.

On Feb. 22, 1944 he married Maxie Holbrook. He was a member of Chestnut Grove United Baptist Church and was a retired laborer from Hensley Nursery. He died in Highland Regional Medical Center, Floyd County, KY, age 83, and was buried in Hackworth Cemetery, Mountain Parkway.

TROY HACKWORTH, was a Corporal with Co. B, 800th Military Police Battalion. He was inducted at Huntington, WV, July 14, 1942 and discharged at Fort Knox, KY on Dec. 23, 1945. He was a Military Policeman and was a qualified Marksman Rifle MI.

He served in New Guinea and received Asiatic-Pacific Theater Ribbon w/Bronze Service Star, Philippine Liberation Ribbon, Good Conduct Medal and WWII Victory Medal.

He was born Sept. 15, 1920 in West Prestonsburg, Floyd County, KY, the son of Charlie and Ollie (Stephens) Hackworth. He married Imogene Hubbard. Troy was a member of Kentucky Farm Bureau, charter member of

Floyd County Farm Bureau, former President of Floyd County Farm Bureau for 31 years and was a Clark Elementary PTA volunteer. He was a meter mechanic for Columbia Gas Company. He died in Floyd County, KY, age 81, and was buried Hackworth Family Cemetery, Station Branch, and Floyd County, KY.

CLAYBORN E. HALBERT, Private First Class, was born to James E. "Bucky" and Ellen Allen Halbert at Printer, KY on Oct. 13, 1924. He entered the U.S. Army in May 1943. Upon completion of basic training at Fort Knox, KY he joined with the 501 Parachute Inf. Regt. Co. D and the 101st Abn. Div. He served in Ardennes, Rhineland and Central Europe. He was wounded during the Battle of the Bulge by gunfire on Nov. 2, 1944. "Matt," as he was known to family, was awarded the WWII Victory Medal, Purple Heart, Bronze Arrowhead, American Theatre Ribbon, EAME Ribbon w/Bronze Stars and the Good Conduct Medal.

DENZIL HALBERT, was a member of the U.S. Army during WWII and achieved the rank of Second Lieutenant. Denzil was inducted on Oct. 7, 1942 and was discharged on July 28, 1946. He was a member of the Medical Administrative Corps. Denzil earned the American Theater Medal, European Theater Medal, China Campaign and the Asiatic Victory Medal.

Denzil along with other local veterans helped organize and charter the American Legion Post 283 of Martin, KY. Denzil was an active member and served as Post Commander for many years until his death in 1996.

MARTIN GREEN HALBERT, Tech Sergeant 4th Grade, son of Martin Green Halbert Sr. and Luna (Martin) Halbert. He served July 17, 1940 - June 21, 1945, WWII. He was with the 24th Inf. Div. and stationed in Hawaii, Australia, Goodenough Island and Dutch New Guinea. He went into the Army at the age of 15 years and 7 months old.

Medals and honors include Asiatic-Pacific Service Ribbon w/Bronze Service Star, American Defense Service Ribbon and Good Conduct Medal.

Married Ruby Slone Sammons and they have children, Martin Greg and Emery Todd Halbert.

MARTIN S. HALBERT JR., entered the U.S. Army on July 17, 1940 during World War II and was discharged on June 21, 1945.

Martin served on foreign ground for two years, 11 months and 16 days with the 24th Inf. He achieved the rank of Technician Fourth Class.

Martin received the Bronze Star Medal for Meritorious Achievement in ground combat in the Asiatic-Pacific Theater of Operation. He also received the Combat Infantry Badge.

EDGAR HALE, born Feb. 13, 1922, at Goodloe, KY. His parents were Susie Stephens Hale and James Hale. He enlisted in the Navy on Oct. 1, 1943 and served during WWII in the South Pacific, specifically on the island of Mactan in the Philippines.

Ratings received were AS, S2C, SIC and EM3C(T). Edgar received an Honorable Discharge from the Navy at the Personnel Separation Center in Bainbridge, MD. in December 1945.

Edgar was re-employed by Princess Elkhorn Coal Co. for whom he had worked as a truck driver. He later became a warehouse man for the same company. After Princess Elkhorn went out of business, he was employed by Banks Miller Supply in Inez, KY, as a warehouse man.

Edgar married Bobby Jean Howard on Jan. 13, 1951. To this union was born three daughters: Gwendolyn, Anita and Edwynna. Ed departed this life on July 19, 1994.

HENRY CLAY HALE, Seaman 1/c, born Dec. 2, 1919, son of James and Susie Hale. He enlisted in the U.S. Navy in the spring of 1943 and served in the Pacific Theater until his discharge Dec. 14, 1945. He saw action throughout the South Pacific, including the invasion of Iwo Jima.

On return to the States after the war, he became involved in Kentucky politics, gaining office as a State Legislator in 1948. He served three two-year terms. He was also elected as the Sergeant-in-Arms of the State Legislator in 1958. He was elected as Sheriff of Floyd County for three terms.

Henry married Winifred Osborne in 1946 and they had seven children and 10 grandchildren.

He was a life-long member of the VFW. Besides his involvement in politics, he owned a construction company and was an avid farmer, owning a farm on Blue River as well as a blue grass farm in Harrison County. He spent many days on his blue grass farm after retirement, tending to his beloved cattle. Ironically he died on his farm while tending to his cattle on Oct. 25, 1990.

IKE HALE, born in 1901 in Floyd County, KY, the son of Charles S. "Doc" and Elizabeth "Betty" Hackworth Hale. He served with B Troop, 121st Squadron, 106th Cavalry Group in Europe, 1944-45. Ike received the Purple Heart. He was never married. He was killed by a train while visiting his niece in Roanoke, VA. He died in 1973, age 72.

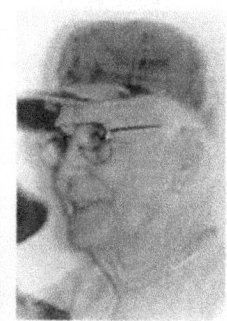

HOMER HALEY, Petty Officer 3rd Class, born Aug. 14, 1925, in Pikeville, KY, son of William and Belle Haley. He enlisted in the U.S. Navy in 1943, completed training at Great Lakes Naval Training Center in Illinois, and was assigned to the ship, LST-523.

He participated in the D-Day Invasion, where his ship was sunk by a mine. He was awarded the Purple Heart for injuries he received in this action. He later was assigned to the ship, LST-543, and participated in many battles with the Pacific Fleet, including liberation of the Philippines and the Okinawa Invasion.

Homer received several awards during his Naval service, including the China Service Medal, American Campaign Medal, Occupational Medal, WWII Service Medal, EAME Campaign Ribbon w/Bronze Star, Asiatic-Pacific Campaign Ribbon w/Bronze Star and the Asia Ribbon. He was discharged Jan. 27, 1946. Homer returned home, then attended Mayo State Vocational School in Paintsville, KY, where he received training in auto mechanics.

Homer's most memorable experience was waking up to a huge explosion and having to tread water in the English Channel until he was picked up by a rescue ship.

He married Faye Branham on Feb. 3, 1945, who passed away Feb. 12, 1999. They had one child, Jack Haley, and one grandchild, Jason Haley, who passed away on May 27, 2002. He is a retired businessman residing in VanLear, KY, home of country music singer, Loretta Lynn.

HOMER HALL, Radio-Tec 3rd Class, USNR, born April 27, 1924, son of Millard F. Hall and Lillie Tackett Hall. He was drafted into the Navy when he was 18 during WWII and received his basic training at the US Naval Training Station in Great Lakes, IL. He was deployed to San Francisco, then to Pearl Harbor.

His first major battle was the Battle for

Midway. He was on the USS *Yorktown* for five days and nights when she was hit by a torpedo and sank. The USS *Wasp* rescued the crew and took them back to Pearl Harbor where he received radio training. He served in the US Naval Air Forces as a radio operator, later transferred to an amphibious unit, and later transferring to the USS *Belleau Wood,* an aircraft carrier. He was in the Asiatic-Pacific Campaign under the command of Admiral Halsey. Homer was in 15 major battles.

His decorations include two Bronze Stars in the Asiatic-Pacific Campaign Ribbon, 12 Battle Stars from the *Belleau Wood* (CVL-24), Philippine Liberation Campaign Ribbon w/2 Bronze Stars and the Presidential Unit Citation (on Oct. 30, 1944 the *Belleau Wood* suffered a direct hit from a Japanese Zeke (a kamikaze) cruising 90 miles off the shores of Leyte Gulf. Homer also received the Purple Heart this day and the Silver Star. He was 30 miles offshore when the A-bomb was dropped and was among the first to go ashore to bring back POWS from Japan. He had many horrifying stories to tell about these missions. He also received the Distinguished Flying Cross Citation from the President of the United States, The Commander of Chief; U.S. Pacific Fleet, C.W. Nimitz. He received an Honorable Discharge on Dec. 25, 1945, saying this was the best Christmas present he ever received.

Homer married his soul mate, Mary Alice Tackett on April 9, 1948. They had seven children (one infant deceased), eight grandchildren, and six great-grandchildren. He was the owner of Hall's Bypro Market, a school bus driver, and delivered bottle gas for many years. Homer was an avid fisherman, he loved working in his garden and in his latter years he loved growing flowers and got immense pleasure from nature. He loved our beautiful mountains and simple way of life. He was a loving, caring father and husband. He retired at the age of 72 to help take care of his wife. After the death of Mary, his health declined rapidly. He suffered severe burns from a house fire. He had developed diabetes and P.T.S.D. All of the stress caused his Parkinson's Disease to worsen and limit his mobility. He died August 17, 2005. He is missed sorely by all he knew.

LUTHER HALL, oldest son of Johnnie Lee and Minnie Davis Hall, entered U.S. Army Jan. 30, 1942 and was discharged Aug. 25, 1945. He served with the 727th Engineering Battalion as a medic with Co. A. They were track builders and bridge carpenters.

They landed Dec 26, 1942 on Algeria and fought through Sicily, from Southern Italy to north of Rome. They were buried in ash when Mt. Vesuvious blew. The Pope came out to greet and bless the troops at Rome. At Naples they shipped to Southern France, fighting and building to Rhineland then into Germany.

Luther died Jan. 26, 1995 and is buried at Battle Creek, MI.

OAKIE HALL, born Dec. 10, 1923 at Honaker, KY, son of Charlie and Margaret Hall. He entered the Army on June 15, 1943 and served with Battery "D" 131st AAA Gun Battalion. He was discharged from service in Munich, Germany as a machine gunner on Nov. 8, 1945. He then re-enlisted and served with Murphy General Hospital and Waltham 54 in Massachusetts as a truck driver.

He was discharged Jan. 26, 1950 and awarded a three Bronze Service Star for campaigns in Northern France, Rhineland and Central Europe, Good Conduct Medal and WWII Victory Medal.

He died June 18, 1982 in Pikeville, KY and is buried in a cemetery at Printer, KY. His children are Michael and Scott Hall of Pikeville, KY.

TOWN HALL, born Nov. 10, 1905 in Floyd County, KY. He enlisted in the U.S. Navy Aug. 5, 1944 and was Seaman 1st Class V-6. Military locations include U.S. Naval Training Station, Simpson, NY; San Bruno, CA; U.S. Naval Hospital, Mare Island, NY; and U.S. Public Health Service, Fort Worth, TX. He was discharged April 20, 1945.

Civilian employment includes Superintendent of Floyd County School System and he also owned and operated a motel in Floyd County. He was married to Hollie B. Hall.

WALTER HALL, born Jan. 28, 1926 at Harold, KY, the son of Richard and Era Conn Hall. He had one sister, Betty. WWII began when he was a teenager in high school and too young for military service. But with the war progressing, he enlisted with the U.S. Marines at the age of 17 in January 1944. After basic training at Camp Lejeune, NC and Parris Island, SC, where he earned a Sharpshooter Medal, he was sent to the South Pacific and saw duty in several locations.

Trained in the use of special weapons and part of the 2nd Anti-Aircraft Artillery Battalion, he was part of the Marine invasion of Okinawa, April 1, 1945. There, he was a searchlight operator with a team assigned to protect an airstrip the Marines had built. After Okinawa, he served for a time with occupation forces in Tientsin, China. He was discharged with the rank of Corporal May 14, 1946.

Walter married his high school sweetheart, Aileen Sellards, June 5, 1946. They had two daughters, Nancy and Rhonda, and five grandchildren. After military service, he and his father opened a furniture and grocery store, but his father died in 1949, leaving him to operate alone. He was gifted as a salesman and, after a time, changed his business to the sale of boats and mobile homes. For several years he operated Hall Marine and Mobile Home Sales in Stanville and Prestonsburg.

He was a devoted family man and avid fisherman who also loved boating and travel. He lived in Betsy Layne but much of his retirement was spent in a motor home or on a houseboat. He passed away May 2, 2002.

WENDELL D. HALL, born April 6, 1925 in Eastern, KY. He enlisted into the U.S. Navy in August 1943 and was stationed aboard USS *Melvin R. Newman* and USS *Cascade* for 18 months. He was also stationed in Hawaii and the South Pacific.

Wendell's most memorable experience throughout the duration of his stay is when he and his crew patched up the destroyer after a Kamikaze suicide plane attack so they could return to Hawaii. He also remembers visiting Japan after the war.

He re-enlisted for one more year in September 1953 and was in England during the Queen's Coronation. He was discharged in March 1946 and March 1953 (respectively) with the rank of FCT1/c.

Mr. and Mrs. Wendell Hall have two children, five grandchildren and four great-grandchildren. His civilian employment was in management. Wendell is retired now and does volunteer work for the Red Cross.

WALKER HAMILTON, Private First Class, born Jan. 27, 1923, son of Robert Lee and Betty Hall Hamilton of McDowell, KY. He enlisted in the Marine Corps on Sept. 24, 1943. He served 10 months with the 4th Marine Division, before being deployed to Titian in the Mariana Islands. He and his fellow Marines made a beachhead landing and fought for control of Titian. After five days of intense fighting, he was shot in the head on June 19, 1944, by friendly fire. He was paralyzed in both legs and the left arm. He had three brain surgeries. He had his first surgery aboard the USS *Solace* on June 20, 1944. The second surgery was done at the U.S. Naval Hospital, in Seattle, WA on Nov. 4, 1944. Here doctors removed bone fragments 2" down into his brain. His third and final surgery was done at Dayton, OH. He was awarded an Honorable Discharge on March 17, 1945.

Doctors said he would never walk again and would be lucky to live for a year. But he beat the odds and lived 59 additional years. He was released from the VA Hospital in Dayton, OH on Oct. 24, 1945, with many honors. He was awarded a Purple Heart, 4th Division Marine Patch, Rifleman, Marksman and numerous other medals.

After returning home he taught himself to walk and drive a car. He married Gorment

Jones on May 8, 1943. They had five children, 13 grandchildren and 19 great-grandchildren.

Even though he was paralyzed he and his wife ran several successful businesses. He joined the church in 1969, where he served as Deacon, was a member of the DAV, the PVA and a Kentucky Colonel.

In 1994 he suffered a stroke that left him immobilized. Through all this he remained a man with high morals and a strong faith. He loved family and friends. He and his wife had 60 years of marriage before his heart finally gave out. He passed away on March 25, 2004. In memory of a loving husband, father and grandfather. *Submitted by his daughter, Patty Qvick.*

JOHN HAMMONS, born Sept. 28, 1907 and enlisted in the U.S. Army with the 581st Med. Coll. Company Rifle Marksman. Stations include Sicily, PI Valley, Naples-Foggia, Rome-Arno and North Apennines. He drove ambulance transporting wounded and fatally wounded to medical units.

Medals include Theatre Ribbon w/5 Bronze Stars per WD Company 33/45, Good Conduct Ribbon per Company 4, HQ, 161st Med. Bn. 45. He was discharged Oct. 20, 1945 with the rank of PFC.

He was a coal miner in civilian life. John married Edna Derossett (Hammons) and they had three children: Carol, Wanda and Peggy, and four grandchildren: Johnathan, Cori, William and Michael. He passed away March 18, 1987.

JAMES ARTHUR HARMON, Sergeant, born June 5, 1923 in Betsy Layne, KY. Enlisted in U.S. Army in August 1940. Assigned to 1st Tank Bn. He was stationed at Fort Thomas, KY; Fort Knox, KY; Fort Dix, NJ; and overseas.

Participated in missions and battles in Naples-Foggia, Rome Arno, Tunisia, Rome, North Africa, Anzio Beach Head. He was wounded in North Africa. Discharged June 30, 1945 with the rank Sergeant. His awards include the EAME Theater Ribbon w/3 Bronze Stars, American Service Medal and Good Conduct Ribbon.

James and Dolly married April 16, 1946 and have five children. James retired as supervisor from Kentucky and West Virginia Gas Co. and is a retired minister, Tom's Creek Free Will Baptist Church. He is currently an active Evangelist.

FRED HARRIS, Sonarman Third Class, born March 5, 1924, the youngest son of Martha Josephine (Kendrick) Harris and John W. Harris of Brandy Keg at Lancer, KY. He entered the U.S. Navy following graduation from Prestonsburg High School in 1943. He was on active duty from Sept. 24, 1943 until May 16, 1946.

After completing basic training at Great Lakes Naval Training Station in Illinois, he was stationed at U.S- Naval Frontier Base at San Pedro, CA. As a sonar operator, he was assigned to monitor the defense of the harbor of Los Angeles, CA. While on duty at nearby Fort MacArthur, he recalls reading the words "War Ends" as they came across the ticker tape when the war with Japan was over.

After his Honorable Discharge, he returned to Floyd County where he joined his brothers in Harris Brothers Construction Co. for the next 35 years. He married Dorothy Fern Leake on Nov. 3, 1948. They have one daughter, Kathy Lynn (married to Danny W. Lowe) and three grandchildren. Fred and Dorothy reside on Little Paint Creek where they have lived for the past 48 years.

PAUL JAMES HARRIS, born Sept. 2, 1925 at Alvin, KY, the son of J.E. "Speed" and Helen Harris. He enlisted in U.S. Army, Infantry Division on May 26, 1945 at Huntington, WV.

He received the World War II Victory Medal and was discharged Dec. 10, 1945 at Fort Benning, GA.

Paul was married to Jeanette Bonor and they had three children. He was self-employed and owned Harris Trucking. He passed away Dec. 20, 1983.

ROBERT E. HARRIS, born March 20, 1927, at Emma, KY, the son of J.E. "Speed" and Helen Harris. He enlisted in the U.S. Air Force Jan. 28, 1946 and was stationed at Camp Atterbury, IN. He served as Clerk General and qualified with the M-1 Carbine 162. He received the WWII Victory Medal.

Pfc. Harris was discharged Aug. 9, 1947 at Camp Stoneman, CA.

Robert was married to Dorothy Burchett and had two children. His occupation was a heavy equipment operation. He passed away Dec. 12, 2004.

JAMES "JIMMY" HENRY HATCHER, born July 14, 1920 at Harold, KY. He enlisted July 14, 1942 as a Private First Class with 45th General Hospital. Tours include Naples-Foggia, Rome-Arno, earning two Battle Stars. He was discharged Dec. 15, 1944. James is now deceased.

SAMUEL KENIS HATCHER, born July 28, 1914, Harold, KY. He enlisted July 31, 1941 and served with the 66th Engineers, Topo Co. with the duty of light truck driver.

He participated in battles and campaigns in Po Valley, Sicily, Naples-Foggia, Rome-Arno and North Apennines, earning five Battle Stars. Discharged Dec. 15, 1944 with the rank Private First Class.

Samuel married Reca Harmon and they have one son, Samuel Hatcher, and two grandchildren, Samantha and David Hatcher. Employed by Kentucky West Virginia Gas Co. He passed away Feb. 25, 1974.

SAMUEL R. "BUDDY" HATCHER, born March 2, 1902 at Allen, KY. He enlisted in the U.S. Armed Services Aug. 18, 1942 with Co. A, 373rd Engineer General Service Regiment. He served in Northern France, Rhineland and Central Europe. He was discharged Dec. 15, 1944 with the rank of 1st Sergeant. Buddy is now deceased.

R.C. HAYES, son of Mary Flanery Hayes, served during WWII and was a German Prisoner Of War. He attended Maytown High School.

ARTHUR W. HAYWOOD, born Feb. 7, 1918 in Hindman to John and Maggie Haywood. He enlisted June 5, 1942 in Fort Thomas as a Private in the U.S. Air Force, 64th AAF. He went through basic training, Airplane Mechanics School, specializing on PBYs and B-24s. He attended Aerial Gunnery School and served as gunnery instructor and combat crew trainer.

Medals and honors received were Good Conduct Medal, Aerial Gunner Wings, Mechanic AF Bar, AAF Aircrew Member and carbine and pistol expert. Just prior to his being shipped overseas, WWII ended and he was discharged Dec. 17, 1945 at Patterson Field AFB, OH with the rank of Staff Sergeant.

He was married to Carlos Maureen Hale (deceased) and has two children, Philip Haywood of Belfry and Rebecca Haywood of Prestonsburg. Arthur is currently living in Prestonsburg where his wife Kathryn is a resident of Riverview Nursing Home.

HARGUS HAYWOOD, Corporal, a Floyd County Native was a member of the 101st Abn. "Screaming Eagles," was one of 12,000 paratroopers to participate in the Battle of the Bulge, the biggest battle the U.S. Army ever fought. The 101st Abn. won their fame by stopping the greatest onslaught in Army history at Bastogne. Heywood lied about his age and enlisted in the Army in 1940 when he was 16.

A combat medic with the 463rd Parachute Field Artillery Battalion, he jumped with the 82nd Abn. Div. into German occupied Sicily in 1943. The Germans surrendered on May 7, 1945, the Allied forces officially claimed victory on May 8th. Hargus made Staff Sergeant and still has his olive green uniform with his Silver Wings above his left breast pocket and multi-colored ribbons below. He is most proud of the Presidential Unit Citation.

SHERRILL HAYWOOD, born Oct. 6, 1914 in Lackey, KY, son of John and Maggie Haywood. He enlisted on April 7, 1942 at Fort Thomas, KY as a Private in the U.S. Army and he served in the 8th Army Air Force and the 31st Air Depot Group, the 329th Supply Squadron and the 16th English Squadron. Haywood first enlisted in 1942 and was discharged on Oct. 6, 1945, but he re-enlisted on April 17, 1948. He recruited in Idaho Falls until July 1950 in Reg. 3 Battalion; he went to Korea with the 2nd Bn. Branch in July 1950 and returned in August 1951 where he was assigned to Fort Riley, KS. In 1951 Haywood transferred to Fort Benjamin Harrison, IN and did recruiting in Indianapolis, IN from 1952-53.

He served during WWII, Korea and Vietnam. He was wounded in action in February 1951 and left for dead, but the medics came by and discovered he was still alive. He woke up in a hospital several days later where he remained until March 1951.

Haywood received the Bronze Star, two Silver Stars, European Theater Service Medal w/6 stars, American Defense Service Medal, EAME Ribbon, and Good Conduct Medal. He was discharged on March 1, 1954 in Port Hamilton, NY with the rank of Master Sergeant.

Haywood was married to Doris Hurley. He died Dec. 13, 1981 at Beaumont Army Hospital and is buried at Fort Bliss National Cemetery.

JOHN G. HEINZE, born Oct. 4, 1925, Prestonsburg, KY. He enlisted Dec. 20, 1943 in the U.S. Army Air Force and was stationed at Scott Field, IL.

Overseas he participated in battles and campaigns in Ardennes and Rhineland. He completed 35 missions over Germany before his discharge on Oct. 30, 1945. Received two Bronze Stars for campaigns, AM w/5 OLCs, American Theater and EAME Theater Ribbons and Overseas Service Bar.

Employed by Bank Josephine, Prestonsburg, KY. He and his wife Barbara have three children: John Jr., Lisa and Gretchen.

FRANK M. HEINZE, born Jan. 29, 1924 in Prestonsburg, KY. He enlisted into the U.S. military on April 9, 1943. He was with the 28th Bomb Squadron, 19th Bomb Group. He attended military schools in Boca Raton, FL. Stations include Truax Field and graduated basic engineering courses, ASTP and City College in New York, NY.

His mission was Air Offensive in Japan. Medals include the Distinguished Unit Medal, w/Bronze Star Cluster, American Theatre Ribbon, Asiatic-Pacific Theatre Ribbon w/ Bronze Star and the Victory Medal. He was discharged March 6, 1946 with the rank of Sergeant.

Frank graduated with an engineering degree. He was employed with the Turner Elkhorn Coal Co. and was unmarried. He died in December 2005.

ARNOLD HERALD, born Jan. 8, 1922 to John Wesley Herald and Alice (Burga) Herald, Prestonsburg, KY. He enlisted in the Army during WWII, Aug. 12, 1942.

He was a truck driver. He was awarded the EAME Theatre Ribbon. Arnold was discharged in January 1945.

He married Phyllis Hyden and they had three children: John Arnold, Clora (sissy) Morgan and Rhoda Hall (deceased). Arnold passed away April 26, 1989. At the time of his death, he was a heavy equipment driver. He and Phyllis are buried Hyden Family Cemetery, West Prestonsburg, KY.

BALLARD CLINTON HERALD JR., born June 23, 1922 at Abbott Creek, Prestonsburg, KY to Ballard and Della R. Herald. Herald volunteered for the Navy in December 1941 and reported for duty Jan.

23, 1942 in Great Lakes, IL. He trained as a Pharmacist Mate First Class and X-ray Dept.

Two years of service was spent in the Navy hospital at Rosneath, Scotland. He also served in the Navy hospitals at Portsmouth, NH, Bethesda, MD, Portsmouth, VA, and Treasure Island, CA. He was discharged in December 1945 with the Good Conduct Medal, Victory Bar, European Theater Operations Ribbon, and American CAOMP.

He moved from Prestonsburg to Cleveland, OH in 1951 and was employed by Ford Motor Co. for 24 years as an instrument repairman. He was a life time member of the American Radio Relay League and a world traveler. He volunteered for several years doing Missionary work in Central America.

He passed away July 28, 1985 and is buried at Davidson Memorial Gardens, Ivel, KY. He never married and is survived by one sister Jean Herald Burke and one niece Della Burke Ormerod, of Prestonsburg, KY.

JOHN L. HERALD, son of Jeff and Osa Herald, was born in 1922 at West Prestonsburg, KY. He was a graduate of Prestonsburg High School and a star football player.

He was inducted into the Air Force at Huntington, WV on Sept. 24, 1942. In 1943, he graduated from the aviation mechanics course at Seymour Johnson Field, NC, the Army Air Force Technical Training Command.

After discharge, he married Anna Louise Hagans and they had one son, William Jefferson. He passed away in 1966 and is buried at Highland Memorial Park, Paintsville, KY.

ROBERT THOMAS "BUSTER" HERALD, born May 12, 1912 to Roland "Coon" Herald and Virginia Sizemore Herald in Prestonsburg, KY. He has one brother, Luther Herald, living in North Carolina. Buster enlisted in the U.S. Army during WWII in August 1942. He was a mechanic and served in New Guinea, South Philippines and Luzon.

He was discharged in December 1945. Buster was overseas for 24 months with rank of Tech Sergeant. His awards were Bronze Arrowood Medal, Meritorious Award-Asiatic Pacific Ribbon w/3 stars, Philippine Liberation Ribbon w/2 Bronze Stars, Good Conduct Medal and WWII Victory Medal.

Buster married Edith Gray and they had one daughter, Dorothy, and one son Robert Thomas. At the time of his death in April 1967, he was employed by H.B. Ranier Construction Co. Buster and Edith are buried Davidson Memorial Gardens, Ivel, KY.

A letter written to *Floyd County Times* in 1945 by Sgt. R.T. "Buster" Herald from New Guinea:

"I get *The Times* every now and then, but when I get it I read every word in it maybe two or three times. I sure wish I could see the old "burg" again soon. We are having it pretty nice over here now, but it was hell for a while. I sure wish that everybody was back at home, but it will be a long time before that will happen. I guess the draft board has got everybody from the looks of the paper and the only ones left are too old or too young. We have showers and a nice place, the tents are all floored and screened and it is nice here, but it is hot as hell and dusty as it can be. I guess this is all I can tell you for tonight, only I hope Doug Hays and Troy Sturgill win. Give them my best wishes."

THOMAS HENRY HERALD, was the youngest child of Jeff and Osa Osborn Herald. He was born in April 1928, West Prestonsburg, KY. After graduating from Prestonsburg High School he enlisted in the U.S. Air Force serving 27 years.

Thomas Henry Herald and son Mark holding picture of Tom's father, Jeff Herald, at age 17 and uncle, Ballard Herald, age 17 at Herald family reunion, Archer Park, Prestonsburg- June 1983.

He married Helen of Paris, France while he was stationed there during WWII. They had five children, each born in different cities or countries. His three sons attended The Citadel Military Academy. He also had two daughters. After his 25 years of service he enlisted for three more years so his oldest son could graduate from a Japanese school.

When he retired from the Air Force he made his home in Marietta, GA. He was a teacher at Chattahochee Technical Institute in Marietta and was also a realtor. He died Aug. 25, 1995.

WILLIAM DOUGLES HERALD, born Nov. 2, 1924, to William and Allie Calhoun Herald, West Prestonsburg, KY. He had one sister, Ellen Herald Horn, (Mrs. Russell Horn). Bill enlisted in the Army in WWII in 1946. The majority of his service was spent in Italy. He received an Honorable Discharge Jan. 7, 1947.

Returning to his home in West Prestonsburg, KY, he was employed by Kentucky-West Virginia Gas Co. for 40 years. He married Josephine Scutchfield, daughter of Darwin and Rebecca Haywood Scutchfield, on Sept. 11, 1945. They have two sons, Larry and Gary, and seven grandchildren. Bill is a life member of Zebulon Lodge, FAA Masons, Shriners, and a member of Community United Methodist Church. He and his wife live in Prestonsburg, KY.

THOMAS MAY HEREFORD JR., Chief Petty Officer, Storekeeper, born Oct. 11, 1914, son of Thomas and Molly Nunnally Hereford. He volunteered in the U.S. Navy in 1943 and completed his basic training at U.S. Naval Training Station, Great Lakes, IL. He served on the USS *Jupiter* based in San Francisco, CA.

Prior to the war, he owned and operated the I. Richmond Company Department Store in Prestonsburg. After the war, he established the Thomas Hereford Company Appliances and Sporting Goods.

Thomas married Inez May Richmond in August 1932. They had three sons: David, Thomas III and John, and six grandchildren. He passed away March 27, 1995 and is buried beside his wife in the Richmond Memorial Cemetery in Prestonsburg. *Submitted by his son, David R. Hereford.*

JESS J. HICKS, May 28 1925-July 27, 1959, son of Wm. and Elsie Hale Hicks, served in the U.S. Army during WWII. He was born at Hipps, KY and married Suzannie Flanery.

WILLIE HICKS, born Aug. 22, 1918 in Hippo, KY, son of Bill and Jemima Hicks. In 1938 he left the area to move to Carrollton, KY where he participated in the Works Project Program to learn automotive/collision repair skills. He remained there until 1941 then lived in Louisville, KY.

In February 1942 he enlisted in the U.S. Army as a result of WWII. He was first stationed at Fort Eustis, VA and the end of 1946 was in Honolulu, HI. During his military career, he reached the rank of Sergeant and was a drill instructor where he helped prepare new recruits to become soldiers before they left for their assignments overseas.

On Nov. 5, 1942 he married Virginia Click and had four children and four grandchildren. He enjoyed success for almost 40 years as an auto-body repairman, first in Salyersville, KY then eventually opening his own business in 1961. In 1963 he moved his business to Graham Street in Prestonsburg, KY and officially opened it as Hicks Body Shop. He retired from his business in 1985.

HENRY LOUIS HOLBROOK, Private, born May 29, 1922. His home was on Middlecreek Road, Prestonsburg, KY. He was the son of Henry F. Holbrook and Alka Adams Holbrook. He graduated from Prestonsburg High School in 1940 and he married Juanita from Indiana.

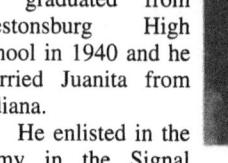

He enlisted in the Army in the Signal Corp and received training at the University of Nebraska, University of Alabama and University of Kentucky. He was taken out of school and sent overseas in September 1944. He was a member of Co. C 262nd Inf. 66th Div. and was killed saving a superior officer on Jan. 7, 1945 while serving in Italy. He was awarded a Purple Heart.

JOSEPH WHEELER HOLBROOK, Private, born April 26, 1913, the son of Henry F. Holbrook and Roxie Alley Holbrook. His home was on Middlecreek Road, Prestonsburg, KY. He graduated from Bonanza High School and worked for Princess Elkhorn Coal Company at David, KY.

He went into the Army and was a member of Co. F 179th Inf. Bn., 49th Div. He received EAME Theater Ribbon w/4 Bronze Stars, Good Conduct Medal, WWII Victory Medal and a Purple Heart.

He was killed in an automobile accident on Dec. 14, 1955. He was married to Essie Joseph of Salyersville, KY.

SELDON F. HORNE, born Feb. 15, 1919 to Mr. and Mrs. James L. Horne. He enlisted Sept. 19, 1943 with the 4th Inf. Unit, trained at Fort Knox, then was transferred to Tyler, TX.

He was then sent overseas. He served in the Army a total of seven months before he was killed in Normandy, France where he was buried until May 1948 when he was then taken to Camp Nelson National Cemetery at Nicholasville. He received the Purple Heart.

He was married to Anna B. Horne Meador. His son is Seldon D. Horne of Prestonsburg. He has one granddaughter Kimberly Dawn Horne of Lexington, KY.

JOHNIE HOWELL, Private First Class, Co. A, 800th Military Police Battalion, served in the U.S. Army from July 11, 1942 until Dec.

13, 1945. He saw action in New Guinea and the Philippines. He received the Asiatic-Pacific Theater Ribbon w/3 Bronze Stars, Philippines Liberation Ribbon, Good Conduct Medal, and WWII Victory Medal.

He was born May 13, 1921, son of Alexander "Alec" and Dorsie Osborne Howell of McDowell, KY. He had three brothers: Rudolph, Ray and Adrian; three half-sisters: Margaret Stumbo, Rosie Thomas and Veda England.

Before entering service, he was a tipple man at Ligon, KY. He married Mary Louise Moore, daughter of Winfield and Callie Moore of Ligon, KY. They had seven daughters: Dorothy Newman, Linda Sue McCoy, Anna Rose Jenkins, Carol McGlothen, Brenda Kay Mullins, Beverly Fay Hall and Kimberly Little.

Johnie worked for the Inland Steel Company as a joy operator in the mines. He and Mary lived in Ligon, Hi Hat, and Wheelwright while they raised their family.

At 43 years of age, he died in his sleep from a heart attack on Aug. 24, 1964. He was buried in the Newman Cemetery at Hi Hat, KY.

COLUMBUS HUBBARD, son of Clyde and Inez Addington Hubbard and the grandson of Reverend Malcom and Lula Kendrick Hubbard and of Monroe "Judge" and Frances Hubbard Addington. Columbus was born in Prestonsburg, Floyd County, KY on Oct. 18, 1928, the third of 15 children born to Clyde and Inez. Columbus  enlisted in the U.S. Army in October 1948. He completed his basic training at Fort Dix, NJ and was assigned to Co. E of the 6th Armored Cavalry Regiment. He served with his regiment in Germany for eight years.

He lived at Camp Dennison, near Milford and was a foreman for Keller's Industries in Cincinnati. Taking a short vacation, he was visiting his mother in Thurman and suffered a heart attack in Wellston while visiting in the home of his sister-in-law, Mrs. Vivian Martin, and family, on Sunday evening. He died en route to the hospital in the Gaskill ambulance and was pronounced dead on arrival at Holzer Hospital in Gallipolis. He was 38. He was buried in Ridgewood Cemetery.

Besides his mother he leaves four children: Phyllis, Charles, Laura and Ivan; and the following brothers and sisters: Joan of Athens, Lula of Kentucky, Betty of Gallipolis, Blain of Jackson Rt. 4, Armine Lambert of Gallipolis, Mae of Kingston, Garry of Cleveland, David and Hazel Dunn of Circleville, Wayne in Korea, Baskum and Opal Sharp of Jackson. *Submitted by Kathy Hubbard Hanlon and cousin, Karen Nelson Marcum.*

JOSEPH HARRIS HUBBARD, born Sept. 16, 1916 in Floyd County, the son of the late Malcolm and Rebecca Harmon Hubbard. He graduated from Prestonsburg High School in 1937 and joined the U.S. Army Air Corps in 1939.

He rose to the rank of Staff Sergeant with the 7th Air Corps, serving with the 19th Pursuit Squadron and the 72nd and 73rd Fighter Squadrons. He was stationed at Wheeler Field, Pearl Harbor, HI, during the 1941 attack and was posted on Midway Island.

He was discharged from the service in 1945, having earned the Legion of Merit for his actions at Midway.

He moved from Prestonsburg to Adrain, MI, in 1947, where he was a supervisor for Stubnitz Green Spring Corporation, until 1977. He was manager for Protec Inc., from 1978-84. From 1984-91 he was employed by the United Postal Service in Winder, GA, and in Washington, GA.

He was a life member of several Michigan and Georgia chapters of American Legion. Am Vets, the VFW, and Pearl Harbor Survivors Association. He was also a member in Adrain of the Dads and Fans Club and Eagles Club. He distinguished himself as the Post Adjutant/Quartermaster in 1992-93 for Post 5899 in Washington, GA, where a memorial service was held in his honor after he died at his home near Washington, GA, during the week of July 4, 1997. He was 80 years old.

He is survived by his children, Joseph H. Hubbard II of Adrain, MI; Leilani Hubbard Ruesink of Three Rivers, MI; Yvonne Brown Hubbard of Charlottesville, VA; Mike Hubbard of Chevy Chase, MD; and Veronica Lynne Hubbard of Annandale, VA; his siblings, Clara Dutko of Columbus, OH; Frances Branham and Jean Hackworth, both of Prestonsburg; and James Bruce Hubbard of Chicago, IL; and 12 grandchildren. He was cremated.

BRUCE HUFF, son of Grover Cleveland and Vilora Slone Huff, served aboard a battleship that prepared the way for the greatest amphibious landing of the Pacific War. Off the coast of Iwo Jima he watched and applauded as the Marines raised the American Flag atop Mount Suribachi. This was captured in a photograph taken by Joe Rosenthal and was used to promote the war effort. It became the most famous photo of WWII.

JOHN E. HUFF, born Feb. 4, 1922 in Prestonsburg, KY to Price and Edna Huff. He enlisted Oct. 27, 1942 as a PFC in the U.S. Army in the Anti-Tank Company, 7th Regt., 3rd Inf. Div. and on Nov. 10, 1943, he was in training in Wheeler, GA.

On Feb. 13, 1943 he embarked from New York and traveled to Casablanca, Africa. He joined the 3rd Div. on Spanish Moroccan border, then to Tunisia. He made an amphibious landing in Sicily before going to Salerno and Maples, Italy and Mt. Cassino. On Jan. 22, 1944 amphibious landing at Anzio then on to Rome.

Amphibious landing in Southern France up the Rhine River Valley to Strassburg to Comar pocket where he was wounded. He was sent to the hospital then returned to his company and crossed the Rhine River to Mannheim, Nuremberg and Munich Berchtesgarden, Hitler's home. He went to Salzburg, Austria, and when the war ended in May 1945, on his way home, he traveled to England aboard the *Queen Elisabeth* en route to the U.S.

He received the Combat Infantryman Badge, Purple Heart, District Unit Citation, Good Conduct Medal, European Theatre Ribbon w/7 Battle Stars and 3 Arrowheads and French Fourragere. His most enduring memory is the time he spent on Anzio Beachhead.

John married Anna L. Huff, they have two daughters, Sandra L. Sandusky and Sherry L. Bruemmer, and four grandchildren. John passed away July 2, 2005.

MONT R. HUFF, having survived the Dec. 7, 1941, attack on Pearl Harbor, went on to serve in the Philippine Islands where some of the bloodiest battles of WWII were fought. Also during his military career, he served with the last active horse cavalry at Fort Meade, MD where he was bugler and played TAPS for soldiers being interred in Arlington National Cemetery. Mont is the son of Grover Cleveland and Vilora Slone Huff of Pippa Passes.

ARTHUR FRANKLIN "ART" HUGHES, born March 6, 1917, in Floyd County, the son of Millard and Josie Wright Hughes. Drafted in 1944 in U.S. Army, trained at Fort Bliss, TX and served during clean-up operations in the Philippines. After about 18 months he was discharged in 1945 with the rank Corporal.

His civilian employment was automobile dealer. He married Oma Josephine May on June 25, 1937. He died Jan. 15, 1991. He had five children: Dolores (Harrington), Dawn (Hicks), Mona (May), Randall Hughes and Brenda (Vanderpool), and 12 grandchildren.

EARL HUGHES, Private, born May 31, 1923, son of Eugene Wallace Hughes and Lillie Rose Blair Hughes.

He enlisted in the U.S. Army in August 1943 and completed basic training in Camp Blanding, FL.

He was shipped to North Africa and served in combat in North Africa, Sicily, Italy and France. He earned the WWII Victory Medal, EAME Ribbon w/3 Bronze Stars, Good Conduct Medal and a Meritorious Unit Award with the 88th Inf. Div. He was discharged in December 1945.

Earl married childhood sweetheart Ruby Lewis Sammons Hughes on March 19, 1943. They have four children: Roger D. Hughes (LT USN Ret.), Ronald H. Hughes (GS13 MSHA Ret.), Deana G. Hughes Newson (Director of Human Resources for Martin Co. Fl. Schools) and Dr. Tonda L. Hughes (University of Illinois Chicago School of Nursing Professor). Earl and Ruby have 10 grandchildren and nine great-grandchildren.

Earl retired from coal mining after a 43-year-career. He is a member of the Wheelwright Lodge F&AM #889 and the Prestonsburg Church of Christ.

CARL S. HUMBLE, born in Dwale, KY. He enlisted in the U.S. Army in April 1944 during WWII. Wounded, he received the Purple Heart. After his discharge in 1947, he worked for Ford Motor Co. Married to Ethel McKinney, they had five children, 17 grandchildren and 15 great-grandchildren.

CHARLES CLIFTON HUMPHREY, born Nov. 27, 1923, Ligon, KY. He enlisted June 30, 1943 in the U.S. Army, serving as Combat Engineer. He was stationed in Fort Thomas, KY, Fort Belvoir, VA, Rome, Southern France, Rhineland, Europe and North Africa.

Memorable experiences include building bridge across Rhine River under fire and D-Day mission.

Discharged March 29, 1946 as Sergeant. His awards include EAME Theater Ribbon w/4 Bronze Stars, Good Conduct, Victory WWII, Distinguished Unit Badge and Bronze Arrowhead.

Charles was the son of Herbert and Nannie Humphrey. He married Fern Stanley Nov. 15, 1947 and they had four children, seven grandchildren and eight great-grandchildren. As a civilian he worked as a coal miner. He passed away May 7, 2005.

EUGENE HYDEN, Tech Sergeant, born Oct. 14, 1921, the son of the late Estil and Eva Hyden. He grew up in Auxier, KY and graduated from Auxier High School in 1940. He was attending Alice Lloyd College when he volunteered for the U.S. Air Force. He completed basic training at Chanute Field, IL. Later he was stationed at Kelly AFB, TX.

When he was deployed overseas he was first stationed in the Philippines, then on Guadalcanal. He was a radio operator in a B-52 bomber. He had completed 49 missions and was on number 50 when his plane disappeared and he was listed missing in action on Nov. 14, 1943. His plane was never found and he was declared dead Jan. 25, 1945. TSgt. Hyden is survived by one sister, Pauline H. Sparks.

JOE TAYLOR HYDEN, Lieutenant, son of Joe K. and Nora E. Allen Hyden. He volunteered for the Marines immediately after Pearl Harbor. He, along with a cousin, William W. "Bud" Hyden, son of William W. and Myrtle Harmon Hyden, joined the service together.

William was later stationed at the Pentagon. Joe Taylor went to Officer Candidate School and served in the South Pacific for the duration of the war. After he returned from the service he married Dixie Lou Ratliff and had four children: Dr. Alan Joe Hyden, Debra Lou Hyden Burke, Terri Sue Hyden Allen, and Joe Taylor "Joey" Hyden II. He also raised, as his son, Dr. Robert David Marshall, son of Buddy Marshall and Dixie Ratliff Marshall Hyden. Bobby was killed during WWII.

Before joining the Marines he attended Caney Creek (Alice Lloyd College). He received his A.B. Degree from U. of Kentucky. He returned to his alma mater, Prestonsburg High where he taught science and coached football.

After his discharge he graduated from U. of Louisville, School of Dentistry. He opened his dental practice in Martin, KY where he lived and raised his family. Joe Taylor died in 1984 and is buried in Davidson Memorial Garden, Ivel, KY.

THOMAS KIT HYDEN, son of Joe K. and Nora E. Allen Hyden. He joined the U.S. Navy in 1939. He was stationed in Kodiak and Nome, Alaska for a time. After Pearl Harbor he was placed on a hospital ship as a Pharmacist's Mate. He also served on the USS *Jacob Jones*. He was wounded when he retrieved a hand grenade and threw it overboard.

He was transferred from the *Jacob Jones* five days before it was attacked and sunk. He married Muriel Rockne and had one son, Thomas John Hyden. Tom was killed in Billings, MT in an auto accident in 1953.

ABB IRICK, served in U.S. Armed Services attached to General Patton's 3rd Armd. Div. He received the Bronze Star Medal, Good

Conduct Medal, American Campaign Medal, EAME Campaign Medal w/Bronze Star, WWII Victory Medal, Combat Medic Badge 1st Awd., Honorable Service Lapel Button and Driver and Mechanic Badge. Abb married Ethel Hall and they had two daughters, Diana and Abby. He is deceased.

VIRGIL ISAAC, born April 9, 1923 at Alphoretta, KY. His parents were Maryland and Anna Compton Isaac. He married Joanna Smith Feb. 3, 1942 and a year later was called to serve his country. Virgil was inducted into the U.S. Army March 25, 1943. He completed basic training at Fort Thomas, KY. Virgil acquired the rank of Sergeant and was with the 492nd Fighter Squadron.

He was shipped overseas and was in on the invasion of Normandy. He was also stationed in Northern France, Ardennes, Rhineland, Central Europe and Air Offensive Europe.

His decorations include EAME Ribbon w/6 Bronze Stars, Good Conduct Medal, Distinguished Unit Badge w/Bronze Star and Belgian-Fourragere. Virgil departed the service at Camp Atterbury, IN with an Honorable Discharge.

After returning home Virgil worked in the coal mines and was a member of the UMWA. He and Joanna had eight children. He passed away on June 14, 1995 and is buried in the family cemetery at Dinwood, KY.

JOHN S. ISON, born Aug. 23, 1918 and enlisted in the U.S. Army. He served with HQ 82nd Armored Medical Battalion of the 12th Armd. Div., Classification T-4. He was stationed at Camp Campbell, KY, Texas, Nashville, England, France and Germany.

His group joined up with General Patton and took Germany. They were the second group to cross the bridge at Remagan. As part of a Medical Battalion, he re-entered parts of France and Germany ahead of armored units (after infantry). John made some lifelong friends in the service.

John was awarded EAME Theatre Ribbons w/2 Bronze Service Stars, American Theatre Ribbon, Good Conduct Medal, WWII Victory Medal, Meritorious Unit Award, GO#28HQ 12th AD and the European Theatre Ribbon. He was discharged Dec. 28, 1945. His civilian employment was in sales, the coal industry, he operated a service station with his brother, and co-owned a car dealership.

On Sept. 20, 1941, John married Helen Price, and had two children, James and Carolyn, and two grandchildren, John Steven and Leslie Anne. John enjoyed working in his church and the Kiwanis organization, camping and fishing. He passed away Oct. 19, 1975.

FREDERICK ALLEN JAMES, Seaman First Class, born Aug. 14, 1927 and served in the U.S. Navy from June 26, 1945 to Aug. 19, 1946. Stationed at NTC Sampson, NY; USS *Shangri-La* and NAS San Diego, CA.

Awards include Pacific Theater Ribbon, American Theater Ribbon and Victory Medal.

As a civilian he was employed with Southern Bell for 33 years. Member of VFW, Floyd County Rescue Squad, Presbyterian Church, Masons, Boy Scout leader, Little League football, Floyd County and Big Sandy Historical Societies.

Married Ruth Hall and has three children: Freddy II, Mary Ann Purvis and Emily Anderson. Married Sue Millian, had one son Matthew. Married Joy Jones.

TOM JAMES, born Aug. 14, 1900. Enlisted Sept. 10, 1943 and served as Carpenters Mate First Class in Pearl Harbor, Honolulu, Hawaii. He was discharged Sept. 10, 1945.

JOE JARRELL, son of Epp and Millie Jarrell, was born on April 28, 1923, Dana, KY. His induction into the Army was on April 8, 1944 at Fort Thomas, KY. He was sent to Camp Ting Hao, Kinming, China. He participated as Private First Class in the India-Burma Campaign, Central Burma Campaign, and China Offensive Campaign.

His occupational specialty was half track driver. This involved hauling personnel, servicing vehicles daily and doing repairs on them.

Some decorations were Asiatic-Pacific Service Medal, Combat Infantry Badge, Good Conduct Medal and WWII Victory Medal. He also was noted for his Carbine Marksmanship, Rifle M-1 Sharpshooter, Bar Cal 30 Marksman, SMG M-3 Expert.

He married Offie Kidd on Dec. 20, 1946 and they raised two sons and one daughter at Dana, KY. He was a self employed coal truck driver. He belonged to Sammy Clark Freewill Baptist Church. He passed away on July 9, 1998.

GARFIELD JOHNSON, son of Tab Johnson, served in the U.S. Army during WWII. He was injured but didn't let it keep him from working as a coal miner for 24 years.

He received several medals including Good Conduct and Marksmanship. He currently lives on Left Beaver with his wife.

Garfield Johnson, Jan. 29, 1943 during WWII.

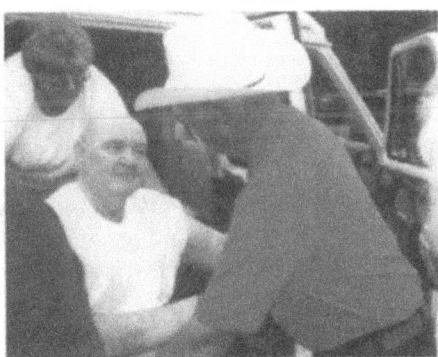

Garfield being lowered into the arms of his brother Jack, who had not seen each other in 24 years. This was taken at the Johnson Family Reunion on Aug. 7, 2004

GROVER JOHNSON, born March 17, 1917, son of James A. and Melvinie McCurry Johnson. He enlisted in the U.S. Army Sept. 24, 1940. He completed his training in California and was then sent to the Ardennes and Rhineland. He was discharged on Oct. 10, 1945 with the rank of Platoon Sergeant 745. He received the Combat Infantryman Badge, EAME Theater Ribbon w/2 Bronze Stars per WD and GO #33/45.

When he returned home he began working as a coal miner for Inland Steel and later Island Creek Coal he retired after 30 years. He was married to Delores Bates Johnson who passed away at an early age. He later married Marie Hall. He has 13 children and many grandchildren and great-grandchildren. Grover passed away on Jan. 19, 1987. He was a member of DAV of Martin, KY.

JACK JOHNSON, son of Tab Johnson, served in WWII. This picture was taken in 1943.

JOHN EPP "DECKER" JOHNSON, son of Tab Johnson, served with the U.S. Army during WWII.

MELVIN JOHNSON, Private First Class, born May 4, 1921, son of Johnny and Mary Alice Johnson. He enlisted in the U.S. Army in 1942, and served 37 months with 100th Chemical Mortar Battalion Army.

He participated in the Battles and

Campaigns of Naples-Foggia, Rome-Arno, North Apennines, and Po Valley. He was discharged from the military services, on Oct. 18, 1945.His decoration includes EAME Ribbon w/4 Bronze Stars and Good Conduct Medal.

Melvin married Zetta Gibson on Nov. 4, 1946, and they started a family which consisted of seven children and eight grandchildren. Melvin worked as a coal miner for many years. He was a kind, loving and caring father and friend. After a long and enjoyable life, he passed away on April 10, 1989.

CHARLIE JONES, born Jan. 29, 1920 in Floyd County, KY, the son of Harrison and Easter Jones. He enlisted in the U.S. Army April 15, 1942 and assigned to Co. I, 8th Inf. as a rifleman.

He saw combat in Normandy, Central Europe, Ardennes and Rhineland. Early in 1945 he was wounded in action and a piece of shrapnel remained in his left thigh for the rest of his life.

He was discharged Aug. 24, 1945. His awards include the Combat Infantry Badge, Purple Heart, OLC and Ribbon w/4 Bronze Stars.

He married Laura Castle Aug. 3, 1942 and they had three children: Charlotte, Charles and Carlos. He worked in the coal mines, moved to Ohio in 1952 where he did factory work. He passed away May 11, 1985, Willard, OH.

JACK G. JONES SR., Sergeant, son of William and Lucy Goble Jones, he served in the U.S. Army Air Corps as a ball turret gunner in B-l7 and B-29 bombers. He served with the 1060th AAF Base Unit and was stationed at Fort Hayes, OH; AAF Ord in Greensboro, NC; AAFTS Sioux Falls, SD; and four weeks at AAF Flex Gney, LV.

Medals include Victory Medal Marksman, Pistol, Sharpshooter, Carbine and Machine Gun, AFF Air Crew Member Badge with Gunner and the American Theatre Ribbon.

Jack married Helen Drake and they had one son Jack Jr. and two grandchildren. Jack was a thoroughbred horse breeder. He raised the horse Henbit, winner of the English Derby. He was a breeder for 35 years.

Jack passed away in July 2002 and is buried in Lexington. He was a member of Central Christian Church and the Keeneland and Lexington Country Club.

WILLIAM JONES, born May 23, 1923 and enlisted in the U.S. military April 16, 1949, serving with 354th Service Company Infantry as a heavy truck driver.

Locations include Fort Thomas, KY; Camp Atterbury, IN; and Central Europe. He was awarded the Marksman Carbine Medal, Combat Infantry Badge, WWII Victory Medal, Good Conduct Medal and EAME Ribbon w/Bronze Star. He was discharged March 15, 1946 with the rank Tech GR 5.

As a civilian, he worked in the mining industry.

CLAUDE D. KENDRICK, born July 30, 1909 at Lancer, KY. He was the son of Everett and Jenny Kendrick. He enlisted in the U.S. Army Nov. 10, 1943 and assigned with the 1374th Engineers Petroleum District Company as a pump operator 220. He was based at Fort Thomas, KY and overseas in the Normandy, Northern France, Rhineland and Central Europe Campaigns.

His citations include EAME Theatre Ribbon w/4 Bronze Stars, Good Conduct Medal and WWII Victory Medal. He was discharged Dec. 10, 1945.

Claude married Zelma Conn and after service they resided in Pontiac, MI where he was employed as an appliance repairman. He passed away March 17, 1965.

DENNIS KIDD, Staff Sergeant, born Dec. 27, 1923 on Prater Creek, Dana, KY, the son of Green B. and Hulda Kidd. He was drafted into the U.S. Army in August 1943, completed his training in Camp Blanding, FL, and served 24-1/2 months in European Theater with the 12th Armor Infantry. He participated in the Battle of Bulge in Komar, France.

During his time in the Army, he was awarded the Infantry Badge, Good Conduct Medal and European Theater Ribbon. Dennis was discharged from the service in October 1946. His most memorable experience was watching the enemy holding white flags, turn themselves in to become Prisoners Of War.

After being discharged, Dennis came home to his wife Alpha and his daughter Sue.

As the years past, Dennis's family grew to eight children, 21 grandchildren, and 24 great-grandchildren. He continues to live on Prater Creek. His occupation throughout his life included coal mining and carpentry work until he became disabled. His main activities now include going to church and preaching the gospel.

GEORGE KIDD, served in WWII.

EPP LAFERTY, Private First Class, born Aug. 5, 1928 in Prestonsburg, KY. He enlisted June 14, 1946 in the Regular Army and spent his time in service as a member of 622nd Military Police Co., touring the countries of Guam, Japan and Germany.

Discharged May 14, 1947 as PFC, he received the WWII Victory Medal and Army of Occupation Medal (Japan).

Upon his return to Floyd County, he operated an automobile service station, drove a TNT truck, transported Floyd County school children as a member of the school district's transportation department and served as Deputy Sheriff of Floyd County. His wife is deceased. He has one daughter Jennifer. Currently at Riverview Nursing Health Care Center, Prestonsburg, KY, he enjoys visiting with family and friends and talking about life in military.

FLOYD LAFERTY, born Sept. 21, 1917, Floyd County, KY was killed in Naples, Italy on Oct. 21, 1943 during WWII. He is buried in the Shepherd Cemetery at Dwale, KY. He was the son of Marion Laferty and Roxie Hamilton. Marion was born in Floyd County, KY Sept. 9, 1878, d. Oct. 10, 1957 and was the

son of Robert Lee "J-Bob" Laferty, born 1856 in Wyoming County, WV and Amanda Prater born about 1858 in Floyd County, KY. Roxie Hamilton died in 1965. *Information from Dr. Bryan Griffith and submitted by Karen Nelson Marcum.*

ABRAN LAFFERTY, Private First Class, U.S. Army, WWII, was born Feb. 12, 1923 at Dwale, KY. He was the son of Jonah "Johner" Lafferty (Laferty) and Fannie Parsons and the grandson of Robert Lee "J-Bob" Lafferty and

Amanda Prater. He died at Dwale, KY July 17, 1990 and is buried in the Shepherd Cemetery at Dwale, KY. *Information from Dr. Bryan Griffith and submitted by Karen Nelson Marcum.*

JOE LAFFERTY, served in the Navy as a Boatswain's Mate 1st Class from 1942-46. During those years he made nine trips to Europe, two trips to the Pacific, and two trips around the world. He served in three invasions which included getting troops off and on half-tracks and onto pontoons under fire. He also served in Oran, North Africa; Anzio Beach Head, Sicily; Salerno, and Naples, Italy. He received two Bronze Stars and one Silver Star.

Joe married Opal Isaac, the couple had three children: Leonard, Jim and Ann.

JOSEPH E. LAFFERTY, born March 7, 1923 was the son of John E. "Monk" Lafferty and Betty Canterbury. His mother died when he was young, and his father remarried to Darcus Wills Branham who helped raise him. He was in the U.S. Navy in WWII and died in 2006 in Raleigh County, WV. His half-brother, Bill Branham Jr., also served in the U.S. Navy in WWII. *Submitted by Karen N. Marcum.*

EDWIN LAYNE, son of Arby and Rebecca Phoebe Scalf, was born July 2, 1923. He was killed in Germany in WWII on June 2nd.

JOHN LEAKE JR., entered the U.S. Army March 16, 1942 and served as EM until Nov. 23, 1942. Commissioned 2nd Lieutenant Nov. 24, 1942, he was assigned to the 80th Inf. Div. where he trained and served throughout WWII.

The 80th became an operational part of Patton's Third Army at St. Lo, France in August 1944 and remained with it thru all four ETO Campaigns. He held numerous positions in 2nd Bn., 319th Inf., 80th Inf. Div. such as Rifle Company Platoon Leader, Executive Officer and Company Commander. He served as Battalion S-3 during most of combat. Also served a short time as Chief Prison Officer at the "War Crimes Trials" in the Nuremberg, Germany during the early stages of the proceedings conducted in 1945-46.

Separated from active duty March 12, 1946 as a Captain, Infantry and accepted an appointment as Captain, Infantry in the Officer's Reserve Corps. He remained active in the Reserve until retirement as a Colonel, Infantry, Nov. 14, 1974 having served a total of 32-1/2 years.

ROBERT LEE, born June 3, 1916 on Stone Coal Creek in Pike County, was the son of Sanford and Lora Lee. He enlisted in the U.S. Army in 1942 and completed basic training at Fort Dix, NJ in 1945. His unit number was 3543 4769/80th Div.

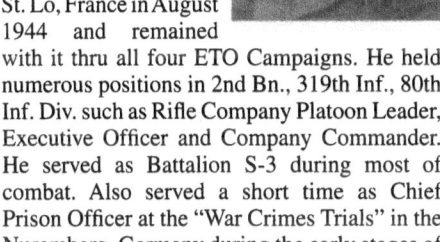

He received awards as a sharp shooter and pistol range. His unit was sent to Dusseldorf, Germany, where he was captured by the Germans and held in prison camp for 12 months. When he returned to the States, he was stationed at Miami Beach, FL and Telehoma, TN.

He received an award for Honorable Discharge for his tour of duty in Germany. After his discharge, he returned to Pike County where he married Mary Ozetta Layne on June 30, 1945. To this union was born nine children, 10 grandchildren, and 15 great-grandchildren.

Robert spent several years working in the coal mines and farming. His hobbies are squirrel hunting and fishing. He lived at Layne Bottom for 57 years until his recent illness. He now resides at Salyersville Health Care and Rehabilitation Center in Salyersville, KY.

ARNOLD LEEDY, born Aug. 12, 1925 to William and Henrietta Leedy of Drift, KY. He enlisted in the U.S. Army as a truck driver and served in New Guinea, Luzon and the Philippines and received the Asiatic-Pacific Theater Ribbon w/3 Bronze Stars, Philippine Liberation Ribbon w/Bronze Star, Good Conduct Ribbon, Bronze Arrowhead and WWII Victory Medal. He was discharged Feb. 28, 1946.

He married JoAnne Williamson and they had four children. JoAnne died in 1958, leaving Arnold to raise the children alone. He met and later married Frieda McMillen, she passed away in 1997. Arnold passed away in March 2000 of congestive heart failure. He is survived by five children, 17 grandchildren and many great-grandchildren. He was truly the hero of his family.

THOMAS RAYMOND LEMASTER, Tech Sergeant 5, born Sept. 1, 1920, son of James Hansford LeMaster, Ashland, KY, and Florence Hereford Reynolds of Prestonsburg. He enlisted in the U.S. Army on Oct. 8, 1942, completed tire repair training in San Antonio, TX and welders' school training in Aberdeen, MD. Prior to deployment, he served 11 months stateside. He served as an automotive mechanic for two years and four months in Europe, Africa, and the Middle East from August 1943 until December 1945. He participated in campaigns in Ardennes, France, and in Central Europe.

He was discharged Dec. 14, 1945. His decorations include WWII Victory Medal, EAME SV Ribbons w/2 Bronze SV Stars, Good Conduct Medal, and Meritorious Award GO 37 HQ CAS 27 Nov. 1944.

Thomas married Mabel Jean Conley on June 14, 1946. They had three daughters and four grandchildren. He was employed by Kentucky West Virginia Gas Co. and worked there as a welder, safety director, personnel director, and land agent. Tom, as he was called by friends and family, died June 16, 2002. *Submitted by Kay LeMaster Wingham.*

FRANK LESLIE, born July 17, 1920 to Crit an Clara May Leslie of Emma, KY. He enlisted in the U.S. Navy in January 1920 as an Apprentice Seaman. He was stationed aboard the *Salt Lake City* for six years.

He served in Pearl Harbor and left three days before the bombing. From there he went to Alaska with a convoy to escort Jimmy Doolittle on the Tokyo Raid. He was also at Iwo Jima and throughout the South Pacific.

He was discharged in 1948 with the rank of Boatswain Mate 1st Class. He was employed with Island Steel and C&O Railroad.

Frank married Hester Woods and they had four children and nine grandchildren. He is now deceased.

LARCIE HENSON LEWIS, Tech, Sergeant, born March 9, 1916, Banner, KY. He enlisted Oct. 29, 1940, was assigned to 10th Regt., 5th Inf. Div., RCTG STA Fort Thomas, KY.

He saw combat in Normandy, Northern France, Ardennes, Rhineland and Central Europe GO 33 WD 45. Memorable was crossing the Rhine and Battle of the Bulge.

Discharged Nov. 6, 1945 as Platoon Sergeant. His awards include Victory Ribbon, Service Stripe, six Overseas Service Bars, American Defense Service Medal, American Theater Campaign Medal, EAME Campaign Medal w/5 Bronze Stars and Purple Heart.

Married Pearlie Mae Miller on Feb. 2, 1946. To this union was born four children: Roger, David and Clyde Preston Lewis, and Connie Mae Roadcap. They have 14 grandchildren and 14 great-grandchildren. Retired from West Virginia Gas Co. He was also a volunteer minister of New Hope Association of United Baptists. He passed away March 24, 1993.

SHIRLEY ADRIAN LEWIS, born March 1, 1919, in Betsy Lane, KY. He was the son of Thomas J. Lewis and Octavia Stratton Lewis. Shirley enlisted in the army on Jan. 30, 1941 and completed basic training at Fort Knox, KY.

He was a Corporal in the 69th Armd. Regt. when he traveled to New York to board the *Queen Mary* headed for Ireland.

From there he was sent to England, loaded artillery on ships and began their descent to Oran, North Africa. As they were in pursuit of their destination, their ship was torpedoed. Once their equipment was replaced they fought the Germans on the front lines. Shirley's tank was "knocked out" and he was taken prisoner. After being held in Tunisia, he boarded a German plane that was shot down, causing them to make a forced landing on the Isle of Sicily. From there they were taken by train to Austria to a concentration camp and then, on to Frankfurt, Germany, where he was held as a POW until the end of the war.

When he was a POW they were given one meal a day, which they ate slowly to make it last. They also hid their rations under their mattresses to keep others from stealing them while they were sleeping.

When he returned to the States he married Nelva Akers on Aug. 13, 1945 and they had two children, Peggy Lewis Rapier and Carolyn Lewis Baldridge Cottengin, and three grandchildren: Matthew Lewis Baldridge (deceased), Kelly Carol Baldridge and Jon R. Rapier. He is a member of Community Methodist Church.

CECIL M. LITTLE, Private First Class, born Feb. 22, 1924, son of Prophet and Ludema (Hall) of Melvin, KY. He was drafted into U.S. Army April 22, 1943, not much is known about his training in the States and where, but his MOS was toxic gas handler. He also qualified as a marksman with the rifle. Cecil stayed for

11 months 12 days before going to Europe where he was placed with the 192 Chemical Depot.

He spent one year eight months and 10 days in Europe and received four Bronze Stars, EAME Theater Ribbon, Good Conduct Medal, WWII Victory Medal. Cecil returned to Fort Knox Separation Center and was discharged Dec. 20, 1945.

After returning to the States he returned to work for C&O Railroad where his dad worked. He met and married Earlene Henson on Feb. 17, 1949, to this union three children were born: Barbara, Darlene and Jeffery. Cecil was laid off at the railroad and moved to Ohio and tried farming (share cropping); that did not work out and he went to Detroit, Michigan and got a job at Dana Corporation then was laid off. He returned to Kentucky with his family and later went to Indiana where he retired.

Cecil always had smile, a joke, and a tale for you. He loved for the family from Kentucky to come and visit and he would take you around Huntington and show you the changes in the town since your last visit. There were many from Kentucky that stayed with him until they found a job and got established enough to move out. He was truly a good man. Cecil passed away Oct. 21, 1989. He had four grandchildren.

TRAVIS LITTLE, born Feb. 22, 1921 in Melvin, KY. He enlisted into the U.S. Army on Oct. 26, 1934. He had basic training at Fort Thomas, KY; served at Fort McPherson, GA, Camp Jackson, SC and Fort Benning, GA; maneuvers at Fort Francis and Warren in Cheyenne WY, Fort Greely, Kodiak, AK, Camp Ripley, MN and Camp Perry, OH. He also attended Army Ranger School, OSC Infantry School, Fort Benning, GA. He graduated as 2nd Lieutenant in October 1942, then was promoted to 1st Lieutenant in 1943.

Transferred to Army Air Corps in Camp Phillips, KS, then to Maxwell Field, Montgomery, AL; transferred to Bainbridge Field, GA where he flew BT-13, BT-13A aircraft.

He was sent for overseas duty in 1944. In May of the same year, he was sent to France as a Platoon Leader with the 2nd Bn., 90th Inf. Div. He was in several battles in Metz, France where he was wounded in the arm and leg by a German grenade. Lt. Little was in the hospital for five months in France and England before being sent to Daytona Beach, FL to a convalescent hospital.

After several months, he was Honorably Discharged in October 1945. He received decorations for Battles in Northern France and Rhineland, citations for EAME Campaigns, Medals w/2 Battle Stars and the Purple Heart.

He married Mildred "Mickey" Ogles and had one daughter Patricia, and one son Robin. His civilian employment was Chief of Maintenance in coal mines. He died July 3, 1998.

BERKLYNN LLOYD MARSHALL, born in Water Gap, KY in 1921, the son of Marvin and Emma Catherine Marshall. He enlisted in the Air Force after college in 1942, completed training at the Southern Signal Corps School at Camp Murphy, FL. Berklynn was a Staff Sergeant in the 598th Air Engineer Squadron 382nd Service Group, his military occupation was radar repairman airborne equipment, and had Carbine Ex: Rifle MM.

He participated in WWII and was decorated with the American Theater Ribbon, Asiatic-Pacific Theater Ribbon w/2 Bronze Stars, Good Conduct Medal and WWII Victory Medal. He was discharged in 1946 but later re-enlisted and participated in the Korean Conflict.

When he returned to the States Berklynn married Audrey Jo Gibson from Wayland, KY. They had two children, three grandchildren, and two great-grandchildren. He was employed as an electronic engineer for AT&T where he worked for 39 years before retiring in 1986. Berklynn was also a Mason for 50 years, an avid HAM radio enthusiast, loved to fish and spend time in his garden. He passed away August 4, 1998 in Decatur, GA where he lived the later part of his life with his wife Audrey.

CHARLES ROBERT "CHARLIE BOB" MARSHALL, was the son of Charles and Florence Marshall of Martin, KY. He volunteered with the U.S. Army Air Force. In the Fall of 1942, Charlie was attending Duke University's Engineering program where he attended classes for only a semester before leaving to serve his country. He was a tail gunner in the B-24 Liberator bomber stationed in England flying numerous missions over Germany. He was killed in action leaving behind his wife Dixie Lou Ratliff and a six-month-old son, Robert David.

JAKE MARSILLETT, born Aug. 25, 1911 in Blue River, KY and entered active service Oct. 22, 1942 at Huntington, WV. His MOS was Military Police 677. He participated in the Italian Campaign, Tunisian and Sicilian campaigns.

He received an Honorable Discharge Jan. 23, 1945 and received the EAME Ribbon w/3 Battle Stars.

He was very proud to have served his Country, and after the war kept his uniform hanging on his bedroom wall for over 30 years.

He married Joyce Robertson and they had 11 children and 31 grandchildren. Jake passed away Aug. 7, 1985 and Joyce on June 12, 1963, both in died Rochester, NY where they had lived for 50 years.

BILL CODY MARTIN, entered the service during WWII and served with the Seabees. He was discharged on Oct. 29, 1945. Bill attended McDowell High School.

CLEM MARTIN, son of Ellis and Lula Hayes Martin, was born in Garrett, KY June 29, 1915. He was educated in Floyd County schools and was among the first graduates of Garrett High School. Clem attended college at Alice Lloyd and Morehead State University in Kentucky where he earned both his BA and MA Degrees in education.  He returned to Floyd County where he spent most of his time as a teacher, a principal and director of curriculum and instruction.

Clem was a veteran of WWII and entered the Air Force April 1, 1943 where he became a Personal Affairs Consultant. He took an airplane mechanics course in Amarillo, TX and received training in Flex Training School in Kingman, AZ. He was listed as a carbine marksman and achieved the rank of Corporal.

Clem earned the American Theater Ribbon, Good Conduct Medal and the WWII Victory Medal. His time of military service was two years, 10 months and 24 days. Clem served his country with true morality and dedication. Upon his Honorable Discharge, Clem returned to Floyd County, KY where he spent the remainder of his life helping to educate Floyd County's youth.

In addition to being a patriotic military man and a dedicated educator, Clem was a devoted son, a loving husband, and a doting father. His daughter, Sharon Martin Lavender, followed in his footsteps in education and is now teaching gifted students in Sampsom County, NC. His widow, Alice O. Martin, a retired teacher, does volunteer work in the schools where Sharon teaches.

Clem Martin passed away Jan. 16, 1985 after suffering a massive heart attack. He was eulogized by Norman Allen, then editor of the *Floyd County Times* as an outstanding leader in education in Eastern Kentucky.

MELVIN BYRON "NICK" MARTIN, PFC (TA), born Jan. 31, 1924, the son of Lee and Katherine Weddington Martin of Wayland, KY. He enlisted in the U.S. Marine Corps (USM CRSS) on May 26, 1943, to serve national emergency years, and was assigned to active duty June 10, 1943.

Weapons Qualification: Rifle Marksman July 29, 1943 and Special Military Qualifications: Automatic Rifleman. Service included (sea and foreign) Pacific area Jan. 13, 1944 - May 2, 1945; MD USS *General Leroy Eltinge*, Sept. 19, 1945 - Nov. 16, 1945;

Battles, engagements, skirmishes, and expeditions include participation in action against the enemy at Roi and Namur, Marshall Islands, Feb. 1, 1944-Feb. 4, 1944; Saipan and Tinian, Marianas Islands June 15, 1944-Aug. 10, 1944; Iwo Jima, Volcano Islands, Feb. 19, 1945 - March 4, 1945. He was wounded in action June 17, 1944 and March 4, 1945. He was Honorably Discharged from the Redistribution Battalion, Camp Lejeune, NC and from the U.S. Marine Corps Reserve on Nov. 30, 1945, with Honorable Service Lapel Button and Purple Heart.

Nick married Josephine Slone Martin on June 19, 1945 and worked as a coal miner for 28 years. To this union were born five children, 10 grandchildren and six great-grandchildren. Nick passed away Jan. 29, 1975, due to complications from a malignant brain tumor surgery.

SHERIDAN MARTIN, Private First Class, born Sept. 3, 1917 at Jump, KY, son of Hasadore "H.D." Martin and Monnie Hughes. He enlisted in the Marine Corps in 1939. He was assigned to the Marine Corps' First Division.

He died on Aug. 14, 1942 on Guadalcanal and is buried in the A.L. Martin Cemetery at Drift, KY. He was awarded the Purple Heart, American Defense Medal, Freedom Medal, Asiatic-Pacific Campaign, and a Presidential Citation.

He was a brother to Sherman Martin, McClellan Martin, Topsy (Lowe) Butler, Norma Jean (Martin) Bone and Nelma (Martin) Hall.

SHERMAN MARTIN, born July 31, 1926 at Jump, KY, son of Hasadore "H.D." Martin and Monnie Hughes. He enlisted on Sept. 6, 1944 at Huntington, WV as S/C in the U.S. Naval Service in the NRS Huntington, USNTS Great Lake, IL, TADCEN Shoemaker, CA, LCS (PAC), USS *Ashland*.

Sherman was discharged March 25, 1946 from the U.S. Personnel Separation Center, Bainbridge, MD. He received the Pacific Theater Ribbon, American Theater Ribbon, Victory Medal and the Philippine Liberation Ribbon. His most enduring memory was visiting Guadalcanal where his brother, Pfc. Sheridan Martin died.

He married Jacqueline Akers on June 3, 1944 at Paintsville, KY. Their children are Kathryn Jean Eldridge, Judith Ann Hale, Sherman Martin Jr., John Frederick Martin and Sheridan Martin. Sherman died April 9, 1997 at Lexington, KY. He is buried in the Sherman Martin Cemetery, Drift, KY.

BILLY MAY, born Dec. 17, 1922 in Cliff, KY. He enlisted in the Army Jan. 21, 1943 and served in the 899th Signal Company, Aircraft Maint. Div., 8th Air Force as radio and aircraft equipment repairman. Locations include Honington, England - EAME Theater.

He had great memories of repairing damaged aircraft after their  return from aerial combat and repairing their radio equipment. Discharged Jan. 29, 1946 as Tec 4. He received the EAME Theater Ribbon, WWII Victory and Good Conduct Medal.

After discharge he was assistant purchasing agent, Princess Elkhorn Coal Co.; purchasing agent, Pocahontas Fuel Corp.; and purchasing agent, the Pittson Co. Billy May is deceased. Survivors are his spouse, Voila Allen May who lives in David, KY; and children, William Jarvis May and Vicki Lynn Gusse.

CHARLES VERNON MAY, Tech 3, was the son of John and Martha "Jackie" (Laven) May. He entered the U.S. Army on April 18, 1942 and was discharged in September 1945. During WWII he served in Europe as an auto mechanic. He served with 3026 Ordnance Co.

He married Dixie Stumbo and they had two children, Charles Graham and Glenn David May. He also had one brother David May and three sisters: Helen Burke, Virginia Allen and Sally Branham. Charles is buried in the May Family Cemetery.

ELIJAH BROWN MAY JR., born in Ashland, KY, Dec. 28, 1923, the son of Elijah Brown May and Mary Barney May. He enlisted in the U.S. Marines on Sept. 24, 1943 and completed basic training and advance training as a telephone man, forward artillery observer at Camp Pendleton, CA.

He was assigned to the Pacific Theater of Operations, where he participated in the Battle of Iwo Jima, and the Occupation of Japan. He received the Pacific Theater Medal w/2 Battle Stars, and qualified for the Sharpshooters Medal with Rifle, Pistol and Machine Gun endorsements. He returned to the United States in 1946 and was separated from service at Camp Lejeune, NC on Feb. 6, 1946. He had attained the rank of Corporal (E-5) at time of discharge.

On Oct. 24, 1942 he was married to Allie Ann Moore. They had five sons, six grandchildren and seven great-grandchildren. He was employed by United Fuel Gas Co. for a few years and was manager of the Francis Shoe Store for 30 years until his retirement in 1989.

He was an Eagle Scout and served as Scoutmaster of Troop 27 of the Boy Scouts of America for 17 years. He helped 35 young men attain the rank of Eagle Scout. He was recognized by the National Boy Scout Council with the Scoutmasters Key and the Silver Beaver Award. He was the First Recipient of the Prestonsburg Woman's Club Award for Work with the Youth of Prestonsburg and Eastern Kentucky. He was a civic leader thru his participation on the Prestonsburg City Council for many years. He was a regional director of Officials for the Kentucky High School Athletic Association and was recognized as an outstanding football and basketball official. He donated his boyhood home "The Samuel May House" to the city of Prestonsburg to be preserved as a National Historical Structure. He passed away on Feb. 16, 2005.

RUSSELL MAY, born May 21, 1921 to Lonnie and Dora Neeley May. During WWII Russell was assigned to the 101st Abn. Div. as a paratrooper and mapmaker. He parachute jumped in Normandy, France, Rhineland and Holland and holds the Purple Heart, Bronze Star, the French and the Belgium Citations.

After returning from the war years in Europe, he founded the May Sign Co. and manufactured signs and installed them in several states. He was married to Eve Bennington and they had three children: Kathy, Jane and Rusty.

In 1972, Russell had the privilege of being tutored by one of Europe's greatest landscape artists, Gerhard Neswadba. In 1973 he sold the sign shop and opened May Art Gallery in Prestonsburg. Russell passed away on May 4, 1990.

WILLIAM HAROLD MAY, born in Garrett, KY on Oct. 3, 1920, the son of Elijah Brown May and Mary Barney May. He attended and graduated from Prestonsburg High School in 1939. Enlisted in the U.S. Army in Baltimore, MD in February 1943 and completed basic training and advanced training at Camp Hann, Riverside, CA. He was then assigned to the 125th Anti-Aircraft Artillery Battalion, which moved to Shreveport, LA, for advanced artillery training which began on July 26, 1943 and continued until Jan. 15, 1944. From Feb. 20, to April 22, 1944 the battalion was stationed at Camp Livingston, LA. The battalion transferred from there by train to Camp Miles Standish, MA, the staging area for the Atlantic Crossing.

On June 30th the battalion packed its gear and traveled to Boston Harbor, where they boarded the troop ship *Mount Vernon* and sailed for England (During the tour of duty in England and Northern Europe, the 125th AAA Battalion managed to shoot down 750 German V-1 and V-2 rockets). On Sept. 20, 1944 the unit traveled from the Romney Marshes to Southampton where they boarded liberty ships and crossed the English Channel to France. They landed on Omaha Beach, Normandy Sept. 23, 1944, several months after the initial D-Day assault. In December 1944, this unit participated as a support unit during the winter offensive of 1944, and was involved in the Battle of the Bulge, the Christmas time assault staged by the German army.

Upon completion of the war, he returned to the United States in late 1945, and was subsequently discharged having attained the rank of Technical Sergeant.

He returned to Prestonsburg and found employment as a sign painter and for many years was employed by May Sign Co., owned by the late Russell May, he continued with the several successor owners of that business until his retirement. He married Lucille Sexton on Aug. 5, 1965. He along with his brother E.B. May Jr. donated their boyhood home, "The Samuel May House," to the city of Prestonsburg to be preserved as a National Historical Structure.

He was very active in church work, being a member of the Community Methodist Church for more than 25 years. He was a Sunday school teacher and served on the administrative board as treasurer until his passing on June 20, 2001.

FLETCHER MAYO JR., born Floyd County, KY in 1928 and entered the U.S. Army during WWII. He later lived in Newport News, VA and worked in a shipyard. He was a brother to Royce Mayo who was in the U.S. Air Force. He died 2001 and is buried in Virginia. *Submitted by Karen Nelson Marcum.*

ROYCE MAYO, WWII, was with the 8th Air Force, B-17, heavy bombardment was stationed in England. From there, he would fly to Germany. He returned to Floyd County, KY and married Garnet Akers. They had five children: Peggy, Danny, Royce Jr., Laura and Sandra.

His brother, Fletcher Mayo Jr., was in the U.S. Army. They were sons of L. (Branham) and Fletcher Mayo Sr.; Fletcher's parents were Sidney and A. (Garrett) Mayo; L. Branham's parents were Sol and Sally (Calhoun) Branham; Sally's fa-

ther was Thomas Calhoun, a CSA Veteran. *Submitted by Karen Nelson Marcum. (Photos from Royce Mayo)*

ANDY "BUSTER" MCCLANAHAN, born Sept. 14, 1912 in Floyd County, KY, was the son of John McClanahan of Chatteroy, WV and Laura Shepherd of Floyd County, KY. He married Stella Warrix, daughter of Add and Josephine Calhoun Warrix. They lived on Bull Creek and raised three children: Anthony, Gardner and Emma Jo.

Buster served as a Private First Class in WWII in the U.S. Army.

He died at the Veterans Hospital in Huntington, WV Feb. 26, 1976, and is buried at Davidson Memorial Gardens Cemetery at Ivel, KY. *Submitted by Karen Nelson Marcum.*

JAMES MCGLATHEN, lived at Salisbury. He attended Martin High School and entered the U.S. Army during WWII. He was killed in action in the Pacific.

TAULBEE MCGUIRE, born Jan. 29, 1919, was the son of Richard McGuire and Ida Banks and had the following siblings: Georgia, Edna, Garnet, Richard Jr. and Grace. He fought in WWII and his tombstone states that he died in 1949, but the family says that he died in the Army and was brought home for burial. He is buried in the George McGuire Cemetery on the Right Fork of Bull Creek, Floyd County, KY.

Taulbee was the grandson of George (born 1850 in Floyd County) and Artie McGuire. He was the great-grandson of Issac McGuire (born 1812 in Tazewell County, VA) and Vandelilah "Dilley" Moore (born between 1820-27, Floyd County, KY).

Seth Marcum, with the help of Roy Branham, dug the tombstone out of the weeds and bushes so that a picture could be taken of it. *Information from Loma Warrix Derossett, Clara Lucille Derossett Garrett and Helena Warrix Nelson and submitted by Karen Nelson Marcum.*

JOE MEADE, Sergeant, born June 26, 1923, the son of James Madison and Mandy Elliott Meade of Printer, KY. He enlisted in the U.S. Army July 1943 and was discharged from Fort Dix, NJ.

He served in Co. L, 14th Inf., 100th Div. and was in combat in Germany and France. He was cut off behind enemy lines and reported missing in action for awhile. His awards include Good Conduct Medal, ETO Ribbon w/2 Battle Stars and Rifleman Badge.

Joe married Rebecca Frances Salisbury Jan. 14, 1946 and they had five children. After his discharge he worked first in coal mines then went to Michigan and worked 32 years for General Motors, retiring from there in 1987. He moved back to Kentucky and became very active with the DAV. He was very proud to have served his country. Joe departed from this life June 10, 2003.

RUSH MEADE, was born in Hi Hat, KY. He enlisted in the U.S. Army Air Force Foreign Technical Division. He was stationed at Camp Atterbury, IN; Hensley Field, Dallas, TX; Lackland Air Force Base, TX; Holloman Field, NM; Bradley Field, Okinawa and Tackinawa, Japan, Hawaii and Greenland with the Pacific AFB, OH. His memorable experiences was the Cuban Crisis.

He was discharged in 1963 with the rank of Tech Sergeant. His awards include Air Force Longevity Service Award Ribbon w/4 Bronze OLCs, Air Force Good Conduct Medal w/2 Bronze OLCs and the Good Conduct Medal w/ Bronze Clasp and four Loops.

Upon returning to civilian life. Rush was service manager for Chevy Olds Dealer in Ohio, Prestonsburg and Hazard. He also worked for the Floyd County Board of Education as a school bus driver.

Rush married Justine Bates in 1955. They had two children and five grandchildren. Sadly, he passed away. May 31, 2001.

SCOTT MEADE, PH3, born on Feb. 25, 1921, was the son of Hibert F. and Laura Hall Meade. Scott was a graduate of McDowell High School and attended Caney Creek Junior College. Scott was drafted into the U.S. Navy in December 1943. After Boot Camp he was assigned to Balboa Naval Hospital in San Diego, CA. While there he trained as a Hospital Corpsman.

He was later transferred to Pearl Harbor, HI. After several months he was transferred to the USS *Capps,* a destroyer, and was there until the end of the war. He received several campaign medals and awards.

After WWII Scott became a mortician and operated a Funeral Home in West Liberty, KY. Later he was employed in the coal industry and the Ford Motor Co.

On Feb. 14, 1942 he married Irene Hensley. They had three sons and seven grandchildren and five great-grandchildren. Scott's three sons also served in the U.S. Navy during the Vietnam era. Scott passed away on Nov. 26, 1979.

DOUGLAS M. "DOUG" MEADOR, born July 9, 1922 at Dock, KY, enlisted Army Air Corps, later USAF, Oct. 29, 1942 at Bremerton, WA. He was stationed at many different locations, both in U.S. and foreign countries, i.e. Central and South America, Caribbean Islands, Japan, Korea, many Pacific Islands, Europe, North Africa and Mid-East.

His military duties included flight engineer, crew chief, mainly on large airplanes. Memorable was flying over and mapping the Andes Mountains in South America; being, perhaps, the last

American to fly out of Pongyang, North Korea; trips to Australia, Berlin, Germany and many other cities of note.

Retired Dec. 31, 1962 at Edwards AFB, CA with rank of Tech Sergeant (E-6). Some of his awards are Good Conduct Medal w/3 clusters, Sharpshooter w/rifle, American Theater, WWII Victory Medal, Korean Theater w/2 Battle Stars, American and Korean Presidential Ribbons and other minor citations.

Doug worked 14 years for post office in Yakima, WA and for 25 years has volunteered in nursing homes. Married 34 years to Anna Belle Horne and has one stepson. They currently reside in west Van Lear, KY.

MACK E. MEADOR, born June 5, 1920 to Melvin J. and Nanny Johnson Meador of Cliff in Prestonsburg, KY.

He entered the US Army Air Corps Div. on April 15, 1942. He served for 12 years overseas in India during WWII and in Korea from 1952-53 earning area service ribbons and Battle Stars, Good Conduct Ribbon, Specialty and Machinist. He was an avid fisherman and loved the outdoors.

GEORGE JEFFERSON MEADOWS, born April 3, 1925, Prestonsburg (Meadows Branch of Bull Creek), son of Joe W. Meadows and Mary Gray Meade. He enlisted in the Navy July 1943 and was stationed at Great Lakes, IL, San Diego, CA, Marshall Islands, Guam, Saipan and Johnson Islands.

Memorable experience was when his ship was torpedoed

and they had to abandon it and spent the night in shark infested waters before being picked up the next day.

Discharged April 4, 1946 as Second Class Boatswainmate. Awards include WWII Ribbon, Asiatic-Pacific Campaign and Stars for battles he was in.

He married in 1947 to Ida Belle Mille and had five children, 17 grandchildren and 22 great-grandchildren. Worked for Ford Motor Co. for 37 years and is now retired. He also had 10 siblings (four now deceased).

ALDO MILLER, born Nov. 11, 1909, Prestonsburg, KY. He enlisted March 16, 1942 in the Army Air Force and was stationed at Camp Atterbury, IN; Fort Thomas, KY; 123 AAF Base

Unit and overseas at Egypt-Lybia, Tunisia, Naples-Foggia and Rome-Arno.

PFC Miller was discharged Sept. 1, 1945. His awards include EAME Theater Ribbon w/4 Bronze Stars and Asiatic-Pacific Theater Ribbon w/Bronze Stars.

After discharge he worked as construction machine operator. Married twice, both deceased. He had one daughter, Mary Lou Miller Lavender and one grandson, Thomas Lavender. After moving to an apartment for seniors, he cleared an area behind the complex which the residents named Miller Park. Aldo passed away Nov. 28, 1983.

CURTIS MELVIN MILLER, born June 22, 1926 at Cliff, KY, was the son of Andrew Jackson Miller and Martha Saunders. He was drafted into the Army when he was 18 years of age. Since he had starting working on ships in New Port News, VA when he was 16, and had experience, he volunteered for the Navy, the Army allowed him to join. He enlisted in December 1944, was a deck hand and the ships fitter on the USS *Pigeon,* which was an AM-374 mine sweeper. He helped build and repair the USS *Houston,* USS *Hornet,* and the USS *Wasp.* He was Honorably Discharged from the Navy as a Seaman Second Class on May 6, 1946.

Curtis married Lenora Cox on May 8, 1944. They had four children: Edith, Edwin Curtis, Sharon Rose and Floyd Andrew "Chris;" five grandchildren and three great-grandchildren.

He made a living for his family working in the coal mines and completed his high school education. He received his GED on June 24, 1970. As his experience and education increased, he became a foreman, mine inspector and before he retired from the coal industry was the Chief Examiner for the Department of Mines and Minerals.

Curtis enjoyed his retirement and always encouraged his children to retire as early as possible so they could do the things they wanted. He loved to garden and could revive a plant that was practically dead. Flowers and vegetables just seemed to flourish under his care. He was a big UK and Cincinnati Reds Fan and rarely missed a game. He was very active in the LDS church and worked tirelessly to help the church grow in this area.

Curtis passed away July 17, 2005. He is greatly missed by his family and friends.

NORMAN MILLER, born May 26, 1924, West Prestonsburg, KY and enlisted April 9, 1943 in the U.S. Marines. Stationed at Marine Recruit Depot, San Diego, CA; Goleta Air Station, CA; Marine Air Station at Eltora, Santa Ana, CA; Eva Marine Air Station, Oahu, territory of Hawaii; assigned to 2nd Marine Div., Camp Lejeune, NC; UN training, Atlanta, GA.

Participated in battle at Palau Island. He was wounded in action Sept. 26, 1944. Discharged May 10, 1966 with rank Gunnery Sergeant. Awards include Asiatic Medal, American Theatre Medal, Victory Medal, Good Conduct Medal, Sharp Shooter Medal and Expert Bayonet.

Norman is the son of the late Ted and Rebecca Wireman Miller. He had two brothers, Lewis Jackson "Jack" and Wilson; three sisters: Minnie (his twin), Ida Belle and Beverly. He first married Evelyn Smith and then Gwen Lee McKenzie with whom he had one daughter Alanna Normay. He also has two stepchildren, Mollette Lafferty and Carol Sherman, and six grandchildren.

He retired from Kentucky Education Department after 30 years of service. He is a member of DAV Chapter 18, lifetime member of VFW 2685, Marine Corps League Chapter 617, American Legion Chapter #17; Vietnam Veterans of America Chapter 214; American Am Vets #98, Kentucky Retired Teachers and Johnson County Retired Teachers. Life member of Zebulon Lodge #273 F&AM, Salyersville Lodge #769 F&AM, Paintsville Lodge #131 F&AM, Fred W. McKenzie Council #98, Paintsville Commandery #48, life member of Prestonsburg Chapter #182 RAM, 32nd KCCH of Lexington, KY. KYCH Pier 25, Louisville, KY and El Hasa Shriner Temple.

THOMAS WILFORD MILLER, born June 16, 1920, at Cliff, KY, the son of Andrew Jackson Miller and Martha Saunders. He enlisted in the Navy Aug. 14, 1940. Tom was an Electrician's Mate and was on the USS *Yorktown* when it was hit on June 7, 1942. He was working in the engine room when a torpedo hit and sunk the aircraft carrier. His friend standing next to him was killed and Tom was left floating in the Pacific Ocean for over two hours waiting to be rescued. He said he saw a ship and starting swimming to it but the people on the ship didn't see him and pulled away before he was able to get their attention.

Tom helped raise the USS *West Virginia* at Pearl Harbor. He participated in the Battle of the Midway. He also served on the USS *Great Lakes,* a destroyer, and on the USS *Passumpsic,* an oiler. He received an Honorable Discharge from the Navy Aug. 13, 1946. His rank was EM2/c when he was discharged. Tom was awarded five Bronze Stars and a Silver Star.

Tom was married to Virginia Mars and had three children: Glenn, Pam and Cindy. After they divorced, he married Patty Tackett and they had two sons, Tom and Jack. He has two grandchildren and one great-grandchild.

He worked for the Standard Oil Co. for 30 some years and lived in Michigan. He was a loader, maintenance personnel, and an operator. After his retirement, he moved to Wise, VA and lived there till he passed away on Feb. 11, 1987.

Tom would visit often and if we weren't home, he'd always leave the message, "Kilroy was here." When we'd ask him what that meant, he'd always tell us to look it up. He was an avid reader and was always joking about something.

FRANCIS MARION MOLES, served in WWII and was stationed at Great Lakes Naval Training Station in Illinois. He was discharged Nov. 21, 1945.

VAUGHN "VON" MOORE, born to Mart and Mandy More of Wayland, KY. He had two sons, Richard and Phillip. Von served in the 4th Medical Division in 1942 and received five Bronze Stars and one Bronze Arrowhead. He was Honorable Discharged in 1945.

WILLIAM WADE MOORE JR., born Aug. 5 1914, at Garrett, Floyd County, KY, son of William Wade and Lura Stafford Moore. He married Versa Hall in 1936 and had two children, Betty Lou and Wade Carroll Moore; three sisters: Grace Moore, Opal Moore Bolen and Mable Moore Hicks.

Sgt. Wade served in the U.S. Army in North Africa, Sicily, Italy, South France, Holland and Germany. He was a five star soldier.

When the war ended Wade came home and went to work for Princess Elkhorn Coal Co. at David, KY, where he worked until retirement.

After retiring Wade made several trips

to Israel, where he studied the bible, having a love for God and his chosen people. He was a licensed photographer, also a ham radio operator - call letters k4gag. Wade died July 24, 1992. *Submitted by Grace Moore.*

ELMER H. MORRISON, born in Wayland, KY on Sept. 15, 1924. He enlisted in the U.S. Army Air Force on Aug. 2, 1943. Elmer was a Technical Sergeant in the 761st Bomb Squadron and 460th Bomb Group. He served as a tail gunner and a radar operator on a B-24 airplane in the European Theater.

He was captured by the Germans and became a Prisoner Of War on March 1, 1945. He was freed by Patton's Army on April 29, 1945. Elmer received two Purple Hearts and other distinguished awards.

Elmer was Honorably Discharged Oct. 3, 1945. He married Florence Best on July 27, 1946. They had one daughter Constance, born in January 1948. Elmer and Florence made Wayland, KY their home, where Elmer served as Postmaster for 29 years. He passed away April 9, 2002.

CHESTER W. MOSLEY, born March 17, 1918 in Gibson, KY to parents of Warnie and Eliza Mosley. He served in the U.S. Army from December 1939 to June 1945 having obtained the rank of First Sergeant with the 3rd Armd. Div., Btry. A 391st Armd. Field Artillery Battalion as an expert gunner.

He was involved in the Battle of the Bulge, the invasion of Normandy and battles in Northern France. Chester's medals included EAME Campaign Medal w/2 Bronze Stars, American Defense Service Medal, American Campaign Medal, WWII Victory Medal and Good Conduct Medal.

On Dec. 27, 1940 Chester and Ruth Sherman Mosley began a marriage lasting 51 years. Together they had five children and 11 grandchildren. He worked as a coal miner for Inland Steel and Island Creek of Wheelwright, KY for 33 years.

Chester was very active with the UMWA serving as president of UMWA Local #5499 and attending several national UMWA Constitutional Conferences. He passed away Jan. 1, 1992.

CHARLES F. MULLINS, Sergeant, born May 1, 1925 at Myra, KY, son of Patton and Mountie Johnson Mullins.

Charles was inducted Aug. 20, 1943, after receiving his basic training, he was placed in the Infantry, Co. G, 135th Inf. Regt. 34th Div. Fifth Army. Med. Combat Infantry. He participated in Anzio Beachhead. He received Purple Heart, three Bronze Stars, Good Conduct Medal, WWII Victory Medal, and was issued the EAME Theater Ribbon. He also received the Sharp Shooter Badge and a Lapel Button. Charles was discharged Dec. 31, 1945.

Charles married Ida Mae Johnson (deceased). They moved to Oakhill, OH, and later moved to Dayton, OH where he retired from the City Maintenance Department. Charles and his son still live in Dayton.

PAUL L. MULLINS, Private First Class, was awarded the Silver Star while serving with the 4th Marines, Reinforced, First Provisional Marine Brigade in action against enemy Japanese forces on Guam, Marianas Islands July 21, 1944.

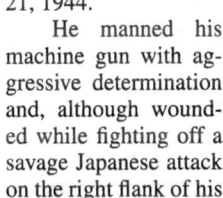

He manned his machine gun with aggressive determination and, although wounded while fighting off a savage Japanese attack on the right flank of his platoon, he continued firing his weapon until he succumbed to his wounds.

ALVIN NELSON, born April 8, 1924, Floyd County, KY, son of Denver Nelson and Lida Shepherd, was killed Dec. 13, 1944 in WWII and was brought home to be buried in the Dwale Cemetery at Dwale, KY. *Submitted by Karen Nelson Marcum.*

JAKE NELSON, son of William Nelson and Mary Clifton and grandson of William James

"John Bud" Reynolds and Emmarita Nelson. His brothers were Milt, Willard and Reynolds. *Submitted by Karen Nelson Marcum.*

MACK NELSON, born in Floyd County, KY, son of Jeff Nelson and Belle Smith. He married Anna Bell Pennington. He served in WWII and later went to live in Arizona. His children are Patty, Mack Preston, Gary, Jack and Carolyn.

SAMUEL "SAM" NELSON, born Aug. 6, 1923, Floyd County, KY to Hiland and Martha Osborne Nelson. He was in the U.S. Navy during WWII.

He returned from the war and married Mildred Steele. Their children are Betty Jewel, Vigis Samuel, Nona Jean, Grady Edward, William Douglas, Brenda Kay (deceased), James David and Zelda Faye. Another son, Robert, died at birth in 1966. Mildred Nelson died Aug. 1, 1981 and is buried in Floyd County. Sam died May 17, 1998.

Sam and Mildred named their oldest son, Vigis Samuel, after Mildred's brother, Vigus Steele, who was killed in action in Germany during WWII. *Submitted by Karen Nelson Marcum.*

TED NELSON, son of Hiland and Martha Osborne Nelson, was born Nov. 24, 1927 in Colonial Hollow, across the river from Prestonsburg, KY. He married Helena Warrix, daughter of Theodore and Hamie Wills Warrix. They had five children: Ted Jr., Ed Arnold, Tommie, Karen and Mary Jo.

Ted served in WWII and had the opportunity to be on Hitler's personal plane after the war. He died Dec. 29, 1992 and is buried in the Richmond Cemetery in Prestonsburg, KY. He was a minister for 40 years and pastor of the Town Branch Church for 35 years. *Submitted by Karen Nelson Marcum.*

WILL NELSON, Tec 5, son of Hiland and Martha Osborne Nelson, was born Sept. 8, 1925 in Floyd County, KY. and served in Germany with the U.S. Army during WWII.

He married Dora Bell Webb and lived at Dickie Town. He died May 1, 2005 and is buried on the Webb Cemetery at East Point, KY. *Submitted by Karen Nelson Marcum.*

ESTILL NEWMAN, Private First Class, served with the 349th Inf., 88th Div., 5th Army in Italy. He began Army service March 21, 1944 and went overseas November 13 of the same year. Estil was the son of W.W. Newman of Melvin and the husband of June Newman.

WILLIAM "BILL" NEWMAN JR., born Aug. 16, 1924, son of Willie and Maxie Newman. He enlisted in the Army in July 1943 and was located first in Fort Thomas, KY, then Fort Sill, OK, Fort Meade, MD, Camp Shanks, NY, Carter Wales, England and St. Austele, England.

He took part in the D-Day invasion of France during WWII and the Liberation of Okinawa in the Pacific.

He returned to the States in Camp Atterbury, IN, where he was discharged from the Army in January 1946. His decorations include Good Conduct Ribbon, Victory Medal, Driving and Mechanic Badge, Carbine Marksman, American Theater Ribbon, European Theater Ribbon, Asiatic-Pacific Theater Ribbon and the French Croix de Guerre w/Bronze Cluster and Bronze Arrowhead.

Bill married Ruby Evelyn Kinney and they have four children, 11 grandchildren and 15 great-grandchildren. Ruby passed away in 1992, after which Bill married Peggy Ratliff of Prestonsburg, KY. Bill has two stepsons and seven step grandchildren.

After coming out of the Army. Bill made a living working in the coal industry in and around the Wheelwright and Melvin, KY area. He worked from early in the morning until late at night. He also worked hard at gardening and raising livestock. His hobbies include hunting and fishing.

Bill, now 80 years old, resides in Prestonsburg, KY with his wife, Peggy.

GARDNER NEWSOM, born in Melvin, Floyd County, KY on Nov. 21, 1922 to Lawrence and Zettie Hall Newsom. He was drafted into the Army Nov. 15, 1943, received basic training at Camp Croft, SC Carolina, and served as a rifle expert for Co. H, 180th Inf. Regt., 45th Div.

Gardner was with the 45th Div. in Anzio, Italy in 1944 where it withstood repeated German assaults against its positions. The unit was sent to Southern France in August of that year. It advanced through Western France reaching the German border by the end of the year. In 1945 his division was in the Rhineland Campaign at the Siegfried Line that took Homburg. The Division crossed the Danube in April 1945 and took Munich on the 30th.

Gardner was Honorably Discharged as a Sergeant on May 17, 1946. He had seven months, 19 days of continental service and one year, three months and 26 days of foreign service. Decorations and citations include EAME Theater Ribbon w/Bronze Star and a WWII Victory Medal.

When he returned home he married Wadie Little and was employed as an electrician for Inland Steel Company in Wheelwright, KY. He passed away on Nov. 16, 1990 leaving his wife and three children.

PHILIP NEWSOME, Technician Fifth Class, Med. Det. 1463 Service Command Unit, Fort McClellan, AL, born Aug. 27, 1906 in Orkney, Floyd, KY, son of Wilson "Wilse" and Henrietta Hopkins Newsome. He was inducted into the U.S. Army Oct. 27, 1942 at Fort Thomas, KY. He specialized as a medical technician 409 and qualified with the 03MM rifle. Philip received a "Good Conduct Ribbon AR 600-68." His Honorable Discharge began Sept. 20, 1945 at Fort McClellan, AL.

Philip married Alpha Mitchell on Dec. 24, 1946 at McDowell, Floyd, KY. He was employed as a coal miner and a member of the Old Regular Baptist Church. He was loved by his many nieces and nephews. Philip died of a heart attack on July 10, 1975 in East McDowell, KY.

BILL OSBORNE, son of Bee and Sallie Allen Osborne, was born at Wayland, KY in 1909. He first married Ethel Webb and had two children, Billie Jean, born 1938 and Charles, born 1940, died 1980. He had two grandsons, Christopher Fannin and Charles Gavin Osborne; and two granddaughters, Carter Lynn and Mitchell Osborne. He later married Emma Harris and Dollie Martin.

Bill entered the Army in September 1942 at Fort Thomas, KY. He served as Sergeant with Btry. A, 216th Coast Arty., Bn. AA from 1942 to July 1945, when he was discharged at Camp Atterbury, IN. He fought in the following campaigns: Sicily, Naples, Foggia, Rome, Arno, Rhineland, Southern France and Central Europe, and was awarded the EAME Theater Ribbon w/6 Bronze Stars and the Good Conduct Medal.

Bill attended Caney College and was a teacher before volunteering for the Army. From 1947 until retirement in 1976 he was a letter carrier at the Prestonsburg Post Office. He died of lung cancer in 1978 at Prestonsburg.

FRANK OSBORNE, born April 24, 1921 to John Patrick and Sarah Alice Delong Osborne. His family lived around the Dickie Town area of East Point. He married Flora Dixon, daughter of Edgar and Jennie Daniels. Frank was in the 12th Armd. Div., 3rd Army under Gen. Patton in WWII. He served from 1941 and 1946 in England, France, Germany, Czechoslovakia and Italy. He now lives at Hager Hill, KY with his wife, Flora.

On the back of this photo is written: "From your husband that loves you more than life itself. To the best wife in the world. I love you ... so bye my little Darling. Take care ... Love forever.

Frank is the great-great-uncle of Seth and Noah Marcum.

DEVERT OWENS, born Aug. 23, 1916 in Raven, KY, enlisted in the U.S. Army April 3, 1945. He served with Co. A, 808th Engr. Avn. Bn. and was stationed in Tokyo Japan. He served as a construction foreman 059. Owens was discharged May 10, 1946 as a Sergeant.

Memorable experiences: The rebuilding of Japan.

He was awarded the Expert Infantryman

Badge, Asiatic-Pacific Campaign Medal, WWII Meritorious Unit Award, Theatre Ribbon, Good Conduct Medal and Victory Medal.

He was married to Vivian Martin Owens and had one son, one daughter, two grandchildren and three great-grandchildren. Civilian employment was spent as Director of Hazard Vocational School and University of Kentucky Professor for 22 years. He passed away in 1988 at his home in Lexington, KY.

MARCUS OWENS, born Oct. 12, 1912 at Raven, KY. He joined the 351st Sqdn., 333rd Air Svc. July 10, 1940. He was stationed in Tunisia, Naples-Foggia-Rome-Arno.

Medals include EAME Theatre Ribbon w/3 Bronze Stars and American Defense Service Medal. He was discharged Sept. 7, 1945 with the rank of Staff Sergeant.

Civilian life found him teaching in the Floyd County School System. He also taught at Alice Lloyd College where he was a supervisor.

Marcus married Inez Rudy Aug. 18, 1941 and they had two sons, Larry who was killed in an auto accident, and Marcus Jr. They have three grandchildren and three great-grandchildren.

BENTON OWSLEY, born July 9, 1907 in Vest, Knott County, KY, the son of Byrd Owsley. He attended Hindman School and enlisted in the USN Dec. 4, 1943. He served in SV 6-USNR. His military locations/stations included NTS Bainbridge, MD USS *Salamonie*; USN Tadcen, Shoemaker, CA; and USS *St. George*. He was discharged Nov. 4, 1945 achieving the ranks of Aviation Equipment Support, Seaman Second Class and Seaman First Class.

Missions/Battles: Asiatic-Pacific, EAME, American Area and Philippine Liberation. He was awarded the Philippine Liberation Medal w/2 Stars.

Civilian employment was in ship building, Dry Dock Company, Newport News, VA and as a miner for David Elkhorn Coal Company in David, KY.

He and his wife, Chloe Branham Owsley (deceased), had six children and 16 grandchildren. They were members of Community United Methodist Church. Being the seventh son of a seventh son, he was believed to be able to heal children suffering with "thrush." Many people asked him to "cure" their children. Benton enjoyed fishing and hunting. He passed away Feb. 2, 1986 in Prestonsburg, KY.

GEORGE ALLEN PATTON, born March 19, 1923 in Langley to Oscar and Lucy Estep Patton. Patton enlisted Aug. 23, 1943 in Huntington, WV as an Apprentice Seaman in the USN.

He served his boot camp at Great Lakes, IL; then was assigned to the newly commissioned destroyer escort *Thomason* 203 at Charleston, SC. He made several convoy runs in the Atlantic waters before transit of the Panama Canal. He sailed the South Pacific, stopping at several islands—some with familiar names but many with strange sounding names; such as Galapagos, Bora Bora, Pago Pago, Samoa, Guadalcanal, Solomon, New Guinea, Wake, Hawaii, Noemfoor, Mindora, Luzon, and the Philippines to name a few. The operations of the *Thomason* were long and strenuous. The ship acted as anti-submarine patrol, radar picket, escort for ships joining and leaving convoys, chased down reported submarine contacts, rescued downed aviators, and maintained armed boat patrol around ammunition ships.

Patton wrote, "We were on our unremitting hunt for enemy submarines en route from Leyte Gulf to Okinawa when we were informed of the Japanese surrender. Our service with the Seventh Fleet completed, we sailed for home. Thoughts of home prevailed during the long, arduous train ride of five days and five nights from California to Maryland. But, it seemed the longest ride of all when I journeyed up the Big Sandy and started looking for familiar landmarks. When the train pulled into the Maytown station, I knew that after almost two and a half years' absence, I was home at last."

Medals and honors Patton received were the American Theater Campaign Ribbon, the Asiatic-Pacific Campaign Ribbon w/3 Bronze Stars and the Philippine Liberation Ribbon w/1 Bronze Star. The most enduring memory of war was that while he was engaged in an anti-submarine patrol off Luzon, his unit discovered, attacked and destroyed a Japanese submarine. He was elated and still recalls the thunderous shouts and cheers of his fellow shipmates.

Patton was discharged Dec. 13, 1945 from Bainbridge, MD with a rank of Coxswain. He is married to Mosaleete Patton. Their children are Elizabeth "Kathy" Halbert of Langley, Paul C. Patton and Jerry A. Patton, both of Prestonsburg. They have nine grandchildren and six great-grandchildren. Patton resides at Langley.

JAMES QUENTIN PINKERTON, born Feb. 3, 1923 in Ivel, KY, enlisted in the U.S. Army Jan. 22, 1943 and served with the 471st AAA Bn., 37th Inf. Div., XIV Corps. Military locations/stations: Camp Wallace, TX; Guadalcanal; Tulagi; Emiru; and New Guinea.

Missions/campaigns included Northern Solomons, Luzon Campaign, Lingayen Gulf, and Clark Field, Manila, Philippine Islands. He was discharged Jan. 10, 1946 as a Private First Class.

Memorable experiences: Various Japanese surrenders. Meeting his sister, Pfc. Marcella M. Pinkerton, 5th Air Force, in Manila, Philippine Islands in July 1945. His gun and crew, he was the gunner of a quad .50 cal machine gun, being "loaned" out to various Army and Marine units throughout the South Pacific. And the gun crew getting no recognition due to the parent division being elsewhere.

He was awarded the Asiatic-Pacific Theatre Medal w/2 Bronze Stars, Philippine Liberation Medal w/2 Bronze Stars, Good Conduct Medal, Victory WWII Medal and Philippine Independence Medal. He also earned the following badges: Rifle Sharpshooter, Bayonet, M-1 and MG.

He is the son of William G. and Olia Bailey Pinkerton. He married Anna L. Davis on March 10, 1951. They have three children, six grandchildren and three great-grandchildren. He is retired from Chesapeake and Ohio Railroad and currently resides in Blaine, KY.

BERT NEWTON PORTER, Electricians Mate, Second Class (T), SV6, USNR, born on Sept. 22, 1918 at Alvin (Emma), KY, son of Bertram Lee Porter and Margery Harris. He enlisted in the USN on April 10, 1944 at Louisville, KY. He received his training at USNTC, Great Lakes, IL. He was stationed in Ames, IA at the Naval Training School for electricity. He served on the USS *Cyrene* which was the flagship of the P.T. Tender squadron, and the USS *Mobjack*. He had knowledge of P.T. boats from top to bottom. It was the tender's job to repair the P.T. boats damaged in action. He fought in the Philippines. He and John F. Kennedy were on a P.T. boat at the same time.

  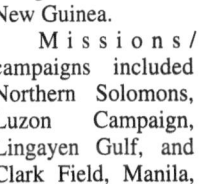

75

He received his Honorable Discharge on Jan. 3, 1946 at USN Separation Center, Great Lakes, IL. His decorations include the Asiatic-Pacific Campaign Medal, American Theatre Medal, Victory Ribbon and Philippine Liberation Medal.

Bert married Malta Sue May on Sept. 22, 1940 in Floyd County. They had one daughter, Madelyn Sue (Porter) Burchett. After being discharged he returned home where he put to use the electrical training he received in the Navy. He worked several different electrical jobs and was a member of the IBEW Union. He and his family ran a bait shop and a fishing supply store called Porter's Bait Shop for years. He loved fishing. He was a member of the VFW and a Shriner. Bert died on Aug. 18, 1996 and is buried in Davidson Memorial Gardens.

JOHN M. PORTER, born June 14, 1926, enlisted in the USAF July 23, 1943. He entered at Wright Patterson AFB, Dayton, OH and served in England, France and Germany. He was discharged March 15, 1946 as a Private First Class.

Memorable experiences: Hospitalized almost immediately after being sent to England. Later learned diagnosis was rheumatic fever resulting in a damaged heart and early demise.

He married Betty Hall Porter on Sept. 23, 1946 and had two children, John R. Porter and Susan P. Wallen, both of Stanville, KY. He was a self-employed automobile dealer. Porter passed away April 28, 1973.

ORVILLE PORTER, served as a Technician 4 in the 227th Repl. Co. during WWII. He was born June 22, 1908 and died Aug. 6, 1971.

He was married to Bess Calhoun, daughter of John Cat Calhoun and Minnie Hignite.

He had two children, Johnny and Margaret (deceased). He is buried on the Wills Cemetery at Water Gap, KY. *Submitted by Karen Nelson Marcum.*

VERNON "BUSTER" PORTER, born Oct. 21, 1924 in Allen, KY, enlisted in the U.S. Army Nov. 17, 1945. He was stationed in Japan. Missions/Battles: WWII.

Memorable Experiences: Devoted citizen of Allen, KY. Served as city councilman and as mayor for one term. Member of Masons, Shriners and a Kentucky Colonel.

His awards and medals include the WWII Victory Medal and Army of Occupation Medal (Japan). He was discharged on Aug. 19, 1948 with the rank of Staff Sergeant.

Civilian employment: Driving truck for Standard Oil for 10 yrs. Ran local Imes Service Station until retirement.

He married Margaret Kendrick Porter on Sept. 15, 1950. They have two sons, Vernon Porter and Randal Porter, both of Allen, KY; three grandsons; three granddaughters; and two great-grandsons. He resided at Allen, KY his entire life. Porter passed away on Nov. 19, 1997.

GEORGE PRATER, USCG, born Feb. 22, 1924 in Floyd County, KY. Graduated from Sheepshead Bay Maritime School in Brooklyn, NY. Served in the Merchant Marines during WWII from 1943-45.

He was the son of Wesley and Sarah Martin Prater of Prestonsburg, KY. Prater was married to Catherine Hager from David, KY and had four children: Gregory, Elaine, Karen (deceased in 1995) and Jeffrey; and six grandchildren: Lindsay, John, Travis, David, Chuck (deceased 2005) and Jenny. He passed away Dec. 29, 1996 in Bradenton, FL.

LACY L. PRATER, born on Aug. 10, 1914 in Floyd County, KY was the son of William and Rhoda Blankenship Prater. He was inducted at Fort Hayes, Columbus, OH on Feb. 5, 1941. He was a Private in the Army Armored Division serving in the Southwest Pacific Theatre.

He was taken prisoner after the fall of Bataan Peninsula and reported as a Prisoner Of War on May 7, 1942 by the Army. He was in the prison war camp Osaka Main Camp, Chikko Osaka # 34-135. He was liberated and returned to service on Oct. 28, 1945.

LUTHER D. PRATER, Lieutenant, born on Oct. 9, 1921 in Myrtle, Floyd County, KY was the son of Newte and Essie Holbrook Prater. He was a graduate of Bonanza High School, attended Caney Junior College, and graduated from the University of Kentucky with a year of post-graduate work. He enlisted in the Air Corps in June 1942.

After leaving Lexington he went to St. Louis, then to Florida and on to San Diego, CA.

He was awarded the Air Medal for shooting down a Japanese plane, the first in his squadron.

He was prominent in the news and discussion by radio commentators of the gigantic America air attack on Formosa. He was quoted in Lowell Thomas Tuesday evening broadcast describing the assault by carrier-based planes on the Japanese stronghold. He shot down three Japanese planes said, "I never dreamed of such confusion. There were Zeros all around us, flying in twos, threes and sixes. I would see a couple of Zekes on somebody's tail and try to shoot one down. Then three or four would get on me."

"Japanese ground batteries opened up with phosphorus shells, sending white tentacles through the sky. Everything happened in a split second."

He flew from the carrier of VAdm. Marc A. Mitscher's seagoing air force. He is now living in California.

WALTER M. PRESTON, Major, born June 12, 1915, the son of Chester and Fannie Preston, in Martin, KY.

He enlisted in the U.S. Army in 1941 and made it his career. He served as unit commander of the field artillery during WWII and participated in the Korean War. In 1957, he spent the last six years of his service involved with Nike missiles at Fort Sheridan, IL until his retirement in 1963.

He then moved to Florida and had a Private business fixing televisions, radios, and anything else that had tubes or transistors. Later, in 1975, he moved to Colorado Springs where years before he had served at Fort Carson, CO.

Walter married Ruth Osborne, daughter of Perry and Mary Osborne of Martin, KY, and had one son, Walter in 1950, and one daughter, Mary in 1954. He had one granddaughter, Alicia, by his son, Walter Perry, who resides in North Carolina.

Walter passed away Dec. 24, 1991, and is survived by his wife, their two children and one granddaughter.

EARNIE RATLIFF, Staff Sergeant, entered the U.S. Army Jan. 14, 1942. He is the son of Allen Ratliff and Jane Patton of Langley, KY. He is pictured with his wife, Olive Wicker.

HENRY C. RATLIFF, born May 6, 1925 in Alphoretta, KY, was inducted into the service Sept. 30, 1943 at Fort Thomas, KY. He served as a mechanic at Fairfield Air Depot in the engineering branch. He was discharged April 30, 1946 as a Private First Class.

His awards/medals include the EAME Service Medal, Good Conduct Medal, American Theater Service Medal and Victory Medal.

JAMES RATLIFF, born Nov. 9, 1922 is the son of Lizzie Bradley and Beverly Lewis Clark Ratliff. He was a graduate of Martin High School and a U.S. Army WWII veteran who was decorated with a Silver Star, Purple Heart and three Bronze Stars.

He was a former officer in the DAV, the American Legion and VFW. James married Dora Ellen Click and they had one son, Terry and three daughters: Linda, Carolyn and Sherry. He is now deceased and buried in his family cemetery at Stephens Branch, Martin, KY.

WILLARD RATLIFF, Private First Class, born May 12, 1915, the son of Henry Ratliff and Rebecca Johnson Ratliff of Blue River, KY. He enlisted in the USMC at Louisville, KY on April 12, 1944. He was in action against the enemy in the Pacific on Okinawa, Ryukyu Islands, and the Occupation of China, WWII. He was a clerk general 055 and auto. rifleman 746.

Willard was issued an Honorable Service Certificate, a Service Lapel Button and a Good Conduct Medal. He was discharged on March 7, 1946 at Camp Lejeune, NC.

Willard attended school at Berea College in 1934. He was interested in clothing merchandising. He was employed by N&W Overall Company, Lynchburg, VA. His territory covered 30 counties in Kentucky and West Virginia. He sold work clothes and sportswear to mining "Company Stores", country dry goods stores, and better Specialty Shops.

Willard married Ruth Boyd and they had two children. They lived at Betsy Layne for many years. After retiring in 1977, they moved to Lexington, KY. He loved to tell of his war experiences and the jungles on Okinawa. Willard died in Lexington in 1992. Ruth deceased in 2004.

EDGAR "BULL" RAY, born Feb. 20, 1919 in Biscuit, KY, enlisted in the U.S. Army Sept. 3, 1942. He was stationed at Camp Butner, NC. Ray was discharged Sept. 1, 1943.

He is married to Pearl Reynolds Ray and has nine children: Lucill, Gary, Roger, Anna Gail, Linda Kay, Dylene, Danny, Edgar Allen and Jimmy; and two grandchildren, Joshua Dean Ray and Nathaniel Dustin Ray. He now loves spending time with his grandson, Joshua Dean Ray, and children. He resides in Beaver, KY.

ROGER REED, born June 8, 1914 at Garrett, KY, the son of Gold Reed and Sarah Patton. He entered the U.S. Army on Oct. 19, 1939 at Fort Thomas, KY with a rank of Private. He asked for field artillery but found himself instead a medic. He served with the 11th Inf. Med. Det., 5th Inf. Div. He was assigned to Fort Benjamin Harrison, IN where he ran the regimental and battalion detachment until 1943 as Private First Class, Corporal, Sergeant, and Staff Sergeant. For most of those years, he was in charge of the 2nd Bn. Aid Station of the 11th Inf. Med. Det.

Roger told that he got tired of the medics and took a lower rank, Private, in order to transfer to the 3451st Ord. QM Co. He was sent overseas and served as a mechanic, Technician Fifth Grade until he became ill and was sent to the Hoff General Hospital in Santa Barbara, CA. He was discharged on March 10, 1944.

He was awarded the Asiatic-Pacific Theater Medal, the American Defense Service Medal, a Lapel Button and the Southwest Pacific Expedition Medal.

He married Olive Vanderpool. His children are Roger, Priscilla, Gary Edsel and Jerry.

REV. AMOS REFFITT, born Jan. 29, 1916, at Blue River, Floyd County, KY, the son of Daniel and Martha (Marsilett) Reffitt. On May 9, 1941 he married Emma Hale, also of Floyd County, KY. They had one daughter, Christenna (Reffitt) Haywood.

Cpl. Tec 5 Amos Reffitt, a WWII Army veteran was inducted into the service on Aug. 19, 1942. He served in the Solomon Islands with Btry. C, 250th Anti-Aircraft Arty. Bn. Battles and campaigns: Northern Solomons.

His decorations and citations include the Asiatic-Pacific Ribbon w/Bronze Star, WWII Victory Medal and Lapel Button. Military Occupational Specialty: Searchlight Crewman. He received a Letter of Appreciation from then President Harry Truman. Amos was Honorably Discharged Jan. 6, 1946. He received no wounds in the battle.

Rev. Amos Reffitt and family have lived in Indiana (Warsaw area) for 53 years. He passed away Aug. 10, 2005 at the age of 89.

EVERETT REYNOLDS, born 1923, the son of Ernest Reynolds and Catherine Shepherd, is a veteran of WWII. He enlisted in June 1941, as a Private with Btry. C, 2nd Field Arty. Bn.

Everett served four years to the end of the war and returned home to Floyd County. Shortly after his return from the war, he married Desmond Hale and together they have five children: Freddie, Jewell, Randy, Jeffrey and Sandi. Everett and his family moved to Pontiac, MI in 1951, where he worked for many years and retired from General Motors.

Everett and Desmond have been happily married for 60 years and currently reside in Benton County, TN. *Submitted by Renee Kyle and Karen Nelson Marcum.*

JAMES BRUCE REYNOLDS, the son of Malcom and Rebecca Harmon Hubbard was born Sept. 3, 1922 in Floyd County, KY. James was married to Roberta Littell on Dec. 30, 1967. James died April 29, 1998 and is buried in the Hubbard Family Cemetery on Spurlock Creek, Prestonsburg, KY.

His father was the son of William James

and Sarah Hubbard. Sarah had two brothers who fought for the Confederate and both were prisoners of war. William M. Hubbard was released. Her brother, Henry Clay Hubbard, was shot and later died in a POW Camp. His remains were not returned to Right Fork of Bull Creek in Floyd County until July 2004.

JOHN BUD REYNOLDS, son of William James Jr. and Rebecca Mayo Reynolds, and grandson of William James Sr. and Rhoda Allen Reynolds, served in the U.S. Army on Corregidor and was captured by the Japanese and held prisoner until he died in 1945.

He was posthumously awarded the following from President Harry S. Truman "In grateful memory of John Bud Reynolds, who died in the cause of his country in the Pacific area Feb. 16, 1945. He stands in the long line of patriots who dare to die that freedom might live and through it he lives in a way that humbles the undertaking of most men. Harry S. Truman, President of the USA."

The John Bud Reynolds Veterans of Foreign Wars (VFW) Post at Martin, KY is named in his honor. His brother Bill, accompanied by his daughters Patty and Jody, and grandson Ethan, accepted on behalf of the Reynolds family the Bronze Medal awarded posthumously in 1986. *Information from Rebecca Funk and submitted by Karen N. Marcum.*

WALTUST REYNOLDS SR., born March 15, 1916 to Dock and Belle Reynolds of Beaver, KY. He joined the U.S. Army during WWII and served in Denver, CO, the South Pacific, New Guinea and the Philippines.

He received the Good Conduct Medal, Meritorious Unit Award and three Bronze Stars. He attained the rank of Technical Sergeant.

Waltust married Marie Reynolds and had two children, Waltust Jr. and Delva Tackett; five grandchildren: Amy Kimbler (and Dale), Mark Tackett, Trenton Tackett, Brad Reynolds and Deven Reynolds; and two great-grandchildren, Bethany Kimbler and Cameron Kimbler.

He was a member of the Samara Old Regular Baptist Church, the Kentucky Colonels and the DAV of Betsy Layne, KY.

CHARLES EDWARD RICE, born June 14, 1921 at Banner, the son of Elmer W. and Nicy Conn Rice. He enlisted in the U.S. Army Aug. 27, 1940. He completed basic training and MP training at Fort Knox, KY, then was transferred to Fort Thomas, KY. He received a severe head injury while helping to apprehend an intoxicated soldier in Cincinnati. He was in a coma for several weeks and spent several months in Walter Reed Hospital in Washington, D.C. recovering from his injuries. He was discharged Dec. 2, 1941 on disability.

Charles Rice married Eleanor Samons in 1942. They had three children and four grandchildren. He worked on the railroad at

Martin and at Russell before moving to Lima, OH in 1951 where he worked for Ford Motor Company. He retired from Ford in 1986. Charles Rice passed away Feb. 4, 1997.

CLAUDE DOUGLAS RICE, Seaman First Class, USNR, WWII, was born Aug. 11, 1927, East Point, KY. After serving his term in the Navy was employed by South Central Bell Telephone Company, Pikeville, KY. He was married to Mildred (Cotton) Horn of Inez, KY. He had three children: Susan Poe Rice, born March 30, 1954, a retired school teacher living on Cedar Creek Rd., Pikeville, KY; Teresa Ann Rice Piper, born Sept. 30, 1955, living in Hunt, NY; and James Claude "Jim" Rice, born Dec. 28, 1962, employed by the U.S. Postal Service, residing in Pikeville.

The last week of Claude's life was spent enjoying a vacation with his family in Columbus, OH. Returning home, he went to Dewey Lake for boating-relaxing and accidentally fell into the lake while refueling his outboard engine. Some portion of the boat or motor struck his body and was unable to retrieve his boat, he drown Aug. 31, 1964.

FRANCIS GORDON RICE, PSG, U.S. Army WWII, was born Aug. 19, 1924 in East Point, KY. He passed away Oct. 25, 1990.

He married Alka Irene George on Jan. 2, 1946. They had one son, Kenneth Gordon Rice, who was born in Germany Aug. 28, 1947 and one daughter, Carolyn Ann, born June 16, 1954. His wife and children all reside in Louisville, KY.

He retired from the Army with 22 years of service and 15 of those years served on foreign soil.

GEORGE A. RICE, Technician 5, born March 21, 1926 at Banner, KY was inducted on Feb. 12, 1945 and entered into active service in the U.S. Army on Feb. 12, 1945 at Huntington, WV. He spent all his time in the U.S. He was attached to the Army Ground Forces Board #2 at Fort Knox, KY. His military specialty was machinist helper. He qualified with the MM M-1 rifle.

He was discharged on Oct. 25, 1946 at Separation Center, Fort George G. Meade, MD. His decorations and citations include WWII Victory Ribbon, Good Conduct Medal and American Theater Ribbon.

George married Jean Dotson. They had four children: Georgenia R. Hall, Lynn R. May, Vicky R. Flannery and Joseph Neil Rice. They also have 10 grandchildren and seven great-grandchildren. George died on Sept. 2, 1993.

JAMES RUSSELL RICE, born Nov. 14, 1919 in East Point, KY, Apprentice Seaman CO 341, USNTC, Sampson, NY, enlisted in the USN May 12, 1944. He was Honorably Discharged with the understanding to return to Curtis Wright, Columbus, OH, building the Navy Helldiver bomber, pre-flight and training ramp.

Russell married Malta Music April 12, 1941. Malta passed away Feb. 13, 2000. They had two children, one son, Clarence Russell, born Jan. 14, 1942 and one daughter, Sharon Kaye Rice Watkins, born Jan. 8, 1953; four grandchildren; and six great-grandchildren.

He had several jobs after the war, last being in the Legal Dept., Kentucky West Virginia Gas Company, Prestonsburg, KY. He retired in 1979 with 25 years of service. After being retired for 26 years he has learned the job of doing the chores; mainly house and lawn; also carving "The Cane With A Brain" has made its home in many states. He has attended and supported The Little Paint First Church of God for 85+ years.

JOHN D. RICE, Private First Class, born July 29, 1922 in Floyd County, KY, the son of Judd and Maggie Music Rice. One of nine children (three others also served in U.S. Army), he was a young farmer and miner before inducted into the U.S. Army during WWII Feb. 11, 1943. He traveled to Beserta, Africa, shortly leaving for Angio Beach Head, Italy in 3rd Inf., Co. I, 15th Regt. where his squadron walked in land mine territory capturing 27 enemy soldiers. June

6, 1944, Normandy Invasion Day, John went to Rome, Italy, trained for the invasion of Marseilles, France until August 15, 8:00 a.m. where he was the first scout to land and clear the beach head, stepped on a land mine at 8:30 a.m. and was rescued several hours later. He spent six months in Army Hospital Georgia and was Honorably Discharged Jan. 13, 1945.

John's decorations include Unit Decoration Fourragere, France, Purple Heart w/2 OLCs, Medal for Meritorious Achievement, Army of Occupation 1945, Victory Medal, Good Conduct Award, EAME Campaign 1941-45, Honorable Service Award, Badge Qualification Combat, Infantryman, Army first award.

John has been married to Marie Perry Rice for 60 years. A devoted husband, father, grandfather, great-grandfather, community and church leader, he spends few idle hours, but gardens, fishes and hikes the hills for cane wood.

SAMUEL ZELLARD RICE, Private First Class, 134th Inf., 35th Div., WWII, was born Dec. 13, 1921, deceased in action Dec. 31, 1944 in the Bels.

He was married to Mary Woods. They had one daughter, Clara Evelyn.

At the time he enlisted in the Army, he was employed by the Inland Steel Coal Company, Wheelwright, KY.

SHIRLEY B. RICE, Technician 4, born Oct. 16, 1919 at Banner, KY. He was inducted on Jan. 20, 1943 and entered into active service of the Army of the U.S. on Jan. 20, 1943 at Fort Thomas, KY. He left for the European Theater on Feb. 12, 1944 and returned to the U.S. on Oct. 6, 1945. He was attached to the 3516th Ord. Auto Maint. group. His military specialty was as a welder. He participated in battles and campaigns in Normandy, Northern France and Central Europe.

He was discharged on Oct. 11, 1945 at Separation Center, Camp Atterbury, IN. His decorations and citations include EAME Theater Ribbon w/3 Bronze Stars, Good Conduct Medal, Meritorious Unit Award Medal and Croix de Guerre Medal.

Shirley married Elizabeth Bartley. They have eight children, eight grandchildren and many great-grandchildren. He died on April 20, 1980.

WILLIE B. RICE, Technician 5, born Aug. 1, 1922 at Banner, KY. He was inducted on Jan. 9, 1943 and entered into active service on Jan. 26, 1943 at Fort Custer, MI. He left for the European Theater on Feb. 10, 1944 and returned to the U.S. on May 13, 1945. He served in the 101st Abn. Paratroops. His military specialty was heavy mortar gunner and qualified as MM w/rifle parachutists. Willie was a Prisoner Of War in Germany for more than six months.

He was discharged on Nov. 28, 1945 at Separation Center, Fort Sheridan, IL. His decorations and citations include Victory Medal American Ribbon, EAME Ribbon w/2 Bronze Battle Stars, two Overseas Service Bars, Good Conduct Medal and Purple Heart Medal.

Willie first married Anna Fenix and then he married Maxie Newsome. He was an elder in the New Life United Baptist Church and was moderator of the New Hope Association. He had three children, five grandchildren and four great-grandchildren. He died on Sept. 17, 1997.

WILLIAM L. ROBERTS, born Aug. 8, 1924 in Emman, KY, enlisted in the U.S. Army Dec. 10, 1942. He served with B Co., 597th Signal Aircraft Warning Bn., as a radio repairman. He was discharged Jan. 7, 1946 as a Technician Fourth Grade.

Military locations/stations were New Guinea and Southern Philippines (liberation of Luzon).

He was awarded the American Theater Medal, Asiatic-Pacific Theater Ribbon w/3 Bronze Stars, Philippine Liberation Medal, Good Conduct Medal and WWII Victory Medal.

He graduated from the University of Miami, FL with an engineering degree. Civilian employment as IBM engineer. He was married to Cecilia and had five children (two sons and three daughters) and nine grandchildren. He passed away Sept. 2, 2005.

EDWARD F. ROBINSON, born in Bevinsville, KY on March 26, 1927, enlisted in the service on May 26, 1945. Branch of Military: training combat with Army Engrs. Div. as demolition specialist and transferred to Quartermaster Corps.

Military locations/stations: Camp Atterbury, IN; Camp Claiborne, LA; Fort Jackson, SC; LeHarve, France; Namur, Belgium; Frankfort, Germany; Bad Nauheim, Germany; Frankfurt, Germany; and Heidelberg, Germany.

Memorable experiences: "When I arrived at European Command Headquarters in Frankfurt, Germany they wanted to assign me at Quartermaster Headquarters as Troops Clerk in Personnel Div. I told them it wouldn't work because I was a country boy and didn't want in a big city. So they sent me to the Continental Base Section Headquarters in Bad Nauheim, Germany. There they assigned me the same job that I was to have in Frankfurt. Bad Nauheim was a small resort town, and for this reason, was not destroyed in the war. I spent one and one-half years there and got a good reputation. Continental Base Section (CBS) was deactivated in early 1947 and I was sent back to Frankfurt to do the very same job that they originally wanted me to do."

"When I first arrived back in Frankfurt, Germany we marched two and one-half miles to work every weekday. My office was located in the Hohenzollern School near the I.G. Farben office building where most offices were. Very seldom was it called off due to weather. We ate breakfast at our company mess hall. We also had a transient mess hall that could be used for lunch or anytime. We rode Street Car #57 about a mile for lunch. My first lunch was the day after I arrived in Frankfurt. I didn't know how to get to the mess hall, so another GI near my age, asked me if I wanted to go with him. I jumped at the chance. So, we got the #57 Street Car and never did arrive at the mess hall. We got several street cars and our Col. Shaller and Capt. Watson were getting worried. Finally, on the way back to the office I mentioned that he must not know much about Frankfurt. He replied, "I thought you did." Turns out he had arrived the day before I did and he also was a country boy."

"In February and March 1948, European Command Headquarters was moved to Heidelberg, Germany, another resort town that was not destroyed."

"I left there for home on June 22, 1948, and arrived home on July 22."

His awards and medals include the American Defense, Good Conduct, Victory and Occupation (Germany). He was discharged on July 21, 1948 as a Staff Sergeant.

Civilian employment was with Turner Elkhorn Mining Company and as postmaster, Langley, KY. He currently resides in Langley and is retired.

GEORGE E. ROBINSON, Sergeant, born June 21, 1917 at East Point, KY. His parents were George and Adaline Music Robinson. George enlisted in the U.S. Army Sept. 11, 1940. He received his training at Fort Thomas, KY as an automotive mechanic.

George served in Normandy, Northern France, Rhineland and Central Europe. His decorations and citations were Theater Ribbon w/4 Bronze Stars, National Defense Service Medal, Expert Marksman and Distinguished Unit Citation.

He married Eva Manuel and they had five children: George, Sue, Tyrone, Billy Ray and Darlene. George died during a mining accident on Feb. 9, 1967.

BLAINE SALISBURY, served in the U.S. Army 1941 to 1945 during WWII. Military locations, stations include New Guinea, Philippines and Japan. He served with the 148th Inf. Bn., 37th Div. He trained at Fort Knox and served at Camp Atterbury. Salisbury had malaria in New Guinea and was in Japan after the bombing.

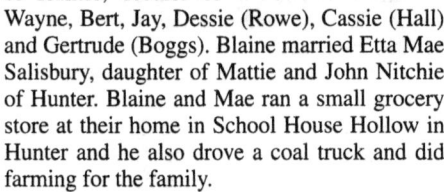

He is the son of Link and May Salisbury of Hunter; brother of Wayne, Bert, Jay, Dessie (Rowe), Cassie (Hall) and Gertrude (Boggs). Blaine married Etta Mae Salisbury, daughter of Mattie and John Nitchie of Hunter. Blaine and Mae ran a small grocery store at their home in School House Hollow in Hunter and he also drove a coal truck and did farming for the family.

He wanted a better future for his family so he went north to find employment. He started working at Goodyear Tire and Rubber Plant in St. Marys, OH in 1954 and then moved his family north. Unfortunately Blaine died in an auto accident in 1957 in St. Marys. Wife, Mae, remained in St. Marys and raised their four children: Anthony (deceased 2003), Frances, Kenneth and Danny.

JAMES L. "BLACKIE" SALISBURY, born March 13, 1926, passed away on May 2, 1970. He was the son of Henry and Ellen (Flanery) Salisbury of Martin.

Everyone knew him as "Blackie." He served as a light machine gunner, having received his Combat Infantryman Badge. He served in Africa and Europe. His commendations include: Army of Occupation Medal (Germany), Good Conduct Medal, Victory Medal and EAME Theatre Service Medal.

After the war, Blackie settled in his home community, the "Cummingsville" section of Martin. He worked for several years at the C&O Railroad. While working at the Price Tipple, he was killed in a derailment accident. Blackie was very popular in the community. He loved to hunt, fish, and trap, and to "tinker" - he took things apart, made things, and fixed things. He married the former Jean Fyffe, remaining together right up until his death. The couple had no children.

In the photo, Pfc. James L. "Blackie" Salisbury is crouching down in a Cummingsville (Martin) street. Behind him is visible the old Beaver Valley Hospital. The two boys with him are his brother, Franklin D. "Sambo" Salisbury and (smallest) their first cousin, Larry Greer.

JOHN Q. SALISBURY, was the son of John and Fannie Francis (Halbert) Salisbury, of Hunter. John Q. was born June 23, 1919. He served in the 438th Troop Carrier Group. He was a radio mechanic and an air crew member, having 'earned his wings.'

Commendations include: American Defense, American Theatre ribbons, EAME Ribbon w/2 Bronze Stars and one Silver Star; Good Conduct Medal, Air Medal w/3 Bronze Clusters, Victory Medal and Distinguished Unit Badge.

He served at Rome/Arno, Southern France, Normandy, Northern France, Ardennes, Rhineland and Central Europe.

After the war, he married the former Pauline Nunemaker, and they had three children: John Allen Salisbury, Bruce Salisbury and Gina (Salisbury) Moore. John Q. worked for many years as an engineer with the C&O Railroad.

In the photo are, left to right: Henry Salisbury, John Q. Salisbury, Blackie Salisbury, Patty Sue Salisbury and Sambo Salisbury.

NORRIS SALISBURY, born Nov. 14, 1927 to Henry and Ellen (Flanery) Salisbury, of Martin. What he related to me, over the years, was that he served as a photographer in the Army Air Corps. He received extensive training while in the service. He told the family at the end of WWII that "the next one will be in a place called Korea, because we've photographed every square inch of that place."

Norris eventually settled in Michigan, marrying the former Ruth Lackey. They had one daughter, Julie. Ruth's daughter by a prior marriage, Gail (Dollahan) Johnsen, was in all respects Norris' daughter, as well.

For additional information, you may wish to contact his sister, Alma Ruth Edwards, at: mountaingirl@myvine.com.

STACY SALISBURY, born April 21, 1915 in Floyd County, KY, enlisted in the U.S. Military Dec. 27, 1944. He was stationed in Camp Blanding, FL and saw action in the Asiatic-Pacific Theatre. He was discharged Feb. 7, 1943 with the rank of Second Lieutenant Staff Sergeant.

His civilian employment included management of restaurant and night clubs.

TED H. SALISBURY, commonly known as "H" Salisbury, served in WWII in Germany (like his brother, Rodney).

He was born Oct. 30, 1927. He grew up in the Cummingsville section of Martin, and later lived there as an adult, right up until the time of his death.

"H" achieved the rank of Corporal. He was a rifleman, and as late as the 1990s could still quote the serial number off of his M-1 rifle. He had an affinity for the German language, picking it up quickly. Because of this, he was used on occasion to accompany/guard German prisoners. He also developed a keen interest in a German girl, whom even in his later years, he never forgot.

"H" was the son of Ted and Lucy (Casebolt) Salisbury, of Martin. He had one daughter, Clara Helen (Salisbury) Marks, currently of Michigan and Arizona.

While in the service, he received the WWII Victory Medal and the Army of Occupation Medal.

After his service to our country, "H" worked for years on the C&O Railroad, then later served as state Alcoholic Beverage Control Agent. He possessed a very colorful, unique personality; and was passionate - being capable of strong personal feelings - sometimes positive, sometimes less so.

GROVER SAMONS, born 1921, died 2000, enlisted in the Army in 1940. He served in England, France and Germany during WWII. He re-enlisted for service in 1944, serving a total of seven and a half years. He received the Bronze Star for bravery in the line of duty.

After serving in the Army he returned home to Minnie, KY with Elfriede Samons, his lovely war bride from Bremerhaven, Germany. He became a merchant and then a coal operator. He and Elfriede have three children: Rita Johanna Samons Daniels of Minnie, Tony Grover Samons of Lexington, and Jody Lee Samons of Minnie. Grover and Elfriede have nine grandchildren and two great-grandchildren.

Grover was an active member of the McDowell First Baptist Church. He loved God, family and country. He was a brave man of honor with a good heart, loved forever by family and friends. *Submitted by Elfriede Samons and Rita Daniels.*

ERMAL CLAY "BUB" SCUTCHFIELD, was born on Nov. 25, 1923, the son of Beckham and Elizabeth Scutchfield at West Prestonsburg.

He enlisted on April 16, 1943 and served two years, nine months and 29 days. He was stationed at NTS Great Lakes, IL and FSS Virginia Beach, VA. He served aboard the USS *David W. Taylor*. He was involved in the Philippine Liberation and Asiatic-Pacific Theater. He received the Victory Medal and American Theater Award. Some ratings held were as, Seaman Second Class, Seaman First Class, RDM Third Class. He received an Honorable Service Discharge.

He married Maurine Harmon on Sept. 27, 1946. They had two children, Sandra Lynn and Orville David. He worked at Inland Steel Mines for 21 years before retiring due to black lung disease. He and Maurine were both baptized on April 7, 1974. He enjoyed working in the church and fishing and hunting.

He passed away in May 1997 after a battle with cancer.

EUGENE "SONNY" SCUTCHFIELD,

was born to Sid and Lula Calhoun Scutchfield. He was employed by Kentucky-West Virginia Gas Company before enlisting in the Army during WWII.

He lost his life in the Battle of the Bulge, Dec. 16, 1944 to Jan. 25, 1945, in Germany.

His body was not returned to his beloved hills or family home on Bull Creek, KY.

ORVILLE THOMAS SCUTCHFIELD,

born March 19, 1922 to Beckham and Elizabeth Scutchfield, West Prestonsburg, enlisted in the Navy in October 1942. He served aboard the USS *Bristol* until it was sunk in the Atlantic Ocean in October 1943. He stayed in the ocean for four hours before being rescued.

Orville Thomas Scutchfield and his bride, Louise Ferguson, taken on their wedding day in april 1944.

He came home on a 30 day survivor's leave in December 1943. Returning he went to Boston where he served aboard the USS *O'Brian*. He returned home in April of 1944 when he married Louise Ferguson. He was then shipped to England before going to Normandy. He was killed when the USS *O'Brian* was hit on June 25, 1944. His body was not returned home until January 1949.

He was awarded the Purple Heart and numerous other awards.

The family received a document "in grateful memory" signed by President Franklin Roosevelt years later after someone found it in an old desk drawer.

PALMER SCUTCHFIELD,

was born Dec. 10, 1910 to Ed and Maggie Johnson Scutchfield. When his father died he helped his mother on the farm raising his many siblings.

Palmer enlisted in the Army during WWII and remained for 15 years. When he returned to his home, with the help of his friends, he erected a large flag pole on Scutchfield Cemetery, Bull Creek Route 80 - the family cemetery. His niece, Josephine Herald, continues the upkeep of the flag since his death in 1998.

He never married. When his health failed, he entered the V.A. Hospital in Wilmore, KY where he passed away on Dec. 8, 1998. He is buried in Scutchfield Cemetery under the flag of which he was so proud.

EDWARD GRAHAM SELLARDS,

born Jan. 8, 1923, at Banner, KY, the son of Jack and Nancy Akers Sellards. He had two brothers and five sisters who called him Graham, but in later years he became Ed to his friends and business associates.

He enlisted in the USN in December 1941, soon after the bombing of Pearl Harbor and the beginning of WWII. His basic training was at the Great Lakes Naval Station in Illinois; then he was sent to Madison, WI, for special radio training.

He was sent to the Central Pacific Islands and saw his first major battle in the invasion of Saipan. As a radio operator, his mission was to direct the Marines in their landing craft toward the perilous beach. He was involved in other invasions - at Peleliu, Tarawa and Iwo Jima - where he remained at sea directing shore traffic by radio. Each of these was a major and hard fought battle. Except for these invasions, much of his duty at sea was aboard a sub chaser.

After his discharge from the Navy in November 1945, he married Betty Jane Ratliff and was both a sales agent and district manager for Commonwealth Insurance Company. They lived for a time in West Virginia and Tennessee before settling down in Barbourville, KY. There he served as a deacon in his church and was active in the Gideon organization. He passed away Nov. 27, 1984.

MILLARD SETSER,

born Jan. 12, 1920 at Edgar, the son of Marion and Lida Burchett Setser. He was inducted into the U.S. Army June 25, 1941 and trained at Fort Knox. His unit, HQ Co., 46th Armd. Inf. Bn., 5th Armd. Div. participated in Normandy and Northern France/Germany campaigns.

He received the American Defense Ribbon, Good Conduct Medal and EAME Theater Ribbon.

He was a member of DAV Chapter 18 at Auxier. Millard was married to Roberta Howell by whom he had four children: Elaine, Justin, Erelene and Judy. He worked in Michigan during the 50s, then as a carpenter in Floyd County until retirement.

He had a passion for bluegrass music and was still playing guitar at age 81. Millard passed away March 22, 2004 at age 84 and was laid to rest at Auxier Relocation Cemetery.

HERSHEL SHELL,

born Feb. 14, 1922 at Bonanza, KY to John and Dora Hackworth Shell, joined the 3C Camp at the age of 16 and stayed there until he was drafted into the U.S. Army in 1942. He entered at Huntington, WV and he separated at Cen Camp, Atterbury, IN with Honorable Discharge.

He was at Luzon and was stationed at another location when Pearl Harbor was attacked. He was discharged on Jan. 11, 1946 with the Asiatic-Pacific Theater Ribbon w/1 Bronze Star, Philippine Liberation Ribbon, Good Conduct Medal and WWII Victory Medal.

He was a heavy equipment operator and mechanic for both strip mining and underground mining. He built roads from Whitesburg to Frenchburg, KY as well as the road to Dewey Lake.

He was married to Elizabeth Mae Burchett who died in 1976. He then married Okiemae Risner. He died on Nov. 7, 2003.

JOHN SHEPHERD,

born Nov. 2, 1917 in Floyd County, KY served in WWII and is buried on the Shepherd Cemetery at Dwale, KY.

He was the son of William "Hoot" Shepherd, born 1883 and Delilah Wallen, born 1888. Hoot was the son of Andrew Shepherd and Emma

Goodman. Delilah Wallen was the daughter of John Wallen and Minerva Nelson. John was the son of CSA soldier, Shelby Wallen, who is buried on the Right Fork of Bull Creek. Minerva's grandfather, George Nelson, born 1812 in Hancock County, TN (later moved to Floyd County, KY), was in the Mexican War.

His brothers and sisters were: Andrew, Lydia, Josie, Ann, Joseph and Goldie.

He married Goldie Clifton and had two daughters, Janice and Bernice. *Submitted by Karen Nelson Marcum.*

PAUL WHEELER SIMMONS, was born July 31, 1917 in Floyd County, KY to John Morgan and Lona Nelson Simmons. He enlisted in the U.S. Army on Feb. 25, 1941 as a Private. He served with the Cryptographic Tech 805 in HQ Co., 1st Signal Bn., 7th Army and 3rd Army.

He served in Algeria-French Morocco, Sicily, Rome-Arno, Rhineland, Southern France and Central Europe.

His medals include the EAME Theater Ribbon w/6 Bronze Stars and Bronze Arrowhead, American Defense Medal and Good Conduct Medal.

His most enduring memory was when he received, decoded and delivered the message "for Patton's Eyes Only." Paul was discharged Sept. 20, 1945 with the rank of Technician 4. Paul is now deceased.

GEORGE W. SIZEMORE, volunteered at age 45 for Army service in August 1942, WWII. George was the son of Flora Sizemore and husband of Meta Ford Sizemore, both of Prestonsburg, KY.

Despite his age, he entered Armored Corps training at Fort Knox, KY and was stationed overseas for 16 months. During the American drive through France, George was wounded and remained hospitalized in England and Ireland until his discharge. He received the Purple Heart.

He is buried in Ford Cemetery, Prestonsburg, KY.

J.P. SKEANS served in the Pacific during WWII.

CARTHEL HALE SMITH, graduated from Prestonsburg High School in 1935 as valedictorian and entered the U.S. Naval Academy at Annapolis, MD in 1940. He was an officer in the USN. He was assigned to the Submarine Service.

Smith went down with his submarine in the South Pacific in WWII.

ARCHIE SNIPES, born on Sept. 16, 1919 in Floyd County, KY, the son of James Thomas "Tommy" and Elizabeth Jane "Lizzie" Leeke Snipes. He was a Private with the Army. He enlisted May 16, 1944 at Fort Thomas, Newport, KY.

He married Eunice Hannah. He died in Piqua Memorial Medical Center, Piqua, and Miami County, OH on April 22, 1993. He was 73.

DARWIN SNIPES, born in 1923 in Floyd County, KY, the son of Joe and Cora Spradlin Snipes. He was a Private in the U.S. Army Infantry. He was inducted in March 1943 and went to England in May.

He died in Normandy, France on June 29, 1944 in infantry action. He was 21. Snipes was buried in July 1944 in Joe Snipes Sr. Family Cemetery, Abbott Creek, Floyd County, KY.

JAMES D. "BUSTER" SPEARS, born March 29, 1927, the son of Myrtle Jane and William K. Spears. He served in the U.S. Army during WWII.

After returning home from the war he moved to Columbus, OH and worked for Temkin Roller Bearing.

James never married and at 29 years old he was killed in a bad truck accident in Louisa, KY Aug. 10, 1956.

FRENCH PRESTON "FP" SPENCER, Seaman First Class, USNR, born Nov. 24, 1925, the son of Alex and Kate (Turner) Spencer. He enlisted in the USN Jan. 19, 1944 as a sophomore in high school. He spent a year in Norfolk, VA transporting troops to various parts of Europe and then in Panama Canal at the Fleet Air Wing Base. He received the American Theater Ribbon and Victory Medal and was Honorably Discharged April 22, 1946.

FP married Loretta Barker on Feb. 20, 1953, and had four children: Rickey, Jeffery (died at birth), Michael and Randy. He divorced and remarried Dorothy Riddle Jan. 6, 1979. FP had eight grandchildren and five great-grandchildren.

FP was employed in maintenance at General Motors and retired in 1980 after 30 years service.

FP had a passion for gardening and loved giving most of what he grew to family and friends. FP enjoyed a good cup of coffee while keeping up with current events from the newspaper or television. He was always known for drinking his coffee from a small cup so it could never get cold. Most people knew FP as an inventor and he created projects around the house. He built a water garden with a backyard garden pathway. FP passed away Dec. 8, 2005.

HERBERT SPRADLIN, born May 18, 1912, the son of Mr. and Mrs. Henry Spradlin. He enlisted in the U.S. Army and served with the 49th General Hospital in the South Pacific, including the Philippines.

He was awarded the Asiatic-Pacific Ribbon w/Bronze Star, among other awards.

He was married to Elva Spradlin and had three sons. Herbert passed away Feb. 16, 1998.

OLVA SPRADLIN, born on Aug. 4, 1922 in Floyd County, KY, the son of Cager and Ducie Hackworth Spradlin. He was a motorcycle mechanic, packer, high explosives ammunitions worker, toolroom keeper, stock clerk, and stock control clerk.

He was seriously wounded and died in Normandy, France in June 1944. He was 21 years of age.

SCOTT SPRADLIN, Technician 4, born July 10, 1925, the son of the late Henry and Florence Brown Spradlin, Myrtle, Floyd County, KY. While still in high school he was drafted in the U.S. Army on Sept. 24, 1943, basic training at Camp Chaffee, AR.

He went overseas and landed in Naples, Italy. He was a Combat Medic, Det. 141st Inf., 36th Div. and received Bronze Arrowhead Medal, WWII Victory Medal, Purple Heart, Bronze Service Stars and Bronze Star Medal w/OLCs. He served as Surgical Technician and also a Medical Technician in Rome-Arno, Southern France, Rhineland and Central Europe.

He returned to Fort Knox, KY and was discharged Dec. 21, 1945. Scott spent 28 days in the V.A. Hospital in Huntington, WV and then went back to high school and graduated in 1946.

He worked for Big Sandy Tobacco Company several years. Married Mary M. Edmonds May 15, 1954. Moved to Pikeville, KY. Worked for Pikeville Oil & Tire, Gulf Oil and then Kentucky-West Virginia Gas Company for 27 years. Retired in 1987.

JOHN H. SPURLOCK, entered the service on Dec. 30, 1942 and was discharged Dec

13, 1944 after being wounded in Germany. He spent three months in the hospital in Germany and returned home in 1945. John was born on Sept. 8, 1922 and passed away Dec. 28, 1992.

CARL STAFFORD, son of Carl and Maxie Fairchild Stafford; husband of Mary Lou Lewis. He has three daughters: Marilyn, Suzanne and Carolyn.

His three sisters are: Mae Fern Stafford Hale, Iris Janet Stafford and Pansy Ruth. Half brothers and sisters are: Lura Stafford Moore, Sofronia Stafford Spradlin, Burl and Byron Stafford. He was born and raised in Paintsville, KY, Johnson County. *Submitted by Mary Lou Stafford.*

VIGIS MILTON STEELE, born Jan. 20, 1923 at Bull Creek, Floyd County, KY to Ernest and Rebecca McGuire Steele. His brothers and sisters were Mildred (who married Sam Nelson), Jean, Ruby and Clyde Steele. His half brother is Harvey Caudill Jr.

He was a Staff Sergeant in the 65th Armd. Inf. Bn., 2nd

Armd. Div., and was killed in action in Germany March 7, 1945. He is buried on the McGuire Cemetery, which is on top of the mountain at the left of the mouth of Shop Branch on the Right Fork of Bull Creek.

His namesake, Vigis Samuel "Sammy" Nelson, along with Seth and Noah Marcum just cleaned his gravesite off. Seth and Noah picked flowers for his grave. *Submitted by Karen Nelson Marcum and Sammy Nelson.*

ALBERT STEPHENS, enlisted in the U.S. Army on Feb. 11, 1943. He was born in Floyd County, KY. His parents were Henry Clay Stephens and Alice Risner. He had two brothers who also were in WWII, Harrison and William "Bill." Bill was killed in action on Luzon April 6, 1945. Albert and Harrison enlisted on the same date. *Submitted by Karen N. Marcum.*

CHARLES WILLIAM STEPHENS, born April 17, 1923, enlisted in the USMCR, April 9, 1943. Military locations/stations include USMCR Recruit Depot, Camp Elliott, CA; USMCR, Seattle, WA; Pacific Area sea service Jan. 25, 1944-Jan. 5, 1946. He served as a rifle marksman and Rifle Non-Commissioned Squad Leader. He was discharged Jan. 28, 1946 as a Corporal.

He participated in action against the enemy at Okinawa; Ryukyu Islands April 1, 1945-April 14, 1945; again May 30, 1945-June 21, 1945. Also participated in the Occupation of Japan Sept. 22, 1945-Dec. 17, 1945.

Memorable experiences: Sept. 22, 1945 to Dec. 17, 1945, Occupation of Japan, kindness of Japanese civilians. Their impoverished condition because of the war. Horrible memories of Battle for Okinawa as member of a replacement company for the 2nd Marine Div.

He was awarded the American Theater Ribbon, South West Pacific Service Ribbon and WWII Victory Medal.

Civilian employment was with Chelsea Fiber Products Company in Chelsea, MI from 1946 until his retirement. He was married to Verglinda Patrick Stephens and had three daughters: Katheryn Stephens (Texas), Joyce Stephens (Michigan) and Janice Stephens (Michigan). Stephens is deceased.

CLAUDE STEPHENS, son of Bob and Minnie Stephens, was born in Floyd County, KY and fought in WWII. He lives in Indiana. *Photo belongs to Nola Stephens Mayo. Submitted by Karen Nelson Marcum.*

CLYDE B. STEPHENS, Technician 5, born April 16, 1924 at Hite, KY, the son of Grover and Minnie Stephens. Stephens enlisted May 26, 1943 at Huntington, WV. He served in the

U.S. Army, 796th AAA Bn., Sp. 10 Armd. Div. He attended a training camp in Stewart, GA; Camp Gordon, GA; then was sent to England to Camp Blackmore, with new equipment, and trained further. He landed on LST at South Hampton. He landed on Omaha Beach; convoyed to Metz, Germany where Patton took his troop to Thiondille and crossed the river north of Metz. On December 15, he moved in convoy with PCB moving north; 16th day in Bastogne, Belgium, under shell fire. On the first half track in 3rd Army to go into Germany, ended up in 7th Army, Garmish Parkerchev.

He was discharged on Feb. 4, 1946 at Camp Atterbury, IN, with the rank of Technician 5. His decorations include the Bronze Star and Presidential Unit Citation. Stephens commented he was glad he didn't get hit or wounded.

Clyde married Eva Stephens. His children are Marla Hall of Martin, Johnny Clyde of Hunter, and Steven Samuel of Martin. He has several grandchildren. He currently resides at Martin.

HARRISON STEPHENS, enlisted in the U.S. Army on Feb. 11, 1943. He was born in Floyd County, KY. His parents were Henry Clay Stephens and Alice Risner. He had two brothers who also were in WWII, Albert and William "Bill." Bill was killed in action on Luzon April 6, 1945. Harrison returned to Floyd County and raised a family. He now resides in Pike County, KY. *Submitted by Karen N. Marcum.*

JOE STEPHENS, born in Floyd County, KY, was the son of Alex Stephens and Emma Johnson. He and his brother, William Stephens, served in WWII.

Joe has a son, Billy Joe, who lives in Nashville, TN. *Info from his sister, Nola Stephens Mayo. Submitted by Karen N. Marcum.*

WILLIAM J. "BILL" STEPHENS, born in Risner, Floyd County, KY April 10, 1906, was the son of Henry Clay Stephens, born Aug. 13, 1869 in Floyd County, and Alice Risner, born Dec. 6, 1886 in Floyd County. Bill was killed in action in WWII on Luzon by mortar shrapnel April 6, 1945.

Bill's father was a former Circuit Court Clerk of Floyd County from 1915 to 1923 and was a Circuit Court Judge from 1939 through 1945. Henry Clay Stephens was first married to Fannie Hicks and had the following children: Alexander, Hiram, Gracie, George W., Charles, John C. and Robert. He married Alice Risner and had nine more children: William J., Albert, Harrison, Frank, Julia, Lillie, Marie and Peggy.

Bill had two brothers who also served in WWII, Harrison and Albert. *Photo belongs to Bill's niece, Nola Stephens Mayo. Submitted by Karen Nelson Marcum.*

WILLIAM STEPHENS, born in 1924 in Floyd County, KY, was the son of Alex Stephens and Emma Johnson. He and his brother, Joe Stephens, served in WWII.

William married Verclinda Patrick. Their three children: Catherine, Janice and Joyce. *Info from his sister, Nola Stephens Mayo. Submitted by Karen N. Marcum.*

HOWARD STICKLER, son of Edward and Mary Salisbury, attended Martin High School and served in the U.S. Navy during WWII.

STEVE H. STOUT, born Jan. 5, 1927, enlisted in the U.S. Army on May 8, 1945 and was stationed in California, Louisiana, New Jersey and Japan. One of his memorable experiences was traveling to Japan and back and getting to see half the world. He traveled 18,000 miles and rode out a typhoon.

His awards and medals include the Pacific Theatre Medal, Japanese Occupation, Good Conduct Medal and the Expert Infantry Emblem. He was discharged in October 1946 with the rank of Corporal.

On Sept. 23, 1946 Steve married Wilda Arrington and they have two children, James Steven and Virginia Marie; two granddaughters, Stephanie and Lesly; one grandson, John; and one daughter-in-law, Carolyn.

Steve was employed with the C&O Railroad and currently resides at Martin, KY.

DENZIL F. STUMBO, Staff Sergeant, entered the service on Nov. 27, 1942. He served as an airplane mechanic/gunner. His duties included maintaining and operating a 50 caliber machine gun on a B-24 Liberator. He was also an aerial engineer.

He flew his required 25 missions in the European Theater of Operations over Germany, then volunteered with his crew to fly five extra missions. He was awarded the Distinguished Flying Cross, Air Medal w/3 OLCs and the Good Conduct Medal. He was discharged Oct. 9, 1945.

He married Eathel L. Patrick and they have one son Danny Stumbo and one granddaughter Angela.

ISSAC STUMBO, born in Floyd County, KY, was the son of Taylor Stumbo and Rhoda Fitzpatrick. He was a veteran of WWII.

He married Nola Stephens, daughter of Alex Stephens. The have a daughter, Sandra. He is deceased. *Photo from Nola Stephens Stumbo Mayo. Submitted by Karen Nelson Marcum.*

JACK STUMBO, entered the U.S. Navy during WWII and served on the *Enterprise*. He was discharged March 9, 1946. Jack attended Martin High School and lived at Salisbury.

JIM STUMBO, Private First Class, born July 8, 1922 at McDowell, KY, the son of Joe Stumbo and Mint Sizemore. He enlisted in the U.S. Army in Huntington, WV. He took his basic training at Fort Hancock, NJ. He was transferred overseas on May 4, 1944 and was assigned to the 29th Inf., European Theater of Operations. He was wounded in action in February 1945 in Germany. He was hospitalized for three months and was then returned to his unit.

He was discharged in October 1945 at Camp Atterbury, IN with the rank of Private First Class. He participated in the battles and campaigns in Northern France, Ardennes, Rhineland and Central Europe. He was awarded the EAME Ribbon w/4 Bronze Stars, Good Conduct Medal, Purple Heart and Combat Infantry Badge. Jim said the war was "terrifying." "It couldn't be any worse. It was like hell on earth."

His children are Jimmy D. Stumbo of Drift, Jerry Ann Standafer of West Liberty, Marietta Adams of Drift and Joe D. Stumbo of Florida. He has six grandchildren and two great-grandchildren.

WALTER L. STUMBO, Private First Class, born Feb. 12, 1926 at McDowell, KY, the son of Lee Stumbo and Annie Mae Hall. He enlisted in the U.S. Army on May 8, 1944 at Fort Thomas, KY. He served in Co. D, 242nd Inf. as a heavy machine gunner.

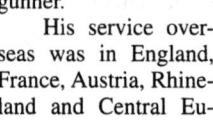

His service overseas was in England, France, Austria, Rhineland and Central Europe. He participated in campaigns/battles in Northern France. His MOS was Special Vehicle Operator.

He was discharged Nov. 14, 1945 at Bruck, Austria. His decorations include the Combat Infantry Badge, Bronze Star, Good Conduct Medal and European Theater Ribbon. After the war he worked as a coal miner.

Walter married Gertrude Turner on Jan. 31, 1948 at McDowell, KY. They had 10 children: Patricia, James, Barry, William, Jackie Darrell, Cheryl, Robert, Teresa, Walter and Jackie Belinda; 20 grandchildren and 11 great-grandchildren. Walter died Oct. 27, 2000 at Versailles, KY.

ARNOLD E. TACKETT, Private First Class, born Dec. 7, 1924, the son of John M. and Mellie Elswick Tackett at Fed, KY. He was drafted into the Army Aug. 16, 1944 while working for Inland Steel at Wheelwright. Arnold completed basic training at Fort Benjamin Harrison, IN then to Camp Atterbury; Fort Blanding, FL; Fort Meade, MD; and Fort Hamilton, NY for deployment to England. From England he was shipped to LeHavre, France where he was placed in the 3rd Army as a machine gunner in the 519th AAA Gun Inf.

Arnold received three Bronze Stars for Ardennes, Rhineland, Central Europe, Combat Infantry Badge, Good Conduct Medal, WWII Victory Medal and Kami Ribbon. He was discharged at LeHavre, France on Oct. 6, 1945 to enlist in the regular Army for a 60-day furlough.

While on furlough he married Alma Mae Little on Dec. 28, 1945 at Melvin, KY. He returned to service as a Commissary Clerk at Fort Lawton, WA and received his second Honorable Discharge May 9, 1947. Arnold and Alma had five children, all of them reside in Floyd County. He was also legal guardian for five other children that lived with them until they moved away for work.

He returned to work for Inland Steel Company Mines; he worked underground until he got his back broken in a haulage accident. He returned to work on the preparation plant as a boiler operator. Inland later sold to Island Creek Coal Company where he retired in 1974.

After retirement he devoted his time to his church and wood working in his small shop. Arnold was an ordained minister in the Joppa Old Regular Baptist Church and was assistant moderator at the date of his death. Arnold was a member of Joppa Church for 45 years. He was also a member of DAV Chapter 128 at Wayland, KY, board member of the Tackett Family Association, and a member of UMWA Local Union 5899 at Wheelwright. Arnold passed away Wednesday, June 29, 1994.

SAMUEL THACKER, born Jan. 8, 1926 at Banner, KY, was the son of Noah and Rosa Thacker. He enlisted in the Army June 10, 1941 at 15 years of age, giving his birth date as Jan. 8, 1923. He was discharged June 6, 1945.

After basic training he served in Alaska and the Aleutian Islands as cannoneer in the 855th Coast Arty. Btry. where he received the Asiatic-Pacific Theater Ribbon and American Defense Service Medal w/Bronze Star.

He married Maxine Laferty May 14, 1947. They had three daughters, one son and four grandchildren. In 1960 he moved his family to Greenup County where he was employed by Armco Steel. He retired after 32 years with Armco. After nine and one-half years of retirement spent fishing, gardening, and enjoying his grandchildren, he died of lung cancer June 21, 1997. Four great-grandchildren have now joined his family.

PAUL WARD THOMPSON, born Oct. 26, 1910 in Stark, KY, enlisted in the service in 1940. He served in the Merchant Marines 1940-42 and in the USN in 1943. Military locations/stations were: training in Cleveland, OH, the Pacific Theater and the South Pacific in WWII.

He participated in the battles of Okinawa and Philippines.

Civilian employment: grocery store proprietor. He was married to Ura Bane Hunt and had one son, Paul Hunt Thompson and three grandsons: Paul Norman, Charle and John Emit. Thompson passed away Jan. 18, 2001.

ARTHUR TIBBS, born Oct. 31, 1924 in Harold, KY, enlisted in the USN Aug. 13, 1943. He served on the USS *Houston*, Sete Terminal, CA and USS PC-812. Tibbs was discharged March 25, 1946 as F1/c.

He was awarded the Victory Ribbon, Asiatic-Pacific Medal w/3 stars and Philippine Liberation Medal w/1 star.

He is married to Charlotte and has five children, 11 grandchildren and five great-grandchildren. He worked for the Caterpillar Corp. until his retirement. Tibbs currently resides in Mentor, OH.

LANGLEY TURNER, Technical Sergeant, born June 12, 1920, enlisted in the U.S. Army Aug. 21, 1940 at Fort Thomas, KY. He was in Co. B, 9th Inf. Div. He was discharged May 27, 1945.

Battles in which he participated in include Algeria-French Morocco, Tunisia, Sicily, Normandy, Northern France and Germany. He was wounded twice while in France.

Turner was awarded seven Bronze Service Stars, two Purple Hearts, Good Conduct Medal, American Defense Service Medal, American Campaign Medal, Presidential Unit Citation, EAME Campaign Medal, Silver Star Medal, WWII Victory Medal, Combat Infantryman Badge (first award) and Honorable Service Lapel Button WWII.

When he returned to the States he got a job with the C&O Railroad where he was employed until he retired. Langley married Violet Sparkman of Dema, KY. They had two children and two grandchildren.

WILLIAM C. "BUSTER" TURNER, born July 4, 1922 at Minnie, KY, the son of William and Lizzie Turner. He was married on June 25, 1942 to Anna Rae Spriggs. He was inducted into the U.S. Army at Fort Thomas, KY, and did his basic training at Fort Hancock, NJ. He was assigned to the 143rd Regt., 3rd Bn., 36th Inf. Div., Company HQ. After basic training he was sent to Camp Upton at Long Island, NY where he guarded the coastline. He was sent to Fort Meade, MD, and then to Camp Pickett, VA, where he was shipped to the European Theater of Operations at Oran, Africa on April 25, 1944. Before he was shipped overseas, his wife gave birth to their first daughter, Bobbie Jo.

He was sent to Italy where he landed on the Anzio Beachhead. Then he was involved in the Invasion of Southern France. On Aug. 29, 1944, he was captured by the Germans. He was held prisoner in Germany until April 26, 1945. He was shipped back to the States and sent to Deshon General Hospital at Butler, PA. He received the Good Conduct Medal, African European Service Medals w/3 Bronze Stars, Sharpshooter - Combat Infantry Badge and two Overseas Service Bars. He was discharged on Oct. 29, 1945.

He returned home to Drift, KY and went to work in the mines. He and his wife had two more daughters, Ruth Ann on July 7, 1946, and Ernestine on April 10, 1951. He retired from the Turner Elkhorn Mining Company in 1985 after working for about 40 years. He now lives at Minnie, KY with his wife of 63 years. They both belong to the Old Beaver Regular Baptist Church. He is a deacon of the church and is actively involved in church work. His first priority is his family and he dolts on his four grandchildren and his six great-grandchildren. At 83 years of age he is reaping the rewards that he deserves for his years of work and service.

JOHN HAYS TURNLEY, born on Oct. 29, 1924 at Wheelwright, KY. His father was John Phinizy Turnley from Galveston, TX. His mother was Narcissa Hays. John is a WWII veteran. He married Maxine Gayheart on Dec. 30, 1950. They had two children, Ricky Alan and Connie Denise Turnley.

John worked for the American Electric Power Company (previously called Kentucky Power Company) for 52 years before he retired. He is still working as a state certified electrical inspector.

He is very active in the John W. Hall Masonic Lodge, Kiwanis Club and other community activities. He has served as the district deputy grand master of the Masons. He has a passion for photography, filming most all community events in the area. He plays golf and is excellent at bowling. He has traveled to many countries and has been an asset to the Martin-Prestonsburg area.

JOE WHEELER TUSSEY, was inducted into the U.S. Army on Dec. 15, 1942 at Fort Thomas, KY at age 20.

From April 12, 1943 to May 8, 1943, Pvt. Joe W. Tussey of Co. E completed the Non-Commissioned Officers Course in Gilroy, CA. Promoted to Staff Sergeant in 1943, Joe was assigned the battle patrol in the 7th Inf. Regt. Joe was awarded the Bronze Star for valor in combat on Nov. 2, 1944 in France. His actions were recognized in a letter dated Jan. 19, 1945, stating the award was "for valorous conduct in action against the enemy."

SSgt. Tussey earned the Purple Heart on Feb. 10, 1945 for wounds received in combat on Jan. 27, 1945.

Because of military censorship, he could not reveal his exact location in correspondence back home. However, in a letter to his mother dated May 10, 1944, he stated he was "somewhere in Italy." He also mentioned that he had visited Casablanca while he was in North Africa earlier.

While in the 7th Inf. Regt. on Jan. 27, 1945 in Houssen, France, he was awarded the Silver Star for gallantry in action. A letter dated May 25, 1945, from Lt. Col. Lloyd B. Ramsey, stated, "You have won the admiration of all officers and men of your regiment, and for your self-sacrifice, courage, and devotion to duty. Your county may well be proud of you."

In letters to his wife, Jewell, dated June and July 1945, he said he was in Salzburg, Austria and Hershfield, Germany and made the following observation. "The 3rd Div. has waited a long time for this. They fought their way up a long trail to Germany than any other American Division, from North Africa, Sicily, Italy, Southern France and Central France. It won't be long until we can be home."

Joe was promoted to technical Sergeant and was Honorably Discharged on Oct. 14, 1945 at Camp Atterbury, IN.

He returned home to Floyd County, KY and like many veterans, began working in the coal mines. After working in the mines for some time, Joe accepted a supervisory position as section foreman for Princess Elkhorn Coal Company. In November 1954, he was injured in a mining accident that severed his spinal cord. After extensive rehabilitation at McGuire's Veterans Hospital in Richmond, VA, Joe began working as a tool dresser for Princess Elkhorn Coal and later for Patsy Coal. He sharpened cutting machine bits, roof bolter bits, and coal drill bits until the mines closed in 1973.

Joe was saved and became a Christian and joined the Highland Avenue Freewill Baptist Church in 1976. Joe served as treasurer of the church until he was ordained as a deacon on June 17, 1979.

He also served as a board member of the David Community Development Corporation, working to bring a municipal water system to David, KY.

He was promoted to eternity on Feb. 14,

1986, leaving Jewell, his wife of 43 years, three children, three grandchildren, and countless friends and loved ones.

CHARLIE VANDERPOOL, the son of William "Bill" and Cordela Sexton Vanderpool of Garrett, KY, served in the U.S. Army and fought in WWII in Germany. He returned home after the war to discover his brother, Sage, was fighting in the Philippines. Charlie re-enlisted, hoping that he would be shipped to the Philippines to fight with his brother, and that is where he was stationed.

Charlie was involved in a jeep accident in 1947. He developed pneumonia and died. His body was brought back to Garrett and he was buried on Stone Coal Creek in Garrett with the rest of his family. He was born Dec. 8, 1917 and died in May or June of 1947.

SAGE VANDERPOOL, born Sept. 1, 1921 to William "Bill" and Cordea Sexton Vanderpool, was a Sergeant in the U.S. Army as a pioneer member of mine laying platoon of an anti-tank company with the 32nd Inf. Regt. in Alaska and Asia for 32 months. He disarmed enemy mines, used magnetic mine detectors to locate and neutralize  mines by removing the fuses. He also spearheaded beach landing and made emergency repair to vehicles.

His medals include the Asiatic-Pacific Theater Ribbon w/4 Bronze Stars, the Philippine Liberation Ribbon w/2 Bronze Stars, Good Conduct Medal and the WWII Victory Medal.

Sage married Dorothy Wells Vanderpool and had three sons to serve in the Vietnam Era. Eddie Darell was wounded in Vietnam, Terry Wendal spent three tours of duty and Larry Elven served stateside.

Sage worked for the AT&T Company until his death on Jan. 1, 1980.

DOUGLAS VAUGHAN, of Prestonsburg was the son of Alma Vaughan. He was on an American ship that was bombed during the Anzio (Italy) landings in January of 1944 where 17 allied ships and nearly 5,000 British and American soldiers died.

GARLAND VAUGHAN, the son of Harry and Fanny Perry Vaughan of Prestonsburg, was a member of the 11th Armd. Div. He was in combat in the Ardennes Forrest in Luxembourg during the Battle of the Bulge and also served in Belgium and the German Rhineland.

He was awarded the EAME Theater Ribbon, WWII Victory Medal and the Good Conduct Medal. Garland received his discharge from military service on Nov. 18, 1945.

He was married to Rebecca Vaughan. He died June 11, 1981.

Pictured are Harry Vaughan (left), Garland Vaughan (right) and Ronald E. Vaughan (front).

HARRY VAUGHAN, the son of William and Stella Vaughan of Prestonsburg, was killed in a vehicle accident on a military base in Tennessee.

Harry Vaughan is pictured on the left, above.

JESS WILLARD VAUGHAN, born Sept. 27, 1918 at Bays Branch to Buren and Cynthia Vaughan, was drafted in Prestonsburg as a Technician 5 CAG for the U.S. Army. Jess was killed in action during WWII on Oct. 28, 1944. He is buried in the Vaughan Cemetery at Bays Branch. He was 26 years old.

CLARENCE D. WALLEN, born Feb. 22, 1923, the son of Lee and Lula Wills Wallen, was lost at sea Oct. 3, 1943 during WWII. He is pictured with his brother, Curtis. Clarence had three other brothers, all of whom were in the service.

CURTIS WALLEN, served in WWII, one of five sons of Lee and Lula Wills Wallen, was in the USN.

JOHN WALLEN, born Sept. 17, 1920, the son of Henry and Johnnie Calhoun Wallen, had five brothers and three sisters, all deceased.

He was inducted into the U.S. Army in 1942

and completed his basic training at Camp Butler, NC. He served 24 months in Europe with Co. B, 92nd Medical Gas Treatment Bn. attached to the 7th Army. He served as messenger, driving a Jeep over 70,000 miles in England, France, Germany, Luxembourg, Belgium, Holland and Austria. He was discharged in December 1945 with rank of Private First Class.

In April 1946 he married Thelma Stephens and had three children. Only one survives, Joyce Ann Wallen, Lexington, KY.

In May 1975 he married Lorena Wells Goble, who had a son, Gary L. Goble, Louisville, KY.

He now has two step grandchildren.

He worked as a heavy equipment operator and retired in 1979.

He is now active in the Oleika Shrine, Lexington, KY, Zebulon Masonic Lodge #273, and DAV Chapter No. 18, Auxier, KY.

RICHARD WALLEN, is one of five sons of Lee and Lula Wallen who served with the U.S. military. Richard was born Feb. 18, 1925 and died April 25, 1992.

He was married to Lois Osborne Wallen.

He served in WWII with the USN.

ALBERT WARD, born Dec. 30, 1912 in Auxier, KY, the son of James William and Sarah Jane Ward. He enlisted in the U.S. Army Aug. 6, 1940. He served as a Private with Co. G, 261st Inf. He was stationed at Fort Knox and spent one year, eight months and five days in foreign service. He was a submachine gun expert and ammunition handler. Ward was discharged Nov. 9, 1944.

He participated in the Asiatic-Pacific Theater and was awarded the Asiatic-Pacific Theater Ribbon.

He had one daughter, Betty Jane. He spent his civilian employment as a miner. Ward passed away April 29, 1983.

CURTIS WARRIX, born June 9, 1920, at Watergap, KY, the son of Adam "Ad" Warrix and Josephine (Calhoun) Warrix, enlisted in the Army at Fort Knox, KY, July 22, 1940. He was shipped to Hawaii Dec. 16, 1941, just nine days after Pearl Harbor. He spent the balance of his military career there, first repairing bomb damage  and later building and maintaining facilities for American troops.

He was discharged Sept. 18, 1945. He was awarded the Asiatic-Pacific Theater Ribbon, the American Defense Service Medal, a Lapel

Button, and qualified as a Carbine Marksman. He was active in veteran's associations and organizations the remainder of his life.

He returned to Watergap, married Minnie (Miller) Warrix, and reared three sons and two daughters. He was a carpenter and cabinetmaker, working for Allen Lumber Company, Pikeville College, and as a self-employed tradesman. He died in December 1991 of leukemia.

WILLIAM FREDRICK WARRIX, born Aug. 23, 1922 to Wiley and Thetra Meadows Warrix, enlisted in the USN Oct. 23, 1942. He was Seaman First Class USNR. He was aboard the cruiser *San Diego*. The crew was a part of the first task force to strike Rabaul, Gilbert Islands, Marshall Islands, Philippines, Formosa, Okinawa and the China coast.

The *San Diego* was out of the States for 17 months without making a liberty port. The *San Diego* crowning achievement was to lead the victorious allies up to Tokyo's front door. The cruiser had taken part in 33 operations in the Pacific War.

Willie received 13 stars for Asiatic-Pacific American area, two stars for Philippines Liberation and Victory Medal. He was discharged Dec. 17, 1945.

He married Maudie Baldridge in 1949 and they had four sons. Willie was an engineer. He was baptized and attended the First Church of God, University Dr., Prestonsburg. Willie passed away in 1994 and is buried in the Warrix Family Cemetery, Jane Brown Branch near Prestonsburg. Maudie still lives in the home they built there.

ZEAN WARRIX, born June 2, 1919 at Bull Creek, Floyd County, KY, died Feb. 28, 1965.

Zean was a Private in Co. E, 33rd Inf. His niece, Helena Warrix Nelson, remembers that she had gone to town with her grandmother, Josephine, and Aunt Gertrude when they saw a soldier on crutches coming toward them. It was Zean. They didn't

know that he was coming home. He'd walked through the swamps for months with his boots on until he'd developed a foot disease.

He had three children: Larry, Eugene, and Kathy.

The photo is of Curtis and Zean Warrix (on right), sons of Add and Josephine Calhoun War-rix. Both sons served in WWII and are buried at Davidson Memorial Gardens at Ivel, KY. *Submitted by Karen Nelson Marcum.*

ROBERT SANDERS WELLMAN, U.S. Army, Technician Third Grade (Sergeant), WWII, was born June 19, 1924 at West Prestonsburg, KY to Felix and Gladys Harris Wellman. He graduated Morehead State College with a BS Degree in Education at the age of 18.

Bob was inducted into the Army July 1, 1942 in Morehead, KY. He qualified as a pistol sharp shooter and a carbon sharp shooter. On Feb. 27, 1944 he departed for the European Theatre, arriving March 10, 1994. He served in the Ardennes and Normandy Campaign (Battle of the Bulge), Northern France, and the Rhineland, for which he received a "Good Conduct" and Victory Medal. In the American Theatre and EAME Theatre, he received four Bronze Stars. On Nov. 17, 1945 Bob departed for the U.S., arriving Nov. 18, 1945. Bob received an "Honorable Discharge" at Bowman Field, Louisville, KY on Feb. 12, 1946.

Next, Bob enrolled in the University of Kentucky Law School, graduated, and practiced law in Prestonsburg, KY. On Feb. 3, 1951, Prestonsburg, KY he married Betty Jean Martin. Betty and Bob had two daughters, Elizabeth Lynn and Nora Lou and later six grandchildren. He became county attorney of Floyd County in the late 1950s.

Bob moved his family to Nashville, TN. He worked for the U.S. Government, becoming Attorney General of the SBA over the State of Tennessee, served both as Regional Counsel and District Counsel; however, after retirement he continued as a Consultant to the U.S. Government. Bob was a former member of the First Methodist Church of Prestonsburg, Calvary Methodist Church of Nashville, TN, and member of Zebulon Lodge No. 273, F & AM. Bob passed away on Oct. 4, 1995 in Nashville, TN.

ARVIL WELLS, Private First Class, born in 1922, enlisted in the U.S. Army on Nov. 24, 1942. He served in the Philippines where he died on May 15, 1945. He received the Asiatic-Pacific Campaign Medal w/2 Bronze Stars and Arrowhead, Bronze Star, Purple Heart, Combat Infantry Badge, Philippines Liberation Medal, Combat Infantry Badge, Philippine Presidential Unit Citation, Good Conduct Medal, WWII Victory Medal and the Honorable Service Lapel Button.

Arvil is buried at Polt D, Row 12, Grave 105 in the Manila American Cemetery, Manila, Philippines. He was the son of Samuel Jefferson and Vicie Goble Wells.

EDWARD WELLS, Staff Sergeant, born Jan. 1, 1918 at Auxier, KY, the son of George and Cora Wells. He enlisted in the Army in 1936 and served for three years at Fort Thomas, KY. He was Honorably Discharged but after a short time he was unable to find employment and decided to re-enlist. He re-enlisted at Pittsburgh, PA on April 27, 1940 and was transferred to Hawaii. He was assigned to I Co., 35th Inf., 25th Div.

He was on active duty when WWII started at Pearl Harbor on Dec. 7, 1941. He participated in battles at Guadalcanal, Vella Lavella, Balete Pass, Luzon, New Caledonia and Manila. He was discharged at Camp Atterbury, IN on July 21, 1945.

His decorations include Honorable Service Lapel Button, WWII, Combat Infantry Badge, Expert Badge w/Bayonet Bar, two Bronze Stars one with an Oak Leaf Cluster, Purple Heart, Good Conduct Medal, President Unit Emblem, American Defense Service Medal w/Foreign Service Clasp, Asiatic-Pacific Campaign Medal w/3 Bronze Stars, WWII Victory Medal and Philippines Liberation Medal. He was awarded the Pearl Harbor Commemorative Medal posthumously.

He married Phyllis Jane Fannin on Feb. 22, 1946. They had three children and four grandchildren. He retired on Jan. 25, 1980 from Ypsilanti Communities Utility Authority, Ypsilanti, MI as a Lab Technician at the Water Treatment Facility. After retirement he and Phyllis moved to Florida where he spent 10 wonderful years. He passed away on Jan. 4, 1990.

EUGENE WELLS, Seaman First Class, born Jan. 8, 1921 in Lancer, KY, enlisted in the USN in March 1941. He served on the USS *Aaron Ward* 483, a Navy battleship. He participated in Bloody Friday at Guadalcanal. Nov. 13, 1942-April 7, 1943 he participated in the battles of Guadalcanal and Tulagi. He was seriously injured.

Memorable experiences: 27 dead crew members, ship sank. They were protecting the future president, John Fitzgerald Kennedy.

His awards/medals include the Purple Heart, Navy Good Conduct Medal, American Campaign Medal, Asiatic-Pacific Campaign Medal and WWII Victory Medal.

He was married to Ollie E. Wells and had seven children and 17 grandchildren. His civilian employment was spent as a mechanic. Eugene passed away July 28, 1995.

GRANT WELLS, born on April 9, 1917 to Samuel Jefferson and Vicie Goble Wells, was a Private in the U.S. Army. He served in WWII in Germany. He spent four years, four months and 11 days and then re-enlisted in 1946 and discharged May 14, 1947. He was a truck driver.

Grant married Ida Salyers Wells and they had 10 children, two of which served in the U.S. military, Grant Jr. in the USMC and Paliegh Marion "Butch" in the U.S. Army. Grant Sr. is buried in the May Cemetery at Martin, KY.

JAMES MILFORD WELLS, Corporal, born Aug. 10, 1926 at Auxier, KY, entered the U.S. Army on June 28, 1945. He served in HQ Section 1580, Area Service Unit at Camp Campbell, KY.

He married Mary Ella Lappin and they had three sons: James, William and Robert.

During his civilian life he was a baseball umpire and basketball referee for the state of Kentucky. He was employed by the Floyd County Board of Education.

ALBERT WHITAKER, born April 16, 1914 in Bonanza, KY died Sept. 15, 2004 served with the 8th Army CE AUS. He enlisted on Oct. 15, 1943 in Huntington, WV. Organization: Philippines, Civil Affairs Unit, 28th HQ. Classification: Technician 5.

Civilian occupation: Albert was a farmer who plowed, cultivated and tended stock on general farms. He drove four horse teams. He also did some rough carpentry work in connection with the farms. Later he delivered mail on a star delivery route. Albert spent several years working in the Ohio steel mills.

Military occupation: Construction Foreman.

Military qualifications: Rifle MM.

Battles and campaigns he participated in include New Guinea, South Philippines (Liberation) and Luzon.

His decorations and citations are the Asiatic-Pacific Theater Ribbon w/3 Bronze Stars, Philippines Liberation Ribbon w/2 Bronze Stars and Victory Medal WWII. He was discharged on Feb. 4, 1946 at Camp Atterbury, IN.

Albert's parents were Caleb and Zella Rice Whitaker. He was married to Mable Greer Whitaker and to Betty Griffith Whitaker.

Albert was a construction foreman who served with the Philippine Civil Affairs Unit #28 in the Asiatic-Pacific Theater for 17 months. He supervised up to 100 civilian laborers in the various processes of building roads, bridges, and dwelling accommodations for troops. Also, Albert supervised the laborers in loading and unloading rations for use by combat troops. He crossed the Equator while aboard the USAT *Noordam*.

JAMES BUCK WICKER, born June 29, 1925 at Estill, KY, enlisted in the USN on Oct. 7, 1943 in the Hospital Corps. His stations include Pensacola and Key West, FL, and Norfolk, VA. He participated in WWII and Korea.

He received the USNR Honorable Service Button and Honorable Service Lapel. He was discharged May 12, 1952.

Civil employment was with General and National Cash Register. He graduated from the University of Kentucky with an AB Degree in Psychology. He had three children: James Jr., Phillip and Devert; and five grandchildren. He passed away Nov. 11, 1997.

OLLIE POWERS WILLS, was born Jan. 20, 1921 in Floyd County, KY to James Hiram Wills and Josie Deanna Jarrell. He was a veteran of WWII and has a son named Freddie Wills.

He has the following siblings: Clayton Edward, Rina Mae and Alberta.

He is the grandson of William Andrew Wills and Luemma Honaker. His great-grandfather, Hiram Wills, was the first Wills to locate in Floyd County and was a Union Civil War soldier.

His mother was the daughter of John Jarrell and Nancy Jane "Nan" Lafferty. Nancy was the daughter of Confederate soldier, James Lafferty, and Sarah Alice Bingham. *Information from Helena Warrix Nelson and Hamie Wills Warrix. Submitted by Karen Nelson Marcum.*

WARREN CARL WOHLFORD, Second Class Gunner's Mate, born May 13, 1923, to John and Mae Osborne Wohlford, enlisted in the USN April 1, 1943. After training in Great Lakes, IL; Pensacola, FL; Dahlgren, VA; and Rhode Island, he was assigned to the USS *Antietam*, a new aircraft carrier. Following a shakedown cruise to

Trinidad, the *Antietam* headed for the Pacific area and later was on its way to participate in an invasion of Japan when the war officially ended.

Warren's special recognitions included the Victory Medal, American Area Campaign Medal, Asiatic-Pacific Area Campaign Medal and Good Conduct Ribbon.

After his discharge in 1946, he worked in a coal-preparation plant until retiring because of health reasons. He married Pamela Vicars in 1955 and they have one daughter and two granddaughters. He is currently a resident of the Eastern Kentucky Veterans Center in Hazard, KY.

Photo is of Warren (center, with earphones) and his gun crew at their station (Quad 5) aboard the USS *Antietam* on Dec. 24, 1945, in Yokosuka, Japan. The *Antietam* had traveled to the Yellow Sea to help escort four Japanese ships to the Yokosuka Navy yard, ships that had failed to surrender after the war officially ended. What a memorable Christmas!

CHARLES WOODY, was in basic training Aug. 24, 1945. He excelled in gunnery that led to being hand picked for a top secret battalion, authorized by the President and the War Department.

He served with the 464th Anti-Aircraft Arty. Wpns. Bn. in China, Burma and India Asiatic-Pacific Theater. The mission was to eradicate Japanese

from China, Burma and India with standing orders, "Take No Prisoners." The 464th CA Abn. was also attached to the 10th Air Force and became the first American based combat unit in China, Burma and India in 1943.

Charles won several medals including the Asiatic-Pacific Battle Ribbon w/3 Bronze Stars, Sharp Shooters Cross in Field Artillery Rifle, Pistol, Sub-Machine Gun and Anti-Aircraft Artillery. As the war ended, he was assigned to the Military Police during the Map Operation. He was shipped home Nov. 2, 1945.

EDWARD E. WRIGHT, born May 15, 1925, the son of George and Nettie (Pitts) Wright. He was drafted during his senior year of high school in July 1943, and sent for six months training at Fort Knox, KY, then to England.

On the 31st of July he was reported missing in action. After three weeks it was then reported that he was killed in action on July 31st. His body was buried in a cemetery in Shilo, France.

The grave and plat was given Pvt. Edward E. Wright Co. E 67th Armored Regt. In July 1948, his remains were returned to Marion Funeral Home in Martin, KY, and he was laid to rest in the Wright Cemetery on Bucks Branch, Martin, KY.

KOREAN WAR

NELSON ROBERT ALLEN, born Oct. 27, 1932 at Hueysville, KY, one of 10 children of Wayne Allen and Mallie Craft. He was a veteran of the USN serving from 1952 to 1956 during the Korean Conflict. He was discharged on Oct. 5, 1960.

He married Carol Lynne Rice. They had one son named Robert Brian Allen. Nelson died on April 28, 2005 at Ashland, KY. He is buried in the Bellefonte Memorial Gardens.

ANDREW BARNETT JR., born Jan. 1, 1927 in West Prestonsburg, KY. He was enlisted in the U.S. Army on Feb. 3, 1955 with the classification 1 Private-2, RA, TC. He was stationed in Stuttgart, Germany. He served a total of six years, seven months and 15 days, two years and 10 months of this was spent overseas.

He then re-enlisted on July 26, 1954 and served three years with the 517th ORD Co. He was stationed at Fort Knox, KY when he received an Honorable Discharge June 9, 1955 with the rank of Corporal.

He received the National Defense Service Medal, American Occupation Medal and German Occupation Medal.

Andrew married Pearl Newsom and was a truck driver in civilian life. He passed away in 1960 after accidental electrocution in Carrie, OH.

GRIELLY BARNETT, born Feb. 20, 1931 in West Prestonsburg, KY. He enlisted in the U.S. Army on Aug. 3, 1948 with the rank of Private First Class (T) RA Arty. Private-1. He served five years, 10 months and 29 days with five years, two months and 23 days spent overseas, believed to be in Germany. He was assigned to signal duty with Btry. A29, AAA Bn. (AW).

His awards include the American Occupation Medal, Korean Service Medal w/3 Bronze Stars, United Nations Medal and the National Defense Service Medal. He was discharged from Fort Knox, KY on Oct. 10, 1954.

In civilian life Grielly was employed with the Ford Motor Company, Ypsilanti, MI.

JULIE DOLORES "DEE" OSBORNE BIEDIGER, First Lieutenant, USAF Nurse Corps, was born Nov. 3, 1934 at Hite, KY, daughter of MD (Crow) Osborne and Allie Taylor Osborne. She graduated from Prestonsburg High School and Louisville General Hospital School of Nursing. She was commissioned to the USAF Nurse Corps  in May 1956 and assigned to Gunter AFB in Alabama. Her next assignment was the 4451st USAF Hospital at Cannon AFB in Clovis, NM. There she met and married fellow officer, Larry Biediger, a Texan, on Feb. 7, 1957. She was assigned to the 388th Tactical Hospital at Etain AFB in Etain, France in March 1957, and was discharged in November 1957.

Dee and Larry had four children when he, a fighter pilot, was listed MIA over North Vietnam on Jan. 29, 1967. She moved her family to San Antonio, TX. Col. Biediger was declared KIA in 1974. Dee then went to work for the Texas Dept. of Mental Health, retiring in 1994. She now has seven grandchildren and still lives in San Antonio.

THOMAS EDWARD BOLLING, son of Walter and Frances Odell Bolling, was killed in action in the Korean War. His body was returned to be buried on the Old Middle Creek Road past West Prestonsburg. He was with the 27th Inf. Regt. Div. of the U.S. Army and was killed on Feb. 16, 1951. He was born in Floyd County, Nov. 10, 1927.

His brother, Walter Karr Bolling, was aboard the USS *Arizona* when it was bombed at Pearl Harbor. His body was never recovered, but there's a memorial stone for him next to his mother's grave. She died Dec. 15, 1971. *Submitted by Karen Nelson Marcum and Helena Nelson.*

CHARLES RAY BOYD, born Feb. 23, 1932 in Wheelright, KY is the son of Ella Rice and Albert George, taking the Boyd name at the age of 6. He enlisted in the U.S. Army on June 10, 1949. He served with the 7th Armd. Cav. He was stationed at Fort Knox, KY; Fort Townsend, WA; Japan; and Korea. He participated in nine battles. He was captured while on patrol and was a POW for 33 months before being released from POW Camp in Pan Mow Jon, South Korea, Freedom Village.

He received the Combat Badge, United   Nations Service Medal, Japanese Occupation, Korean Service Medal w/1 Silver Star and four Bronze Stars, Defense Service Medal, two Good Conduct Medals and two Purple Hearts.

Charles Ray married the love of his life, Louisa Burchett, on May 18, 1958 and they raised three sons and one daughter. He is a member of the United Food Commercial Worker of Dayton, OH and is now retired as Second Vice President.

JOHN I. BRADBURY, born Sept. 9, 1929 in Belleville, IL enlisted in the USN July 20, 1949. He attended the U.S. Naval Academy from 1949-53. Military locations, stations include Duke University ROTC; Norfolk, VA; Monterey, CA; Newport, RI; Long Beach, CA; and Honolulu, HI. He was an executive officer on several sea assignments.

Bradbury participated in battle off Wonsan Harbor, Korea 1953-54. He was discharged July 1973 with rank of Commander.

He was married to Mary Day and they have three sons: David, Bill and John. He married second to Nina Zack. Bradbury has 10 grandchildren.

Civilian employment as salesman, real estate agent and life insurance salesman. He passed away July 28, 2005.

RAYMOND A. BRADBURY, born June 19, 1928 in Stoke-on-Trent, England. He entered the USAF on Jan. 31, 1951. He completed basic training as an airman at Lackland AFB near San Antonio, TX. He was assigned to Class 51-28 as an aviation cadet at Ellington AFB in April 1951 to train as an aerial navigator. He completed and graduated as a Second Lieutenant with Navigator Wings on Nov. 20, 1951.

Bradbury was assigned to B-26 crew trainings at Langley AFB, VA before going to Korea as a member of a four-man flight crew. He flew in the nose of B-26 bombers as a navigator bombardier. He completed 55 combat missions over North Korea and returned to the U.S. in August 1952. His next assignment was as a navigation instructor at Ellington AFB near Houston, TX. He fulfilled his three year service obligation on Nov. 24, 1954 receiving an Honorable Discharge.

Raymond married Clara Blackburn on Nov. 28, 1951. They have two children, Philip and Barbara; three grandchildren; and two great-grandchildren.

He was a mining engineer graduate from West Virginia University before entering the military and returned to the mining profession in December 1954. He worked in Illinois, West Virginia and mostly in East Kentucky. He held various management positions and retired as President of Martin County Coal Corporation on Dec. 31, 1992. Raymond A. Bradbury is retired and living in Lexington, KY. He is a member of the Lexington Rotary Club.

BILLY R. BURCHETT, Major, born Dec. 21, 1926, son of Willie Lee and Anna Burchett. He was drafted into the Army in April 1945, completed basic training at Fort Polk, NC and served in the Philippines until Japan surrendered. He was transferred to Japan where he served with the Occupational Forces until he was discharged from service on Dec. 1, 1946.

When he returned home he attended Eastern Kentucky University where he enrolled in the Reserve Officers Training Corps, and was commissioned a Second Lieutenant in the Army in 1950.

He was called back into service in 1951 and was sent to Korea where he served as Battery Executive Officer and later Battery Commander, of Btry. "B," 955th Field Arty. Bn.

He participated in several battles and was awarded the Bronze Star.

He returned home in February 1953 and remained in the Army Reserve until he was transferred into the Retired Army Reserve in 1968.

After returning home he married Shelby Rowe. She passed away Sept. 2, 1989. He is retired from the Columbia System. He enjoys golf and fishing.

BILL BURGA JR., U.S. Army, 1st/23rd Inf., 2nd Inf. Div., Korea 1967-68. He was born April 22, 1946, son of Bill and Alta Burga. He was in the military from October 1966-February 1972. His basic training was in Fort Campbell, KY, where he served for four months. His advanced infantry training was in Fort Ord, CA, where he served for four months. His artillery training was in Fort Sill, OK for four months. He was in Korea October 1967-October 1968.

He has one son, Jeff and is married to Kathy. He is the great-grandson of Thomas H. Amburgey/Burga.

GEORGE BUSH, son of Judge and Roberta Bush, was born Feb. 20, 1936. He entered the U.S. Army in April 1953. He attended basic training at Camp Picket, VA. After basic training he was stationed at Fort Bragg, NC where he worked as a medic while he assisted the dentist and worked in the hospital. He was discharged in May 1956.

George has five children and three stepchildren: Diane Sexton, George David Bush, Denver Bush, Denise Little, Debbie Combs and Clarence Davis, Carla Davis and Chuck Davis.

ARLEN CALHOUN, Private, U.S. Army in the Korean War. He was born in Floyd County, KY Sept. 9, 1926 and was the son of Elza Calhoun and Dona Wallen. Arlen died May 21, 2000 and is buried on the Calhoun Cemetery.

Arlen married Wanda Goble.

His mother, Dona Wallen, was the daughter of John Wallen and Minerva Nelson. John was the son of Civil War soldier, Shelby Wallen and Susannah Hale. Minerva was the daughter of Civil War soldier, Alexander Clark and Emmarita Nelson.

His father, Ezra Calhoun, was the son of Thomas Benton "Dode" Calhoun and Ellen Merritt. His grandfather was Thomas Calhoun, a Civil War soldier. Ezra and Dona Calhoun are buried at West Prestonsburg, KY.

Arlen had the following siblings: Graham married Mildred Pennington; Opal married Hobert Younce; Blanche married John Younce; Lomie married Morrow Hatfield; and Easter Belle married Ervin Slone. *Submitted by Kathy Hubbard Hanlon and Karen Nelson Marcum.*

BUD CALHOUN, born on Dec. 28, 1928 at Watergap, KY. He was the son of Dewey (Calhoun) Goodman and Nannie Wallen Calhoun Baldridge. He was in the Army in the 576th Armd. FA Btry. and served in Korea where he was a POW for 90 days.

He was a Corporal in the Army and received the Korean Service Medal w/2 Bronze Stars, Good Conduct Medal, United Nations Service Medal and National Defense Service Medal.

He was married first to Elsie Hamilton Calhoun in May 1949. She preceded him in death and he later married Wanda Stewart Calhoun on July 24, 1996. Bud and Elsie had two children, Budalene and Larry. He had four grandchildren and eight great-grandchildren.

Bud was a heavy equipment operator for Island Creek Coal Company for 39 years and a life member of the DAV Chapter 18 at Auxier and most important a Christian. He died on July 11, 2005 at Highlands Regional Medical Center in Prestonsburg.

JAMES B. "BILLY" CHAFFINS, born July 31, 1929 at Rock Fork, son of Dave Chaffins and Minta Inmon. He was a retired clerk, formerly employed with Conley Food Store. He was an Army veteran of the Korean War.

He died on Oct. 20, 1993 at Wayland, KY. He is buried on the Coburn-Inmon Cemetery at Garrett, KY.

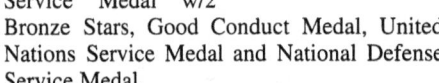

RUSSELL CLARK, Corporal, born Jan. 13, 1932 at Grethel, KY to Goldie and John Calvin Clark. He enlisted in the U.S. Army in 1952 and completed basic training at Fort Campbell, KY with the 101st Abn. He was then sent to Fort Meade, MD where he attended Cooking and Baking School. He was stationed there and in the field for the remainder of his time. He was discharged in 1955.

Russell married Sue Simpkins on Sept. 27, 1958 and had two sons. He was self-employed in Ohio and Kentucky. The last 36 years of his life, he was the first one to sell gasoline on Branhams Creek and the first to operate a snack bar. He loved to work in his yard and garden. He passed away April 9, 2002.

HOWARD L. CLINE, born April 2, 1931 in Prestonsburg, KY. He enlisted into the U.S. Army Aug. 1, 1956 and was stationed in Fort Smith, AK and Stuttgart, Germany. However, he was not in combat, he transported officers around Germany.

Mr. Cline's most memorable experience is going to Germany. He was discharged Jan. 1, 1958 with the rank of Private First Class.

He was formerly married to Francis Bush from Lawrence County, KY and has two daughters, Colene (Gerald) Brunton and Kimberly (Ron) Fritz; and three grandchildren.

After the military, he worked as a machinist with Techniglas for 38 years.

He currently resides in Lithopolis, OH and enjoys retirement along with horseback riding and fishing.

GEORGE EVERETTE CONN JR., Private, born July 9, 1928, was the son of George and Ruth Layne Conn of Ivel, KY. He worked with his father doing construction work until Army service. He enlisted in the Army on June 5, 1951 and trained at Fort Knox during the Korean Conflict. His significant duty assignment was HQ H&S Co., 29th Air. He was separated from the Army July 13, 1953.

He married Betty Jean Goble in July 1954 and they had two sons, Steve (mines and minerals inspector) and Rick (Kentucky State Trooper) who was awarded a medal for Heroism in gas line explosion at Ivel, KY.

He had three grandchildren: Nicholas, Andrew and Madison. George passed away July 16, 1985 and is buried in the family cemetery at Ivel, KY.

BILLY A. COOLEY, born Sept. 11, 1933 in Langley, KY. He enlisted in the military and served with the 28th MP Co., 28th Div. He was stationed in Kansas, Indiana and Germany. The one thing he remembers the most about his military experience is how bad the food was! He was discharged in 1953 with the rank of Private First Class.

After serving his Country, he returned

to civilian life and worked in the mining and factory industries. He is now retired and currently living in Emma, KY.

ROSS HALBERT "BUD" COOLEY, born Dec. 16, 1929 in Northern Floyd County, KY. He enlisted in the U.S. Army Nov. 5, 1953 at Ashland, KY. He attended Engineer School for nine weeks in 1954. Discharged Oct. 25, 1955 at Camp Chaffee, AR as a Private First Class and transferred to USAR.

He was awarded the Korean Service Medal, United Nations Service Medal, National Defense Service Medal and Good Conduct Medal.

Bud was married to Ina Abbott and had four children: Debbie, Phyllis, Steve and Greg. He was a Floyd County school board member for 12 years. He received his BS Degree from Morehead College. He worked for Johnson Coal Company in bookkeeping. Bud passed away Aug. 8, 1983.

HARRY VINCEL COOLEY, born Feb. 18, 1939 in Prestonsburg, KY to Otis and Viola May Cooley. He enlisted in the USAF in 1956, completed his basic training at Lackland AFB in Texas. From there he went to Francis E. Warren AFB in Cheyenne, WY, where he became a communications center specialist. He later served at Elmendorf AFB in Alaska. He enjoyed the beautiful land of Alaska. His last station was Donaldson AFB in Greenville, SC, where he met his wife, June Madison Cooley. He served there until his duty was over, Airman Second Class. He received an Honorable Discharge on March 9, 1960.

He then returned to Prestonsburg. He worked at several different jobs, his last one being Columbia Gas, where he retired. He was also a member of The Floyd County Rescue Squad.

He has experienced bad health in the past five years, but continues to enjoy his family, friends, and his church, Community Methodist, where he is a charter member. The Cooleys have two sons, Timothy, who was also in the Air Force, and Daniel. They also have three grandsons, one granddaughter, and one great-granddaughter.

RICHARD CRISP, Sergeant, born March 13, 1930 in Hite, KY, son of Caner and Laura Compton Crisp. He enlisted in the Regular Army on July 4, 1951. His 16 weeks training was at Fort Belvoir, VA. He served in Korea from November 1951 until November 1952. He served as a medic in an infantry platoon, 7th Div., 32nd Inf. Regt., 3rd Bn., 1st Plt.

Awards: Korean Presidential Unit Citation, Commendation Ribbon w/Medal Pendant, United Nations Service Medal, Korean Service Medal w/4 Battle Stars, National Defense Medal, Bronze Star, Combat Medical Badge and Good Conduct Medal.

Sgt. Crisp served on Heart Break Ridge, KumWa Valley and Triangle Hill. His company crossed the 38th parallel line between South and North Korea. They stayed about 20 miles beyond the 38th line for months.

While stationed at Yuma, AZ Test Station, he was selected as Platoon Sergeant of the Month.

Released from service in June 1954. Served five years in inactive Reserve duty and was discharged in June 1958.

Civilian employment: Natural Gas Compressor Station, Langley, KY. He is now retired and preaching God's word. He has two Doctrine Degrees in Bible. Crisp resides in Banner, KY.

BOBBY CURNUTTE, born Oct. 3, 1931 in Auxier, KY. He enlisted in the U.S. Army Jan. 30, 1952 and served with the 101st Abn. Div. He was stationed at Fort Sam Houston, HQ Co., 4006 ASU RC. He served in Germany with Btry. B, 517th Armd. FA Bn., APO Bremerhaun, Germany for nine months. He was discharged Jan. 9, 1954 as a Corporal.

He was awarded the Sharpshooter Medal.

Curnutte was a coal miner for 36 years. He married Alice May Wireman Oct. 7, 1950 and has three children and one grandchild. He was a life member of the DAV and VFW. He enjoyed fishing and hunting. Curnutte passed away June 28, 2004.

LLOYD DANIELS JR., Technical Sergeant, born July 27, 1933, son of Lloyd and Louberta Daniels. He enlisted in the U.S. Army in 1951, completed paratroop training at Fort Benning, GA, and served 23 months in Korea with RA Inf., Co. A, HQ Bn., 2128th ASU STA COM. He participated in the Battle of Pork Chop Hill.

When he returned to the States he was stationed at Fort Knox, KY and was part of the Honor Guard during the 1954 Kentucky Derby. Lloyd was discharged Aug. 1, 1954.

His decorations include the Combat Infantry Badge, United Nations Service Medal, Korean Service Medal w/2 Bronze Campaign Stars, National Defense Service Medal and Good Conduct Medal.

Lloyd married Joyce Hopson on April 18, 1954. They had five children and eight grandchildren. He was employed as a neon tube bender for May Sign Co. until he fell two stories while repairing a sign. He was an avid fisherman. A frequent jokester, he once caused a "Big Foot" scare in Lancer Bottom. Lloyd was the recipient of the 13th lung transplant at UK Medical Center July 8, 1993. He passed away Nov. 1, 1994.

ALTON DELONG, Private First Class, USMC, entered the service Jan. 31, 1952. He was separated from the service on Jan. 16, 1954, San Francisco, CA.

His medals include the National Defense Service Medal, United Nations Service Medal and Korean Service Medal.

Alton was born at Edgar, KY March 16, 1930, son of James Harvey DeLong and Eva Setser DeLong. He married Perleen Hayes of Adams, KY Sept. 14, 1951, daughter of Howard and Elva Short Hayes of Adams, KY. They have two children, Linda and Steven.

He attended Sowards Creek School and graduated from Prestonsburg High School. After service he lived in Columbus, OH and retired from Owens-Illinois. Alton died July 6, 1988 and is buried at Columbus, OH.

ARLAND DELONG, Corporal, U.S. Army, entered at Fort Knox, KY May 16, 1951 and was discharged Feb. 15, 1954. His assignment was Special Services, 98th General Hospital in Munich, Germany.

He is the son of James Harvey DeLong, a veteran of WWI and Eva Setser DeLong. They lived on Dicks Creek until Dewey Lake was built. He moved to Lawrence County, KY, where he met and married Gloria

Faye Salyer, daughter of Minyard Salyer, a WWI veteran and Beulah Williams Salyer of Blaine, KY. They made their home at Adams, KY where they still live. They are the parents of Gerald L., Gregory Lee, Adrian Bruce and Angela Anita; and grandparents of Samantha, Matthew, Brenton, Amy, Jason and Ryan.

He walked to his first school at Sowders Creek, rode a horse to Prestonsburg High School, graduating in 1947, taught school and retired from Columbia Gas. He is currently serving his sixth term as Republican member of the Lawrence County Board of Elections.

ROBERT DEMPSEY, of Blue River was a POW in the Korean War. He was in the U.S. Army in A Co., 38th Inf. Regt., 2nd Inf. Div. and was the son of Moss and Nora Dempsey, born Jan. 1, 1931. He was declared missing Feb. 12, 1951. His family was given his award of the Purple Heart w/OLC.

This is the first war casualty that I remember. We went to church with his father when I was a child. His parents never got over his loss. I remember his father requesting prayer for his son at each church service through the years. I also remember thinking that it must be an awful thing to not know whether your son was dead or alive. This was when I was just a small child. His father thought he was alive and was a prisoner. The parents died without knowing what happened to Robert.

I was in the Floyd County Justice Center a year or so ago and was speaking with Cheryl Tussey Shepherd. There was also a young man present with the last name of Dempsey so I asked him if he knew Moss Dempsey. It turned out that he was a relative of Robert who was a POW. That young man told me that Robert's body had been found and identified by DNA. I never was able to get any more details, but I remember thinking, "I've wondered about Moss Dempsey's son for about 50 years and am glad his remains were found. I just wish his parents could have known." *Submitted by Karen Nelson Marcum.*

RICHARD DILLOW, Corporal, born June 13, 1932, in Ligon, KY, son of Eddie and Myrtle Dillow of Ligon, KY. He enlisted in the Army Oct. 5, 1949, completed basic training at Fort Knox and was at Fort Bliss, TX. When the Korean War started, he was shipped to Fort Lewis, WA, then to Japan, then to Korea. He served with HQ & HQ Co., 21st Regt., 24th Inf. Div.

He participated in the spring, fall, and winter offense above the 38th parallel in Korea.

His decorations include the United Nations Service Medal, Korean Service Medal w/2 Bronze Campaign Stars, Combat Infantry Badge, Army Occupation (Japan) Medal and Good Conduct Medal.

Memorable experiences: Being a staff driver for a full Colonel which allowed him to see a lot of Japan.

Richard was discharged in 1953. He went back to work at the Clear Branch Mining Co. for one week, then moved to Detroit, MI. He was employed at Cadillac Motor Car Div. where he retired in 1988 after 35 years of service. He married Melda Mitchell in 1953 and they had a son, Kim and a daughter, Karen. They also have three grandchildren: Justin, Caleb and Kaitlain.

Richard has been involved in the prison and jail ministry since 1988. He is now the President of Christ's Jail Ministry, Inc. and the Assistant Chaplain at county jail in Ann Arbor, MI. He enjoys playing golf.

DOYLE ROSS DINGUS, born in Martin, KY on Jan. 31, 1931. He entered the Officer Candidate School of the USN (USNR) on March 6, 1953 and attended the U.S. Naval Postgraduate School in Monterey, CA. He worked at the Fleet Weather Central in Washington, D.C. and finally served as the Meteorological Officer on the USS *Saipan* based in Pensacola, FL. He was Honorably Discharged on July 19, 1956.

Doyle participated in a search and rescue mission of the USS *Saipan* following a disastrous hurricane in Mexico. He also considers his work at the Fleet Weather Central memorable.

Following his service in the Navy he obtained Bachelor, Master's and PhD Degrees in electrical engineering, worked in private industry, and in civil service at Eglin AFB. He now enjoys retirement and teaching courses in electronics at the University of West Florida in Fort Walton Beach. *Submitted by Helen H. (Mrs. Doyle R.) Dingus.*

ERNEST PHILIP "BUD" DINGUS, Sergeant, born Jan. 15, 1930 at Martin, KY, the son of Ray and Mousie Dingus.

He enlisted in the Marines on Feb. 25, 1948

and completed his training in Camp Lejeune, NC. His weapons qualification was marksman-carbine. His military specialty was power shovel and crane operator. His service included serving in Vieques, PR and also in Kool, Japan and Korea.

Battles included participation in the capture and securing of Seoul, Korea. Also engaged in the Wonsan-Hungnam against enemy forces in South and Central Korea.

Medals included Korea Service Medal and Good Conduct Medal. He was Honorably Discharged on Feb. 24, 1952.

Ernest married Justine Caudill on June 4, 1954. They had three children and six grandchildren.

He was employed at McLouth Steel Corp. in Trenton, MI before retiring in 1985 with 31 years of service. He died on Jan. 14, 2004 at the age of 74 of a heart attack.

JAMES DINGUS, the first son of Lacy and Pauline Shepherd Dingus, was born March 16, 1939 at Hite, KY. He joined the U.S. Army April 3, 1956. After completing basic training at Fort Leonard Wood, OK, he was assigned to an artillery unit as a truck driver at Fort Sill, OK. After a short tour in Germany, he returned to the States and was again assigned to Fort Sill, OK. James was given a disability discharge from the Army on March 11, 1959 with the rank of Specialist Fourth Class.

He moved to Mansfield, OH and was employed by General Motors until he retired in 1995. He married Shirley Crockett on Nov. 9, 1962. He and Shirley had five children, one daughter and four sons. They all live in the Mansfield area. After his first wife passed away, he married Elsie Daily in October 1994. James passed away on March 17, 2003 after a short battle with cancer. He is buried in the Stallard Cemetery in Carter County, KY.

GLENN MCCLELLAN DIXON, born Sept. 1, 1933 in Van Lear, KY, enlisted into the USAF on June 10, 1952. He was stationed at Sampson AFB, Shepherd AFB, K-9 AFB, Kirkland AFB, New Mexico and Korea. He was a flight engineer and mechanic on B-26 light bomber during the Korean War. He was discharged June 9, 1956.

Glenn married Roberta Wiley on April 20, 1957. They have two sons and three grandsons. After serving his country, he was employed in

the mining industry. Glenn is now enjoying retirement and currently lives in David, KY.

JOHN RICHARD "DICKIE" DIXON, Airman, born Sept. 25, 1935 to Glen and Ann Dixon, enlisted in the USAF in 1953. He completed basic training at Lackland AFB, San Antonio, TX, served at Lowry AFB, Denver, CO. He took Air Police training and was chosen to guard President Eisenhower while in Denver.

From there he was sent to Landsburg AFB Landsburg, Germany. He played basketball for the Base Team and also threw the javelin.

He won the National Defense Service Medal and Good Conduct Medal. He was Honorably Discharged in September 1957.

After returning to the States, John married Carol Elking on Sept. 8, 1957. The couple left for Paris, TX where he had a basketball scholarship at Paris Junior College. He was inducted into the Hall of Fame on Nov. 10, 1990. They have three children and six grandchildren.

He got into sales after college and stayed in sales until his death on July 10, 2005. He was last employed by AFLAC Insurance Company and was loved and respected by all who knew him. He was a devout Christian and drove a church bus for 20-25 years bringing children and adults to church and Sunday school.

GARLIN ELLIOTT, served in the U.S. Marines during Korean War.

PAUL S. EPLING, Corporal, born Oct. 20, 1929 at Logan, WV, son of William and Nellie Epling. He enlisted in the U.S. Army on July 3, 1951, 3rd Armd. Div. in Fort Knox, KY where he completed his basic training. He then completed eight weeks of cook school training. He

served 18 months in Japan at Camp Hakatta. He worked as meat market manager while in Japan. After serving his time in Japan he was transferred to Fort Campbell and was discharged May 29, 1953.

He received a Good Conduct Medal.

He served in the Reserves for six years after his discharge and received a Honorable Discharge.

Paul married Queenie Epling on Aug. 25, 1955. They have one daughter, Pamela Epling Reid, and two granddaughters, Rachel Reid Clark and Courtney Jaye Reid They also have one great-grandson, Peyton Curtis Clark.

Paul was self-employed and owner of a grocery store, car dealership and gas station. He is retired now and enjoys his family, sports, friends and church. He is a member of the Betsy Layne Church of Christ.

WILLIAM JOSEPH FANNIN, born in the coal mining camp of Glo in Floyd County, KY on Aug. 20, 1934, the youngest son of Joseph Thomas Fannin and Olive Margaret Rice. He was named Billy Joe Fannin at birth, but changed his name to William Joseph Fannin in September 1975.

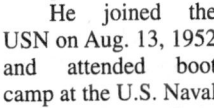

He joined the USN on Aug. 13, 1952 and attended boot camp at the U.S. Naval Training Center, Bainbridge, MD for recruit training. Upon completion he was assigned to the Naval Hospital Corps School at Bainbridge in January 1953. He graduated from the school in May 1953 and became a Qualified Hospital Corpsman. He was assigned to the U.S. Naval Hospital, Bethesda, MD.

He was transferred to the U.S. Naval Hospital, Annapolis, MD that is located on the grounds of the Naval Academy. His enlistment expired and he was discharged on Aug. 19, 1955. He decided to re-enlist in the Navy and returned to active duty in January 1956. The following is a list of duty stations during his 21 year career:

2nd Marine Div. in Camp Lejeune, NC in January 1956.

USNAS, Jacksonville, FL in July 1957.

Medical Department Administration School in Portsmouth, VA in July 1959.

Marine Corps Base, Camp Pendleton, CA after graduation in June 1960.

3rd Marine Div. in Okinawa to report in October 1961.

1st Medical Bn., 1st Marine Div. in Camp Pendleton, CA in November 1962.

U.S. Naval Hospital, Bainbridge, MD in August 1964.

USS *Harry E. Yarnell* (DLG-17), Norfolk, VA in July 1967.

USS *Springfield* (CLG-7), Norfolk, VA in February 1968.

U.S. Naval Station Dispensary, Norfolk, VA in October 1968.

Naval Inshore Warfare Command Staff, USNAB, Little Creek, VA in 1970.

William retired from Naval service in April 1973 and had attained the rank of Senior Chief Petty Officer.

SYLVESTER FRANCIS, U.S. Army, served during the Korean War. He is the son of Bill and Julia Yerrace Francis Sr.

CLAUDE GEARHEART, born in Hueysville, KY to Willie and Ada Gearheart on July 12, 1930. Claude enlisted in the U.S. Air Force at the age of 19 and served in Korea and two terms in Vietnam. Claude was trained as a draftsman and aerial photography. He spent 23 years in the Air Force and received the National Defense Service Medal and a Good Conduct Medal.

Claude married Sue and had two sons, Willie James and Claude Anthony, and one daughter, Barbara. He passed away in 1987.

DONALD HAROLD GOBLE, Sergeant, born on Dec. 26, 1927 at Prestonsburg, KY. He entered into active service in the Army on March 5, 1951 at Portsmouth, OH. He was in the ERC Inf., 2nd Army.

He was discharged March 6, 1953 at Separation Center, Fort Jackson, SC. He served in the Army from March 5, 1951 until being discharged on March 6, 1953.

ROBERT HOMER HACKWORTH, Technical Sergeant, Co. I, Armored School, inducted at Ashland, KY on June 17, 1952 and was discharged at the Transfer Station, Fort Knox on March 16, 1954. He was an instructor.

He severed in Korea and received the Korean Service Medal w/2 Bronze Campaign Stars, United Nations Service Medal, National Defense Service Medal and CCM. He received the Korean War Service Medal in 2004.

Born on Oct. 12, 1929 in Myrtle, Floyd County, KY, the son of Bruce and Sula Howell Hackworth. On Aug. 21, 1954 he married Betty J. Bays. He was a car loader for Stevens Coal Company, Christensburg, KY. He died at his home on Left Fork Abbott Creek, Floyd County, KY. He was 53. He was buried in Mark

Meade Cemetery, Left Fork of Abbott Creek, Myrtle, KY.

ROBIE HACKWORTH, retired USAF, instructor pilot at Craig AFB, September 1954. 2nd Lt. Robie Hackworth, formerly of the Middle Creek Road, was the first Floyd Countian to be graduated as a jet fighter from a USAF Flying Training School. He used to fly over Granny Branch in Prestonsburg, Floyd County, KY. He was a Colonel in the Air Force. He had quite a prestigious record. He was involved in a small way in the space program and was attaché to the Ambassador in Peru.

He lived in Madison, AL and married Virginia June Evans. He died in Madison County, AL on Nov. 11, 1996 and he was 65.

CHARLES EVERETT HAGER, born Aug. 25, 1932 to Everett and Hallie Hager of David, KY. He enlisted in the USAF June 5, 1952. He was with 14th Material Sqdn. (ADC), Aberdeen Proving Grounds, MD. He served in the Korean War.

He earned the Korean Service Medal w/2 Bronze Stars, United Nations Service Medal, National Defense Service Medal and the Good Conduct Medal. He was discharged June 4, 1956 as Airman Basic.

He was employed at Princess Elkhorn Coal Company, David, KY. Charles married Rue Hemmie Childers on June 28, 1969. He and Rue are active members of the Middle Creek Baptist Church, where Charles serves as deacon and sings in the choir. Rue sings as part of a trio and they serve their Lord faithfully.

EDGEL TRUMAN HALL, Army Specialist 4 (T) (E-4), Infantry, birth certificate states he was born July 24, 1935 in Floyd County, KY to Beverly and Mella Newsome Hall. His service records state he was born July 24, 1933. Inducted at Ashland, KY on April 17, 1952.

Served in the Korean Campaign, receiving the Korean Service Medal w/2 Bronze Stars, a Bronze Star Medal w/"V" Device, a Good Conduct Medal, a United Nations Service Medal, a National Defense Medal and a Combat Infantry Medal.

Edgel was in the Army eight years, nine months, eight days, with four of those years in Korea. His last duty and assignment was in Co. "O," 1st BG, 22nd Inf. at Fort Lewis in Washington. He received an Honorable Discharge on Jan. 24, 1961.

GARY S. HALL, born Sept. 30, 1937 in Montezuma, IN. He enlisted into the Air National Guard Air Force, Fort Wayne, IN in 1956 and served during peacetime. He received an Honorable Discharge Jan. 4, 1963 with the rank of Airman Third Class.

He was married in 1958 and had four daughters and 10 grandchildren. During his civilian life he was a heavy equipment operator. Sadly, Gary passed away on Jan. 10, 2002.

KELLY HALL, youngest son of Johnnie Lee and Minnie Davis Hall, born at Dwale, KY April 9, 1939. He entered the USN April 1956 and retired in June 1979. He served 20 years in submarine services. Kelly now lives in Mountain Home, AR.

RICHARD "DICKIE" GARY HALL, born Oct. 16, 1941 in Floyd County, KY. He married Peggy Gayle Wright, daughter of Elder Kaney and Maggie Wright. They had two children, Jane Elizabeth and Richard Ashley. Dickie was a veteran Airman Second Class of USAF.

He died on Aug. 25, 2005 and is buried on the Wright Family Cemetery on Water

Gap Road. *Submitted by Peggy Hall and Karen Nelson Marcum.*

TAYLOR DOUGLAS HARRIS, born Oct. 18, 1932, the son of J.E. "Speed" and Helen Harris, enlisted in the USAF Feb. 28, 1952. He went to New York for basic training. He then went to Aberdeen, MD and Wichita Falls, TX where he attended Aircraft School. He was transferred to Lockbourne AFB, Columbus, OH where he was assigned to  Strategic Air Command where he was Crew Chief at KC97F air to air refuel and traveled to many countries. He was awarded Airman of the Month. He was discharged Feb. 27, 1956 and was active duty until 1960.

Taylor married Florene Conn. They have two children and reside at Cow Creek. He owns Harris Diesel Services, Inc. at Martin where he works with his son.

EDDIE HOPKINS, born April 25, 1930 at Topmost, KY, enlisted in the USAF on Dec. 31, 1947 where he served in the Aircraft Fire and Reserve Service. He was located in several stateside and various overseas assignments throughout his 20 years of military service.

Missions and battles include indirect involvement in the Korean and Vietnam conflicts. He was involved in several aircraft crashes that included near death experiences through rescue attempts.

Mr. Hopkins received several medals and awards over his 20 year span of service. He was discharged on Oct. 31, 1968 with the rank of Master Sergeant.

Civilian employment includes Federal Government Inspector for 12 years and as a strip mines driller with the Betsy Layne Coal Company for 10 years.

He is married to Virginia Reed Hopkins and has two children, one stepson, four grandchildren and two step-grandchildren. He currently resides in Prestonsburg, KY. Being 75 years old, his activities are limited. However, he is living a life that is worthy of a Heavenly home which is most important to him.

BILL H. HOWARD, born in Prestonsburg, KY on Sept. 26, 1930 to J.H. Howard and Nell Burchett Howard of Cow Creek. He grew up in Prestonsburg and attended Prestonsburg Elementary from 1937 to 1944 and Prestonsburg High School 1944 to 1949. After graduation, he was employed by the Kentucky State Highway Engineering Department until he enlisted in the USAF on Sept. 21, 1951 during the Korean War. He was dispatched to Sampson AFB in Albany, NY. There he completed  basic training and was transferred to Lawson School for medical assistants in Los Angeles, CA where he studied from 1951 to 1952 and received his Degree as an X-Ray Technician and was applied the title of Senior Radiographic Specialist. During this time he married Barbara Branham on Dec. 28, 1951, the daughter of John P. Branham and Lura Fraley Branham of Bull Creek. He was then assigned to the 95th Tactical Hospital Strategic Air Command at Biggs AFB in El Paso, TX until 1955. On Jan. 8, 1954 their first child, Barbara Lynn Howard, was born at William Beaumont Army Hospital. In 1955 he separated from the Air Force and was transferred to the Air Force Reserve where he obtained an Honorable Discharge in September 1959 and was awarded the National Defense Service Medal.

While he was a Reservist, he entered Pikeville College under the GI Bill and attended from September 1955 to 1958 and then on to the University of Kentucky from 1958 to 1959.

After college, he was employed by Kentucky West Virginia Gas Co. from 1959 to 1963. During this time their second daughter,

Debra Kay, was born on Sept. 6, 1960. On April 1, 1963 he was employed by the Prestonsburg City Utilities as Assistant Superintendent to Mr. Dick Davis. On Jan. 1, 1974 he was promoted to Superintendent and was licensed by the State of Kentucky as a water treatment plant operator and waste water treatment plant operator. He retired from Prestonsburg City Utilities Commission on Sept. 30, 1995 after 32-1/2 of service.

On Aug. 25, 1979 Debra Kay married Gregory Carl Dixon of David, KY. They have two sons, Jonathan Howard Dixon born March 5, 1982 and Gregory Adam Dixon born Jan. 7, 1985. On Aug. 30, 1980 Barbara Lynn married William F. Moyer from Pennsylvania. They have two children, their first, a daughter, Lauren Ashley Moyer born Oct. 24, 1985 and John William Moyer born July 7, 1996.

Civic organizations: Prestonsburg Lodge #293 IOOF (Independent Order of Odd Fellows), 1979-80 elected as 144th Grand Master of Kentucky and honored to place wreath of flowers on the Unknown Soldiers Grave in Arlington Cemetery, Washington, D.C. in May 1980; Zebulon Lodge #273, Master Mason Third Degree and 32nd Degree accepted Scottish Rights Free Masonry; Kentucky Colonel 1963, appointed by Governor Bert T. Combs; member East Kentucky Water & Waste Water Association, Past President - received Eugene Nicholas Award for Outstanding Service 1997; Board of Prestonsburg Church Housing Authority, Chairman of Board five years; Floyd County Chamber of Commerce, board member, elected President 1986-87 and elected to Floyd County Chamber of Commerce Hall of Fame 1995; Jenny Wiley Fish and Game Club; member First United Methodist Church Prestonsburg; appointed to Floyd County First Utility Commission - Judge Paul Hunt Thompson April 8, 1999; and member Cow Creek Fire Department, Tax Advisory Board.

BILLY HOWARD, son of Pauline Shepherd Dingus joined the Army Dec. 7, 1948. He was awarded the Silver Star for the following action in the Korean War.

On Sept. 27, 1950 Cpl. Billy Howard was deployed with the 1st Cav. Div. in Korea near Hamhung-ni about 100 miles deep in enemy territory. The task force was ambushed by 10 enemy tanks supported by infantry. When the ambush occurred, Cpl. Howard, driver for the Task Force Commander, realized the need for immediate action. He unhesitatingly and voluntarily mounted a two and a half ton vehicle and parked it broadside across the highway over which the enemy tanks were advancing. Heedless of his personal safety and the heavy volume of fire, he remained in the truck, which by now was riddled with bullets, until it was effectively placed to block the road. His personal bravery and selfless devotion to duty delayed the approaching enemy long enough to enable friendly tanks to arrive, engage and destroyed the enemy tanks.

While stationed in Germany he married Gisela "Shelia." They have one daughter, Barbel.

After serving tour in Vietnam, he was assigned to Fort Benning, GA, retiring Sept. 1, 1969 with pay grade E7.

HERBERT HUMPHREY JR., born March 13, 1935 in Ligon, KY, the son of Herbert and Nannie Humphrey. He enlisted in the U.S. Army Dec. 8, 1954 and served as a tank crewman. His military locations, stations were Fort Knox, KY and Fort Lewis, WA. He was discharged Dec. 7, 1956 as a Corporal.

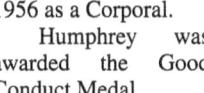

Humphrey was awarded the Good Conduct Medal.

He is currently in the heating and cooling business in Columbus, OH.

JAMES WILLIAM HUMPHREY, born April 7, 1928 in Ligon, KY, the son of Herbert and Nannie Humphrey. He enlisted in the U.S. Army July 17, 1952 at Fort Knox, KY. He served in Mt. Fuji, Japan and as Tank Commander in Korea. He was with the 6th Div. Tank Bn. and 24th Inf. Div. Humphrey was discharged June 24, 1954 as Staff Sergeant.

He was awarded the Korean Service Medal w/1 Bronze Campaign Star, United Nations Service Medal, National Defense Service Medal and Good Conduct Medal.

Memorable experiences: His division was involved with taking care of prisoners.

He married Pauline Stanley May 5, 1947 and has one daughter, three grandchildren and two great-grandchildren. Civilian employment as supervisor for manufacturing plant. He is currently retired and resides in Hilliard, OH.

ALLEN LEE "ATCH" HYDEN, Staff Sergeant, a son of Joe K. and Nora E. Allen Hyden. Allen was inducted into the U.S. Army in 1950-51 and served in Korea for eight and one-half months in the 2nd Div., 23rd Regt. He went to Japan from Fort Knox, KY and then to Korea.

He married Peggy Dyer (deceased) and had two daughters, Peggy Lee Hyden Wysong and Marian Kit Hyden.

CHARLES DOUGLAS HYDEN, born May 6, 1931 at Johns Creek, KY, enlisted in the U.S. Army on Nov. 12, 1952 as a Corporal with the 3rd Div. He was located at Camp Gordon, Fort Knox and spent one year in Korea with H Co., 3rd Bn., 11th Cav. Regt.

His awards include Cavalry Infantry Badge, Korean Service Medal w/2 Bronze Stars, United Nations Service Medal and the Good Conduct Medal. He was discharged on Nov. 11, 1954.

Charles was the son of Harry and Lucy Hall Hyden. He married Margaret Hughes in 1954 and they had six children. He worked at Pike Electric. Charles passed away Dec. 8, 1978.

JESSE JAMES JOHNSON, served in with the U.S. Marines during the Korean War.

JAMES L. LAFERTY, Sergeant, born Jan. 24, 1935, the son of Anderson and Hazel Daniel Laferty. He enlisted in the Army on April 9, 1957 and completed basic training at Aberdeen Proving Grounds and served in Frankfurt, Germany. He was an Ammo Specialist Fourth Class. He was discharged on March 31, 1963.

His decorations included the Good Conduct Medal.

James married Thelma Spears on Nov. 9, 1971. They had three children (one died at birth) and one grandson. He was employed as a clerk for the U.S. Postal Service. James loved to hunt and fish. He passed away on Oct. 17, 1992.

ADRIAN LAFFERTY, born June 6, 1929 in Prestonsburg, KY, the son of Jerry and Lula DeRossett Lafferty. He was drafted into the U.S. Army in 1951, completed troop training at Fort Knox, KY, and served 24 months active duty in Germany with the 82nd Recon., 2nd Armd. Div. as a scout. He returned to the States on May 10, 1953 and served five years Ready Reserve as a Sergeant. He was discharged on May 16, 1958. His most memorable experience was coming home and seeing his wife-to-be who had waited for his return.

Adrian was married to Wanda Jean Hunt from May 20, 1953 until her death on Oct. 10, 2005. They had two daughters and two grandchildren. He began work as a spread superintendent for construction companies involved in natural gas and water pipelines, in Eastern Kentucky and Southwestern Virginia. He owned his own company, Mountain Pipeline Inc., from 1980-99 when he retired. He is a 32nd Degree Mason and a member of the Oleika Shrine Temple in Lexington, KY. He served as Deacon at the First Baptist Church in Prestonsburg, KY and he is a Kentucky Colonel. He is a charter member of the Virginia Gas & Oil Association. He enjoys reading history, current affairs and news, watching college sports and playing the banjo. He continues to make his home in Prestonsburg.

ROY L. LAYNE, Corporal, 23-year-old son of the Reverend and Mrs. Carol Layne of Betsy Layne, KY, was killed in action with the 19th Inf. Regt., October 9, in Korea after nine months of Army Service.

Before entering the Armed Forces, he attended Betsy Layne High School. After graduation, he found employment with the C&O Railway Company as telegraph operator. He was known as one of the community's finest young men. He was survived by his parents; one brother, Robert; and two sisters, Lucille and Ruth.

BIRKEY L. LEWIS, born Aug. 1, 1931 at Woods (Banner), KY, the son of Elder K. and Jessie Dillon Lewis. He enlisted in the USMC on Nov. 8, 1951 and was stationed at Parris Island, SC. He later transferred to Camp LeJeune, NC and served in Cuba, Haiti and Puerto Rico  as a radio operator during the Korean War. He earned the National Defense Service Ribbon and obtained the rank of Lance Corporal at the time of his Honorable Discharge on Nov. 5, 1953.

Upon his return from the Marines, he attended Mayo State Vocational School for his welding certificate. He married Rebial Garrett and they have one child, Janice L. Justice. Birkey worked as a welder and mechanic in the 70s and 80s. He became disabled in 1990 after a work related accident. He is an Ordained Minister with the Brandy Keg Freewill Baptist Church.

CLARENCE FREDRICK MARTIN, Private First Class, son of the late Cary and Ina Martin was born Nov. 20, 1931. He enlisted in the Army Oct. 4, 1949.

After basic training at Fort Knox, he was trained as a Stevedore at Fort Lawton, WA. Upon completion he served with the 156th Trans. Co. at Port Whittier, AK for 18 months. From there he was sent to Camp Leroy Johnson, New Orleans, LA. From there he was sent to Fort Eustis, VA and on to Newfoundland where he served six months. He then went to Camp Kilmer, NJ and then to Camp Leroy Johnson to be discharged on Jan. 16, 1953.

He earned the Good Conduct Medal and the National Defense Service Medal.

He married Emma Lou Taylor on Dec. 28, 1950. They now live near Prestonsburg, KY. They have two children, Mary Lou Bailey and Freddy Martin. They also have four grandchildren and five great-grandchildren.

PAUL NEWTON MARTIN, Master Sergeant, son of Cary and Ina Martin was born on June 9, 1929. He entered the Army May 16, 1951. Arriving in Korea, February 1952, he was a tank driver in the Heavy Tank Co., 15th Inf. Regt.

He earned the Korean Service Medal w/2 Bronze Stars, United Nations Service Medal, Good Conduct Medal, National Defense Service Medal and Overseas Service Ribbon. He served with distinction in the 15th Inf. in Korea and received a Certificate from Col. Richard Stilwell. Col. Stilwell wrote on the back "Good luck and good hunting."

Separated from the Army on Feb. 13, 1953, he then served in the 364th Engr. Co. Reserve Unit in Prestonsburg until his Honorable Discharge July 20, 1961.

Paul died Dec. 12, 2001 at Highlands Medical Center of heart related problems. Paula Sue Layne, daughter; Heather Ousley, granddaughter; Mrs. Marvin Music, sister; and Clarence Martin, brother, survive.

TANDY MARTIN, born on Sept. 30, 1930 in Printer, KY, enlisted in the U.S. Army on Sept. 29, 1951 and received four months training at Fort Knox, KY. He was stationed with the 7th Army for eight months and the 15th Constabulary Sqdn. Border Patrol for eight months at Bamburg, Germany. He also had border patrol on the East-West border.

Mr. Martin received the Good Conduct Medal and the Occupational Medal (Germany). He was discharged on Sept. 9, 1953 with the rank of Corporal.

CHARLES WILLIAM MCGUIRE, Private First Class (T), born March 1, 1932 at Water Gap, KY, entered into active service in the Army of the U.S. on Jan. 22, 1952 at Columbus, OH. His most significant duty assignment was with Med. Co., 224th Inf. Regt. APO.

He received the Korean Service Medal w/3 Bronze Stars, United Nations Service Medal and the Combat Infantry Badge. He was discharged on Oct. 5, 1953 at Separation Center, Camp Atterbury, IN.

CHARLES MEADOWS, Corporal, born March 25, 1928, to Henry and Mary (Hurd) Meadows, was drafted Jan. 3, 1951 into the U.S. Army. He completed basic and infantry training at Fort Knox, KY and served two and one-half months at Camp Fuji, Japan (South Camp) followed by eight and one-half months in Korea

with Co. "A", 25th Div., 14th Inf. Regt. maintaining defense positions around Pork Chop Hill, Heartbreak Ridge, Punch Bowl and others.

Upon returning to the States, he was stationed at Fort Knox through Oct. 7, 1952 then, Ready Reserve until discharged in 1957.

Mr. Meadows' decorations include: the Combat Infantry Badge, Army Occupational Medal (Japan), United Nations Service Medal and Korean Service Medal w/2 Bronze Campaign Stars. In 1980 he was commissioned a Kentucky Colonel.

Charles married Helen Buchannon on March 26, 1958. They had three children and six grandchildren. He was employed as a coal miner. He has been with the DAV for more than 25 years and presently an active member of the 18th Chapter on Auxier, KY.

BILLIE JOE MILLER, the son of Clyde and Hester Miller of Prestonsburg, KY was a Squad Leader in the 2nd Bn. HQ of the 31st Regt. in Korea. His citations include Silver Star, National Defense Service Medal, Korean Service Medal, Combat Infantry Badge and the United Nations Service Medal.

After military service in 1965, he moved to Lexington, KY where he worked in construction. He married Geneva Abner in 1968. Sadly, Billie Joe passed away Dec. 23, 1983.

LEWIS J. MILLER, born July 22, 1932 to Ted and Rebecca Wireman Miller, enlisted into the U.S. Army on Sept. 13, 1952. He was stationed at Fort Meade, MD. He received basic training at Camp Pickett, VA. He received eight weeks of medical training at Percy Jones Army Hospital in Battle Creek, MI. He was discharged on Sept. 13, 1954.

Lewis married Pearl Dunbar and they had one daughter, Emily. He worked for the Ford Motor Company for 36 years and is now retired and active in the American Legion, Eagles and is a 40 year Mason in Northville, MI.

WILSON MILLER, born Jan. 7, 1935 in West Prestonsburg, KY, enlisted in the U.S. Army on Dec. 6, 1954. He was an Army tank driver with the 6th AC, 7th Army. He was stationed at Fort Knox, KY and Fort Benning, GA with the 3rd Inf. Div. He was also stationed in Straibins, Germany with the 6th AC, 7th Army and was border patrol on the Czechoslovakian border and received the Good Conduct Medal. He was discharged Dec. 7, 1956 with the rank of E-4 Third Class.

Mr. Miller married Martha Quinton in 1960. They have two sons and three grandchildren. He retired from General Motors where he worked as a pipe fitter for 34 years.

He and Mrs. Miller currently live in Swarts Creek, MI and spend their winters in Florida playing golf.

CHARLIE MITCHELL, Sergeant, born May 27, 1930, son of Robert Lee and Arminia Mitchell. He enlisted in the Army Aug. 28, 1952 and completed infantry training at Indian Town Gap, PA.

He then shipped out to Korea where he served over 13 months with E 5 Co. 10th Inf. 7th Div., 17th Regt. He participated in several major battles including Pork Chop Hill were he was wounded twice (both shoulders and both legs) on July 8, 1953.

When he returned to the States in 1954 he was hospitalized at Fort Knox, KY and was later Honorably Discharged.

His decorations include the Korean Service Medal, Combat Infantry Badge, Good Conduct Medal, Two Purple Hearts, U.S. Service Medal and two Bronze Stars.

Charlie married Phylistene Newsome, July 6, 1954, and they have 10 children, 10 grandchildren, seven step grandchildren, and six step great-grandchildren. Charlie worked in the steel industry and the coal industry. He was an avid outdoorsman until his health began to fail. He and his wife still reside in Floyd County at Grethel, KY.

RAY MOORE, Staff Sergeant, USAF, born March 9, 1929, in Garrett, KY, the son of Kendall and Girvie Moore. He enlisted in the Air Force in August 1950, completed basic training in San Antonio, TX, then attended Petroleum Production School in Caven Point, NJ. He spent two years in Japan and Iwo Jima during the Korean War.

He returned to the States and was stationed at Moody AFB in Valdosta, GA. Ray was discharged in August 1954. He was awarded the Korean Service Medal, United Nations Service Medal, Good Conduct Medal and the National Defense Service Medal.

Ray married Ruby Smith of Sassafras, KY on April 11, 1953. They had two sons and two grandsons.

After his discharge, he attended the University of Kentucky receiving a BS Degree in electrical engineering. He was employed in Louisiana on offshore drilling oilrigs for the Schlumberger Company for three years. He then moved to Tennessee where he worked for 28 years for the Tennessee Valley Authority.

After his retirement in 1988, Ray spent his time fishing, hunting, and watching his grandsons grow up. He passed away in January 2000 at the age of 70. He was laid to rest in Jeff, KY.

EUGENE MULLINS, Staff Sergeant, son of Troy and Italy Mullins of Garrett, KY served in the USMC with 1st Marine Div., 5th Marines. He was a Korean War veteran.

His medals include the National Defense Service Medal, Presidential Unit Citation, Korean Service Medal w/3 Battle Stars, United Nations Service Medal and Good Conduct Medal.

He was a brother to Paul Mullins.

JOHN A. NEELEY, of Cliff, KY enlisted in the USAF on Oct. 11, 1951. He was stationed at numerous U.S. bases as well as England, France, Korea and Vietnam. He was involved with Airlift Operations during 1968 and the Khesahn siege attempted by the North Vietnamese army. He enjoyed his tours in England and Hawaii.

He was awarded Small Arms Expert Ribbon, Good Conduct Medal w/3 devices, Air Force Service Ribbon w/5 devices, Air Force Commendation Medal w/4 devices, Air Force Outstanding Unit Award w/2 devices, National Defense Medal, Vietnam Service Medal, Vietnam Gallantry Cross, Vietnam Campaign Medal, Air Force Meritorious Service Medal and the Bronze Star Medal.

Retired CMSgt. John Neeley of the 15th Supply Sqdn. was named the Air Force Outstanding Supply Civilian Junior Manager of the Year 1993 highlighted a career of excellence in customer service. The award recognized his superb leadership skills and dedication to quality customer service. He attended a formal awards ceremony at the Pentagon.

He was discharged Nov. 1, 1978 with the rank of Chief Master Sergeant. He worked in private and civil service from 1978-96. He married Brenda Bartlett (Neeley) in 1955, they have two sons and five grandchildren and currently live in Honolulu, HI. He is retired and enjoying his family.

REBEL NELSON, born Feb. 1, 1933 to Homer and Pearle J. Nelson of Prestonsburg, KY was the oldest of 10 children. He enlisted on April 17, 1953 in the U.S. Army. He was stationed in Hawaii, Japan and Korea. He received basic training at Fort Knox, KY.

He made many friends in the Army, two in particular and stayed in touch after he was discharged on March 22, 1955 with the rank of Sergeant. He loved his post in Hawaii and often remarked on how beautiful it was.

He received the National Defense Service Medal, Korean Service Medal, Vietnam Service Medal and Good Conduct Medal.

Before entering the Army he was a truck driver. After discharge, he attended Mayo Vocational College where he studied auto body technology. Upon graduation he owned and operated a body shop where he trained his four younger brothers: Homer Jr., Johnny, Walter and Ronnie, the art of auto body work.

Rebel married Madlene Hobrook and they had three children: Ricky, Randy and Sandy. Before his death on Dec. 9, 2001, he loved hunting and spending time at his cabin at Cave Run, KY and racing. He was a Dale Earnhart fan and he loved getting together with family members.

KERMIT NEWSOME, Airman 1/c, born Aug. 28, 1935, son of Bert and Nellie (Hamilton) Newsome. He enlisted in the Air Force in 1953 and took his basic training at Sampson AFB in Geneva, NY, completing in December 1953. He was then sent to Fort Snelling in Minneapolis, MN where he was assigned to the Crash Rescue Squad.

Sent overseas to the island of Iwo Jima and he will never forget the caves they stayed in to survive the typhoons. Upon his return, he was sent to Bedford AFB, MA. He was discharged in September 1957 and received three medals for his service.

Kermit and Barbara married on Sept. 4, 1954. They had two sons (both deceased) and daughter Loretta, who was born while he was stationed at Fort Snelling. They now reside at McDowell, KY. He is a retired coal miner.

CHARLES VICTOR "PETE" NITCHIE, served in the U.S. Army April 1956 to April 1958 as a Private First Class in the Infantry, 8th Army, 1st Bn. in Germany. He took basic training at Fort Carson, CO, spent 14 months in Germany and then went to Fort Dix and trained troops on the firing range during his last three months in service.

He left Hunter to work in Ohio, Illinois and Michigan, before deciding to move back to Kentucky. Pete and his wife, Phyllis, currently reside in Pikeville, KY. They have one daughter who is married and three grandchildren.

He is the son of Mattie and John Nitchie, and brother to Earnest "Sam", Minnie, Clara Cross and Mae Salisbury.

WELDON OAKLEY, of Garrett, KY is a graduate of Garrett High School class of 1949. He was barely 17 years old when he joined the U.S. Army and served in Korea, building pontoon bridges. He retired with the Alcoa Company and is the widower of former teacher, Peggy Bowling.

One of Mr. Oakley's most memorable experiences is when he saw Gen. Douglas MacArthur while working on the bridges.

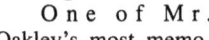

Today Mr. Oakley is a proud member of the "Chosin Few," an organization made up of the men who were at the Chosin Reservoir when the Chinese came over the Manchurian border and pinned them down. He still proudly flies the American Flag everyday.

DONALD W. OSBORNE, son of Maryland and Allie Taylor Osborne, was born at Hite, KY on Aug. 17, 1930.

He enlisted in the Army in 1947, was stationed at various U.S. bases, and discharged in 1950. In February 1951, he re-enlisted and served in Korea with the 15th Inf. until March 1952 when he was reassigned to Germany and was discharged in 1954. He joined the USAR in 1957 and served as First Sergeant with Prestonsburg and Pikeville units until retirement in 1990.

His medals include Meritorious Service Medal, Korean Service Medal w/4 Bronze Stars, United Nations Service Medal, Combat Infantry Badge, Army Commendation Medal, Good Conduct Medal, Korean War Service Medal, Army Reserve Medal, National Defense Medal and Army Reserve Achievement Medal w/3 OLCs.

Osborne married Drema May in 1955. They have three children and four grandchildren.

He was Postmaster at Prestonsburg when he retired in 1991 after 35 years with the Postal System. He and Drema live at Prestonsburg.

FRANKLIN D. OSBORNE, Sergeant Major, U.S. Army (Ret.), born on Nov. 11, 1936, the sixth child of Maryland Osborne and Allie Osborne Anderson.

He enlisted in the U.S. Army in December 1953. After basic training at Fort Knox and advanced training at Fort Benning, he was sent to Korea and pulled two tours with the 2nd Inf. Div. In 1958 his older brother, CSM Ronald Osborne, now deceased, persuaded him to transfer to the 2nd Armd. Training Regt. Later, they both were First Sergeants in the 3rd Armd. Div. in Germany, and while he was attending the newly established Sergeant Majors Academy as a member of its first class, his brother was promoted to Sergeant Major and reassigned to the Academy as an instructor. They both later served as Sergeant Majors at posts within 50 miles of each other in Germany.

His tour in Vietnam was as advisor to the Vietnamese Armor Forces. He spent six months with the 2/10 Armd. Cav. Troop and six months with the 1/5 Tank Co. While he was with the Tank Co., his younger brother, 1st Sgt. James "Merle" Osborne (Ret.), arrived in Vietnam and they saw each other often.

On Nov. 11, 1965, his cavalry troop made three attacks on a reinforced Viet Cong regiment at Cu Chi, and was surrounded each time having to fight their way out. They lost almost half the troop that day but with the help of over 30 strikes from the USAF and eight Army helicopters they were able to prevail. That is one Veteran's Day he will definitely never forget! It was also his birthday and the day his second daughter, Lisa, was born in Ashland, KY. Later he was decorated for valor in that battle.

His military decorations and awards are: Meritorious Service Medal w/OLC, Bronze Star Medal w/V Device, Combat Infantry Badge, Parachutist Badge, National Defense Service Medal w/OLC, Republic of Vietnam Campaign Medal w/2 Bronze Stars, Armed Forces Expeditionary Medal, Army Commendation Medal w/4 OLC, Vietnamese Cross of Gallantry w/Bronze Star, Vietnamese Cross of Gallantry w/Palm, Korean Service Medal, United Nations Service Medal, Good Conduct Medal w/7 awards and Master Tank Gunner Award.

He married Carolyn Sue Evans of Ashland, KY in 1960. They have two daughters, Crystal, who served 12 years as Intelligence Officer in the U.S. Army and is now a Major in the USAR, and Lisa. Both girls are attorneys, of which he is extremely proud since he was a high school dropout. They also have one granddaughter, Shelby.

After 24 years of active military service, he retired in 1977 and worked 19 years with the U.S. Postal System in Sarasota, FL where he and Carol have made their home.

JAMES MARYLAND "MERLE" OSBORNE, Master Sergeant, son of Maryland Osborne and Allie Osborne Anderson, entered the U.S. Army two days after his 17th birthday, on Nov. 19, 1957. After basic training at Fort Knox, he was stationed for two years at a NIKE Air Defense Missile Base in Michigan. Upon re-enlistment, he was sent to Military Intelligence School and spent the remainder of his 20-year military career in various positions in the intelligence field.

Osborne's overseas service included Korea, Japan, Germany and Vietnam. Most of his 31 months (two and one-half tours) in Vietnam was spent in psychological warfare assignments, working in Special Operations with various Marine Corps, Air Force, Army Infantry and Special Forces units. He considers the Vietnam tours to be the most important and rewarding service of his career. Other significant assignments included duty with the U.S. Military Liaison Mission to the Soviet Forces in East Germany and serving as company First Sergeant in Frankfurt, Germany.

After 20 years of military service, Osborne retired from the Army as a Master Sergeant in 1978.

Decorations and awards received by Osborne include the Meritorious Service Medal, Bronze Star Medal, Air Medal, Combat Aircraft Crewman Badge, Army Commendation Medal w/3 OLCs, Navy Commendation Medal, Good Conduct Medal, Vietnam Service Medal w/5 Campaign Stars, National Defense Service Medal, Army of Occupation Medal, Meritorious Unit Citation and Presidential Unit Citation.

Upon retirement from the Army, Osborne attended and graduated in 1980 from Eastern Kentucky University with an accounting degree. He began a second career as an accountant, holding several positions in both government and private practice.

Now retired, Osborne lives with his wife, Margie, and granddaughter, Amber, at Mays Branch in Prestonsburg.

JAMES PERRY "PEDO" OSBORNE, born at Martin, KY on July 22, 1929, the son of Perry and Mary Skeans Osborne. He had one brother, Jackie and three sisters: Ruth, Jean and Pauline.

James entered the Army at Fort Knox on June 13, 1951. After basic training he was assigned to Co. A, 64th Heavy Tank Bn., 3rd Inf. Div. in Korea. He served one year in Korea and received the Korean Service Medal w/2 Bronze Campaign Stars and the United Nations Service Medal. He returned to Fort Knox and was discharged March 12, 1953.

After military service James worked at various jobs in Floyd County, and was married twice, first to Marie Hall and then to Maude Compton. He had no children and both marriages ended in divorce. He now resides in his family's home place at Martin.

JANICE LEE "JAN" OSBORNE, the daughter of Maryland and Allie Taylor Osborne of Hite, KY, graduated from Martin High School in Floyd County and Memorial Hospital School of Nursing in Huntington, WV.

Her first job as an RN was at Paintsville Hospital in Johnson County.

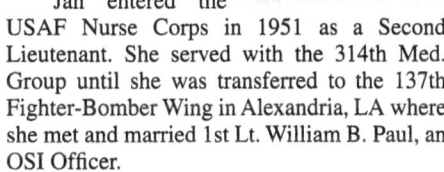

Jan entered the USAF Nurse Corps in 1951 as a Second Lieutenant. She served with the 314th Med. Group until she was transferred to the 137th Fighter-Bomber Wing in Alexandria, LA where she met and married 1st Lt. William B. Paul, an OSI Officer.

After their discharge Jan and Bill settled in Atlanta where Bill practiced law and served with the Georgia National Guard JAG Corps. Jan worked for a few years as an RN at Grady Memorial Hospital. They had three children: Alan, Shannon and Jennifer and now have six grandchildren. They are retired and live in Conyers, GA.

RONALD B. OSBORNE, born 1932, died 1998, son of Maryland and Allie Taylor Osborne of Hite, KY, enlisted in the Army in March 1948.

He served in Alaska, Korea, Panama, Vietnam (where he was wounded) and Germany. He served as Command Sergeant Major in Germany and at Fort Hood, TX until he retired in 1977.

Medals and awards received during his long military career include Meritorious Service Medal, Purple Heart, Bronze Star w/V Device, Legion of Merit, Combat Infantry Badge, Korean Service Medal w/4 Bronze Stars, United Nations Medal, National Defense Medal, Vietnam Service Medal w/3 Bronze Stars, Army Commendation Medal, Vietnam Cross of Gallantry, Good Conduct Medal w/3 clasps and Unit Award for Valor.

In 1951, Osborne married Rhoda Lafferty, born 1934, died 2000, of Prestonsburg. They had three sons: Donald, Robert and Clifton, all now living in Texas, and one granddaughter, Caitlin.

CSM Osborne died in September 1998 of Multiple Myeloma, a cancer caused by exposure to Agent Orange while serving in Vietnam.

PHILLIP PARSONS, US Army Feb. 17, 1955 to July 18, 1961, Korea and Vietnam. He died while on active duty.

RUSSELL STEPHEN PARSONS, born Feb. 16, 1932 in Allen, KY, was the son of the late Allie Smith Parsons and Frank Parsons. He was inducted into the U.S. Army on Jan. 8, 1953 and trained at Camp Breckenridge with the 101st Abn. Div. He fought in the battle zones of Korea and received his Honorable Discharge Dec. 10, 1954.

Prior to his military service, he worked as a painter for the McJunkin Supply Company in Allen, KY. After his return, he worked in various maintenance positions, one of which was with the Floyd County Board of Education.

Russell married Madge Slevins on Oct. 5, 1963. They had one son, Michael, in 1965. His family was a priority in his life. He enjoyed woodwork and light gardening and served as lay minister for the Methodist Church. He passed away at home on the evening of Nov. 22, 1985.

CHARLES GOMAN PATTON, of Hueysville, KY was born Nov. 4, 1933. He served in the military from 1956-58 and was stationed in Korea. His rank was Specialist 3.

Patton was married to Emogene Slone Patton and they had five children: Susan J.P. Salisbury, Jeffery P. Patton, Charlotte B.P. Case, Melanie L.P. Turner and Belinda C.P. Fitch.

His parents are Russell and Maggie Conley Patton.

DONALD RAY PATTON, born June 4, 1944 in Prestonsburg, KY, joined the USMC Feb. 1, 1965. He was assigned to GD Co. HQ, Marine Corps, 4th Marine Corps Dist., Arlington, VA. He was a rifleman. He attended the Marine Non-Commissioned Officers and Individual Protective Measures at MCI in Washington, D.C. He was a nuclear accident assistant.

He received the National Defense Service Medal, Presidential Unit Citation, Good Conduct Medal, Silver Star Medal, Vietnamese Cross of Gallantry, Vietnamese Campaign Medal and the Vietnamese Service Medal w/1 Star. He was discharged Feb. 10, 1969 with the rank of Sergeant.

He passed away March 22, 1970 and is buried on Mining Branch on Campbell Cemetery. *Submitted by Karen Marcum.*

JAMES PRATER, born Feb. 24, 1932 in Hueysville, KY, was the son of Harvey and May Reed Prater. He was a USAF Korean War veteran.

He married Ruth Ann Slone Prater and they had four sons: Donald, James, Greg and Mike; four stepsons: Arnold, Arthur, Harold and Bruce; and six daughters: Rebecca, Sandra, Eliza, Vickie, Pamela and Barbara. James passed away April 1, 2006.

ROY O. RATLIFF, the beloved husband of Eulene Hamilton Ratliff, was born Jan. 15, 1929, in Martin, the son of the late McFarland "MF" Ratliff and Hazel Turner Ratliff. He passed away Oct. 16, 2004.

Roy graduated from Martin High School in 1945, where he was a member of the Purple Flash basketball and baseball teams. He attended Pikeville College and Georgetown College where he was a member of the Kappa Alpha fraternity (KAs). He also attended Broadcasting School in Nashville, TN. Roy was a retired radio broadcaster (Rockin' Roy) with WDOC and WPRT, a salesman, and businessman. He was a member of the 1st Assembly of God at Martin, Sergeant First Class U.S. Army veteran of the Korean War 1951-53, a member of the 364th Engr. Co. Army Reserve Unit, the American Legion Post 283, a charter member and first Post Commander of the American Veterans (AMVETS) Post 27 and a Kentucky Colonel.

Roy was blessed with the gift of voice. His love for talking about family, genealogy, sports, music, his and Eulene's travels, history, cooking, and politics was wonderful. But talking about our Heavenly Father and our Lord Jesus Christ was his greatest love. Roy loved to cook and he was famous for his chili on Red, White, Blue Day and his holiday hams. He passed all these gifts on to his family, which we are thankful.

In addition to his wife, Eulene, he is survived by one son, Rory Gregory (Lola Brashear); four daughters: Sherry Lorraine, Regina Robin (Zenith Hall), Cecelia Hazel, and Jimmie Eulene (Steve Slone); seven grandchildren: Jason, Jeremy Roy (Victoria), Stephanie, Kelley, Steven Glen, Sarah, and Laura; and two brothers, James Burns (Lorraine) Ratliff, and Blake Ratliff. *We love you, R.O.R and Daddy, and dearly miss you. Eulene, Sherry, Greg, Robin, Cecelia, Jamie and families.*

GOLD REED JR., Medical Technician, born Aug. 6, 1932 at Hueysville, KY, was the son of Gold Reed and Sarah Patton. He enlisted on Nov. 20, 1952. He served in the AMEDS of the USAR as a medical technician in Co. G in the Korean War. He was discharged on Nov. 7, 1954 at Fort Knox.

His decorations include the Good Conduct Medal and Corporal Stripes.

Gold married Hazel Chaffins. His children are Malessia (Reed) Rister, Jesse Reed, Gregory Reed, Randy Reed, all of Garrett, KY, and Berniece (Reed) Hamilton of Langley, KY.

He died April 16, 1975 at the Veterans Hospital in Lexington, KY. He is buried in the family cemetery at Hueysville, KY.

THOMAS REYNOLDS, Sergeant, entered the U.S. Army on March 8, 1951 during the Korean War.

He received the Combat Infantry Badge, Korean Service Medal w/Bronze Star, Army of Occupation Medal (Japan) and the UN Service Medal. He received an Honorable Discharge on Oct. 29, 1956

Thomas was born Jan. 4, 1929, the son of James and Frankie (Slone) Reynolds. He married Marietta Halbert on Oct. 15, 1951.

JOE ERMEL ROBERTS, Corporal, 2nd Marine Air Wing, was born March 29, 1930 on Gunstock Fork of Spurlock near Printer, Floyd, KY to Marion and Sophie Spurlock Roberts. His childhood was shared with a brother, Brighan and sisters: Ola B., Nola and Ida.

On Sept. 6, 1951 during the Korean War, Joe was inducted into the Marine Corps. His basic training was at Parris Island, SC. From Parris Island he was moved to Cherry Point, NC and promoted into the 2nd Marine Air Wing. From Cherry Point he moved to Puerto Rico where he helped build an airstrip. This airstrip was used by troops going to Korea. Joe returned to Camp Lejeune, NC. He was "Honorably Discharged" Sept. 6, 1953.

Joe married Ruth Martin on Nov. 21, 1953 at Drift, Floyd, KY, and they are the parents of Ricky Roberts and Rita Jo Roberts Slone. Joe now has three grandchildren and two great-grandchildren.

JAMES F. ROWE, born in 1934 at Pumpkin Center, KY, the son of Rev. Charlie and Clora Rowe. He attended school in Wayland, Little Paint and Prestonsburg. In 1952, before finishing school, at 17, he enlisted in the USAF. He took basic training at Sampson AFB, NY. He was selected to attend school at Sheppard AFB, TX for advanced training in aircraft and engine maintenance.

His first assignment was Donaldson AFB, SC.

In 1955 and 1956 he completed a tour in Germany and France. He was stationed at Homestead AFB, FL; Presque Isle, ME; Clinton Sherman AFB, OK; Wright Patterson AFB, OH; and Seymour Johnson AFB, NC. He was a launch crew member with SAC'S 702nd Strategic Missile Wing, this was the first mobile launched (SNARK) intercontinental missile site in the U.S. located at Presque Isle, ME.

He was a crew chief for several years on the C-47, C-45, T-11 and B-25 before being selected for the missile field. On Tues., Nov. 2, 1958 he was the crew chief on Homestead AFB's last B-25 aircraft that were being phased out and taken to Davis-Monthan AFB, AZ to retire.

Married to Patricia Jean Turner from Garrett, they have two children, four grandchildren and three great-grandchildren. He retired from the USAF in 1973. He and his wife reside in Winchester, KY.

RODNEY SALISBURY, son of Ted and Lucy (Casebolt) Salisbury, was born March 10, 1930. He served as a clerk typist in the war in Germany. His commendations included the Occupation Medal (Germany) and the Good Conduct Medal.

After the war, Rodney never married. He became a teacher and after some work in Floyd County, eventually settled in Michigan. There he taught until he retired.

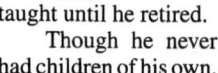

Though he never had children of his own, there were at least two that were like daughters to him, his niece, Clara Helen (Salisbury) Marks, and his cousin, Charlene (Davis) Bush.

Rodney loved to 'talk' and though he lived many miles from his Floyd County home, he always kept up with everything going on here. He loved this place, and these people - especially his family.

GARY H. SALYERS, born Sept. 12, 1935 in Orkney, KY. He was drafted Oct. 27, 1954 into the U.S. Army and had basic training at Fort Knox, KY. He was a Private First Class and served in Fort Sam Houston, TX as a Cook and Mess Sergeant. He was discharged Oct. 26,

1956. He re-enlisted with the U.S. Army Jan. 11, 1958 and had basic training at Fort Knox and Fort Bliss, TX. He then went to Korea with the 1st Cav. Div. in 1959, then went back to Fort Bliss, TX where he was discharged on Jan. 11, 1961.

He married Janice Bently in 1960. After serving in the U.S. Army, he attended school and became a heavy equipment operator. Gary owns and operates Salyer Grading in Powell, OH where he has been in business for 40 years. He and Janice have three daughters: Jennifer Lynn, Jessice Leigh and Jacinda Lois and three grandchildren. They celebrated their 45th wedding anniversary.

JOE ROBERT SCALF, son of Violet Runyon Scalf and Ervin Scalf, he was born June 10, 1929.

He was killed during the Korean War on Feb. 13, 1951. Buried with military honors at the Scalf Cemetery, on Buffalo Creek, Endicott, KY.

ALTON W. "DOCK" SCUTCHFIELD, born Sept. 3, 1931 to Beckham and Elizabeth Scutchfield, Prestonsburg, KY. He enlisted in the Army in March 1949 and served as an Army engineer doing his basic training at Fort Knox, KY. He was then sent to Fort Worden, WA and served with the 532nd Engr. Boat and Shore Regt. They performed maneuvers in Hawaii and Puerto Rico.

He married Goldie Meadows on March 29, 1950. They moved to Ypsilanti, MI, where they raised three sons and a daughter. They now have seven grandchildren, two step-grandchildren and four great-grandchildren.

He retired from Ford Motor Company on Jan. 1, 1991 after 36 years of service. He has belonged to First Freewill Baptist Church of Ypsilanti since February 1957, serving for many years as the Sunday school bus driver. Goldie passed away on Sept. 17, 2002 after a battle with cancer. He still lives in Ypsilanti, MI.

WILLIAM H. "BILL" SCUTCHFIELD, born to Darvin and Rebecca Haywood Scutchfield Jan. 5, 1934, enlisted in the Army during the Korean War.

Bill had one brother and three sisters. He was an underground coal miner working in Knott and Breathitt counties after his discharge for the Army.

Bill married Vivian Thacker and they had one daughter, Debbie.

His favorite pastime was riding his Harley Davidson motorcycle.

Bill accepted the Lord and was baptized several years before his death May 14, 2003.

He was buried in Scutchfield Family Cemetery on Bull Creek.

JACK BUFORD SELLARDS, born Aug. 21, 1932, at Banner, KY, a son of Jack and Nancy Akers Sellards. He had two brothers and five sisters. Having lost his mother at the age of 8, he was living with his brother, David Estill, in Castro Valley, CA, and attending Hayward High School when he enlisted in the USMC. It was Oct. 29, 1949, and he was 17. He had basic training in San Diego and was assigned to the Marine Guard Detachment at the Naval Air Missile Test Center in Point Mugu, CA.

After the Korean War began, he was sent to the Fleet Marine Force in the Pacific in 1951, then to Japan where he was a Military Police. Trained in communications, he became a special courier delivering high priority messages between Japan and Korea. He returned to the States and was discharged in April 1952.

His military training was put to use as a civilian and he worked for a time as a TV repairman in Monroe, MI, before opening his own shop there.

He moved to Barbourville, KY in 1964 and operated Jack's TV and Appliance shop for 39 years, retiring in 2004. He has five grown children and lives with his wife, Peggy, in Corbin, KY, where he is an active member of Gideons International.

BALLARD LEE SHEPHERD, Sergeant, born July 6, 1939. His father was Brice Shepherd and his mother was Lulu Shepherd of David, KY.

Sgt. Shepherd enlisted in the Army in November 1956. His sole purpose for joining the Army was to be adventurous, to see the world, and to do good for his nation. When Ballard joined the Army he was only 17 years old. He was in the military for six years, 10 months and 11 days.

During his time in the military he was stationed in Germany when the Berlin wall was built, he was also in during the Dominican Republic, and the Cuban Crisis.

Some interesting places that Ballard was stationed to were as follows: Germany, Alaska, state of Washington, Fort Campbell, Fort Bragg and Fort Knox. Sgt. Shepherd received airborne training and was in the 101st and 82nd Abn. Div. Ballard, at the time of discharge, was a Sergeant and had received his Jump Wings and Presidential Citation.

After being discharged from the Army years later he became an active member in the Big Sandy Chapter 18 DAV. He has been a member of this Chapter for 27 years and has been the Commander for seven years.

Ballard Shepherd married Phyllis Fulton in August 1979. They had three children and he had three from a previous marriage. He also has six grandchildren. As a civilian he worked many years as a mechanic running his own business.

Now that he is retired he spends his leisure time, when he's not helping the DAV, going fishing and hunting.

Phyllis was also in the Army in the Woman's Army Corps or WAC. She joined this division in June 1969.

ELZIE SHEPHERD JR., son of Elizie and Trennie Hall Shepherd, was the grandson of Johnnie Lee and Minnie Davis Hall. He served in the U.S. Army in Germany and Korea. He is now deceased.

DAN DAY SLONE, born in Lackey, KY enlisted in the U.S. Army July 20, 1954 and served with the Signal Corps. Military locations, stations were Darmstadt Germany and Fort Knox, KY. He was discharged July 10, 1957 with rank of Sergeant.

His awards/medals include the National Defense Service Medal, Army of Occupation

101

Medal (Germany) and the Good Conduct Medal.

Memorable experiences: He had a twin brother, Van Ray Slone, who joined first. He could not let his brother go alone so he joined and caught up with his brother at Ashland, KY.

He married Arminda M. "Dolly" Potter and had two children, Danny and Deana; and two grandchildren, O.J. and Crystal. He was a successful insurance salesman for Lincoln Life for 16 years making staff manager and district manager. Then he worked 20 years with his own bread route.

He is married to Geneva Whitaker now after his wife of 40 years died. Dan and Geneva go to church and are active in the church. He enjoys golf and bowling. He loves helping his fellow man.

RALPH "JACK" SLONE, of Langley, KY served in the military from September 1952-54 in the Korean War. His rank was Sergeant. He was wounded April 18, 1953 in Korea.

Jack's medals include the United Service Medal, Korean Service Medal, two Silver Stars, Combat Infantry Badge, Purple Heart, National Defense Service Medal and Good Conduct Medal.

He is the son of Emery Slone and Julie Bailey Slone.

VAN RAY SLONE, born June 30, 1937 in Lackey, KY, enlisted July 20, 1954 and served in the U.S. Army, RA, Sig. C. His military locations, stations were Fort Knox, KY and Darmstadt Germany. He was discharged July 2, 1957 as Corporal.

Slone was awarded the National Defense Service Medal and Army of Occupation Medal (Germany).

Memorable experiences: Was fortunate to train and serve alongside his twin brother, Dan Day Slone.

Civilian employment was with the Ford Motor Company in Bedford, OH as a lineman and was an underground miner for many years. He was married to Lillie Faye Marsillett and had two children, Chicita L. Callihan and Vanessa Scott; and four grandchildren: Lakita Faith Lykins, Joshua Corey Scott, Travis Jerell Scott and William Van-Douglas Callihan.

Slone passed away Oct. 10, 2005 and is buried in the Davidson Memorial Gardens.

His greatest enjoyment during the last two years of his life was attending and serving in worship services at the Auxier Freewill Baptist Church. He also enjoyed various activities with his family.

WALTER M. "BUDDY" SLONE, Tech Sergeant E-5, born Dec. 21, 1947, the son of Charlie and Nancy Slone. He volunteered for the draft in August 1967 and completed his basic, AIT and armor school training at Fort Knox, KY. He was shipped to Korea and served with the 7th Div. A Troop 2/10 Cavalry. He was in Korea when North Korea captured one of our Navy ships, the USS *Pueblo*.

He volunteered to go to Vietnam in 1968 and served with the 9th Inf. Div. 2/47 Recon at Camp Bearcat, north of Saigon until the 9th Div. moved south of Saigon into the Mekong Delta. He was sent to sniper school and returned to his unit 2/47 Recon. Walter was involved in many combat operations, air mobiles, search and destroy missions, night ambushes and also operated with the Navy swift boats. They would drop them off and pick them up a few days later if they survived the mission.

Discharged at Fort Lewis, WA in 1969. His decorations include the Silver Star, three Bronze Stars w/V, four Army Commendations w/V, Purple Heart, Combat Infantry Badge, Good Conduct Medal, National Defense Medal, Vietnam Service Medal, Vietnam Campaign Medal, Vietnam Cross of Gallantry, Korean Armed Forces Expeditionary Medal and Korean Service Medal.

The bad part of the war was when he returned home to Betsy Layne to learn that two of his friends had been Killed in Action in Vietnam, Jeff Mulkey and Kenny Blackburn. He enjoyed spending time with them at Fort Knox, KY in a bowling alley before he shipped out to Korea in 1967 – that was their last meeting and that day will never be forgotten by William.

Walter married Bonnie Stevens, daughter of Ervin and Georgia Stevens of Harold, KY. They have two children, Buddy and Georgina, and four grandchildren. He is employed by Ford Motor Co. as skilled trades journeyman tool & die welder. Walter likes to work on old cars and travel. He is a life member of the DAV, VFW and VVA; he's also a Shriner and member of Hillbilly Clan #21 Detroit.

WALTER E. SNAVELY, Sergeant Major, born March 14, 1928 to Joe and Glenice Snavely. He enlisted in the U.S. Army in 1949 and completed training at Fort Knox, KY. He

served one tour of duty in Germany and returned home where he joined the Reserve and started work for W.W. Grimm's Meat Company.

He met and married Arnita Compton in 1954. He went to work for Stuckey's store/gas chain in Abingdon, VA, then moved to manage a Stuckey's store in Petersburg, VA. He remained in the Reserve and in 1956 returned to active duty. He retired Aug. 1, 1974, after 20 years of service.

Walter's decorations include the Bronze Star Medal, Meritorious Service Medal, Army Commendation Medal w/OLC, Good Conduct Medal, Fifth award, Army Occupation Medal Germany, National Defense Service Medal w/ OLCs, Vietnam Army Medal w/4 Service Stars, Vietnam Campaign Medal, Meritorious Unit Commendation Expert Missileman Badge and Sharpshooter Badge-M-14 Rifle.

Walter and Arnita had two children, Charles Gobel Snavely and Nena J. Snavely Biliter, and two grandchildren, Christopher Snavely and Katheryn I. Snavely. He also had a sister, Wilma Messer, and a brother, Andrew J. Snavely.

He enjoyed retirement spending time playing golf, working at the church and being with family and friends.

Walter E. Snavely passed away Jan. 31, 1999.

BILL CLAUDE SPEARS, born Nov. 9, 1924 in Edgar, KY, the son of John Walker and Nina McGuire. He enlisted in 1958 at Prestonsburg, KY as a Private in the U.S. Army. He was a heavy equipment operator. Spears was discharged in 1951 with the rank of Private.

Bill died on Sept. 20, 1961 on Auxier Road in a car accident. He is buried in the Davidson Memorial Gardens, Ivel, KY.

ALEXANDER LACKEY "ALEX" SPENCER JR., Private, born on Jan. 12, 1931 at Eastern Kentucky, son of Alexander Lackey Spencer Sr. and Katherine Turner. Alex graduated from Maytown High School in 1950.

He was drafted into the Army in 1953 while he was a teacher and principal at Wayland Grade School. He served with Co. B of the 78th AFA Bn. at Wackerheim, Germany. He worked as a typist for the supply department for instructors of Troop Information and Education. He graduated from Pikeville College in 1960 and received his Master's Degree from Miami University in Ohio in 1975.

Alex was discharged in 1956. Alex married Caroline Jean Price on March 25, 1960 at Norwalk, OH. They have one son André Gerard Spencer, and daughter-in-law, Kathy Lynn (Clark) Spencer; and two grandchildren, Trevor Alexander and Tyler Andrew Spencer.

ROGER A. SPRADLIN, Sergeant First Class, 179th Regt., 45th Inf. Div., completed basic training at Indiantown Gap, PA. He served in Korea from 1952-53 and received three Bronze Stars. He was involved in the Heartbreak Ridge, Old Baldy, Cherwon Valley and Lukes Castle. He served in a Rifle Platoon then months later transferred to Supply Sergeant in A and B Companies.  He obtained permission from the Pentagon and Washington to rewrite Property Books for Co. A (which has never been done). He had to "beg, borrow and steal" for the equipment (jeeps, trucks, etc.) but he "got what he needed one way or the other."

Upon returning to the USA, he was transferred to transportation in Fort Eustas, VA, and the Inspector General Office. He did inspections for the post until his discharge. He married Helen Sue Colvin Spradlin and they have three children: Pamela, Leslie and Gregory. Roger retired from Columbia Gas after 37 years. He and Helen Sue are active members of the Community United Methodist Church. They reside at Mays Branch in Prestonsburg, KY.

DELMAR STEWART, born in Honaker, KY enlisted in the U.S. Army in October 1955. He served in Germany and was discharged in October 1958 as a Corporal.

He is married to Joene Keathley and has one child and two grandchildren. Stewart currently resides in Harold, KY and is working, traveling and enjoying his grandchildren.

DENVER STEWART, born in Honaker, KY enlisted in the U.S. Army in 1953. His military locations, stations were Fort Smith, AR and Germany. He was discharged in 1960 as a Staff Sergeant.

Stewart had four children and nine grandchildren. He is deceased.

MARION THACKER, born March 2, 1928, at Banner, KY, to Noah D. and Rosa (Click) Thacker.

Mr. Thacker attended school at Banner, KY, until the sixth grade and then went to Martin, KY where he graduated from the high school in 1947.

He worked in the coal mines for a time and then enlisted in the U.S. Army. He took his basic training at Fort Campbell, KY. In June 1950 he was sent to Japan and on July 5, 1950, he was sent to Korea. On July 16, 1950, he suffered his first injury when he received several bullet wounds. On Aug. 10, 1950, he received severe burns from a bullet exploding the gasoline tank of his vehicle. After spending a short time in the hospital in Tokyo, Japan, and the hospital in Hickman AFB in Hawaii, he spent approximately 15 months in Bethesda Naval Hospital due to several burns he received in Korea.

He graduated from the University of Kentucky with a Degree in Mechanical Engineering in 1957. He was employed by the Bureau of Reclamation, living first in Kabab, UT until housing was built in Page, AZ. This work was involved with the construction of the Glen Canyon Dam. This is also where he met and married Donna Boswell. The couple were married in Page, AZ, on Nov. 1, 1959. In August they transferred to Grand Island where Marion continued to work for the Bureau of Reclamation until his retirement in July 1985.

Thacker received the following medals: three Purple Hearts, Bronze Star, Korean Service Medal, Occupation Medal, National Defense Service Medal and three other medals.

He passed away in March 2004. He has one son, Craig and one daughter, Kathryn.

JAKE R. THOMAS, born in Garth, KY on July 9, 1928 he graduated from Prestonsburg High School with the class of '47 and entered the U.S. Army in January 1951. Cpl. Thomas was slightly wounded Oct. 14, 1951, but was back at the front two days later. Five days later he was killed.

Thomas received the Purple Heart and was a Private First Class.

He was the son of Lawrence and Ruth Thomas. He had three sisters: Gertie, Ethel and Mrs. Robert Wilcox; and three brothers: Arnold, William and Ralph Douglas.

JOE P. TURNER, born Dec. 20, 1926 at Hueysville, KY to Green and Dora Turner, enlisted in the U.S. Army in March 6, 1945, and later on Aug. 14, 1950 with the 64th Field Arty. Bn., 858 Order, Korea.

Turner received the WWII Asiatic-Pacific Campaign Medal, WWII Victory Medal, Army Occupation Medal, Korean Conflict, Korean Service Medal w/1 Bronze Star. He was discharged Dec. 12, 1946 with the rank of Sergeant, and the second time on Dec. 5, 1951.

He married Blanche Allen Turner and they have one son, Darwin and two grandchildren. Joe now lives in Greenup County.

DAVID KELSE "TOBE" VAUGHAN, born May 28, 1930 in Cliff, KY enlisted in the U.S. Army Dec. 29, 1952. He was stationed in Fort Dix, NJ with the 269th Ord. Det. (WUR). He was discharged Dec. 13, 1955 as Private First Class.

He was awarded the Occupation Medal (Germany) and National Defense Service Medal.

Civilian employment was with the Spurlock Food Service. He was the son of T.J. and Nell Harris Vaughan. He passed away in September 1957.

GEORGE S. VAUGHAN, born at Prestonsburg, KY on Sept. 16, 1928. His parents were T.J. Vaughan and Nell Harris Vaughan.

He was drafted into the U.S. Army on Jan. 3, 1951 and was stationed at Fort Devens, MA. He was discharged on Jan. 9, 1953. His rank was Private First Class.

George and Laura Goble were married on May 16, 1951. They have two daughters, Cheryl and Kristal. They have one beautiful granddaughter, Nikki Bradley.

George worked as a mine mechanic for 27 years. He then worked as a field representative for United Mine Workers of America for eight years before retiring.

He passed away Nov. 16, 1996.

JOHN E. VAUGHAN, born Oct. 3, 1930 in Prestonsburg, KY the son of David J. Vaughan and Orbie Prater Vaughan.

In May 1948 he graduated from Prestonsburg High School and received a scholarship from the Princess Elkhorn Coal Company at David, KY to attend the University of Kentucky. He played football and basketball in high school.

In March 1952 he married Betty Jean Layne of Betsy Layne, KY. In June 1953 he received a BS Degree in Mining Engineering from the University of Kentucky and was commissioned a Second Lieutenant in the USAFR; having taken the Reserve Officers Training Corps Program (ROTC) while at UK.

In November 1953 he was called to active duty in the USAF.

December 1954 he received his Pilot Wings upon completing the USAF Jet Fighter Pilot School at Laredo AFB, TX. He was assigned to the Military Air Transport Service, transitioned to four engine aircraft (C-124), and stationed at Dover AFB, DE. At Dover the duty involved flying cargo to Thule, Greenland; Iceland, England, Europe, Turkey, Pakistan and other locations.

In July 1957 he was assigned to the Air Force Institute of Technology (AFIT) at Wright-Patterson AFB, OH as a student.

1958 he was integrated into the Regular Air Force Officer Corps.

March 1959 he received his BS Degree in Aeronautical Engineering from AFIT. Assigned to the Air Research and Development Command (ARDC) as an aeronautical engineer involved in aircraft procurement programs of relatively small liaison type aircraft to meet USAF and Army requirements.

In October 1962 he resigned his Regular USAF commission, left active duty, and accepted a commission in the USAFR at the same rank, Captain.

August 1971 he was assigned to a USAFR unit as a pilot flying C-119 and C-123 aircraft.

In September 1981 he was assigned to the Retired Reserve List as a Lieutenant Colonel.

RONALD E. VAUGHAN, was 5 years old when the photograph was taken. His parents were David J. and Orbie Prater Vaughan of Prestonsburg. He graduated from high school in Prestonsburg in 1956. He enlisted in the USAF and took basic training at Lackland AFB in San Antonio, TX. He was sent to F.E. Warren AFB in Cheyenne, WY for training in communications. After completing training he was assigned to Germany for three years and was stationed at Sembach AB; Rheine-Main AB; HQ 12th Air Force at Ramstein, Germany; Giebelstadt AB; and USAFE HQ in Wiesbaden Germany. He was discharged upon his return to the U.S.

He entered Morehead State College in 1960 and received an AB Degree in Education, earned a Master's Degree from Xavier University and a Doctorate Degree from West Virginia University. He worked for 37 years in Ohio's public schools, 31 years of his work was in administration.

BILLY D. WALLEN, Private First Class, the son of Mattie and Ollie Wallen, was born April 9, 1931. He enlisted in the U.S. Army in 1949 and served two years, one of which was the Korean War. He was stationed at Fort Lewis, WA with the 2nd Div. Co., 38th Arty.

After discharge, Billy returned to Floyd County and worked for Kentucky-West Virginia Gas Company for 35 years. He married Doris Smith in 1949. They had four children, two of which are deceased, Lydia and Brenda Wallen who are twins. He is survived by his wife, Doris; two daughters, DaveAnne Spangle and Deborah Wright; seven grandchildren; and 10 great-grandchildren.

Billy loved and raised horses, hunted and fished. He was very patriotic and belonged to the DAV, American Legion and VFW. Billy passed away July 4, 2003 after a long fight with heart disease and cancer.

JAMES ALEX "JIM" WALLEN never returned from the Korean War. His date of loss is listed as July 25, 1950. He was listed as a POW. After he was missing for four years, he was declared dead. He was a Private First Class E3 with the D Co., 5th Regt. Inf., 1st Cav. Div. of the U.S. Army. He was discharged from the Army and then re-enlisted. He re-entered into active duty on March 29, 1946 at Saipan with the 62nd Aircraft Control and Warning Sqdn. He operated field radio sets to locate and follow aircrafts and reported positions by phone.

He liked being in service while in Japan. Re-enlisted to return to Japan and was sent to Korea when the war broke out.

He was born Nov. 27, 1928 in Floyd County, KY to Ollie Wallen and Mattie McGuire. His niece, Daveann Wallen Spangler, gave me his history. She said that she'd found a picture of him on the cover of *Life Magazine*, Vol. 20, Aug. 14, 1950, that had been folded up and saved by his mother.

Clara Lucille Garrett told me that Jim stopped by to tell her mother, Loma Warrix Derossett, that he was going away but "would come back and marry that pretty little Meadows girl (Mary) and was going to be a United Baptist preacher." *Submitted by Karen Nelson Marcum.*

SAMUEL WALLEN, born Dec. 4, 1927 to Lee and Lula Wallen of Floyd County, KY, served in the Korean War. *Submitted by Karen Marcum.*

WOODROW WALLEN, son of Lee and Lula Wills Wallen, was born June 30, 1932 in Floyd County, KY. He served in the Korean War.

He married Ruth Emily Wallen and had five sons, all of which served with the U.S. military, three in WWII, two in the Korean War and one lost at sea. *Submitted by Karen Marcum.*

MELVIN WEBB, born in Wayland, KY enlisted in the USAF in December 1954. He was stationed at Shaw AFB, Sumter, SC. He was discharged Dec. 21, 1962 as Airman First Class.

Civilian employment was with National Mines and Bizzack Waco Scaffold in Cleveland, OH. He is married to Priscilla (Coleman) Webb and has one daughter, Cheryl May and two granddaughters, Kelly and Victoria. He currently resides in Allen, KY and enjoys hunting and fishing. He is a NASCAR fan.

BOBBY W. WELLS, Specialist 2 (E-5), born Sept. 15, 1933, one of the seven sons of George Wash and Cora Bell Goble Wells, who were veterans of the U.S. military. He enlisted in the U.S. Army in March 1954, completed basic training at Fort Knox, KY, and advance training at the Army Security Agency Training Center at Fort Devan, MA. He went from Fort Devan to Arlington Hall Station, VA, then the home of the National Security Agency, where he received more training. From Arlington Hall, he was sent to Germany, where he spent the next 26 months working as a communications security analyst in Heidelberg and various other locations in Germany and France.

He returned to Fort Dix, NJ in February 1957, where he was separated from the Army and was officially discharged from the Army eight years later.

His decorations include Sharpshooter Medal, National Defense Service Medal, Germany Occupation Medal and Good Conduct Medal.

Bobby married Herbie Jean Banks on Aug. 28, 1959. They had three children. He graduated from Morehead State University, and spent 27 years in the Floyd County School System. After retiring from teaching, he spent the next 15 years operating a company called The Question Well. That company sold academic team questions to schools in 40 states and two foreign countries. He is presently retired, but stays active by producing historical and genealogical material on Floyd County and Eastern Kentucky.

Bobby and Herbie live at 110 Burke Avenue, Prestonsburg, KY 41653, where they have lived at this same location most of their married life.

BILL BUCK WRIGHT, son of George and Nettie Pitts Wright, was born Aug. 2, 1930. He volunteered for military service in 1950 and spent four weeks in the States, then was sent to Korea, assigned to 23rd Inf. Regt., Co. G, 6th Mechanical Calvary.

He was on a hill when he was wounded by machine gun fire. He could not use his leg because circulation was cut off from his foot. He was dragged down the hill by a young soldier. They were almost to the medical aid station when the young soldier was shot in the mouth. He never saw the young soldier at the medic station. They amputated his leg just below his knee, but gangrene took over and he was flown to Bethesda Naval Hospital for further surgery. He was given last rites and told his box was waiting outside for him.

His memory of the flight was knowing sometimes and then not knowing for periods of time. In the Naval Hospital in Bethesda, MD, his leg was again amputated hoping to get all the gangrene poison which left about six inches for an artificial limb to be made for him. His condition was critical and the family was asked to come to be with him. During his recuperation, a nurse with an artificial leg taught him to use one foot.

Vietnam

LARRY WAYNE ADKINS, born Jan. 22, 1946, at Wheelwright, KY, son of Bryan and Christine Adkins. He enlisted April 1966 at Prestonsburg, KY as a basic trainee in the USAF, in the Personnel Research Laboratory. He spent 28 days in basic training at Lackland AFB in Texas. His brother, Maurice and he pulled basic training together.

He was discharged in March 1970 at San Antonio, TX, with a rank of Buck Sergeant. Medals and honors he received were the National Defense Medal, Marksmanship Medal, Good Conduct Medal and Air Force Medal.

He is married to Shirley Adkins. Their children are Kim Castle and Shelly Tackett.

JAMES LYNN ALLEN, born Feb. 24, 1947, son of James E. and Violet Coburn Allen. He went into military service Aug. 6, 1968. He took his basic training at Fort Bragg, NC and assault helicopter training at Fort Eustis, VA.

He went to Vietnam January 1969 and was assigned to 128th Assault Helicopter Co. on March 18, 1969. He was injured when his helicopter was shot down on the Cambodian border. He was medivaced to Japan and later transferred to the 55th Avn. May 1969 in Seoul, Korea. His medals include: Combat Infantry Badge, Vietnam Service Medal, Purple Heart, Combat Flight Medal, National Defense Badge and Korean Service Medal.

James married Gloria Mae Allen and they have two sons and five grandchildren. He is now employed by the family business, J.E. Allen Drilling and Construction Co.

VERNON L. ALLEN, Command Sergeant Major, born Jan. 12, 1939 at Drift, KY, son of Graden and Margaret Allen. He enlisted in the U.S. Army in 1958, completed basic training and combat engineer training with the 2nd Engrs. Bn., at Fort Benning, GA, and served 12 months in Vietnam with the 617th Engr. Co. (Panel Bridge). He received several missions to construct bridges; one mission required the construction of a 170-foot bridge, the longest unsupported bridge in Vietnam.

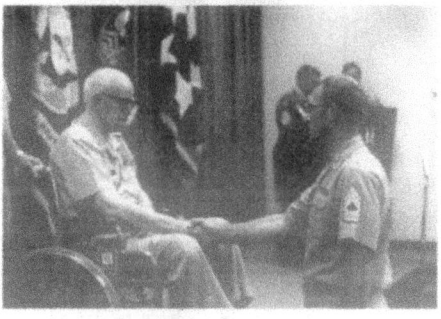

Gen. Omar Bradley greets MSG Vernon Allen at the Sergeants Major Academy in Fort Bliss, TX in 1979.

His decorations include: Legion of Merit, Meritorious Service Medal, Army Commendation Medal, National Defense Medal, Vietnam Campaign Medal, Republic of Vietnam Cross of Gallantry w/Palm, Vietnam Civil Actions Medal, Army Services Ribbon, Drill Sergeant Badge and Good Conduct Medal with 10th Award.

Vernon married Ingeborg H. Karl on June 26, 1962. They had two children and three grandchildren. He retired from the Army Oct. 31, 1988, then worked as a Civil Service employee for an additional 14 years. He retired again on May 31, 2004 with a total of 44 years in the Federal Government, to the state of Missouri.

STEPHEN ALEX ANDERSON, son of Alex and Allie Osborne Anderson, was born at Hite, KY in Floyd County. He was drafted into the Army on Dec. 8, 1970, during the Vietnam War, and completed basic training at Fort Knox on Feb. 19, 1971. He received advanced individual training at Fort Sill, OK from where he was shipped to Germany to serve with C Btry., 5th Bn., and 77th Field Arty. He was a missile crewman at Grafenwhor on the Czechoslovak border, and also served on the Island of Crete off the coast of Greece. He was awarded the National Defense Medal and the M-16 Sharpshooter Medal. He was discharged on Nov. 30, 1972 and returned to Floyd County to work as a carpenter.

Anderson was married to Ilene Moore of Garrett, KY and they had two children, Ethan, born 1985 and Lindsey, born 1987. He is now retired and resides at Hite.

JAMES L. BAKER, son of Goldie and Creed Baker, was born in 1948 in the Floyd County community of Johns Creek. He was in the U.S. Army for two years. He later moved to California and is married with children.

TOMMY GAYLE BENTLEY, born Dec. 5, 1947 at McDowell, KY. Drafted into the Army on Jan. 25, 1968. Tour completed Jan. 23, 1970. Served with sergeant missile system as a sergeant missile crewman with the Army Artillery. Stationed at Fort Jackson, SC for basic training. From there he was sent to Fort Sill, OK for AIT training in sergeant missile. From Fort Sill he was sent to Vicensa, Italy where he served with B Btry., 5th Bn., 30th Arty. Duties included transporting and helping assemble and fire the missile. All information other than that is classified and he can't disclose anymore. Served in the NATO forces under SETAF (Southern European). All went well with his military experience except once; they were put on red alert for nine days when Russia invaded Yugoslavia in 1969. That was kind of scary for a few days.

He made lots of friends in his two years of service and still keeps in touch with most of them. Last year he visited his best friend in South Dakota and they had a very nice time in the four days he stayed with him.

He received the Good Conduct Medal, National Service Ribbon and Expert Rifleman Medal. He was prompted to Private E-2 out of basic training, put E3 out of AIT and Specialist Fourth Class on Dec. 3, 1968. Left his military career as Specialist Fourth Class (or Corporal).

After his military, he was married on Jan. 8, 1971 to Sandra Morgenstern. They were blessed with three kids: Cheryl Kay, born March 6, 1975; Charles Leroy, born July 29, 1977; and Alan Gayle, who was stillborn Aug. 21, 1982. Later divorced in 1997 and married to Terry Carver May 9, 1998. Currently lives in Columbus, OH and has since June 9, 1963.

He worked in a machine shop for five years as a crankshaft grinder and later changed to operating heavy equipment. In December 2004, he became eligible for retirement. However, he really loves his work and will continue until 2009 and then retire and travel the USA to visit all his "ARMY BUDDIES."

O. SAM BLANKENSHIP, born April 5, 1947 in Columbus, OH. His parents were Oscar and Bertha Estep Blankenship of Thelma, KY. He graduated from Franklin Heights High School in 1965 and enlisted in the Marine Corps Dec. 8, 1965.

Sam served two tours of duty in Vietnam where he was awarded three Purple Hearts and numerous other medals. He was Honorably Discharged March 8, 1968.

Upon his return he completed both his Bachelor's and Master's Degrees in business and accounting. He married Cathy Young and fathered three sons and a daughter: Steven, Lisa, Matthew and Andrew. After Cathy's death he married Jeanne Burke. They have two granddaughters and three grandsons. He is currently employed with Edward Jones Investments of Prestonsburg.

JACKIE M. BOOTH, born on March 18, 1948 in Whitehouse, KY enlisted in the USAF in 1967. His father, Monroe Booth, served in the U.S. Army in WWII. Jack served in Japan, Germany and San Angelo, TX.

He received the following medals and decorations: National Defense Service Medal, Air Force Good Conduct Medal (1967-70), AFM 900-3, SO GB-557, DAF (1968). Jack was a Security Policeman ABR77130 compl-67. In 1971 Jack was released from active duty with honorable service.

Jack married Diane Smith from Phelps, KY. They have lived in Prestonsburg, KY for over 30 years. Jack and Diane have two sons, Thurman L. Booth, currently serving the U.S. Army 15 years, and Jessie M. Booth of Dana, KY. They have three grandchildren and three step-grandchildren. Jack is a wonderful father and papaw. He now works as a security guard at Massey Energy. Jack likes to work outside, fish and garden.

BOBBIE DONALD BURCHETT, born Jan. 14, 1959 at Endicott, KY. He enlisted in the U.S. Army as a Specialist 5 with the Army AUS AGC and later transferred to Co. A, 12th Bn., 5th Bde. USAARMC.

He received the National Defense Service Medal Expert Badge (rifle). He was discharged Feb. 12, 1971.

THOMAS D. BURGA, Sergeant, born March 25, 1946, son of Bill and Alta Burga. He enlisted in the U.S. Army. Served in the 573rd Supply and Service Co. He was in Vietnam February 1968-February 1969.

Thomas married Drema Ray and has two daughters and one granddaughter. He retired from General Motors in Michigan where he currently lives.

BILLY CALHOUN, Private First Class E-3, born May 25, 1941 on Town Branch, Floyd County, KY. He inducted into the Army on Nov. 1, 1963 at Ashland, KY.

He served in AUS UNASGD. He was transferred to USAR, Fort Gordon, GA. His last duty assignment was Stu Co. S USASESCS 3rd U.S. Army. He was Honorably Discharged on Nov. 5, 1965. He died on April 15, 2004.

JAMES W. CAMPBELL, born April 5, 1946 to Paul and Mildred Campbell of Weeksbury, KY. He enlisted in the U.S. Army in 1965. He trained at Fort Devens, MA and was shipped out to Vietnam in July 1966 and served as Infantry Squad Leader with the 196th Inf. Bde. and the 4th Inf. Div. and never lost a man in battle. He had operations in Attleboro, Gadstien, Cedar Falls and Junction City in 1966.

He returned to the States and was a Drill Sergeant at Fort Knox, KY for 15 months. Mr. Campbell remembers the time he was going to the aid of a company of men where he found a few still alive.

His decorations include the Vietnam Service Award, the National Defense Medal, the Good Conduct Medal and the Combat Infantry Badge.

James married Gail Humphrey on Nov. 30, 1968. They have two children and eight grandchildren. He was employed as a coal miner and is now retired.

ELVA CASE, served in the U.S. Army in Vietnam, 1962-65.

ROBERT DARRELL CASTLE, Aviation Maintenance Administrator 2, born May 23, 1945, son of James M. Castle and Marjorie Stambaugh Castle. He graduated from the University of Kentucky in 1968. He holds a Master's in Psychometry (1982) and a Master's in Counseling (2000) from Eastern Kentucky University. He is employed at Mountain Comprehensive Care Center, Prestonsburg.

He enlisted in the USN in October 1968. He completed boot camp at Great Lakes, IL and Electronic School at FATULANT, NAS, Jacksonville, FL. He was attached to RVAH-6, Vigilante Sqdn., at NAS Albany, GA. He was deployed twice to the coast of Vietnam aboard the USS *Kitty Hawk* (1970) and aboard the USS *America* (1972). He was a member of CAG 8 and CAG 11, Task Force 77. He served two tours off the coast of North and South Vietnam as part of a photo reconnaissance squadron, 1970-72. He was discharged from the USN Aug. 10, 1972 at NAS Albany, GA.

Robert married Henrietta Jane Montgomery, daughter of Henry C. and Glennora Wells Montgomery June 15, 1966 at Auxier, KY. They have one son, Robert Darrell Castle II, who lives in Nicholasville, KY.

CHAD RONDAL CAUDILL, born March 6, 1939 to Henry C. and Madge Huff Caudill. He retired from the USAF where he served as an air traffic controller and was instrumental in the launch of Apollo II.

As a Technical Sergeant, he and his men were sent to Cape Kennedy, FL to control the departure and arrivals of helicopters carrying dignitaries to and from NASA headquarters such as President Lyndon B. Johnson and Vice President Agnew. He was also active in USAF Mobile Communications and traveled extensively in the U.S. and foreign countries.

Sgt. Caudill passed away on Feb. 13, 2005. The graveside services were performed by the Wright Patterson AFB of Dayton, OH.

THOMAS HOWARD CESCO, born in Tram, KY Feb. 4, 1949. Enlisted in the U.S. Army May 28, 1968. Classification and Division: RA UNASGD PV1. He was stationed in Germany and Vietnam. Discharged March 26, 1971.

His awards and medals include the National Defense Service Medal, Vietnam Service Medal and Vietnam Campaign Medal.

Cesco is the son of Otto Cesco and Elizabeth Blackburn Cesco. He has four brothers and sisters: Forrest, Ottis, Glenda and Debbie. He married (first) Glenna Fannin Cesco and (second) Sadie Dotson Cesco and has one son, Terry Wayne Cesco. Civilian employment as car salesman and construction worker. Cesco died Dec. 17, 2005.

GREGORY B. CLARK, born Feb. 7, 1950 at Prestonsburg, KY, son of Bernard and Peggy Clark. He enlisted in the Army on May 17, 1970 in Ashland, KY with a rank of E-1. He served with the 2nd 94th, attached to the 101st Arty. unit. He trained at Fort Bragg, NC and completed AIT at Fort Sill, OK. From there, he was sent to Vietnam where he pulled a 13-month tour of duty.

Because he had less than six months left in the service, he was discharged from the Army in November 1971 at Fort Knox, KY with the rank of E-4. Clark said that what he remembers most about the Vietnam War is "not knowing who you were really fighting."

He and his wife, Berniece, live in Floyd County, KY.

PHILLIP R. COLEMAN, Private First Class, born Feb. 10, 1945, son of Guy and Rusha Collins Coleman (both deceased). Now survived by nine siblings.

Graduated from Wayland High School in 1963. Because of the Vietnam War the draft was in full force so Phillip was drafted in the spring of 1966.

The basic training was "only" about eight weeks and then the military put a gun in his hand and shipped him off to Vietnam. He landed there in September but his stay was not long. He was killed Oct. 29, 1966. He served with Co. F, 8th Inf., 4th Inf. Div.

His awards/medals include the Purple Heart.

Phillip was athletic, full of life, loved music and playing the drums. They sneaked from their mom and danced in the Wayland Fountain. He broke up a fight at the Martin Youth Center so it's hard to understand why he died fighting.

"The Good"... they do die young. Phillip has been greatly missed by his friends and family.

THOMAS H. COOK, born on Oct. 27, 1944 in Paintsville, KY. He enlisted in the USMC on March 28, 1963 and was stationed at Parris Island, SC; Camp LeJeune, NC; Camp Pendleton, CA; and Canoi Bay, HI. Missions and battles include Dominican Republic, Vietnam, Jack Stay, CO, Apache I & II among others.

Mr. Cook's most memorable experiences include traveling to Spain, Portugal, Puerto Rico, Hawaii, the Philippine Islands and Japan.

He received the Good Conduct Medal, Combat A&F Ribbon, Presidential Unit Citation, Combat Action Ribbon, National Defense Service Medal, Armed Forces Expeditionary Service Medal, Vietnam Service Medal w/2 Bronze Stars, Republic of Vietnam Meritorious Unit Citation (Gallantry Cross), Vietnam Campaign Medal and the Rifle Expert Badge w/3-years Bar.

Mr. Cook was employed with Bell South. He married Brenda Wilcox Cook and has three children: Thomas Jr., Timothy and Kandi; and one grandson, Jacob Cook. He is retired and enjoys fishing, hunting and gardening.

ALBEN RICHARD COOLEY, born Nov. 13, 1938 in Wayland, KY. He enlisted into the U.S. Army where he was a Private First Class in the 5th Inf. He was stationed in Fort Carson, CO. He was discharged on Dec. 28, 1967 and was formerly married to Doris Dingus.

In civilian life, Mr. Cooley was employed with the Kentucky-West Virginia Gas Co. He passed away May 17, 1999.

DANNY DINGUS, Staff Sergeant, born July 21, 1945 in Hite, KY. He is the son of Lacy and Pauline Dingus. He enlisted in the U.S. Army in August 1962 and completed basic training at Fort Knox, KY. He was stationed at Graffton, IL; Baumholder, Germany; Phu Loi, Vietnam; Fort Hood, TX; Chu Lai, Vietnam; Fort Eustis, VA; Da Nang, Vietnam; and Fort Carson, CO. He was discharged July 31, 1972.

Danny's many decorations include Combat Infantry Badge, Vietnam Campaign Medal w/60 Device, Vietnam Service Medal w/6 Bronze Service Stars, Bronze Star Medal w/3 OLC, Army Commendation w/2 OLC, Purple Heart Istole, The Air Medal, the Good Conduct Medal w/1 OLC and six Overseas Service Bars.

Danny married Linda Sue Jullirate May 27, 1968 in Williamsburg, VA. They have three children and four grandchildren. He was employed by International Harvester and the U.S. Post Office in Fort Wayne, IN also Dana Spicer Axle, Syracuse, IN, before retiring in August 2005. Sadly, his wife Linda Sue, passed away in May of 1993.

MITCHELL DINGUS, USMC (Ret.), born Dec. 3, 1946 at Hite, KY, son of Lacy and Pauline Shepherd Dingus. He attended school at Martin for 10 years. After graduating from Larwill High School in Larwill, IN in May 1965, he enlisted in the USMC at Fort Wayne, IN. After Marine boot camp at San Diego, CA he was assigned the MOS of 2311, Ammunition Technician.

Mitch was then deployed to Camp Hauge, Okinawa where he worked in the Okinawa Ammo Storage Depot for six months. He then received orders for the Marine Ammo Storage Dump at Da Nang, Vietnam. After seven months in Vietnam he rotated back to Okinawa and volunteered for another six months of duty on Okinawa. Promoted to Corporal.

Upon returning to the States he was stationed at Camp Pendleton, CA. He then volunteered for security duty in the Panama Canal Zone, where he escorted Cuban and Russian ships through the Canal.

He volunteered to go back to Vietnam for a 13-month tour of duty. While on leave he got married to his first wife, Linda Baker, his high school sweetheart. He was promoted to Sergeant before being discharged at Marine Corps AS El Toro, CA in April 1969.

After 89 days of civilian life he re-enlisted in the Marines and was stationed at Camp Lejeune, NC with the 2nd Bn., 6th Marines. While at Camp Lejeune he attended the Military Intelligence Analyst Course in Maryland, and became the assistant to the battalion's intelligence chief.

His next assignment was with the 2nd Bn., 4th Marines on Okinawa as their Intelligence Chief. He was promoted to Staff Sergeant and assigned to Fort Huachuca, AZ as an instructor for the Army's Intelligence Center and School. There he married for the second time to his present wife of 32 years, Connie Lee Casselberry. After a three-year tour of duty with Intelligence Center and School he was selected to become a Marine recruiter in Zanesville, OH where he was promoted to Gunnery Sergeant.

His next assignment was Intelligence Chief for HMM 165 in Kaneohe Bay, HI. After three years in Hawaii, he was assigned to train the Marine Reserves at Glenview NAS, Glenview, IL. Promoted to Master Sergeant.

His last duty station was with the G-2 of the Fleet Marine Force Norfolk, VA. He retired from the Marines in August 1986.

He now lives with wife, Connie, in New Concord, OH. Their daughter, Michelle, is a physical therapist in Knoxville, TN and son, Travis, is a customer service representative with Time Warner Cable. Dennis, a son by his first marriage, works in the medical field.

Decorations, medals, badges, citations and campaign ribbons awarded to Mitch are as follows; National Defense Service Medal, Vietnam Service Medal w/4 stars, Vietnam Campaign Medal w/6 devices, Navy Commendation w/V, Presidential Unit Citation, Sea Service Deployment Ribbon w/star, Marine Corps Expeditionary Medal w/star, Army Commendation Medal, Humanitarian Service Medal, Good Conduct Medal w/6 stars, two Meritorious Mast, Rifle Expert Badge and Pistol Expert Badge.

ROBERT BRUCE DINGUS, born July 5, 1948 in Hite, KY, the eighth child of Lacy and Pauline Shepherd Dingus. He attended school at Martin for nine years, graduating in 1966 from Larwill High School, Larwill, IN.

He enlisted in the U.S. Army Nov. 7, 1966 while still in high school. After Army basic training he attended wheel vehicle mechanic training at Fort Knox, KY. His MOS was 62J20 general construction mechanic. He served in Vietnam from Oct. 7, 1967 to Aug. 27, 1968. Upon returning to the States he was assigned to HHC, 1st Bn. USAEBS, 1st Army, Fort Belvoir, VA. He was Honorably Discharged Nov. 6, 1969 with the rank of Specialist 5 which he was promoted to June 6, 1969. He returned to Whitley County, IN and began employment with LML Corporation in Columbia City, IN.

He re-enlisted in the Army Oct. 13, 1970 and was sent back to Vietnam where he served from Oct. 31, 1970 to May 29, 1972. Upon returning to the States he was assigned to HHC, 52nd Engr. Bn., HQ, FORSCOM Fort Carson, CO. He was Honorably Discharged with the rank of Specialist 5 on Oct. 13, 1970.

He was a member of the Columbia City VFW Post and North Manchester American Legion Post.

He married Deborah Hoover. They had one child, Natasha Ann Dingus, born Feb. 23, 1979, died Aug. 27, 1980.

Robert Bruce Dingus died Sept. 29, 1998 in Columbia City, IN. He is buried at Boonville Cemetery, Richland Township, Pierceton, IN. He is survived by a son, Dustin Cody Creech.

His decorations, medals, badges, commendations and campaign are as follows: Army Commendation Medal w/OLC, Purple Heart, Good Conduct Medal, National Defense Service Medal, Vietnam Service Medal w/4 Bronze Service Stars, Vietnam Campaign Medal w/device (1960), three Overseas Service Bars and Rifle Expert Badge.

MARSHALL ENDICOTT, Private E-1, born June 23, 1955 to Wanda and Thomas Endicott. He enlisted in the U.S. Army in 1974 and completed paratrooper training at Fort Knox, KY and served only four months.

He returned home from Fort Knox, where he was stationed upon getting an Honorable Discharge. Even though he liked the Army, and wanted to stay on, problems with his feet caused him to be hospitalized.

Marshall moved to Columbus, OH and worked as a meat cutter. Marshall married Gloria Taylor and they have two sons, Kyle and Shawn. They now live in Marysville, OH and works for Honda. He has had surgery on his feet.

WOODROW FOLEY, born Oct. 21, 1942 to Cora and Lemule Foley. He enlisted in the USAF where he served for four years.

After returning home he married wife, Julia, and had four daughters. He died of cancer

May 19, 1993 in Palesteen, IN where he lived and worked in his later years.

DANNY FRANCIS, son of Bill and Julia Yerrace Francis Jr. Served in the USMC in the Vietnam War.

DONALD D. FRANCIS, Gunnery Sergeant, USMC, served in the Vietnam War. He is the grandson of Bill and Julia Francis Sr.

LARRY FRANCIS, Specialist 4C, U.S. Army, served during the Vietnam War. He is the grandson of Bill and Julia Francis Sr.

FRANKLIN RAY GEORGE, USN, born Dec. 5, 1948, son of Grant and Estelle George. He entered from Hi-Hat, KY, August 1967-August 1969. His training was at Great Lakes, MI. Rank E-5, station at Norfolk, VA on the Atlanta Fleet, ship flag, Service Squad 4, with a two star Admiral aboard.

He married Dorothy in Texas and he works for Gulf Chemical in Freeport, TX and currently lives in Freeport, TX. He has four step children and six step grandchildren.

JIMMY DOUGLAS GEORGE, USAF, born Sept. 27, 1945, son of Grant and Estelle George. He entered from Hi-Hat, KY, August 1965-June 1969. Rank E-4. His boot camp training was in San Antonio AFB, then stationed at McCoy AFB, Orlando, FL. During that time he was transferred overseas, every six months, where he was stationed in Guam and Thailand, twice. He flew as an airplane pilot and also worked as a mechanic on airplanes.

He married first, Patty and has one daughter. His married his second wife, Karen, from

Texas and has two sons. His oldest son, James, will be sent to Iraq in the next two months. He is a highway construction worker and lives near Angleton, TX.

OLMA DAVID GEORGE, U.S. Army, born Sept. 25, 1947, son of Grant and Estelle George. He entered the service from Hi-Hat, KY Nov. 4, 1966-Oct. 25, 1968. His training was at Fort Bragg, NC, then sent to Fork Sill, OK for training in artillery. Rank 3-5, shipped to California then to Vietnam, where he was placed on front line in combat, during his two year stay in Vietnam.

He married Rhonda and has two daughters and one son and has five grandchildren. He is retired as an electrician and lives in Bradford, OH and has a cabin near the Cumberland Lake, KY where he enjoys fishing.

ROGER DEAN GEORGE, Staff Sergeant, born April 21, 1948, son of Grant and Estelle George. He entered from Hi-Hat, KY September 1961-August 1969. He was stationed in San Diego, CA. Served in Vietnam for 13 months as a Military Recruiter, then he was in Okinawa for two months.

He married Ramona and has two daughters and one son, and two grandchildren. Currently works for General Motors and lives in Miami County, OH.

WILLIAM HENDERSON GEORGE, USMC 1828 587, Fort Meade, MD. He was born Jan. 5, 1939, son of Grant and Estelle George. He enlisted in the Marines February 1959 and discharged February 1963. He was stationed at Parris Island during training, then to Guanaco, VA for his office training. He was stationed at Washington, D.C. at the Ana Costa NAS as security duty for President Eisenhower's helicopter.

He married Ann Mae Young. He is retired from General Motors, Dayton, OH and currently lives here in Dark County, OH.

R. RAY GIBSON JR., born Jan. 7, 1942 in Wayland, KY. Enlisted June 21, 1963. Military bases: Lackland AFB, TX - basic training; Lowry AFB, CO - Technician School; McConnell AFB, KS - 23rd TAC; Nellis AFB, NV - 4521 A&E Maint. Sq.; Yokota AFB, Japan - 441st Combat Support Group; and Korat RTAFB, Thailand - 388th Tactical Fighter Wing. Duty: Fire Control (radar) Systems technician on the F-105 Thunderchief fighter/bomber aircraft.

Memorable experiences: Seeing the Bob Hope's Christmas show, 1966, and being home with the family to see the telecast of his show and laughing when he saw himself and buddies on television. Touring the cities of Tokyo and Bangkok, seeing their people and its sounds are memories for life. A funny one was watching "I Love Lucy" in Japanese. Everyday was a memorable experience; it was a day closer to going home.

His awards/medals include the Air Force Outstanding Unit Award, Vietnam Service Medal w/1 cluster (1966), Air Force Good Conduct Medal, National Defense Service Medal and Air Force Small Arms Expert Marksman Ribbon. Discharged Jan. 11, 1967 with rank of Airman Second Class.

Married Judith Lee Frances on Sept. 12, 1964. They have three daughters, two grandsons and one granddaughter. They reside on the north coast of Ohio in Mentor-On-The-Lake, OH. Retired from Bailey Meter Co., Wickliffe, OH. Now he is working as an instructor for Mentor school's Latch-Key Program. Most of his time revolves around family, which he cherishes and enjoys very much.

JACKIE L. GOBLE, Sergeant First Class, born Sept. 6, 1936 in Lancer. He enlisted in the service in 1954 with four tours in Germany and two tours in Vietnam. Military locations, stations: twice at Fort Leonard Wood and one at Fort Campbell, KY. He served with the combat engineers. He participated in eight Tet Offensives in Vietnam.

His awards/medals include the Vietnam Cross of Gallantry, Combat Infantry Badge (first award), Vietnam Campaign Medal, Bronze Star Medal w/2 Bronze OLCs w/V device, Purple Heart, Good Conduct (fifth award), National Defense Service Medal and Vietnam Service Medal. He retired from service in 1976 with rank of Sergeant First Class E-7.

He has one brother who served 20 years in the Army, one brother who served 20 years in the USAF and a brother-in-law who served 20 years in the Air Force. They all retired with rank of E-7.

Goble retired from Dupont in Mississippi and now resides in Auxier, KY. He enjoys traveling and fishing.

RAYMOND CURTIS "DANK" GOBLE, Specialist 5, born March 14, 1947 in Dinwood, KY, son of Raymond Ross Goble and Violet Little. He enlisted in the U.S. Army on Aug. 4, 1966. He completed basic training at Fort Knox, KY and advanced training at Fort Belvoir, VA. He was transferred back to Fort Benning, GA in April 1967. He transferred to Thailand, December 1967. He served one year in Thailand and then transferred back to Fort Benning, GA in December 1968, where he was an instructor at the Officer Candidate School, until receiving an Honorable Discharge on Aug. 8, 1969.

While at Fort Benning he met and married Nina Joyce Green on Dec. 7, 1967. They have one son, two daughters and eight grandchildren. He retired April 1, 2005, from the U.S. Post Office, as a Postmaster. He and his family live at 827 Lee Road 2017, Phenix City, AL 36870. He currently works part time at the Mail Bag.

ROY HACKWORTH, a Private with Co. M, QMS Bde. He was discharged at Fort Lee, VA on Nov. 24, 1971. He was qualified rifle marksman.

He was born on Jan. 25, 1951 in Floyd County, KY and was the son of Rebel and Julia Reffett Hackworth. He married Patsy Pruitt.

PAUL DONALD HAGANS, Langley, KY served 1969-71, stationed in Germany. Rank: Sergeant E-5.

He was born Aug. 6, 1948. He is married to Deborah Kay Sammons and has one son, Paul Matthew Hagans. His parents are Wayne and Mae Hagans.

JAMES E. HAGER, Specialist 4, U.S. Army, born in Logan County, WV Aug. 24, 1940. Enlisted March 9, 1966 and was discharged Feb. 21, 1968. Served at Fort Knox, KY; Fort Leonard Wood, MO; and with the 814th Engr. Co. in Germany as a construction machine operator building bridges.

He is the son of Mr. and Mrs. Everett Hager of David, KY. Hager attended Eastern State College at Richmond, KY.

He now resides in Fayetteville, NC. Hager has one daughter, Shyla and two grandchildren, Jamie and Lyric.

LOWELL GEORGE HAGER, born Oct. 11, 1934, was the son of Everett and Hallie Hager of David, KY. He enlisted in the U.S. Army in January 1957 to "see the world" and spent the rest of his enlistment behind a desk as a clerk/typist. He was discharged in January 1959 with the rank of Private.

He was killed in a car accident in Johnson County, KY five months upon returning to home. Lowell was never married, but left behind a loving family.

DENNIS CLARK HALL, son of Elva and Gen Hall, grandson of Johnnie Lee and Minnie Davis Hall. Served in the U.S. Army in Vietnam. He now resides in Marshall, MI.

CLYDE RANDAL "RANDY" HARMON, Private, served with the 5th Surgery Hospital. He was inducted at Ashland, KY

June 12, 1969 and discharged at Fort Knox, KY June 11, 1971. He was a Medical Specialist.

Randal received the National Defense Service Medal.

He was the son of Clyde Patrick and Anna Lee Hackworth.

DONALD M. HARRINGTON, born June 19, 1936 in Columbus, OH, and reared in Prestonsburg by his parents, Hoover and Julia Harrington.

Drafted into the U.S. Army in 1960 and retired in 1985 at the rank of Sergeant Major. Served one tour of duty in Korea and two tours in Vietnam (1965-66 and 1968-69). He ended his career as an instructor with the ROTC Department at Ouachita Baptist University in Arkadelphia, AR, where he still lives.

After his retirement, he worked for 16 years as an alcohol safety coordinator.

He married the former Dolores Hughes of Prestonsburg July 13, 1957.

DONALD HENSLEY, joined the Armed Forces on July 16, 1965 and was discharged April 21, 1967. He served with the USARV, Special Troops APOB 96307.

He received the Marksman Rifle, M14, National Defense Service Medal, Vietnam Service Medal, Vietnam Campaign Medal and Mechanics Badge w/1 bar.

DONALD V. HORNE, Specialist 4, born Nov. 4, 1946, son of Woodrow and Clarice Horne. He was drafted into the U.S. Army in 1968. Completed advanced infantry training at Fort Ord, CA. Served 12 months in Vietnam with Co. B, 4th Bn., 23rd, 25th Inf. Div.

He participated in many battles around Nu Baden and Ho-Chimen Trail.

When he returned to the States he was stationed at Fort Hood, TX and was part of a tank experiment. He was discharged July 10, 1970.

His decorations include the Combat Infantry Badge, National Defense Service Medal w/ stars, Republic of Vietnam Medal, Bronze Star Medal, two Purple Hearts w/OLC, two Army Commendation Medals w/V Device and Oak Leaf Cluster.

He is married to Freeda C. Horne and has two daughters, Tonya and Rhonda; and one grandson, Alex. He owned and operated Right Beaver Ready-Mix for 30 years in Lackey, KY. He is now disabled.

HAROLD DEE HUGHES, born at Bucks Branch, Martin, KY and he attended Martin Elementary and Martin High School. He served two terms in Vietnam where he was wounded in an ambush. While crossing the Viet Kong River, his patrol boats were sunk with mortar rounds. He woke up in the hospital in Japan.

ROGER D. HUGHES, Lieutenant, USN (Ret.), born Feb. 7, 1944, son of Earl Hughes and Ruby L. Sammons Hughes. He enlisted in the USN in July 1962. He was promoted from E-1 to E-7 prior to receiving his commission in December 1975. He served aboard the USS *South Carolina* and USS *Independence*. He was maintenance chief in Attack Sqdn. 43 and maintenance material control officer in Patrol Sqdn. 23. He earned the Navy Achievement Medal, the National Defense Medal, the Navy Expeditionary Medal, both Presidential and Navy Unit citations, Good Conduct Medal w/2 Bronze Stars and Sea Service Ribbon w/3 Bronze Stars. He retired in January 1985.

Roger married Nancy L. Meade Hughes March 8, 1998. They have three children and eight grandchildren. He received a BSEE Degree from the University of Louisville and worked for Lockheed Martin as a test engineer prior to final retirement. He is a member of the Wheelwright Lodge F&AM #889 and the Prestonsburg Church of Christ.

WILLIAM S. "SAM" HUMBLE, born in Martin, KY enlisted in the U.S. Army in 1961. He was stationed at Fort Bragg, NC and served as a paratrooper. He was discharged in 1964 with rank of Corporal.

Sam is married to Bonnie Stewart and has three children and seven grandchildren. Civilian employment was with General Motors. He currently resides in Milan, MI and enjoys hunting, fishing, gardening and his grandchildren.

CLINTON RAY HUMPHREY, born Sept. 5, 1949 in Ligon, KY. He was enlisted Dec. 9, 1970 into the U.S. Army at Fort Knox, KY where he was a clerk-typist. Tour of duty was Vietnam.

Decorations include: National Defense, Vietnam Service and Campaign Medal, and Army Commendation Medal.

Clinton was discharged July 31, 1972 and was married to Kathy Humphrey. He worked in the heating and cooling business.

Clinton is the late son of Herbert and Nannie Humphrey.

CARL LEE JARRELL, serviced in the USAF enlisting March 17, 1961. He was born Oct. 30, 1940, son of Epp and Millie Jarrell of Dana, KY.

He served four years working as service transportation and ran heavy equipment on flight lines, changing engines on B47 aircraft. He completed basic training at Lackland AFB in San Antonio, TX. He was then sent to Lincoln AFB at Lincoln, NE with the 307th Field Maint. Sqdn. Sac. He received the Good Conduct Medal.

He was married to Sharon Fryzek in January 1965. They had one daughter. He lived in Nebraska and Michigan before returning to the Prestonsburg area in 1977. He retired from Goble Excavating in 1999 due to health reasons. He currently resides in Auxier, KY.

JAMES MANFORD JARRELL, was born on March 2, 1944, the son of Epp and Millie Jarrell at Dana, KY.

While living in Ypsilanti, MI he was drafted in 1965 into the Army. He did his basic training in Fort Knox, KY. He served in Vietnam as front line Supply Sergeant taking supplies to men at the front line combat zones. He served for over two years.

He returned to Ypsilanti, MI, working at Hydr-Matic. He married Ruby Wakeland and they had one son.

While enjoying the summer at the Ford Lake he rescued two men from drowning.

He passed away May 12, 1973 in a car accident.

DONNIE RAY JOHNSON, Specialist 4, born Nov. 21, 1949 at Melvin, KY, son of Robert Lee and Alpha Jean (Little) Johnson. He was drafted into the U.S. Army in 1969, received basic training at Fort Knox, KY and AIT training in Fort Sill, OK, and served 14 months in South Vietnam with C Btry., 1st Bn., 92nd Field Arty. Air Mobile. He participated in the Tet Offensive of 1969 and 1970. The unit moved a total of 39 times in support of the infantry and other artillery units. When he returned to Seattle, WA he was discharged from the U.S. Army on Dec. 15, 1970. His decorations were the National

Defense Medal, Vietnam Service Medal, Vietnam Campaign Medal, two Overseas Bars and Army Accommodations Medal.

Donnie married Debra Kay Jones on June 4, 1971. They had one daughter. He was employed by several coal companies and the U.S. Dept. of Labor, MSHA. Donnie has retired and presently lives at Bevinsville, KY.

He and his wife enjoy camping, wood working and visiting area flea markets.

JIMMIE JOHNSON, born April 10, 1943 at Hi Hat, KY. He enlisted in the U.S. Army Sept. 18, 1969 and was certified in CBR training and RVN training. He re-enlisted while with Section III Ch5, AR 601-208 SPN 313 in Phu Bai, Vietnam. He was reassigned to Co. A, 5th Bn., 101st Abn. "Screamin' Eagles." Jimmie was involved

with the Tet Offensive Attack on Saigon and has many stories and amazing photos of his tours of Vietnam. May 15, 1972 is his discharge date.

He received many citations and commendations for service including two Overseas Bars and the Vietnam Campaign Medal. He is truly a testimony to the brave men and women who served in the Vietnam War.

KENNETH JOHNSON, son of Tab Johnson, served with the U.S. military during the Vietnam War.

Kenneth and his wife Georgie.

LARRY DOUGLAS JOHNSON, son of Garfield Johnson, served with the U.S. Army during the Vietnam War in 1966.

LOWELL JOHNSON, Specialist 4 E-4, born Sept. 4, 1948, son of Melvin and Zetta Johnson. He enlisted in the U.S. Army in 1967 and served six months in Vietnam with RA Inf., Co. A, 4th Bn., 9th Inf., APO. He participated in the search and destroy operation in the vicinity of Tan Long, Republic of Vietnam.

On the afternoon of Jan. 4, 1968, he was wounded and passed away. He was an exemplary soldier who died while serving his country. His decorations include the Bronze Star Medal, Purple Heart and Good Conduct Medal for meritorious service in connection with military operations.

Lowell's family included four brothers and two sisters. Hobbies included hunting and fishing. He was a kind, loving and caring son, brother and friend.

FAIRLEY JONES, SPC4-Corporal, born to Della and Foster Jones Oct. 17, 1945, Grethel, KY. He entered the Army in November 1966 in Detroit, MI. He received basic training at Fort Ord, CA, then was sent to A-Burg Base, Germany where he served 18 months and 26 days. Upon being Honorably Discharged he returned home to work in the auto industry in Michigan and later was a truck driver in the coal industry in Kentucky. He married Lola Vene Mitchell April 21, 1973. The couple still resides at Grethel in Floyd County, KY.

EDGAR KIDD, served in the U.S. Navy, 1960-64, Vietnam.

GEORGE KIDD JR., served in Vietnam.

RONNIE LEEDY, born April 17, 1944, the son of Tolva and Nancy Akers Leedy. He enlisted in the U.S. Army in September 1962. After basic training at Fort Knox, KY he was

stationed at Fort Snelling AFB in Minnesota the rest of his enlistment. He was discharged as a Private First Class on Sept. 13, 1965.

His awards were Sharpshooter and Missileman Badge.

He married Doris Justice on Aug. 24, 1968. They have three children and no grandchildren. Ronnie works for the Floyd County Fiscal Court as a heavy equipment operator.

LARCIE D. LEWIS, born in Prestonsburg, KY enlisted in the U.S. Army March 6, 1967. Basic training was at Fort Knox, KY in 1967. Military locations/stations include Btry. C, 5th Bn., 56th Arty., Dillsboro, IN 1967-69 and HHC, USAG, Fort Wainwright, AK 1969-71. He was discharged March 6, 1971 with rank of Specialist 5 E-5.

Memorable experiences: Earthquake 6.7 on scale in Alaska, winter survival at -60° for three weeks (has seen 105° in the summer, -70° in the winter with -110 chill factor).

He earned Expert Badges - M1 carbine, .45 pistol and M14.

He was a welder for 28 years and was disabled in 2002. He married Charlene Hicks on May 31, 1967 and has four children and six grandchildren. He currently resides in East Point, KY and enjoys woodworking.

JIMMY RAY MARCUM, born in Lawrence County, KY to Everett and Callie Fannin Marcum but moved to Floyd County in 1957 as his father worked for the C&O Railroad. He entered the USN in 1968 and was discharged in 1972. He was stationed in Jacksonville, FL and then in San Diego, CA at Miramar. He served two tours in Vietnam on the USS *Ranger,* an aircraft carrier, and was also in Japan and the Philippines. He came back to Kentucky to begin college and had to go back to San Diego shortly thereafter to be discharged from the USN.

He married Karen Nelson in 1970. They have one son, Jimmy R. "Blue" Marcum II, a daughter-in-law, Krissy Hall Marcum, and two grandsons, Seth and Noah. They live in Floyd County where he has worked for the CSX Railroad for 32 years. *Submitted by Karen Nelson Marcum.*

LOWELL DOUGLAS MARCUM, of Allen, KY did two tours of duty in Vietnam in the U.S. Army. He was a Sergeant. He volunteered for another tour to keep his younger brother, Jimmy, from having to go. On the day Lowell returned from Vietnam through Travis AFB in California, his brother, Jimmy, left from Travis AFB  heading for two tours in Vietnam. They both passed through that day but didn't get to see each other.

He later married Ruth Karen Francis and has a son, Lowell Douglas "Dougie" Marcum. They reside at Allen, KY. He worked for the CSX Railroad. *Submitted by Karen Nelson Marcum.*

RALPH MARCUM, son of Everett and Callie Fannin Marcum, of Allen, KY served in the USAF in Okinawa, Japan from 1961 through 1965. He was with the 498th Tactical Missile Group. He was one of four sons of Everett and Callie who served in the military forces of the U.S. of America.

He returned and married Gloria Gibson of Maytown. They moved to Greenup County and raised their two daughters, Jeanne and Michelle. Ralph retired from Armco Steele. *Submitted by Gloria Marcum and Karen Nelson Marcum.*

CHARLES E. "CHUCK" MAY, born December 1946 to E.B. May Jr. and Allia Moore May. He graduated Prestonsburg High School and Morehead State University and received his Doctorate from University of Kentucky. Chuck married Lynn Gray and they have two sons. Matthew is a major in the USAF and Patrick is employed with Dell Computers in Texas.

Chuck is a retired Captain with the USAF. With his civilian employment they have lived in several states, but are in the process of moving back to Kentucky.

DENNIS MCCOWN, born Sept. 2, 1944 in Ligon, KY, one of the twin sons of Curtis and Thelma McCown. His twin's name is Glennis. He was drafted into the Army Sept. 29, 1965 and discharged July 3, 1967.

He served in the U.S. Army, one year in Massachusetts and one year in Vietnam. He was with the 196th Light Inf. Bde., 4th Bn., 31st Inf. He was in many patrols and ambushes and also a lot of battles in Vietnam, including Operation Junction City and Attleboro.

He received the Army Recommendation Medal.

He was a Sergeant and Honorably Discharged in 1967. Now he and his brother, Glennis, both reside in Michigan.

GLENNIS MCCOWN, born Sept. 2, 1944 in Ligon, KY, one of the twin sons of Curtis and Thelma McCown. His twin's name is Dennis. He was drafted into the Army Sept. 29, 1965 and discharged July 3, 1967.

He served in the U.S. Army, one year in Massachusetts and one year in Vietnam. He was with the 196th Light Inf. Bde., 4th Bn., 31st Inf. He was in many patrols and ambushes and also a lot of battles in Vietnam, including Operation Junction City and Attleboro.

He received the Army Recommendation Medal and the Vietnam Gallantry Cross w/ Bronze Star for heroic action on Feb. 28, 1967.

He was a Sergeant and Honorably Discharged in 1967. Now he and his brother, Dennis, both reside in Michigan.

SCOTTY E. MEADE, Aviation Anti-Submarine Warfare Op. 2, born March 17, 1943. He graduated from McDowell High School in 1961 and enlisted in the USN.

He was a combat aircrewman and radar operator on EC121-K aircraft from 1962 until 1965. He re-enlisted in 1965 and was assigned to Patrol Sqdn. Six. While in VP-Six he served as radar operator and in flight technician on P3-A type aircraft. He made anti-submarine patrols in the Pacific area, including Alaska, Midway Island, Guam, Philippine Island, Japan and Korea. During this period he also was involved in Operation Market Time patrols off the coast of Vietnam.

After duty with VP-6 he was assigned as an instructor with FAETUPAC in San Diego, CA, where he taught anti-submarine techniques.

He received the following medals: Aircrew Wings, (two) Navy Unit Citations, (two) Good Conduct Medals, Vietnam Service, Navy Expedition Medal (Korea 1968) and National Defense Medal.

Scotty is retired from Anheuser Busch. He married Mable Owens of Columbus, OH in December 1965. They have three children and four grandchildren.

WENDELL MEADE, Specialist 5, born Nov. 16, 1941 in Amba, KY, son of Annie and Willie Meade. He was inducted into the Army in 1966 and sent to Fort Sam Houston, TX for medical specialist training. He courageously served in the battle zones of Vietnam, earning the Distinguished Service Cross, which was presented to him by Vice President Humphrey and General Westmoreland. In May 1967 he was wounded, earning the Purple Heart.

He returned to Floyd County in October 1967 and married Nellie Parsons in January 1968. They were blessed with a daughter, son and eventually, a treasured son-in-law.

Though his occupations varied, he was dedicated to his role as a Church of Christ minister. His faith, the reason for his conscientious objector status, sustained him throughout his life. He passed away Feb. 25, 2005 at the VAMC in Lexington of an Agent Orange related cancer.

JOHN DAVID MERRITT, Technical Sergeant, born Aug. 26, 1940 in Emma, KY to Dean Robert and Wilma Leslie Merritt. He graduated from Prestonsburg High School and entered the Air Force. He served on Cam Rahn Bay, the Philippines and Seoul, Korea.

John married Lauren Deanna Martin in Tampa, FL. They had two children who still reside in Florida. They are Deanna Leslie Merritt Bouchillon and David Winfield Merritt. He is survived by four grandchildren. They are John Philip Packer, Danielle Lauren Bouchillon, Jessica Dean Bouchillon and Dean Jarrod Merritt, all of Florida. His brothers and sisters were Clara Deanna May of Martin, KY; Rhonda Howard and Delores Reichenbach of Prestonsburg, KY; and Curtis Merritt of Gunlock, KY. One brother, Robert Taylor Merritt, formerly of Allen, KY, passed away March 6, 1988, in Lexington, KY.

John was an avid hunter and fisherman while growing up in Emma. He enjoyed fishing in Florida. He mentioned he wanted to retire in Floyd County, but suffered a brain aneurysm and passed away in Korea, Aug. 8,

1976. His body was interred in the Garden of Memories Cemetery, Tampa, FL. His memory lives on. *Submitted by his sister, Delores Merritt Reichenbach.*

LARRY M. MOSLEY, born Oct. 20, 1946 at Martin, KY. His parents were Chester W. and Ruth O. Mosley. Larry was inducted into the U.S. Army in June 1966, completing his basic training at Fort Jackson, SC. He later completed AIT at Fort Sill, OK specializing in artillery.

He was stationed in Dexheim, Germany at the Anderson Barracks from October 1966 to May 1968. His classification was Army AUFCED demolition expert. Larry also qualified as expert with both rifle and pistol. Larry's medals were National Defense Service Medal, Good Conduct Medal and he received an Honorable Discharge. He obtained the rank of E-5 Specialist with Co. B, 12th Engr. Bn.

After living briefly in Michigan, Larry returned to Kentucky. He worked as an electrician for the coal mining industry. He retired in 2001 and enjoys spending time fishing and hunting.

He has three daughters and seven grandchildren. Larry currently resides at Melvin, KY.

CHARLIE MUSIC, born Feb. 3, 1944. He enlisted in the U.S. Army as a radio teletype operator. He was stationed in Fort Knox, Fort Gordon, Fort Meade, Germany and Vietnam. He earned the Vietnam Service Medal, National Defense Medal, Republic of Vietnam Campaign w/device, Vietnam Campaign Medal w/ Overseas Service Bars and the Good Conduct Medal. He was discharged June 29, 1977 with the rank of Specialist 4.

Charlie's civilian employment was with American Standard maintenance department for 33 years. He is retired now and is a deacon in the Auxier Free Will Baptist Church. He is also Fire Chief with the Auxier Volunteer Fire Department and enjoys Crappie fishing in Alabama.

GRADY NELSON, son of Hiland and Martha Osborne Nelson of Floyd County, KY.

He served in the U.S. Army and was stationed in Germany. He had four brothers: Sam, Will, Jack and Ted, who all served in WWII. His brother, Jack, also served with the U.S. Army. *Submitted by Karen Nelson Marcum.*

JACK NELSON SR., born on March 8, 1935 in Floyd County, KY was the son of Hiland and Martha Osborne Nelson. He was a Private First Class (E3) USAR discharged June 30, 1973.

On Aug. 1, 1964 when he was 29, he first married Annis Gertrude Craft. On Oct. 7, 1983 when he was 48, he second married Edna Carol Hackworth Prater. He was a heavy equipment operator for the Floyd County Road Department. He was a member of the Town Branch Enterprise Baptist Church. He attended school in Floyd County, KY and took welding at Mayo Vocation School.

He was killed in a dozer accident on Left Fork of Abbott Creek after the 1984 flood. He was working a mudslide near Henderson Bays when the dozer jumped out of gear. He was 49 years old. He was buried in the Osbourn Cemetery, Hagar Hill, KY.

PHILIP R. "PHIL" NELSON, born May 23, 1934 at Paintsville, KY, the son of Lula Meade Nelson and George Nelson. He later moved to Prestonsburg, KY.

He entered the U.S. Army in August 1956. Basic training was at Fort Chaffee, AR. He was then flown to Germany and stationed with the 7th Army attached to the 29 Transportation Co., a helicopter division made up of H19 and H34 troop carriers. They were located just outside of Stuttgart in West Germany. While there he was Company Clerk, his office was on the back of a two and one-half ton Army truck. The company was 100% mobile - they could pack and leave within one hour to go to any downed helicopter. He spent 45 days TDY in Munich. Phil was in Germany for about 19 months. He then served in a reserve unit in Prestonsburg, KY. While in the Reserve, his Commanding Officer was C.J. McNally and his First Sergeant was Don Osborne.

Phil married Emma Thomas (now deceased) and they had two sons, John and Kevin Nelson. Phil is now married to Marena Watson Hale and resides at Martin, KY.

TOM NELSON, son of Ted and Helena Warrix Nelson of Prestonsburg, was born in 1949 and served in the U.S. Army from 1968-71.

He is married to Earlene Newsome Nelson and they have four children: Paige, Kristi, Josh and Alison.

VIGIS SAMUEL "SAMMY" NELSON, son of Sam and Mildred Steele Nelson, served in the U.S. Army where he was stationed in Kitzingen, West Germany from Aug. 11, 1970 through March 11, 1972. His discharge date was Aug. 10, 1976. His mother and grandmother did not want him to go to Germany as his uncle and namesake, Vigis Steele, was killed there during WWII at the age of 22.

Cleaning off the grave of his uncle, Vigus Steele, killed in WW II.

He later married Theresa Blackburn. They had three sons. The oldest, Lewis Samuel Nelson, was born Sept. 23, 1978 and died Oct. 3, 1978. His other two sons are Dustin and Robert "Robby." *Submitted by Karen Nelson Marcum and Sammy Nelson.*

EARNEST SAMUEL NITCHIE, served in the U.S. Army Sept. 28, 1966 to Aug. 4, 1968; basic training at Fort Benning, GA; served with 83rd Armd. Div. one year and Armored Cavalry one year. Served in Vietnam August 1967 to August 1968.

He and his wife, Marilyn, live in Ada, OH. They have three children and nine grandchildren.

He is the son of John and Mattie Nitchie of Hunter. Lived in Hunter and graduated from eighth grade at Martin before moving to Ohio with his family. He is the brother of Charles Victor "Pete," Minnie, Mae Salisbury and Clara Cross.

CLARENCE MICHAEL OSBORNE, Sergeant, son of Edgar and Dorothy Rone Osborne, was born Jan. 20, 1944 at Maytown (Langley) KY. He attended three years of school at Maytown and then moved with his family to Payne, OH where he graduated from Payne Public School.

He entered the U.S. Army on Jan. 21, 1965 and went to Fort Knox, KY for basic training. He was in Branch B, 1st Battalion 10th Artillery. He served in Stuttgart, Germany and was discharged in April 1967. He has two children, Christopher Michael and Anita Gayle Osborne, and two grandchildren.

DENNIS OSBORNE, of Ivel, KY was born in Dayton, OH July 28, 1948. He was drafted into the military in April 1968. He served two years after a tour of Vietnam and was discharged in April 1970.

He married Wanda Goble of Ivel and moved to Lebanon, OH where he lived for five years and moved back to Kentucky in 1975. Dennis and Wanda have two children, Brian and Kristy, and four grandchildren.

He operated a body shop for almost 25 years. Now he and Wanda operate a small fiberglass business at Ivel that produces Foxcrofth Insulated Doghouses. In his spare time he enjoys fishing and riding his Harley Davidson motorcycle.

CHARLES RAY "BUCK" OWENS, born in Knott County, KY March 26, 1947. He enlisted in the USN July 6, 1966; classification, AO3; division, GV. He served aboard USS *Yorktown* (CVS-10), homeport Norfolk, VA. Military locations: Boston, MA; Scotland; England; South America; aboard ship in the Atlantic Ocean; crossed Equator - Arctic Circle.

His awards/medals include the National Defense Service Medal and Good Conduct Medal. Date of discharge was April 16, 1970 as an E4.

Civilian employment with Kentucky West Virginia Gas Co. (meter inspector). He is married to Elizabeth Rowe Owens and has one child, Angela Owens Williamson and two grandchildren, Emily Elizabeth and Hevin Nicole. His hobbies are camping, fishing and hunting.

PAUL CALVIN PATTON, born on April 22, 1948 in Paintsville, KY. He was enlisted into the U.S. Army in October 1969 as a Specialist E-4, Fixed Station Communications. He was located at Fort Knox, KY; Fort Monmouth, NJ; and the Vietnam Police Action.

Missions he participated in were Top Secret Communications. Mr. Patton received several awards and accommodations for his efforts in Vietnam.

He is the son of George and Mosaleete Patton of Langley, KY. George was married to Sandra Lihoski of Pennsylvania and Sharon Reed Patton of Prestonsburg and has five children, three sons and two daughters; 12 grandchildren; and 11 great-grandchildren.

Paul currently lives in Lexington and is self-employed in communications.

CLAUDE B. RATLIFF, the son of Olive Wicker Ratliff, enlisted in the U.S. Army in October 1972. Then, Kentucky National Guard-Army Reserve in 1979. He is a Military Police Officer. Completed basic training at Fort Knox and Advanced MP training at Fort Campbell.

Claude married Reginia Maciag July 20, 1972 and they have one child, Jeremy. He graduated from Eastern Kentucky University with a BSW Degree. He was discharged in 2006 with the rank of Staff Sergeant E-6.

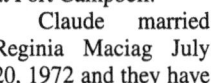

Civilian employment is with the Kentucky State Department, Assistant Coordinator of Veterans Programs. Claude enjoys woodworking and gardening.

KENNETH W. RATLIFF, born Nov. 16, 1950 at Martin, KY, son of Olive Wicker Ratliff. He enlisted in the U.S. Army Nov. 29, 1967 with the 25th Inf. Div. He is basic C-10-5, advance D-2-1 Fort Knox ACO 2nd, 34th Armor Vietnam, stations include Chu Chi, Tay Nimh. He was discharged Nov. 27, 1970.

He was also in the Kentucky National Guard from 1974-85.

His awards include the Vietnam Service Medal, Vietnam Campaign Medal w/2 Overseas Bars, two Bronze Stars, Army Commendation Medal and Combat Infantryman Badge.

Kenneth married Sheilah Jones on May 26, 1973. Sheilah is a teacher at Duff Elementary. They have one daughter, Nikki and two grandchildren, Isabella and Therese. Kenneth is a retired coal miner, now enjoying woodworking, gardening and playing banjo and guitar.

GOBLE REED JR., born Nov. 27, 1935 in Hippo, KY, was in the U.S. Army in intelligence analyst/counterintelligence. Military stations include Fort Knox, KY; Aberdeen, MD; East Chicago, Gary, IN; 8th Army Korea; Fort Hood, TX; Vietnam; Offutt AFB, Omaha, NE; USPAC Hawaii; Thailand; Panama Canal Zone; Germany; and West Point, NY. Tour of duty in Vietnam was 24 months.

Mr. Reed's most memorable experience while in the military is when he met his wife of 40 years, Martha Woods Reed. They spent two and one-half years honeymooning in Hawaii.

His awards and medals include the Bronze Star Medal, Joint Service Commendation Medal (third Oak Leaf Cluster), Army Commendation Medal (first Oak Leaf Cluster), Meritorious Service Medal, Good Conduct Medal (seventh award), National Defense Service Medal, Korea Service Medal, 1 Overseas Bar (four), Overseas Service Ribbon (four), Army Service Ribbon, Vietnam Campaign Medal w/60 Device, Driver and Mechanic Badge, and M16, M1 and M14 Sharpshooter Badge.

Military training includes parts specialist, intelligence analyst, emergency medical care, chemical (CBR), ballistic missile, staff course, and Honeywell 6000 Data Management System.

Goble Reed Jr. is the son of Goble and Rebecca Hughes Reed. He currently lives in Waco, TX.

CHARLES WAYNE REICHENBACH, Sergeant E-5, born July 8, 1946 in Mt. Sterling, KY, son of Carl and Nancye Reichenbach. He was drafted into the U.S. Army on Sept. 4, 1969. His basic infantry and radio operators training was at Fort Knox, KY.

After his training he served nine months in Schwabisch Gmund, Germany in HQ Btry. of the 4th Bn., 41st Field Arty. of the 7th Army. He received a Top Secret Clearance and rapidly attained the rank of Sergeant, E-5. He was involved in high level coded communications in this Pershing nuclear missile unit. In this unit he was awarded the Pershing Professional Badge.

In early December 1970, he reported to Quang Tri, Vietnam to the most northern U.S. military unit stationed in South Vietnam on the DMZ. He was assigned to the "Pioneers" of the 1st Bn., 11th Inf., 1st Bde., 5th Mecz. Inf. Div. The Pioneers were a walking infantry unit air assaulted by helicopter to secure enemy held territory and to serve as a security force at many firebases.

He was among the first 10 men air assaulted from Quang Tri to Khe Sanh in late January 1971. Their assignment was to secure the old Khe Sanh airfield now in enemy territory until armored and engineering units could arrive. This operation was called Dewey Canyon II. He also continued near the border with Laos in a follow up operation called Lam Son 719. This operation secured the roads and territory in Northern and Western South Vietnam for the South Vietnamese army to invade Laos to break up supply lines. He was awarded the Bronze Star and Army Commendation Medal.

He returned to his wife, the former Delores Merritt of Emma, KY. He continued his job as a civil engineer for the Kentucky Highway Department retiring in 2002. They have lived in Prestonsburg, KY since 1981. They have two sons, Jason and Justin, and a grandson, Lucas.

GARY LEE RICE, Private, USMC, received the Purple Heart during the Vietnam War. Gary was born Jan. 29, 1948 and died April 10, 1985.

Gary is buried just past the Junction of US 23 and Route 80 at Bull Creek on the left side of the road inside a fenced cemetery. *Submitted by Karen Nelson Marcum.*

JACKIE DAVID RICE, born April 21, 1941 in Prestonsburg, KY. He enlisted in the U.S. Army Oct. 20, 1962 and served with Co. C, Special Troops, USA ARMC. He was stationed in Fort Knox, KY. Rice was discharged Sept. 15, 1968 as a Private E-2.

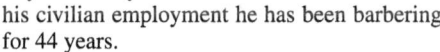

He is the son of Raleigh and Dialphia Rice and is married to Phyllis Ousley Rice. In his civilian employment he has been barbering for 44 years.

MONTIE DELANO RICE, born July 23, 1938 in East Point, KY, enlisted in the USAF in February 1961. He served as an Airman First Class with HQ Sqdn. Military locations, stations include Lackland AFB, San Antonio, TX; Shepherd AFB, Wichita Falls, TX; and Lockbourne AFB, Columbus, OH. He was discharged in February 1964.

Rice was awarded the Good Conduct Medal.

He is married to Barbara Blackburn and has two daughters, Monica Rice and Melissa Madden; and one granddaughter. He is retired from Bell South Telephone Company. Current activities: enjoying retirement.

SID RICHARDSON, born in Grand Raven, MI on Sept. 25, 1939, enlisted in September 1959 in the USN Underwater Weapons Div. Military locations include NAD West Lock, HI; NAS Sanford, Philippines; and NOF Yokdoquka, Japan.

He received the Good Conduct Medal w/cluster and Vietnam Support. He was discharged in December 1967.

Mr. Richardson was employed with General, Otis Doyer, Tissen Elevator companies for 34 years. He and his wife, Myrtle (Hall) Richardson have seven children: Jon, Laura, Dan, Cindy, Lisa, Gary and Heather; 10 grandchildren; and two great-grandchildren. He resides at Hager Hill, KY and enjoys hunting and fishing.

ELLIS ROBINSON, born May 27, 1945 at Dwale, KY, enlisted in the U.S. Army July 1964 as Specialist 4. He served at Fort Knox, Fort Benning, Japan and Vietnam as a field crewman communications paratrooper and carried machine guns and grenade launchers in the Vietnam Conflict for 13 months.

He received the Army Commendation Medal and Expert Firing Medals. He was discharged in November 1967.

He was employed in the plumbing, painting and electrical industries. He married Denise Robinson and enjoys gardening and yard work.

LLOYD H. ROBINSON, born Feb. 16, 1948 in Marshall, MI, enlisted in the U.S. Army Feb. 26, 1968 as an airborne paratrooper. His military locations, stations include Fort Knox; Fort Gordon, GA; Fort Benning, GA; Parat Chu Chi Vietnam; Long Benh and Ben Hoa. He participated in the Tet Offensive. Robinson was discharged Sept. 16, 1969 as E-4 Specialist.

Memorable experiences: His best friend, Leslie Rosecrans. He was killed three days before wounded along Cambodian Border.

His awards/medals include the Purple Heart, Combat Infantry Badge, Bronze Star, Army Accommodation Medal and Vietnam Ribbons.

Civilian employment: American Standard, Prestonsburg, KY; Roberts & Schaefor Construction Co., Chicago, IL; and Associate Electric Coop. Inc., Moberly, MO. His family includes Tara Reed Robinson and Amanda Robinson. He currently enjoys bowling, fishing, going to church, and serving or doing for others.

GARY ROSE, born April 4, 1946 to the late Orville and Myrtle Rose of Hi Hat, KY, enlisted into the USN in 1964, completed basic training at Fort Knox and Fort Dix, NJ. Gary's first assignment was with the 3rd Inf. at Fort Myers, VA where he served in the Honor Guard. In 1965, he was sent to Vietnam where he served one year with Co. A, 1st Bn., 18th Inf. of 1st Inf. Div. (Big Red One). He achieved the rank of Sergeant E-5.

Gary's MOS was 11 B 20, light weapons infantryman and he served as an automatic rifleman and squad leader in Vietnam.

His decorations include the Combat Infantry Badge, Vietnam Service Medal, National Defense Service Medal, Vietnam Campaign Medal, Presidential Unit Citation and the Good Conduct Medal.

He was Honorably Discharged in 1967 and later married Yulanda Lucas. They have three children and four grandchildren. Gary was employed by the Kentucky State Police for 32 years and is now retired.

JOHN B. RUNYON, born Aug. 30, 1942 at Pikeville, KY, enlisted in the U.S. Army Feb. 24, 1964 and served with the Army Engineers, 65th Army Postal Unit. His military locations, stations were Fort Belvoir, VA and Grafenwohr Germany. He was discharged Feb. 24, 1967 as Specialist Fourth Class.

On July 2, 1984 he enlisted in the USAR, Combat Engineers, Pikeville, KY where he served for 11 years and eight months. He was discharged in March 1995 as Sergeant First Class E-7.

In March 1995 he enlisted in the Army Kentucky National Guard, Combat Engineers in Prestonsburg, KY. He retired Aug. 30, 2002 as Sergeant First Class after 21 years in the military.

His awards/medals include the National Defense Medal, Good Conduct Medal and Army Achievement Award.

Civilian employment as a mine inspector. He currently resides in Dana, KY.

ANTHONY R. "TONY" SALISBURY, served in the U.S. Army from 1965 to 1967 with the Military Police and served in Italy during the Vietnam War.

He is the son of Blaine and Mae Salisbury, who left Hunter in 1954. Blaine went north to find work and ended up in St. Marys, OH at the Goodyear Plant. Unfortunately Blaine died in an auto accident in 1957 in St. Marys. Wife, Mae, remained in St. Marys and raised their four children: Anthony (deceased 2003), Frances, Kenneth and Danny.

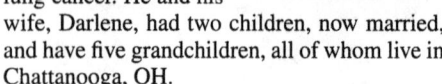

Tony passed away at the age of 57 from lung cancer. He and his wife, Darlene, had two children, now married, and have five grandchildren, all of whom live in Chattanooga, OH.

DANNY SALISBURY, served in the U.S. Army a few months from 1971 to 1972 and received a medical discharge due to complications with his shoulder.

He and his wife, Valerie, reside in St. Marys, OH and have two children and three grandchildren.

He is the son of Blaine and Mae Salisbury who left Hunter in 1954. Blaine went north to find work and ended up in St. Marys, OH at the Goodyear Plant. Unfortunately Blaine died in an auto accident in 1957 in St. Marys. Wife, Mae, remained in St. Marys and raised their four children: Anthony (deceased 2003), Frances, Kenneth and Danny.

KENNETH "DALE" SALISBURY, served in the USN from 1967 to 1971. He served in Vietnam; served on USS *Blue* and USS *Chicago*; attaining the rank BT 2 (E-5).

He currently lives in St. Marys, OH with his wife, Nancy, and has three married children and six grandchildren. He works at Goodyear in St. Marys.

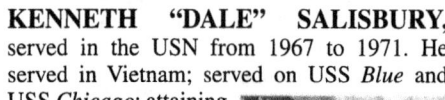

Dale is the son of Blaine and Mae Salisbury, who left Hunter in 1954. Blaine went north to find work and ended up in St. Marys, OH at the Goodyear Plant. Unfortunately Blaine died in an auto accident in 1957 in St. Marys. Wife, Mae, remained in St. Marys and raised their four children: Anthony (deceased 2003), Frances, Kenneth and Danny.

LAWRENCE SALISBURY, born July 2, 1950 to Paul F. and Nellis Laferty Salisbury. He entered the Navy in 1968 and served until 1972. He was in Vietnam from July 1970 to July 1971.

ORVILLE DAVID SCUTCHFIELD, born on Nov. 28, 1948 to Ermal "Bub" and Maurine Scutchfield. He followed in his father's footsteps when he enlisted in the USN on Oct. 19, 1969.

He was stationed at the NS at Newport, RI. He also served aboard the USS *Charles P. Cecil* (DD-835). He received the National Defense Service Medal. He received an Honorable Discharge and was in Naval Reserve.

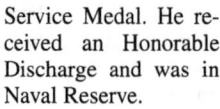

He married Donna Griffith and they had one son, Bryan. David moved to Warsaw, IN and worked at Dalton Industries before retiring in 2000 due to medical problems. He currently resides at Prestonsburg, KY.

ALLEN FRANKLIN SHELTON, Specialist 4, born Aug. 14, 1947, of Drift, KY, son of Loraine Whitt Shelton and Eugene Shelton. He entered the U.S. Army Feb. 8, 1968, and completed his AIT at Fort Polk, LA. He served seven months in the jungles of Vietnam with the 1st Bn., 8th Inf., 4th Inf. Div.

He was injured in combat on Jan. 30, 1969 and was retired with physical disability June 30, 1970. His decorations include: Vietnam Service Medal w/2 Bronze Service Stars, Purple Heart, Army Good Conduct Medal, Overseas Bars (two), Republic of Vietnam Civil Actions Honor Medal First Class Unit Citation Badge, Republic of Vietnam Gallantry Cross w/Palm Unit Citation Badge and Combat Infantryman Badge.

Allen married Ruth Dingus of Martin, KY on Feb. 5, 1970 and they have three children and one granddaughter.

Allen was employed by National Mines Corp. of Wayland, KY for many years. For the last several years he has enjoyed turkey hunting and fishing.

TERRY EUGENE SHELTON, Builder Chief Petty Officer (BUC), USN Seabees (Ret.), born Dec. 24, 1945, son of Eugene Shelton and the late Loraine Whitt Shelton. Enlisted Dec. 29, 1965 with six weeks boot camp in Great Lakes, IL. Reported aboard the USS *Munser* (ATF-107) in February 1966 until September 1969. The ship was homeported in San Diego, CA. While aboard the USS *Munser* they made two deployments to Adak, AK. Deployed

to Vietnam and accomplished several missions. Was on standby to retrieve the USS *Peblo*. This picture made front page of "*All Hands*" as the look out in 1968. Transferred to Naval Weapons Station, Yorktown, VA. Discharged April 1971.

Re-enlisted October 1973 through October 1988 in the USN Seabees. Homeported out of Gulf, MS. Seabees are the construction of the Navy. Their moto is "Can Do." When the Navy or Marines need something constructed the Seabees are sent to do the job. The Seabees made life worth living, made dreams come true.

He received five Good Conduct Awards, M16-A1 Rifle Expert Medals, 45 Pistol Expert Medal, Navy Expeditionary Medal, Navy Battles "E" w/3 'E's, Meritorious Unit Commendation Ribbon, Vietnam Service Medal w/2 Bronze Stars, Vietnam Campaign Medal, National Defense Service Medal/Sea, plus several awards, letters and commendations.

Married Brenda J. Franklin May 25, 1974. Favorite pastime is deer hunting and fishing.

PHYLLIS FULTON SHEPHERD, wife of Ballard Lee Shepherd, joined the Woman's Army Corps (WAC) in June 1969.

RALPH WHEELER SHEPHERD, born in 1938 and died in 1969, served in the U.S. Army in Germany. His family was Paul David and wife, Jessica Lee Shepherd, and grandchildren Jeremy Paul and Courtney Alison Shepherd.

JERRY SIMPSON, born Nov. 2, 1946 in Williamson, VA. He was in the U.S. Army and was stationed in Fort Knox, Fort Polk, Fort Bragg and the U.S. Army Morta, KY. Mr. Simpson was an embalmer in the U.S. Army Mortuary.

Upon his discharge on Feb. 8, 1970, he went on to pursue a career in mortuary science with several funeral homes throughout the Big Sandy Area. He is a member of the Disabled American Veterans.

JOE R. SKEENS, born Oct. 21, 1943, son of Joe "Jay" Skeens and Virginia M. Akers. He served in the U.S. Army from April 21, 1961 to April 20, 1964. He served two tours in Berlin, Germany during the Berlin Crisis while the wall dividing East and West Berlin was being built and was with Operation Big Lift. He was a Medical Specialist with the 2nd Armd. Div. He has one daughter, Tammy, and a granddaughter, Hanna.

Joe started looking for his great-grandfather's grave, George

Skeens, a Civil War veteran many years ago. He searched for 10 years before finding him buried in Oldtown, Greenup County, KY. The information was not on his military papers. Since his search for his great-grandfather began, he has written 16 volumes of *Cemetery Books of Eastern Kentucky Cemeteries* as well as 17 other books with historical information concerning this area. *Photo from Joe Skeens. Submitted by Karen N. Marcum.*

EUGENE SPARKMAN, 62, of Minnie, died Sunday, December 5, at the McDowell Appalachian Hospital, following a short illness.

He was born Sept. 10, 1937, in Knott County, the son of the late Irvin Sparkman and Hazel Slone Sparkman. He was a retired Kentucky West Virginia Gas Company warehouse employee and a U.S. Army veteran.

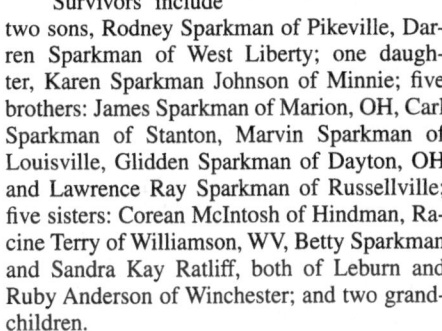

He is survived by his wife, Anna Dean Williams Sparkman.

Survivors include two sons, Rodney Sparkman of Pikeville, Darren Sparkman of West Liberty; one daughter, Karen Sparkman Johnson of Minnie; five brothers: James Sparkman of Marion, OH, Carl Sparkman of Stanton, Marvin Sparkman of Louisville, Glidden Sparkman of Dayton, OH and Lawrence Ray Sparkman of Russellville; five sisters: Corean McIntosh of Hindman, Racine Terry of Williamson, WV, Betty Sparkman and Sandra Kay Ratliff, both of Leburn and Ruby Anderson of Winchester; and two grandchildren.

TIMOTHY WADE SPARKS, son of Albert and Betty Lou Shepherd Sparks. Grandson of Elizie and Trinnie Shepherd. Great-grandson of Johnnie Lee and Minnie Davis Hall. He served in the USN aboard USS *Woodrow Wilson*. He now resides in Connecticut.

BONNIE STEWART, served in the USMC in 1961-62 at Cherry Point, NC. She was discharged in 1964 with the rank of Corporal.

Civilian employment is as Senior Vice-President of IBA State Beauty College.

Bonnie married William S. Humble and they have three children and seven grandchildren. She enjoys traveling, gardening, sewing, reading and spending time with the grandchildren. She now lives in Milan, MI.

LARRY EDWARD STRATTON, born on April 16, 1944 in Prestonsburg, KY, the son of Edward and Celia Stratton of Ivel.

He enlisted in the Army in May 1965. Larry was stationed both in Fort Knox, KY and Cleveland, OH. He was sent to Okinawa, Japan, where he served during the Vietnam War, until returning home in 1968. Upon completion of his service he was an E5, Non-Commissioned Officer.

Married on Thanksgiving Day 1966, Larry and his wife, Gwendolyn, have three daughters and four grandchildren. He was employed by CSX Transportation as a locomotive engineer from 1971 until his retirement in 2004.

Larry currently resides in Ivel where he devotes his time to his parents and his grandchildren. He enjoys biking and fishing and loves to entertain others with tales of his days spent in the Army.

LINDSEY STRICKLIN, born Nov. 8, 1943 to Pat and Maggie Hatfield Stricklin of Lancer, KY. He enlisted in the U.S. Army April 4, 1963, trained at Fort Knox with Army Unit RA-ACG and U.S. Army Administration Center, St. Louis, MO. He completed specialist school in Fort Ord, CA. He served in Korea as a mail clerk. He received the Good Conduct Medal and Marksman Badge (M-14 Rifle). He was Honorably Discharged April 1, 1969.

Lindsey first married Sandra Farrow and they had three children: Mike, Earl and Salley. Then, married Elaine Setser of Prestonsburg. He was a construction foreman in Greenville, SC. He enjoyed gardening, fishing and hunting. He was a member of Mercy Christian Outreach, Piedmont, SC. He passed away June 6, 2000. He is buried in Rose Hill Cemetery, Piedmont, SC.

CHARLES LOY STUMBO, born in Whitesburg, KY, was the son of Valta and William "Bill" Stumbo. He was raised in McDowell, KY by his god-parents, June and Paul Hopkins of Doty Creek, McDowell, KY.

His most memorable experience was being a proud veteran and serving his Country. He also enjoyed and loved playing baseball.

He enlisted in the Army July 14, 1964 in Ashland, KY. He was trained in Fort Benning, GA. He served in the service for 23 months. He was in the Vietnam War. His awards and medals were the National Defense Medal, Marksman Rifle, Vietnam Service Medal and Good Conduct Medal. His rank achieved was Private First Class E-3 (P). He was discharged July 10, 1969 with an Honorable Discharge.

Charles married Patricia Isaac of Martin, KY Aug. 22, 1970. They had one son, Charles "Kevin" Stumbo, and two grandchildren, Lauryn and Cameron of Martin, KY.

Charles was a coal miner for 28 years and enjoyed it until he became disabled in 1994. He passed away May 5, 1998 and is now resting in the Isaac Cemetery at Dinwood, Martin, KY.

GREGORY R. STUMBO, Buck Sergeant E-5, born Aug. 29, 1947, is the son of Granville and Clova Stumbo. He was drafted into the U.S. Army on May 13, 1968 at Fort Knox, KY where he spent one year for basic training, Armor AIT Armor NCO School and OJT. He went on to Vietnam with the Blackhorse, 11th Armd. Cav. where he was wounded and received the Combat Infantry Badge, Bronze Star, Purple Heart, Vietnam Service Medal, National Defense, Vietnam Campaign Ribbon, Gallantry Cross w/palm, eight Bronze Campaign Stars for ever major battle, Good Conduct Medal, Sharp Shooter Medal and four Unit Citations. He was discharged on April 24, 1970.

Greg married Kathy Shannon on Sept. 21, 1968. They have three children and eight grandchildren. He was employed as a coal industry repairman for 28 years.

He resides in Drift, KY and he is a disabled veteran and is into woodcrafts, church and fishing.

JACK STUMBO, served in U.S. Army from August 1959 through December 1962. He was in Berlin, Germany April 1960 through April 1961 and Frankfurt, Germany April 1961 through April 1962. He was with the U.S. Army Security Agency.

He served in Vietnam April 1962 through December 1962 with the 351st U.S. Army Asia Recon

Group. Discharged December 1962 as Specialist First Class E-6.

FRANK SWEENEY, born March 1, 1938, enlisted in the U.S. Military in 1950. He served with the HQ Co., HQ Command FORSCOM as an Armor Recon Specialist and Armor Crewman. Stations include Vietnam, Germany and Fort Riley, KS.

He received a Bronze Star w/V, Army Commendation Medal w/OLC, Air Medal, Good Conduct Medal, National Defense Medal, Combat Infantry Badge, Republic of Vietnam Campaign Ribbon, Republic of Vietnam

Cross of Gallantry, Expert Rifle Marksman 45 cal. Pistol and the Aircraft Crewman Badge. He was discharged March 31, 1978.

DAVID LEE TACKETT, son of Newberry and Pearl Hall Tackett, grandson of Johnnie Lee and Minnie Davis Hall. Served in the U.S. Army in Vietnam. He now resides in Marshall, MI.

ANCEL JAMES TERRY, from Allen (Dwale), KY, was in the Army. He went to Vietnam in September 1970 and was killed in April 1971. He was a Corporal when he died of land shrapnel injuries.

He was brought home, had a military funeral and is buried in Davidson Memorial Gardens, Ivel, KY. He was not married and left no children. *Submitted by friend, Freda Campbell.*

PAUL HUNT THOMPSON, born Sept. 26, 1946 in Sharpsburg, KY enlisted in the USMC Infantry/Logistics, 1st Marine Div. He had basic training at Parris Island, SC and infantry training at Camp Geiger, SC. He was with the 3rd AMTRAC Bn., 1st Marine Div. in Vietnam. He was discharged in January 1969 as a Sergeant.

Thompson participated in numerous combat operations in conjunction with Infantry Battalion of the 1st Marine Div., primarily with 1st Bn., 1st Marine Regt.

His awards/medals include the Navy Unit Citation, China Service Medal, U.S. Vietnam Service Medal w/3 Campaign Stars, South Vietnam Medal, Presidential Unit Citation, Good Conduct Medal, Rifle Sharpshooter and Pistol Expert.

Civilian employment: grocery store proprietor, Floyd County Sheriff and Floyd County Judge Executive.

Thompson has three sons: Paul Norman, Charlie and John Emit; one stepson; one stepdaughter; and eight grandchildren: C.C., Frankie, Tyler, Mollie, Kierra, Megan, Paul Zach and Emma. He currently resides in Wheelwright, KY and enjoys camping.

NICKEY D. TURNER, enlisted in the USMC during his senior year in college and after receiving his degree and completing boot camp was commissioned a Lieutenant.

In 1972 he founded a bank in Sterling, VA and at the age of 32 became the youngest bank president in the U.S. Nick is President of WSC Holdings, Inc. and Chairman of Washington Securities Corporation in Chevy Chase, MD. He is an Adjunct Professor of Finance for three universities and serves on the Senate Finance Committee of National Louis University where he is a Fellow.

A graduate of Maytown High, Bowling Green Business University, he received his Master's from National Louis University. He is a Kentucky Colonel and one of the few recipients of the Patrick Henry Award presented by Virginia Governor Gilmore.

Nick met Corene Gibson, a McDowell High graduate, at college. They were married in 1960 and live in Vienna, VA. They have one son and two grandsons.

Nick is the son of the late Jake Turner Jr. and James E. Allen and Violet Coburn Allen.

EDDIE DARRELL VANDERPOOL, Sergeant, born Aug. 7, 1947 to Sage and Dorothy Wells Vanderpool of Weeksbury, KY. He enlisted into the U.S. Army on Nov. 16, 1966. He was wounded in Vietnam and is totally disabled. Sgt. Vanderpool received the National Defense Medal, Republic of Vietnam Campaign Medal w/60 device, Air Medal, Purple Heart, Bronze Star Medal w/device, Combat Infantry Badge, one Officers Service Bar, VCOFG, Vietnam Service Medal w/5 CC, Expoval Badge M-16 Rifle, M60MG MKMoval Badge, M-14.

Eddie married Dian Ashcraft and had a daughter, Kathy Marie. He and Dian later divorced and he then married Robin Wade and they have three daughters. Lisa Marie, married Jeff Castle and they have a son named Ty. Shana Kie and Selena Lyne Vanderpool are both studying medicine.

Eddie was discharged on Aug. 20, 1975. He worked for AT&T and construction.

LARRY EDWIN VANDERPOOL, born June 15, 1949 to Sage and Dorothy Wells Vanderpool of Weeksbury, KY. He served in the U.S. Army during Vietnam. However, he did not go to Vietnam, he spent two years in the service.

Larry married Lisa Blackburn. They had one daughter, Lindsay. Larry and Lisa divorced and he later married Dorcie Betten from New York. They had two sons, Travis Sage and Kyle John Vanderpool.

Larry was an expert rifleman. After he was discharged he worked in construction. Larry passed away in 2004. He was the grandson of William "Bill" and Cordela Sexton Vanderpool.

TERRY WINDELL VANDERPOOL, born Feb. 2, 1951 to Sage and Dorothy Wells Vanderpool of Weeksbury, KY, enlisted into the U.S. Army on March 17, 1969 and served three tours of duty in Vietnam.

His military locations and stations include CMD XVIII Airborne Corps TUSA. He was a Private First Class.

He received the National Defense Service Medal, Vietnam Service Medal and the Vietnam Campaign Medal w/device 60.

Terry married Ardella Tilly and they have two children, Dionne Elizabeth and Scott David Vanderpool. Dionne married Lorn Eliffson and they have two children, Alyssa and Christian. Scott married Angela Chancy and they have a daughter, Makala.

Terry worked in construction after his discharge on Oct. 18, 1972. He now resides in Chillicothe, OH.

PAUL R. WELLS, born May 5, 1931 in Kentucky, enlisted in the USAF Oct. 11, 1952. Military locations, stations include Nellis AFB, NV; Thule Greenland; Orlando, FL; Sewart AFB, TN; Lompoc, CA; Fairbanks, AK; and Keesler AFB, Biloxi, MS. He served in Vietnam.

Wells was discharged Jan. 11, 1972 as Senior Master Sergeant. He passed away Aug. 16, 1992.

RAYMOND EUGENE WRIGHT SR., born Dec. 3, 1948 at Drift, KY, the son of Raymond Wright and Hattie Howell. He was a retired U.S. Army Master Sergeant and Vietnam veteran.

He was awarded the National Defense Service Medal, Armed Forces Expeditionary Medal, Vietnam Campaign Medal, Vietnam Service w/2 Campaign Stars, Army Commendation Medal, Meritorious Service Medal, Overseas Service Ribbon, Overseas Service Bar, Good Conduct Medal and the Army Achievement Medal.

He was a retired Pentecostal pastor of New Testament Christian Church. He married Victoria J. Holder. He and Victoria were the parents of Raymond Eugene Wright Jr. of Clarksville, TN; two daughters, Victoria Ray Wright of Woodlawn, TN and Angela Wright Bowman of Covington, KY. He died on May 4, 2006 at Blanchfield Army Hospital, Fort Campbell, KY and is buried in the Lucy Hall Cemetery, McDowell, KY.

DESERT STORM/GULF WAR

MOSES JOE FRASURE JR., born Dec. 8, 1967 at Martin, KY, son of Moses Frasure Sr. and Roberta Newsome. He enlisted in the Navy on Dec. 27, 1987 at Beckley, WV. He went to boot camp in San Diego, CA and then completed "A" School. He was assigned to serve aboard the USS *LaMoure County*. He was stationed in San Diego, CA; in Norfolk, VA; and later in Sugar Grove, WV. Frasure was part of Desert Storm and his ship was the only one that unloaded troops and equipment during the conflict.

He was discharged on Dec. 16, 1995. He earned the National Defense, the Kuwaiti Liberation and Sea Service medals. He was also awarded the Expert Rifle and Pistol and Battle "E" medals. He received two Good Conduct Medals.

Moses married Pamela Faye Bradley in September 1988 at Wayland, KY. They are the parents of Amanda Kathryn Frasure, Brooke Nicole Frasure and Moses Reece Frasure.

BARRY JOHNSON, son of Larry Johnson, joined the U.S. Army in 1993.

DESERT STORM

THURMAN L. BOOTH, Sergeant First Class, born in Circleville, OH, on May 29, 1970. He is the son of Jack and Diane Booth, and grandson of Monroe Booth.

He entered the U.S. Army in September 1990 and served with the 4th Bn., 5th Air Defense Arty. Regt. as a Vulcan crew member during "Operation Desert Storm." He currently holds the MOS of 14J40. His assignments include: 4-5 ADA Fort Hood, TX; 2-6 ADA Fort Bliss, TX; 4-3 ADA Larson Barracks, Kitzingen, Germany; ADA Btry., 3rd ACR Fort Carson, CO; Alpha Btry. Operations Group Fort Irwin, CA; 1-44 ADA Fort Hood, TX; and 1-44 AMD Fort Bliss, TX. He is currently the Platoon Sergeant for Sensor Plt.

He has held positions as Vulcan driver, crewman for the ground based sensor (now the 14J MOS), Bradley driver, gunner, track Commander, Observer Controller and Platoon Sergeant.

His awards and decorations include Meritorious Service Medal, Army Commendation Medal (fourth OLC), Army Achievement Medal (eight OLCs), Army Good Conduct Medal (fifth knot), National Defense Service Medal (two Bronze Stars), Armed Forces Expeditionary Medal, South West Asia Service Medal, Global War on Terrorism Service Medal, Armed Forces Service Medal, Non-Commissioned Officers Professional Development Ribbon (#3), Army Service Ribbon, Overseas Service Ribbon, NATO Medal, Kuwait Liberation Medal (Saudi Arabia), Kuwait Liberation Medal (Kuwait), Drivers Badge (track) and German Marksmanship Badge (Bronze). He is a member of the Honorable Order of Saint Barbara and the prestigious Sergeant Audie Murphy Club.

Thurman's military education includes: 16R Vulcan Crewmember, 14S Avenger Crewmember, 14R Bradley Crewmember, 14J Ground Based Sensor Operator, PLDC, BNCOC, ANCOC, NTC Observer Controller, Infantry Basic Refresher Course, UCOFT Trainer/Instructor, Bradley Crew Evaluator, Combat Lifesaver, Medical Specialist Sustainment (232 hours) and numerous other courses.

Thurman married Norma Medina of Mexico City in August 1993. They have two beautiful children, Kevin who is 9 and Melany is 2 years old. Thurman is currently and proudly serving in El Paso, TX.

BARRY D. CONLEY, born Nov. 21, 1969 in Martin, KY, graduated from Allen Central High School in 1987. He joined the USAF in 1988. From May 1988 to October 1988 he attended military basic training and security police technical school at Lackland AFB in San Antonio, TX and Air base ground defense school at Fort Dix, NJ. Afterwards he was assigned his permanent duty station at Grand Forks AFB, ND. While there his duties consisted of missile field patrols and security and protection of all personnel involved.

He also served during the entire Gulf War (Desert Shield and Desert Storm) though never going overseas.

He received the Good Conduct Medal and the National Defense Service Medal for service during the Gulf War. He was Honorably Discharged in March 1992 at the rank of E-4 Senior Airman.

He currently resides in Martin, KY and is a life member of the DAV.

GARY DOTSON, graduated from Prestonsburg High School in 1976. He attended Eastern Kentucky University and received a BS Degree in Police Administration. He received his commission as a Second Lieutenant and began service in the U.S. Army in April 1981. His first assignment was with the 3rd U.S. Infantry (The Old Guard).

He served in numerous staff and leadership positions during eleven years of active duty. His assignments included: Ft. Benning, GA, Ft. Myers, VA, Ft. Knox, KY, Ft. Wainwright, AK, and Ft. Harrison, IN. In Sept. 1992 he departed active duty and returned home to Prestonsburg where he continues to serve in the Army Reserves. In 1998 he transferred from the Infantry to the Military Police. In 2002 he received a one year recall to active duty where he served with US Central Command, MacDill AFB, FL.

He currently is the Chief of Prestonsburg Fire Department and a member of the Middle Creek Volnteer Fire Department. He is the son of Elsie Dotson and the late Mitchell Dotson.

JAMES HENRY "JIMBO" HALE, Lieutenant Colonel, born Aug. 19, 1948, son of Henry C. and Winifred Hale, Blue River. He enlisted in the USAF in 1972, completed Officer Training School and pilot training in Texas. He remained in Texas and served two tours as an instructor pilot before spending 12 years in the F-4 Phantom Fighter Aircraft. Those locations in the F-4 included Germany and California. He retired from the USAF in 1992.

His decorations include the Aerial Achievement Medal w/2 OLCs for participation in Operation Desert Storm, Meritorious Service Medal w/2 OLCs, Southwest Asia Service Medal, Air Force Commendation Medal, Combat Readiness medal w/1 OLC and the National Defense Medal.

Jimbo married Sandra Stephens in 1969. They have one son, James Jr., who is a Lieutenant in the USN. Jimbo is still living his childhood dream - flying high performance fighter aircraft as an "agressor" pilot against USN aircraft.

He works for a company based in Quincy, IL although he lives in Durango, CO.

ERNEST "ERNIE" LAFFERTY, son of Ernie and Emma Jo McClanahan Lafferty, served in the U.S. Army, 4th Mechanized Inf., 68th Armd. Div. from 1986-88. His grandfather, Andy "Buster" McClanahan, was a WWII Veteran. They lived on Bull Creek in Floyd County, KY. *Submitted by Karen Nelson Marcum and Ernest Lafferty.*

JACK NELSON JR., born on June 10, 1968 in Prestonsburg, Floyd County, KY. He was the son of Jack Nelson Sr. and Annis G. Craft. He was a member of the Prestonsburg National Guard for four years.

On Dec. 10, 1989, when he was 21, he married Beverly R. Griffith. He had a daughter named Misty Dawn Rozella. On Aug. 22, 1990, when he was 22 years old, he died at Dixie Heights in Prestonsburg, KY. He was buried in Osborne Family Cemetery, Hager Hill, KY.

JAMES BRENT REED, Staff Sergeant, from Drift, KY, born May 11, 1960, son of James L. and Shelby Reed and brother of: Janet R. Johnson, Pippa Passes, KY; Deborah Ann Reed, Lexington, KY; and Robert Alan Reed (USN), San Diego, CA. He attended McDowell Elementary School. Graduated high school from Millersburg Military Institute and attended Prestonsburg Community College, Alice Lloyd College and Morehead State University. He married Brenda Hudnell of Reynoldsburg, OH and they have one daughter, Sarah Elizabeth.

He enlisted in the U.S. Army in 1979 and completed Military Police training at Fort McClellan Military Reservation in Alabama. He was assigned to Aberdeen Proving Grounds, Aberdeen, MD.

After completion of his tour of duty he entered the Army Reserves and served in South Carolina, Bardstown, KY and Pikeville, KY. While in the reserves he was called to active duty and served in the Gulf War 'Desert Storm' in Saudi Arabia. He was awarded several medals and service awards.

He worked in restaurant management for Applebee's, Greenwood, SC and Columbia, SC; Steak and Ale, Columbia SC and Greenville, SC; O'Charley's, Richmond and Lexington, KY; and Longhorn Steak House, Charleston, WV and Cincinnati, OH. He then entered the insurance business as an agent for The Horace Mann Company in Cincinnati, OH. He passed away in February 2003.

JOHN B. RUNYON II, born Aug. 20, 1969, enlisted in the Army Reserve in 1987 as a Military Recruiter and is currently stationed in Atlanta, GA.

He received Recruiter of the Year award as well as the National Defense, Good Conduct and Army Achievement Award.

SFC Runyon is still on active duty. He is married to Sherry Branham and they have one son, William John Runyon. He enjoys playing golf.

NIKKI RATLIFF SALUNGA, Lieutenant, USN, attended Wayland Elementary School where she graduated as valedictorian in 1988, and then attended the June Buchanan School where she graduated as valedictorian in 1992. Throughout her schooling, Nikki played basketball and was named top rebounder in the state of Kentucky at one point during the 1991-92 season.

She received an appointment to the U.S. Naval Academy where she graduated with merit with a BS Degree in Political Science in 1996. She was commissioned a Naval officer and served on active duty in the USN for five years and three months, as well as two years and nine months in the inactive Naval Reserve.

During active duty, Nikki served onboard two combat destroyers, USS *Hayler* (DD-997) and USS *Mahan* (DDG-72), and also served as Operations Officer at Assault Craft Unit Two in Norfolk, VA.

Her brief but distinguished Naval career included three deployments overseas, where Nikki's ship participated in major international operations in the Persian Gulf, Red Sea, and the Adriatic Sea.

She earned one Navy Commendation Medal, three Navy & Marine Corps Achievement Medals, an Armed Forces Expeditionary Medal, a Meritorious Service Medal, and qualified as sharpshooter in both rifle and pistol.

After Naval service, Nikki attended law school at the University of Virginia. She is now an attorney and resides in Richmond, VA with her husband and daughter. Nikki is the daughter of Kenneth and Sheilah Ratliff.

CARL EDWARD STEELE, born Oct. 17, 1955 at Betsy Lanyne, KY, son of Carl and Meblein Steele. He enlisted in the Navy in September 1978 at Lexington, KY.

He served aboard the USS *Enterprise* and the USS *Mercy* Hospital Ship. He served aboard the *Mercy* as a doctor during the Gulf conflict.

He is a Commander, assigned to a USN Hospital in Oakland, CA.

IRAQI FREEDOM

BRIAND ANDREW BROWNING, son of Steven and Cheryl Browning; grandson of James and Lavada Hall Browning; and great-grandson of Johnnie Lee and Minnie Davis Hall. He is now serving in USMC.

MICHAEL ELLIOTT, served in the Army in Iraq.

BOB FRANCIS, Corporal, U.S. Army, grandson to Bill and Julia Francis Sr.

WILLIAM TONY FRANCIS, Corporal, U.S. Army, grandson to Bill and Julia Francis Sr.

WM. MICHAEL GUNTER, born June 1, 1967, the son of Al and Judith Gunter in Union City, TN. Moved to Prestonsburg, KY in 1973. Graduated from Prestonsburg High School in 1985, Prestonsburg, KY.

Joined the Air Force and was a Presidential Honor

Guard, stationed at Bolling AFB, Washington, D.C. for four years, then became a Secret Service officer at the White House. He has belonged to the elite counter sniper unit for the past 15 years and travels with the President all over the world.

CHRISTOPHER HALL, son of James and Rhonda Hall; grandson of Aaron and Wanda Hall; and great-grandson of Johnnie Lee and Minnie Davis Hall. Now serving in the USN aboard USS *Chaffer*.

GREGORY WINN HAYES II, Journalist 3, USN, grandson to Bill Francis Jr.

TIM L. HYDEN, born Aug. 22, 1972, enlisted into the USAR on Feb. 8, 1991. He also enlisted into the U.S. Army on Jan. 28,

1996, where he was combat engineer with the 101st Abn. Div.

Military stations include the USAR, Pikeville, KY for five years; Fort Riley, KS for three and one-half years; Fort Hood, TX for five years; and at present, Fort Campbell, KY.

Sweeping for land mines following a mine strike.

Missions include deployment to Saint Kitts West Indies, aided in reconstruction after a major hurricane in 1993. He was deployed with the 4th Inf. Div. to Iraq for Operation Iraq Freedom in 2003. He aided in the capture of Saddam Hussein in Operation Red Dawn in Adwar, Iraq, as well as capturing many of the former Baath Party Members. He was also involved in destroying millions of tons of explosives found in Iraq.

One of Mr. Hyden's most memorable experiences is crossing the border into Iraq to be welcomed by the Iraq citizens waving and cheering as they entered the country.

Awards and medals include five Army Commendation Medals, four Army Achievement Medals, two Good Conduct Medals, one Army Reserve Achievement Award, two National Defense Service Medals, one Iraq Campaign Service Medal, one Global War on Terrorism Medal, two Non-commissioned Officers Professional Development Medal, one Army Service Ribbon, and one Army Reserve Overseas Service Ribbon.

Tim is the son of the late Charles D. Hyden and Margaret D. Hyden and married Debbie Jarrell on July 8, 1991. They currently live in Clarksville, TN where he is still serving in the U.S. Army 101st Abn. Div. with the rank of Staff Sergeant.

MATTHEW MAY, Major, 30-year-old son of USAF Sgt. Charles and Lynn Gray May, is currently serving in the USAF. Matthew is at present training pilots in Little Rock, AR.

His grandfather, E.B. May Jr., was in the USMC, WWII veteran who served in Iwo Jima. His other grandfather, Manis Gray, was a paratrooper with the USAF. His great-grandfather was Walter K. Boling who served in WWI, his son (Matthew's uncle) is entombed on the USS *Arizona* at Pearl Harbor. His other uncle, Thomas, was killed in Korea.

Matthew is the third generation to proudly serve in the U.S. Armed Services.

EDWARD BRANDON MCDONALD, Captain, son of Carl Jeffery and Mary Nelson McDonald, was commissioned in the U.S. Army as a Second Lieutenant. Soon after he was sent to Signal Officer Basic School and then became 2nd Plt. leader, A Co., 307th Signal Bn. at Camp Carroll in support of the U.S. Troops.

He received the Army Commendation Medal, Certificates of Achievement and Commanders Coins of Excellence.

Brandon was promoted to First Lieutenant and ordered to Schofield Barracks, HI to serve with 1st Bn., 14th Inf. Regt.'s Signal Officer (S-6) where he received the Army Commendation Medal w/OLC.

Brandon was reassigned to the post of Executive Officer of the Global Command and Control Systems at Fort Shafter, HI. On Aug. 1, 2001 he was promoted to Captain.

Edward was Honorably Discharged in 2001 and graduated from the University of Louisville Law School in May 2005 and was sworn in as an attorney in Frankfort.

He re-enlisted in the Army as a JAG Officer Captain and is stationed in Fort Hood, TX. *Submitted by his aunt, Karen Nelson Marcum.*

STEFAN MORGAN, born Sept. 3, 1984 to Rick and Stephanie Healy Morgan. He enlisted in USN, Special Clearance Team I. He served 19 months in the Bahamas.

He has earned the Overseas Defense Medal, National Forces Services Medal, National Expeditionary Medal, Expert Rifle Medal, Expert Pistol Medal, Global on Terrorism Medal and Global on Expeditionary Medal.

He is a deep sea diver and a mammal trainer.

Stefan is still serving our country at the Naval Sub Base in Coronada, CA. His most memorable experience was coming home to loved ones after being in the Bahamas.

Stefan is the grandson of Shag and Shirlee Branham of Prestonsburg, KY.

ROBERT ALAN REED, SGT-2-E5 from Drift, KY, son of James L. and Shelby Reed and brother of: Janet R. Johnson, Pippa Passes, KY; James Brent Reed (U.S. Army veteran), deceased; and Deborah Ann Reed, Lexington, KY. He attended McDowell Elementary School. Graduated High School from Millersburg Military Institute and attended Prestonsburg Community College. He is married to Edith Patterson from Neon, KY and currently resides in San Diego, CA. He has one son, Robert William Scott and one daughter, Katelyn Lauren.

He enlisted in the USN on June 6, 1989. On his first tour of duty he completed training at Great Lakes Training Center and AME-2 training at Millington, TN (Honors) and was assigned to Cecil Field in Jacksonville, FL, VFA 106, VFA 203.

After his first tour of duty was complete he was general manager for Chuckie Cheese's restaurants in Columbus, GA; Nashville, TN; and Lexington, KY.

He re-entered the Navy and on his second tour of duty he completed sonar tech school in San Diego, CA (Honors) and the Navy Command Counselor Career School (Honors). He is currently assigned to the USS *Shiloh* (CG-67) in San Diego, CA.

His awards and medals include: 'C' Service Deployment Medal, Navy Good Conduct Medal, Global War on Terrorism Service Medal, Battle E Award, Rifle Marksman Award, Joint Meritorious Award in Support of Tsunami Victims and Humanitarian Service Award in Support of Tsunami Victims.

JARRED STEPHENS, age 22, Military Police Officer in the U.S. Army, (presently serving in Iraq at the time of this photo) is a 1999 graduate of Prestonsburg High School. He is the son of Denise and Graham Stephens of Prestonsburg, the grandson of Denver Osborne and the late Doris Osborne of Hi Hat, KY and the late Darb and Caroline Stephens of Prestonsburg, KY.

STEPHANIE HYDEN WERRICK, Sergeant, was born July 14, 1981 in Prestonsburg, KY. She is the daughter of Danny and Judy Setser of Prestonsburg, and Charlie Hyden of Minnie, KY. Her grandparents are Millard and

Roberta Setser, Doug and Margaret Hyden of Prestonsburg and Bill and Bonie Brown of Saginaw, TX. She graduated from South Floyd High School in 1999 and attended Morehead State University.

Stephanie enlisted in the U.S. Army in November 2000, trained in Fort Jackson, SC and Fort Campbell with the 101st Abn. "Screamin' Eagles" HQ. She was deployed to Kuwait in February 2003 in Operation Iraqi Freedom. She drove most of the 700 miles to Mosul, Iraq.

She is currently stationed at Camp Falcon, Fox Co., in Operation Enduring Freedom and will return from Baghdad in January 2007.

UNKNOWN

JOHN WESLEY BREWER, son of Lonnie and Doris Brewer. He served in the USAF. He now resides in Creston, OH.

HENRY OWEN BREWER, son of Lonnie and Doris Hall Brewer and grandson of Johnnie Lee and Minnie Davis Hall. He served with the USN. He now resides in Pittsburgh, PA.

DWAYNE ELLIOTT, served in the U.S. Army.

JAMES ESTIL GARRETT, son of Willard and Fanny Mae Hall Garrett and grandson of Johnnie Lee and Minnie Davis Hall. He served in the USN. Garrett now resides in Piketon, OH.

MARTIN LUTHER GARRETT, son of Willard and Fanny Mae Hall Garrett and grandson of Johnnie Lee and Minnie Davis Hall. He served in the U.S. Army and now resides in Lake Alford, FL.

DONAHUE HALBERT, son of Ed and Rhonda Flanery Halbert, served the U.S. Army for 20 years. After retiring he opened a gun shop in Maytown.

JAMES ALAN HALL, son of Aaron and Wanda Hall and grandson of Johnnie Lee and Minnie Davis Hall. He served in the USN.

His last assignment was serving aboard the Presidential yacht *Sequoia*. He now resides in Great Falls, MT.

RICHARD ALLEN HALL, USN, son of Kelly Hall and grandson of Johnnie Lee and Minnie Davis Hall. He retired after 20 years in submarine service. He now lives in Vancouver, WA.

RUSSELL HALL, son of Aaron and Wanda Hall and grandson of Johnnie Lee and Minnie Hall. He served in the USN. Russell now resides in Scappoose, OR.

KENYON JAMES HOPKINS, son of Don and Brenda Shepherd Hopkins and grandson of Elzie and Trinnie Shepherd. He is the great-grandson of Johnnie Lee and Minnie Davis Hall. He served in the U.S. Army with the 25th Inf. Div. He now resides in Marshall, MI.

ELMER RAY JOHNSON, son of Grover Johnson, served with the U.S. Marine Corps.

EDWARD "BILL" LAFERTY, son of Aurthe and Alma Laferty. He is married to Ruth Ousley.

GREGORY DALE LANIER, son of Ken and Minnie Garrett Lanier; grandson of Williard and Fanny Garrett; and great-grandson of Johnnie Lee and Minnie Davis Hall. He served in the USN. He now resides in West Virginia.

EVERETT MARCUM JR., son of Everett and Callie Fannin Marcum of Allen, KY served in the U.S. Army.

He later married Margaret Luxmore and has three children: William, Anita and Matthew. He worked for the CSX Railroad and now lives in Oneida, TN. *Submitted by Karen Nelson Marcum.*

LESTER PARSONS, unknown.

GERALD WILLIAM SHEPHERD, son of James L. Shepherd, served in the USN. Grandson of Elzie and Trinnie Shepherd. He was the great-grandson of Johnnie Lee and Minnie Davis Hall.

JAMES LEE SHEPHERD, U.S. Army, was the son of Elzie and Trinnie Shepherd. He was the grandson of Johnnie Lee and Minnie Davis Hall. He now lives in Marshall, MI.

JOHN DAVID TACKETT, son of David Lee and Nancy Tackett; grandson of Newberry and Pearl Tackett; and great-grandson of Johnnie Lee and Minnie Davis Hall. He served with the 101st Abn. Rangers. He now resides in Virginia.

ALL VETERANS GAVE SOME
THESE VETERANS GAVE ALL

WORLD WAR I

HARRIS ARNETT	JAMES H. COLLINS	SAM DILLON	TIP GAYHEART	LAMUEL HAYNES	VESTER M. GOWAN	ELIJAH THOMPSON
GRADE BURCHETT	WILLIAM M. COX	BUD ENDICOTT	EDWARD D. HALL	ELI JOHNSON	LEONARD PALMER	GARLAND W. WELLS
REUBEN CALVIN CLARK	JESSE COYER	JOSH FIFE	GEORGE GARLAND HARRIS	LYNDON EARL LANGLEY	GEORGE VISCENZE TASSONE	

WORLD WAR II

BENJAMIN AKERS	CHARLES CLEVENGER	QUENTIN HALL	CHESTER JOHNSON	AUDRY MIDDLETON	LAWRENCE PORTER	MARTIN L. SMITH
EUGENE ALEXANDER	KERMIT CLICK	ROY HALL	EDGEL JOHNSON	BALLARD B. MILLS	HOMER POWELL	DARWIN L. SNIPES
CHESTER A. ALLEN	JAMES K. COLLINS	HERSHEL HAMILTON	ESTILL JOHNSON	CHARLES MOORE	LEE PRATER JR.	ENNIS SPRADLIN
HENDERSON W. ALLEN	PALMER COLLINS	LEE HAMILTON	THURMAN JOHNSON	CHARLES MOORE	RAYMOND RACKLEY	VIGIIS M. STEELE
MARION ANDERSON	MORRISON COMBS	RALPH C. HARRIS	DANIEL JONES	FRANK MOORE	RUSSELL O. RATLIFF	ASHLAND P. STEPHEN
LEE BAKER	CURTIS CONN	CARL LUCIAN HAYES	MILLARD A. JONES	PALMER MOORE	NORMAN REED	BILL STEPHENS
HARRY WILFORD BENNER	JAMES H. CRISP	WILLIS HICKS	CHARLES E. JORDAN	ROBERT MOSLEY	JOHN B. REYNOLDS	OLLIE J. STURGILL
ARNOLD BENTLEY	WILEY C. ELLIOTT	EUGENE HINTON	ADRON JUSTICE	PAUL L. MULLINS	SAMUEL Z. RICE	AMOS TACKETT
RICHARD BINGHAM	EMERSON C. ESTEP	HENRY LEWIS HOLBROOK	WATT KEATHLEY	DENVER MUSIC	JOHN W. RING	JAMES TACKETT
ELMER BLACKBURN	TOMMY J. FAIRCHILD	CHARLES HOPPER	WARREN A. KOONTZ	ALVIN NELSON	BILL ROBERTS	DAN TERRY
JACK LINVELL BLACKBURN	RANDALL FANNIN	SELDON HORNE	FLOYD LAFFERTY	EUGENE OPPENHEIMER	AMOS ROBINSON	ANDY THACKER
WALTER KARR BOLLING	R.C. FITZPATRICK	JAMES HORTON	ROBERT C. LAMBERT	HERMAN L. ORSBON	RUSSELL ROBINSON	HILLARD TUTTLE
JAY B. BRANHAM	ANTHONY FRASURE	ARNOLD HOWARD	RAY V. LAWSON	ADAM OUSLEY	ROBERT L. RUNNELS	DOUGLAS VAUGHN
CHARLES E. BROOKS	HERSHEL DOUGLAS FRAZIER	DANIEL HOWARD	HERBERT W. LAYNE	MITCHELL OUSLEY	WINTER G. RUNYON	HARRY W. VAUGHN
ROY L. BURCHWELL	JOE W. GARRETT	FRANK EUGENE HUBBARD	MALCOLM B. LAYNE	OLLIE OUSLEY JR.	ASTER L. SALISBURY	JEFF WILLARD VAUGHN
AUBURN CALHOUN	FRANK GAYHEART	ARBIE HUNT	C. ROBERT MARSHALL	CLYDE D. PATRIDGE	JAMES T. SALISBURY	CLARENCE DOUGLAS WALLEN
CHARLES H. CAMP	BERT GOBLE	CHARLES E. HUNTER	SANDY MARTIN JR.	CLYDE R. PATTON	EUGENE SCUTCHFIELD	GEORGE E. WEBB
DARVIN CAUDILL	GEORGE GOODMAN	JAMES W. HURD	SHERIDAN MARTIN	JESS PENNINGTON	ORVILLE T. SCUTCHFIELD	ARVIL WELLS
ORVILLE CHAFFINS	ELMER HALL	EUGENE HYDEN	DICK F. MAYO	CLARENCE PERRY	MATHEW SHORT	HERBERT WHITAKER
LOUIS WOODROW CHILDERS	FOSTER HALL	FRANK HYDEN	JAMES E. McGLOTHEN	HOMER S. PHAUP	CURTIS L. SIZEMORE	FRED WILLIAMS
JOHN CLARK	JIMMIE N. HALL	JAMES F. HYDEN	RUSSELL E. McPEEK	GLENN PINKS	CARTHEL SMITH	EDWARD E. WRIGHT
LAWTON E. CLARK	MARION HALL	BEN JARRELL	AUGUST MEADE	HARRY PORTER	DOUG SMITH	JOHN H. YOUNG
				GARLAND PATTON		

KOREAN WAR

JIMMIE ALLEN	WILLIE L. COLLIER	GLENN FRASURE	RANDOLPH HAYES	RALPH KIDD	CLYDE D. SPRADLIN	JAMES A. WALLEN
THOMAS E. BOLLING	RUSH F. CRUM	DONALD D. GIBSON	BRISON HOWARD	ROY L. LAYNE	SAMUEL T. STUMBO	CECIL H. WATSON
CHARLES D. CARTT	ROBERT DEMPSEY	HENRY E. GIBSON	FRANKIE B. HUGHES	DONALD H. ROOP	STERLING D. TACKETT	DENVER LEE WELLS
LESLIE D. CLICK	PEARL G. DEROSSETT	CLYDE HAMILTON	ROBERT L. JOHNSON	JOE R. SCALF	JAKE R. THOMAS	
ELMER ROY CLIFTON	HENRY A. DUDDLESON	JAMES M. HARRISON				

VIETNAM WAR

ARVEL DEWITT AKERS	DANNY BLEVINS	LAWRENCE EDWARD CLARK	BALLARD R. CONNERS JR.	DONALD RAY HAYWOOD	LOWELL JOHNSON	BILLY JAY PITTS
JORDAN A. BELCHER	ANDREW JACKSON CAMPBELL	TERRY WALKER CLIFTON	DAVID E. GAYHEART	BILLY RAY HUNTER	W. H. JONES III	ANCIL JAMES TERRY
WILLIAM K. BLACKBURN	VICTOR CALHOUN	PHILLIP RODNEY COLEMAN	DONALD HALL	ANDY JOHNSON JR.	JEFF MULKEY	

DONATED BY BIG SANDY CHAPTER 18 D.A.V.

FLOYD COUNTY, KENTUCKY VETERANS DISCHARGES

Name	Disc. Date	Book	Page
Absher, Jack A.	25-Oct-1949	10	131-132
Ackerman, John E.	3-Mar-1972	11	552
Acree, Creed	21-Nov-1950	6	483
Adams, Bernard	11-Jun-1947	2	154
Adams, Deward	14-May-1950	2	351
Adams, Ellis	24-Nov-1947	2	122
Adams, Fred J.	6-Jul-1949	3	78
Adams, Garland	31-Dec-1949	6	320
Adams, James Edward	21-Mar-1947	2	206
Adams, Junior	11-Jul-1971	11	468
Adams, Larry	23-Aug-1971	11	485
Adams, Mildren	4-Mar-1959	8	151
Adams, Otto	30-Dec-1950	7	109
Adams, Ross L.	12-Mar-1959	8	182
Adams, Roy Lee	7-Feb-1974	12	94
Adams, Tommy Neil	10-Mar-1975	13	124
Adams, William W.	28-Mar-1950	4	474
Addis, James R.	15-Apr-1950	11	104
Addis, Larry Dean	3-May-1978	12	173
Adkins, Alex	8-Oct-1949	3	298
Adkins, Bertee	1-Feb-1975	13	129
Adkins, Billie	8-Oct-1972	11	596
Adkins, Cecil C.	14-Oct-1949	11	7
Adkins, Charles R.	23-Dec-1949	4	178
Adkins, Chester Lee	29-Jul-1976	13	279
Adkins, Clarence	7-Dec-1949	4	15
Adkins, Clifford	3-Oct-1949	3	294
Adkins, Darrell Allen	26-Sep-1973	12	37
Adkins, Denver Eugene	31 June 1969	12	18
Adkins, Donald Everette	12-Jul-1974	13	7
Adkins, Dugan	15-Oct-1949	3	329
Adkins, Earl	21-Jul-1948	6	577
Adkins, Earl	12-Mar-1950	6	578
Adkins, Elvie	12-Feb-1957	11	89
Adkins, Evan D.	4-Feb-1950	4	381
Adkins, Gary Wayne	11-Oct-1970	11	412
Adkins, George	14-Mar-1974	12	105
Adkins, George Everett	29-Jan-1950	5	502
Adkins, Gerald Shannon	2-Sep-1965	11	116
Adkins, Jerry Lance	22-Apr-1957	7	439
Adkins, John G.	27-Apr-1972	11	565
Adkins, Johnie	22-Jun-1945	2	282
Adkins, Kenneth Eugene	24-Feb-1960	8	189
Adkins, Millard	18-Mar-1950	4	451
Adkins, Orgie	17-Jun-1949	2	313
Adkins, Orville	21-Nov-1949	3	535
Adkins, Patrick	4-Dec-1949	3	631
Adkins, Ralph	13-Sep-1949	3	209
Adkins, Ralph	19-Dec-1949	4	51
Adkins, Ray	3-Sep-1964	10	105
Adkins, Ronald Craig	7-Sep-1971	11	487
Adkins, Thurman	15-Jul-1947	2	43
Adkins, Tom Francis	5-Jun-1956	7	187
Adkins, Tramble	5-Jan-1948	2	53
Adkins, Willard	6-Sep-1949	6	375
Adkins, Willie	14-May-1950	6	284
Adkins, Willis Gene	27-Jul-1997	14	226-227
Africa, William	19-Jul-1922	1	84
Akers, Adren A.	20-Aug-1956	11	316
Akers, Avery	20-Apr-1950	5	256
Akers, Benjamin Morgan	9-Feb-1975	13	126
Akers, Bobby C.	31-Mar-1972	11	550
Akers, Carl	26-Aug-1949	3	210
Akers, Charles	2-Jul-1960	9	277
Akers, Curtis	26-Jan-1950	5	167
Akers, Daniel	28-Nov-1949	6	238
Akers, Daniel	19-Nov-1950	6	237
Akers, David R.	30-Jan-1950	4	333
Akers, Dewey	15-Aug-1949	3	134
Akers, Eddie	14-May-1950	6	461
Akers, Elder	21-Jul-1949	3	148
Akers, Elijah	31-Oct-1945	1	135
Akers, Elijah	31-Oct-1945	1	615
Akers, Ervin	4-Nov-1949	3	448
Akers, Eugene	28-Sep-1963	5	85
Akers, Eugene	28-Sep-1963	9	252
Akers, Evan	18-Dec-1949	4	210
Akers, Evan Fonce	26-Jan-1950	5	154
Akers, Everett Leonard	1-Nov-1949	5	17
Akers, Everett Leonard, Jr.	30-Jul-1969	11	473
Akers, Forrest Rose	31-Oct-1949	5	40.5

Name	Disc. Date	Book	Page
Akers, Francis	10-Oct-1950	5	432
Akers, Francis A.	8-Jan-1950	4	132
Akers, Fred	19-Oct-1949	3	360
Akers, Hubert	2-Nov-1949	3	441
Akers, James Eugene	3-Dec-1970	11	422
Akers, Jimmy Lee	11-Nov-1971	11	506
Akers, John	30-Nov-1950	5	422
Akers, Kenneth Howard	12-Apr-1958	8	291
Akers, Lee	5-Jun-1949	3	31
Akers, Leroy	16-Aug-1950	9	326
Akers, Lowell Keith	1-Jun-1977	13	335
Akers, Noah	23-Oct-1949	5	471
Akers, Noah Carson	23-Aug-1973	12	25
Akers, Orbie	22-Jan-1950	4	242
Akers, Ranson	7-Nov-1949	3	479
Akers, Simon	17-Dec-1949	5	105
Akers, Simon	17-Dec-1949	11	55
Akers, Ted Lee	16-Dec-1949	5	111
Akers, Thomas	30-Jan-1948	2	24
Akers, Thurman	2-Feb-1950	4	312
Akers, Vance L.	3-May-1976	12	164
Akers, Vance Lee	29-Apr-1972	12	164
Akers, Vance Lee	29-Apr-1972	12	318
Akers, Vinson Dwayne	15-Dec-1993	14	102
Akers, Walter	25-May-1952	7	87
Akers, Wilburn	17-Nov-1950	6	268
Akhlaghi, Ahmad Reza Ahadi	24-Jun-1998	14	244
Alexander, Alfred R.	30-May-1947	2	50
Alexander, George S.	15 Dec. 1945	4	42
Allen, Wick	22-Nov-1949	3	600
Allen, Alex V.	29-Nov-1949	4	380
Allen, Anthony Nichols	25-Sep-1973	12	36
Allen, Ballard Hall	6-Aug-1961	9	28
Allen, Barbara V.	17-Jun-1993	13	436
Allen, Barbara V.	4-Jul-1995	14	196-197
Allen, Blucher, Jr.	24-Oct-1949	2	458
Allen, Carl Edward	19-Oct-1972	11	355
Allen, Carl W.	3-Dec-1949	4	143
Allen, Cleaster	9-Aug-1949	6	325
Allen, Corey Bart	8-Feb-2005	15	53
Allen, Curtis Thomas	6-Mar-1957	7	465
Allen, Danny Lee	17-Feb-1976	13	241
Allen, David D.	1-Jun-1969	11	376
Allen, Dewey	24-Jun-1949	3	52
Allen, Edgel	7-Nov-1949	4	125
Allen, Elmo Benton	2-Apr-1958	12	258
Allen, Felix W.	27-Apr-1949	3	20
Allen, Floyd B.	16-May-1957	15	122
Allen, Floyd B.	28-Sep-1963	15	112
Allen, Floyd B.		15	121
Allen, Fred	13-May-1923	1	253
Allen, George Dewey	9-Dec-1949	5	80
Allen, Glen Roger	19-Feb-1977	13	309
Allen, Glenn D.	28-Sep-1949	3	255
Allen, Grover Morris	9-Jun-1950	5	486
Allen, Haden	16-Sep-1949	3	384
Allen, Henry	23-Sep-1949	3	481
Allen, Herman	7-Feb-1950	6	472
Allen, Hollie	23-Jul-1949	4	370
Allen, Hubert Gene	20-Jan-1971	11	259
Allen, James	3-Nov-1949	3	444
Allen, James Alex	8-Feb-1966	11	145
Allen, James Litton	23-Aug-1949	11	87
Allen, James Lynn	7-Mar-1974	12	100
Allen, James P.	29-Oct-1925	1	242
Allen, Jarvis	19-Oct-1948	2	358
Allen, Jerry	14-Oct-1949	3	548
Allen, Jewel Day	14-Mar-1950	5	211
Allen, Joe Edward	8-Jul-1956	7	208
Allen, Joe K.	22-Jan-1950	4	330
Allen, Kenneth Raymond	20-Nov-1958	8	111
Allen, Kermit	20-Oct-1949	6	326
Allen, Lorn	6-Dec-1970	11	200
Allen, Nelson Robert	6-Oct-1964	11	130
Allen, Oliver C.	26-Jun-1949	3	62
Allen, Oliver E.	16-Nov-1949	5	505
Allen, Oliver K.	2-Jul-1954	7	96
Allen, Oscar	13-Nov-1949	3	514
Allen, Ralph E.	22-Mar-1950	9	24
Allen, Ralph J.	12-Jan-1950	4	145
Allen, Ray	18-Sep-1949	3	381

Name	Disc. Date	Book	Page
Allen, Ray V.	9-Jun-1951	7	18
Allen, Robert	27-Jan-1951	6	349
Allen, Robert E.	17-Jan-1949	2	273
Allen, Ronald Douglas	25-Jun-1975	13	164
Allen, Roscoe	18-Dec-1949	5	104
Allen, Roy	24-Oct-1945	2	3
Allen, Rudolph	14-Jan-1918	1	164
Allen, Rudolph	15-Jul-1922	1	163
Allen, Rudolph	3-Oct-1923	1	165
Allen, Russell Sage	12-Jan-1972	11	529
Allen, Sidney Earl	29-Jun-1970	11	221
Allen, Taggett	23-Jan-1958	7	477
Allen, Teddy Darrell	11-Jan-1976	13	230
Allen, Thomas	31-Oct-1949	3	395
Allen, Thomas	2-Dec-1950	6	212
Allen, Thomas J.	11-Apr-1950	4	491
Allen, Thomas Jacob, Jr.	5-Jan-1968	11	308
Allen, Thomas, Jr.	5-Jan-1972	11	562
Allen, Vernon	10-Oct-1949	4	23
Allen, Volney Dameron	16-Mar-1950	14	299
Allen, Volney Dameron	16-Mar-1950	14	301
Allen, Wayne P.	5-Dec-1948	2	258
Allen, William	19-Apr-1949	2	298
Allen, William	19-Apr-1949	6	5
Allen, William	16-Nov-1949	3	523
Allen, William C.	22-Jan-1950	4	272
Allen, William Grover	27-Jun-1960	8	282
Allen, William K.	12-Apr-1950	7	108
Allen, William K.	4-Mar-1979	13	424
Alley, Elbie	27-Aug-1949	3	152
Alley, Elmer	29-Nov-1949	4	18
Alley, James Edward	19-Mar-1950	5	423
Alley, Joe	10-Jul-1923	1	73
Alley, John	24-Sep-1949	6	536
Alley, Keith Shannon	27-Oct-1959	8	221
Alley, Lee	3-Dec-1921	1	10
Alley, Neil	11-Apr-1978	14	140
Alley, Orris	8-Dec-1950	6	223
Amburgey, Brody	30-Dec-1949	6	607
Amburgey, Olin	10-Jan-1950	9	279
Amburgy, Curtis Ray	11-Nov-1974	13	77
Amburgy, Robert V.	21-Nov-1958	8	121
Amburgy, William H.	23-Oct-1947	2	348
Anderson, Alex	17-Jul-1946	2	211
Anderson, John Franklin	6-Dec-1959	8	245
Anderson, John Marvin, Sr.	19-Nov-1949	5	45
Anderson, Lonnie	8-Jan-1950	4	141
Anderson, Phillip Lee	10-Apr-2002	15	30
Anderson, Ralph Leonard	15-Mar-1976	13	247
Anderson, Richard Charles	30-Nov-1958	8	115
Anderson, Robert C.	16-Sep-1960	8	307
Anderson, Stephen A.	1-Dec-1976	13	297
Anderson, Willie Clarence	4-Jan-1970	11	161
Archer, Arthur Johns, Jr.	19-Jan-1950	5	138
Archer, William T.	2-Sep-1949	3	171
Arnett, Charles	27-Jan-1950	6	35
Arnett, Clark	25-Oct-1957	7	425
Arnett, Johnny	10-May-1973	13	266
Arrowood, John	23-Jan-1950	9	253
Arrowood, Larry G.	10-Sep-1967	11	240
Artrip, Arnel	5-Dec-1949	6	54
Artrip, Carlos	23-Jun-1947	2	193
Atkinson, Elbert	2-May-1949	6	401
Auxier, John	19-Jan-1953	6	641
Auxier, Regina Lynn	24-Nov-1988	12	285
Babb, Owen, Jr.	4-Oct-1949	5	2
Babb, Walter	18-Sep-1949	3	234
Babbs, Hugh	12-Feb-1953	6	643
Baca, Senforoso Andres	15-Oct-1978	14	97
Baca, Senforoso Andres	29-Apr-1992	14	96
Bailey, Amos A.	18-Oct-1949	4	255
Bailey, Ben F.	8-Dec-1922	1	230
Bailey, Chester P.	16-Dec-1949	5	482
Bailey, Darrell S.	22-Oct-1974	11	343
Bailey, David	28-Oct-1949	6	15
Bailey, Delmas	13-Sep-1951	6	597
Bailey, Delmont G.	20-Jan-1950	15	125
Bailey, Grover	1-Feb-1950	10	112
Bailey, Henry	8-Nov-1949	4	308
Bailey, Henry D.	19-Oct-1969	11	209
Bailey, Joe Dean	13-Jul-1976	13	276

Name	Disc. Date	Book	Page
Bailey, Joe L.	6-Sep-1949	3	178
Bailey, Norman L.	17-Dec-1974	13	83
Bailey, Paul Hager	29-Nov-1956	7	257
Bailey, Ralph	1-Apr-1950	4	479
Bailey, Robert	26-Aug-1950	6	51
Bailey, Robert L.	18-Feb-1975	13	110
Bailey, Robert Lowell	16-Dec-1974	15	103
Bailey, Sidney E.	22-Jan-1950	4	223
Bailey, Vern M.	27-Nov-1949	4	80
Bailey, Ward	15-Aug-1950	6	493
Baker, Bill Jr.	21-Feb-1957	7	328
Baldridge, Ance	11-Jan-1950	5	468
Baldridge, Belve	11-Dec-1949	4	91
Baldridge, Bernard	4-Nov-1949	3	469
Baldridge, Carl	14-Jan-1950	6	143
Baldridge, Clifford	8-Aug-1950	6	31
Baldridge, Delmar Ray	18-Aug-1959	8	281
Baldridge, Denver	23-Jul-1950	5	515
Baldridge, Dexter	11-Sep-1949	6	201
Baldridge, Earl	16-Feb-1950	6	170
Baldridge, Earnest	19-Oct-1949	3	357
Baldridge, Earnest	27-Oct-1949	5	64
Baldridge, Harold L.	30-Dec-1953	8	321
Baldridge, Harold L.	11-Oct-1973	12	42
Baldridge, John W.	1-Sep-1955	7	146
Baldridge, Leonard	13-Dec-1949	4	376
Baldridge, Luther J.	2-Oct-1948	2	302
Baldridge, Monroe	14-Feb-1950	6	485
Baldridge, Nelson Ray	30-Nov-1961	9	44
Baldridge, Ollie J.	29-Oct-1949	5	22
Baldridge, Robert	17-Aug-1949	3	168
Baldridge, Robert	16-Sep-1959	14	143
Baldridge, Robert	19-Oct-1965	14	144
Baldridge, Robert	29-Mar-1967	14	142
Baldridge, William	15-Nov-1949	3	525
Baldridge, Willie A.	18-Jun-1923	1	92
Baldridge, Willie L.	12-Jul-1923	1	197
Baldridge, Willie L.	27-Sep-1949	4	637
Ball, Donale B.	4-Dec-1949	3	594
Ball, Lafon	22-Oct-1949	3	359
Ball, Printess L.	7-Jul-1949	5	431
Ball, Richard D. Jr.	5-Apr-1949	4	621
Ball, Richard D. Jr.	4-Nov-1949	4	440
Ballenger, Donald C.	27-Dec-1967	11	433
Banks, Arthur	4-Mar-1950	4	421
Banks, Delmer	26-Sep-1958	8	92
Banks, Frank	1-Aug-1925	1	93
Banks, George E.	15-Apr-1951	7	78
Banks, George E.	15-Apr-1951	10	41
Banks, Harrison	1-Feb-1960	10	43
Banks, Harry A.	8-Jul-1966	11	302
Barnes, Calvin Cecil	28-Sep-1957	8	51
Barnes, John J.	6-Sep-1950	5	248
Barnett, Andrew Jr.	10-Jun-1959	9	244
Barnett, Darby Ray	5-Feb-1970	11	377
Barnett, George Edward	31-Dec-1953	9	142
Barnett, Grielly	15-Oct-1958	9	18
Barnett, Harold	15-Mar-1950	6	309
Barnett, Walter	1-Jan-1959	8	138
Barnett, Walter Jr.	8-Feb-1973	11	615
Barnett, Willard	6-Dec-1950	12	279
Barnette, Carmel C.	8-Mar-1974	12	103
Barsbon, John	18-May-1923	1	33
Bartley, Buford	22-Oct-1949	3	509
Bartley, Hobart	12-Dec-1973	12	295
Bartley, Hobert	12-Dec-1973	12	72
Bartram, Frank Jr.	16-Dec-1949	6	488
Bartrum, Gordon L.	19-Dec-1971	13	397
Bartrum, Thomas H.	26-Jun-1978	13	368
Bartrum, Walter C.	29-Dec-1075	13	224
Bates, Cephas	8-Dec-1946	2	92
Bates, Charles	7-Feb-1947	2	344
Bates, Clyde	2-Mar-1948	2	93
Bates, Clyde Edward	6-Sep-1972	11	350
Bates, Dallas	7-Jul-1966	14	164
Bates, Dallas	7-Jul-1966	14	262
Bates, Dallas	6-Aug-1969	14	163
Bates, Dallas	22-Mar-1971	14	263
Bates, Darrell Wayne	22-Jan-1970	11	374
Bates, Earnest Jr.	28-Mar-1950	4	475
Bates, Garvis	13-Dec-1949	5	97
Bates, Jake	28-Oct-1949	6	93
Bates, John W.	10-Oct-1949	5	475
Bates, Julius Caesar	3-Oct-1959	8	280

Name	Disc. Date	Book	Page
Bates, Julius Caesar	11-Dec-1965	11	333
Bates, Julius Caesar	11-Dec-1969	11	365
Bates, Julius Caesar	1-Dec-1975	13	367
Bates, Lawrence	27-Dec-1949	4	93
Bates, Lester Jr.	28-May-1984	12	229
Bates, Lester Jr.	28-May-1984	12	230
Bayes, Gordon	16-Dec-1949	8	94
Bayes, Ronald B.	8-Dec-1950	7	137
Bayes, William David	6-Jan-1971	11	421
Bayless, Homer	14-Oct-1923	1	75
Bays, Billy	12-Mar-1952	6	565
Bays, Elbert	14-Sep-1949	3	213
Bays, Erman	10-Oct-1949	3	363
Bays, Joe W.	2-Jul-1950	4	640
Beckelheimer, Mort	22-Apr-1923	1	214
Becker, Leland Sears	18-Jan-1923	1	149
Becker, Margaret S.	25-Dec-1949	4	430
Begley, Sydney	11-Oct-1922	1	152
Belcher, Jack Edward	18-Oct-1949	5	12
Belcher, John D. Jr.	19-Jan-1950	4	237
Belcher, John W.	1-Jul-1949	3	66
Belcher, Johnny M.	26-Jun-1974	13	16
Belcher, Johnny R.	21-Feb-1980	13	405
Belcher, Marion E.	14-Jul-1947	2	311
Belcher, Robert G.	3-Mar-1983	13	431
Bell, Robert David	27-Sep-1973	12	40
Bellamy, Billie	26-Jan-1950	14	151
Benedict, Joseph	25-Jan-1950	7	73
Benedict, Joseph	12-Jan-1951	7	72
Benjey, Robert	15-Oct-1949	3	349
Bentley, Adrian E.	24-Jan-1954	7	371
Bentley, Allen	11-Sep-1949	6	111
Bentley, Carl Eugene	12-Sep-1963	9	187A
Bentley, Danny	2-Feb-1975	13	107
Bentley, David Charles	4-Apr-1974	13	10
Bentley, David Charles	13-May-1974	13	41
Bentley, Delmar	29-Jul-1949	3	117
Bentley, Earl	12-Sep-1947	2	82
Bentley, Elberson E.	14-Nov-1949	5	32
Bentley, Elmer	18-Dec-1949	4	234
Bentley, Elmer	1-Dec-1950	5	439
Bentley, Emert	20-Dec-1949	5	205
Bentley, Estil Jr.	30-Jan-1977	13	306
Bentley, Fair Jr.	29-Oct-1969	11	356
Bentley, George	17-Jan-1950	4	235
Bentley, Isam	24-Nov-1949	10	136
Bentley, John	13-May-1949	3	23
Bentley, John	8-Nov-1949	3	531
Bentley, Larry	26-Jul-1974	13	25
Bentley, Lloyd	4-May-1950	6	394
Bentley, Luttral	9-Nov-1949	3	478
Bentley, Mance	12-Jan-1950	4	614
Bentley, Marion	11-Oct-1957	7	422
Bentley, Norman R.	13-Aug-1978	13	362
Bentley, Norman W.	5-Dec-1949	4	485
Bentley, Stanton Ray	25-Jun-1996	14	192
Bentley, Trent	15-May-1950	6	99
Bentley, Troy	23-Oct-1947	9	337
Bentley, William Henry	2-Jul-1979	14	79
Bentley, Winfred	22-Sep-1949	6	92
Benton, Shirley M.	14-Jan-1954	7	58
Berger, Charles	18-Feb-1973	11	618
Berger, Joe J.	11-Nov-1947	2	34
Berger, Stanley W.	8-Jun-1973	13	365
Berger, Steve	26-Sep-1949	3	248
Berger, Steve Warren	27-Jun-1970	11	400
Berger, Steve Warren	27-Jul-1970	11	399
Berkley, Robert E.	12-Jan-1959	8	139
Bettis, Terry Lee	4-Sep-1968	11	307
Beverly, Clyde	7-Jun-1949	6	149
Bevins, Carl Thomas	15-Jul-1975	13	168
Bevins, James Larry	9-Mar-1961	9	4
Bibbe, James Douglas	6-Oct-1959	8	211
Bickford, Paul	29-Oct-1949	3	451
Billips, Edward Lee	15-Jul-1975	13	171
Billips, John Franklin	15-Nov-1956	7	248
Bingham, Dave	6-Oct-1949	3	328
Bingham, Reed C.	12-Jan-1950	11	74
Bingham, Sam	7-Oct-1949	3	280
Birchfiield, David	19-May-1950	5	513
Blackburn, Adrian	23-Mar-1950	5	255
Blackburn, Alvin	2-May-1977	13	331
Blackburn, Amos	2-Nov-1948	2	242
Blackburn, Amos D.	31 Nov 1971	13	206

Name	Disc. Date	Book	Page
Blackburn, Bennie	30-Jan-1949	3	18
Blackburn, Bill J.	26-Mar-1950	5	228
Blackburn, Charles	27-Sep-1949	3	296
Blackburn, Clyde	24-Jun-1949	3	22
Blackburn, Clyde	30-Nov-1949	3	607
Blackburn, Cody Dwight	22-Mar-1995	14	23
Blackburn, Cody Dwight	22-Mar-1995	14	231
Blackburn, Colonel J.	22-Nov-1950	6	381
Blackburn, Colonel J.	22-Nov-1953	10	26
Blackburn, Craig Emberton	16-Aug-1995	14	200
Blackburn, Crit	27-May-1923	1	121
Blackburn, Curtis Talmadge	7-Mar-1975	13	123
Blackburn, Curtis Talmadge	7-Mar-1975	14	3
Blackburn, Delmon	20-Sep-1949	3	246
Blackburn, Delmon L.	1-Mar-1976	13	245
Blackburn, Edgar	10-Dec-1949	4	27
Blackburn, Elmer O.	1-Feb-1957	7	326
Blackburn, Elster E.	23-Nov-1971	11	522
Blackburn, Everett	22-Oct-1949	2	432
Blackburn, Floyd	28-Sep-1949	3	245
Blackburn, Frank	11-Nov-1948	5	465
Blackburn, Gomer C.	28-Jun-1946	10	208
Blackburn, Gomer Cecil	28-Jan-1965	10	207
Blackburn, Homer	16-Oct-1949	3	430
Blackburn, Howard D.	24-Jan-1950	4	466
Blackburn, Jacky K.	23-Dec-1974	13	90
Blackburn, Jacky K.	23-Dec-1974	15	71
Blackburn, Jacky K.		15	68-70
Blackburn, Jacky K.		15	74-75
Blackburn, James E.	13-Oct-1949	12	170
Blackburn, Joe D..	9-Nov-1977	12	156
Blackburn, John	1-Nov-1949	6	380
Blackburn, John H.	16-Oct-1974	13	58
Blackburn, Lindsay	31-Aug-1971	11	484
Blackburn, Lloyd R.	29-Mar-1950	5	222
Blackburn, Micheal Douglas	3-Nov-2006	15	83-84
Blackburn, Ollie	14-Jan-1950	4	215
Blackburn, Otis	6-Sep-1949	3	195
Blackburn, Raymond	5-Dec-1949	3	618
Blackburn, Southie	21-Jan-1950	6	123
Blackburn, Tom	8-Nov-1949	3	500
Blackburn, Troy	19-Jan-1950	4	296
Blackburn, Troy	19-Jan-1950	12	183
Blackburn, Troy W.	15-Nov-1972	13	398
Blackburn, Vernon	18-Oct-1949	3	356
Blackburn, Warren G.	2-Feb-1950	4	310
Blackburn, Willard Sr.	7-Jul-1949	3	84
Blackburn, William C.	22-Dec-1949	4	81
Blahnik, John R.	12-Jul-1949	3	93
Blair, Billy	26-Jan-1951	10	32
Blair, Eugene	2-Jan-1950	6	76
Blair, Gregory A.	20-Jul-1975	13	173
Blair, John D.	27-Jul-1965	11	96
Blair, Roland	21-Aug-1947	2	98
Blair, Virgie	28-Apr-1948	2	367
Blair, William Earl	28-Aug-1975	13	290
Blankenship, Carl	2-Dec-1949	6	199
Blankenship, Condy	27-Jun-1958	8	118
Blankenship, George P.	26-Dec-1949	14	154-155
Blankenship, George P.	29-Dec-1949	11	328
Blankenship, Odis D.	7-Dec-1949	6	109
Blankenship, Randy E.	17-Dec-1976	13	229
Blevins, Glen	15-Jan-1970	11	373
Blevins, Gustave N. Jr.	9-Jun-1949	3	37
Blevins, Mike H.	5-Apr-1949	9	322
Blevins, Mike H.	5-Apr-1949	9	325
Blevins, Mike H.	10-Nov-1955	9	320
Blevins, Myrl D.	16-Nov-1949	9	259
Blevins, Myrl D.	15-May-1951	9	260
Blevins, Tony Milford	15-Aug-1983	12	257
Boggs, Hassele	5-Oct-1953	7	33
Boggs, Hasselle N.	2-Jun-1956	7	181
Boggs, Paul H.	29-Mar-1949	3	9
Bolen, Edmon Emerson	2-Aug-1956	7	225
Bolen, Lloyd	15-Jan-1949	2	271
Boling, Walter Karr	23-Aug-1923	9	328
Bolton, Joe Rodney	18-Nov-1976	12	305-306
Bonar, Henry Jr.	24-Apr-1964	9	228
Booth, Jackie Marion	13-Mar-1975	12	310
Booth, Monroe	7-Nov-1949	8	12
Booth, Oakie	10-May-1950	4	559
Booth, Oakie	10-Sep-1956	7	219
Booth, Oscar H.	29-Dec-1949	7	32
Booth, Phillip Gene	28-Aug-1974	13	37

Name	Disc. Date	Book	Page
Borders, Douglas E.	21-May-1951	11	27
Borders, Jack	7-Feb-1950	6	26
Borders, Paul D.	22-Oct-1949	10	209
Boudle, Jacinda Dawn	1-Feb-2002	15	33
Boudle, Paul Bernard	1-Oct-1995	14	170
Boudle, Shane Bernard	18-Nov-2001	15	29
Bowe, Wallace E.	24-Feb-1950	6	82
Bowling, Lonzo Jay	7-Apr-1968	12	24
Bowling, Richard	12-Dec-1947	2	152
Bowling, Robert William	1-Jul-1999	14	284
Boyd, Albert Jr.	16-Mar-1950	5	252
Boyd, Alex	24-Jun-1949	3	60
Boyd, Arley	9-Oct-1949	3	565
Boyd, Arley	5-Apr-1950	4	495
Boyd, Ballard C.	9-Sep-1949	3	187
Boyd, Barry Lynn	30-Apr-1975	13	145
Boyd, Charles R.	8-Oct-1957	7	412
Boyd, Charley	8-Feb-1950	4	359
Boyd, Clifford	11-Mar-1950	4	443
Boyd, Coley Douglas	26-Feb-1950	12	167
Boyd, Earnest	26-Jan-1947	2	61
Boyd, Floyd	8-Oct-1956	8	23
Boyd, Floyd	2-Aug-1960	10	67
Boyd, Frank	15-Aug-1951	6	516
Boyd, Harry Randall	9-Sep-1976	13	286
Boyd, Henry Bascom	12-Nov-1975	13	207
Boyd, James W.	30-Mar-1950	4	470
Boyd, James W.	30-Mar-1950	10	80
Boyd, Jerry	15-Jun-1951	6	429
Boyd, John	10-Feb-1988	15	90
Boyd, Kenneth John	17-May-1962	9	77
Boyd, Kessie	27-Jun-1949	3	59
Boyd, Lloyd	8-Oct-1956	8	24
Boyd, Orbie	17-Nov-1949	3	513
Boyd, Otis	15-Oct-1949	5	245
Boyd, Randy	5-Dec-1982	13	429
Boyd, Sandy	8-Oct-1974	12	200
Boyd, Thomas	31-Jan-1950	5	543
Boyd, Tommy Joe	10-Feb-1974	14	59
Boyd, Wilford	9-Jan-1950	4	113
Boyd, Wilford	16-May-1957	7	341
Boyd, Wilford	30-Oct-1960	10	55
Boyd, Willard	6-Nov-1949	7	362
Boyd, William B.	14-Aug-1923	10	5
Boyd, William I.	24-Jan-1950	5	546
Braddock, Eddie	14-Apr-1947	2	191
Braddock, William F.	11-Dec-1949	5	106
Braddock, William F.	11-Dec-1949	11	122
Bradley, Alex	21-Mar-1950	6	467
Bradley, Bernis	15-Feb-1950	6	83
Bradley, Bernnie	17-Jun-1949	3	69
Bradley, Clyde	7-Aug-1960	9	332
Bradley, Eli	12-Aug-1948	2	336
Bradley, Gardis	16-Dec-1956	7	269
Bradley, George E.	20-Oct-1971	13	357
Bradley, Glenn H.	13-Mar-1974	12	104
Bradley, Gliden	3-Aug-1949	3	125
Bradley, Gorman Jr.	21-Jun-1978	13	359
Bradley, Green	24-Jun-1923	9	324
Bradley, Hansel S.	1-Oct-1963	9	200
Bradley, Harlen Eugene	15-Nov-1956	7	249
Bradley, James Daniel	22-Aug-1963	9	182
Bradley, John L.	5-Jun-1924	1	112
Bradley, John L.	5-Jun-1924	12	251
Bradley, Rudolph	2-Jun-1964	9	273
Bradley, Sam	17-Apr-1978	12	172
Bradley, Scott Duglas	23-May-1978	12	176
Branham, Andrew	27-Jul-1923	1	37
Branham, Astor J.	4-Jun-1959	8	177
Branham, Bill Jr.	9-Jan-1950	5	125
Branham, Burnard	13-Jan-1950	5	141
Branham, Burnard	13-Jan-1950	5	175
Branham, D.C.	8-Jan-1959	8	137
Branham, David	21-May-1956	7	202
Branham, Dee	3-Nov-1949	3	462
Branham, Dee	2-Dec-1950	7	31
Branham, Earl	17-Sep-1949	3	211
Branham, Earl H.	17-Dec-1949	5	249
Branham, Earsel	21-Dec-1949	6	605
Branham, Estille J.	17-Nov-1949	4	155
Branham, Ezra	2-Aug-1956	9	289
Branham, Frank B.	3-Jan-1950	4	116
Branham, Gary Allen	13-Feb-1975	13	117
Branham, Gene Paul	4-Jul-1957	7	352
Branham, Goble Jr.	11-Oct-1956	7	315
Branham, Harold F.	29-Sep-1948	2	231
Branham, Jack I. Jr.	4-Oct-1949	5	83
Branham, James D.	25-Dec-1949	4	277
Branham, James R.	19-May-1959	8	172
Branham, Jay	11-May-1947	2	41
Branham, John	25-Jun-1923	1	247
Branham, John Jr.	6-Mar-1955	7	229
Branham, Junior W.	26-Jan-1950	5	420
Branham, Lloyd	16-Oct-1974	13	61
Branham, Lyman C.	1-Nov-1972	11	608
Branham, Okla	2-Sep-1949	6	6
Branham, Paul J.	7-Dec-1958	9	264
Branham, Richard L.	22-Mar-1970	11	205
Branham, Robert C.	31-Jan-1950	5	463
Branham, Stephen Elliott Jr.	23-Apr-1997	14	222
Branham, Sylvia M.	16-Aug-1947	2	129
Branham, Taulbee Jr.	29-Dec-1967	14	13
Branham, Theop	5-Nov-1949	6	367
Branham, Thomas	24-May-1949	3	27
Branham, Troy L.	10-Aug-1951	14	289-294
Branham, Troy L.		14	61
Branham, Troy Lee	6-Feb-1977	14	60
Branham, Turner	13-Oct-1958	11	614
Branham, William Jr.	6-Sep-1963	10	110
Branson, John A.	9-Jun-1974	13	11
Bray, Lawrence Jr.	2-Jan-1950	4	104
Breeding, Esrom	15-Oct-1949	5	9
Breeding, Esrom	15-Oct-1949	10	24
Breeding, Lester	3-Nov-1957	7	429
Breeding, Paul	13-Dec-1949	9	356
Breeding, Steven	1-Jul-2005	15	64
Breeding, William H.	1-Nov-1962	9	131
Brewer, James D.	14-Dec-1949	5	100
Brickford, David	18-Sep-1949	3	223
Brock, James E.	22-Feb-1955	7	218
Broglin, Clell	14-Aug-1947	2	109
Brookover, Harry E.	23-Mar-1950	5	456
Brookover, Ira E.	10-May-1923	1	155
Brown, Andy	4-Jan-1923	1	220
Brown, Billy E.	3-May-1956	7	179
Brown, Cecil G.	26-Mar-1957	7	316
Brown, Charles E.	14-Dec-1977	13	352
Brown, Charles Evert	20-Jan-1958	12	286
Brown, Charley	27-Oct-1949	3	435
Brown, Clifford	10-Nov-1970	11	199
Brown, Danny Lee	6-Jul-1975	13	174
Brown, Dennis	9-Jan-1959	12	233
Brown, Douglas	15-Mar-1950	6	50
Brown, Edgel	15-Mar-1967	12	281
Brown, Edgel	8-Nov-1970	12	282
Brown, Edward K.	16-May-1923	1	211
Brown, Ellis	12-May-1970	14	104
Brown, Harlis	14-Dec-1955	7	244
Brown, Harry	31-Jan-1950	10	76
Brown, Harry	23-Jun-1951	10	77
Brown, Herbert	1-Feb-1953	6	620
Brown, Herman	28-May-1956	7	180
Brown, Kevin Robert	31-Jul-1998	14	248
Brown, Lloyd	14-Dec-1961	9	53
Brown, Lovel	12-Oct-1949	6	273
Brown, Lovel	3-Jan-1951	6	274
Brown, Lovel C.	17-Apr-1958	9	23
Brown, Menida	21-Jan-1923	1	54
Brown, Parris	15-Aug-1920	1	138
Brown, Paul V.	25-Apr-1976	13	264
Brown, Robert L.	24-Jan-1947	2	63
Brown, Robert L.	27-Oct-1948	2	335
Brown, Samuel C.	5-Feb-1923	1	114
Brown, William D.	7-May-1979	12	297
Brown, Willie	5-Sep-1922	1	602
Brown, Willis Dean	16-Jul-1971	11	477
Brunk, Floyd	15-Nov-1949	3	498
Bryant, Danny Lee	15-Sep-1974	13	42
Bryant, Danny Lee	15-Sep-1974	12	319
Bryant, Earl	13-Oct-1961	9	38
Bryant, Edd	24-Oct-1956	9	199
Bryant, Eli	13-Dec-1949	4	11
Bryant, Eugene	16-May-1946	2	168
Bryant, Fred	27-Feb-1959	8	150
Bryant, James W.	15-Dec-1949	4	138
Bryant, Roger Dean	10-Aug-1977	12	160
Bryant, William L.	23-Oct-1973	12	50
Buckley, John K.	2-Nov-1949	9	296
Buckley, John K.	14-Dec-1950	9	308
Bumgardner, James	31-Oct-1949	3	440
Bunting, Robert V.	22-Jan-1950	4	256
Bunting, Thomas	29-Dec-1950	6	250
Burchell, George	17-Nov-1949	3	541
Burchell, Jay	11-Jan-1950	6	68
Burchett, Albert	6-Feb-1950	10	81
Burchett, Ames	12-Jan-1923	1	17
Burchett, Andrew J.	30-May-1955	4	415
Burchett, Andrew J.	3-Sep-1957	7	397
Burchett, Arrie	7-Nov-1948	2	312
Burchett, Belvard	27-Nov-1949	3	591
Burchett, Billy	2-Dec-1950	6	549
Burchett, Bobbie D.	13-Feb-1975	13	383
Burchett, Clyde B.	13-Dec-1949	5	155
Burchett, Dave	27-Apr-1921	1	256
Burchett, Dave	10-Jun-1923	1	257
Burchett, Dewey	25-Jan-1949	2	275
Burchett, Dick	28-Oct-1948	2	235
Burchett, Fred C.	8-Jan-1950	4	349
Burchett, George	7-Jan-1950	6	276
Burchett, Glen	17-Dec-1950	6	573
Burchett, Hansford	26-Apr-1960	9	250
Burchett, Harold C.	7-Jun-1964	9	350
Burchett, Jake	23-May-1923	1	22
Burchett, James L.	30-Sep-1947		
Burchett, Kenneth	11-Apr-1976	13	259
Burchett, Randolph	23-Apr-1948	2	337
Burchett, Rebecca	19-Jan-1948	2	67
Burchett, Robert	19-Oct-1949	3	362
Burchett, Robert White	5-Jun-1956	7	199
Burchett, Roland L.	13-Jan-1950	4	301
Burchett, Thomas	30-May-1923	1	244
Burchett, Thomas E.	11-Oct-1957	7	424
Burchett, Thomas E.	11-Oct-1957	7	459
Burchett, Wade	23-Feb-1950	6	29
Burchett, Willard R.	31-Aug-1949	4	102
Burchett, Willie A.	14-Apr-1985	13	445
Burchett, Willie M.	8-Dec-1950	9	334
Burchett, Woodrow J.	5-Sep-1972	11	230
Burchfield, David	9-Aug-1981	13	421
Burga, Bill	26-Aug-1949	3	147
Burga, Bill	26-Aug-1949	12	207
Burga, Ollie Jr.	23-Apr-1950	4	533
Burga, Thomas D.	14-Nov-1973	12	59
Burga, Thomas Jr.	28-Sep-1949	3	253
Burgess, Vernon	15-Nov-1949	11	335
Burke, Charles E.	7-Jan-1950	4	150
Burke, Charles E.	7-Jan-1950	12	287
Burke, Charles Edward	15-Dec-1970	14	33
Burke, Charles Evert	13-Nov-1954	12	288
Burke, Charles Stephen	16-Feb-2002	15	31
Burke, Douglas	16-Oct-1949	3	358
Burke, Edgar	18-Dec-1949	5	108
Burke, Edmund R. Jr.	23-Dec-1962	9	151
Burke, Edmund R. Jr.	7-Feb-1966	11	155
Burke, Gordon R.	27-Aug-1972	11	582
Burke, Hayden M.	22-May-1978	12	182
Burke, Hern D.	1-Apr-1950	4	498
Burke, Hern D.	6-Apr-1953	6	639
Burke, Jimmy	21-Sep-1961	9	34
Burke, Joe E.	23-Jan-1950	4	264
Burke, John F.	7-Jun-1949	3	33
Burke, John W.	19-Jan-1950	4	206
Burke, Mitchell D.	3-Sep-1949	3	172
Burke, Orville	19-Jul-1954	4	639
Burke, Pat	16-Sep-1973	12	33
Burke, Paul	8-Dec-1949	4	49
Burke, Paul	8-Dec-1949	9	5
Burke, Raymond	20-Oct-1949	3	495
Burke, Richard Lee	1-Mar-1993	14	50
Burke, Roland	8-Aug-1971	11	478
Burke, Ronald	2-Nov-1972	11	605
Burke, Ronnie Thomas	14-Sep-1969	14	53
Burke, William N.	4-Nov-1961	9	46
Burke, Winston	11-Mar-1949	4	519
Burke, Winston	27-Nov-1950	6	520
Burkett, Charles C.	27-Nov-1948	2	251
Burkett, James A.	29-Apr-1949	3	17
Burkett, Jeff	25-Mar-1950	6	245
Burkhart, Roy	31-Jan-1950	6	101
Burton, Franklin H. Jr.	2-Oct-1949	6	48
Burton, Hobert	30-May-1923	1	219
Burton, Leffie	12-Jan-1950	4	298

Name	Disc. Date	Book	Page
Bush, Jackie Donald Jr.	15-Feb-2004	15	48
Bussey, Rufus	30-Jan-1947	2	31
Butcher, Harmon	8-Apr-1951	6	469
Butcher, Sam	30-Jan-1947	2	20
Butler, Crystal Lynn	18-Jan-2005	15	54
Butler, James Henry	24-Dec-1975	12	334
Butler, Warren	26-Jan-1950	6	141
Cade, Jerome	6-Jun-1951	11	34
Caldwell, Beckem	12-Oct-1949	3	339
Caldwell, Morris, E.	23-Dec-1949	5	150
Calhoun, Bert	2-Nov-1949	6	290
Calhoun, Billy	6-Nov-1969	11	358
Calhoun, Bradis	9-Feb-1950	12	134
Calhoun, Chester	14-Jan-1950	4	191
Calhoun, Chester	22-Jan-1958	8	264
Calhoun, Denver	18-Jun-1949	6	28
Calhoun, Estill	7-May-1964	9	225
Calhoun, Ishmael	27-Aug-1950	7	122
Calhoun, Ishmael	27-Aug-1950	9	254
Calhoun, James	9-Jul-1957	7	408
Calhoun, James	16-Jul-1958	8	53
Calhoun, James K.	23-Jul-1950	7	17
Calhoun, James K.	28-May-1953	7	2
Calhoun, John	15-Aug-1949	3	140
Calhoun, Junior	21-Dec-1950	7	119
Calhoun, Kenneth	10-Oct-1961	9	172
Calhoun, Lester	26-Nov-1972	14	12
Calhoun, Lewis L.	29-Oct-1949	4	499
Calhoun, Marvin	26-Nov-1949	6	346
Calhoun, Ray	9-Nov-1949	4	111
Calhoun, Raymond	27-Nov-1946	2	51
Calhoun, Woodrow	18-Dec-1949	9	271
Callahan, William R.	1-Dec-1949	4	618
Callahan, William T.	13-Dec-1949	4	450
Calton, Hargis	18-Apr-1947	2	204
Cambpell, Lugene	23-Jun-1949	6	436
Campbell, Billy E	11-Jul-1973	15	43
Campbell, Billy E.	13-Feb-1968	15	43
Campbell, Daniel	22-Mar-1967	14	183
Campbell, Deeve	11-Jan-1950	6	439
Campbell, Earl	29-Oct-1949	6	69
Campbell, Edgle	13-Mar-1951	7	170
Campbell, Elmo	10-Jan-1950	5	213
Campbell, Henry M.	7-Jun-1972	11	338
Campbell, James	19-Dec-1949	4	177
Campbell, James Garnard	27-Sep-1997	14	232
Campbell, James W.	28-Sep-1972	14	18
Campbell, John	7-Nov-1949	3	489
Campbell, John	15-Nov-1949	6	422
Campbell, John	19-Nov-1950	6	287
Campbell, Lugene	21-Apr-1951	6	437
Campbell, Overton	18-Nov-1949	6	371
Campbell, Ray	11-Dec-1949	6	564
Campbell, Ronald V.	26-Jul-1971	11	296
Campbell, Thomas Chandler	27-Feb-1957	7	327
Cannon, Earl C.R.	18-Jul-1958	11	78
Cannon, Hugh L.	1-Aug-1960	10	33
Capellie, Peter J.	19-Jan-1950	4	241
Carey, James E.	15-Apr-1951	7	29
Carlton, Clyde C.	30-Oct-1949	4	263
Carlton, Clyde C.	30-Nov-1950	7	69
Carlton, Clyde C.	20-Nov-1951	7	70
Carlton, James	16-Sep-1949	6	618
Carpenter, Charles	11-May-1951	6	517
Carr, Ambers	12-Jan-1950	4	453
Carr, Elwood	16-Oct-1961	9	45
Carr, Frank	24-May-1949	6	299
Carr, Lum	30-Mar-1951	9	222
Carr, Lum	15-Nov-1957	9	226
Carr, Tomie	12-Oct-1949	3	399
Carr, Winston	24-Sep-1949	3	259
Carroll, Amos	12-Jul-1946	8	326
Carroll, Amos	31-Mar-1948	2	148
Carroll, Carmell	4-Mar-1975	13	121
Carroll, Clayton	28-Aug-1949	3	153
Carroll, Theodore E.	16-Jan-1974	11	30
Carroll, Timothy L.	12-Nov-1979	13	403
Carroll, Will	27-Jul-1979	12	335
Carter, James J.	11-Mar-1950	6	408
Cartmell, Billie W.	19-Mar-1958	8	28
Carver, Robert L.	28-Jun-1950	4	636
Case, Andy	27-Oct-1959	11	140
Case, Bert	14-Nov-1949	11	107
Case, Bert	14-Feb-1951	11	106
Case, Charlie	21-Dec-1950	6	590
Case, Clive	1-Aug-1957	7	373
Case, Clive D.	13-Aug-1978	13	363
Case, Dallas	16-Nov-1949	3	597
Case, Elba	29-Jun-1951	6	313
Case, Hursel	19-Jun-1949	3	45
Case, Johnny	30-Dec-1949	5	139
Case, Larry B.	1-Feb-1975	13	98
Case, Phillip Lee	23-Nov-1967	11	258
Cassady, Austin	20-Feb-1950	6	409
Castle, Anthony R.	20-Mar-1974	12	112
Castle, Bennie	13-Jun-1961	9	10
Castle, Clifford C.	7-Nov-1949	5	449
Castle, Ellis Jr.	8-Jun-1961	9	32
Castle, Freddie J.	1-Aug-1960	9	154
Castle, Harold C.	19-Aug-1956	7	364
Castle, Ira	25-Sep-1947	2	54
Castle, Jimmy R.	17-Nov-1977	12	157
Castle, John M.	25-Mar-1923	1	51
Castle, John W.	3-Apr-1957	10	10
Castle, Larry D.	6-Nov-1975	13	204
Castle, Millard W.	2-Dec-1949	5	116
Castle, Roger L.	25-Jun-1970	11	393
Castle, Vernis G.	11-Nov-1972	11	603
Caudill, Bennie	13-Jun-1961	9	10
Caudill, Claude	24-Jan-1950	4	274
Caudill, Delmas	4-Oct-1949	4	343
Caudill, Donal	8-Oct-1956	7	233
Caudill, Earl	24-Jul-1949	6	86
Caudill, Earl	1-Dec-1949	6	479
Caudill, Earl	5-Dec-1950	6	376
Caudill, Eddie C.	27-Feb-1970	12	166
Caudill, Edward	20-Mar-1950	10	38
Caudill, Edward	23-Nov-1950	6	226
Caudill, Edward	1 April 1947	10	134
Caudill, Elmer L.	24-Oct-1956	7	236
Caudill, Elmer R.	13-Oct-1961	9	37
Caudill, Estill	18-Feb-1950	6	198
Caudill, Fhirow	12-Mar-1950	5	217
Caudill, Fhirow	15-Jul-1956	7	188
Caudill, Franklin E.	10-Apr-1968	11	15
Caudill, Hetric	14-May-1951	6	487
Caudill, Hetric	2-Aug-1956	14	51
Caudill, James E.	14-Mar-1977	13	318
Caudill, Jarlies Warne	4-Aug-1955	7	140
Caudill, Johnny M.	23-Feb-1975	13	122
Caudill, Kimber	Sept 1945	9	97
Caudill, Milton	26-Oct-1949	6	542
Caudill, Peat	8-Oct-1949	4	622
Caudill, Ralph	30-May-1950	10	89
Caudill, Ralph	30-May-1950	10	90
Caudill, Ross	14-Feb-1950	4	576
Caudill, Toy	29-Jul-1947	2	131
Caudill, Walter S.	13-Apr-1961	9	70
Cavins, James O.	20-Jul-1949	3	104
Cavins, Kermit D.	17-Aug-1949	3	146
Cavins, Kermit D.	15-Oct-1974	13	60
Centers, Charles	23-Apr-1969	14	77
Cesco, Thomas H.	27-Mar-1975	13	132
Charles, Henry	3-Jul-1949	6	478
Charles, Landon	13-Aug-1956	11	131
Chatman, Foster	12-Sep-1949	3	188
Cheek, Adam E.	11-Feb-1923	1	19
Cherren, Charles Jr.	19-Nov-1950	10	20
Childers, Albert D.	2-Dec-1956	8	22
Childers, Archer F.	11-Apr-1973	11	326
Childers, Conrad D.	17-Feb-1971	11	435
Childers, Frank	17-Oct-1947	2	106
Childers, Frank	17-Oct-1949	6	404
Childers, James	27-Nov-1951	1	3
Childers, James	3-Oct-1040	6	43
Childers, James M. Jr.	16-Nov-1949	12	126
Childers, Samey R.	1-Dec-1949	6	197
Childers, William H. Jr.	26-Dec-1949	4	88
Chullen, John L.	6-Jan-1972	11	526
Chullen, Claris Ann	10-Dec-1970	11	583
Chullun, John	19-Jan-1950	5	446
Clair, Luther R.	24-Aug-1962	9	96
Clark, Andrew J.	30-Jan-1950	4	345
Clark, Bernard N.	6-Apr-1950	5	265
Clark, Bruce	4-Jan-1950	6	315
Clark, Carmel	29-Dec-1949	6	443
Clark, Charlie W.	21-Jun-1950	4	604
Clark, Douglas	25-Nov-1949	3	536
Clark, Dutch	19-Mar-1974	12	111
Clark, Earnie	16-Dec-1973	12	75
Clark, Eddie L.	4-Mar-1975	13	177
Clark, Edford	26-Jan-1950	14	203
Clark, Edford L.	26-Jan-1950	4	486
Clark, Edward	5-Jun-1923	1	130
Clark, Fed	14-Oct-1949	3	346
Clark, George E.	20-Jun-1950	4	606
Clark, Gregory B.	18-Nov-1975	13	209
Clark, Henry	2-Jul-1950	5	332
Clark, Irvin	2-Aug-1949	3	121
Clark, Isaac L.	20-Sep-1956	7	312
Clark, James	16-Sep-1949	3	199
Clark, James E.	7-Dec-1949	5	89
Clark, James M.	26-Mar-1950	4	482
Clark, James R.	24-Sep-1956	7	375
Clark, Jessie	13-Nov-1923	10	138
Clark, Joe A.	18-Feb-1950	4	389
Clark, Joe C.	10-May-1970	12	302
Clark, John B.	30-Jan-1950	5	157
Clark, John G.	30-Jan-1974	12	89
Clark, Kermit E.	19-Jul-1949	3	102
Clark, Ralph	16-Dec-1949	5	462
Clark, Rexford	22-Apr-1927	11	250
Clark, Rexford	4-Nov-1931	11	249
Clark, Rexford	7-Dec-1934	11	248
Clark, Rexford	25-Dec-1934	11	247
Clark, Rexford	28-Jan-1938	11	246
Clark, Russell	9-Dec-1958	8	123
Clark, Rutherford B. Jr.	24-Apr-1949	3	19
Clark, Thurman	7-Feb-1950	4	356
Clark, Wayne Wright	23-Oct-1969	12	309
Clark, William L.	2-Dec-1948	2	296
Clarke, John B.	18-Feb-1923	1	12
Clatworthy, Bobby	30-Apr-1959	8	167
Clay, Carl Edward	19-Aug-1957	7	437
Clemons, Joel H.	16-Jul-1975	13	170
Clevenger, Aubert E.	25-Sep-1947	2	17
Click, Alroy	21-Jul-1958	8	300
Click, Billy Joe	16-Jun-1958	12	337
Click, Carl V.	14-Oct-1964	10	137
Click, Clarence A.	13-Nov-1949	4	170
Click, George	22-Nov-1949	6	227
Click, George H.	12-Mar-1958	8	46
Click, Ira R.	21-Apr-1968	11	149
Click, Isaac R.	8-Jan-1950	4	115
Click, James G.	13-Apr-1957	7	347
Click, Jobie	15-Nov-1948	11	5
Click, Lummie Jr.	8-Aug-1974	14	4
Click, N.D.	5-Oct-1970	11	191
Click, Raymond D.	24-Jun-1954	7	94
Click, Robert H.	8-Aug-1957	7	398
Click, Thurman	26-Feb-1950	4	434
Click, William B.	23-Sep-1976	13	285
Clifton, Charles W.	16-Nov-1949	7	296
Clifton, Charles W.	17-May-1951	7	295
Clifton, Dave E.	8-Nov-1948	11	93
Clifton, Fanna	19-Aug-1949	6	612
Clifton, Felmer R.	30-Aug-1956	7	386
Clifton, James	12-Jul-1949	6	116
Clifton, John P.	6-Dec-1949	4	8
Clifton, Johnny P. Jr.	1-Jan-1963	12	109
Clifton, Michael A.	31-May-1976	13	270
Clifton, Terry W.	21-Nov-1972	12	3
Clifton, Terry W.	21-Nov-1972	12	289
Cline, Eugene	18-Nov-1949	5	53
Cline, Eugene	18-Nov-1949	5	450
Cline, James B. Sr.	8-Jun-1948	2	190
Cline, S.E.	24-Aug-1960	9	310
Cline, Vadis R.	3-Mar-1950	4	438
Coakley, Dana Robert	22-Sep-1965	11	105
Coburn, Arthur	27-Nov-1949	5	67
Coburn, Arthur	27-Nov-1949	5	522
Coburn, Edgar	15-Oct-1949	3	332
Coburn, Elisworth G.	27-Oct-1949	3	555
Coburn, Garmon	4-Jan-1951	6	271
Coburn, Joe E.	1-Jun-1953	7	239
Coburn, John	22-Oct-1949	3	373
Coburn, Willie O.	8-Apr-1923	1	56
Cochrane, George C. Jr	14-Mar-1956	8	20
Cole, Charles	5-Jun-1973	11	339
Cole, F.D.	19-Dec-1950	6	617
Cole, John M.	11-Feb-1950	9	341
Cole, Leonard	16-Jan-1950	4	276

127

Name	Disc. Date	Book	Page
Coleman, Robert B.	19-Nov-1975	13	216
Collett, Allen M.	19-Oct-1948	10	25
Collier, Denver L.	8-Oct-1956	7	320
Collier, Earl	18-Aug-1958	8	145
Collier, Okie Jr.	22-Mar-1950	4	573
Collier, Ovie	1-Dec-1952	6	616
Collier, Ovie Jr.	23-Oct-1949	10	173-174
Collier, Ovie Jr.	17-Dec-1952	10	175
Collins, Paul	17-May-1959	8	175
Collins, Adrian N.	12-Jan-1959	8	135
Collins, Arthur	19-Dec-1949	4	85
Collins, Can C.	24-Dec-1973	12	79
Collins, Carl	22-Nov-1950	6	196
Collins, Carnlee	1-Jan-1950	5	128
Collins, Charles R.	27-May-1973	12	49
Collins, Charlie	9-Dec-1948	2	276
Collins, Chester	31-Jan-1950	4	408
Collins, Chester	31-Jan-1950	11	67
Collins, Cornelius	30-Oct-1949	7	118
Collins, Cornelius	16-Nov-1950	6	293
Collins, Dan	20-Jan-1924	1	208
Collins, Denver	30-Jun-1950	6	372
Collins, Eddie F.	10-Jun-1975	13	157
Collins, Edward	21-Jan-1959	11	102
Collins, Ellsworth H.	17-May-1950	4	578
Collins, Emil A.	4-Jul-1971	11	467
Collins, Emma A.	25-Oct-1949	5	14
Collins, Ernest	22-Aug-1947	6	410
Collins, Everette W.	18-Oct-1948	2	303
Collins, Frank	17-May-1923	1	87
Collins, Garfield	11-Jul-1922	9	292
Collins, Gerney D.	15-May-1978	12	174
Collins, Glen	27-Nov-1946	2	85
Collins, Glen	12-Sep-1956	9	274
Collins, Glen D.	20-Sep-1971	11	491
Collins, Grover M.	4-Dec-1967	11	176
Collins, Hascue	28-Feb-1951	9	290
Collins, Hassel	24-Oct-1948	2	234
Collins, Hollie	27-Jan-1950	6	308
Collins, James	13-Jan-1950	6	558
Collins, James	19-Dec-1973	12	78
Collins, James E.	23-Dec-1953	7	62-63
Collins, John	8-Dec-1946	2	40
Collins, John B.	30-May-1973	12	9
Collins, John D.	30-Dec-1947	2	28
Collins, John W.	14-Jun-1949	3	268
Collins, Johnny D.	13-Nov-1974	13	70
Collins, Joseph	9-Nov-1949	3	487
Collins, Junior	14-Jun-1950	5	467
Collins, Kermit L.	18-Dec-1961	9	50
Collins, Lloyd W.	19-Oct-1949	5	5
Collins, London	5-Jun-1949	10	85
Collins, Malcom	1-Dec-1949	3	596
Collins, Malcom H.	7-May-1923	1	23
Collins, Marion	16-Jul-1947	2	164
Collins, Martin Jr.	29-Jun-1962	9	86
Collins, Mont	13-Sep-1945	2	39
Collins, Ollie	6-Feb-1950	4	418
Collins, Paul H.	17-Jan-1966	12	127
Collins, Ralph	7-Jul-1949	6	341
Collins, Ray	3-Mar-1950	5	188
Collins, Ray	15-Dec-1955	8	10
Collins, Raymond	31-Jul-1975	13	180
Collins, Thomas	3-Jan-1923	1	195
Collins, Tommy J.	9-Aug-1965	11	103
Collins, Walter S.	9-Dec-1951	5	480
Collins, William	28-Jul-1951	6	486
Collins, William L.	28-Jul-1947	2	84
Collins, Woodrow	15-Dec-1949	4	50
Combs, Arby	2-Oct-1947	2	1
Combs, Bert T.	20-May-1950	11	124
Combs, Billie	5-Dec-1949	3	625
Combs, Carmel	17-Dec-1949	4	43
Combs, Cleon K.	10-Jul-1947	2	286
Combs, Cotriel	29-Nov-1949	4	12
Combs, Earl	23-Dec-1949	7	16
Combs, Edmond Lee	27-Apr-1969	14	153
Combs, Harry	20-May-1949	6	135
Combs, James	15-Mar-1973	11	620
Combs, James	15-Mar-1973	13	356
Combs, John G.L.	22-Oct-1949	3	389
Combs, Kristina Marie	10-Aug-2006	15	78
Combs, Kristina Marie	15-Jul-2007	15	88
Combs, Paul C.	15-Feb-1950	4	409
Combs, Thomas S.	9-Dec-1949	4	2
Combs, Townsell A.	7-Jan-1950	5	132
Combs, Virgie	26-Jul-1948	5	540
Combs, Walter	13-Dec-1949	4	47
Comer, Kieran John	4-Aug-2005	15	66
Compton, Ashland	5-Jan-1950	4	136
Compton, Burgess	4-Feb-1923	1	174
Compton, Charles	8-Jul-1949	6	328
Compton, James	14-Aug-1949	3	135
Compton, Jordan Tyler	2-Apr-2009	15	113-114
Compton, Marvin	29-May-1952	6	581
Compton, Omery D.	11-Oct-1956	7	227
Compton, Tommy L.	3-Nov-1964	10	146
Compton, William J.	16-May-1960	8	271
Compton, William S.	14-Mar-1974	13	272
Comstock, Bobby M.	14-Apr-1950	4	493
Comstock, Carl	27-Mar-1923	1	103
Comstock, Gene P.	1-Apr-1959	8	225
Comstock, Robert I.	3-Mar-1976	13	244
Conley, Augusta G.	25-Jun-1956	7	192
Conley, Baird	19-Jan-1950	4	218
Conley, Barry Dean	31-Mar-1996	14	185
Conley, Ben	13-Sep-1949	5	13
Conley, Bert	13-Dec-1949	4	58
Conley, Cecil	13-Aug-1949	3	132
Conley, Clifford	15-Jul-1949	3	97
Conley, Clifford	2-Mar-1954	11	264
Conley, Clifford	21-Jun-1958	11	265
Conley, Clifford	13-Aug-1961	11	267
Conley, Clifford	1-Sep-1967	11	266
Conley, Earlen	5-Aug-1979	14	22
Conley, Ellis R.	11-Nov-1949	5	33
Conley, Eucker	5-Mar-1950	5	203
Conley, Franklin	4-Jan-1923	1	4
Conley, George	22-Jan-1951	6	432
Conley, Grannis B.	23-Jun-1949	3	58
Conley, Grover B.	13-May-1949	3	21
Conley, Henry C.	7-Sep-1970	11	407
Conley, Henry M.	28-Apr-1950	5	441
Conley, Herman	7-Nov-1949	3	563
Conley, Herman	13-Mar-1950	4	467
Conley, Hubert	16-Sep-1949	9	291
Conley, Jackie L.	24-May-1962	9	78
Conley, Jackie L.	29-Jul-1966	11	329
Conley, Jackie L.	29-Jul-1974	13	417
Conley, Jackie L.	1-Nov-1978	13	371
Conley, Jackie L.	1-Nov-1978	13	420
Conley, James D.	17-Jul-1949	3	107
Conley, James P.	19-Mar-1950	4	567
Conley, Larry D.	5-Jun-1975	13	155
Conley, Leck	5-Dec-1922	1	8
Conley, Lewis H.	5-Jul-1949	3	89
Conley, Michael O.	20-Dec-1973	13	340
Conley, Neve	31-Mar-1965	11	251
Conley, Paul D.	17-Sep-1951	9	33
Conley, Rickey D.	6-Mar-1979	13	378
Conley, Temen J.	12-Apr-1950	5	250
Conley, Theodore L. Jr.	22-Aug-1950	5	442
Conley, William P.	11-Nov-1949	4	118
Conley, Willie	3-Jul-1947	7	97
Conley, Woodrow	1-Dec-1949	3	629
Conn, Aaron R.	8-Mar-1950	4	437
Conn, Albert	13-Feb-1975	13	105
Conn, Barbara	23-Jun-1950	6	7
Conn, Bennie G.	25-Sep-1958	11	90
Conn, Bryce	21-Sep-1974	13	44
Conn, Carl	6-Oct-1949	3	290
Conn, Charles	9-Jan-1950	6	403
Conn, Crit	19-Apr-1951	7	46
Conn, David I.	1-Jul-1972	11	342
Conn, Dewey	20-Oct-1949	4	407
Conn, Eddie	11-Oct-1949	3	417
Conn, Emmit E.	6-Apr-1950	5	264
Conn, Eursel D.	5-Oct-1962	9	108
Conn, Frank	27-Oct-1949	3	484
Conn, Fred R.	3-Feb-1950	4	334
Conn, Garland D.	24-Sep-1961	9	35
Conn, George	26-Jun-1949	3	67
Conn, George Jr.	18-Dec-1956	7	354
Conn, Harold	30-Sep-1951	6	541
Conn, Hershel	9-Jan-1957	7	280
Conn, Jackie	22-Nov-1973	12	64
Conn, James A.	15-Jan-1948	2	86
Conn, Jim	13-Jan-1951	6	272
Conn, Joe H.	13-Dec-1949	4	221
Conn, John L.	16-May-1957	7	334
Conn, Johnie B.	3-Dec-1948	2	261
Conn, Junior	18-May-1950	6	85
Conn, Maryland Jr.	3-Sep-1947	2	11
Conn, Noah	12-Oct-1949	3	322
Conn, Norman	15-Aug-1949	3	138
Conn, Paul	27-Jun-1971	11	292
Conn, Paul D.	20-Dec-1962	13	205
Conn, Ranal	3-Mar-1973	11	619
Conn, Sammie	13-Oct-1947	2	181
Conn, Samuel	7-Nov-1949	3	534
Conn, Travis	31-Aug-1949	3	212
Conn, Troy R.	21-Jun-1974	13	18
Conners, Thomas B.	4-Apr-1951	12	137
Connors, Ballard F. Sr.	16-Nov-1949	3	512
Connors, James Paul	4-Jan-1950	12	248
Connors, James Paul	4-Jan-1950	9	257
Connors, James Paul	4-Jan-1950	12	247
Connors, Printis	7-Nov-1950	6	175
Connors, Thomas	20-Oct-1949	3	392
Connors, William	29-Sep-1949	3	251
Contie, Fudie J.	15-Feb-1949	3	4
Cook, Curtis L. Jr.	20-Jul-1971	11	476
Cook, Henry W.	10-Oct-1949	6	464
Cook, James R.	12-May-1964	9	241
Cook, Otis D.	9-Jan-1959	8	132
Cook, Phillip D.	20-Mar-1972	11	543
Cook, Raymond	5-Nov-1957	7	434
Cook, Roy	27-Jan-1947	2	55
Cook, Sam	21-Oct-1948	2	233
Cook, Spencer	9-Nov-1949	5	26
Cook, Spencer	9-Nov-1949	5	514
Cook, Thomas Henry	30-Jun-1971	14	40
Cook, Willia E.	22-May-1975	13	154
Cooley, Alvin R.	9-Jan-1972	11	252
Cooley, Dave	7-Nov-1949	3	486
Cooley, Donald D.	5-Apr-1972	11	553
Cooley, Dorlen	22-Oct-1950	6	163
Cooley, Edward	23-Apr-1950	4	27
Cooley, Harry V.	10-Mar-1964	12	145
Cooley, James	28-Jun-1949	3	88
Cooley, James J.	18-Nov-1949	5	57
Cooley, James J.	18-Nov-1949	11	2
Cooley, Jerry T.	19-Jan-1977	13	302
Cooley, Joe	8-Feb-1950	6	343
Cooley, Joe	8-Dec-1956	7	262
Cooley, Kenneth R.	7-Sep-1961	9	106
Cooley, Paul G.	2-Dec-1949	4	243
Cooley, Robert G.	13-Apr-1948	2	199
Cooley, Robert L.	2-Dec-1973	12	82
Cooley, Savage W.	30-Nov-1949	4	121
Cooley, William	9-Sep-1949	3	179
Cooper, Glen	27-Nov-1949	5	71
Cooper, Glen	27-Nov-1949	5	519
Cooper, Jackie D.	12-Jul-1968	11	172
Cooper, Mickey M.	21-Jul-1956	7	206
Cooper, Rex Clayton	13-Jul-1962	9	92
Cooper, Victor	29-Nov-1951	6	548
Copley, George W. Jr.	31-May-1950	6	416
Corbin, Carl D.	24-Nov-1949	5	52
Cordial, Ennis	28-Oct-1947	2	329
Cordial, Raymond	5-Jun-1949	3	32
Cornett, Clinton	21-Dec-1949	5	518
Cornett, Kelly	30-Jun-1949	15	109
Cornett, Phil	21-Dec-1947	11	94
Cornette, Astor L.	9-Aug-1971	11	231
Cornette, Howard	12-May-1957	7	353
Cottrell, Frederick	15-Nov-1949	3	515
Cottrell, Frederick R.	15-Nov-1949	11	143
Couch, Carter M.	21-Dec-1949	4	628
Cox, Luther	6-Nov-1949	3	559
Cox, Willie	25-Nov-1949	4	128
Coy, Francis M.	5-Feb-1950	4	385
Crabtree, Roe	19-Oct-1949	3	443
Crabtree, William C.	19-Jan-1951	5	435
Craft, Eddie F.	22-Jan-1923	1	203
Craft, Eddie M.	29-May-1964	10	34
Craft, Edgar V.	6-Oct-1955	7	204
Craft, Harris A.	10-May-1961	9	14
Craft, Paul R.	7-Nov-1957	7	432
Craft, William	8-Jul-1950	6	19
Craft, William	24-Jul-1951	6	470
Craft, William R.	8-Jun-1959	8	178

Name	Disc. Date	Book	Page
Craft, Willis	18-Dec-1947	2	49
Crager, Dennis F.	27-Oct-1956	7	259
Crager, Donald R.	2-Nov-1966	12	55
Crager, Donald R.	8-Nov-1971	12	52
Crager, Donald R.	12-Mar-1973	12	53
Crager, James	17-Oct-1949	6	247
Crager, Ralph L.	8-Dec-1961	9	56
Crager, Roy E	18-Oct-1973	12	54
Crain, Donald J.	21-Jun-1956	7	185
Crain, Donald J.	21-Jan-1960	8	254
Crain, Robert Franklin	5-Jun-1971	5	311
Crawford, Arvel R.	25-Sep-1974	13	43
Crawford, Charles	7-Mar-1950	5	204
Crawford, Delzie	8-Feb-1950	10	151-152
Crawford, Foster	23-Oct-1964	10	179
Crawford, Paul	5-Mar-1957	7	321
Crider, Andrew J.	19-May-1959	8	174
Crider, Charles A.	15-Sep-1971	11	315
Crider, Claudith S.	4-Jun-1978	12	181
Crider, Gaylord	5-Dec-1949	4	20
Crider, Millard	17-Feb-1957	7	383
Crider, Sam	29-Nov-1949	6	95
Crider, William J.	11-Jul-1971	11	227
Crider, Woodman	10-Nov-1949	6	441
Crisp, Arthur	9-Oct-1956	7	255
Crisp, Clarence	30-Sep-1949	3	261
Crisp, Clarence H.	5-Nov-1949	4	536
Crisp, Curtis	4-Nov-1949	7	115
Crisp, Dennis	2-Dec-1976	13	296
Crisp, Earnest	20-Apr-1950	4	507
Crisp, Earnest Jr.	20-Apr-1975	13	138
Crisp, Edward	21-Aug-1949	3	145
Crisp, Everett	18-Jun-1949	3	48
Crisp, Everett	6-Jan-1950	4	139
Crisp, Everett M.	5-May-1976	13	268
Crisp, Felix	15-Apr-1923	1	190
Crisp, Frank	24-Jun-1923	1	194
Crisp, Grover B.	21-Mar-1923	1	100
Crisp, Harry H.	24-Sep-1948	2	328
Crisp, Herman	26-Jun-1950	6	270
Crisp, James	15-Oct-1949	3	370
Crisp, James K.	8-May-1949	2	365
Crisp, James K.	27-Jan-1950	11	142
Crisp, Kendell	3-Nov-1951	5	484
Crisp, Lee	27-May-1923	1	122
Crisp, Lewis	9-Dec-1921	1	607
Crisp, Obie	15-Feb-1950	4	400
Crisp, Ray	20-Apr-1950	4	512
Crisp, Richard	4-Jun-1958	8	37
Crisp, Sherman D.	26-Oct-1972	11	602
Crisp, Sol	6-Oct-1949	3	294
Crisp, Tracy	15-Sep-1950	6	360
Crisp, Verden	28-Oct-1948	2	254
Crisp, Walter	7-Oct-1949	6	63
Cross, Agis S.	12-Sep-1947	2	137
Crum, Bill	25-Jan-1950	6	440
Crum, Billy G.	19-Mar-1959	10	4
Crum, Billy G.	19-Mar-1959	12	45
Crum, Billy G.	19-Mar-1959	12	188
Crum, Billy G.	20-May-1962	12	190
Crum, Billy G.	1-Oct-1966	12	46
Crum, Carl	8-Jan-1950	4	619
Crum, Clifford	8-Jan-1960	8	263
Crum, Daniel	24-Dec-1949	4	105
Crum, Daniel F.	26-Oct-1959	10	79
Crum, Donald B.	16-Jan-1950	4	360
Crum, Earnest	17-Dec-1949	6	357
Crum, Ellis	5-Nov-1957	9	280
Crum, Elsworth Lee	17-Aug-1974	14	246
Crum, Fonzo	7-Oct-1949	11	80
Crum, Frank	23-Apr-1947	2	79
Crum, Haskel	24-Sep-1949	3	229
Crum, Isaac	5-Jun-1924	1	61
Crum, James R.	18-Aug-1958	9	231
Crum, Marvin	3-Sep-1969	14	44
Crum, Marvin	1-Sep-1973	14	58
Crum, Merlin	19-Nov-1950	6	193
Crum, Oscar	18-May-1923	1	205
Crum, Robert	23-Feb-1923	1	68
Crum, Robert	14-Oct-1949	3	420
Crum, Robert L.	25-Dec-1945	11	3
Crum, Russell	24-Sep-1949	3	237
Crum, Sol Jr.	20-Jan-1950	4	251
Crumb, James	27-Nov-1921	1	605

Name	Disc. Date	Book	Page
Crumb, James	27-Nov-1921	1	618
Cummings, Steven C.	7-Feb-1972	11	548
Curnutte, Bobbby	10-Jan-1958	8	130
Curnutte, Orvel	18-Oct-1949	3	364
Curry, Charles	22-Jan-1950	6	535
Curry, Charles	19-Jan-1951	6	534
Curry, Dawson	7-Feb-1957	11	65
Curry, Forrest S.	15-Jun-1960	8	276
Curry, James R.	20-Dec-1964	10	178
Curry, John P.	15-Jan-1959	8	133
Curry, Ronald K.	13-Jul-1960	8	288
Curry, Roy	1-Jun-1972	11	566
Dailey, Kermit E.	19-Apr-1972	11	556
Dailey, Kermit Eugene		15	107
Dale, Jesse	29-Jul-1923	1	241
Damron, Charles T.	5-Dec-1949	4	68
Damron, Claude J.	7-Oct-1959	8	214B
Damron, Donald C.	4-Jan-1949	2	279
Damron, John Jr.	2-Dec-1963	9	202
Damron, Kenneth R.	22-Nov-1949	3	528
Damron, Ralph	15-Dec-1967	11	255
Damron, Ralph	24-Dec-1975	13	218
Damron, Robert A.	31-Aug-1947	2	105
Damron, Veirgis	18-Jan-1949		
Damron, William B.	26-Sep-1949	6	96
Damron, Willis	26-May-1965	11	60
Daniel, Roscoe	20-Apr-1964	9	234
Daniels, Augustus Basil	3-Jun-1923	7	266
Daniels, Bee	9-Aug-1944	2	133
Daniels, Charles	14-Jul-1952	7	80
Daniels, Charles C.	20-May-1946	2	145
Daniels, Charles E.	9-Jun-1974	13	8
Daniels, David L.	11-Jul-1949	11	76
Daniels, Earl J.	24-Nov-1949	3	566
Daniels, Edward	2-Oct-1949	3	271
Daniels, Elmer	3-Nov-1949	5	43
Daniels, Everett A.	2-Jun-1958	8	48
Daniels, Floyd E.	1-Oct-1976	14	258
Daniels, Floyd Kenneth	28-Oct-1950	10	147
Daniels, Graden	22-Sep-1949	3	231
Daniels, James B.	28-Aug-1955	7	145
Daniels, James D.	8-Apr-1961	9	1
Daniels, James H.	2-Apr-1974	14	36
Daniels, James Larry	2-Aug-1958	8	67
Daniels, Lloyd, Jr.	10-Jan-1950	4	227
Daniels, Mack R.	20-Dec-1949	5	137
Daniels, Paul V.	3-Apr-1976	13	255
Daniels, Raymond L.	28-Feb-1950	5	184
Daniels, William	7-Dec-1949	4	205
Davidson, John A.	9-Jan-1950	4	207
Davidson, Preston	26-Jan-1923	1	79
Davis, Arvin G.	10-Dec-1927	1	80
Davis, Arvin G.	17-Dec-1949	5	438
Davis, Clyde E.	14-Jan-2008	15	98
Davis, Dylan Wayne	1-Aug-1949	5	226
Davis, Edgel	21-Mar-1960	8	265
Davis, Elmer L.	25-May-1949	3	25
Davis, Floyd	5-Aug-1967	15	63
Davis, Gene Douglas	4-Feb-1950	6	494
Davis, James	6-Jul-1951	6	502
Davis, James	3-Dec-1968	11	151
Davis, James H	13-Feb-1975	13	102
Davis, Jerry W.	23-Sep-1949	3	285
Davis, Joe	17-Apr-1953	7	27
Davis, John H.	19-Feb-1972	11	549
Davis, Marshall	17-Feb-1950	4	388
Davis, Rady	16-Apr-1973	11	630
Davis, Ralph, Jr.	14-Jun-1953	7	13
Davis, Ray C.	30-Oct-1957	9	351
Davis, Ray E.	25-Jun-1949	3	56
Davis, Raymond	24-Nov-1959	0	240
Davis, Richard W.	7-Feb-1950	4	588
Dawhare, Edward	5-May-1979	14	256
Dawson, Deal	21-Apr-1971	11	279
Dawson, Harold T.	1-Feb-1947	14	109
Dawson, James	7-Jul-1950	6	56
Day, Billy S.	13-Sep-1957	7	405
Day, Billy S.	27-Jun-1957	7	349
Day, Carl W.	26-Mar-1971	11	440
Day, Gary L.	20-Aug-1970	11	402
Day, Larry G.	26-Sep-1949	3	278
Deal, George	7-Feb-1950	6	150
Deal, Parris	28-Oct-1949	7	130
Deboard, James	25-Apr-1971	11	281
Deboard, Kenneth R.			

Name	Disc. Date	Book	Page
Debord, Ralph	3-Oct-1949	3	301
Decker, Virlen	25-Jan-1923	1	216
DeCoursey, Amerida G.	22-Oct-1949	5	436
Decoursey, Ernest E.	15-Aug-1950	12	152
DeLong James	25-Dec-1922	1	104
DeLong, Kennis	10-Feb-1947	2	147
DeLong, Oral	10-Nov-1949	5	31
DeLong, Russell	29-Jul-1949	3	115
Dempsey, Arnold E.	16-Oct-1965	11	115
Dempsey, Chester	22-Jul-1948	9	315
Dempsey, Harlan L.	28-Oct-1958	8	200
Dempsey, Harry G.	3-Oct-1957	4	416
Denny, Roy R.	21-Jan-1950	5	193
Derossett, Ashland	8-Jan-1950	4	174
Derossett, Christopher C.	21-Feb-1950	5	168
Derossett, Degarmo	14-Dec-1956	7	263
Derossett, Donald C.	22-Feb-1950	5	268
Derossett, Earl D.	3-May-1977	13	323
Derossett, Earl R.	15-Oct-1973	11	499
Derossett, Frank	6-Dec-1923	1	91
Derossett, Greeway	12-Jun-1949	3	626
Derossett, Harold E.	24-Feb-1975	13	175
Derossett, Jack	23-Jan-1950	5	142
Derossett, Jake	11-Feb-1923	1	171
Derossett, James	6-Nov-1949	3	488
Derossett, James	21-Dec-1949	4	79
Derossett, James K.	1-Dec-1949	3	36
Derossett, James N.	3-Sep-1957	7	396
Derossett, Joe	20-Jan-1950	4	303
Derossett, John B.	11-Aug-1963	9	171
Derossett, Joseph	12-Feb-1951	6	323
Derossett, Larce	19-Nov-1949	3	550
Derossett, Merion	17-Feb-1955	7	150
Derossett, Michael F.	15-Jul-1975	13	167
Derossett, Paul G.	8-Nov-1956	7	243
Derossett, Sam Naymon	3-Sep-1957	7	396
Derossett, Silas	17-Jun-1949	6	40
Derossett, Theodore	18-Dec-1950	6	233
Derossett, Theodore R.	1-Nov-1949	7	26
Derossett, Thomas J.	19-Oct-1949	9	349
Derossett, Thomas J.	11-Apr-1975	13	142
Derossett, Will	25-Jan-1923	1	85
Derossett, William T.	14-Oct-1963	9	194
Deskiins, Wells	8-Dec-1949	3	623
Deskins, Arnold L.	27-Jul-1949	3	116
Deskins, Arthur, Jr.	14-Nov-1976	13	294
Deskins, Henry	25-Oct-1949	3	383
Devol, Bernard J.	24-Oct-1949	6	9
Dewese, William A.	31-Mar-1921	1	109
Dials, Clarence F.	6-Feb-1958	7	481
Dials, Hargus	15-Feb-1950	4	525
Diles, Edward	23-Jun-1933	2	287
Diles, Edward	12-Sep-1947	2	149
Dillion, Calvin	13-Jan-1950	4	300
Dillion, Calvin	1-Jan-1973	11	624
Dillion, James H.	11-Nov-1974	13	71
Dillion, Lee	12-Dec-1922	1	7
Dillion, Phillip	25-Mar-1948	2	179
Dingus Blanche	28-Mar-1950	6	477
Dingus, Blanche E	10-Jan-1949	7	100
Dingus, Blanche E	10-Jan-1949	9	245
Dingus, Charles D.	19-Jan-1972	12	201
Dingus, Charles D.	19-Jan-1972	12	294
Dingus, Charles P.	23-Feb-1950	4	448
Dingus, Edward S.	8-Sep-1949	7	115
Dingus, Ernest	25-Feb-1956	11	12
Dingus, Henry	30-Oct-1949	3	442
Dingus, Herbert K.	19-Apr-1955	7	133
Dingus, Jack G.	20-Oct-1958	8	98
Dingus, James O.	1-Feb-1959	9	285
Dingus, Joseph	20-Sep-1949	3	244
Dingus, Kent R.	14-Jul-1983	15	86
Dingus, Mark H.	22-Jan-1970	11	372
Dingus, Ralph W.	14-Feb-1976	13	236
Dingus, Richard L.	6-Apr-1950	5	267
Dingus, Sam P.	5-Jun-1924	1	117
Dingus, Samuel P.	16-Feb-1948	2	15
Dingus, Thomas G.	19-Dec-1949	4	439
Dingus, Wayne D.	29-Oct-1970	11	626
Dingus, William J.	15-Mar-1950	4	444
Dixon, Albert	10-Jan-1950	6	384
Dixon, Carl	25-Oct-1949	3	422
Dixon, Glenn M.	10-Jun-1960	8	214
Dixon, James	16-Sep-1949	6	62

Name	Disc. Date	Book	Page
Dixon, Marvin, Jr.	14-Jan-1965	10	189
Dixon, Mervil	13-Nov-1949	6	42
Dodd, Charles	23-Sep-1949	6	178
Dodd, Willis	20-Sep-1949	6	177
Dodds, Matthew E.	24-Nov-1922	1	18
Donahoe, Michael	25-Feb-1974	12	98
Donahoe, Patrick	7-Nov-1974	13	68
Dorton, Earnest C.	15-Sep-1971	11	498
Dotson, Edgar T.	23-Jan-1950	4	240
Dotson, George A.	19-Jun-1974	13	12
Dotson, Greely	1-Dec-1949	5	81
Dotson, James D.	22-Mar-1976	13	250
Dotson, James L.	14-Sep-1949	3	205
Dotson, Lewis	14-Oct-1949	3	307
Dotson, Lewis D.	8-Jan-1950	4	153
Dotson, Mitchell	2-Feb-1950	5	162
Dotson, Willard	18-Jul-1971	11	293
Dove, Paul V.	20-Dec-1964	13	14
Draughn, Homer	16-May-1957	7	452
Dudleson, Buster	9-Jan-1950	8	289
Dudleson, Larry M.	17-Sep-1972	11	599
Dudleson, Larry Russell	22-Nov-1994	14	145
Duff, Edmond	21-Aug-1951	9	342
Duff, Freeman	6-Sep-1960	8	312
Duff, James A.	31-Oct-1957	8	66
Duncan, Charley	9-Feb-1972	11	537
Duncan, Roy R.	28-Aug-1974	13	40
Dunnagan, John	18-Nov-1969	11	156
Dusina, James T.	9-Mar-1972	11	541
Dusina, Jerry D.	13-Jun-1971	11	289
Dye, Ed	29-Oct-1949	3	407
Dye, Martin Woodrow	20-Mar-1994	14	121
Dye, Rabon	16-Dec-1971	11	528
Dye, Rabon	16-Dec-1971	14	8
Dye, Tilton	28-May-1972	15	10
Dyer Donald	23-Dec-1943	11	85
Dyer, Donald A.	20-Jul-1949	11	86
Dyer, Joseph E.	20-Dec-1949	4	219
Ealey, Sam	11-Jun-1949	6	58
Eden, Bert	29-Oct-1952	6	622
Edena, Willie R.	18-Nov-1949	9	281
Edwards, Hales	30-Jul-1923	9	348
Edwards, Lloyd R.	2-Jul-1950	4	627
Elder, Larry Eugene	23-Mar-1965	11	59
Elkins, Andrew T.	9-Oct-1956	7	480
Elkins, Billy R.	17-Jan-1950	4	209
Elkins, Laurence T.	27-Jul-1956	7	360
Elkins, Ralph	20-Oct-1949	3	348
Elkins, Richard	24-Apr-1950	4	517
Elliott, Barzell F.	1-Jul-1905	1	140
Elliott, Edmond	10-Apr-1958	8	50
Elliott, Edmond	10-Sep-1961	9	39
Elliott, Forrest	12-Dec-1950	6	260
Elliott, Francis Jr.	18-Mar-1958	8	14
Elliott, Garlin	10-Aug-1955	9	191
Elliott, James Jr.	21-Dec-1950	6	332
Elliott, James O.	31-Jan-1958	7	486
Elliott, Jesse	24-Jun-1949	3	54
Elliott, John P.	14-Aug-1947	2	73
Elliott, John T.	28-Feb-1950	5	177
Elliott, Linda Jean	8-Oct-1984	14	264
Elliott, Linda Jean	8-Oct-1984	14	266
Elliott, Linda Jean	8-Oct-1984	14	268
Elliott, Robert W.	30-Dec-1922	1	2
Elliott, Ronald	9-Oct-1974	13	64
Elliott, Russell	21-Dec-1949	6	266
Elliott, Russell	17-Dec-1950	6	261
Elliott, Vernon H.	8-May-1974	13	2
Elliott, Wilburn Jr.	9-Jul-1978	13	381
Elliott, Willie H.	11-Jun-1974	13	13
Elliott, Willie J.	8-Jan-1947	1	141
Ellis, Johnny	1-Nov-1950	6	172
Ellis, Tilden R.	17-Aug-1961	9	21
Elswick, Clayton	15-Sep-1959	8	213
Elswick, Elmer	23-Dec-1947	2	342
Elswick, Hershel	27-Apr-1958	8	158
Elswick, Luther	19-Nov-1922	1	101
Elswick, Luther	17-Nov-1922	10	188
Endicott, Otto	3-Nov-1949	3	460
Endicott, Ralph Dwayne	6-Oct-1996	14	201
England, Grover	30-Mar-1950	9	269
England, Robert E.	2-Jul-1972	11	573
England, Robert V.	1-Sep-1949	10	141
England, Thomas Clifford		11	125

Name	Disc. Date	Book	Page
Epling, Paul S.	7-May-1957	8	11
Epling, William T.	1-Mar-1923	1	98
Epling, William T.	1-Mar-1923	1	239
Estep, John Lewis	1-May-1997	14	242
Estep, Wallace Jr.	11-Dec-1949	4	5
Estep, William	9-Aug-1950	6	18
Estridge, Willon	30-Jul-1949	6	81
Evans, Hatler	2-Apr-1957	8	155
Evans, Herbert	1-Apr-1923	1	236
Evans, James	24-Apr-1947	2	134
Evans, James P.	16-Aug-1961	9	117
Evans, James R.	13-Dec-1949	4	416
Evans, John	28-Nov-1949	3	581
Evans, Willard	11-Dec-1922	1	224
Everidge, Charles	26-Aug-1956	10	204
Faine, George E.	5-Feb-1950	9	352
Faine, William H.	5-Feb-1950	2	76
Fairchild, Chester A.	20-Oct-1947	2	119
Fairchild, Dennis	3-Jul-1949	3	101
Fairchild, Johnie	2-Oct-1949	6	386
Falestead, James Ray	16-Sep-1972	11	223
Fannin, Billy	3-Jul-1949	3	507
Fannin, Billy J.	19-Aug-1959	8	203
Fannin, Billy L.	24-Dec-1957	7	482
Fannin, Charles R.	19-Nov-1959	8	233
Fannin, Ernest A.	8-Jan-1950	4	179
Fannin, Glen	7-Dec-1949	3	627
Fannin, John	8-Jul-1948	2	202
Fannin, John D.	21-May-1950	4	565
Fannin, Otto	12-Jan-1923	1	125
Fannin, Otto Walker Jr.	8-Sep-1960	8	310
Fannin, Thomas	29-Oct-1949	3	503
Fannin, William Thomas	28-Mar-1975	13	136
Farmer, Billy	11-Feb-1950	5	169
Farmer, Eldridge	17-Aug-1956	11	312
Farmer, James E.	1-Oct-1935	2	33
Farrell, Paul	5-Jan-1994	14	105
Fenix, Ray	15-Sep-1957	7	401
Ferguson, Benjamin D.	25-Mar-1954	11	39
Ferguson, Benjamin D.	25-Mar-1954	8	199
Ferguson, Charles D.	8-Oct-1958	8	241
Ferguson, Claude S.	11-Mar-1968	12	144
Ferguson, Claude S.	9-Mar-1972	13	301
Ferguson, John	25-Nov-1949	3	527
Ferguson, John M.	5-Mar-1956	9	94
Ferguson, Leonard R.	25-Dec-1967	11	256
Ferguson, William H.	19-Nov-1949	9	156
Ferguson, Willis Dean	27-Jun-1958	8	45
Ferrari, Louis	13-Aug-1965	11	88
Ferrell, Alonzo	3-Jul-1949	3	105
Ferrell, Gadis	9-Apr-1947	6	168
Ferrell, Gladis F.	9-Apr-1947	2	357
Ferrell, Hobert	11-Mar-1947	2	184
Ferrell, Hubert	3-Dec-1949	6	125
Fields, Chester L.	15-May-1959	11	99
Fields, Elmer G.	2-Jul-1950	11	120
Fields, Okie	30-Sep-1947	2	182
Fife, Earl	28-Nov-1949	10	126
Finey, Jack	3-Feb-1950	5	186
Fitch, Donald W.	8-Jan-1950	4	154
Fitch, Gordon E.	27-Jun-1966	11	241
Fitch, Jack	9-Jan-1923	1	55
Fitch, Paul	21-Jan-1955	7	113
Fitzpatrick, Carl	25-Jan-1950	7	74
Fitzpatrick, Carl	20-Nov-1952	7	76
Fitzpatrick, Franklin	13-Jun-1974	13	22
Fitzpatrick, Henry D.	28-Jul-1947	2	167
Fitzpatrick, Henry D. Jr.	8-Jan-1950	4	208
Fitzpatrick, Isaac	26-Sep-1947	11	214
Fitzpatrick, James D.	30-May-1949	3	35
Fitzpatrick, Paul Thurman	11-Feb-1965	12	150
Fitzpatrick, Sam H.	4-Jan-1950	4	109
Fitzpatrick, Steve	8-May-1923	1	64
Flack, Harold B.	19-Jan-1923	10	45
Flanery, Dave M.	5-Jan-1950	4	202
Flanery, Herschel Beverly	11-Aug-1966	11	157
Flanery, Isaac	9-Jul-1949	3	90
Flanery, Jessie C.	7-Oct-1968	11	192
Flanery, Roy L.	26-Sep-1949	11	56
Flanery, Thomas R.	27-Sep-1959	8	252
Flanery, Vernon	3-Jul-1950	9	530
Flannery, Aaron Dwaine	10-Jan-1999	14	257
Flannery, Burnis	4-Feb-1950	4	348
Flannery, James M.	25-Mar-1923	1	240

Name	Disc. Date	Book	Page
Flannery, Paul V.	15-Sep-1975	13	192
Flannery, William Edward	13-Jun-1975	13	165
Flannery, William T.	3-Nov-1974	13	282
Fleming, John Paul	13-Oct-1993	14	186
Floyd, John Velvin	10-Jan-1974	14	116
Foley, Hansford	3-Sep-1949	3	173
Foley, James	9-Feb-1950	4	338
Foley, Willie	30-Dec-1948	2	268
Ford, Edgar K.	8-Nov-1949	5	30
Ford, Willie R.	12-Jan-1923	1	14
Foster, Billie	5-Dec-1949	3	630
Foster, Emmitt	26-Jun-1957	7	365
Fouts, Arnold	21-Jan-1950	4	363
Fouts, Clyde	5-Dec-1949	6	322
Fouts, Clyde	20-Nov-1950	6	316
Fouts, Hershell	12-Mar-1957	7	471
Frady, Claude P. Jr.	11-Jun-1949	3	103
Frady, Noble	13-Mar-1949	3	5
Frady, Samuel W.	20-Dec-1949	4	92
Fraley, Ben Jr.	22-Nov-1949	3	553
Fraley, Beryl D.	29-Apr-1950	5	263
Fraley, Billy	8-Feb-1957	7	288
Fraley, Challie	22-May-1949	3	22
Fraley, Don	6-Nov-1949	6	65
Fraley, Elmer	3-Jul-1949	3	375
Fraley, Inez F.	1-May-1947	2	290
Fraley, Jack D.	8-Jan-1950	4	304
Fraley, Jack F.	29-Oct-1946	2	40
Fraley, Lewis	4-Dec-1949	3	617
Fraley, Meryl E.	25-Mar-1950	4	531
Fraley, Paul	6-Oct-1949	10	168
Fraley, Phillip E.	4-Dec-1970	11	416
Fraley, Raymond B.	1-Feb-1950	4	471
Fraley, Robert L.	18-Oct-1972	13	351
Fraley, Thomas D.	21-Jun-1979	13	400
Fraley, Thomas Douglas	21-Jul-1983	15	20
Francis, Bill J.	19-Dec-1948	2	260
Francis, Danny F.	4-Nov-1973	13	186
Francis, Dennis	22-Dec-1949	4	253
Francis, Donald D.	5-Oct-1970	11	318
Francis, Fredrick	27-Apr-1950	6	373
Francis, Fredrick	4-Apr-1951	6	374
Francis, Jack F.	4-Nov-1965	11	121
Francis, John P.	19-Jun-1962	11	394
Francis, John P.	4-May-1969	11	395
Francis, Larry E.	15-Jun-1975	13	160
Francis, Nells J.	26-Jan-1950	5	163
Francis, Oscar	1-Feb-1950	4	332
Francis, Otis M.	3-Dec-1949	5	59
Francis, Sylvester	10-Mar-1957	7	322
Francis, Sylvester	11-Sep-1960	10	145
Francis, Truly	6-Feb-1950	5	164
Frasrue, Harlis N.	16-Sep-1965	12	193
Frasure, Andrew	25-Dec-1949	7	68
Frasure, Arnold L.	13-May-1950	4	598
Frasure, Clarence	9-Jul-1972	11	294
Frasure, Deevie R.	4-Mar-1948	2	274
Frasure, Delmar	12-Sep-1971	11	493
Frasure, Edwin P.	21-Sep-1949	4	71
Frasure, Elmer R.	2-Jan-1950	5	476
Frasure, George S.	29-Apr-1945	5	500
Frasure, Harlis N.	16-Sep-1952	12	191
Frasure, Harlis N.	16-Sep-1959	12	194
Frasure, Harlis N.	16-Sep-1969	12	192
Frasure, Harlis N.	16-Sep-1972	13	387
Frasure, Harlis N.	16-Sep-1976	13	388
Frasure, Harlis N.	1-May-1979	15	385
Frasure, James H.	30-May-1947	2	25
Frasure, Keith Allen	30 June 1987	12	313
Frasure, Kelly	12-Dec-1949	4	28
Frasure, Martin	16-Dec-1949	4	176
Frasure, Melvin	22-Nov-1923	1	77
Frasure, Moses	17-Dec-1999	14	306
Frasure, Paul	1-Dec-1978	13	374
Frasure, Randall	27-Feb-1974	12	99
Frasure, Wade	18-Oct-1949	3	345
Frasure, Walter	1-Sep-1949	3	180
Frazier, Clyde	13-Dec-1949	5	124
Frazier, Elkaner	13-Jan-1950	4	415
Frazier, Glenn O.	8-Dec-1959	9	42
Frazier, Glenn O.	13-Dec-1963	11	25
Frazier, Hager	3-Feb-1949	3	41
Frazier, Jack	10-Dec-1949	7	132
Frazier, Jack	10-Dec-1950	11	10

Name	Disc. Date	Book	Page
Frazier, James A.	18-Apr-1947	2	110
Frazier, James M.	7-Dec-1948	4	117
Frazier, John	4-Apr-1950	6	23
Frazier, John G.	28-Jan-1974	12	88
Frazier, Lee	13-Oct-1949	3	338
Frazier, Lois E.	11-Sep-1957	7	407
Frazier, Orris E.	5-Aug-1965	11	389
Frazier, Russell M.	7-Nov-1956	7	238
Frazier, Sherrill	30-Jan-1949	2	278
Frazier, Theodore	22-Nov-1949	3	532
Frazier, William B.	28-Aug-1957	7	384
Freman, Dow	12-Dec-1926	1	191
Friedman, Adolph Richard	9-Jan-1959	8	146
Friedman, Edward Michael	1-Jan-1958	7	468
Friend, Tilden B.	14-Jan-1950	4	186
Friend, Tilden B.	16-Aug-1955	12	211
Frisby, David	10-Jun-1949	3	46
Frisby, Ferrell R.	29-May-1949	3	28
Frye, Charles K.	21-Sep-1949	9	303
Fugate, Donald R.	19-Nov-1959	8	293
Fugate, Elbert	15-May-1951	6	579
Fugate, Franklin P.	11-Mar-1970	11	385
Gallagher, David E.	23-Sep-1949	4	526
Garcia, Renee Karen	26-Mar-1999	14	275
Gardner, Billy E.	5-Jun-1961	9	9
Garland, Smiley	3-Sep-1949	3	162
Garrett, Camden	23-Sep-1949	3	230
Garrett, Douglas	7-Oct-1950	6	263
Garrett, George D.	8-Dec-1974	13	79
Garrett, Herbert	5-Oct-1949	3	287
Garrett, John	6-Aug-1922	1	179
Garrett, Leonard	18-Apr-1950	6	60
Garrett, Stewart	23-Nov-1949	3	537
Garrison, John Sidney Jr.	20-Dec-1975	13	217
Gayheart, Arnold E.	25-Jun-1949	3	143
Gayheart, Bobby L.	27-Apr-1963	9	148
Gayheart, Chip	13-Dec-1949	6	103
Gayheart, Dewey	1-May-1923	1	212
Gayheart, Dewey	1-May-1924	1	213
Gayheart, Dial	9-Jul-1949	3	110
Gayheart, Elisha	6-Apr-1950	5	260
Gayheart, General	12-Sep-1949	6	71
Gayheart, Goffery Sherril	28-Feb-1971	11	437
Gayheart, Jackie M.	27-Mar-1977	13	320
Gayheart, Ralph C.	5-Jul-1971	11	463
Gayheart, Redford	6-Feb-1950	6	147
Gayheart, Roy	25-Jun-1950	4	610
Gayheart, Salem	7-Sep-1949	6	310
Gayheart, Willie	6-Jan-1950	8	324
Gearheart, Billy J.	8-Sep-1975	13	191
Gearheart, Buncie J.	30-May-1950	4	579
Gearheart, Dale	29-Jul-1950	6	84
Gearheart, Don	20-Aug-1958	10	101
Gearheart, Don	19-Sep-1960	10	102
Gearheart, Edward	31-Aug-1949	7	103
Gearheart, Edward	15-May-1951	6	570
Gearheart, Norman	16-Mar-1964	9	229
Gearheart, Orris	7-Nov-1947	7	71
Gearheart, Paul	29-Aug-1971	11	490
Gearheart, Rexford	4-Sep-1972	11	612
Gearheart, Walter F.	18-Feb-1957	7	305
Gearheart, Wootson	27-Nov-1921	1	610
Gee, Arthur	7-Feb-1950	5	444
George, Charles R.	10-Nov-1975	13	203
George, Clyde	6-Feb-1950	6	17
George, Clyde N.	26-Mar-1957	7	314
George, Edward	25-Dec-1949	6	88
George, Malcolm D.	7-Jan-1950	4	163
George, Thomas E.	27-Jan-1950	9	284
George, Willard C.	23-Oct-1949	5	20
George, Willie	17-Jan-1950	9	270
Gibson, Amos	29-Jul-1976	13	281
Gibson, Byrne	13-May-1949	6	324
Gibson, Charles Douglas Jr.	8-Nov-2001	15	27-28
Gibson, Charles L.	25-Jul-1957	7	374
Gibson, Clarence	25-Jul-1949	7	90
Gibson, Claude	2-Jun-1970	11	392
Gibson, Darwin	24-Sep-1953	7	37
Gibson, Donald E.	10-Jul-1962	9	130
Gibson, Donald E.	30-Mar-1966	11	165
Gibson, Earl	26-Jun-1966	14	146
Gibson, Edward C.	4-Dec-1951	5	481
Gibson, Ernest	5-Dec-1949	5	93
Gibson, Ernest	10-Jan-1950	4	634

Name	Disc. Date	Book	Page
Gibson, Ernest R.	1-Feb-1967	11	14
Gibson, Ernest Ray	1-Apr-1980	14	10
Gibson, Farley	30-Dec-1949	8	38
Gibson, Forest D.	20-Nov-1974	13	120
Gibson, Gary L.	10-Oct-1974	13	52
Gibson, Gordon	9-Jan-1961	9	217A
Gibson, Grover	18-May-1977	13	327
Gibson, Henry	10-Dec-1949	4	34
Gibson, Henry D.	29-Oct-1949	4	112
Gibson, Jack	11-Oct-1949	4	413
Gibson, Jack	16-Sep-1956	7	336
Gibson, James G.	2-Sep-1955	8	85
Gibson, James G.	2-Sep-1958	8	84
Gibson, Johnny E.	7-May-1975	13	150
Gibson, Leroy	11-Feb-1950	5	170
Gibson, Lon C.	25-Apr-1976	13	263
Gibson, Marvin W.	19-Feb-1958	8	4
Gibson, Millard	3-Nov-1949	3	449
Gibson, Mont Jr.	14-Sep-1949	3	201
Gibson, Ollie	9-Nov-1949	3	613
Gibson, Ray	22-Jun-1949	3	92
Gibson, Ray	18-Oct-1949	3	376
Gibson, Robert T.	9-Jun-1965	11	64
Gibson, Ronnie G.	27-Oct-1967	11	274
Gibson, Russel	10-Mar-1950	7	32
Gibson, Stanley W.	4-Feb-1988	12	259
Gibson, Theodore	31-Jan-1964	10	97
Gibson, William David	30-Oct-1973	12	51
Gibson, William H.	27-Dec-1949	4	249
Gibson, Willie	16-Oct-1977	13	342
Gilbert, Lloyd	24-Oct-1947	2	36
Gilbert, William Robert Jr.	11-Feb-1960	8	260
Gillespie, John D.	22-Feb-1973	11	622
Gillium, Elmer Eugene	3-Mar-1955	7	117
Gillum, Beach	16-May-1977	2	113
Gillum, Charles	15-Jan-1951	6	553
Goble, Archie D.	27-Jan-1955	10	129
Goble, Arthur F.	2-Feb-1950	4	340
Goble, Bert	11-Jun-1959	8	186
Goble, Bill	21-Nov-1949	5	37
Goble, Billy	11-Jun-1952	6	585
Goble, Billy Van	12-Mar-1959	14	175
Goble, Charles A.	23-Nov-1950	9	84
Goble, Charles A.	7-Jan-1950	9	85
Goble, Clarence	24-Jun-1949	6	67
Goble, Darrell Travis	25-Jan-1998	14	250
Goble, Delman	20-May-1950	5	470
Goble, Donald H.	9-Feb-1951	8	188
Goble, Donald H.	7-Mar-1957	7	299
Goble, Earnest	6-Nov-1949	10	104
Goble, Elder V.	24-Jun-1975	132	162
Goble, Elijah	24-Aug-1949	3	149
Goble, Estill	6-Dec-1949	4	1
Goble, Floyd E.	18-Dec-1922	1	154
Goble, Frank	2-Dec-1949	3	595
Goble, Frank E.	2-Nov-1949	4	271
Goble, Freddie A.	17-Feb-1970	12	119
Goble, Garnet	4-Mar-1948	2	368
Goble, Gary D.	1-Jan-1975	13	113
Goble, George	13-Mar-1947	2	151
Goble, George W.	22-Apr-1959	8	159
Goble, Grady T.	22-Jun-1975	13	161
Goble, Grnest L.	6-Nov-1949	5	27
Goble, Hershel	29-Mar-1950	4	480
Goble, Howard	3-Oct-1956	10	157
Goble, Jackie L.	4-Oct-1962	9	114
Goble, Jacob Claude	17-Jul-2002	15	34
Goble, Jacob Claude	17-Jul-2002	15	67
Goble, James	18-Apr-1951	6	563
Goble, James	20-Apr-1950	6	562
Goble, James B.	25-Oct-1949	3	421
Goble, James C.	3-Aug-1949	5	180
Goble, James C.	1-Mar-1950	5	180
Goble, James E.	17-Apr-1950	5	258
Goble, James P.	26-Oct-1971	11	263
Goble, John	30-May-1923	1	192
Goble, John	14-Oct-1924	1	193
Goble, John	2-Aug-1949	3	120
Goble, John H.	22-Oct-1949	3	398
Goble, Larry R.	31-Jan-1976	13	235
Goble, Leonard	29-Dec-1949	4	165
Goble, Leonard H.	21-Jan-1958	7	479
Goble, Lloyd	4-Nov-1960	9	175
Goble, Loie	17-Nov-1957	7	442

Name	Disc. Date	Book	Page
Goble, Loie Jr.	17-Nov-1957	7	484
Goble, Lon F.	3-Jun-1923	1	223
Goble, Oakie	29-Jul-1948	2	208
Goble, Raymond	12-Aug-1949	3	131
Goble, Raymond	29-Dec-1949	4	167
Goble, Raymond	8-Jan-1950	4	158
Goble, Raymond R.	23-Feb-1950	15	123-124
Goble, Richard	14-Jun-1949	3	42
Goble, Robert M.	16-Dec-1949	6	336
Goble, Ronnie	12-Jan-1950	6	264
Goble, Ruben	12-Jun-1952	8	227
Goble, Ted	2-Dec-1949	4	35
Goble, Thomas R.	21-Apr-1950	5	473
Goble, Timothy Ray	9-May-1974	14	14
Goble, Vernon	26-Apr-1949	6	207
Goble, Victor V.	28-Apr-1975	13	261
Goble, Virgil	28-Feb-1950	4	427
Goble, William, Jr.	11-Nov-1972	11	607
Goble, Woodrow W.	9-Jun-1950	4	599
Goff, Herbert	24-Feb-1950	5	232
Goins, Mablein	25-May-1959	14	278
Goodman, Albert	29-Jan-1923	1	1
Goodman, Claude Vernon	8-Dec-1973	15	115
Goodman, Danny L.	29-Dec-1980	13	410
Goodman, Dave	31-May-1948	2	189
Goodman, Dewey	15-Jan-1948	2	60
Goodman, Earl	24-Dec-1948	2	263
Goodman, Neilus	28-Dec-1949	4	582
Goodman, Oscar	11-Jan-1950	4	169
Goodman, Sammy Allen	31-Jul-1966	15	100
Goodman, Thomas W.	10-Feb-1950	4	369
Goodwill, Roger	31-Aug-1975	14	119
Gore, Cecil E.	4-Feb-1953	7	410
Gore, Charles A.	20-Jun-1949	3	47
Gore, William	15-Oct-1949	3	330
Gore, William H.	11-Jan-1950	4	172
Gray, Amos	30-Mar-1949	3	8
Gray, Charles	29-Dec-1950	6	555
Gray, David Ashley	16-Mar-1997	14	220
Gray, Galloway	1-Feb-1923	1	166
Gray, Jack R.	27-Mar-1973	11	625
Gray, Lisa Ann	3-Aug-1997	14	228
Gray, Manis E.	1-Jul-1949	3	65
Gray, Raymond H.	20-Jan-1950	10	21
Gray, Richard F.	17-Dec-1962	9	126
Greathouse, Eddie	13-Apr-1977	13	321
Greathouse, Forrest D.	22-Aug-1979	13	402
Green, Albert	24-Mar-1950	4	534
Green, Cecil	17-Oct-1949	4	347
Green, Cecil	15-Mar-1951	6	418
Green, Elmo	17-Sep-1957	7	473
Green, Henry C.	12-Dec-1948	2	257
Green, John H.	6-Oct-1949	4	535
Green, Monroe	5-Sep-1948	2	221
Green, Newt Jr.	1-Jan-1948	2	212
Green, Perry Jr.	12-Oct-1949	7	566
Green, Perry Jr.	16-Jul-1957	7	370
Green, Tarnacey	13-Jun-1958	8	80
Green, Woodrow	8-Sep-1947	2	115
Greene, Billy	6-Sep-1972	11	349
Greene, Glenn	1-Nov-1956	7	235
Greene, Herbert	5-Jul-1949	3	71
Greene, Joseph	9-Sep-1946	2	160
Greer, Eddie	1-Nov-1949	3	446
Greer, Ishmel	10-Nov-1949	3	493
Greer, Paul B.	8-Mar-1957	7	300
Greer, Paul William	12-Nov-1974	14	20
Griffith, Arnold Ray	17-Dec-1970	11	417
Griffith, Bob	11-Aug-1949	3	159
Griffith, Donald S.	2-Dec-1949	10	99
Griffith, James Louis	17-Dec-1968	11	380
Griffith, James Michael	15-Dec-1975	13	215
Griffith, Keith Rondall	2-Apr-1975	13	135
Griffith, Keith Rondall	2-Apr-1975	13	146
Griffith, Norman	1-Aug-1968	11	166
Griffith, Paul	4-Nov-1952	6	608
Griffith, Rayful	25-Jul-1958	8	77
Griffith, Raymond Jr.	15-Jul-1971	11	474
Griffith, Robert	21-Jan-1951	6	303
Griffith, Russell Eugene	14-Mar-1956	7	158
Griffith, Wayne Randle	18-Dec-1956	7	270
Grigsby, Rolan	4-Dec-1949	12	131
Grimm, William	9-Oct-1958	8	104
Grinstead, James D.	28-Feb-1957	12	268

Name	Disc. Date	Book	Page
Grinstead, James D.	27-Mar-1962	13	443
Gross, Ralph	19-Sep-1974	13	48
Gullett, Larry F.	19-May-1971	11	282
Gullett, Ronald L.	2-Feb-1970	11	174
Gunnell, Ballard	18-Jun-1923	1	231
Gunnell, Harvey	13-Nov-1952	6	610
Gunnell, Harvey R.	21-Jul-1957	7	379
Gunnell, James	3-Jan-1923	1	5
Gunnell, James	10-Oct-1949	3	388
Gunnell, Walter	16-Feb-1950	4	396
Gunnels, Charles	1-Dec-1977	13	349
Gunnels, James E.	1-Apr-1963	9	146
Gunnels, Millard Edward	29-Sep-1971	11	497
Gunter, Joe E.	3-Apr-1955	7	149
Habern, Henry	9-Jan-1950	6	90
Habern, John E.	21-Aug-1958	8	87
Habern, Lawrence J.	19-Jan-1950	2	245
Hackworth, Cash	30-Jan-1923	1	6
Hackworth, Earl	10-Nov-1949	3	473
Hackworth, Ernest	1-Dec-1949	3	587
Hackworth, Harrison	18-May-1922	1	604
Hackworth, Jerry	15-Mar-1950	6	1
Hackworth, Junior	18-Nov-1949	3	570
Hackworth, Maynard	10-Jan-1950	5	136
Hackworth, Robert H	7-Mar-1958	8	95
Hackworth, Roy	25-Nov-1975	13	213
Hackworth, Thomas D.	14-Dec-1949	4	61
Hackworth, Thurman	3-May-1946	2	102
Hackworth, Troy	24-Dec-1949	4	134
Hagans, Jack	19-Apr-1951	6	389
Hagans, Paul D.	9-Jan-1975	13	92
Hagans, Ralph N.	9-Aug-1972	11	584
Hagans, Rondal C.	2-Dec-1946	2	315
Halbert, Anthony Emanule	16-Mar-1995	14	158
Halbert, Claude	19-Dec-1958	8	125
Halbert, Clayborn	7-Jan-1950	4	352
Halbert, Dan	6-Jan-1950	4	149
Halbert, Denzil	25-Jul-1949	12	273-274
Halbert, Denzil	29-Jul-1950	12	271
Halbert, Denzil	29-Jul-1950	12	275-276
Halbert, Denzil	1-Apr-1951	12	270
Halbert, Denzil	1-Jan-1957	12	269
Halbert, Herman	29-Aug-1949	6	463
Halbert, Joe E.	1-Nov-1966	13	444
Halbert, John H.	6-Jul-1961	12	165
Halbert, Martin	22-Jun-1949	10	108
Hale, Billy D.	21-Apr-1955	9	237
Hale, Billy D.	21-Apr-1958	9	238
Hale, Charles G.	25-Aug-1961	9	27
Hale, Chester W.	8-Jan-1950	4	123
Hale, Clarence E.	2-Jun-1971	11	454
Hale, Claude	10-Dec-1949	7	22
Hale, Claude	21-Jan-1950	4	261
Hale, Edgar	18-Dec-1949	5	503
Hale, Edgar	18-Dec-1949	5	102
Hale, Edward E.	15-Dec-1949	5	98
Hale, Estill	9-Nov-1949	6	491
Hale, Estill	31-Aug-1961	9	36
Hale, Evert	30-Nov-1949	3	584
Hale, Fred	15-Dec-1949	4	290
Hale, Harry Eugene	25-Jan-1968	11	299
Hale, Henry C.	15-Dec-1949	5	95
Hale, Herman	2-Feb-1964	9	174
Hale, Jack	21-Apr-1971	11	461
Hale, Jackie D.	11-May-1975	13	148
Hale, James L.	20-Feb-1958	8	247
Hale, James N.	20-Jul-1949	3	109
Hale, Lawrence	30-Nov-1949	3	599
Hale, Richard	1-Apr-1947	2	128
Hale, Samuel V.	17-Jan-1923	1	196
Hale, Warnie	14-Aug-1949	3	133
Hale, Warren S.	14-Jun-1923	9	267
Hale, Warren S.	13-Jul-1925	9	266
Hale, William A.	15-Nov-1973	12	62
Haley, Homer	28-Jan-1950	5	521
Halfhill, Charles Thomas Jr.	4-Feb-1975	13	99
Halfhill, Michael Gene	8-Dec-1978	13	372
Hall, Adrian L.	4-Feb-1950	4	343
Hall, Albert	19-Nov-1949	6	363
Hall, Albert	16-Mar-1951	6	364
Hall, Ambrose S.	7-May-1922	1	128
Hall, Andrew J.	29-Oct-1948	2	236
Hall, Archie	18-Oct-1949	3	310
Hall, Arlie	15-Oct-1949	3	455
Hall, Arnold	1-Apr-1949	3	13
Hall, Arnold	29-Jan-1978	14	38
Hall, Astor	20-Nov-1949	3	556
Hall, Audis R.	5-Dec-1950	6	216
Hall, Ballard E.	15-Feb-1950	4	433
Hall, Bert	8-Nov-1949	3	456
Hall, Bert T.	4-Apr-1947	2	111
Hall, Bill III	23-Sep-1947	2	81
Hall, Bill M.	13-Nov-1969	11	360
Hall, Bill M.	1-Nov-1973	12	65
Hall, Billy H.	7-May-1957	7	330
Hall, Billy J.	1-Nov-1948	2	237
Hall, Billy J.	24-Mar-1972	11	555
Hall, Birchell Cooledge		11	272
Hall, Blaine	3-Oct-1946	3	266
Hall, Bob	3-Apr-1950	5	231
Hall, Bob	22-Apr-1959	11	19
Hall, Bobby	6-Apr-1950	5	246
Hall, Bobby N.	27-May-1971	11	453
Hall, Carlos L.	16-Feb-1950	4	399
Hall, Carlos R.	12-Oct-1971	11	502
Hall, Carnelius	28-Aug-1949	10	42
Hall, Carol Lynne	5-Mar-1981	15	12
Hall, Cecil	16-Nov-1949	7	3
Hall, Cecil	13-May-1951	7	4
Hall, Cecil	13-May-1951	6	448
Hall, Cecil	9-Sep-1973	14	45
Hall, Charles	10-Dec-1949	3	634
Hall, Charles E.	14-May-1951	5	454
Hall, Charles E.	8-Oct-1958	8	114
Hall, Charles E.	23-May-1973	12	6
Hall, Charley	16-Jan-1923	1	13
Hall, Charlie	15-Jun-1959	8	184
Hall, Clarence E.	4-Dec-1968	11	195
Hall, Cleadus	17-Sep-1972	11	592
Hall, Cletis C.	26-Aug-1959	8	207
Hall, Clifford	2-Sep-1949	2	325
Hall, Clyde	29-Dec-1950	6	314
Hall, Damon	8-Jan-1975	13	91
Hall, Darrell B.	16-Jun-1971	11	317
Hall, Dave B.	23-Oct-1947	2	163
Hall, Delmas L.	8-Aug-1971	11	475
Hall, Delmer	25-Oct-1950	9	263
Hall, Denver B.	24-Feb-1949	7	49
Hall, Donald J.	29-Sep-1975	13	196
Hall, Ed	23-Nov-1947	2	270
Hall, Ed	18 June 1919	1	217
Hall, Edgar H.	15-Sep-1949	3	208
Hall, Edgar R.	31-Jan-1958	8	168
Hall, Edgar R.	31-Jan-1964	9	219
Hall, Edgar Ray	31-Jan-1964	14	85
Hall, Edgel T.	25-Jan-1965	12	204
Hall, Edward	2-Oct-1947	2	207
Hall, Edward	22-Oct-1949	3	405
Hall, Eldon Gardner	10-Jan-1974	12	110
Hall, Eldon Gardner	7-Sep-1977	13	338
Hall, Ellis	1-Oct-1935	2	187
Hall, Ellis	6-Jan-1950	6	97
Hall, Elmer	24-Jan-1950	4	267
Hall, Emil B.	14-Sep-1949	5	240
Hall, Ernest	10-Feb-1950	4	477
Hall, Estil	19-Jul-1949	6	100
Hall, Eugene	6-May-1950	4	551
Hall, Evan	22-Apr-1947	2	171
Hall, Frank	2-Oct-1949	4	564
Hall, Fred	27-Oct-1949	3	404
Hall, Fred	25-Jul-1951	6	509
Hall, Gary W.	13-May-1976	13	267
Hall, Glenden K.	15-May-1957	7	367
Hall, Gregory A.	28-Dec-1983	12	219-220
Hall, Guy F.	25-Aug-1948	5	216
Hall, Harry W.	15-Dec-1949	11	100
Hall, Harry W.	15-Dec-1949	5	117
Hall, Haskell	4-Feb-1950	4	461
Hall, Hezzie	18-Mar-1950	8	268
Hall, Hillard	9-Jun-1949	3	34
Hall, Homer	14-Apr-1949	3	43
Hall, Homer	26-Dec-1949	5	146
Hall, Homer	4-Nov-1956	12	199
Hall, Howard	9-Jan-1951	5	469
Hall, Isaac Jr.	26-Oct-1949	7	361
Hall, Isaac N	9-Jul-1959	8	297
Hall, Ishmael	10-May-1946	10	17
Hall, Ivan E.	12-May-1959	9	12
Hall, J. Lee	30-Jan-1957	7	293
Hall, J. Lee	16-Sep-1960	11	238
Hall, James	6-Jun-1949	2	306
Hall, James	27-Nov-1949	6	191
Hall, James	3-Nov-1950	6	188
Hall, James	20-Dec-1951	6	640
Hall, James	28-Dec-1953	9	333
Hall, James A.	11-Jul-1959	8	196
Hall, James D.	15-Jul-1979	13	395
Hall, James Dwayne	15-Jul-1979	15	62
Hall, James K.	31-Dec-1958	8	127
Hall, James K.	27-Jul-1976	13	277
Hall, James L.	28-Jan-1960	11	9
Hall, James M.	7-Nov-1959	8	243
Hall, James R.	24-Feb-1954	7	123
Hall, James W.	25-May-1956	8	191
Hall, Jay	4-Sep-1947	2	91
Hall, Jay	12-Jul-1948	2	201
Hall, Jeff	15-Apr-1958	8	34
Hall, Jerry E.	26-Apr-1973	11	628
Hall, Jerry Jr.	26 Apr 1 957	9	58
Hall, Jimmy R.	18-Feb-1976	12	187
Hall, John	28-Jan-1946	2	331
Hall, John	29-Sep-1948	2	226
Hall, John	7-Sep-1947	2	177
Hall, John F.	4-Oct-1973	12	44
Hall, John G.	10-Apr-1950	4	489
Hall, John Jr.	8-Jul-1949	3	85
Hall, John M.	16-Feb-1923	1	198
Hall, Johnnie	5-Oct-1949	6	414
Hall, Junior	16-Sep-1949	3	225
Hall, Junior	11-Dec-1950	6	633
Hall, Kellard	30-Sep-1949	3	269
Hall, Larry	20-Mar-1974	12	113
Hall, Lee	5-Apr-1948	2	158
Hall, Leon	22-Feb-1977	14	11
Hall, Leonard	10-Mar-1950	5	189
Hall, Leonard	24-Dec-1963	9	218
Hall, Leonard	1-May-1967	11	239
Hall, Leonard	6-Feb-1972	11	536
Hall, Lloyd	3-Nov-1960	9	55
Hall, Lloyd Henry	1-Jan-1985	14	194
Hall, Luther	26-Aug-1949	3	151
Hall, Mack D.	13-Jul-1972	11	577
Hall, Malcom	1-Jul-1948	11	321
Hall, McDonell	14-Jan-1950	4	488
Hall, McKinley	25-Jul-1947	6	106
Hall, McKinley	18-Apr-1956	7	217
Hall, McKinley	9-Oct-1956	11	48
Hall, Melvin	4-Dec-1949	5	84
Hall, Melvin J.	1-Apr-1974	12	118
Hall, Merlin	6-Nov-1949	3	540
Hall, Michael	24-Apr-1975	13	141
Hall, Michael E.	3-Jul-1995	14	162
Hall, Ned	11-Dec-1973	12	70
Hall, Norman	10-Dec-1957	7	463
Hall, Oglevee C. Jr.	22-Jul-1947	1	144
Hall, Omer	29-Aug-1958	8	136
Hall, Orville	4-Feb-1950	4	321
Hall, Orville	10-Mar-1965	11	119
Hall, Owney C.	8-Mar-1950	5	202
Hall, Palmer	14-Oct-1949	3	314
Hall, Paul	31-Dec-1975	13	221
Hall, Paul R.	28-Oct-1949	3	400
Hall, Randolph	19-Apr-1960	4	515
Hall, Raymond	15-Aug-1971	11	297
Hall, Raymond C.	9-Jul-1950	4	626
Hall, Raymond D.	8-Jan-1950	4	124
Hall, Raymond D.	10-Mar-1983	13	432
Hall, Raymond E.	12-Mar-1975	13	130
Hall, Reuben	4-May-1959	9	360
Hall, Richard	14-Jun-1958	10	100
Hall, Richard G.	8-Oct-1967	12	67
Hall, Robert	13-Oct-1949	3	309
Hall, Robert	12-Nov-1949	3	542
Hall, Robert	23-Jul-1952	6	594
Hall, Ronald S.	10-Aug-1971	11	494
Hall, Roy	29-Apr-1959	8	169
Hall, Rush	2-Oct-1949	6	355
Hall, Russell D.	16-Dec-1960	9	96
Hall, Russell L.	12-Mar-1950	11	46-47
Hall, Shadrick	3-Oct-1949	3	302
Hall, Sid	13-Sep-1949	3	196
Hall, Stanley B.	15-Nov-1973	12	58

Name	Disc. Date	Book	Page
Hall, Sternley G.	1-Aug-1959	8	201
Hall, Steven W.	27-Mar-1976	13	252
Hall, Sylvester	27-Nov-1949	3	544
Hall, Taylor	8-Apr-1923	2	153
Hall, Terry D.	25-Sep-1974	13	49
Hall, Thomas D.	31-Dec-1980	13	411
Hall, Thomas L.	31-Jan-1974	12	19
Hall, Tommy R.	30-Jun-1972	11	572
Hall, Town	21-Apr-1949	2	299
Hall, Town	9-Mar-1972	11	546
Hall, Truman	15-Dec-1974	13	84
Hall, Thomas S.	9-Sep-1973	12	32
Hall, Vardie	25-Aug-1947	2	114
Hall, Victor	25-Nov-1950	6	208
Hall, Wade	19-Dec-1949	5	499
Hall, Wallace R.	8-Feb-1950	4	346
Hall, Ward	6-Feb-1950	4	368
Hall, Wendell D.	23-Mar-1950	5	238
Hall, Wesley L.	4-Apr-1950	5	239
Hall, Wid Jr.	10-Oct-1958	9	213
Hall, Willard	25-Jan-1950	4	597
Hall, William P.	24-Jun-1949	3	61
Hall, William R.	18-Jan-1962	9	81
Hall, Willie	31-Jan-1950	6	416
Hall, Willie F.	18-Nov-1949	5	41
Hall, Woodrow W.	10-Dec-1949	5	99
Hamby, Caleb H.	17-Oct-1949	12	303-304
Hamby, Jerry D.	1-Jan-1970	14	149
Hamilton, Alona Corinne	1-Aug-2001	15	22
Hamilton, Billy G.	3-Nov-1960	8	304
Hamilton, Bud K.	1-Sep-1958	10	172
Hamilton, Butler	2-Oct-1956	9	62
Hamilton, Carter	22-Sep-1974	13	50
Hamilton, Charles	20-May-1952	7	154
Hamilton, Charles B.	11-Dec-1969	11	190
Hamilton, Charles T.	29-Oct-1949	4	224
Hamilton, Charlie	24-Aug-1947	9	276
Hamilton, Charlie	18-Jan-1950	4	232
Hamilton, Charlie	31-Jan-1950	4	318
Hamilton, Clarence	3-Dec-1949	3	586
Hamilton, Clyde Junior	31-Dec-1969	11	204
Hamilton, Danny	8-Feb-1977	13	305
Hamilton, Delmer	20-Feb-1958	8	3
Hamilton, Elijah	12-Jan-1950	4	156
Hamilton, Elmer C.	22-Jan-1957	7	284
Hamilton, Emitt	19-May-1959	8	171
Hamilton, Ervin Thomas	17-Apr-1959	8	163
Hamilton, Ervin Thomas Sr.	20-May-1963	9	155
Hamilton, Eugene	26-Mar-1950	5	263
Hamilton, Eugene	13-Dec-1950	6	230
Hamilton, Foster	27-Dec-1949	4	284
Hamilton, Glen D.	2-Oct-1977	13	341
Hamilton, Gretho	5-Apr-1975	13	179
Hamilton, Hearsel	30-May-1954	5	523
Hamilton, Henry	15-Oct-1949	3	311
Hamilton, Henry	18-Oct-1949	3	310
Hamilton, Henry	10-Jan-1950	4	357
Hamilton, Hillard	2-Oct-1949	4	288
Hamilton, Homer	10-Dec-1949	6	630
Hamilton, Homer	23-Jan-1950	4	230
Hamilton, Ira B.	21-Nov-1959	8	244
Hamilton, James	30-Oct-1949	3	431
Hamilton, James W.	23-Oct-1949	4	583
Hamilton, John W.	27-Jan-1950	4	287
Hamilton, Kenis	28-Jul-1952	7	38
Hamilton, Kenis	8-Oct-1953	7	39
Hamilton, Linda G.	16-Mar-1952	7	172
Hamilton, Linda G.	12-Sep-1979	13	414
Hamilton, Melvin	18-Sep-1949	3	224
Hamilton, Melvin Jr.	3-Aug-1972	11	581
Hamilton, Minnis	10-Jan-1952	5	501
Hamilton, Oscar C.	18-Oct-1949	5	6
Hamilton, Phillip Lavon	30-Jan-1970	11	206
Hamilton, Ranold R.	31-Mar-1950	7	42
Hamilton, Ranold R.	16-Feb-1953	7	44
Hamilton, Ray	9-Jan-1950	4	162
Hamilton, Raymond	24-Dec-1949	4	106
Hamilton, Roy J.	31-Jan-1949	10	9
Hamilton, Russell	31-Oct-1957	7	433
Hamilton, Sie	29-Sep-1921	1	613
Hamilton, Thomas	11-Oct-1949	3	317
Hamilton, Thomas Jr.	14-Jan-1971	11	423
Hamilton, Tolby	25-Aug-1949	3	160
Hamilton, Tracy	3-Oct-1949	6	187
Hamilton, Victor	20-Sep-1949	3	235
Hamilton, Virgil	20-May-1949	3	26
Hamilton, Walker	18-Mar-1949	2	319
Hamilton, Walker	27-Dec-1960	9	2
Hamilton, Wall	21-Dec-1949	10	192
Hamilton, Webster	18-Feb-1950	4	563
Hamilton, Wilber	23-Aug-1949	3	191
Hamilton, Wilber L. Jr.	1-Oct-1966	11	212
Hamilton, Wilber Lee Jr.	17-Aug-1960		
Hamilton, Willie	24-Dec-1958	8	170
Hamilton, Willie	18-Sep-1960	13	138
Hammond, Albert	25-Jan-1950	6	33
Hammond, James	25-Sep-1949	3	236
Hammonds, William T.	2-Nov-1948	2	284
Hammons, John	21-Oct-1949	8	246
Hammons, John	21-Oct-1949	11	331
Hampton, Bennie	18-Nov-1949	3	517
Hampton, Ed	26-Jul-1923	1	245
Hampton, Estill	8-May-1947	1	143
Hampton, Hassel	9-Jan-1950	9	265
Hampton, Jesse	10-Oct-1949	3	297
Hancock, Bobby R.	21-Jan-1962	13	315
Hancock, Bobby R.	19-May-1966	13	316
Hancock, Clyde F.	19-Jan-1956	7	200
Hancock, Lawrence	4-Sep-1949	3	207
Hancock, Oscar	1-Nov-1949	9	358
Hancock, Roger L.	23-Apr-1979	13	382
Hancock, Thomas E.	7-Mar-1955	11	591
Hancock, Thomas J.	18-Apr-1907	1	227
Hancock, Thomas J.	13-Feb-2003	1	228
Handshoe, Blaine	8-Feb-1977	13	307
Handshoe, Floyd	31-Jan-1950	6	393
Handshoe, Jay	30-Mar-1976	13	254
Handshoe, Kermit	1-Dec-1949	5	66
Handshoe, Kermit	1-Dec-1949	10	201
Handshoe, Milton	15-Nov-1949	12	231
Hanger, George R.	18-Feb-1950	4	460
Hansford, Donald E.	22-Apr-1958	8	35
Hardee, Robert	4-Dec-1949	6	267
Hardee, Robert	6-Nov-1950	6	262
Hardwick, James S.	2-Feb-1966	11	144
Hardwick, John D.	18-Aug-1974	13	31
Harkins, Walter S. III	21-Sep-1949	4	529
Harkins, Walter S. III	20-Apr-1950	4	528
Harless, Eizie W.	5-Jan-1971	11	527
Harless, Oakey C.	25-Oct-1957	7	423
Harless, Winfred D.	29-Sep-1971	11	495
Harlow, Roy Franklin	1-Feb-1980	14	63
Harman, Arch	18-Jul-1923	1	49
Harmon, Charles	15-Jun-1951	6	428
Harmon, Clyde Randal	12-Jun-1975	13	187
Harmon, Clyde Randal	12-Jun-1975	13	193
Harmon, Dolie C. Jr.	10-Sep-1949	3	183
Harmon, Ernest	8-Nov-1949	3	538
Harmon, Fred	21-Jan-1950	6	224
Harmon, Herman	27-Mar-1950	6	46
Harmon, James Jr.	30-Oct-1957	7	430
Harmon, James Jr.	6-Oct-1972	11	595
Harmon, Jimmy D.	11-Dec-1971	11	521
Harmon, Leonard	20-Aug-1945	2	222
Harmon, Paul W.	15-Nov-1957	8	8
Harmon, Ronnie	23-Feb-1975	13	111
Harmon, Tommy	17-Feb-1975	13	108
Harmon, William	14-Nov-1949	3	583
Harper, Fred	14-Oct-1957	7	438
Harrington, L.B.	4-Dec-1949	5	520
Harris, Allen E.	17-Jan-1957	7	278
Harris, Andrew Jackson	4-Sep-1967	11	434
Harris, Bill	8-Jun-1959	8	180
Harris, Bill N.	7-Oct-1953	7	5
Harris, Bobby R.	27-Jul-1960	9	134
Harris, Dock	24-Jul-1962	9	129
Harris, Donald E.	9-Apr-1964	9	240
Harris, Estill	6-Jan-1948	2	9
Harris, Irvin	9-Dec-1949	4	16
Harris, John E.	24-Nov-1948	2	250
Harris, John H.	21-Nov-1973	11	295
Harris, John K.	11-Jul-1949	3	98
Harris, Kelse	8-Feb-1972	11	262
Harris, Paul	17-Dec-1950	6	232
Harris, Paul J.	11-Dec-1949	10	176
Harris, Paul J.	17-Dec-1950	10	177
Harris, Raymond	21-Sep-1947	2	157
Harris, Robert	10-Aug-1951	6	503
Harris, Robert M.	29-Jul-1971	12	239
Harris, Walter	30-Jun-1923	1	94
Harris, William R.	18-Apr-1960	9	262
Harris, William T.	29-Oct-1974	13	65
Harvel, Charles	27-Oct-1949	5	79
Harvel, Thurman Joe	14-Nov-1949	5	36
Hatcher, Bernard Beckham	30-Nov-1953	10	63
Hatcher, Bernard Beckham	14-Mar-1963	10	64
Hatcher, James	29-Nov-1949	3	572
Hatcher, Sam K.	31-Aug-1949	3	161
Hatcher, Samuel R.	22-Oct-1949	3	408
Hatfield, Curtis	12-Jul-1957	7	366
Hatfield, Isadore	11-Dec-1947	4	401
Hatfield, Jerry	8 Nov 1971	13	205
Hatfield, Joe W.	28-Jul-1956	7	216
Hatton, Cecil	11-Jan-1948	2	83
Hatton, Ruffard A.	31-Oct-1949	5	516
Hawkins, James F.	27-Apr-1971	11	348
Hayden, Charles I.	16-Dec-1973	12	73
Hayes, Carl	14-Jan-1950	6	421
Hayes, Carl	27-Feb-1951	6	342
Hayes, Carl	25-Jul-1958	8	63
Hayes, Carl L.	6-Jun-1948	10	60
Hayes, Clarence	7-Jul-1949	3	83
Hayes, Claude	28-Oct-1949	6	506
Hayes, Clyde	20-Mar-1950	4	458
Hayes, Earrit Mirl	6-Oct-1949	5	533
Hayes, Glenn	19-Oct-1949	3	350
Hayes, Gordon	15-Dec-1960	14	147-148
Hayes, James	9-Dec-1975	13	223
Hayes, James C.	28-Nov-1957	7	441
Hayes, James R.	4-Jun-1949	3	29
Hayes, James R.	13-Oct-1949	6	194
Hayes, Marion, Jr.	4-Feb-1950	6	219
Hayes, Paul E.	20-May-1947	2	339
Hayes, Paul E.	26-Nov-1949	4	501
Hayes, Paul E.	2-Aug-1950	7	98
Hayes, Paul E.	2-Nov-1969	11	458
Hayes, Russell	16-Aug-1977	12	149
Hays, Lawrence	11-Oct-1949	4	457
Haywood, Arthur W.	18-Dec-1949	4	130
Haywood, Billy H.	6-Nov-1968	11	159
Haywood, Calvin	23-Aug-1950	6	39
Haywood, Charles	23-Feb-1951	6	413
Haywood, Charlie	12-Feb-1947	2	245
Haywood, Grover C.	2-Jan-1949	3	3
Haywood, Jobe	28-May-1923	1	31
Hazelett, Seibern K.	11-May-1977	13	328
Heardl, William D.	8-Jan-1950	9	247
Heasley, Charles W.	13-Aug-1955	7	242
Heinze, Frank	7-Mar-1950	4	436
Heinze, John	31-Oct-1949	3	490
Helton, Raymond	2-Oct-1962	9	109
Henderson, Bennie Howard	20-Dec-1973	12	117
Henderson, Berchel Jay	10-Jul-2008	15	104-105
Henderson, Donald	27-Dec-1976	13	300
Henderson, Poe	24-Nov-1949	3	578
Henderson, Ray H.	8-Jun-1972	11	568
Henegar, William	16-Jan-1951	6	356
Henry, Roy R.	11-Apr-1972	11	277
Henry, William	2-Aug-1949	6	490
Hensley, Donald	22-Apr-1971	11	444
Hensley, Irby	17-Jul-1923	1	258
Hensley, Laton C.	20-Dec-1949	4	392
Henson, Bob	29-Aug-1961	9	31
Henson, Clifford	25-Feb-1958	10	35
Henson, Dennis	16-Dec-1975	13	222
Henson, Sandy	16-Jun-1978	13	375
Hents, Pinion	22-Jun-1923	2	169
Hereford, Thomas May Jr.	21-Mar-1950	5	218
Herron, James	7-Feb-1957	3	311
Hewitt, Homer	26-Oct-1955	7	232
Hewitt, Homer E.	8-Jul-1923	1	132
Hibbitts, Donnie	16-Dec-1951	6	545
Hicks, Allen	7-Mar-1923	1	238
Hicks, Arnold	10-Jan-1950	4	192
Hicks, Arville	23-Oct-1955	10	86
Hicks, Aubrey	3-Dec-1949	3	609
Hicks, Bernice	3-Dec-1949	6	540
Hicks, Bert	23-Apr-1953	7	77
Hicks, Billie	24-Aug-1971	11	479
Hicks, Brownie	7-Feb-1950	4	364
Hicks, Burlin	22-Feb-1949	6	345
Hicks, Burnice	23-Jun-1951	6	526

133

Name	Disc. Date	Book	Page
Hicks, Carl	6-Sep-1949	6	465
Hicks, Carl	6-Nov-1950	6	195
Hicks, Charles	20-Jun-1950	6	450
Hicks, Charles	10-Apr-1951	6	451
Hicks, Claude	17-Feb-1949	6	424
Hicks, Daniel	12-Jan-1923	1	233
Hicks, Daniel	12-Jan-1923	1	76
Hicks, Daniel Jr.	7-Oct-1949	4	524
Hicks, Donald	29-Jun-1956	7	207
Hicks, Donovan	20-Nov-1956	7	261
Hicks, Douglas	28-Apr-1971	11	285
Hicks, Doyle	23-Jan-1968	11	152
Hicks, Ecil	18-Jan-1950	6	174
Hicks, Eddie S.	4-Nov-1958	8	105
Hicks, Elize	8-Jan-1950	4	142
Hicks, Elliott	17-Nov-1947	2	5
Hicks, Ermal Edmon	23-Jan-1964	15	81-82
Hicks, Eugene	24-Sep-1956	7	307
Hicks, Glen	18-Aug-1954	9	359
Hicks, Glen	10-Oct-1957	5	537
Hicks, Greeley	12-Nov-1949	6	338
Hicks, Hamsel	19-Dec-1957	7	446
Hicks, Hansel	11-Oct-1950	5	477
Hicks, Hansel	Oct-1946	9	316
Hicks, Hubert	25-Dec-1949	4	133
Hicks, James	24-Mar-1953	7	45
Hicks, Joe	25-Oct-1970	11	243
Hicks, John	18-Dec-1949	6	632
Hicks, Johnie	22-Jul-1949	3	166
Hicks, Johnie	22-Jul-1949	4	616
Hicks, Kenneth	21-Jul-1975	13	172
Hicks, Larry A.	22-Nov-1973	12	68
Hicks, Larry E.	10-Mar-1977	13	319
Hicks, Leonard	21-Jul-1949	3	106
Hicks, Milton	21-Feb-1923	1	102
Hicks, Orville	2-Jan-1932	9	278
Hicks, Orville	6-Nov-1949	11	137
Hicks, Patrick	18-Oct-1949	7	86
Hicks, Patrick	1-Oct-1953	7	87
Hicks, Preston	28-Oct-1949	5	21
Hicks, Ralph	2-Dec-1959	8	248
Hicks, Ray B.	27-Jan-1956	7	464
Hicks, Roy	23-Jun-1949	8	283
Hicks, Sherrill	8-Mar-1971	11	436
Hicks, Smith	22-Jan-1956	7	174
Hicks, Vester	31-Jan-1963	10	149
Hicks, Vester	18-Oct-1964	10	150
Hicks, Virgil	24-Oct-1957	7	466
Hicks, Wayne	8-Aug-1958	8	78
Hicks, Wayne	22-Aug-1964	10	135
Hicks, Wendell S.	15-Jun-1967	11	224
Hicks, Willie	14-Dec-1949	6	104
Higgins, Chester	1-Nov-1963	11	77
Hil, Ricky	30-Nov-1978	13	373
Hill, Alex	26-Jan-1923	1	83
Hill, Alex L.	26-May-1921	1	82
Hill, Billy	30-Jun-1953	7	15
Hill, George	16-Dec-1946	10	171
Hill, James	3-Jul-1950	5	460
Hill, John H.	29-Oct-1949	3	397
Hill, Paul	13-Dec-1949	6	430
Hill, Tom	18-Feb-1923	1	15
Hill, Tom	18-Feb-1923	1	86
Hinkle, Earl	25-Jul-1949	3	267
Hinkle, Kenneth	14-Sep-1959	8	229
Hinton, Bill	27-Sep-1949	3	276
Hitchcock, Paul	15-Jul-1963	9	185
Hitchcock, Robert	5-Nov-1948	2	238
Hnsley, John	13 June 1919	1	150
Hobbs, Joe	28-Oct-1949	3	476
Hobbs, Parker	4-Oct-1949	3	291
Hobbs, Raymond	30-Dec-1949	4	183
Hobbs, Zollie	14-Jan-1950	4	184
Hobson, Earl	7-Oct-1949	3	323
Hobson, James	18-Dec-1922	1	180
Hobson, Joe	13-Jul-1923	9	268
Hogsed, Carl	12-Sep-1949	2	227
Hogsed, Clyde	19-Dec-1949	11	92
Holbrook, Albert	7-Oct-1951	7	88
Holbrook, Charles	7-Nov-1957	7	474
Holbrook, Charles	8-Nov-1963	9	230
Holbrook, Edmund Androx	17-Jun-1956	7	184
Holbrook, Ellis	9-Oct-1956	7	272-273
Holbrook, Floyd Joseph	11-Dec-1973	12	69
Holbrook, Glenn	18-Oct-1962	12	206
Holbrook, Grover	18-Jul-1923	1	237
Holbrook, Grover	18-Jul-1923	1	199
Holbrook, James Carl	14-Jul-1965	11	95
Holbrook, Jessie	18-Feb-1947	2	295
Holbrook, Joseph	12-Jan-1950	6	108
Holbrook, Kerry	11-Oct-1977	13	344
Holbrook, Mark	8-Jan-1976	13	226
Holbrook, Remus Darrel	7-Oct-1976	13	291
Holbrook, Tilsman Jr.	6-Nov-1962	9	116
Holbrook, William P.	13-Jan-1950	4	180
Holbrook, Woodrow	13-Dec-1949	4	94
Holbrooks, Vonden	23-Oct-1949	4	611
Holland, John Thomas	17-Nov-1995	14	172
Holman, Edward	11-Dec-1973	12	71
Holmes, Alvin	21-Dec-1949	5	176
Holt, John	13-Jan-1950	6	592
Holt, John	1-Feb-1951	6	600
Holt, John	16-Jan-1956	7	160
Holt, Mason	5-Nov-1975	13	200
Holt, Monnie	2-Jul-1951	6	568
Holt, Nelson	30-Aug-1949	2	326
Holt, Raymond	1-Jan-1950	10	19
Holt, Willie	10-Oct-1947	2	172
Homes, Gordon	27-Nov-1951	5	478
Honaker, Chester	24-Sep-1949	3	239
Honaker, William	16-Nov-1949	3	519
Hondel, Robert	16-Mar-1964	9	173
Hondel, Willis	2-Sep-1956	7	220
Honeycutt, Charlie	20-Aug-1956	7	212
Honeycutt, Ernest	14-Nov-1956	7	246
Honeycutt, Malcom	23-Feb-1947	2	139
Hood, Robert Lee	4-Sep-1975	15	106
Hoover, Bert	13-Nov-1949	4	53
Hoover, Corporal H.	4-Mar-1948	2	223
Hoover, Elmer	25-Oct-1957	7	428
Hoover, George	16-Oct-1949	4	459
Hoover, Johnnie	17-Nov-1949	7	111
Hoover, Ray	24-Feb-1947	2	332
Hoover, Willie B.	13-Jul-1971	11	469
Hopkins, Eugene	25-Aug-1950	9	294
Hopkins, Roger Dean	9-Feb-1997	14	205-206
Hopkins, Ronnie D.	30-Mar-1971	11	283
Hopper, Harry Benjamin Jr.	31-Oct-1949	5	234
Hopper, Joseph M.	3-Nov-1957	7	435
Hopson, Alex W.	19-Jul-1956	7	201
Hopson, Everett	8-Jan-1950	4	166
Hopson, Jimmie R.	13-Sep-1962	9	103
Hopson, Lee D.	12-Aug-1969	11	184
Hopson, Palmer	2-Feb-1972	11	324
Hopson, Samuel	21-Nov-1949	5	46
Horn (Honn), Myrvin	8-Dec-1960	8	319
Horn, Bascom Jr.	5-Oct-1972	11	605
Horn, Carl	20-Aug-1958	8	74
Horn, Carl D.	12-Jun-1983	13	430
Horn, Donald	4-Jul-1951	6	523
Horn, Guy R.	4-Jun-1964	9	300
Horn, Harry	12-Mar-1964	9	176
Horn, Joe W.	9-Feb-1950	4	344
Horn, Johnie	10-Jan-1980	13	404
Horn, Morton	11-Mar-1948	2	354
Horn, Otto	17-Mar-1950	4	463
Horn, Steward	17-Apr-1950	4	509
Horne, Carl	1-Jul-1958	8	62
Horne, Carl T.	3-Oct-1949	3	288
Horne, John D.	22-Apr-1974	13	6
Horne, Walter	29-Sep-1949	6	282
Horner, Elmer	3-Feb-1950	5	158
Horton, Nathaniel	11-Feb-1923	1	9
Houchins, Charles	6-Jul-1949	3	72
Howard, Bill H.	23-Sep-1959	8	210
Howard, Chalmer	12-Apr-1974	13	5
Howard, Charles	29-May-1962	11	61
Howard, Eugene	9-May-1958	8	30
Howard, Garry G.	4-Mar-1969	11	323
Howard, Glenda Lee	31-Aug-1995	14	295-296
Howard, Gold	17-Feb-1954	7	75
Howard, Gold	17-Feb-1954	10	181
Howard, Hager	18-Dec-1949	4	362
Howard, Harold J.	1-Oct-1963	10	56
Howard, Harry	16-Apr-1959	8	173
Howard, Harvey	6-Sep-1949	3	157
Howard, Homer	11-Oct-1961	9	59
Howard, Jackie	21-Nov-1975	13	212
Howard, James	26-Sep-1949	6	280
Howard, Morgan	4-Dec-1956	8	42
Howard, Patrick	22-Dec-1922	1	43
Howard, Ray	5-Dec-1949	4	24
Howard, Sam	5-Dec-1949	4	67
Howard, Willard	18-Sep-1947	4	558
Howell, Astor	7-Nov-1949	5	23
Howell, Billy	5-Jun-1977	13	330
Howell, Chester	17-Jan-1951	6	473
Howell, Chester	1-May-1957	8	141
Howell, Davie Jr.	23-Dec-1946	4	96
Howell, Dennie	10-Oct-1973	12	43
Howell, Edgar	26-Aug-1947	2	343
Howell, Edward	9-Dec-1969	11	363
Howell, Elisha	6-Jul-1951	10	119
Howell, Emit	9-Dec-1950	6	561
Howell, Emitt	22-Dec-1950	6	259
Howell, Frank	25-Sep-1949	3	250
Howell, Frank	25-Sep-1949	6	112
Howell, Fred	9-Mar-1923	12	197
Howell, Harvey	31-Oct-1949	3	463
Howell, James	15-Dec-1975	13	239
Howell, James Elmer	17-Jan-1957	14	110
Howell, Jarvey	24-Jun-1923	1	222
Howell, Jerry	8-Jun-1972	11	570
Howell, Joe Jr	14-Dec-1949	4	428
Howell, John	8-Apr-1947	2	90
Howell, Johnie	14-Dec-1949	4	552
Howell, Joseph	29-Jan-1923	1	249
Howell, Manford	4-Nov-1976	14	229
Howell, Milford	19-Apr-1957	7	389
Howell, Morgan	23-Feb-1923	1	181
Howell, Nancy Paulene	1-Mar-1995	14	254
Howell, O.C.	27-Feb-1950	4	423
Howell, Oval	2-Dec-1948	2	375
Howell, Paris	20-Oct-1971	11	505
Howell, Reed	1-Jan-1950	6	281
Howell, Sam	13-Nov-1923	1	234
Howell, Tom	3-Nov-1949	3	468
Howell, Willie	17-Jan-1922	1	255
Howell, Willie	13-Jan-1957	7	411
Howell, Willie	1-Jan-1958	7	483
Howell, Willie	15-Oct-1974	13	55
Howes, Raleigh	9-Mar-1956	12	141
Howes, Raleigh	1-Jan-1964	12	140
Hsoson, Glennen	19-Mar-1950	5	214
Hubbard, Bill	7-May-1923	12	133
Hubbard, Charles	14-Oct-1947	4	329
Hubbard, Charles	27-Jan-1950	4	328
Hubbard, Clifford	5-Sep-1949	3	242
Hubbard, Jack	7-Oct-1949	3	365
Hubbard, James	20-Feb-1950	5	98
Hubbard, James	6-Aug-1967	11	233
Hubbard, Joseph	10-Sep-1949	3	192
Hudson, John	13-Oct-1949	6	334
Hudson, John	1-Feb-1969	11	319
Huff, Canton	23-Mar-1974	12	115
Huff, Clifford	13-Mar-1958	5	7
Huff, Ershel	19-Aug-1949	6	218
Huff, Grover	22-Apr-1950	4	550
Huff, John	15-Oct-1949	3	377
Huffman, Eugene	7-Feb-1950	4	472
Huffman, John Albert	23-May-1950	5	474
Hughes, Alex	27-Jan-1950	5	485
Hughes, Arthur	22-Jan-1976	13	231
Hughes, Arthur F.	14-Jan-1950	4	193
Hughes, Buford	16-Jan-1951	6	296
Hughes, Charles	15-Mar-1950	4	449
Hughes, Clarence	5-Jan-1972	11	525
Hughes, Dewey	26-May-1947	2	26
Hughes, Donald	19-Jul-1961	9	26
Hughes, Earl	14-Dec-1949	10	74
Hughes, Ephriam	31-Oct-1949	3	545
Hughes, Eugene	15-Aug-1974	13	34
Hughes, George	7-Jan-1950	4	394
Hughes, Granville	4-Dec-1949	3	589
Hughes, Henry	10-May-1962	9	76
Hughes, Hugh	10-Nov-1949	4	44
Hughes, Jobe	14-Oct-1949	3	434
Hughes, Johnnie	11-Nov-1948	2	249
Hughes, Kenneth Ray	21-Nov-1973	14	107
Hughes, Millard	29-Apr-1951	6	431
Hughes, Ronald	16-May-1976	13	269
Hughes, Willard	8-Dec-1958	8	144

Name	Disc. Date	Book	Page
Hughes, Woodrow	11-Oct-1950	6	138
Hull, Bobby	18-Dec-1974	13	86
Humphrey, Charles C.	30-Mar-1950	14	165-166
Humphrey, Charles C.	30-Mar-1950	14	167168
Humphrey, Charles C.	29-Mar-1953	14	169
Humphrey, Clinton Ray	1-Aug-1976	15	41
Humphrey, James William	25-Jun-1958	8	58
Humphries, Herbert Jr.	8-Dec-1960	9	82
Hunt, Arco	22-Aug-1964	12	336
Hunt, Curtis	15-Nov-1949	3	516
Hunt, Darvin	31-Jan-1950	4	386
Hunt, Deames	14-Dec-1949	4	120
Hunt, Donald	7-Jan-1950	4	502
Hunt, Edward	8-Dec-1950	6	231
Hunt, Elmer	30-Nov-1949	3	590
Hunt, Ernest	22-Oct-1949	3	391
Hunt, Erschel	19-Aug-1950	6	107
Hunt, Franklin	2-Sep-1949	3	169
Hunt, Monty	25-May-1922	1	611
Hunt, O.C.	3-Dec-1949	3	616
Hunt, Troy E.	10-Nov-1970	11	198
Hunt, Velmer	30-Jan-1974	14	99
Hunt, Willie	14-Dec-1949	4	31
Hunter, Arnold	18-Oct-1949	10	73
Hunter, Charles	26-Aug-1949	3	336
Hunter, Claude	8-Aug-1947	2	117
Hunter, Columbus	12-Jan-1960	10	203
Hunter, Delmar	11-Nov-1949	4	323
Hunter, Newl	7-Nov-1949	4	577
Hunter, Oliver	13-Dec-1949	5	96
Hunter, Ora	10-Feb-1947	1	142
Hunter, Robert P.	15-Feb-1957	7	290
Hunter, Rupert A.	14-Nov-1947	2	107
Hunter, Steven	20-Nov-1975	13	208
Hunter, Thomas	5-Nov-1949	6	449
Hunter, Webster	9-Nov-1949	3	465
Hunter, Woodrow	23-Apr-1951	8	298
Hurd, Connie	17-Nov-1975	13	211
Hurd, Marcus	6-Oct-1949	6	358
Hurd, Milan	18-Mar-1923	1	111
Hurd, Oscar	15-Apr-1947	2	215
Hurd, Rudolph	3-Aug-1949	3	150
Hurd, Shular	27-Nov-1961	9	60
Hurst, Luther	22-Mar-1950	5	539
Hurt, Earnest	26-Oct-1949	8	32
Hurt, Earnest	12-Feb-1951	8	33
Hurt, Estill	23-Sep-1949	3	308
Hurt, Willard	27-Aug-1947	2	101
Hutchinson, Eugene Rodney	5-Aug-1965	11	82
Hutchinson, Garland	9-Nov-1949	3	423
Hyden Ephraim	12-Dec-1974	13	78
Hyden, Alex	30-Mar-1947	6	599
Hyden, Carl	20-Jun-1963	9	160
Hyden, Charles	12-Nov-1958	8	119
Hyden, Charles	21-Mar-1968	12	171
Hyden, Darvin	19-Jun-1963	9	163
Hyden, Floyd	4-Mar-1953	6	627
Hyden, Glen	26-Apr-1962	9	141
Hyden, Henry	5-Aug-1957	8	157
Hyden, Jesse	26-Jul-1950	5	498
Hyden, Joe T.	19-Jan-1950	2	347
Hyden, Oscar	13-Sep-1977	13	337
Hyden, Oscar Jr.	20-Feb-1968	11	314
Hyden, Thomas	7-Apr-1951	5	490
Imes, Melvin	29-Oct-1949	5	421
Inmon, Buford Cap	29-Oct-2000	15	13
Irick, Leonard	27-Nov-1949	5	69
Irish, Robert	19-Mar 1956	7	215
Isaac, Howell	31-Jan-1950	6	501
Isaac, Jonah	3-Oct-1958	8	99
Isaac, Randal	22-Sep-1978	13	366
Isaac, Russell	22-Mar-1967	11	208
Isaac, Tommy	11-Oct-1981	13	423
Isaac, Tony	29-Dec-1957	7	458
Isaac, Virgil	29-Oct-1949	12	185
Isaac, Virnes	10-Aug-1950	10	1-2
Isaacs, William Jr.	5-Jan-1959	8	129
Ison, Delbert	25-Nov-1947	2	6
Ison, Delbert	24-N0v-1943	11	33
Ison, John	29-Dec-1949	4	101
Issac, Boge	11-Jun-1948	2	247
Issac, Lee, Jr.	2-Oct-1947	2	124
Issacs, Clyde	4-Jul-1984	12	223
Jackson, Arlie	12-Jun-1975	13	156
Jackson, Dennis	12-Jan-1974	12	85
Jackson, Dwight	1-Mar-1984	12	221
Jackson, Handy	19-Sep-1979	14	273
Jackson, John	18-Jan-1950	10	22
Jacobs, Adam	6-Dec-1949	5	82
Jacobs, Columbus	7-Nov-1949	7	285
Jacobs, Elmer	13-Jan-1948	2	138
Jacobs, Elmer	12-Feb-1951	6	352
Jacobs, Russell	12-Nov-1949	6	391
James, Doris	21-Nov-1971	11	514
James, Jerome	25-Aug-1974	13	39
James, Tom	2-Sep-1949	2	324
Jarrell, Ambers	11-Feb-1947	2	62
Jarrell, Carl	17-Mar-1971	11	325
Jarrell, Charley	5-Oct-1949	3	293
Jarrell, Charlie	24-Dec-1922	1	127
Jarrell, Curtis	29-Nov-1949	5	90
Jarrell, Fred	1-May-1970	11	457
Jarrell, Fred	3-May-1970	11	170
Jarrell, George Henry	13-Feb-1975	13	104
Jarrell, Harvey	5-Jun-1922	1	21
Jarrell, Joe	13-Oct-1949	6	155
Jarrell, Joe	9-Nov-1950	6	202
Jarrell, John	10-Jan-1970	12	147
Jarrell, Leo	19-Oct-1961	9	40
Jarrell, Odis	30-Dec-1949	10	156
Jarrell, Odis	4-Dec-1952	10	155
Jarrell, Raymond Michael	28-May-1979	13	390
Jarrell, Sam	23-Oct-1947	2	175
Jarrell, Troy	21-Jul-1975	13	175
Jarrell, Virgil	18-Jan-1950	6	329
Jarvis, Estill	23-Dec-1949	5	173
Jarvis, James	5-Jun-1982	13	425
Jervis, Clinton	29-Mar-1950	4	504
Jervis, Curtis	12-Dec-1949	4	30
Jervis, Ellis	22-May-1957	7	340
Jervis, Jeff	22-Sep-1922	1	29
Jervis, Thomas Jefferson	25-May-1960	8	275
Jervis, Walter	18-Nov-1949	3	505
Jervis, Woodrow	4-Sep-1949	3	190
Jessie, Charley	14-Nov-1949	4	48
Jewell, Randy	16-Aug-1979	12	195
Jewell, Randy	16-Aug-1979	13	399
Johncox, Virginia A.	9-Dec-1949	4	22
Johns, Ferdie C.	17-Feb-1949	3	353
Johns, John	14-Dec-1950	6	251
Johns, Ross	21-Aug-1947	5	199
Johnson, Alvis	23-Nov-1949	5	50
Johnson, Arlen	23-Dec-1949	5	140
Johnson, Arthur	22-Oct-1956	5	231
Johnson, Bob	26-Feb-1959	11	112
Johnson, Burinda	4-Dec-1947	11	4
Johnson, Carl	5-Nov-1948	2	244
Johnson, Cecil	10-Sep-1949	5	538
Johnson, Charles	19-Jan-1978	12	175
Johnson, Charlie	17-Mar-1950	5	417
Johnson, Charlie	2-Nov-1950	7	287
Johnson, Clarence	8-Dec-1950	6	275
Johnson, Cline	11-Jan-1972	11	254
Johnson, Clyde	23-Jul-1947	2	95
Johnson, Columbus	18-Jan-1950	6	566
Johnson, Crit	9-Feb-1950	4	361
Johnson, Curtis	30-Oct-1949	7	110
Johnson, Curtis	21-Aug-1963	9	184
Johnson, Daniel	21-Oct-1947	2	72
Johnson, Danny	30-Jul-1975	13	275
Johnson, Darvin	3-Feb-1950	4	371
Johnson, David	9-Sep-1978	13	369
Johnson, Dennis	18-Jan-1950	5	133
Johnson, Dingus	7-Dec-1949	7	176
Johnson, Donald	17-Jul-1974	13	24
Johnson, Donnie	16-Dec-1974	13	82
Johnson, Earl	2-Oct-1949	6	144
Johnson, Earl	10-Jan-1965	11	415
Johnson, Edison	4-Jun-1975	13	158
Johnson, Edward	20-Nov-1952	6	609
Johnson, Elmer	28-Oct-1973	12	56
Johnson, Elmer	25-Jun-1974	13	23
Johnson, Ernest	17-Dec-1949	4	64
Johnson, Estill	25-Oct-1949	3	518
Johnson, Everett	27-Nov-1949	5	68
Johnson, Foster	14-Oct-1949	3	318
Johnson, Gardner	3-Aug-1949	3	144
Johnson, Garfield	30-Apr-1948	5	16
Johnson, Gary	11-Nov-1969	11	359
Johnson, Gordon	7-May-1972	11	197
Johnson, Grover	11-Oct-1949	9	246
Johnson, Henry	11-Nov-1949	6	395
Johnson, Hobert	27-Sep-1971	11	496
Johnson, Homer	31-Jan-1950	4	339
Johnson, Homer	15-Dec-1950	6	236
Johnson, Homer	4-Sep-1958	8	83
Johnson, Hubert	20-Jun-1950	4	603
Johnson, Hubert Frantz Jr.	22-Sep-1957	7	404
Johnson, Iberay	30-Jun-1949	3	70
Johnson, James	28-Nov-1948	43	168
Johnson, Jesse	1-Apr-1956	8	113
Johnson, Jimmie	8-Aug-1962	9	127
Johnson, Jink	26-May-1975	12	252
Johnson, Joe	8-Dec-1947	2	143
Johnson, John E.	17-Dec-1949	5	200
Johnson, John J.	23-Apr-1923	1	58
Johnson, John R.	29-May-1949	2	318
Johnson, Johnny	23-Dec-1973	12	80
Johnson, Johnny Scott	15-Nov-2000	15	15
Johnson, Keene	5-Nov-1969	11	362
Johnson, Kendrick	23-May-1950	4	569
Johnson, Larry	27-Jun-1974	13	26
Johnson, Layne	8-Aug-1973	12	97
Johnson, Lem J.	11-Dec-1949	5	425
Johnson, Leo	24-Nov-1949	5	491
Johnson, Levi	5-Aug-1950	11	23
Johnson, Luther	8-Dec-1961	14	100
Johnson, Luther Jr.	30-Jan-1977	13	304
Johnson, Miller Lewis	14-Nov-1958	8	106
Johnson, Ova	23-Dec-1949	4	638
Johnson, Paul	11-Feb-1970	11	378
Johnson, Percy	20-Dec-1972	13	355
Johnson, Ray	21-Jul-1976	13	278
Johnson, Robert	2-Aug-1951	6	513
Johnson, Ronnie	9-Jul-1975	13	166
Johnson, Russell	30-Nov-1949	3	428
Johnson, Russell	28-Nov-1949	3	573
Johnson, Stanley	28-Jun-1950	4	613
Johnson, Sylvan	31-Jul-1949	3	129
Johnson, Thomas	5-Dec-1972	11	610
Johnson, Tilden	31-Dec-1949	4	100
Johnson, Tom Jr.	22-Nov-1952	7	10
Johnson, Verlin	9-Aug-1949	3	219
Johnson, Vernon	15-Jan-1950	4	228
Johnson, Vernon B.	12-Apr-1973	11	627
Johnson, Virgil	21-Nov-1949	3	549
Johnson, Wayne	11-Feb-1950	4	365
Johnson, Wilford Jr.	27-Jul-1959	8	232
Johnson, Willie Brooks	17-Oct-1970	11	193
Johnson, Willie Ray Jr.	5-Apr-1967	11	406
Jones, Burnis	5-Oct-1949	3	304
Jones, Carl	31-Dec-1949	6	27
Jones, Clark	28-Sep-1949	3	605
Jones, Clynard	6-Feb-1957	7	391
Jones, Deward	25-Sep-1949	6	288
Jones, Earl	17-Oct-1949	11	132
Jones, Edgar	30-Jul-1949	4	286
Jones, Elmer	24-Apr-1949	2	300
Jones, Elva	7-Apr-1950	4	514
Jones, Fred	26-Nov-1963	10	107
Jones, Gregory	17-Mar-1974	12	108
Jones, Gregory Randall II	2-Jul-2004	15	50
Jones, Jack	15-Feb-1950	4	395
Jones, John Kelly	30-Nov-1957	11	123
Jones, Johnny	5-Aug-1972	11	580
Jones, Loa	7-Jan-1958	7	454
Jones, Manis	28-Nov-1949	3	602
Jones, Melvin	10-Oct-1949	3	312
Jones, Michael	8-Jun-1972	11	340
Jones, Ola	26-Apr-1951	6	397
Jones, Paul	6-May-1963	9	149
Jones, Paul	1-May-1967	11	298
Jones, Pete	24-Apr-1947	2	23
Jones, Randall	3-Dec-1969	11	153
Jones, Robert	8-Oct-1949	10	130
Jones, Robert	1-Jan-1950	6	411
Jones, Robert	25-Feb-1968	11	391
Jones, Ronald	11-Jun-1972	11	288
Jones, Shelby	27-May-1950	4	572
Jones, Silver	26-Sep-1947	2	317
Jones, Tivis N.	29-Oct-1952	7	84
Jones, Wiley	8-Sep-1960	8	303

Name	Disc. Date	Book	Page
Jones, William	16-Mar-1950	6	400
Jordan, Paul	30-Jun-1950	4	624
Joseph, Denvil	7-Nov-1949	3	520
Joseph, Herman	7-Aug-1971	11	313
Joseph, Hershel	25-Jul-1973	12	22
Joseph, Maryland	7-Jul-1963	14	132
Joseph, Maryland	10-Sep-1966	14	131
Joseph, Maryland	12-Apr-1972	14	130
Joseph, Maryland	15-Mar-1978	14	129
Joseph, Maryland	3-Oct-1982	14	128
Joseph, Maryland	9-May-1989	14	127
Joseph, Raymond	21-Aug-1949	3	139
Joseph, Raymond	7-Nov-1973	13	20
Joyce, Jay	30-Oct-1949	6	162
Judd, Arthur	1-Dec-1963	10	53
Judd, Lester	28-Mar-1978	12	169
Justice, Aaron	1-Mar-1951	6	559
Justice, Carl	1-Nov-1949	3	472
Justice, Charles	9-Oct-1949	9	137
Justice, Doffie	20-May-1951	14	260
Justice, Jack	19-Dec-1949	5	123
Justice, Kennith Ray	5-Oct-1972	14	98
Justice, Virgil Joseph	13-Mar-1950	10	71
Keathley, Brian Patick	10-Jul-1995	14	160
Keathley, Donald Ray	10-Feb-1972	14	24
Keathley, Henry	20-Dec-1950	6	256
Keathley, Jackie	17-Nov-1957	7	469
Keathley, James	17-Dec-1949	4	70
Keathley, James L. Jr.	31-Jan-1958	8	5
Keathley, Joe	29-Nov-1950	6	229
Keathley, Leroy Hamilton	15-Apr-1970	14	199
Keathley, Samuel G.	17-Dec-1970	14	101
Keathley, Samuel Green	4-Jul-1967	11	228
Keathley, Ted	18-Dec-1949	4	73
Keathley, Teddie	3-May-1974	11	306
Keathley, Walker	13-Feb-1957	7	289
Keene, Bobby	26-Jun-1974	13	17
Keene, Ernest Jr.	30-Apr-1976	13	262
Keene, Joseph	8-Jan-1950	9	83
Keenon, George Hamilton	1-Jan-1952	5	487
Keeton, Max	19-Nov-1949	5	38
Kendrick, Claude	11-Dec-1949	4	21
Kendrick, Claude	10-Jan-1970	11	367
Kendrick, Claude L.	1-Jan-1973	14	27
Kendrick, Ernest	15-Oct-1956	9	249
Kendrick, Franklin	19-Nov-1967	11	171
Kendrick, Gary R.	10-Jan-1974	14	49
Kendrick, John	31-Aug-1949	3	206
Kendrick, Marvin	23-Apr-1956	12	240-241
Kendrick, Ronald	17-Oct-1974	13	62
Kendrick, Vernon	20-Feb-1947	2	37
Kendrick, William	3-Nov-1949	4	425
Kendrick, William	26-Apr-1975	13	144
Key, James R.	1-Sep-1965	15	16
Key, Jimmy Ray	15-Jul-1986	14	305
Kidd, Alexander	24-Apr-1947	2	56
Kidd, Bobby	30-Jun-1977	13	334
Kidd, Carmel	30-Aug-1950	11	169
Kidd, Carmel	2-Mar-1951	7	114
Kidd, Charlie	9-Jan-1959	8	128
Kidd, Christopher Alan	4-Sep-2002	15	36
Kidd, Clarence	26-Nov-1964	10	158
Kidd, Dennie	19-Oct-1950	6	318
Kidd, Donald	22-Mar-1979	13	379
Kidd, Edgar	8-Feb-1946	8	64
Kidd, Edward	18-May-1955	7	135
Kidd, Everett	23-Oct-1955	7	153
Kidd, George Jr.	16-Nov-1981	14	282-283
Kidd, Gregory	12-Mar-1979	13	377
Kidd, Henry	7-Dec-1959	14	233
Kidd, Henry	11-Dec-1963	10	124
Kidd, James	3-Nov-1949	3	467
Kidd, James	11-Feb-1975	13	106
Kidd, Jerry	24-Apr-1973	11	629
Kidd, Jettie L.	31-Oct-1949	3	453
Kidd, Luther	26-Sep-1949	7	12
Kidd, Luther	27-Dec-1950	7	11
Kidd, Miles	7-Dec-1950	6	235
Kidd, Rufford	31-Jul-1947	2	71
Kidd, Willie	14-Feb-1950	4	398
Kilbourne, Dave	25-Sep-1946	2	45
Kilburn, Joe	19-Apr-1948	11	430
Kilgore, Craig	6-Mar-1972	13	56
Kilgore, Craig	13-Oct-1974	13	57

Name	Disc. Date	Book	Page
Kilgore, Craig Edwin	6-Mar-1972	14	15
Kilgore, Craig Edwin	13-Oct-1974	14	16
Kilgore, Glen	7-Jan-1950	6	190
Kilgore, Granham	8-Nov-1949	3	601
Kilgore, Sylvester Ray	2-Jun-1950	5	419
Kilgore, Sylvester Ray	2-Jun-1950	5	428
Kimbler, Robert	28-Aug-1957	7	382
King, Burbage	29-Oct-1948	2	232
King, Franklin	23-Aug-1970	11	403
King, Joseph	24-Jan-1950	4	311
King, Leon	29-Mar-1963	15	51
King, Leroy	11-Sep-1962	9	138
King, Newman	1-Jul-1949	3	81
King, Romeo	8-Oct-1972	11	597
King, Waverly	13-Jan-1950	5	110
King, Willie	14-Jan-1950	4	315
Kingsley, Paul	14-Feb-1950	5	525
Kinzer, Bayliss	18-Oct-1962	9	112
Kinzer, James	16-Dec-1948	5	78
Kiser, Albert	21-Dec-1949	4	74
Kiser, Elmer	4-Oct-1957	7	413
Kiser, Tory	25-Nov-1949	3	577
Kitchen, John	31-Dec-1956	7	294
Knott, Lewis Jr.	12-Aug-1950	10	16
Knott, Lewis Jr.	5-Feb-1952	10	11
Lackey, James	6-Jun-1974	13	9
Laferty, Avran	27-Mar-1950	9	187
Laferty, Buford	18-Sep-1964	10	193
Laferty, Charles	26-Feb-1959	8	149
Laferty, Clarence	1-Nov-1966	11	234
Laferty, Clinton	7-Dec-1971	11	260
Laferty, Colonel	9-Jan-1956	7	163
Laferty, Donald	7-Aug-1974	13	29
Laferty, Donald	19-Oct-1976	12	210
Laferty, Halleck T	30-Oct-1949	4	54
Laferty, Herman	8-Jul-1965	11	79
Laferty, James	9-Apr-1963	9	144
Laferty, James W	28-Jan-1949	4	596
Laferty, Lucien	5-Oct-1949	3	289
Laferty, Otis V.	27-Oct-1949	3	91
Laferty, Stewart	24-Oct-1958	8	97
Lafferty, Adrian	9-May-1957	8	295
Lafferty, Adrian	9-May-1957	12	234
Lafferty, Adrian	16-May-1962	12	235
Lafferty, Ashland	11-Aug-1949	3	194
Lafferty, Bascom	4-Apr-1957	10	143
Lafferty, Bradis	18-Sep-1963	9	188
Lafferty, Clyde	5-Aug-1961	9	16
Lafferty, Curtis	13-Mar-1950	5	241
Lafferty, Darrell	4-Feb-1950	4	327
Lafferty, Darwin	9-Jan-1950	6	145
Lafferty, Donald	18-Nov-1959	9	162
Lafferty, Donald	17-Jun-1963	9	161
Lafferty, Earl	25-Aug-1949	3	158
Lafferty, Elmer	23-Feb-1977	13	310
Lafferty, Epp Jr.	25-Oct-1951	6	524
Lafferty, Ernest	17-Apr-1960	12	142
Lafferty, Ernie Floyd	16-Oct-1992	14	72
Lafferty, Galloway	6-Dec-1949	4	4
Lafferty, George	12-Apr-1950	6	340
Lafferty, George L.	26-Nov-1957	9	186
Lafferty, Jeannie	11-Jan-1979	13	376
Lafferty, Jesse Jr.	19-Nov-1956	7	245
Lafferty, Joe	6-Dec-1949	5	87
Lafferty, Joe	6-Dec-1949	4	506
Lafferty, Johnie	12-May-1950	5	549
Lafferty, Leo	25-Sep-1949	3	247
Lafferty, Lonzo	11-Dec-1949	4	9
Lafferty, Lucian Jr.	12-Feb-1974	12	96
Lafferty, Virgil	11-Dec-1950	7	131
Lafferty, Willie	23-Jul-1971	11	471
Lafferty, Woodrow	22-Dec-1949	6	412
Laffferty, Bill	20-Aug-1947	2	59
Langley, Henry	26-Apr-1923	1	44
Langley, Raymond	5-Dec-1949	9	255
Latham, Luther	23-Mar-1949	3	6
Laven, Luttrell	26-Oct-1949	3	415
Laven, Russell	6-May-1950	4	556
Lawson, Albert	6-Jul-1971	11	291
Lawson, Clovis	11-Nov-1950	7	102
Lawson, Fieldery	22-Mar-1950	4	481
Lawson, Freeman	15-Jul-1958	8	56
Lawson, Garnie	17-Jul-1958	8	54
Lawson, Gary	24-Jan-1972	11	532

Name	Disc. Date	Book	Page
Lawson, Gary Lee	15-Jun-1969	14	188
Lawson, Herbert	28-Jan-1949	3	11
Lawson, Lonie	25-Jun-1963	9	165
Lawson, Okie	23-Nov-1970	11	414
Lawson, Orville	12-Feb-1950	4	375
Lawson, Quillen	20-Nov-1974	13	73
Lawson, Richard	26-Mar-1959	8	160
Lawson, Rondell D.	2-Oct-1962	14	78
Lawson, Rondell D.	1-Oct-1966	14	66
Lawson, Sonnie Darrell	12-May-1969	11	334
Lawson, Teddie	21-Aug-1972	11	346
Lawton, Hunter	7-Jun-1971	11	489
Lay, Fred	3-Oct-1949	5	10
Layne, Archer	7-Nov-1949	3	499
Layne, Bertram	25-Apr-1947	2	166
Layne, Billy	16-May-1951	6	522
Layne, Donald Howard	8-Oct-1958	8	94
Layne, Ed	7-Nov-1947	2	66
Layne, Fred	8-Jan-1950	4	194
Layne, Harry	5-Oct-1949	6	89
Layne, Henry	6-Sep-1949	3	174
Layne, Hubert	1-Feb-1950	4	322
Layne, Jake	13-Feb-1950	7	25
Layne, James Roger Jr.	17-Jul-1956	7	197
Layne, Jimmy George	25-Jan-1973	13	422
Layne, Leland	28-Jul-1949	5	119
Layne, Marvin	16-Mar-1950	5	493
Layne, Otis	31-Aug-1949	3	204
Layne, Roscoe	31-Jan-1950	4	320
Layne, Scott	10-Oct-1966	11	441
Lee, Claude	21-Jan-1950	5	196
Lee, Daniel	24-Jul-1950	10	185
Lee, Robert Terry	29-Sep-1994	14	139
Lee, Stanley Everett	5-Aug-1993	14	138
Leedy, Arnold	19-Feb-1950	6	254
Leete, Martin	6-May-1947	2	94
LeMaster, Frank	24-Dec-1956	7	275
LeMaster, George	1-Dec-1949	10	18
LeMaster, Millard	12-Apr-1963	9	145
LeMaster, Paul	26-Jun-1957	7	353
LeMaster, Payne	29-Apr-1948	5	496
LeMaster, Thomas	15-Dec-1949	4	233
LeMaster, Wayne	24-Jan-1950	6	59
Leslie, Alfred	14-Feb-1952	6	556
Leslie, Allen	21-May-1949	3	24
Leslie, Claude	2-May-1950	5	547
Leslie, David	2-Apr-1949	3	10
Leslie, Don	31-Dec-1950	6	252
Leslie, Edward	15-Sep-1948	11	110
Leslie, Edward	22-Feb-1956	11	111
Leslie, Frank	28-Dec-1950	10	92
Leslie, Frank	16-Sep-1958	10	93
Leslie, Howard	7-May-1957	7	377
Leslie, Kenneth	5-Dec-1974	13	80
Leslie, Ollie	17-Feb-1974	12	95
Leslie, Ollie J.		15	58
Leslie, Ralph	4-Apr-1957	7	357
Leslie, Samuel	26-Jan-1950	6	336
Leslie, Samuel J.	19-Aug-1949	7	136
Lewis, Albert	10-Jan-1950	4	200
Lewis, Birkey	6-Nov-1957	8	284
Lewis, Birkey	8-Nov-1963	10	165
Lewis, Chester	20-Aug-1958	8	82
Lewis, Cordie	10-Jan-1923	1	66
Lewis, Elder	18-Jul-1923		
Lewis, Eugene	20-Apr-1950	10	27
Lewis, George	12-Dec-1957	11	129
Lewis, Harvey	21-Feb-1923	1	65
Lewis, Irvin	17-Nov-1922	1	62
Lewis, Jackie Jr.	3-Dec-1967	11	384
Lewis, John	20-Feb-1950	6	646
Lewis, John	23-Nov-1952	6	645
Lewis, John H.	3-Feb-1950	7	50
Lewis, John H.	12-Jan-1956	8	202
Lewis, Larcie	7-Nov-1949	6	110
Lewis, Larcie	3-Mar-1975	13	114
Lewis, Malcom	29-Nov-1949	3	611
Lewis, Ollie	13-Jan-1950	4	248
Lewis, Roscoe	5-Jun-1973	11	336
Lewis, Ross	19-Mar-1957	7	310
Lewis, Rudolph	3-Dec-1949	3	633
Lewis, Sam	12-Dec-1949	4	41
Lewis, Samuel	11-Aug-1949	6	455
Lewis, Shirley	30-Sep-1949	3	257

Name	Disc. Date	Book	Page
Lewis, Thomas	28-Dec-1949	4	270
Likens, Joe	28-May-1922	1	81
Likens, Tolva	21-May-1951	12	198
Likens, Tolva	21-May-1951	12	202
Litafik, Gaza	9-Feb-1950	10	14
Litteral, Frank	26-May-1964	9	256
Little, Alex	25-Oct-1949	10	87
Little, Alvin Jr.	19-Dec-1949	2	153
Little, Billy	10-Oct-1971	11	500
Little, Carlos	23-May-1977	13	329
Little, Cecil	21-Dec-1949	4	268
Little, Chester	2-May-1971	11	464
Little, Chester	5-May-1977	13	324
Little, Chester Darrell	22-Dec-2001	14	298
Little, Collier	20-Feb-1950	5	443
Little, Donald	31-Jan-1952	6	552
Little, Donald Charles	21-Dec-1958	8	142
Little, Earl	6-Mar-1968	11	270
Little, Earnest	30-Nov-1949	3	588
Little, Fred	11-Oct-1949	3	334
Little, Fred Jr.	11-Jan-1972	11	257
Little, Glen Edward	25-Aug-1974	14	75
Little, Holly	16-May-1958	8	234
Little, James	18-Sep-1947	2	77
Little, James	12-Jan-1951	7	67
Little, Jerry	10-Apr-1974	12	120
Little, Johnny	16-Jan-1956	8	183
Little, Larry G.	16-Dec-1972	14	56
Little, Larry Gene	15-Oct-1970	14	55
Little, Larry Gene	14-Dec-1971	14	57
Little, Larry Gene	23-Jul-1974	14	54
Little, Lavonis	16-Dec-1956	7	264
Little, Mike	29-Jul-1950	10	113
Little, Mikey	2-Nov-1949	7	66
Little, Ralph	27-Nov-1962	9	123
Little, Raymond	18-Oct-1964	11	1
Little, Robert	3-Sep-1959	8	208
Little, Sean Lee	3-Apr-2000	15	1
Little, Sylvester	11-Oct-1971	11	504
Little, Virgil	6-Nov-1962	9	115
Little, Virgil	1-Nov-1966	11	245
Little, Willie	21-Sep-1956	10	109
Little, Willis	17-Dec-1974	13	87
Little, Willis	2-Dec-1977	12	162
Lockwood, James	4-Oct-1957	7	455
Lockwood, Richard	5-Feb-1950	6	130
Logan, Stanley	8-Nov-1949	10	94
Long, Elmer	14-Dec-1949	5	135
Lovely, Mark	20-Mar-1962	10	44
Lowe, Lloyd	6-Dec-1973	12	227
Lucas, Arthur	23-Sep-1949	7	167
Lucas, Kenneth Ray	31-Dec-1970	14	32
Lucas, Marvin	25-Sep-1949	6	117
Lumpkins, Charles	20-Jan-1958	7	478
Lumpkins, Charles	5-Jun-1961	9	347
Lumpkins, Dennie	23-Feb-1977	12	196
Lykens, Joe Jr.	13-May-1953	7	177
Lynch, Jess	25-Aug-1947	2	125
Lyons, Bruce	6-Dec-1949	10	40
Lyons, Freddy Edward	19-Dec-1983	15	87
Lyons, Harry	3-Oct-1946	2	345
Lyons, Harry	3-May-1950	2	371
Lyons, Harry	3-May-1950	4	594
Lyons, James	16-Jan-1950	4	554
Lyons, James	25-Sep-1973	12	38
Lyons, John	20-Jul-1923	1	116
Lyons, Richard	12-May-1960	8	273
Lyons, William	17-Mar-1950	5	210
Mack, Herman Jr.	1-Dec-1948	2	252
Maggard, Charlie	29-Jan-1950	11	75
Mann, Orban	2-Jul-1959	10	47
Mann, Walter	2-Aug-1974	13	28
Manns, Earl	12-Dec-1949	6	157
Manns, Edward	11-May-1959	11	84
Manns, Jerry	19-Oct-1974	13	74
Manns, Roy	14-Aug-1978	12	228
Manuel, Arnold Alvis Jr.	16-May-1971	11	449
Manuel, Roger	12-May-1975	13	151
Marcum, Lloyd	29-Dec-1977	13	348
Marcum, Lowell Douglas	4-Dec-1973	12	66
Marcum, William	26-Oct-1949	3	416
Marshall, Albert	17-Nov-1949	5	47
Marshall, Arthur	10-Jan-1950	5	146
Marshall, Arthur	27-Sep-1950	6	121

Name	Disc. Date	Book	Page
Marshall, Bennie	12-Mar-1950	6	249
Marshall, Berklynn L.	28-Mar-1950	4	503
Marshall, Clifford B.	15-Mar-1950	4	518
Marshall, Dock	2-Nov-1949	6	192
Marshall, Edga	1-Apr-1953	6	637
Marshall, Fred	22-Apr-1946	1	353
Marshall, Glen	30-Apr-1973	12	2
Marshall, Palmer	29-Nov-1949	4	108
Marshall, Raymond	11-Dec-1949	4	147
Marshall, Ronnie	26-Dec-1949	9	327
Marshall, Virgil	10-Apr-1950	5	251
Marsillett, Smith	23-Apr-1950	4	520
Marsillett, Tobie	25-Sep-1949	3	324
Marsillett, William Henderson	18-Mar-1975	13	131
Martin, Adam	15-Jul-1947	2	297
Martin, Ballard	13-Jul-1970	11	183
Martin, Bermon	5-Dec-1947	2	362
Martin, Bermon	6-Sep-1950	6	189
Martin, Bernard P.	23-Nov-1949	12	29
Martin, Bernard P.	31-Dec-1950	6	353
Martin, Bernard P.	31-Dec-1950	12	30
Martin, Bernard P.	5-Jun-1954	12	28
Martin, Bernard P.	10-Aug-1973	12	31
Martin, Bill C.	30-Oct-1949	5	19
Martin, Billy	21-Jan-1950	5	145
Martin, Billy Keith	29-Jan-1975	14	52
Martin, Blaine	29-Oct-1949	4	26
Martin, Bolten	11-Dec-1949	6	255
Martin, Canton	21-Oct-1949	4	629
Martin, Chalmer R.	1-Mar-1983	14	106
Martin, Clarence	17-Jan-1957	7	281
Martin, Claude	15-Feb-1970	11	383
Martin, Clem	20-Nov-1949	7	34
Martin, Clem	19-Feb-1950	4	397
Martin, Coley	24-Nov-1947	2	262
Martin, Columbus B.	13-Jun-1950	4	600
Martin, David	13-Jan-1970	11	242
Martin, Don	2-Jul-1950	5	510
Martin, Donald	15-Sep-1957	7	400
Martin, Earl	12-Dec-1949	4	266
Martin, Earl P.	31-Jan-1950	7	99
Martin, Eugene	7-Mar-1950	6	78
Martin, Eugene	4-Nov-1950	6	383
Martin, Eugene	23-May-1951	6	480
Martin, Fred	4-Apr-1947	4	161
Martin, Gaylord	6-Jan-1972	11	530
Martin, Gherard	13-Nov-1949	6	498
Martin, Gherard	18-Mar-1951	6	497
Martin, Gomer	5-Feb-1924	9	287
Martin, Gomer R. Jr.	14-Dec-1950	9	286
Martin, Gregory	10-Jan-1950	4	390
Martin, Grover	28-Apr-1971	11	446
Martin, H. G.	8-Jul-1950	5	492
Martin, Harold D.	9-Aug-1961	9	19
Martin, Harry	20-Oct-1949	3	615
Martin, Harry	20-Oct-1949	10	84
Martin, Hawley	7-Nov-1949	6	642
Martin, Henry Jackson	30-Jan-1972	14	76
Martin, James	29-Jan-1947	11	109
Martin, James	31-Dec-1949	11	613
Martin, James C	7-Jan-1958	7	457
Martin, James E.	12-Jan-1971	11	420
Martin, Jerry	12-Oct-1972	11	598
Martin, Jerry Jay	12-Oct-1972	14	238-239
Martin, Joel	14-May-1923	1	148
Martin, John	18-Nov-1921	1	67
Martin, John B.	22-Dec-1949	4	580
Martin, John B.	22-May-1969	11	445
Martin, Julius C.	17-Dec-1963	9	205
Martin, Kermit	1-Aug-1976	13	280
Martin, Lester	12-Sep-1949	3	413
Martin, Lowell	20-Aug-1964	11	163
Martin, Luther	26-Jan-1950	5	166
Martin, Melvin	1-Dec-1949	5	70
Martin, Miles	21-Jun-1923	1	89
Martin, Mitchell	27-Feb-1950	5	182
Martin, Muriel	10-Nov-1949	4	532
Martin, Neb Lamar	5-Mar-1957		
Martin, Neb Lamar	15-Feb-1962	11	98
Martin, Noah	6-Feb-1950	6	73
Martin, Paris	27-Feb-1946	1	136
Martin, Paul	14-Feb-1957	7	301
Martin, Ralph Randall	17-Apr-1962	11	175
Martin, Raymond	9-Sep-1949	4	635

Name	Disc. Date	Book	Page
Martin, Richard Harold	24-Jun-1960	9	11
Martin, Roger	15-Dec-1973	12	74
Martin, Rondell Lynn	27-Apr-1997	14	221
Martin, Sherman	26-Mar-1950	5	227
Martin, Tandy	10-Sep-1957	14	86
Martin, Theodore	22-Jun-1953	10	83
Martin, Tom Jr.	22-Jul-1953	7	19
Martin, Troy	2-Jul-1950	6	24
Martin, Troy D.	13-Jan-1950	5	130
Martin, Vernon	16-Nov-1949	6	74
Martin, Wade	23-Jun-1950	6	102
Martin, Walter J.	13-Jan-1950	4	562
Martin, Willam H.	3-Feb-1950	4	403
Martin, William	2-Oct-1949	3	284
Martin, William	25-Feb-1950	6	588
Martin, William James	28-Jan-1968	11	273
Martin, William L.	20-Feb-1950	5	190
Martin, William M.	12-Jul-1970	11	396
Martin, Willie	23-May-1949	3	50
Martin, Willie	17-Feb-1950	6	333
Maryland, Joseph	9-May-1989	12	290-291
Matheson, James	12-Feb-1950	5	187
Mathews, Austin	21-Jun-1954	5	524
Mathews, Omar	27-Jul-1949	6	173
Mathews, Willis Jr.	11-Jan-1960	8	259
Mature, George	14-Nov-1949	6	243
May, Albert	20-Nov-1949	3	585
May, Billy	30-Jan-1950	4	280
May, Billy J.	7-Aug-1951	11	36
May, Billy Johns	5-Mar-1957	7	302
May, Burns	9-Aug-1920	1	172
May, Cecil G.	16-Jan-1950	4	231
May, Charles V.	28-Oct-1949	8	329
May, Clarence	19-Oct-1949	3	378
May, Claude M.	4-Aug-1949	12	146
May, Clyde G.	5-Oct-1949	5	382
May, Colonel	10-Oct-1947	8	214A
May, Donald G.	12-Oct-1960	10	72
May, Edgar R.	8-Mar-1950	4	568
May, Edward E.	29-Nov-1949	5	55
May, Edward E.	29-Nov-1949	10	70
May, Elijah Brown Jr.	3-Feb-1950	9	118A
May, Elijah Brown Jr.	3-Feb-1950	9	118B
May, Fred	5-Jan-1944	7	91
May, Gardis H.	8-Oct-1956	8	187
May, Gordon J.	19-May-1950	5	517
May, James A.	5-Aug-1956	7	394
May, James A.	6-Sep-1957	7	393
May, John	19-Feb-1922	11	24
May, Robert	25-Dec-1947	12	298
May, Robert D.	24-Oct-1954	11	135
May, Robert L.	12-Sep-1923	1	32
May, Robert L.	23-Dec-1947	2	80
May, Thomas C.	22-Jan-1950	4	226
May, William F.	1-Dec-1977	13	407
May, William J.	17-May-1957	8	309
May, William James Jr.	6-Jun-1956	7	203
May. Claude	4-Aug-1949	12	19
Mayewski, Raymond J.	30-Mar-1949	7	56
Mayewski, Raymond J.	23-Nov-1949	7	55
Maynard, Boyd T.	4-Jul-1977	12	148
Maynard, Ernest J.	4-Oct-1958	9	323
Maynard, Griffith	27-Oct-1949	5	75
Maynard, Joseph	21-Nov-1949	3	562
Maynard, Joseph	10-Mar-1977	13	314
Maynard, Julius	13-Jan-1950	4	420
Mayo, Dennis E.	25-Apr-1972	11	558
Mayo, Fletcher Jr.	5-Oct-1951	3	636
Mayo, Henry L.	10-Apr-1923	11	173
Mayo, Jacob	11-Apr-1947	2	136
Mayo, Royce	11-Nov-1949	6	45
McCarty, Burns Jr.	29-Sep-1952	7	211
McCarty, Burns Jr.	21-Jun-1956	7	210
McCarty, Fred	16-Apr-1948	2	323
McCarty, Malcolm	5-Nov-1947	2	127
McCarty, Wallace Lee	4-Feb-1964	9	216
McClanahan, Andy	8-Nov-1949	3	511
McClanahan, Joe	18-Jul-1949	3	100
McCoart, John Jr.	24-Jan-1923	10	153
McCoart, Mac Arthur	3-May-1972	11	561
McComas, Arthur	23-Oct-1923	10	115
McComas, Edwin	19-Mar-1950	5	215
McCowan, Dennis	4-Jul-1971	11	465
McCowan, Glennis	4-Jul-1971	11	466

137

Name	Disc. Date	Book	Page
McCown, Bert	9-Dec-1949	6	131
McCown, Herman	26-Apr-1947	4	585
McCown, John	14-Jan-1950	4	214
McCoy, Charles	16-Nov-1949	11	139
McCoy, Estill	2-Nov-1947	2	78
McCoy, Gene	19-Apr-1959	7	323
McCoy, Jack Lee	7-Aug-1958	8	68
McCoy, James	22-Jun-1970	11	225
McCoy, Ruebush B.	6-Sep-1949	3	176
McDavid, Charles	17-Sep-1949	4	402
McDavid, Howard	13-Jan-1950	4	405
McDonald, Charles	19-Nov-1949	6	504
McDonald, Charles	10-Jun-1951	6	505
McDowell, James William	6-Feb-1950	5	183
McFannin, Vonnie	27-Aug-1957	7	456
McGarey, Lloyd	18-Dec-1950	6	634
McGarey, Raymond	5-Mar-1950	5	247
McGuire, Basil	10-Sep-1945	6	631
McGuire, Basil	24-Dec-1949	6	200
McGuire, Billie	6-Dec-1955	7	195
McGuire, Charles	6-Oct-1957	7	449
McGuire, Dave	4-Feb-1923	1	27
McGuire, Eura	20-May-1949	4	593
McGuire, Frank	22-May-1923	1	115
McGuire, Howard	19-Dec-1948	2	269
McGuire, Jack	10-Jun-1923	1	71
McGuire, James	18-Sep-1949	11	419
McGuire, John	17-Nov-1947	2	195
McGuire, John	14-Oct-1955	7	152
McGuire, Lillian	14-Jun-1951	5	457
McGuire, Taulbee	28-Jun-1949	4	282
McGuire, Taulbee	25-Oct-1952	6	638
McGuire, Tom	14-Dec-1922	1	160
McGuire, Tom	5-Feb-1950	11	20
McHenry, Allen	1-Apr-1972	11	557
McKee, Glen	27-May-1947	2	14
McKenzie, George	12-Jun-1951	6	489
McKenzie, Robert	8-Dec-1960	8	314
McKenzie, Willard	31-Dec-1960	8	322
McKinney, Arnold	31-Jul-1975	13	178
McKinney, Bill	31-Mar-1947	2	198
McKinney, Burnie	22-Jun-1983	13	433
McKinney, Charles	29-Nov-1950	6	234
McKlnney, Charles Graham	20-Feb-1978	13	418
McKlnney, Charles Graham	1-May-1980	13	419
McKinney, Edgar	24-May-1973	12	7
McKinney, Harry	6-Jun-1957	7	388
McKinney, Henry	6-Jun-1946	4	98
McKinney, Hillard	25-Aug-1950	6	32
McKinney, James	10-Oct-1960	11	54
McKinney, James	1-Feb-1962	14	141
McKinney, Kenneth	22-Oct-1974	13	63
McKinney, Kenneth	4-Jul-1978	14	28
McKinney, Oliver	8-Nov-1948	2	246
McKinney, Oscar	20-Sep-1949	3	263
McKinney, Stoney	29-Sep-1974	13	76
McKinney, William	11-Jun-1923	1	209
McKinzie, Austin	1-Dec-1950	6	239
McKinzie, Willard	31-Dec-1960	14	5
McKinzie, William	28-Jan-1965	10	194
McNally, Charles	3-May-1959	8	65
McNeil, John Charles III	27-Aug-1969	11	202
McPeeks, Lester	4-Feb-1959	8	143
McSurley, Fred	23-Feb-1950	5	194
Mead, Don	19-Mar-1950	5	209
Mead, Terry G.	14-Dec-1977	13	351
Meade, Alma J.	26-May-1959	8	185
Meade, Astor	16-Sep-1949	5	531
Meade, Ben	6-Jun-1982	13	426
Meade, Billy Tom	1-Apr-1979	14	39
Meade, Bobby Joseph	1-Mar-1984	14	120
Meade, Cecil	5-Jan-1950	4	182
Meade, Charles E.	29-Nov-1962	9	121
Meade, Charles E.	29-Jul-1966	11	185
Meade, Charles E.	14-Apr-1996	14	288
Meade, Claude E.	20-May-1971	11	455
Meade, Columbus B.	10-Feb-1950	5	161
Meade, Delbert	14-Nov-1974	13	69
Meade, Delbert	14-Nov-1974	14	177
Meade, Donald	1-May-1950	10	48
Meade, Donald L.	2-Jun-1949	3	38
Meade, Eugene	10-Mar-1947	10	30
Meade, Eugene	15-Feb-1950	4	602
Meade, Everett	25-Nov-1949	4	217
Meade, Foster	8-Apr-1950	4	484
Meade, Gary R.	17-Oct-1974	13	66
Meade, Harland	25-Aug-1947	2	89
Meade, Ishmael T.	19-Nov-1949	5	74
Meade, Jake	13-Jan-1950	6	36
Meade, Jerry	18-Sep-1949	3	216
Meade, Jessee W.	16-Sep-1969	1	612
Meade, Joe	27-Oct-1949	10	95
Meade, Joe	11-Dec-1950	10	96
Meade, Joe C.	14-Dec-1922	1	42
Meade, John P.	26-Jun-1949	7	79
Meade, Kermit	3-Oct-1949	3	270
Meade, O.C.	3-Apr-1950	5	233
Meade, Ray	19-Apr-1956	7	461
Meade, Ray	15-Jan-1958	7	462
Meade, Raymond	10-Jan-1951	6	339
Meade, Rush	4-Oct-1953	7	65
Meade, Rush	4-Oct-1953	7	57
Meade, Rush	5-Jan-1958	7	475
Meade, Samuel G.	24-Jan-1950	4	292
Meade, Scott	9-Jan-1950	5	115
Meade, Teddy	7-May-1970	11	390
Meade, Thomas	4-Dec-1949	4	17
Meade, Tine	26-Oct-1949	3	437
Meade, Vernon	8-Nov-1949	3	501
Meade, Walter	15-Sep-1957	14	81
Meade, Warren G.	5-Oct-1972	11	594
Meade, Wendell	3-May-1972	11	559
Meade, Wesley	21-Sep-1957	14	193
Meade, William M.	23-Jun-1925	1	99
Meade, William R.	14-Jan-1950	4	424
Meade, Wilse	24-Jul-1949	3	112
Meade, Winifred	18-Nov-1949	3	580
Meador, Dock	2-Mar-1950	4	426
Meador, Henry	24-Jul-1923	1	41
Meador, Melvin	12-Jan-1923	1	28
Meadows, Blake Roger Jr.	6-Feb-1946	12	331
Meadows, Brett Eric	9-Jan-1999	14	261
Meadows, Charles	8-Oct-1956	7	283
Meadows, Charles	21-Jan-1958	7	485
Meadows, Cottrell	5-May-1957	7	331
Meadows, Dennis	15-Nov-1949	7	120
Meadows, Dennis	15-May-1951	6	417
Meadows, George	5-Apr-1950	5	453
Meadows, Jack	13-Dec-1949	6	295
Meadows, James	14-Jun-1957	7	344
Meadows, James	5-Oct-1962	9	111
Meadows, Ora	12-May-1949	14	108
Meadows, Paul	11-Mar-1950	4	447
Meadows, Ray	19-Mar-1950	10	162
Meadows, Roy	10-Feb-1985	13	439
Meadows, Todd Wesley	2-Jul-1999	14	285
Meagher, Thomas	2-Jun-1947	7	355
Medlock, Harold	1-Apr-1978	13	370
Meeks, Marty	12-Feb-1992	12	330
Mekolites, Stanley Jr.	5-Oct-1952	8	72
Mellon, James	14-Jan-1950	5	143
Merritt, Billie	22-Sep-1949	3	265
Merritt, Jack	14-Oct-1921	1	609
Merritt, Joe	12-Jan-1950	4	229
Merritt, Rexford	25-Nov-1948	2	248
Merritt, Robert	16-Oct-1949	5	1
Messer, Coet	11-Nov-1948	2	369
Messer, James B.	19-Oct-1956	7	237
Messer, Luther	13-Jul-1947	10	6
Messer, Paul D.	23-Oct-1949	4	555
Messer, Ralph	27-Aug-1950	5	451
Metcalf, Gary	5-Feb-1979	13	380
Milam, Timothy	15-May-1983	13	434
Miller, Adam	1-Oct-1959	9	321
Miller, Aldo	2-Sep-1949	3	177
Miller, Bill	28-Dec-1957	7	447
Miller, Billie J.	18-Oct-1957	7	445
Miller, Billy J.	9-Oct-1947	2	188
Miller, Curtis Melvin	7-May-1950	15	3-4
Miller, Edgar R.	18-Jan-1921	5	534
Miller, Estill	24-Sep-1949	6	166
Miller, Freddie	25-Dec-1957	5	451
Miller, Freddie	31-Jan-1964	9	214
Miller, Gary R.	12-Jan-1975	13	94
Miller, George	5-Sep-1947	2	203
Miller, Green	9-Dec-1956	7	343
Miller, Joe	22-Dec-1949	6	2
Miller, Joe W.	17-Apr-1957	7	348
Miller, John	10-Jun-1952	6	583
Miller, John Franklin Jr.	22-Apr-1962	12	321
Miller, John Franklin Jr.	23-Aug-1965	12	320
Miller, Jonas L. Jr.	3-Jan-1949	4	110
Miller, Larry Shawn	19-Oct-2007	15	96-97
Miller, Luther Eugene	4-Nov-1959	15	35
Miller, Norman	11-May-1953	7	6-7
Miller, Thomas W.	14-Aug-1950	10	7
Miller, Vergil	21-Apr-1948	2	350
Miller, William	25-Oct-1949	3	401
Miller, William R.	21-Dec-1949	4	76
Miller, Wilson	7-Dec-1960	8	316
Mills, Alonzo	7-Jun-1970	8	198
Mills, Euian C.	9-Oct-1949	3	327
Mills, Jerry R.	18-Feb-1994	14	198
Mills, Jimmy	2-Mar-1969	11	210
Mills, Oscar	2-Mar-1969	11	301
Mills, Oscar	2-Mar-1969	11	327
Mims, Albert	18-Jan-1950	5	109
Minix, Hobert	21-Dec-1921	1	59
Minix, Jewel D.	11-Nov-1949	4	316
Minix, Paul R.	28-Jun-1966	11	180
Mitchell, Carl	23-Mar-1950	5	219
Mitchell, Chandos L.	18-Oct-1949	3	342
Mitchell, Charles	15-Jan-1951	6	283
Mitchell, Charlie	26-Jun-1958	9	330
Mitchell, Claude	17-Jan-1951	6	298
Mitchell, Drexel	2-Jul-1956	7	209
Mitchell, Earl	23-Nov-1949	3	564
Mitchell, Howard	1-Feb-1956	7	162
Mitchell, Howard	1-Feb-1956	7	186
Mitchell, John	13-Oct-1949	3	335
Mitchell, John	15-Mar-1950	6	127
Mitchell, Maurice	22-Apr-1950	6	158
Mitchell, Moses	24-Jun-1923	1	156
Mitchell, Orville	31-Dec-1949	8	238-239
Mitchell, Roy L.	6-Jul-1971	11	310
Mitchell, Steven	1-Mar-1996	14	307
Mitchell, Toy	25-Jan-1951	6	297
Mocklar, Martha	5-Apr-1960	11	11
Molden, Linda Marie	20-Dec-1977	15	19
Moles, Francis	22-Nov-1949	5	56
Moles, George	26-Aug-1949	5	497
Mollett, Alvin	15-Dec-1973	12	77
Montgomery, Bill Henry	17-Apr-1968	11	284
Montgomery, Elson	13-Feb-1950	4	391
Montgomery, Henry	13-Aug-1949	2	322
Montgomery, Jeff	13-Nov-1947	2	178
Montgomery, Thomas Eugene	16-Feb-1975	13	118
Moore, Alton	8-Nov-1949	6	124
Moore, Arnold	20-Jun-1948	2	266
Moore, Arthur	13-Oct-1949	6	128
Moore, Arthur	6-Feb-1950	4	432
Moore, Bascom	23-Oct-1949	4	455
Moore, Bubby E.	2-Feb-1950	5	147
Moore, Carl	19-Jan-1975	13	96
Moore, Carl J.	17-Jul-1964	10	65
Moore, Carlos	11-Feb-1974	12	93
Moore, Carmel	30-Jan-1950	5	455
Moore, Charles W.	27-Feb-1962	9	69
Moore, Clabe	12-Mar-1950	9	357
Moore, Clarence	10-Oct-1949	6	151
Moore, Cletis	11-Aug-1960	8	320
Moore, Clinton D.	31-Oct-1963	9	198
Moore, Curtis	15-Dec-1949	6	327
Moore, David L.	17-Jun-1959	8	181
Moore, Dempsey	15-Dec-1950	7	140
Moore, Dickey	14-Dec-1922	1	47
Moore, Donald	16-Aug-1949	12	338-339
Moore, Duran	15-Mar-1950	7	121
Moore, Earl	3-Aug-1947	2	35
Moore, Earl E.	27-Jun-1963	9	166
Moore, Ed R.	13-Mar-1957	10	122
Moore, Ed R.	28-Oct-1958	10	120
Moore, Ed R.	2-Nov-1959	10	121
Moore, Edgel	18-Oct-1946	2	32
Moore, Edgle	13-Dec-1949	4	19
Moore, Edsel L.	6-Oct-1959	12	179
Moore, Edsel L.	17-Sep-1963	12	177
Moore, Edsel L.	10-Aug-1969	12	178
Moore, Edsel L.	2-Jun-1978	12	180
Moore, Estell C.	8-Dec-1949	4	135
Moore, Fred	2-Jan-1948	2	210
Moore, Gilver	31-Oct-1949	3	433

Name	Disc. Date	Book	Page
Moore, Greenville	25-Sep-1947	5	198
Moore, Herschell	28-Sep-1956	7	221
Moore, James	26-Mar-1965	11	21
Moore, James E.	15-Nov-1949	4	595
Moore, Joe Chester	12-Feb-1950	10	199
Moore, John	13-Oct-1949	6	387
Moore, John E.	26-Nov-1958	10	46
Moore, Kellcie	27-Sep-1923	9	208
Moore, Kenneth L.	23-Jun-1971	11	460
Moore, Lenna B.	21-Feb-1923	1	88
Moore, Leslie	22-Nov-1949	3	529
Moore, Melvin	28-Nov-1948	9	217
Moore, Millie	15-Jan-1950	4	278
Moore, Palmer	21-Jul-1950	6	21
Moore, Ray	11-Aug-1958	8	69
Moore, Richard Lee	1-Jul-1962	9	91
Moore, Rodney	4-May-1974	12	125
Moore, Rodney O.	11-Apr-1974	12	123
Moore, Rody	7-Aug-1975	13	182
Moore, Thomas	27-Apr-1953	6	648
Moore, Virgie	11-May-1977	13	326
Moore, Virgil	13-Nov-1949	4	56
Moore, Vone	20-Sep-1949	3	217
Moore, William Jr.	25-Sep-1949	3	258
Moore, Willie	16-Mar-1950	6	139
More, Belvie	27-Aug-1946	2	281
Morefield, James T.	31-Mar-1959	14	122
Morgan, James	19-Mar-1948	2	155
Morgan, Phillip	25-Sep-1951	6	647
Morgan, Robert	30-Aug-1925	11	196
Morison, Harold	8-Oct-1949	4	539
Morison, Roger	24-Dec-1949	4	541
Morris, Arthur L.	17-Aug-1949	3	141
Morris, Larry	24-Jan-1984	14	247
Morris, Larry (correction to DD)	12-Jul-1981	14	248
Morris, Melvin	20-Jan-1976	13	233
Morris, Winford M.	20-Jul-1961	9	15
Morrison, Jack	29-Oct-1949	3	471
Morrison, Jack C.	26-Oct-1959	8	224
Morrison, Ruben	18-Nov-1949	3	530
Morrison, Thomas	13-Feb-1950	6	142
Morrison, Wilson	16-Oct-1949	6	53
Morrow, Lawrence	15-Nov-1949	3	496
Moscrip, James	20-Oct-1949	5	112
Mosley, Arnold	17-Jan-1964	9	209
Mosley, Bobby	3-Sep-1973	12	63
Mosley, Charles Wesley	22-Apr-1971	14	25
Mosley, Chester	24-Jun-1949	3	54
Mosley, Curtis	17-Jan-1950	4	260
Mosley, Dennis	9-May-1973	12	4
Mosley, Donnie	2-Feb-1972	11	538
Mosley, Gene H.	6-May-1965	11	58
Mosley, Gordon	7-Jun-1964	9	261
Mosley, Kinnel	5-Jul-1949	3	73
Mosley, Larry	19-May-1972	11	564
Mosley, Mathew Bill	12-Nov-1998	14	255
Mosley, Ray	18-Jul-1957	7	358
Mosley, Robert	14-Feb-1950	6	547
Mosley, Robert Jr.	8-Apr-1951	6	544
Mosley, Tharp	7-Oct-1949	6	137
Mulkey, Henry	19-Oct-1964	10	154
Mulkey, Julius	3-Feb-1973	12	296
Mulkey, Keith	27-Jun-1977	12	217
Mulkey, Roscoe	11-Feb-1950	6	475
Mullett, James	4-Dec-1947	2	349
Mullett, Paul	11-Dec-1949	4	314
Mullett, Roy	28-Oct-1984	13	437
Mullett, Roy E.	11-Sep-1949	3	185
Mullins, Alpha	24-Mar-1947	2	374
Mullins, Arnold Lee	23-Mar-1970	14	73
Mullins, Bobby	11-Oct-1951	6	546
Mullins, Burnis	20-Apr-1950	4	522
Mullins, Carlton	17-Dec-1974	13	88
Mullins, Carlton	11-Jun-1987	12	253
Mullins, Charles	29-Aug-1966	11	189
Mullins, Charles	13-Dec-1973	12	76
Mullins, Charles C.	27-Aug-1962	9	101
Mullins, Charles E.	4-Nov-1958	8	117
Mullins, Christopher	17-May-2009	15	117
Mullins, Clarance	5-Mar-1957	8	86
Mullins, Clark	7-Jul-1950	10	68
Mullins, Claude Margis	13-Mar-1963	15	38
Mullins, Claude Margis	21-Jun-1977	15	37
Mullins, Danny	20-Jan-1975	13	97

Name	Disc. Date	Book	Page
Mullins, Duval	17-Mar-1947	2	21
Mullins, Emzy	19-Apr-1948	2	180
Mullins, Eugene	4-Aug-1951	14	126
Mullins, Eugene	25-Dec-1957	7	450
Mullins, Frank	1-Feb-1975	13	100
Mullins, Harold	2-Oct-1949	5	16
Mullins, Hatler	17-Oct-1960	9	120
Mullins, Hilbert	31-Aug-1949	3	170
Mullins, Jim	30-Mar-1975	13	133
Mullins, Joe R.	30-Dec-1965	11	141
Mullins, Luther	8-Nov-1961	9	41
Mullins, Michael Shane	28-Sep-1993	14	88
Mullins, Ralph	5-Sep-1971	11	235
Mullins, Ronnie	6-Apr-1976	13	256
Mullins, Steve	12-Feb-1947	2	161
Mullins, Sylvester	25-Jun-1923	1	45
Mullins, Terry	15-Oct-1974	13	59
Mullins, Walter	21-Jan-1950	5	129
Mullins, William	1-Feb-1951	6	614
Mullins, William Carl	22-Jun-1954	12	135
Mullins, Johnnie	14-Apr-1959	12	168
Mundy, Thomas	17-Mar-1949	5	178
Munson, Frederic	13-May-1951	6	515
Mur[hy, Mitchell	31-Aug-1970	11	341
Murdock, Charles Aaron	4-Jun-1981	14	23
Murphy, Donald	8-Dec-1960	8	318
Murphy, John	7-Feb-1957	7	309
Murphy, Pauline	9-Apr-1950	2	364
Murray, George	27-Sep-1946	2	100
Music, Alvin C.	7-Mar-1949	5	3
Music, Alvis	20-Oct-1949	3	352
Music, Bill	12-Feb-1950	4	377
Music, Billy	22-Apr-1973	11	278
Music, Billy H.	14-Oct-1959	8	219
Music, Bobby R.	20-Apr-1956	8	59
Music, Bobby R.	8-Aug-1957	8	60
Music, Charles	30-Jun-1971	11	462
Music, Charles Donald	30-Jun-1968	14	30
Music, Claude	13-Oct-1949	5	39
Music, Darwin	16-Jan-1950	9	204
Music, Darwin	28-Mar-1951	9	203
Music, David	20-Sep-1979	13	401
Music, Elmer J.	3-Oct-1947	2	185
Music, Frank E.	28-Jul-1957	7	369
Music, Frank E.	28-Apr-1959	8	161
Music, Frank Jr.	3-Feb-1971	11	431
Music, Franklin D.	30-Sep-1963	9	193
Music, Graham	10-Jun-1949	3	57
Music, Graham	4-May-1951	7	20
Music, Jay K.	15-Sep-1957	7	403
Music, Jerry A.	21-Aug-1973	12	23
Music, Leonard	16-Jul-1975	13	183
Music, Max R.	26-Mar-1965	11	22
Music, Ralph	11-Sep-1956	14	253
Music, Theodore	23-Apr-1973	1	167
Music, Thomas	4-Jan-1956	7	159
Music, Thomas Henry Jr.	9-Apr-1974	13	27
Music, Tom E.	12-Aug-1965	11	128
Music, Tom H.	15-Dec-1949	5	94
Music, William	11-Dec-1949	4	496
Musick, Otis	26-Nov-1949	5	51
Mynhier, Raymond	31-Oct-1949	3	418
Mynhier, Walter	20-Oct-1949	3	344
Napier, Alvin	5-Jun-1924	1	137
Napier, Canton Livingston	5-Mar-1963	9	140
Neeley, Chester	29-Jun-1949	3	63
Neeley, John B.	19-Jan-1950	4	246
Neeley, Marion	1-Aug-1987	11	83
Neese, James P.	13-Aug-1958	14	202
Nelson, Billy	22-Sep-1960	8	299
Nelson, David Wayne	16-Feb-1994	14	118
Nelson, Eugene	17-Oct-1947	2	27
Nelson, Eugene	16-Jun-1953	8	1
Nelson, Grady	27-Mar-1966	14	103
Nelson, Henry	16-Feb-1962	9	63
Nelson, Jack	19-Jun-1949	9	251
Nelson, Jake	5-Oct-1953	10	200
Nelson, Jeff Jr.	5-May-1949	5	4
Nelson, Mack	30-Mar-1950	6	550
Nelson, Rebel	23-Mar-1959	10	111
Nelson, Reynold	13-Jan-1950	9	248
Nelson, Ted	5-Aug-1951	9	6
Nelson, Vigus S.	12-Mar-1976	13	242
Nemet, Elmer	3-May-1950	4	543

Name	Disc. Date	Book	Page
Nesbit, Judge	15-Apr-1923	1	26
Newberry, Clarence	8-May-1941	2	289
Newberry, Clarence	1-Feb-1945	2	288
Newman, Cecil	28-Jan-1976	13	234
Newman, Clenon	4-Nov-1947	2	265
Newman, Clyde	12-Jun-1949	4	561
Newman, Earl	24-Dec-1958	8	195
Newman, Edgar	2-Mar-1977	13	313
Newman, Estille	1-Jan-1950	4	126
Newman, Fred	17-Mar-1950	4	454
Newman, Gomer	21-Jul-1949	10	91
Newman, Harvie G.	27-Nov-1949	6	602
Newman, Hint Jr.	14-Dec-1949	4	60
Newman, Kevin	18-Nov-2005	15	72-73
Newman, Kevin	8-Sep-2007	15	93-94
Newman, Kevin	8-Sep-2007	15	95
Newman, Oliver	30-Oct-1946	2	327
Newman, Orby	13-Dec-1949	4	59
Newman, Richard	6-Apr-1978	12	189
Newman, Tivis	28-Sep-1949	4	487
Newman, Willard	22-May-1963	9	168
Newman, Willard	1-Jun-1967	11	261
Newman, William	20-Jan-1950	10	184
Newsom, John Henry		9	283
Newsom, Sterlon	14-Jul-1957	9	43
Newsom, William	13-Nov-1922	1	147
Newsome, Allred	23-Sep-1958	8	101
Newsome, Andy	5-Jul-1953	7	14
Newsome, Andy L.	18-Jul-1923	1	129
Newsome, Andy L.	21-Jan-1969	11	203
Newsome, Anthony	14-Nov-1949	10	161
Newsome, Anthony	5-Sep-1951	6	312
Newsome, Arnold	16-Jan-1975	13	95
Newsome, Avery	13-Nov-1949	9	355
Newsome, Avery	20-May-1951	9	354
Newsome, Ballard	15-May-1951	6	576
Newsome, Ballard	21-Jan-1952	6	554
Newsome, Ballard	17-Oct-1956	7	230
Newsome, Chester	29-Aug-1947	4	335
Newsome, Conrad	3-Jun-1959	8	179
Newsome, Conrad	10-Feb-1966	11	150
Newsome, Curtis	2-Oct-1949	6	265
Newsome, Darvis	11-Sep-1974	13	45
Newsome, Earl	16-May-1950	12	215
Newsome, Edward	6-Jun-1957	9	227
Newsome, Edward	6-Jun-1957	10	140
Newsome, Elmer	10-Jan-1950	5	144
Newsome, Epp	9-Mar-1923	9	297
Newsome, Estill	2-Feb-1970	11	379
Newsome, Everett	13-Oct-1947	4	609
Newsome, Everett	4-Oct-1961	12	184
Newsome, Gardner	18-May-1950	9	336
Newsome, George	2-Sep-1971	11	488
Newsome, Harlin E.	20-Aug-1952	6	596
Newsome, Hershal	27-Nov-1949	3	551
Newsome, John	8-Jul-1958	12	151
Newsome, Millard	23-Oct-1947	2	294
Newsome, Minis	20-Oct-1957	7	431
Newsome, Noah	13-Dec-1949	7	190
Newsome, Palmer	26-Jan-1957	10	167
Newsome, Philip	21-Sep-1949	3	232
Newsome, Ralph	27-Dec-1970	11	253
Newsome, Raymond	7-Nov-1948	2	240
Newsome, Riley Jr.	29-Oct-1972	11	601
Newsome, Robert T.	25-Oct-1961	9	54
Newsome, Teddy	3-Sep-1947	2	338
Newsome, Town	9-Dec-1950	9	215
Newsome, Worlie	15-Oct-1949	6	184
Newsome, Z.L.	11-Feb-1960	8	258
Nichols, Henry	11-Nov-1949	3	466
Nickles, Arnold	18-Jul-1971	11	477
Nidiffer, Paul	13-Jan-1950	10	133
Noakes, John Henry	13-Jul-1963	15	45
Noakes, John Henry	13-Jul-1969	15	46
Noakes, John Henry	14-Jul-1969	15	47
Noakes, John Henry	3-Aug-1972	15	44
Noble, Adam	9-Sep-1957	7	392
Nolen, Charles	9-Nov-1949	5	25
Norris, William	27-Nov-1949	4	630
Nuckles, Boyd	22-Nov-1949	3	560
Nunnery, Albert	22-Jul-1950	12	213
Nunnery, Byron	25-Nov-1949	3	575
Nutter, John	16-Feb-1947	6	569
Oakley, Austin	20-Jan-1950	5	495

139

Name	Disc. Date	Book	Page
Obroff, Fred	8-Oct-1957	4	414
O'Bryan, James	12-Jun-1973	12	11
O'Bryan, Orville Jackson	2-Dec-1946	2	156
Oppenheimer, Karl	9-Apr-1950	4	510
Oppenheimer, Karl	12-Jan-1960	8	253
O'Quin, Lacey	18-Nov-1949	11	186
O'Quinn, Danny	25-Sep-1973	12	34
Orsborn, Tilmon	27-May-1949	2	308
Orsborne, Avis	25-Sep-1949	6	38
Osborn, Bill	9-Mar-1951	6	471
Osborn, Emery	14-Oct-1954	7	337
Osborn, Evel	11-Nov-1949	6	47
Osborn, Howard Ray	9-Jul-1951	9	67
Osborn, Howard Ray	8-Jul-1953	9	65
Osborn, Howard Ray	8-Jul-1956	9	66
Osborn, Howard Ray	1-Feb-1962	9	64
Osborne, Bill	5-Aug-1949	3	123
Osborne, Bobby	11-Dec-1958	11	57
Osborne, Burl	9-Mar-1950	5	230
Osborne, Carmel	21-Dec-1956	7	267
Osborne, Carmel	7-Aug-1987	12	256
Osborne, Charles	30-Sep-1949	6	134
Osborne, Charles	10-Apr-1950	6	574
Osborne, Christopher	17-Feb-2005	15	56-57
Osborne, Dave	12-Aug-1947	9	312
Osborne, Dennis	27-Mar-1974	12	116
Osborne, Donald	9-Jan-1958	7	453
Osborne, Donald W.	24-Jun-1954	7	95
Osborne, Estille	5-Nov-1949	6	8
Osborne, Everett	23-Sep-1949	6	52
Osborne, Franklin D.	8-Dec-1960	8	315
Osborne, Freeman	23-Jul-1951	8	466
Osborne, Gary	8-May-1974	6	1
Osborne, Gary Franklin	8-May-1974	14	9
Osborne, Herbert R.	3-Dec-1949	6	366
Osborne, Hiram M.	20-Jun-1908	9	340
Osborne, Hodley	6-Nov-1949	3	470
Osborne, James	9-Mar-1950	12	83
Osborne, James	9-Mar-1950	12	84
Osborne, James	13-Mar-1957	7	395
Osborne, James	27-Mar-1960	8	266
Osborne, James	10-May-1967	11	220
Osborne, Jesse	12-Dec-1961	9	164
Osborne, John	2-Apr-1946	2	42
Osborne, John D.	13-Jan-1970	11	162
Osborne, John M.	1-Oct-1925	11	50
Osborne, John P.	8-Aug-1960	9	80
Osborne, Johnnie	17-Jul-1947	2	46
Osborne, Joseph	18-Jan-1950	4	211
Osborne, Kenneth	1-Dec-1949	6	10
Osborne, Lester	24-May-1947	7	124
Osborne, Luther	13-Nov-1950	6	331
Osborne, Noah	26-Oct-1949	6	291
Osborne, Norman	12-Dec-1949	6	213
Osborne, Otis	5-Dec-1949	4	46
Osborne, Paulie	18-Mar-1957	7	325
Osborne, Paulie	10-Nov-1959	8	267
Osborne, Raymond	30-Sep-1947	2	130
Osborne, Repts	10-Aug-1949	3	136
Osborne, Romie Gene	3-Jul-1956	7	196
Osborne, Ronald	24-Mar-1954	7	81
Osborne, Ronald	22-Aug-1957	7	385
Osborne, Rufus	16-Apr-1958	8	18
Osborne, Rufus	6-Apr-1960	8	270
Osborne, Russell	19-Oct-1949	4	523
Osborne, Scotty	12-Feb-1981	13	413
Osborne, Stallard	15-Mar-1966	11	160
Osborne, William	21-Jan-1948	2	65
Osborne, William	7-Jul-1969	11	216
Osborne. Harold Barness	10-Jan-1950	5	206
Ousley, Bennie	1-Jan-1967	11	432
Ousley, Bennie	1-Jan-1970	11	371
Ousley, Billie	13-Aug-1947	2	304
Ousley, Burnis	22-Aug-1958	8	89
Ousley, Charles	25-Oct-1970	11	244
Ousley, Clarence	5-Dec-1972	11	611
Ousley, Dennie	13-Feb-1975	12	214
Ousley, Dennie	13-Feb-1975	13	101
Ousley, Earl D.	21-Jan-1960	14	276-277
Ousley, Edgel	14-Sep-1964	10	166
Ousley, Emit	30-Oct-1949	7	144
Ousley, Emit	11-Nov-1950	6	206
Ousley, Eric	1-Sep-1976	13	283
Ousley, Everette	17-Apr-1957	7	324

Name	Disc. Date	Book	Page
Ousley, Gary	16-Nov-1975	13	210
Ousley, Harold D.	18-Jul-1972	14	112
Ousley, Harold D.	12-Jul-1976	14	111
Ousley, Herbert	13-Dec-1950	6	37
Ousley, Herbert	25-Feb-1958	11	361
Ousley, Jack	6-Oct-1971	11	352
Ousley, Jimmie	5-Feb-1971	11	438
Ousley, Jimmy Paul	6-May-1997	14	223
Ousley, Jobe	26-Sep-1947	2	10
Ousley, Jobie	12-Mar-1975	13	127
Ousley, Melvin	16-Jul-1953	7	23
Ousley, Orville	23-Mar-1950	4	469
Ousley, Raleigh	16-Nov-1949	5	35
Ousley, Richard	7-May-1973	13	393
Ousley, Richard	26-Jun-1979	13	392
Ousley, Shirley	6-Nov-1949	6	169
Ousley, Troy	20-Sep-1974	13	46
Ousley, William	12-May-1971	11	447
Ousley, Zeb	15-Jan-1950	4	185
Owens, Larry James	12-Jun-1968	11	287
Owens, Bobby Ray	4-Sep-1974	14	37
Owens, Charles	21-Feb-1947	7	297
Owens, Devert	11-May-1950	4	601
Owens, Earnest	22-Feb-1950	4	422
Owens, Ellery	27-Mar-1975	13	134
Owens, James	16-Nov-1969	12	8
Owens, Marcus	8-Sep-1949	3	386
Owens, Odis Lee	29-Jul-1956	8	44
Owens, Robert	18-Feb-1950	4	410
Owens, Ronnie	18-Feb-1976	13	238
Owens, Toba Madison	22-Aug-1975	13	188
Owens, Virgil	10-Sep-1949	7	54
Owens, Virgil	16-Sep-1952	7	53
Owens, Walter	25-Jun-1948	2	200
Owsley, Benton	5-Nov-1949	5	427
Owsley, Dewey	19-Apr-1949	3	14
Owsley, James	15-Mar-1973	11	621
Owsley, Jerry J.	21-Feb-1950	5	208
Owsley, Russell	25-May-1949	3	127
Pack, Donald	12-Feb-1950	5	545
Pack, Glenn	6-Feb-1950	5	548
Pack, Stanley	30-Mar-1987	12	246
Page, Allard	4-Jan-1923	11	168
Page, Danny Ray	14-Oct-1974	14	240-241
Page, Otis	27-Oct-1949	3	450
Paige, Garlie E.	9-Dec-1950	9	329
Paige, James Estil	20-Jul-1957	7	419
Pappas, Charles	7-Jun-1953	7	8
Parker, Donald David	2-Aug-1979	14	114
Parrigan, Edmond C.	25-Jun-1949	4	262
Parrott, Henry	6-Jun-1947	2	228
Parrott, Henry	17-Sep-1948	2	301
Parson, Ed	22-May-1950	4	570
Parson, Oscar	4-Dec-1950	6	228
Parson, Skip	23-Jun-1974	13	15
Parsons, Archie	5-Jul-1949	6	209
Parsons, Bill	27-Sep-1964	10	125
Parsons, Donald	4-Sep-1975	13	189
Parsons, Estill	24-Oct-1949	5	44
Parsons, Frank	10-Aug-1949	3	128
Parsons, Jim	12-Jun-1923	1	162
Parsons, Orville	4-May-1971	11	448
Parsons, Saint	7-Jul-1958	11	117
Parsons, Tom	5-May-1950	5	544
Partt, John	21-Nov-1949	3	571
Patierno, Albert	29-Jan-1950	6	240
Patierno, Earl	12-Dec-1948	2	340
Patierno, Earl	31-Dec-1948	4	506
Patrick, A.B.	8-Oct-1949	7	128
Patrick, Andy	15-Nov-1949	6	164
Patrick, Asbury	12-Mar-1950	6	510
Patrick, Buster	26-Dec-1949	4	148
Patrick, Cassie	4-Oct-1949	5	61
Patrick, Dewey	10-Nov-1949	6	253
Patrick, Georgia	22-Oct-1949	7	127
Patrick, Glenn	29-Apr-1956	8	279
Patrick, Henry	28-Mar-1923	1	63
Patrick, Jack	3-Jul-1949	3	74
Patrick, James	7-Dec-1949	6	278
Patrick, James	24-Oct-1950	6	279
Patrick, James Jr.	10-Dec-1950	6	551
Patrick, Oscar	4-Mar-1947	2	186
Patrick, Tory	9-Oct-1949	3	483
Patten, John A.	19-Mar-1950	4	435

Name	Disc. Date	Book	Page
Patton, Alonzo	15-Jan-1923	1	36
Patton, Alonzo	9-Nov-1949	3	508
Patton, Ancel	12-Oct-1969	11	357
Patton, Billy	28-Sep-1959	9	135
Patton, Carmel	25-Jun-1950	4	607
Patton, Charles	3-Oct-1947	2	58
Patton, Charles W.	3-Oct-1947	12	322
Patton, Charley	4-Apr-1923	1	16
Patton, Charlie	21-Mar-1949	3	215
Patton, Chester	25-Oct-1949	3	427
Patton, Clyde	20-Jan-1950	4	337
Patton, Darwin	24-Apr-1947	2	57
Patton, Don	17-Apr-1974	13	441
Patton, Don	31-Mar-1977	13	442
Patton, Donald	16-Nov-1949	3	522
Patton, Donald	11-Feb-1973	11	616
Patton, Earl	15-Feb-1950	4	383
Patton, Elmer	14-Nov-1949	7	345
Patton, Estill	6-Jul-1949	3	76
Patton, Floyd	1-Dec-1949	6	129
Patton, Gene	17-Sep-1958	8	108
Patton, George	14-Dec-1949	5	113
Patton, Herbert	19-Sep-1949	3	220
Patton, Hobert	30-Dec-1949	4	197
Patton, James	13-Apr-1923	1	46
Patton, Joe	14-Dec-1949	5	122
Patton, John Wiley	27-Sep-1976	14	29
Patton, Johnie	28-Sep-1949	3	303
Patton, Marcus	2-Dec-1949	10	128
Patton, Martin C.	7-Dec-1948	2	256
Patton, Palmer	7-Dec-1949	5	88
Patton, Paul	28-Jan-1976	13	240
Patton, Paul E.	18-Feb-1957	11	80
Patton, Ralph	13-Jul-1970	11	179
Patton, Rhodes	14-Jul-1970	11	404
Patton, Russell	27-Dec-1949	4	259
Patton, Thomas	14-Mar-1923	1	184
Patton, Thomas A.	27-Nov-1949	5	63
Patton, William	3-Nov-1949	4	129
Patton, William	6-Nov-1975	13	202
Patton, Willie	23-May-1923	1	48
Paxton, Aileen	24-Oct-1955	8	192
Payne, Clarence	29-Sep-1949	3	374
Payne, Clarence	29-Sep-1949	3	396
Payne, Edward	5-Aug-1956	7	193
Pebley, Earl	10-Feb-1925	1	226
Pebley, Wiad G.	6-Mar-1949	4	285
Pelphrey, Clark	16-Nov-1949	4	557
Pendrey, Gerald E.	19-Mar-1950	5	212
Perkins, John Daniel	20-Nov-1925	13	214
Perkins, Leon	6-Dec-1949	4	13
Perkins, Leon	6-Dec-1949	9	272
Perkins, Ralph		9	306
Perkins, Terry	5-Jan-1975	13	89
Perry, Clarence Archer	19-Dec-1962	14	243
Perry, Harry	2-Feb-1956	7	306
Perry, James	26-Dec-1949	6	136
Perry, Kellos T.	19-Feb-1919	4	159
Perry, Leonard	17-Apr-1950	6	348
Perry, Saul	16-Jul-1923	1	151
Perry, Thomas	29-Dec-1949	4	90
Peters, Bill Junior	21-Jan-1950	5	134
Peters, Calvin	18-Mar-1950	6	105
Peters, Frank	18-Dec-1949	4	69
Peters, Roy	20-Jun-1946	2	108
Pezzarossi, John	23-Jan-1950	4	283
Phillips, Emuail James	27-Oct-1949	11	17
Phillips, Owen	28-Mar-1947	2	74
Pickle, Frank	19-Aug-1949	6	542
Picklesimer, Estill	10-Mar-1950	4	445
Pinion, Hints	24-Jun-1923	1	126
Pinion, Willie	15-Nov-1950	6	508
Pinion, Willie	5-Feb-1951	6	507
Pitts, Adis	20-Mar-1951	6	365
Pitts, Curtis	20-Jul-1950	6	3
Pitts, Glennis	29-Aug-1971	11	481
Pitts, Joe	8-Aug-1922	1	603
Pitts, John	30-May-1963	9	158
Pitts, John	1-Apr-1967	11	213
Pitts, Richard	19-Feb-1975	13	116
Pitts, Shade	14-Sep-1971	11	535
Platkus, Stanislaw	16-Mar-1950	6	434
Poe, Bennie	18-Feb-1923	1	120
Poe, Elbert	23-Dec-1949	6	474

Name	Disc. Date	Book	Page
Poe, Georgie	8-Jan-1950	6	601
Poe, Isom	31-Oct-1949	6	70
Poe, Joe	23-Jul-1959	9	90
Poe, Joe P.	10-May-1962	9	89
Poe, John	21-Nov-1950	6	511
Poe, Johnny	9-Nov-1947	7	35
Porter, Bert	4-Jan-1950	5	119
Porter, Bert	4-Jan-1950	11	136
Porter, Billy	11-Jul-1979	13	391
Porter, Bobby	27-Nov-1949	6	258
Porter, Bobby	6-Nov-1950	6	257
Porter, Noah	7-Mar-1923	1	187
Porter, Noah	7-Mar-1923	1	229
Porter, Noah Jr.	29-Nov-1949	6	458
Porter, Noah Jr.	5-May-1951	6	457
Porter, Orville	17-Nov-1949	3	506
Porter, Thomas	8-Apr-1957	11	368
Porter, Virgil	28-Dec-1949	4	95
Porter, William	3-Dec-1974	13	81
Poteet, Charles	16-Nov-1949	6	351
Poteet, James	4-Aug-1951	7	104
Poteet, James	16-Dec-1957	7	448
Potter, James	8-Sep-1949	10	142
Potter, James M.	18-Feb-1980	13	406
Potts, David	18-Mar-1971	14	150
Powell, Arnold	24-Nov-1949	3	543
Powell, William	18-Apr-1923	1	107
Powell, William	17-Feb-1959	8	148
Powell, William R.	19-Oct-1972	15	127
Powell, William Ray	19-Oct-1969	15	127
Powers, Charles	28-Sep-1951	7	89
Powers, Elbert	11-Feb-1957	8	49
Powers, James	12-Jan-1961	8	327
Prater, Acy	27-Nov-1958	11	118
Prater, Adus	12-Oct-1949	5	8
Prater, Adus	12-Oct-1949	5	224
Prater, Arnold	9-Dec-1950	6	269
Prater, Carnie	9-Mar-1950	4	468
Prater, Charles	25-Mar-1953	7	85
Prater, Charlie	21-Oct-1949	3	361
Prater, Chillie	28-Feb-1946	2	8
Prater, Clarence	26-Oct-1960	12	16
Prater, Clyde	8-Jan-1950	4	151
Prater, Dennis	29-Nov-1949	3	567
Prater, Dillard	13-Jun-1962	9	93
Prater, Dockie	14-Dec-1949	5	192
Prater, Donald	8-Aug-1969	12	238
Prater, Donald	13-Jun-1976	12	237
Prater, Earl	10-Sep-1949	3	181
Prater, Earl	15-Jan-1950	4	236
Prater, Elex	1-Dec-1950	6	361
Prater, Feely	16-Dec-1949	5	165
Prater, Frank	9-Aug-1949	4	353
Prater, Gardis	26-Sep-1963	9	197
Prater, Gene	24-Jun-1962	9	104
Prater, George	5-Jan-1950	4	114
Prater, Haskell	16-Jan-1950	4	198
Prater, Henry	19-Dec-1922	1	50
Prater, Henry	18-Mar-1976	13	246
Prater, Herbert	5-Aug-1949	3	218
Prater, Herbert	12-Feb-1950	4	483
Prater, James G.	24-Dec-1959	8	251
Prater, Jim	16-Jun-1949	2	310
Prater, Jimmie	13-Jul-1949	3	113
Prater, John	14-Jul-1961	9	20
Prater, Johnie	3-Jan-1950	6	146
Prater, Lee	8-May-1977	13	325
Prater, Lee Jr.	10-Dec-1948	9	318
Prater, Leonard	29-Aug-1958	8	81
Prater, Lonie	19-Oct-1949	3	340
Prater, Lundy	3-Nov-1949	9	338
Prater, Malc	6-Dec-1949	4	99
Prater, Mitchell	4-Dec-1949	4	617
Prater, Murl	19-Sep-1956	9	353
Prater, Newman	14-May-1923	1	90
Prater, Newte	23-Apr-1923	1	70
Prater, Ogil	26-Sep-1958	8	262
Prater, Oscar	24-Dec-1949	4	175
Prater, Ray	18-Feb-1950	4	589
Prater, Robert S.	16-Feb-1950	5	191
Prater, Rufus	11-Jun-1958	8	43
Prater, Sol	22-Aug-1945	2	70
Prater, Talt	11-Jan-1950	4	187
Prater, Walter	3-Jan-1950	6	225

Name	Disc. Date	Book	Page
Prater, Warnie	31-Dec-1946	11	575
Prater, Warnie	31-Mar-1947	11	574
Pratt, Elbert D.	17-Dec-1971	11	520
Pratt, Jay	9-Dec-1948	2	255
Pratt, Woodroe	13-Jan-1950	5	131
Preston, Curtis	30-Sep-1949	3	260
Preston, Herbert	22-Nov-1949	3	526
Preston, Herbert	24-Jul-1972	14	35
Preston, Ishmael Jr.	17-Aug-1974	13	32
Preston, Jay	22-Nov-1949	5	54
Preston, Jay	22-Nov-1949	5	511
Preston, Johnie	12-Oct-1949	9	305
Preston, Nichols	13-Aug-1963	9	242
Prewitt, Martin A.	4-Feb-1923	1	40
Prewitt, Martin A.	Name Only	1	38
Price, Annie	27-May-1948	2	353
Price, Billie	29-Aug-1950	6	426
Price, Dennis	6-Sep-1973	12	61
Price, Harold	12-Aug-1949	4	152
Price, James Cecil	21-May-1977	15	116
Price, Phillip	10-Jun-1976	13	271
Price, Steve	7-Jul-1995	14	161
Puckett, Hubert	17-Nov-1949	5	459
Pugh, David Boyd	3-Jul-1998	14	272
Quinlan, Arthur Jr.	23-Mar-1950	4	592
Rainey, Johnie	5-Nov-1949	12	128-129
Rainey, Tommy	22-Aug-1974	13	36
Rains, Jackie	30-Apr-1958	9	119
Ramey, George	28-Dec-1949	5	195
Ramey, James R.	11-Dec-1958	9	17
Ramey, John	11-Nov-1949	5	512
Ramey, Thomas	23-Aug-1961	9	29
Ramey, Willie	26-May-1959	8	215
Ramey, Willie	20-Apr-1971	11	443
Ransburg, Rudolph	20-Feb-1960	8	261
Ransdell, Marvin	16-Aug-1923	1	177
Ratcliff, John	29-Jan-1950	4	299
Ratcliff, Thomas	29-Jun-1962	9	88
Ratliff, Arnold	14-Jan-1950	4	302
Ratliff, Billy	5-Sep-1959	8	230
Ratliff, Charles	4-Dec-1949	5	172
Ratliff, Chester	3-Feb-1948	2	44
Ratliff, Chester L.	16-Mar-1966	11	167
Ratliff, Claude	18-Dec-1979	13	409
Ratliff, Cleo	9-Aug-1949	3	274
Ratliff, David	18-Jul-1982	12	209
Ratliff, Denzil	16-Oct-1947	2	217
Ratliff, Edgel	18-Feb-1970	6	381
Ratliff, Edgel	18-Feb-1970	11	381
Ratliff, Edward	24-Jun-1954	7	93
Ratliff, Eugene	18-Jan-1961	8	328
Ratliff, George	26-Sep-1949	3	240
Ratliff, Glen	20-Nov-1973	13	416
Ratliff, Henry	1-May-1950	6	160
Ratliff, James	26-Dec-1949	6	159
Ratliff, Jess	8-Dec-1949	5	72
Ratliff, John	6-Jun-1962	9	210
Ratliff, Kenneth	28-Nov-1974	13	75
Ratliff, Langley	15-May-1949	9	275
Ratliff, Luther	1-Mar-1953	6	626
Ratliff, Luther G.	31-May-1958	8	36
Ratliff, Marlin	12-Apr-1950	4	492
Ratliff, Millard	28-Jun-1949	3	64
Ratliff, Oliver	21-Oct-1949	3	368
Ratliff, Ollie	3-Dec-1949	4	540
Ratliff, Otis	8-Dec-1949	5	73
Ratliff, Robert	31-Mar-1976	13	253
Ratliff, Rondell	31-Dec-1968	11	158
Ratliff, Rudy	9-Nov-1949	5	29
Ratliff, Terry	6-Jul-1970	11	226
Ratliff, Thomas	20-Jun-1949	3	44
Ratliff, Tom	8-Aug-1949	3	126
Ratliff, Trubie	23-Jul-1949	9	335
Ratliff, Woodrow	29-Aug-1976	12	300
Ratliff, Woodrow	26-Nov-1979	12	299
Ray, Beekle	23-Oct-1949	4	581
Ray, Benton	23-Mar-1950	4	465
Ray, Benton	23-Mar-1950	7	61
Ray, Billy Lee	3-Jul-1998	14	245
Ray, Gilbert	19-Jan-1950	4	250
Reed, Andrew	25-Sep-1949	3	275
Reed, Boyd	24-Mar-1950	11	134
Reed, Clyde Lamonte	25-Feb-1998	14	237
Reed, Don	16-Mar-1960	8	272

Name	Disc. Date	Book	Page
Reed, Estill	17-Dec-1949	4	86
Reed, Goble Jr.	10-Sep-1964	10	123
Reed, James	13-Jan-1950	6	205
Reed, Jerry	26-Jan-1970	11	375
Reed, Kelly	17-Jul-1949	3	124
Reed, Robert	11-Nov-1945	1	616
Reed, Robert	7-Jan-1960	8	290
Reed, Roger	11-Mar-1948	2	307
Reed, William	9-Jul-1949	3	99
Reed, Worley	22-Jun-1923	1	52
Reedy, Denver	1-Jan-1962	9	52
Reffett, Henry	25-Oct-1949	3	394
Reffett, Virgil	17-Jan-1950	4	429
Reffitt, Amos	7-Jan-1950	4	131
Reffitt, Ellis	22-May-1947	2	183
Reffitt, Elmer	9-Oct-1947	2	205
Reffitt, Frank Dean	15-Oct-1976	13	292
Reid, Roy	30-Jul-1950	6	10
Reitz, Henry	14-Feb-1950	4	530
Reynolds, Andrew Jackson	28-Oct-1960	8	71
Reynolds, Andrew Jackson	19-Feb-1962	9	190
Reynolds, Arnold	14-Jun-1957	7	351
Reynolds, Charlie	21-Oct-1949	6	204
Reynolds, Charlie	9-Oct-1950	6	203
Reynolds, Dennis	13-Jul-1970	11	181
Reynolds, Earl	3-Sep-1949	3	163
Reynolds, Edgar	19-Jul-1950	7	155
Reynolds, Edgar	2-Dec-1952	5	504
Reynolds, Emit	17-Apr-1950	4	575
Reynolds, Ernest	18-Jul-1923	1	159
Reynolds, Everett	14-Jul-1949	3	94
Reynolds, Garr Vondas	9-Sep-1960	9	7
Reynolds, Gotto	27-Oct-1960	9	110
Reynolds, Herbert	4-Sep-1975	13	190
Reynolds, Herbert Ray	4-Sep-1975	15	118
Reynolds, Homer	16-Apr-1950	9	343-344
Reynolds, James	15-Jan-1978	13	353
Reynolds, Joe	16-Nov-1922	2	230
Reynolds, John	28-Mar-1947	2	112
Reynolds, Johnny	14-Aug-1975	13	184
Reynolds, Lewis	21-Oct-1947	2	19
Reynolds, Lewis	23-Sep-1976	13	287
Reynolds, Raymond	6-Nov-1958	8	107
Reynolds, Riley	26-Oct-1950	7	166
Reynolds, Roland	26-Jul-1956	11	71
Reynolds, Ronald	12-Jun-1975	13	169
Reynolds, Thomas	11-Dec-1956	7	476
Reynolds, Waltrust	5-May-1952	6	580
Reynolds, William	23-Nov-1949	3	574
Rice, Charles	3-Dec-1945	2	104
Rice, George	26-Oct-1950	6	165
Rice, Harold	30-Jul-1950	11	51-52
Rice, Howard	20-Sep-1971	11	345
Rice, James	16-Oct-1958	8	96
Rice, James L.	20-Nov-1956	7	247
Rice, James V.	27-Feb-1959	8	156
Rice, John	14-Jan-1949	3	379
Rice, John Jr.	25-Jul-1950	2	352
Rice, John V.	28-Nov-1949	5	60
Rice, Kenneth	1-Dec-1949	6	25
Rice, Luther J.	8-Dec-1949	4	14
Rice, Orville	4-Feb-1949	10	13
Rice, Randolph	30-Nov-1949	6	454
Rice, Raymond	8-Jun-1949	3	87
Rice, Reginald	30-Oct-1960	10	206
Rice, Sam	19-Oct-1949	3	367
Rice, Shirley	12-Oct-1949	3	337
Rice, Thomas	21-Oct-1949	3	369
Rice, William	4-Oct-1965	11	114
Rice, Willie B.	29-Nov-1949	4	387
Richardson, James	2-Aug-1949	6	625
Richmond Robert	9-Sep-1976	13	284
Richmond, Everett	24-Sep-1949	3	254
Richmond, Everett H. Jr.	24-Sep-1949	4	584
Ricker, James	8-May-1925	12	260
Rickman, Richard	11-Aug-1975	13	181
Ridener, Freddy	1-May-1964	9	235
Ridner, Freddy	10-Apr-1960	9	236
Rife, Russell	25-Dec-1951	6	539
Riley, Issac Jr.	22-Jul-1955	7	440
Riley, Thomas	28-May-1922	1	602
Riley, Thomas	28-Mar-1949	3	7
Risner, Curtis Garland	13-Aug-1973	14	19
Risner, Gary	3-Apr-1986	15	23

Name	Disc. Date	Book	Page
Risner, Gary	13-Jul-1991	15	25
Risner, Gary	19-Feb-1993	15	24
Risner, James	5-Oct-1949	3	300
Risner, James L.	26-Oct-1949	11	38
Risner, James L.	15-May-1974	13	219
Risner, James W.	2-Nov-1949	10	59
Risner, James W.	22-Nov-1950	10	58
Risner, James W.	28-Jan-1954	10	57
Risner, Warren	18-Mar-1950	4	586
Risner, William	25-Jul-1949	3	122
Rister, Clarence	1-Dec-1958	8	116
Rister, Edgar	5-Sep-1971	11	237
Roache, Paul	31-Jul-1950	4	297
Roark, Fess	5-Jan-1950	4	140
Roark, James Jr.	11-Nov-1949	3	491
Roberts, Charles	14-Jun-1973	12	10
Roberts, Daimetta	1-Dec-1949	3	622
Roberts, Everett	18-Jul-1923	1	134
Roberts, Everett	18-Jul-1924	7	51
Roberts, Fred	18-Aug-1924	1	250
Roberts, George	12-Jan-1923	1	25
Roberts, Herman	9-Dec-1956	7	368
Roberts, James	3-Nov-1949	3	480
Roberts, James Denver	13-Aug-1969	14	46
Roberts, Jerry	2-Feb-1972	11	534
Roberts, Joe M.	1-Aug-1965	15	32
Roberts, Larry Carlton	13-May-1978	15	91-92
Roberts, Leo	25-Jan-1958	7	470
Roberts, Leonard	22-Nov-1950	11	16
Roberts, Samuel	22-Oct-1949	3	402
Roberts, William	25-Jul-1949	3	592
Roberts, William H.	14-Feb-1959	8	193
Roberts, William L.	8-Jan-1950	4	358
Roberts, William W.	12-Aug-1960	8	292
Roberts, Willie R.	16-Jan-1950	4	307
Roberts, Willie V.	10-Mar-1947	1	218
Roberts, Willie V.	10-Mar-1947	2	378
Robinette, Carl Langley	20-Nov-1949	5	49
Robinette, Glenn	30-Jul-1955	7	205
Robinette, Orville Shirley	18-Nov-1949	5	48
Robinson, Abe	11-May-1944	10	23
Robinson, Abe	28-Sep-1949	3	262
Robinson, Bascom	3-Feb-1922	1	607
Robinson, Billie	16-Nov-1949	6	496
Robinson, Billie	19-Nov-1950	6	214
Robinson, Billie	20-Dec-1950	6	495
Robinson, Billie	15-Sep-1959	8	217
Robinson, Charles	4-Dec-1949	3	612
Robinson, Clarence Jr.	24-Dec-1952	11	401
Robinson, Clarence Ray	8-Mar-1974	12	102
Robinson, Claude	31-Aug-1971	11	486
Robinson, Earnest	26-Sep-1949	8	90
Robinson, Edward F.	20-Oct-1949	9	239
Robinson, Edward F.	22-Jul-1952	9	242
Robinson, Edward Fain	21-Aug-1955	9	243
Robinson, Ellis Wayne	8-Nov-1971	11	512
Robinson, Elza L. Jr.	18-Jan-1950	4	295
Robinson, Ezra	28-Jan-1950	4	293
Robinson, Floyd	19-Jan-1950	4	384
Robinson, George E.	20-Oct-1949	9	346
Robinson, George Washington	24-Oct-1958	8	102
Robinson, George Washington Jr.	28-Jan-1960	8	255
Robinson, Harmon	26-Nov-1947	2	132
Robinson, Herman	29-Sep-1949	8	165
Robinson, Herman	29-Sep-1950	8	164
Robinson, James Edward	16-Dec-1979	14	74
Robinson, John	20-Oct-1949	6	557
Robinson, John	19-Feb-1951	6	344
Robinson, John D.	21-Sep-1949	4	382
Robinson, John H.	20-Oct-1949	4	273
Robinson, Lewis Jr.	29-Oct-1949	7	60
Robinson, Lewis Jr.	16-Oct-1952	7	59
Robinson, Lloyd Henry	1-Oct-1973	12	39
Robinson, Luther	25-Jun-1958	8	47
Robinson, Luther	13-Oct-1960	8	306
Robinson, Mars	31-May-1951	6	423
Robinson, Mars	6-Apr-1959	8	301
Robinson, Paul Edgar	14-Jan-1969	11	154
Robinson, Ronald	10-Jan-1950	6	118
Robinson, Tommie Atlas	15-Mar-1962	9	61
Robinson, Wess	12-Jan-1923	1	11
Rodebaugh, John S.	12-Oct-1949	3	347

Name	Disc. Date	Book	Page
Rodgers, Rastus	20-Oct-1947	2	144
Rodgers, Virgie	18-Feb-1947	2	330
Rogers, Charlie	1-Nov-1949	10	62
Rogers, Harrison	2-May-1947	2	123
Rollins, James	21-Nov-1974	13	72
Rone, Elwood	26-Sep-1949	6	604
Roop, Adis	19-Nov-1949	3	620
Roop, Ambers Jr.	18-Aug-1950	5	509
Roop, Billy	17-May-1970	11	217
Roop, Donald	29-Oct-1959	8	228
Roop, Keith	13-Nov-1969	11	218
Roop, Tommy	29-Oct-1970	11	409
Rorrer, Guy Jr.	6-Apr-1952	7	41
Rose, Delbert	3-Aug-1949	6	362
Rose, Earl	19-Apr-1949	3	14
Rose, Eugene	17-Oct-1973	12	48
Rose, Francis	3-Feb-1950	4	406
Rose, Gary	20-Aug-1968	11	482
Rose, Harold	20-Feb-1950	4	414
Rose, Howard	11-Mar-1950	5	472
Rose, John	28-Dec-1949	4	119
Rose, Morgan	23-Oct-1949	3	406
Rose, Orville V.	16-Dec-1949	5	101
Rose, William Kent	31-Jan-1971	14	224
Roseberry, James	8-Apr-1949	6	75
Roseberry, Thomas	9-Aug-1957	7	381
Ross, Ledford	16-May-1971	11	451
Ross, Ledford	2-Sep-1980	12	249
Ross, Wheeler	5-Dec-1949	4	29
Rossi, Joe	17-Jan-1958	7	472
Rowe, Amos	23-Oct-1952	7	223
Rowe, Amos	16-Sep-1956	7	222
Rowe, Charles	13-Nov-1956	7	241
Rowe, Claude	30-May-1923	1	106
Rowe, Delmer	12-Feb-1964	11	320
Rowe, Kermit	15-Oct-1949	3	380
Rowe, Lonnie	29-Apr-1958	8	27
Rowe, Rans J.	11-Sep-1949	11	72
Rowe, Virgil	13-Dec-1949	6	294
Rowe, William	8-Aug-1962	9	95
Rusmussin, Hans	10-Jul-1923	1	96
Russell, Paul	10-Oct-1949	3	341
Russo, Johnathan Andrew	3-Jun-2000	15	40
Russo, Jonathan Andrew	2-Feb-2003	15	40
Ryan, George D. Jr.	20-Dec-1949	4	87
Ryan, Milton	15-Sep-1947	2	16
Sabo, Thomas	7-Aug-1972	12	114
Salem, Wilma	28-Sep-1961	9	99
Salisbury, Alfred	8-Mar-1957	7	317
Salisbury, Ashland	6-Dec-1949	6	119
Salisbury, Bert	29-Oct-1952	3	403
Salisbury, Blaine	21-Oct-1949	3	412
Salisbury, Clyde Russell	2-Dec-1955	8	9
Salisbury, Cola	3-Feb-1948	2	356
Salisbury, Colan Lee	16-Jul-1972	11	576
Salisbury, Ervin	14-Aug-1952	6	593
Salisbury, Ervin	25-Oct-1957	12	284
Salisbury, Frank	6-Dec-1957	7	443
Salisbury, George	4-Jun-1923	1	173
Salisbury, German	24-Nov-1949	6	80
Salisbury, Gordon	21-Aug-1947	2	355
Salisbury, Gordon	21-Aug-1947	6	91
Salisbury, Harold	2-Jun-1950	6	388
Salisbury, Herbert G.	20-Jan-1950	11	68
Salisbury, Herbert G.	15-Sep-1948	2	224
Salisbury, Herbert G. Jr.	29 April1 955	10	54
Salisbury, Herbert Gene Jr.	19-Oct-1972	11	600
Salisbury, Jack D.	11-Dec-1949	4	144
Salisbury, James	20-Mar-1950	6	22
Salisbury, James	5-Nov-1950	6	220
Salisbury, James L.	20-Jul-1950	7	417
Salisbury, James O.	7-Dec-1959	10	191
Salisbury, Jay	19-Jan-1948	2	192
Salisbury, Jay	14-Oct-1949	3	554
Salisbury, Joe	5-Oct-1963	8	216
Salisbury, Joe J.	6-Apr-1951	10	61
Salisbury, John Q.	6-Nov-1949	3	582
Salisbury, Lackey	28-Aug-1924	1	182
Salisbury, Lee	30-Jan-1950	6	55
Salisbury, Lloyd	11-Jan-1957	7	318
Salisbury, Marvin Jr.	6-Apr-1962	14	189
Salisbury, Noris	18-Aug-1968	11	178
Salisbury, Oliver	27-Nov-1949	3	569
Salisbury, Ray	11-Feb-1950	6	72

Name	Disc. Date	Book	Page
Salisbury, Robert	23-Jan-1948	4	281
Salisbury, Robert L.	4-May-1974	13	3
Salisbury, Rodney	21-Aug-1957	7	380
Salisbury, Stacy	8-Feb-1947	7	101
Salisbury, Teddy	12-Aug-1951	10	144
Salisbury, Tom	22-Jul-1923	1	221
Salisbury, Vernon	6-Oct-1949	3	282
Salisbury, Vernon Jr.	16-Sep-1970	14	90
Salisbury, Vernon Jr.	17-Sep-1973	14	91
Salisbury, Vernon Jr.	14-Jul-1974	14	94
Salisbury, Vernon Jr.	18-Feb-1975	14	92
Salisbury, Vernon Jr.	21-May-1978	14	93
Salisbury, Vernon S.	16-Dec-1963	9	206
Salisbury, Wayne	10-Jan-1950	4	494
Salmons, Leonard	14-Apr-1946	9	302
Salmons, Melvin	18-Jan-1950	6	623
Salts, Oakie	31-Aug-1947	10	127
Salyer, Clarence	21-Dec-1960	8	325
Salyer, Herman	12-Dec-1956	8	237
Salyer, Paul	20-Mar-1977	13	322
Salyer, Paul E.	18-Mar-1948	2	170
Salyers, Ellis	7-Mar-1949	3	2
Salyers, Franklin	2-Feb-1964	9	211
Salyers, Harold	10-May-1962	9	79
Salyers, Jay	24-Jun-1923	1	105
Salyers, Melvin	21-Dec-1965	11	138
Salyers, Oscar	25-Aug-1963	9	209A
Sammons, Archie	6-Apr-1976	13	258
Sammons, Bascom	20-Dec-1922	1	158
Sammons, Charles Casey	23-Sep-1972	14	17
Sammons, Dallas D.	9-Jul-1950	6	133
Sammons, David	28-Mar-1976	13	257
Sammons, Earl	15-Jan-1958	7	467
Sammons, Jack Jr.	29-Jul-1956	7	228
Sammons, Leonard	23-Sep-1949	3	228
Sammons, Lloyd	3-Oct-1959	8	222
Sammons, Lonnie	21-Apr-1951	6	406
Sammons, Marvin	9-Jun-1969	11	229
Sammons, Robert	21-Mar-1957	7	333
Sammons, Ward	19-Dec-1952	7	9
Samons, Beverly	5-Jun-1924	1	188
Samons, Casey	11-Feb-1950	4	446
Samons, David	12-Apr-1976	13	265
Samons, David Jr.	15-Jul-2000	15	2
Samons, Eugene	26-Jul-1951	7	43
Samons, Green	23-Mar-1950	4	456
Samons, Green	24-May-1957	7	339
Samons, Henry	14-Oct-1949	3	319
Samons, Herbie	13-Oct-1946	2	64
Samons, Hezie	5-Feb-1950	4	325
Samons, Ivory	18-Feb-1950	6	369
Samons, Jay	5-Dec-1949	4	25
Samons, Kirly	20-Nov-1977	12	161
Samons, Lester	25-Nov-1949	3	561
Samons, Lowell	21-Feb-1963	9	136
Samons, Malcolm	16-Aug-1957	7	378
Samons, Manis	7-Feb-1965	11	37
Samons, Michael Keith	3-Jun-1987	14	182
Samons, Richard	17-Aug-1950	5	529
Samons, Roe	12-Mar-1975	13	128
Samons, Ronald	25-Jan-1974	12	87
Samons, Rupert	10-Mar-1974	12	122
Samons, Terry	23 July 1971	13	176
Sanders, Earnest Jr.	14-Feb-1964	9	307
Sanders, James	7-Jan-1970	6	366
Sanders, Leighton	7-Jan-1970	11	366
Sayers, Leonard John	30-Oct-1969	14	302
Sayers, Leonard John	30-Oct-1974	14	303
Sayers, Leonard John	1-Dec-1999	14	304
Scalf, Billy	7-Oct-1962	9	153
Scalf, Charles	3-Jul-1951	9	207
Scalf, Earl	13-Mar-1950	5	235
Scalf, Jackie D.	20-Nov-1961	15	14
Scalf, John	22-May-1957	7	338
Scalf, Roland	13-Feb-1950	6	447
Scarberry, Paul Vernon	15-Apr-1975	13	139
Scott, Arthur	6-Oct-1949	3	313
Scott, Ashland	7-Sep-1949	3	184
Scott, Burl	2-Dec-1972	11	609
Scott, Carl	8-Aug-1978	13	361
Scott, Donald	5-Dec-1978	13	389
Scott, Earnest	13-Dec-1949	11	69
Scott, Earnest	3-Mar-1953	11	70
Scott, Edgar	24-Nov-1949	4	78

Name	Disc. Date	Book	Page
Scott, George	18-Aug-1974	13	35
Scott, Gordon Raymond	1-Nov-1975	14	31
Scott, James	5-Nov-1959	8	231
Scott, James L.	2-Mar-1956	14	235
Scott, James Lewis	27-Sep-1961	14	236
Scott, John	16-Apr-1962	9	157
Scott, Junior	5-Oct-1949	9	204A
Scott, Otis	1-Oct-1949	2	360
Scott, Otis	25-Jan-1951	6	433
Scott, Ralph Randall	13-Dec-1956	7	265
Scott, Raymond	26-Jul-1951	6	499
Scott, Richard	16-May-1960	8	274
Scott, Theodore	11-Jun-1949	3	39
Scott, Thomas	21-Oct-1976	13	293
Scott, Thomas Dale	1-Oct-1993	14	89
Scott, Verlie	5-Dec-1956	7	260
Scott, Willis	3-Dec-1946	6	167
Scruggs, William	27-Feb-1949	6	114
Scutchfield, Ermal Clay	9-Feb-1950	5	185
Scutchfield, Orville David	7-Oct-1973	12	47
Scutchfield, Scott Beecher	14-Jul-1971	11	470
Scutchfield, Talmage	7-Dec-1922	1	246
Sellards, Ben	28-Apr-1950	6	87
Sellards, Carl Ray	11-Dec-1969	14	80
Sellards, Eddie	31-Dec-1949	5	120
Sellards, Jack	19-Apr-1956	7	183
Senters, Clyde	4-Feb-1950	5	152
Senters, William	24-Dec-1950	6	289
Senters, Willis	23-Dec-1949	4	244
Setser, Arvin	12-Dec-1949	4	52
Setser, Calvin Gene	17-Nov-1971	11	513
Setser, Cleetis	26-Oct-1949	3	387
Setser, Henry	25-Dec-1949	4	75
Setser, Henry	13-Mar-1957	8	212
Setser, Jake	24-Mar-1947	1	206
Setser, Jake	24-Mar-1947	2	377
Setser, Jake	24-Mar-1947	12	186
Setser, Millard	6-Feb-1949	2	283
Setser, William David	25-Jun-1974	14	113
Sexton, Abraham L.	8-Nov-1949	6	185
Sexton, Birchel	1-Oct-1966	11	194
Sexton, Curtis	16-Aug-1950	6	44
Sexton, Delbert	8-Apr-1958	8	15
Sexton, Elkana	6-Nov-1949	5	541
Sexton, Jason Donald	16-Jun-2004	15	49
Sexton, Larry	14-Jan-1975	13	93
Sexton, Leonard	19-Feb-1958	8	2
Sexton, Marvin	26-Sep-1958	8	91
Sexton, Marvin	1-Dec-1964	10	190
Sexton, Mickey Ray	19-Sep-1966	14	7
Sexton, Perry	17-Jul-1923	1	119
Sexton, Raymond	8-Jul-1949	3	86
Sexton, Richard	29-Nov-1955	7	147
Sexton, Thomas	20-Feb-1957	11	113
Sexton, Wendell	12-May-1964	9	251
Shannon Charles	21-Jul-1952	6	595
Shannon, Donald	8-Dec-1977	13	247
Shannon, Raymond	10-Jan-1950	5	121
Sheffield, James	19-Jul-1923	1	97
Shell, Charles J.	2-Jan-1980	15	129
Shell, Charles James	26-Aug-1975	15	128
Shell, Frank	8-Nov-1949	15	130-131
Shell, George O.	31-Oct-1949	4	291
Shell, Herbert	30-Apr-1950	4	538
Shell, Hershel	12-Jan-1950	8	302
Shell, Johnnie	6-Apr-1965	11	29
Shell, Luther	9-Oct-1949	4	289
Shelton, Allen	30-Jun-1974	13	21
Shelton, Douglas	10-Mar-1972	11	544
Shelton, Eddie	18-Feb-1970	11	382
Shelton, Estile	3-Jun-1947	12	307-308
Shelton, Terry	30-Apr-1975	13	147
Shelton, Terry	1-Nov-1992	14	42
Shelton, Virgil	28-Nov-1978	13	440
Shephard, Benjamin Elbert	15-Jan-1959	8	140
Shepherd, Abe	29-Jun-1923	11	215
Shepherd, Alex	12-Jan-1950	4	216
Shepherd, Arlen	20-Aug-1957	11	182
Shepherd, Arnold	17-Apr-1950	5	257
Shepherd, Belva	5-Feb-1957	7	298
Shepherd, Calvin	28-Oct-1949	6	378
Shepherd, Calvin	11-Jan-1970	11	370
Shepherd, Charles	17-Mar-1950	6	492
Shepherd, Coy	8-Oct-1949	3	424
Shepherd, Denton	22-Nov-1976	13	295
Shepherd, Dial	22-Apr-1958	8	25
Shepherd, Eddie	6-Jan-1976	13	227
Shepherd, Edgiel	27-Jul-1949	3	111
Shepherd, Everett Ray	5-Oct-1964	10	180
Shepherd, Forrest	21-Aug-1955	7	279
Shepherd, Frank	13-Dec-1949	4	222
Shepherd, Gary	13-Jan-1976	13	228
Shepherd, Gordon	23-Oct-1968	11	309
Shepherd, Henry	6-Nov-1974	13	67
Shepherd, High	10-Oct-1974	13	53
Shepherd, Israel	7-Feb-1950	4	341
Shepherd, James	27-Apr-1951	7	21
Shepherd, John	21-Jun-1947	2	142
Shepherd, John Ed	22-Dec-1949	5	508
Shepherd, John Wayne	26-Aug-1999	14	281
Shepherd, Kirk	22-Oct-1949	3	385
Shepherd, Max	7-Jun-1973	12	15
Shepherd, Melvin	8-Sep-1949	6	317
Shepherd, Mitchell	21-Jun-1974	13	14
Shepherd, Mitchell	8-Aug-1979	13	396
Shepherd, Oakie	6-Oct-1959	14	159
Shepherd, Ralph	24-May-1989	12	292
Shepherd, Richard	20-Nov-1949	6	482
Shepherd, Robert	1-Feb-1950	4	305
Shepherd, Robert	20-Nov-1950	6	186
Shepherd, Rocky	11-Oct-1949	3	474
Shepherd, Thomas	20-Nov-1949	7	47
Shepherd, Thomas	20-Nov-1953	7	48
Shepherd, Tony	30-Oct-1956	7	253
Shepherd, Tramble	28-Oct-1970	11	410
Shepherd, Tramble	28-Oct-1970	12	315
Shepherd, Wheeler	1-Dec-1958	8	120
Shepherd, Wilce	1-Nov-1949	5	65
Shepherd, William	8-Jan-1951	5	434
Shepherd, Woots	16-Apr-1950	11	53
Sherman, Clyde	7-Oct-1949	3	461
Sherman, Harry	30-Mar-1951	5	452
Sherman, Jack	24-Oct-1949	6	531
Sherman, Jack	31-Oct-1950	6	532
Sherman, Woodrow	9-Jan-1947	2	341
Shields, Jay	18-Mar-1950	6	468
Shipley, Larry	4-Jun-1972	11	567
Shipley, Warren	28-Apr-1950	4	623
Shipman, Charles	21-Feb-1950	6	644
Shipman, William	6-Oct-1949	3	547
Short, Richard Francis	21-Mar-1994	14	135
Shrewsberry, Shurl	1-Aug-1956	7	198
Shufflebarger, Henry A. Jr.	14-Dec-1949	4	560
Simmons, Paul	21-Sep-1949	3	227
Simpson, Harold	11-Jun-1975	14	286-287
Simpson, Jerry	7-Feb-1974	12	90
Simpson, L.T.	15-Sep-1949	3	200
Simpson, Pat	14-Sep-1970	11	408
Singleton, Ewell	29-Dec-1949	4	537
Singleton, Henry	8-Jul-1923	10	103
Sizemore, Billie	9-Sep-1958	12	159
Sizemore, Brandon Merle	15-Dec-2005	15	76
Sizemore, Danny Craig	13-Aug-1995	15	101-102
Sizemore, Edward	4-Feb-1950	4	313
Sizemore, George W.	13-Jun-1949	3	40
Sizemore, Herbert	10-Nov-1949	3	494
Sizemore, Hubert	27-Oct-1949	3	414
Sizemore, Joe	27-Oct-1948	2	243
Sizemore, John	18-Dec-1949	6	132
Sizemore, Millard	20-Sep-1949	7	168
Sizemore, Millard	9-Feb-1951	7	169
Sizemore, Rolland	23-Nov-1953	7	92
Skeans, Elliott	11-Mar-1937	12	86
Skeans, Floyd	5-Sep-1974	12	124
Skeans, Joe	1-Apr-1971	11	452
Skeans, Leonard	3-Dec-1957	11	35
Skeans, Robie	19-Jan-1950	4	269
Skeans, Sol	23-Mar-1950	5	221
Skeans, Taylor	29-Jun-1949	3	137
Skeens, Joe	21-Apr-1971	11	280
Skeens, John C.	7-Nov-1960	8	323
Skeens, Stephen Joseph	14-Dec-2006	15	85
Skiles, Billy	8-Sep-1970	11	405
Skiles, Chester	18-Sep-1957	9	125
Skiles, Gary	7-Jan-1970	11	369
Skiles, William	26-Dec-1949	4	462
Slade, Edgar	22-Mar-1922	1	248
Sloan, Alex	18-Mar-1946	2	219
Sloan, Alex	23-Jun-1977	13	155
Sloan, David	22-Apr-1950	5	259
Sloan, Delbert	8-Nov-1949	3	504
Sloan, Henry	18-Feb-1971	11	517
Sloan, Homer G.	21-Nov-1982	13	428
Sloan, Howard	6-Nov-1949	3	539
Sloan, James	25-Jun-1958	9	258
Sloane, Hugh	4-Jan-1950	4	225
Slone, Adrian	29-Apr-1959	8	162
Slone, Allen	9-Nov-1949	3	606
Slone, Arnie	18-May-1971	11	450
Slone, Bennie	31-Oct-1950	6	153
Slone, Billy Fred	11-Oct-1970	11	413
Slone, Bobby Selton	14-Jul-1971	14	65
Slone, Brewie	7-Dec-1949	4	355
Slone, Burnice	19-Mar-1950	7	372
Slone, Charlie	5-Mar-1956	7	173
Slone, Clarence	22-Oct-1949	4	37
Slone, Curtis	19-Mar-1952	6	567
Slone, Danny	3-Aug-1972	11	579
Slone, Dennis Keith	17-Dec-1995	14	178
Slone, Denver	10-Oct-1958	9	212
Slone, Donald	4-Dec-1958	8	110
Slone, Earl	7-Dec-1949	3	619
Slone, Elbert	5-Feb-1950	9	345
Slone, Ellis	3-Dec-1958	9	298
Slone, Elmer Jr	22-Sep-1974	13	51
Slone, Ernest	16-Jan-1961	8	256
Slone, Eulis	31-Oct-1949	3	436
Slone, Everett	15-Aug-1949	6	382
Slone, Garfield	24-Jun-1923	1	215
Slone, George	9-Oct-1950	9	288
Slone, Green J.	20-Apr-1950	12	324
Slone, Harry	17-Oct-1971	11	501
Slone, Has	1-Feb-1950	4	309
Slone, Herman	20-Nov-1950	6	215
Slone, Hillard	23-Jun-1964	10	6
Slone, Homer	2-Dec-1948	2	309
Slone, Howard	16-Dec-1949	9	301
Slone, Ike	18-May-1950	4	574
Slone, Irvin	16-Jan-1950	4	252
Slone, James	8-Dec-1960	8	317
Slone, James E.	2-Jun-1950	5	418
Slone, James Marvin	14-Oct-1970	14	47
Slone, John	25-Nov-1949	6	462
Slone, Larry	7-Jan-1971	11	442
Slone, Michael	2-Dec-1992	14	64
Slone, Monroe Jr.	23-Jan-1961	9	51
Slone, Paul B.	25-Apr-1956	7	376
Slone, Paul D.	5-Oct-1961	9	220
Slone, Ralph J.	13-Sep-1958	8	112
Slone, Ralph N.	17-Sep-1958	10	37
Slone, Ralph N.	31-Aug-1961	10	36
Slone, Raymond	12-Feb-1951	6	512
Slone, Raymond	30-Aug-1957	10	205
Slone, Richmond	25-Nov-1949	3	558
Slone, Ronald	2-Oct-1974	13	54
Slone, Roscoe	25-Aug-1960	8	296
Slone, Shirley Ray	6-May-1971	14	125
Slone, Tim	16-Oct-1949	4	508
Slone, Tivis B.	5-Feb-1947	11	232
Slone, Toby Dean	16-Apr-1996	14	187
Slone, Van Ray	3-Jul-1961	9	107
Slone, Vernon K.	8-Aug-1973	12	20
Slone, Wilford	24-Oct-1956	8	190
Slone, William	6-Nov-1949	6	350
Slone, William Jr.	17-Aug-1921	12	132
Slone, William P.	29-Oct-1949	9	105
Slusher, Henry	22-Mar-1957	7	313
Smallwood, Arthur J.	1-Nov-1949	10	51
Smallwood, Arthur J.	25-Dec-1950	10	50
Smallwood, Arthur J.	11-Dec-1953	10	49
Smallwood, Edward	4-Jan-1950	4	127
Smallwood, Freddie James	20-Aug-1963	9	190
Smiderle, Lillian F.	16-Jul-1970	14	69
Smiley, Donald	13-Aug-1963	9	183
Smiley, Ermon	29-Nov-1950	6	481
Smiley, Raymond	16-Dec-1949	5	107
Smith, Arthur	26-Nov-1948	2	272
Smith, Bill	26-Mar-1950	6	615
Smith, Blueford	28-Oct-1949	6	179
Smith, Carl	4-Jul-1949	4	521
Smith, Carter	27-May-1975	13	152
Smith, Charles	14-Jan-1950	4	513

Name	Disc. Date	Book	Page
Smith, Donald	5-Oct-1959	8	220
Smith, Earl	1-Jun-1949	4	419
Smith, Estill Jr.	25-May-1961	9	8
Smith, George	22-Dec-1949	14	270
Smith, James	29-Aug-1949	3	155
Smith, James	21-Nov-1949	6	182
Smith, James C.	14-Dec-1950	7	30
Smith, Jimmy	26-Sep-1973	12	35
Smith, Joseph	8-Jul-1958	8	206
Smith, Nicholas William	28-Sep-2004	15	52
Smith, Paul G.	28-Feb-1950	5	225
Smith, Ronald	23-Nov-1958	8	122
Smith, Russell Lee	6-Feb-1979	14	70
Smith, Ryan Arthur Thomas	10-Jul-1996	14	190
Smith, Virgie	9-Dec-1948	2	357
Smith, Waldo W.	9-Oct-1949	5	242
Smith, Willard	12-Mar-1950	10	202
Smith, William	23-Dec-1949	10	98
Smith, William	14-Jan-1950	6	61
Smith, William	14-Jan-1950	6	64
Smith, William R.	24-Nov-1957	10	187
Smith, William R.	28-Dec-1963	10	183
Smith, Woodrow	7-Nov-1949	6	66
Smith, Woodrow	16-Nov-1949	11	28
Smock, Chester	3-Jan-1950	4	107
Smock, Roy	14-Dec-1949	4	55
Snavely, Walter	18-Oct-1956	7	292
Snell, Robert	14-Jan-1950	4	173
Snipes, Archie	6-Oct-1949	6	49
Snipes, Joseph	13-Jan-1950	4	164
Snoddy, Theodore	19-Nov-1949	3	524
Snyder, Allen	13-Aug-1958	8	76
Sole, Gladys	17-Jul-1949	2	320
Souylerette, Reginal Roy	19-Nov-1961	9	48
Spalding, Burhan	3-Apr-1949	3	12
Sparkman, Elmer	6-Sep-1956	14	136
Sparkman, Kinnel	21-Feb-1923	1	201
Sparkman, Kinnel	21-Feb-1923	2	293
Sparkman, Paul	18-Mar-1976	13	248-249
Sparkman, Willa	21-Mar-1971	11	439
Sparks, Abe	29-Jul-1956	8	57
Sparks, Orville	15-Oct-1949	3	354
Spaulding, Raymond	21-Sep-1947	2	18
Spears, Bill	13-May-1955	10	69
Spears, Broadus	1-Jul-1949	3	77
Spears, Chadwick	12-Sep-1949	3	186
Spears, Curtis	9-Feb-1953	6	624
Spears, Donald	1-Dec-1971	11	515
Spears, Elvie	23-Jun-1947	2	176
Spears, Foster	6-Apr-1947	2	159
Spears, Frank	28-Sep-1922	1	24
Spears, Frank	28-Sep-1922	1	157
Spears, Glenn Berlin	7-Aug-1979	15	8
Spears, Green	8-Jan-1950	4	157
Spears, James	28-Apr-1951	6	398
Spears, John	9-Jan-1949	8	257
Spears, Joseph	25-Aug-1959	8	204
Spears, Lloyd	29-Oct-1949	3	409
Spears, Mexico	4-Jul-1949	3	80
Spears, Orville	20-Dec-1949	4	66
Spears, Raymond	28-Jul-1949	2	316
Spears, Rell	18-Mar-1923	1	146
Spears, Thomas	11-Sep-1949	3	214
Spence, Willard	4-Nov-1949	11	63
Spencer, Bruce	11-Mar-1947	6	619
Spencer, David Lee	4-Jun-1981	14	137
Spencer, French Preston	23-Apr-1950	15	132-133
Spencer, French Preston	23-Apr-1950	15	134
Spencer, James Otto	11-Dec-1969	11	364
Spencer, Lee	22-Jun-1923	1	259
Spivey, Claude	19-Jun-1949	3	51
Spradlin, Bennie	29-Sep-1951	6	518
Spradlin, Billie	24-Dec-1949	4	254
Spradlin, Billy	31-Dec-1956	7	276
Spradlin, Billy L	7-Oct-1958	8	93
Spradlin, Cager	13-Nov-1921	1	604
Spradlin, Charles	16-Dec-1962	9	139
Spradlin, Charles Ronald	29-Aug-1972	15	119
Spradlin, Charles S.	4-Feb-1968	11	271
Spradlin, Clay	5-Jun-1951	6	425
Spradlin, Darwin M.	7-Mar-1951	12	263
Spradlin, Dwight	5-Nov-1949	5	28
Spradlin, Henry	12-Nov-1949	11	133
Spradlin, Herbert	27-Oct-1949	3	382
Spradlin, Hershel	20-May-1951	6	419
Spradlin, Jack	5-Mar-1959	8	154
Spradlin, John	28-Mar-1947	2	38
Spradlin, John	30-Sep-1949	4	220
Spradlin, John C.	5-May-1923	1	69
Spradlin, John H.	11-Jun-1922	10	12
Spradlin, John S.	11-Dec-1949	5	86
Spradlin, Lee	22-Apr-1947	2	29
Spradlin, Lewis	16-Oct-1949	6	120
Spradlin, Oscar	20-Dec-1956	7	268
Spradlin, Roger	31-Oct-1957	7	436
Spradlin, Scott	22-Dec-1949	4	63
Spradlin, Thomas	18-Dec-1949	5	126
Spradlin, William	7-Dec-1949	6	527
Spradlin, William	13-Dec-1950	6	528
Spradlin, William A.	4-Apr-1948	2	165
Spradlin, Willie	2-Dec-1958	10	117
Spreitzer, Doris	22-Aug-1957	8	134
Spriggs, Bill	30-Jan-1945	2	135
Spriggs, John	21-Jan-1950	6	445
Spriggs, Millard	14-Oct-1949	6	390
Spriggs, Thomas	11-Dec-1971	11	593
Spriggs, Wheeler	1-Sep-1950	7	126
Springer, Clinton	25-Jan-1976	13	232
Sprinkler, William	10-Aug-1966	11	188
Spurlock, Denver	5-Nov-1972	15	7
Spurlock, Hobert	5-Aug-1951	7	116
Spurlock, Homer	8-Dec-1949	3	632
Spurlock, James	30-Jan-1966	11	146
Spurlock, James T.	25-Nov-1949	4	160
Spurlock, John	22-Nov-1949	3	598
Spurlock, John C.	1-Jan-1959	8	152
Spurlock, Ottis	9-Jan-1950	4	478
Spurlock, Theodore	30-Mar-1948	9	273A
Stacy, James	12-Jul-1984	12	225-226
Stambaugh, Bob	3-May-1957	7	332
Stambaugh, Donald	26-Sep-1973	12	41
Stambaugh, Glen	6-Jan-1959	8	131
Stambaugh, James	24-Jun-1970	11	222
Stamper, Damron	25-Sep-1949	3	241
Stamper, Samuel	15-May-1950	4	631
Stamper, Walter	19-Nov-1949	3	552
Stancil, Cecil	21-Nov-1949	3	546
Stancil, Harold	3-Feb-1950	4	404
Stancil, Harris	15-Jan-1949	4	411
Stanford, Eugene	17-Dec-1952	6	635
Stanford, Eugene	16-Sep-1957	8	124
Stanford, Howard	5-Feb-1948	2	48
Stanley, Arthur Douglas	20-May-1969	11	347
Stanley, Carl	3-Mar-1963	9	147
Stanley, Chiles	23-Sep-1949	5	7
Stanley, David	14-Jan-1963	9	128
Stanley, Dingus	6-Apr-1950	4	519
Stanley, Earl Junior	25-Apr-1967	11	211
Stanley, Eula M.	14-Aug-1947	2	363
Stanley, Gary	25-Oct-1977	13	345
Stanley, Gene	10-Apr-1960	9	23
Stanley, Haskell	1-Dec-1949	5	77
Stanley, James	30-May-1949	4	212
Stanley, Joe	10-Oct-1957	7	460
Stanley, Joe W.	11-Jul-1961	9	74
Stanley, Leonard	27-Oct-1949	3	411
Stanley, Oscar	25-Mar-1948	2	146
Stanley, Ricky	25-Jan-1977	13	336
Stanley, Sambo	10-Mar-1946	2	216
Stanley, Scott	12-Jan-1950	4	213
Stanley, Thomas	23-Jul-1950	6	4
Stanley, Thomas J.	3-Jan-1950	4	122
Stanley, Warren	22-Oct-1949	3	390
Stanley, Willard	28-Oct-1945	2	88
Stansifer, Benjamin Franklin	17-Jan-1950	5	197
Stapleton, Stevie	17-Mar-1974	12	107
Stapleton, Terry Webb	17-Feb-1975	15	100
Steele, Carl	22-Dec-1969	15	26
Steele, Clyde	26-Sep-1949	3	249
Steele, John	23-Feb-1923	1	30
Steele, Roger	20-Jan-1950	4	247
Steele, Carl	22-Dec-1969	14	82-84
Stegall, John	26-Oct-1925	11	305
Stegall, Joseph	22-Oct-1950	10	88
Stephens, Albert	12-Oct-1949	4	6
Stephens, Billy	3-Sep-1962	9	100
Stephens, Charles	3-Feb-1950	5	151A
Stephens, Clarence	9-Jul-1946	2	373
Stephens, Clay	21-Sep-1947	2	196
Stephens, Cledis	29-Apr-1957	7	329
Stephens, Clyde	28-Jul-1947	2	366
Stephens, Clyde	5-Feb-1950	4	350
Stephens, Darb	22-Nov-1950	9	317
Stephens, Donald	26-Mar-1970	11	387
Stephens, Edgar	12-Jun-1946	11	62
Stephens, Ervin	3-Dec-1950	6	221
Stephens, Eugene	21-Dec-1949	10	114
Stephens, Ezra	5-Jan-1950	4	190
Stephens, Floyd	18-Oct-1949	3	299
Stephens, Frank	13-Dec-1976	13	299
Stephens, George	10-Dec-1951	7	143
Stephens, George	23-Jan-1958	8	52
Stephens, Gorman	5-Nov-1971	11	507
Stephens, Harrison	30-Oct-1949	3	425
Stephens, Herbert	30-Jun-1951	6	530
Stephens, Ira E.	23-Aug-1949	3	142
Stephens, Ira E.	7-Nov-1949	3	475
Stephens, Jackie	6-Jun-1964	9	304
Stephens, James	4-Sep-1947		
Stephens, Joe	5-Oct-1949	3	320
Stephens, Johnny	18-Nov-1951	6	589
Stephens, Marcy	31-Dec-1949	6	307
Stephens, Mark Andrew	1-Dec-1996	14	195
Stephens, Orville	2-Aug-1932	1	614
Stephens, Oscar	12-Jan-1951	6	292
Stephens, Paul M.	12-Sep-1972	11	585
Stephens, Robert	31-Aug-1947	2	264
Stephens, Robert Jr.	10-Aug-1949	4	336
Stephens, Robert L.	23-Nov-1961	9	47
Stephens, Rubin	25-Jun-1953	11	6
Stephens, Thomas	11-Jan-1971	11	276
Stephens, Willard	14-Sep-1949	3	202
Stephens, William	5-Apr-1923	1	178
Stephens, Woodrow Jr.	4-Mar-1988	3	1
Stephenson, Greely	8-Apr-1923	9	295
Stewart, Carl	21-Aug-1963	10	169
Stewart, Edwin	22-Feb-1950	4	442
Stewart, Frank	10-Aug-1953	7	36
Stewart, Harold	8-Oct-1956	7	234
Stewart, Harry Dean	23-Jan-1977	13	303
Stewart, James	2-Apr-1950	4	476
Stewart, Ogden	8-Sep-1948	2	334
Stewart, Okey	10-Oct-1949	3	321
Stewart, Robert	31-Dec-1949	5	236
Stewart, Robert Lee	8-Feb-1985	14	115
Stewart, Roger	24-Sep-1957	7	409
Stewart, Woodrow	22-Jun-1949	3	53
Stickler, Howard	17-Apr-1950	5	253
Stidham, Everett	29-Dec-1949	6	14
Stidham, Russell McCathy	29-Aug-1960	8	311
Stiles, Gomer	21-Feb-1950	5	458
Stiles, Gomer	12-Dec-1951	6	537
Stiles, Wilbur	14-Aug-1923	1	168
Stilton, Paul	4-Sep-1947	12	328
Stilton, Paul	20-Jan-1953	12	327
Stone, Curtis	26-Oct-1949	3	410
Stone, Harrison	12-Dec-1915	1	617
Stone, James	21-Apr-1950	5	494
Stone, Ronald	28-Oct-1962	9	113
Storie, Theodore	19-Feb-1950	4	511
Stout, Steve	13-Oct-1950	6	148
Stover, Thoney	12-Jan-1950	4	199
Stratton, Arley	29-Apr-1950	5	266
Stratton, Billy	6-Nov-1957	8	100
Stratton, Bobbie	6-Aug-1959	8	205
Stratton, Charley	20-Sep-1949	3	221
Stratton, Clayton	26-Oct-1949	3	419
Stratton, Deward	29-Oct-1947	2	30
Stratton, Donald	4-Nov-1952	6	611
Stratton, Grover	29-Jun-1949	3	79
Stratton, Herbert	16-Mar-1950	4	452
Stratton, Isaac	23-Dec-1949	4	372
Stratton, Jackie	9-Nov-1953	7	105
Stratton, Jackie	27-Apr-1959	10	78
Stratton, Jake	24-Nov-1949	10	159
Stratton, James Jr.	20-May-1975	14	95
Stratton, James P.	12-Jan-1950	4	196
Stratton, James T.	8-Jun-1971	11	290
Stratton, John	12-Dec-1950	11	81
Stratton, John T.	8-Jul-1958	9	282
Stratton, Larry	20-May-1972	11	571
Stratton, Leon	27-Apr-1963	9	152

Name	Disc. Date	Book	Page
Stratton, Roy	1-Aug-1960	8	308
Stratton, Sparrel	16-Apr-1950	4	516
Stratton, Theodore	30-Jan-1950	4	258
Stratton, Wade	31-Mar-1951	7	134
Stratton, Windell	23-Feb-1951	5	440
Stricklen, Lindsey	2-Apr-1970	11	388
Stumbo, Ancil	1-Mar-1977	12	301
Stumbo, Beckman	4-Apr-1947	4	326
Stumbo, Bill H.	8-Mar-1959	8	153
Stumbo, Britt Isom	14-Aug-2000	15	6
Stumbo, Charles	6-Jul-1970	12	216
Stumbo, Claude	15-Nov-1950	6	301
Stumbo, Claude	9-Nov-1952	6	302
Stumbo, Collins	7-Jan-1950	5	127
Stumbo, Curtis	9-Aug-1949	6	20
Stumbo, Denzil	10-Oct-1949	4	279
Stumbo, Edward	17-Dec-1949	4	497
Stumbo, Ellsworth H.	29-Oct-1949	3	426
Stumbo, Erman	25-Nov-1948	11	40
Stumbo, George	13-Feb-1923	1	131
Stumbo, Gregory	11-Apr-1974	12	121
Stumbo, Harlan	1-Sep-1961	11	428
Stumbo, Harlan	1-Sep-1967	11	426
Stumbo, Harlan	1-Nov-1970	11	429
Stumbo, Harlan Ray	26-Aug-1955	11	427
Stumbo, Herman C.	16-Jan-1972	11	531
Stumbo, Isaac	2-Dec-1949	6	460
Stumbo, Isom	14-Aug-1949	3	243
Stumbo, Jack	10-Mar-1950	5	426
Stumbo, Jack	28-Dec-1969	11	201
Stumbo, Jimmy	20-Aug-1971	11	480
Stumbo, Joel	14-Oct-1970	11	411
Stumbo, John Jr.	6-Dec-1950	6	217
Stumbo, John M.	16-Nov-1949	5	34
Stumbo, John M.	16-Nov-1949	7	107
Stumbo, Johnny	17-Feb-1977	13	308
Stumbo, Larry J.	24-Aug-1971	11	492
Stumbo, Lee	22-Feb-1923	1	118
Stumbo, Lee	22-Feb-1923	1	185
Stumbo, Lloyd	16-Dec-1949	5	437
Stumbo, Loran	10-Nov-1951	6	603
Stumbo, McArthur	12-Aug-1973	12	21
Stumbo, Orris D.	18-Jun-1960	8	287
Stumbo, Perry N.	13-Dec-1963	9	221
Stumbo, Samuel	14-Jul-1957	11	41
Stumbo, Ted	9-Nov-1949	3	485
Stumbo, Tracy	24-Oct-1974	13	85
Stumbo, Vernon	18-Aug-1974	13	33
Stumbo, Walter	15-Nov-1949	6	385
Stumbo, Wentz	24-Oct-1949	5	18
Sturgill, Adam	9-Jan-1956	8	6
Sturgill, Aner	12-Nov-1949	5	40
Sturgill, Arthur	20-Dec-1957	8	166
Sturgill, Charley	4-Feb-1950	4	306
Sturgill, Clephis	9-Oct-1949	4	587
Sturgill, Earnest	10-Feb-1950	4	354
Sturgill, Edward	14-Dec-1949	10	28
Sturgill, Gene	22-Sep-1949	3	256
Sturgill, Harlie	13-Mar-1950	12	244
Sturgill, Harlie	14-Mar-1950	12	243
Sturgill, James	16-Nov-1948	10	210
Sturgill, Joe	11-Dec-1922	1	235
Sturgill, Monroe	8-Oct-1949	3	292
Sturgill, Norman	9-Dec-1949	4	45
Sturgill, Robert	13-Aug-1948	2	218
Sturgill, Robert Irvan	20-Dec-1956	7	271
Sturgill, Ronnie Gene	10-Apr-1974	14	219
Sullivan, James	24-Apr-1958	11	30
Sutphin, Sidney	25-Sep-1967	7	406
Sutton, Ed	24-Jun-1923	1	176
Sweeney, Frank	1-Apr-1982	14	43
Sweeney, Starlin	17-Mar-1958	8	39
Sword, Charles	22-Oct-1963	9	195
Sword, Christopher Columbus	20-Feb-1975	13	112
Sword, Ernest	16-Jul-1957	8	26
Sword, Russ	2-May-1973	12	1
Symon, David	23-Sep-1976	13	288
Symon, David Harold	23-Sep-1976	14	26
Tackett, Andrew	12-Dec-1948	11	13
Tackett, Andy	29-Oct-1949	3	429
Tackett, Arnold	10-Nov-1949	12	153
Tackett, Arnold	10-May-1951	12	154
Tackett, Arnold	1-Dec-1956	7	342
Tackett, Arthur	30-Oct-1947	2	22
Tackett, Arthur	1-Aug-1956	7	194
Tackett, Benjamin	14-Jan-1950	6	41
Tackett, Bobby G.	5-Sep-1971	11	236
Tackett, Bobby P.	10-Aug-1978	13	364
Tackett, Carl	28-Aug-1963	10	148
Tackett, Charles	31-Oct-1949	11	49
Tackett, Charles	18-Oct-1950	6	152
Tackett, Charlie	26-Sep-1947	2	197
Tackett, Charlie	14-Mar-1950	12	139
Tackett, Chester	14-Apr-1972	11	554
Tackett, Claude	21-Jan-1950	4	238
Tackett, Clifford	30-Jul-1949	3	114
Tackett, Clifford	9-Dec-1949	4	40
Tackett, Clifford	8-Mar-1957	10	160
Tackett, Curtis	1-Mar-1972	11	540
Tackett, Delzie	6-May-1957	7	335
Tackett, Denzil	18-Dec-1949	5	447
Tackett, Donald B.	7-Nov-1968	11	322
Tackett, Dorpha	12-Jan-1969	11	164
Tackett, Douglas	24-Apr-1951	6	392
Tackett, Earl	22-Feb-1950	5	483
Tackett, Edmond	1-Feb-1949	2	280
Tackett, Elmer	21-Mar-1952	6	584
Tackett, Elwood	16-Jan-1954	5	524
Tackett, Elzie	26-Apr-1956	7	175
Tackett, Emitt	15-Dec-1949	5	536
Tackett, Evan	4-Jan-1950	4	204
Tackett, Everett	23-May-1949	2	305
Tackett, Ezra	13-Dec-1949	4	373
Tackett, Forrest	15-Nov-1956	7	258
Tackett, Foster	3-Feb-1950	4	324
Tackett, Freddie	4-Nov-1975	13	201
Tackett, Gary	10-Jan-1975	13	159
Tackett, Herbert	6-Dec-1962	9	124
Tackett, Herman	1-Jul-1970	14	21
Tackett, Ishmael	26-Jun-1960	8	313
Tackett, J.B.	26-Aug-1949	3	157
Tackett, James	8-Oct-1964	10	182
Tackett, James Jr.	7-Dec-1949	4	7
Tackett, Joe	7-Feb-1950	4	571
Tackett, Joseph	2-Aug-1923	1	202
Tackett, Joseph	17-Nov-1949	3	502
Tackett, Joseph Jr.	26-Jan-1950	4	319
Tackett, Kenneth	24-Nov-1949	3	510
Tackett, Larry D.	30-Apr-1975	13	149
Tackett, Larry R.	7-Feb-1974	12	92
Tackett, Lester	3-Jan-1950	4	103
Tackett, Linville	18-Oct-1949	3	393
Tackett, Logan	16-Oct-1949	4	412
Tackett, Lynn	12-Sep-1972	11	590
Tackett, Marvin	31-Oct-1958	8	109
Tackett, Noah	27-Feb-1959	8	147
Tackett, Paul	17-Sep-1974	13	47
Tackett, Pearl	22-Jun-1949	3	118
Tackett, Raymond	1-Nov-1949	6	241
Tackett, Raymond	21-Oct-1950	6	543
Tackett, Raymond	4-Dec-1950	6	242
Tackett, Richard	29-Aug-1949	3	603
Tackett, Richard	8-Nov-1949	3	492
Tackett, Richard	24-May-1957	10	39
Tackett, Robert	14-Dec-1956	7	291
Tackett, Robert L.	18-Aug-1974	13	38
Tackett, Rodney Gene	21-Nov-1995	14	176
Tackett, Roy L.	29-Jan-1961	8	330
Tackett, Ura	3-Aug-1972	12	12
Tackett, Victor	10-Sep-1958	8	197
Tackett, Walk L.	26-Oct-1972	11	344
Tackett, Wallace	30-Aug-1953	7	28
Tackett, Walton	6-Apr-1950	5	223
Tackett, William	1-Oct-1961	11	219
Taylor, Allen	27-Nov-1949	3	557
Taylor, Alvin	22-Nov-1949	5	34
Taylor, Bill	15-Aug-1958	8	88
Taylor, Charles Homer	23-Feb-1973	14	62
Taylor, Corbette	24-Apr-1950	14	184
Taylor, Ellis Beecher	15-Jun-1966	12	14
Taylor, Goble	11-Nov-1955	7	148
Taylor, Joe	5-Aug-1953	7	24
Taylor, Linda Jean	8-Oct-1984	14	264
Taylor, Linda Jean	8-Oct-1984	14	266
Taylor, Linda Jean	8-Oct-1984	14	268
Taylor, Troy	11-Sep-1951	7	112
Taylor, William	3-Jul-1979	12	250
Tendziegloski, Roman	11-Oct-1949	6	183
Terry, Clarence	30-Aug-1957	7	387
Terry, Irettes	15-Jun-1951	6	438
Terry, Irettes C.	15-Dec-1949	6	442
Terry, Jack	29-Nov-1976	13	298
Terry, James	14-Apr-1950	6	67
Terry, Joe Jr.	6-Dec-1949	4	464
Terry, John J.	18-Jan-1950	4	265
Terry, Quentin	26-Jan-1950	10	164
Terry, Thomas	12-Nov-1950	6	484
Thacker, Eugene	23-Aug-1960	14	234
Thacker, Frank	7-Oct-1949	6	407
Thacker, Homer	20-Jan-1950	5	114
Thacker, Marion	1-Nov-1955	7	156
Thacker, Noah Dewey Jr.	16-Oct-1949	5	11
Thacker, Rufus	13-Nov-1950	6	456
Thacker, Samuel	7-Jun-1949	3	49
Thacker, Virgil	19-Apr-1951	6	476
Thomas, Douglas	4-Apr-1979	13	400
Thomas, Harold	8-Apr-1965	11	42
Thomas, Harold	8-Apr-1967	11	207
Thomas, John	26-Oct-1986	13	447
Thomas, Lawerence	28-Sep-1923	9	361
Thomas, Millard	2-Oct-1949	3	283
Thomas, Oid	14-Oct-1947	2	2
Thomas, Robert	26-Oct-1986	13	448
Thomas, William	27-Jan-1951	6	347
Thomas, William	2-Apr-1951	6	396
Thompson, Agriss	13-Nov-1921	1	606
Thompson, Donald Martin	2-Mar-1980	14	191
Thompson, Gale	28-Nov-1949	6	629
Thompson, Gale	22-Nov-1950	6	628
Thompson, John	21-Oct-1947	2	12
Thompson, Johnny	28-Feb-1973	12	312
Thompson, Leslie	3-May-1962	9	233
Thompson, Leslie	25-Mar-1964	9	232
Thompson, Paul	4-Jan-1973	12	13
Thompson, Russell	18-Jan-1950	4	239
Thompson, Ted	14-Dec-1961	9	49
Thompson, Thomas Burton Jr.	1-Feb-1963	9	132
Thornsberry, Earl	2-Apr-1975	13	140
Thornsberry, Ed	14-Dec-1949	7	129
Thornsberry, George	27-Nov-1949	5	174
Thornsberry, Jackie	27-Apr-1976	13	260
Thornsberry, Jeffery Miles	30-Nov-2002	15	39
Thornsberry, Jeffery Miles	30-Nov-2002	15	39
Thornsberry, Johnnie	10-Jul-1946	2	75
Thornsberry, Lawerence J.	9-Jul-1970	11	398
Thornsberry, Olby	17-Jan-1950	10	75
Thornsberry, Phillip	31-Mar-1992	12	332
Thornsberry, Salmer	1-Jul-1950	4	466
Thornsbury, Gordon	25-Jan-1972	11	533
Thorpe, Ollie J.	13-Nov-1949	11	311
Tibbs, Arthur	26-Mar-1950	5	220
Tieche, Thomas	8-Apr-1956	7	420
Tieche, Thomas	9-Jan-1957	7	421
Tincher, Lonnie	15-Dec-1971	11	518
Tipton, Larry D.	1-Aug-1965	11	97
Trimble, James	19-Dec-1961	9	57
Trimble, Jerry R.	6-Aug-1962	9	181
Triplett, Eyvind	1-Apr-1962	9	73
Triplett, Eyvind Ray	3-Apr-1958	8	19
Triplett, Hollie	4-Dec-1949	4	351
Triplett, James	23-Dec-1971	11	524
Triplett, Virgie	16-Sep-1947	2	87
Triplett, Willie A.	1-Nov-1949	3	459
Trusty, Alvin	15-Dec-1947	2	126
Trusty, Arnold	30-Jun-1922	1	35
Trusty, R.B.	2-Oct-1952	6	606
Tufts, Carl L.	31-Oct-1949	4	203
Tufts, Curtis W.	19-Jun-1950	5	445
Tufts, John David Jr.	4-Mar-1950	5	527
Tufts, William Randall	4-Apr-1973	11	332
Turner, Alfred	26-May-1977	13	332
Turner, Andy	16-Nov-1922	2	7
Turner, Bill	4-May-1970	11	300
Turner, Billy J.	2-Mar-1959	8	176
Turner, Clarence	20-Feb-1972	11	539
Turner, Edgar	10-Sep-1947	1	145
Turner, Edgar	8-Jul-1949	3	82
Turner, Ezra	4-Mar-1950	4	505
Turner, Freddie	21-Apr-1949	5	243
Turner, Green	26-Feb-1923	1	254
Turner, Hatler	18-Apr-1950	4	591
Turner, Hershel	2-May-1946	2	99

Name	Disc. Date	Book	Page
Turner, James	30-Sep-1949	6	126
Turner, Joe	13-Dec-1950	6	244
Turner, John	1-Oct-1949	6	319
Turner, John	22-Nov-1949	3	579
Turner, John	8-Jan-1951	6	321
Turner, Johnathan	2-Nov-1972	11	606
Turner, Novis	12-Oct-1919	3	333
Turner, Orvil	9-Jan-1950	9	339
Turner, Orville	1-Jan-1950	4	189
Turner, Oscar	5-Aug-1949	3	167
Turner, Paul	13-Sep-1957	8	79
Turner, Phillip	13-Mar-1974	12	106
Turner, Richard L.	14-Feb-1950	4	417
Turner, Shannon	26-Jan-1950	6	337
Turner, Shiron	2-Mar-1975	13	119
Turner, Tennyson	24-Oct-1958	8	103
Turner, Terry	18-May-1972	11	569
Turner, Thomas	21-Feb-1923	1	204
Turner, Vance	15-Jan-1950	9	299
Turner, William	6-Jul-1972	11	617
Turpin, Harry L. Jr.	6-Nov-1949	4	632
Tussey, Frank V.	7-Apr-1950	5	277
Tussey, Fred	6-Dec-1949	3	621
Tussey, Gordon	26-Feb-1950	6	354
Tussey, Gordon J.	5-Nov-1973	12	57
Tussey, Harmon	6-Jul-1950	4	633
Tussey, Ike	25-Mar-1947	2	69
Tussey, Iseral	16-Jan-1948	2	68
Tussey, Joe	5-Oct-1949	3	306
Tussey, Lindsey	19-Dec-1922	1	186
Tuttle, Burlan	15-Apr-1947	2	103
Tuttle, Ellis	29-Aug-1957	7	399
Tuttle, Forrest Jr.	19-Oct-1972	14	117
Tuttle, Granett	12-Sep-1972	11	587
Tuttle, Virgle	10-Jul-1949	11	32
Underwood, Frank	20-Sep-1949	3	351
Underwood, Grady	11-Nov-1962	9	223
Underwood, Harvey	8-Nov-1962	9	224
Van Horn, Phenious	20-Mar-1953	8	226
Van Horn, Phenious	16-Apr-1959	8	209
Vance, Doffey	2-Dec-1949	4	342
Vance, Hayes Jr.	24-Jun-1975	13	163
Vance, James	13-Sep-1949	3	193
Vance, James M.	14-May-1986	12	277
Vance, James Michael	24-Jun-1981	14	157
Vance, Jesse	24-Jun-1923	1	110
Vance, Jesse J.	15-Nov-1949	3	497
Vance, Joe	7-Nov-1949	3	610
Vance, Kellie	15-Oct-1921	1	60
Vance, Robert	9-Feb-1948	6	598
Vance, Stuart Edwin	11-Feb-1975	14	68
Vance, Thurman	18-Feb-1950	4	590
Vance, Thurman	15-Aug-1951	6	515
Vance, William	27-Jan-1950	7	214
Vance, William	24-Jan-1953	7	251
Vance, William J.	31-Oct-1956	7	250
Vanderpool, Colin	1-Mar-1966	11	148
Vanderpool, Danny Lee	19-Jun-1973	12	17
Vanderpool, Edsel	15-Feb-1948	2	13
Vanderpool, Edsel	15-Apr-1950	2	346
Vanderpool, Elliot	24-Jan-1950	9	313
Vanderpool, Elliot	16-May-1956	9	293
Vanderpool, Herman	29-May-1969	11	337
Vanderpool, Mario	20-Nov-1949	5	76
Vanderpool, Oscar	16-Jun-1949	6	113
Vanderpool, Ottis James	7-Nov-1949	5	62
Vanderpool, Pete	7-May-1923	1	57
Vanderpool, Raymod	11-May-1968	11	269
Vanderpool, Talmadge	21-Oct-1949	3	372
Vanderpool, Wesley Paul		15	61
Vanhoose, Billy	15-Oct-1975	13	199
Vanhoose, Edmund	27-Mar-1951	6	521
Vanhoose, Graber	30-Nov-1949	10	15
Vanhoose, Herman	9-Jan-1925	1	53
Vanhoose, Ralph	29-Aug-1957	7	390
Vanover, Jack	26-Feb-1974	14	101
Varney, Paul Edward Jr.	1-Aug-2001	15	21
Vaughn, Clyde	16-Sep-1949	6	181
Vaughn, David	14-Dec-1959	8	249
Vaughn, Garland	19-Nov-1949	6	171
Vaughn, George	10-Jan-1957	8	250
Vaughn, Glenn	21-Mar-1972	11	551
Vaughn, Jake	4-Feb-1949	11	18
Vaughn, Martin	3-Nov-1950	6	161

Name	Disc. Date	Book	Page
Vaughn, Ronald	11-Nov-1963	9	201
Vaughn, William	31-Oct-1949	3	608
Vaughn, Atlas	31-Dec-1950	6	527
Vicars, George W.	30-Oct-1973	11	354
Vicars, Hubert	21-May-1951	6	571
Vicars, James	12-Mar-1950	5	207
Vicars, Rex David	7-Dec-1992	14	1
Vincent, Billy	22-Jul-1958	8	61
Vincent, Billy	12-Aug-1971	11	483
Vincent, John	12-Oct-1953	7	40
Vinson, Richard Fletcher Jr.	29-Jul-1963	9	169
Vogel, Carol	27-Jul-1980	12	212
Waddle, Joe	14-Dec-1949	4	32
Waddle, Kyle Ray		15	59-60
Waddle, Willie	2-Dec-1949	10	31
Waddles, Diamond	6-May-1963	9	150
Waddles, Elzie	6-Jul-1947	7	64
Waddles, Howard	1-Aug-1960	9	3
Wade, Paul	21-Nov-1978	13	386
Wadkins, Monroe	23-Sep-1949	3	226
Wadkins, Nero	5-Dec-1949	4	3
Wakeland, Estell Winfred	5-Feb-1950	5	179
Wakeland, Estell Winfred	8-Mar-1950	5	181
Walk, Ray R.	12-Aug-1946	2	118
Walker, Clifford	8-Aug-1958	8	75
Walker, Darvin	9-Apr-1959	13	198
Walker, Denman	16-Jan-1949	6	122
Walker, Guy	20-Oct-1949	4	39
Walker, John	14-Jul-1963	9	167
Walker, William	8-Jun-1923	1	210
Wallace, Ernest	1-Aug-1955	7	142
Wallace, Franklin	24-May-1961	9	30
Wallace, Harry	5-Jun-1961	9	22
Wallace, James	26-Jan-1950	4	331
Wallace, James S.	22-Dec-1949	10	3
Wallen, Billy	31-Jul-1955	9	331
Wallen, Buster	2-Oct-1955	7	226
Wallen, Earnest	9-Jan-1951	6	446
Wallen, Edward	18-Jun-1973	14	42
Wallen, Edward	11-Mar-1974	15	42
Wallen, Edward	23-Jan-1979	14	2
Wallen, Ernest	12-Sep-1949	3	189
Wallen, George	11-Feb-1950	7	83
Wallen, J.B.	10-Dec-1954	7	359
Wallen, Joe	12-Feb-1948	12	130
Wallen, John	25-Dec-1949	4	500
Wallen, Johnnie	12-Jan-1950	4	257
Wallen, Leo	15-Jan-1950	4	181
Wallen, Leo	17-Sep-1955	10	29
Wallen, Lewis	24-Sep-1949	4	84
Wallen, Monroe	25-Jan-1950	6	500
Wallen, Odias Gene	9-Feb-1966	14	181
Wallen, Odias Gene	1-Apr-1968	14	179
Wallen, Ollie	14-Jul-1949	3	95
Wallen, Oscar Jr.	7-Mar-1973	11	623
Wallen, Paul R.	9-Oct-1947	2	141
Wallen, Shawn Dale	1-Sep-1994	14	259
Wallen, Wendell	18-Aug-1974	13	30
Wallen, William	11-Oct-1922	1	153
Wallen, William Tavis	18-Apr-1974	14	48
Wallen, Willie	22-Nov-1949	6	368
Wallen, Woodrow	9-Dec-1959	8	242
Walls, Henry	27-Jul-1948	2	209
Walters, Bob	5-Apr-1962	9	72
Walters, Clifton	5-Jan-1950	4	137
Walters, John	24-Mar-1982	12	222
Walters, Junior	12-Oct-1949	10	82
Walters, Marvin	27-Aug-1949	3	156
Walters, Marvin	23-Aug-1953	11	43
Walters, Marvin	26-Aug-1956	11	44
Walters, Marvin	18-Dec-1960	11	45
Walters, Robert D.	18-Sep-2000	15	18
Walters, Robert Dwayne	18-Sep-2000	15	18
Walters, Russell	16-Dec-1949	4	83
Walters, Victor	21-Dec-1949	4	77
Walters, Wayne	10-Sep-1975	13	220
Ward, Albert	10-Nov-1948	2	241
Ward, Arthur	16-Feb-1961	9	68
Ward, Bennie	5-Dec-1948	2	253
Ward, Billy	6-Oct-1975	13	197
Ward, Donald	1-Dec-1971	11	516
Ward, Elmer	19-Aug-1956	7	213
Ward, Freddie Dean	22-Mar-1968	11	275
Ward, John	24-Jun-1923	1	95

Name	Disc. Date	Book	Page
Ward, John Jr.	24-Oct-1957	7	427
Ward, Mitchell	4-Sep-1949	3	182
Ward, Otis	18-Nov-1949	3	533
Ward, Perry	10-Oct-1958	8	218
Ward, Ray	10-Dec-1949	4	38
Ward, Raymond	15-Aug-1960	8	294
Ward, Raymond	15-Aug-1960	10	170
Ward, Richard	9-Oct-1951	5	480
Ward, Ronald	5-Mar-1972	11	545
Ward, Sonny	13-Oct-1949	3	355
Ward, William	10-Oct-1949	3	477
Ward, Winfred	13-Sep-1949	3	203
Warman, John Bell	18-Nov-1949	5	42
Warman, Leo Ted	18-Aug-1958	8	70
Warrens, Donald	9-May-1958	8	29
Warrens, Donald	31-Jul-1964	10	118
Warrens, Earl	11-Aug-1949	6	285
Warrens, Willie	14-Sep-1949	3	272
Warrix, Charles C.	1-Aug-1967	11	286
Warrix, Charles Clay	13-Aug-1963	9	170
Warrix, Curtis	19-Sep-1949	3	238
Warrix, Floyd	2-Jul-1945	2	96
Warrix, Frank	25-Aug-1947	2	52
Warrix, William	18-Dec-1949	5	103
Warrix, Zean	3-Oct-1949	3	277
Watkins, Cecil	13-Jul-1970	11	187
Watkins, Edmond Jr.	6-Dec-1995	14	174
Watkins, Elmer	5-Dec-1949	10	139
Watkins, Everett	13-Mar-1957	7	311
Watkins, Kenneth	26-Sep-1963	9	189
Watkins, Oscar	11-Nov-1949	5	507
Watkins, Rondle	13-Feb-1950	4	378
Watkins, Teddy Junior	14-Jan-1993	14	124
Watsell, Ray R.	19-Dec-1949	4	441
Watson, Cecil	3-Feb-1953	6	621
Watson, Clayton	13-Mar-1951	6	560
Watson, Donald	5-Mar-1972	11	547
Watson, John	24-Dec-1949	4	97
Watson, Paul	3-Jan-1950	10	196
Watson, Paul	3-Jan-1950	10	197
Watson, Sidney	11-Jan-1950	6	377
Watson, Vaughn	7-Mar-1975	13	317
Watson, Willie	21-Mar-1968	12	163
Watson, Willie	25-Jul-1974	13	354
Watts, Jessie	27-Sep-1949	6	427
Watts, Larry	10-Mar-1983	13	435
Watts, Richard Anderson Jr.	27-Oct-1977	13	346
Waugh, Dencil	12-May-1972	11	563
Weaver, Benjamin Lloyd	19-Jul-1978	13	360
Webb, Alfred	4-May-1951	6	405
Webb, Arnold	7-Jan-1950	4	188
Webb, Billy	24-Jun-1971	11	459
Webb, Donald	23-Jun-1969	11	177
Webb, Glen	26-Mar-1976	13	251
Webb, Glenn	21-Sep-1980	12	208
Webb, Hobert	13-May-1974	13	4
Webb, James	16-Dec-1949	6	533
Webb, James A.	17-Dec-1971	11	519
Webb, James E.	3-Jan-1951	9	309
Webb, James O.	20-Jul-1926	12	136
Webb, Kaynard	11-Dec-1949	4	33
Webb, Kenneth	20-Jun-1976	13	273
Webb, Ralph	11-Sep-1949	4	490
Webb, Ronald	7-Oct-1949	3	305
Webb, Roy Jonathan	28-Nov-1983	14	133
Webb, Roy Jonathan	1-May-1994	14	134
Webb, Talt	19-Nov-1906	9	207
Webb, Walter	20-Oct-1949	3	445
Webb, Walter	5-Jun-1963	9	159
Webb, Willie	30-May-1923	1	123
Weddington, Alex	2-Nov-1949	3	457
Weddington, Grant Jr.	24-Apr-1950	5	261
Weddington, Harry	28-Mar-1951	4	473
Weddington, Joe	23-Jan-1950	5	151
Weddington, William	27-Apr-1923	1	133
Wellman, Edward Alan	5-Jun-1997	14	225
Wells, Alton	22-Dec-1949	4	82
Wells, Andrew	24-Mar-1923	1	252
Wells, Andrew	24-Apr-1924	1	78
Wells, Andrew	24-Apr-1924	1	251
Wells, Bill	4-Jun-1922	1	189
Wells, Billie	13-Aug-1951	16	514
Wells, Carl	26-Mar-1950	5	430
Wells, Darrell	16-Jun-1969	11	456

Name	Disc. Date	Book	Page
Wells, Denver	3-Nov-1950	6	180
Wells, Edward	22-Jul-1949	3	108
Wells, Eugene	2-Feb-1947	2	174
Wells, Eugene	24-Nov-1949	5	58
Wells, Ferman	10-Apr-1950	5	244
Wells, Forrest	9-Jun-1952	6	582
Wells, Freddie	1-Dec-1957	7	444
Wells, George	14-Sep-1949	3	233
Wells, Grant	12-Dec-1948	2	267
Wells, Harry	1-May-1973	12	5
Wells, Haskel	2-Jul-1957	7	350
Wells, Homer	26-Jun-1950	4	605
Wells, Homer	16-Feb-1975	13	109
Wells, Jack	7-Dec-1949	6	246
Wells, Jack	12-Dec-1950	6	248
Wells, James	10-Dec-1951	6	538
Wells, James D.	10-Feb-1963	9	133
Wells, James E.	22-Sep-1948	2	225
Wells, Junior	19-Aug-1957	7	418
Wells, Leland	24-May-1950	10	195
Wells, Mary	11-Aug-1947	2	150
Wells, Melvin	9-Jan-1950	5	429
Wells, Melvin	9-Jan-1950	10	106
Wells, Milford	29-Oct-1950	6	176
Wells, Millard	22-Jun-1923	2	229
Wells, Orville	5-Feb-1947	2	97
Wells, Otis	18-Jan-1948	2	214
Wells, Palmer	20-Oct-1949	3	366
Wells, Paul	2-May-1962	9	75
Wells, Richard	13-Jan-1950	6	154
Wells, Ronald R.	17-Sep-1964	11	386
Wells, Sammie	14-Aug-1960	10	52
Wells, Samuel	16-May-1950	5	528
Wells, William	8-Dec-1950	6	277
Wells, William	19-Nov-1956	7	256
West, Charles	5-Mar-1974	13	438
West, Willie	11-Mar-1950	6	13
West, Willie	7-Aug-1950	6	11
West, Willie	7-Aug-1950	6	12
Westbrook, Virgil	16-Feb-1948	7	426
Whicker, Christoper Reed	9-Jan-2001	15	17
Whitaker, Cledis	8-Oct-1949	3	315
Whitaker, Cleveland	18-Mar-1923	1	34
Whitaker, Edgel	6-Nov-1949	3	447
Whitaker, Estill	8-Oct-1949	6	34
Whitaker, Johnny	3-Apr-1950	5	229
Whitaker, Nero	15-Oct-2002	7	157
Whitaker, Robert	22-Sep-1949	10	186
Whitaker, Willie	26-Feb-1922	1	605
White, Bobby	2-Aug-1962	9	102
Whitt, Allen	1-Dec-1952	6	613
Whitt, Arnold	12-Nov-1949	12	316-317
Whitt, Danny Neil	28-Feb-1991	12	311
Whitt, Denzil	1-Apr-1950	4	615
Whitt, Ed	5-Apr-1957	11	66
Whitt, Frank	3-Dec-1949	3	604
Whitt, Robert	6-Feb-1957	8	31
Whittaker, Charlie	6-Oct-1949	3	279
Whitten, Robert	8-Jun-1955	7	282
Wicker, Carl	21-Mar-1948	2	333
Wicker, Fonza	5-Feb-1923	1	243
Wicker, Garland	28-Jun-1949	3	68
Wicker, James	13-Oct-1949	3	326
Wicker, Kendell	3-Jun-1951	7	82
Wicker, Ronald	10-Feb-1975	13	103
Wicker, Willie	15-Nov-1949	3	568
Wilburn, Phil	3-May-1972	12	203
Wilcox Ursal	24-Jan-1957	7	303
Wilcox, Donald	16-Oct-1949	5	526
Wilcox, Etta	1-Jun-1961	9	13

Name	Disc. Date	Book	Page
Wilcox, Randall Dwight	29-Apr-1992	12	340
Wilcox, Woodrow	1-Mar-1950	4	431
Wildman, Robert W.	1-Oct-1977	12	158
Wiley, Carl	6-Jul-1949	3	96
Wiley, Ernest	20-Dec-1949	5	156
Wiley, Gary	11-Jan-1965	10	198
Wiley, Jimmie	16-Apr-1965	11	127
Wiley, Jimmy	16-Apr-1961	11	126
Wiley, Vencil Herald	15-May-1956	7	178
Wilkinson, Garland	19-Feb-1950	4	393
Williams, Amos	20-Nov-1947	2	314
Williams, Charles	10-Sep-1953	7	106
Williams, Delmer	1-Sep-1950	6	379
Williams, Don	5-Jun-1956	5	532
Williams, Donnie	22-Aug-1975	13	185
Williams, Everett	26-Jun-1951	7	52
Williams, Everett	20-Aug-1953	13	427
Williams, Forrest	24-Sep-1949	3	264
Williams, Henry	6-Aug-1921	1	170
Williams, Henry	25-Jun-1923	1	169
Williams, James	2-Apr-1923	1	200
Williams, James	9-Jul-1952	6	586
Williams, John	23-Nov-1960	10	116
Williams, Josh	24-Jan-1923	1	175
Williams, Maurice	27-Mar-1949	4	620
Williams, Mitchell	25-Jun-1974	13	19
Williams, Noah	21-Apr-1919	3	16
Williams, Palmer	11-Jul-1950	5	448
Williams, Ralph	15-Nov-1949	4	57
Williams, Sammy L.	12-Sep-1972	11	586
Williams, William	28-Dec-1950	6	306
Williamson, Bill	28-Apr-1951	6	399
Williamson, Bobby	9-May-1956	7	182
Williamson, Charles Dewayne	23-Feb-1976	14	67
Williamson, Gordon	12-Feb-1950	4	366
Williamson, Howard	5-Oct-1949	3	281
Williamson, James	11-Feb-1951	7	139
Williamson, James L.	5-Dec-1949	7	138
Williamson, Marshall	30-Jun-1970	11	397
Williamson, Marshall	16-Apr-1975	13	394
Williamson, Oliver	15-Dec-1949	4	65
Williamson, Ronnie	19-Nov-1977	12	264
Williamson, Ronnie	19-Nov-1977	12	265
Williamson, Ronnie	20-Aug-1983	12	266
Williamson, Ronnie	20-Aug-1983	12	267
Williamson, Ronnie	14-Mar-1988	12	261-262
Willis, Warner	13-Sep-1956	7	254
Wills, Charles	31-Aug-1973	12	26
Wills, Clayton	29-Nov-1962	9	122
Wills, Ollie	25-Sep-1949	3	324
Wills, Randall	2-Oct-1975	13	195
Wills, Randall	20-Nov-1980	13	415
Wills, Ronald Eugene	28-Jun-1978	15	77
Wills, Susan	6-Jun-1948	2	194
Wills, William	16-Sep-1975	13	194
Wilson, Elmon	30-Mar-1923	11	108
Wilson, Larry Wendell	5-May-1982	14	71
Wilson, Michael	31-Jul-1972	11	578
Wilson, Pete	11-Dec-1949	4	195
Wilson, Rex	12-Feb-1951	6	572
Wilson, Trimble	29-Jul-1956	7	189
Wirghtson, Arthur	22-Apr-1950	4	553
Wise, Thomas	10-Jan-1974	12	81
Wnek, Jimmy	1-Dec-1971	11	523
Wohlford, John	30-Jul-1950	5	424
Wohlford, Warren Carl	16-Apr-1950	5	254
Wood, Denver Dale	17-Aug-1982	14	41
Wood, Denver Dale	17-Aug-1982	14	41
Woods, Carl	15-Aug-1947	6	459
Woods, Clarence Jr.	18-Mar-1975	15	89

Name	Disc. Date	Book	Page
Woods, Corbett	9-Apr-1951	6	591
Woods, Dennie	4-Apr-1950	5	237
Woods, Elmer	5-Feb-1961	8	329A
Woods, John	13-Nov-1951	6	529
Woods, John H.	12-Feb-1968	11	26
Woods, Ray	31-Dec-1949	4	625
Woods, Vernon Ray	20-Feb-1976	13	384
Woods, Willard	15-Sep-1949	3	198
Woody, Charles Jr.	3-Nov-1949	3	452
Woody, Donald	19-Dec-1949	4	317
Wooten, Roderick Allen	23-May-1995	14	156
Workman, Burns	30-Aug-1949	6	140
Wright, Benjamin	10-Mar-1977	13	312
Wright, Billy	4-Jun-1951	6	444
Wright, Burnis	22-Mar-1950	5	464
Wright, Burns	13-Dec-1948	2	259
Wright, Charlie	1-Jun-1950	5	304
Wright, Edgar	24-Mar-1940	1	139
Wright, Edgar	14-Apr-1953	12	280
Wright, Edgil	11-Jan-1950	6	16
Wright, Ell	4-Mar-1973	11	330
Wright, Grover	30-Dec-1958	8	126
Wright, Hagar	26-Sep-1949	3	286
Wright, Harry	16-Nov-1973	12	60
Wright, Henry	20-Nov-1922	1	225
Wright, Henry	18-Dec-1949	4	72
Wright, Jack	18-Feb-1968	11	268
Wright, James	1-Jun-1984	12	224
Wright, James H.	11-Mar-1949	4	612
Wright, Lee	30-Jul-1946	9	314
Wright, Lee	14-Feb-1950	4	374
Wright, Otis	16-Dec-1949	4	62
Wright, Ralph	28-Sep-1949	5	15
Wright, Randall	3-Oct-1976	13	289
Wright, Raymond	14-Nov-1950	10	66
Wright, Roy	27-Jan-1977	13	339
Wright, Sterling	25-Jul-1949	4	171
Wright, Willie	18-Mar-1923	1	39
Wright, Willie Jr.	14-Jan-1950	4	146
Wyatt, George	21-Dec-1948	2	321
Wyatt, Richard	6-Nov-1948	2	239
Wyatt, Tipton	4-Mar-1975	13	125
Wyskiver, Gary Lee	20-Oct-1971	11	503
Yates, Andrew	8-Mar-1923	1	232
Yates, Andy	22-Sep-1949	6	30
Yates, Corbet	15-Feb-1950	4	379
Yates, Edward	18-Nov-1949	3	576
Yates, Howard	18-Nov-1949	4	367
Yates, Joe	18-Feb-1952	5	488
Yates, Kermit	31-Oct-1949	3	454
Yates, Martin	12-Oct-1949	3	316
Yates, William	8-Jan-1957	7	277
Yates, William J.	15-May-1955	7	402
Yates, William J.	17-Apr-1962	9	71
Yelder, George Thompson	3-Apr-1975	13	137
Yonts, Thomas	22-Aug-1973	12	27
York, Earl	28-Jun-1949	11	31
Younce, Joe	2-Oct-1947	9	319
Younce, John	9-Nov-1949	3	614
Younce, Ricky	13-Jul-1988	12	278
Younce, Wendell	4-Aug-1970	11	304
Young, Charles	26-Jan-1950	4	275
Young, Chester	23-Sep-1949	3	273
Young, Gordon Craig	12-Jun-1977	14	87
Young, Ricky	13-Jul-1988	12	278
Yount, Martin	27-Jul-1949	4	201
Zemo, Kenneth Edward	13-Jul-1978	14	6
Zetz, Louis Lukie	13-Sep-1955	11	73
Zetz, Rudolph	17-Feb-1950	11	101

Remember Their Bravery

Honoring those who served our country and those who gave their lives to maintain our freedom

Bank with First Commonwealth Bank, we have the products to suit your every banking need.

1st First Commonwealth Bank
Member FDIC

(606) 886-2321
Toll Free 877-886-6777
www.myfcb.com

- Free Checking
- Savings
- Online Banking
- Online Bill Pay
- Keep In Touch
- IRA
- Mortgage Loans
- Consumer Loans
- Auto Loans
- Home Equity Line of Credit
- Commercial Loans
- Commercial Lending
- Health Savings Accounts

EQUAL HOUSING LENDER

We're Here For You!

First Guaranty Bank

First Guaranty Bank locally owned and operated. With two locations to serve you.

Directors/ Owners

Julius Martin – Chairman
J. Clint Martin – CEO
Greg Stumbo

Charles Johnson –CEO
Joe Burchett
Tommy N. Hall

North Lake Drive
Prestonsburg, Kentucky
41653

P.O. Box 888
36 Main Street
Martin, Kentucky 41649

No fine print.
FREE CHECKING

- No monthly service fee
- Unlimited check writing
- **FREE** VISA® Check Card
- **FREE** Online Banking & Bill Pay

Boyd, Carter, Floyd, Greenup, Johnson, Magoffin, & Pike Counties

www.cnbonline.com
866.462.BANK

 Member FDIC

The Bank for Your Life.

The Elk Horn Coal Company, LLC
544 South Lake Drive
Prestonsburg, KY 41653
Phone No. (606) 886-2330

Elk Horn proudly supports with Floyd County veterans

FLOYD COUNTY FISCAL COURT
149 South Central Avenue-Suite 9
Prestonsburg, Kentucky 41653

Telephone (606) 886-9193
TDD 810-648-6056

Fax (606) 886-1083
E-mail flcofc@yahoo.com

From left: David Layne, Larry Foster Stumbo, Gerald Derossett, Judge Executive Paul Hunt Thompson, James Alan Williams, Keith Bartley, and Jackie Owens.

Floyd County Fiscal Court is committed to providing safe, decent
And affordable housing for low-income clients with special needs.

Hall Funeral Home is one of the leading funeral homes in eastern Kentucky. Located in Martin, Kentucky in Floyd County, it is the epitome of caring service. Family owned and operated, it has become a symbol of trust and friendship.

Its origin dates back to 1947 as Hall Brothers Funeral Home, when two brothers, John C. Hall and Birchell Hall began their commitment to the community. After Birchell's retirement, John opened Hall Funeral Home in newly built, comfortably designed funeral home. With the help of his two sons, Hall Funeral Home becomes one of the premier services in the area. Since John's passing, his sons, Tommy and John C. Hall, Jr., have made a commitment to continue providing honest, affordable and quality

James H. Daniels
9-3-1934 — 6-3-2002
Founder Floyd County Historical & Genealogical Society

Prestonsburg
"Star City" of Eastern Kentucky

Nestled in the mountains, Prestonsburg is a small town with an uptown personality. Offering live entertainment & sports, historical sights and recreational resorts, Prestonsburg is the ideal destination for a fun family visit!

* Archer Park * Court Street Shopping * Floyd County Justice Center *
* Jenny Wiley Theatre * Jenny Wiley Pioneer Festival *
* Jenny Wiley State Resort Park * Lancer Park * May House *
* Mountain Arts Center *
* Ranier Racing Museum * River Park

"Prestonsburg - A great place to visit; an even better place to live!"
- Mayor Jerry Fannin

MAC - Home of Kentucky Opry

A Family-Style Show Featuring Country Music, Gospel, Pop, Bluegrass, Comedy & Dancing

Summer Season Shows:
Friday, June 30; Friday, July 7; Friday, July 14;
Friday, July 21; Friday, July 28; Friday, August 4;
& Saturday, September 2
ALL SHOWS: 8:00 PM
Call for pricing.

MAC will also present this Summer -
Billy Currington, George Jones,
Billy Ray Cyrus, Percy Sledge,
Charles Johnson & the Revivers,
& The Singing Cookes

Call 886-2623 for tickets
or Toll-Free 1-888-MAC-ARTS
for updates to schedule: www.macarts.com

Prestonsburg
The Star City of Eastern Kentucky

Prestonsburg is nestled in the scenic foot hills of Eastern Kentucky and is the #1 destination for motor coach travel. The evening family music entertainment is professional and diverse. Daytime attractions are filled with cultural and heritage charm. Our Convention & Visitors Bureau handles every visit with down home mountain style hospitality.

Evening Entertainment

Mountain Arts Center
1,050 seats, state-of-the-art lights & sound

Jenny Wiley Theatre
Three Off-Broadway-Type Musicals each Summer

The Kentucky Opry

Saturday nights in the MAC – "Best local show this side of the Smokey Mountains"

The Legend Of Jenny Wiley

MUSIC MAN footloose

Daytime Attractions

Loretta Lynn's Homeplace

Mayo Church

East Kentucky Science Center

Other attractions include: Van Lear Coal Mining Museum, David Crafts, Historic May House
Motels: Jenny Wiley State Resort Park, Holiday Inn, Comfort Suites, Microtel, Super 8
Restaurants: Jerry's, Billy Ray's, May Lodge, Cloud Nine, Senior Citizens Center

Prestonsburg Convention & Visitors Bureau

Kentucky UNBRIDLED SPIRIT

Now Open! RANIER RACING MUSEUM!!   1-800-844-4704
www.prestonsburgky.org 113 South Central Avenue, Prestonsburg, Kentucky, 41653

Index

A

Abbott–91
Abner–97
Adams–35, 37, 62, 84
Addington–63
Adkins–35, 37, 38, 51, 105
Adkinston–7
Africa–33
Akers–23, 33, 38, 68, 69, 70, 81, 101, 111, 116
Alien–9
Allen–23, 24, 33, 34, 38, 39, 43, 48, 54, 58, 64, 69, 74, 78, 89, 95, 103, 105, 118
Alley–18, 50, 62
Amburey–43
Amburgey–24, 39, 90
Ames–9
Anderson–30, 32, 37, 40, 65, 98, 99, 105
Argelite–45
Arrington–84
Arrowood–40
Ashcraft–118
Atkin–6
Atkinson–6, 7
Austin–4, 21
Auxier–6, 7, 8, 26
Ayers–24

B

Bacon–9
Bailey–40, 75, 96, 102
Bailey-Bamer–40
Baisden–32
Baker–6, 105, 108
Baldridge–23, 27, 30, 32, 34, 40, 41, 68, 87, 90
Baldrige–33
Ball–40
Bamer–40
Banks–70, 104
Bannon–28
Barker–7, 54, 82
Barnett–7, 12, 89
Barney–69, 70
Bartlett–98
Bartley–79, 152
Bates–6, 24, 65, 71
Bays–43, 93
Beaty–8
Bellamy–53
Benaugh–9
Benge–6
Bennington–70
Bently–101, 105
Benton–44, 45
Berger–40
Berry–34, 43
Best–73
Betten–118
Bevins–8
Biediger–89
Bigley–34
Biliter–102
Bingham–29, 35, 43, 45, 48, 88
Blackburn–28, 41, 89, 102, 107, 113, 115, 118
Blair–64
Blankenship–7, 12, 41, 76, 106
Blevins–7
Blumer–6
Blythe–8
Boggs–41, 80
Bolen–41, 72
Boling–121
Bolling–11, 12, 41, 89
Bone–69
Bonor–60
Booker–25
Booth–41, 106, 119
Boswell–103
Bouchillon–112
Bouney–6
Bowling–6, 98
Bowman–118
Bowyer–23
Boyd–47, 42, 77, 89
Bradley–12, 34, 56, 77, 89, 103, 119
Bragg–8
Branham–18, 34, 42, 43, 46, 51, 52, 55, 63, 67, 69, 70, 71, 75, 94, 120, 121
Brashear–100
Brewer–122
Brooks–9
Broughton–28
Brown–6, 8, 9, 38, 43, 57, 82, 122
Browning–120
Bruce–9
Bruemmer–63
Brunton–90
Bryant–24, 41
Bryson–8
Buchannon–97
Bullock–16
Burchett–11, 24, 27, 28, 41, 43, 60, 76, 81, 89, 94, 106, 149
Burchetts–8
Burchfield–35
Burek–6
Burga–24, 43, 61, 90, 106
Burge–6
Burgess–6, 43
Burgy–29
Burke–4, 11, 12, 18, 43, 44, 61, 64, 69, 106
Burkett–48
Burks–32
Burns–6, 7, 8
Burton–55
Bush–6, 7, 90, 100
Bustle–9
Butler–7, 23, 24, 69

C

Caines–6
Calhoun–24, 29, 32, 34, 37, 44, 54, 62, 70, 76, 86, 87, 90, 106
Callihan–44, 45, 102
Cameron–6
Campbell–36, 43, 50, 51, 106, 118
Cane–9
Canterbury–67
Carrol–45
Carson–9
Carver–106
Case–99, 106
Casebolt–80, 100
Cassady–6
Casselberry–108
Castello–35
Castle–6, 45, 49, 66, 105, 106, 118
Castner–8
Caudill–7, 11, 24, 31, 83, 92, 107
Cesco–52, 107
Chaffins–45, 90, 100
Chafin–30
Chancy–118
Chandler–6, 8
Chaplin–10
Childers–6, 7, 20, 31, 45, 94
Chumley–11
Citizens National Bank–150
Clark–6, 12, 25, 27, 31, 32, 34, 43, 45, 46, 47, 54, 90, 93, 102, 107
Click–41, 46, 56, 62, 77, 103
Clifton–73, 82
Cline–46, 90
Coats–42
Coburn–39, 45, 47, 105, 118
Cockrells–8
Coleman–46, 104, 107
Collins–7, 12, 34, 36, 46, 52, 107
Collinsworth–37
Colvin–103
Combs–7, 24, 29, 32, 47, 56, 90
Compton–64, 91, 99, 102
Comstock–44
Conley–6, 26, 47, 67, 99, 119
Conn–42, 47, 54, 59, 66, 78, 90, 94
Connelly–6, 8
Conners–42
Connors–48
Conry–51
Cook–27, 56, 107
Cooke–7
Cooley–25, 34, 48, 91, 107
Cooper–7
Corder–55
Cordill–7
Cornett–7
Cornwallis–8
Correll–34, 49
Cottengin–68
Cotton–78
Couch–30
Cox–6, 72
Crabtree–7
Craft–32, 39, 89, 113, 120
Crager–25, 48
Craig–8
Craine–13
Crawford–9, 11, 48
Crayfast–9
Creech–108
Crisp–47, 91
Crockett–92
Croft–7
Cross–98
Crow–89
Crum–6, 18
Culbertson–8
Cummings–11
Cunningham–8
Curnutte–49, 91

D

Dailey–7
Daily–92
Dale–35
Daniel–95
Daniels–4, 21, 34, 37, 74, 80, 91, 154
Davidson–23, 25, 33, 34, 35, 36, 49
Davis–6, 35, 40, 49, 59, 75, 90, 94, 100, 101, 109, 117, 118, 120, 122
Day–7, 89
Decker–35
DeLong–35, 49, 91
Delong–74
Demmitt–9
Dempsey–92
Derefield–52
DeRossett–46, 49, 50, 96
Derossett–34, 54, 60, 71, 104, 152
Desert–8
Diamond–27, 28
Dickerson–50
Dillard–9
Dillon–36, 96
Dillow–92
Dils–24, 26
Dingus–11, 25, 50, 51, 92, 95, 107, 108, 116
Dixon–37, 74, 92, 93, 95
Dollahan–80
Dollarhide–32
Dolle–18
Donaphan–9
Doniphan–9
Donohue–23
Dorton–6
Dotson–56, 57, 78, 107, 119
Drake–66
Draper–23
Dunbar–97
Duncan–30
Dunn–63
Dupuy–8
Dutko–63
Dyer–95
Dysart–8, 9

E

Easton–35
Edmonds–82
Edwards–51, 80
Elam–43
Eldridge–9, 69
Eliffson–118
Elking–51, 93
Elk Horn Coal Company–151
Ellington–7
Elliot–51, 54
Elliott–8, 11, 26, 71, 93, 120, 122
Ellis–7
Elswick–84
Ely–8
Endicott–36, 108
England–51, 63
Epling–35, 37, 93
Estep–75, 106
Evans–7, 9, 94, 98
Eve–8
Everidge–9

F

Fairchild–6, 51, 83
Fannin–35, 40, 51, 52, 87, 93, 107, 111, 112, 122
Farrow–117
Faulkner–8
Fee–9
Fenix–79
Ferguson–6, 81
Ferrell–52
Fields–52
Figuiere–45
Finney–30
First Commonwealth Bank–148
First Guaranty Bank–149
Fishback–9
Fitch–55, 99
Fitzgerald–6
Fitzpatrick–6, 7, 23, 52, 84
Flanery–25, 35, 52, 53, 56, 60, 62, 80, 122
Flanigan–11
Flannery–6, 78
Flatwood–6
Flint–32
Floyd County Fiscal Court–152
Floyd County Historical Society–4
Floyd County, Kentucky Veterans Discharges 124
Flutz–33
Foley–108
Ford–7, 11, 82
Foster–9, 50
Fouts–53
Fraley–6, 53, 94
Frances–109

Francis–6, 11, 22, 53, 34, 93, 108, 112, 120
Franklin–116
Frasure–37, 53, 119
Frazier–25, 29, 53
Frederick–9
Fritz–90
Fryzek–110
Fugitt–54
Fulton–101
Funk–78
Fuqua–8
Fyffe–80

G

Gardner–54
Garfield–25
Garland–6, 23
Garrard–8
Garrett–26, 29, 34, 36, 37, 54, 70, 71, 96, 104, 122
Garriott–11
Gayheart–39, 85
Gearhart–54
Gearheart–24, 29, 32, 37, 54, 93
General Howell–17
George–26, 31, 78, 89, 108, 109
Gholson–9
Gibson–9, 27, 54, 55, 66, 68, 109, 112, 118
Gilbert–8
Gilespie–23
Gilliam–42
Giltner–28
Goble–17, 26, 43, 55, 56, 66, 86, 87, 90, 93, 103, 104, 109, 114
Goforth–32Goodman–26, 32, 56, 82, 90
Gortney–50
Graham–6
Gray–26, 56, 61, 71, 112, 121
Grayson–8
Green–109
Greer–31, 56, 80, 88
Griffith–32, 52, 66, 88, 116, 120
Grigsby–56
Gross–54
Gunter–120
Gusse–69

H

Hackworth–26, 27, 35, 37, 56, 57, 58, 63, 81, 82, 93, 94, 109, 110, 113
Hagans–61, 109
Hager–8, 55, 76, 94, 109
Haggins–24
Hagins–7
Halbert–25, 58, 75, 80, 100, 122
Hale–11, 25, 26, 31, 58, 61, 62, 69, 77, 83, 90, 113, 119
Haley–58
Hall–6, 10, 13, 23, 26, 27, 32, 33, 34, 35, 37, 38, 41, 47, 54, 55, 58, 59, 61, 63, 64, 65, 68, 69, 71, 72, 74, 76, 78, 80, 83, 84, 94, 95, 99, 100, 101, 111, 115, 117, 118, 120, 122, 149, 153
Hall Funeral Home–153

Ham–9
Hamilton–6, 7, 33, 38, 59, 66, 90, 98, 100
Hammond–24
Hammonds–31
Hammons–10, 28, 29, 60
Hampton–8
Hancock–46
Haney–6
Hanlon–10, 26, 28, 29, 44, 63, 90
Hannah–26, 57, 82
Hanshoe–54
Hanson–44
Hardwick–6
Harmon–49, 52, 57, 60, 63, 81, 109
Harrington–63, 110
Harris–6, 11, 60, 74, 75, 87, 94, 103
Hart–9, 11
Harvie–8
Harwell–7
Hatcher–4, 60
Hatfield–31, 90, 117
Hawkins–9
Hawks–30
Hayes–25, 56, 60, 69, 91, 120
Hays–62, 85
Haywood–11, 27, 30, 35, 60, 61, 62, 77, 101
Healy–121
Heard–12
Heinze–61
Heizer–28
Henderson–9
Henry–52
Hensley–6, 10, 71, 110
Henson–68
Herald–11, 12, 28, 43, 61, 62, 81
Hereford–27, 62
Herold–27
Herrell–6
Hershberger–45
Hicks–27, 34, 35, 49, 62, 63, 72, 83, 111
Higgins–27
Hignite–26, 28, 44, 76
Hill–11, 31
Hinchman–28
Hitchcock–6
HMS Mauretania–13
Hobrook–98
Hobson–11
Hockaday–9
Holbrook–12, 43, 48, 57, 62, 76
Holder–118
Hollander–8
Holt–7
Honaker–32, 88
Hoover–108
Hopkins–6, 35, 38, 74, 94, 117, 122
Hopson–11, 91
Hord–8, 9
Horn–62, 78
Horne–62, 71, 110
Houghton–9
Howard–7, 56, 58, 94, 95, 112
Howe–7
Howell–25, 35, 52, 62, 81, 93, 118
Howrton–7
Hubbard–10, 26, 28, 29, 44, 57, 63, 77, 90
Huddlesgon–9

Hudnell–120
Huff–63, 107
Huffman–39
Hughes–56, 63, 64, 69, 95, 110, 114
Humble–64, 110, 117
Humphrey–64, 95, 106
Hunt–24, 44, 85, 96
Hunter–52
Hurd–96
Hurley–61
Hurst–7
Hyden–20, 44, 46, 61, 64, 95, 120, 121

I

Inmon–45, 90
Irick–64
Isaac–64, 67, 117
Isbell–11
Ison–65

J

Jackson–7, 8, 9, 28
Jacobs–6
James–65
Janes–7
Jarrell–44, 65, 88, 110. 121
Jenkins–63
Jennings–8
Jervis–28
Jillson–8, 9
Johnsen–80
Johnson–7, 15, 24, 31, 34, 35, 37, 38, 44, 48, 52, 65, 73, 77, 81, 83, 95, 110, 111, 117, 119, 120, 121, 122, 149
Jone–7
Jones–6, 27, 35, 47, 60, 65, 66, 111, 114
Joseph–62
Jullirate–107
Justice–6, 7, 28, 96, 111

K

Karen–70
Karl–105
Keathley–103
Keatings–35
Keene–42
Keenon–11
Keeton–7
Keller–9
Kelly–6, 7, 11
Kendrick–27, 28, 31, 41, 55, 60, 63, 66, 76
Kennon–11
Kidd–65, 66, 111
Kilgore–8
Kimbler–78
King–7
Kinney–74
Kirk–7
Kitchen–6, 51
Korreck–55
Kouns–9
Kulby–7
Kyle–36, 77

L

Lacey–9
Lackey–25, 80
Laferty–29, 66, 84, 95, 116, 122
Lafferty–32, 43, 66, 67, 72, 88, 6, 99, 120
Lambert–63
Langley–35
Lanier–122

Lappin–88
Lapsley–8
Larkin–6
Laven–69
Lavender–69, 72
Layne–11, 42, 67, 90, 96, 103, 152
Leake–36, 60, 67
Lee–6, 27, 28, 67, 120
Leedy–67, 111
Leek–36
Leeke–82
Leftwich–8
LeMaster–67
Lennemann–52
Lesley–6
Leslie–42, 67
Lewis–6, 7, 23, 24, 36, 67, 83, 96, 111
Lihoski–114
Littell–77
Little–22, 56, 63, 68, 74, 84, 90, 109, 110
Lockheart–29
Long–42
Love–8
Lovelady–6
Lowe–60, 69
Lucas–115
Luxmore–122
Lykins–102
Lyon–6
Lytle–38

M

Maciag–114
Madden–115
Madison–91
Mann–43
Manuel–4
Marciano–56
Marcum–6, 10, 19, 23, 24, 25, 26, 27, 28, 29, 30, 31, 32, 34, 36, 37, 41, 43, 44, 54, 56, 63, 66, 67, 70, 71, 73, 74, 76, 77, 78, 82, 83, 84, 87, 88, 89, 90, 92, 94, 100, 104, 111, 112, 113, 115, 117, 120, 121, 122
Marks–80, 100
Mars–72
Marshall–6, 26, 29, 31, 64, 68
Marsillett–10, 68, 77, 102
Martin–6, 11, 24, 29, 31, 47, 48, 58, 63, 68, 69, 74, 75, 76, 87, 96, 100, 112, 149
Massey–32
Matthews–6
May–7, 27, 28, 29, 34, 43, 44, 46, 48, 63, 69, 70, 76, 78, 91, 98, 104, 112, 121
Maynard–7, 24
Mayo–31, 70, 78, 83, 84
McCarty–8
McClanahan–70, 120
McCombs–34
McCown–25, 112
McCoy–63
McCurry–65
Mcdonald–121
McDowell–9
McFarland–32
McGeorge–7
McGill–45
McGilton–8

Mcglathen–70
McGlothen–63
McGuire–7, 11, 29, 36, 37, 70, 71, 83, 96, 102, 104
McIntosh–117
McKenzie–72
McKinney–45, 64
Mckinzie–7
McMillen–67
McNally–113
Meade–12, 23, 71, 110, 112, 113
Meador–36, 62, 71
Meadows–36, 71, 87, 96, 101, 104
Means–8
Medina–119
Meek–8
Merritt–18, 90, 112, 115
Messer–102
Mille–71
Miller–25, 44, 67, 71, 72, 87, 97
Millian–65
Mills–6
Mims–7
Minix–30
Mitchell–38, 74, 92, 97, 111
Moler–36
Moles–72
Montgomery–7, 106
Moore–6, 27, 29, 37, 38, 51, 63, 70, 72, 80, 83, 97, 105, 112
Morgan–6, 23, 25, 28, 29, 61, 23, 121
Morgenstern–106
Morris–23
Morrison–8, 29, 31, 73
Mosley–26, 73, 113
Motyl–39
Moyer–95
Mulkey–102
Mullins–6, 7, 24, 32, 37, 63, 73, 97
Murphy–8
Murray–6
Music–10, 29, 34, 40, 43, 56, 78, 79, 96, 113
Musick–24, 29, 30

N

Neal–31
Neeley–37, 53, 70, 97
Nelson–8, 9, 10, 14, 23, 24, 25, 26, 27, 28, 29, 30, 32, 34, 36, 37, 41, 44, 45, 46, 54, 56, 63, 66, 70, 71, 73, 74, 77, 82, 83, 84, 87, 88, 89, 90, 92, 94, 98, 104, 111, 112, 113, 115, 120, 121, 122
Nesbitt–27
Nevile–8
Newman–55, 63, 74
Newsom–46, 74, 89
Newsome–48, 74, 79, 94, 97, 98, 119
Newson–64
Nichols–37
Nitchie–80, 98, 113
Nolen–6
Normay–72
Norris–9
Norton–6
Nunemaker–80
Nunnally–62

O

Oakley–98
Odell–41, 89
Ogles–68
Ormerod–43, 61
Osborne–7, 23, 25, 29, 30, 37, 41, 48, 58, 63, 73, 74, 76, 86, 88, 89, 98, 99, 105, 113, 114, 121
Ousley–96, 115, 122
Owens–57, 74, 75, 112, 114, 152
Owsley–75

P

Packer–112
Parrot–52
Parsons–66, 99, 112, 122
Patchen–34, 40
Patrick–6, 7, 20, 34, 39, 84
Patterson–121
Patton–11, 23, 24, 25, 29, 33, 75, 77, 99, 114
Paul–99
Pearl Harbor–11
Peary–25
Pelfrey–7
Pennington–11, 45, 73, 90
Percifield–9
Perkins–6
Perry–33, 79, 86
Peterson–11
Phillips–6
Pigman–7, 32
Pinkerton–75
Piper–78
Pitts–6, 88, 104
Poage–8, 9
Poe–30
Pogue–9
Polly–7
Porter–6, 36, 75, 76
Poteet–23
Potter–7, 102
Powers–31
Prater–35, 37, 48, 66, 76, 100, 104, 113
Pratt–6
Preston–6, 76
Prestons–8
Prestonsburg–155, 156
Prewitt–7
Price–8, 30, 65, 102
Pruitt–109
Purvis–65
Pytts–6

Q

Queen Mary–17
Quinton–97
Qvick–60

R

Rainer–11
Ramey–7, 47
Ramsey–8, 85
Ransdell–11
Rapier–68
Rasnake–30
Ratcliffe–64
Ratliff–7, 25, 27, 50, 64, 68, 74, 77, 81, 100, 114, 117, 120
Ray–77, 106
Reed–9, 30, 38, 54, 56, 77, 94, 100, 114, 115, 120, 121
Reedy–38
Reffett–109
Reffitt–77
Regem–6
Reichenbach–112, 113, 114
Reid–93
Repasky–40
Reynolds–36, 50, 67, 77, 78, 100
Rice–5, 16, 24, 29, 30, 51, 78, 79, 88, 89, 93, 115
Richardson–115
Richmond–30, 62
Riddle–82
Risner–34, 40, 81, 83
Rister–100
Roadcap–67
Roberts–9, 24, 36, 79, 100
Robertson–68
Robinson–8, 26, 56, 79, 115
Rockne–64
Romans–28
Rone–114
Rose–115
Rosecrans–115
Ross–30
Rowe–41, 80, 90, 100, 114
Rudy–75
Ruesink–63
Runyon–115, 120

S

Salisbury–33, 41, 46, 71, 79, 80, 84, 98, 99, 100, 115, 116
Salunga–120
Salyer–8, 92
Salyers–8, 40, 88, 100
Sammons–58, 64, 109, 110
Samons–78, 80
Sanders–31
Sandusky–63
Saunders–72
Scalf–7, 30, 33, 37, 46, 67, 101
Scalfin–7
Schutchfield–12
Scott–102
Scutchfield–12, 18, 26, 62, 81, 101, 116
Seabourn–6
Sellards–30, 33, 59, 81, 101
Sergent–30
Setser–35, 49, 81, 91, 117, 121
Sexton–6, 25, 70, 86, 90, 118
Shaller–79
Shannon–117
Sharp–63
Shell–36, 57, 81
Shelton–116
Shepherd–21, 36, 51, 53, 70, 73, 77, 81, 92, 95, 101, 107, 108, 116, 117, 122
Sheppard–11
Sherman–28, 72, 73
Shivel–11
Shores–38
Short–91
Sibert–9
Simmons–42, 82
Simpkins–90
Simpson–9, 116
Sizemore–36, 40, 50, 61, 82, 84
Skeans–30, 82, 99
Skeens–23, 27, 30, 31, 116, 117
Slevins–99
Slone–6, 41, 63, 69, 90, 99, 100, 101, 102, 117
Smallwood–8
Smith–6, 11, 32, 64, 72, 73, 82, 97, 99, 104, 106
Smothers–7
Snavely–102
Snipes–82
Sorensen–54
Spangle–104
Spangler–104
Sparkman–24, 85, 117
Sparks–45, 64, 117
Spears–34, 46, 82, 95, 102
Spencer–4, 25, 31, 37, 40, 56, 82, 102
Spradlin–11, 24, 26, 33, 35, 37, 82, 83, 102
Spriggs–85
Spurlock–11, 12, 82, 100
Stafford–8, 72, 83
Stambaugh–26, 106
Standafer–84
Stanley–27, 53, 64, 95
Stapleton–6, 41
Stapp–7
Steele–73, 83, 113, 120
Stephens–34, 35, 53, 57, 58, 83, 84, 119, 121
Stepp–7
Stevens–7, 102
Stevenson–7
Stewart–7, 28, 37, 90, 103, 117
Stickler–84
Stidham–7
Stone–35
Stout–84
Stransky–33
Stratton–6, 9, 67, 117
Stricklin–117
Strothers–8
Strugill–50
Stumbo–26, 37, 38, 47, 48, 63, 69, 84, 117, 149, 152
Sturgil–41
Sturgill–29, 62
Sullivan–6, 7
Swanson–7
Sweeney–37, 117

T

Tackett–25, 27, 31, 37, 46, 58, 59, 72, 78, 84, 105, 118, 122
Taylor–27, 29, 31, 55, 96, 98, 99, 108
Terry–117, 118
Thacker–6, 84, 101, 103
Thomas–63, 103, 113
Thompson–38, 85, 118, 152
Thorn–9
Thornsberry–26
Tibbett–9
Tibbs–85
Tilly–118
Trans-Star Ambulance–157
Trant–7
Trimble–28
Triplett–9, 11
Trotta–11
Trout–7
Tuggle–31
Turner–6, 7, 29, 31, 37, 40, 48, 54, 82, 84, 85, 99, 100, 102, 103, 118
Turnley–85
Tussey–30, 85, 92

U

USS O'Brien–12

V

Vance–9
Vanderpool–63, 77, 86, 118
Van Bibber–24
Van Hase–6
Van Hoose–6
Vaughan–31, 37, 86, 103, 104
Vaughn–29
Vest–29

W

Wade–118
Wadkins–6, 7, 30
Wages–7
Wakeland–110
Walker–6, 38
Wallen–12, 19, 20, 25, 26, 29, 31, 32, 40, 41, 44, 76, 81, 82, 86, 90, 104
Walsh–7
Walter–47
Ward–6, 7, 9, 37, 86
Warfield–47
Waring–8
Warix–37
Warrick–32
Warrix–32, 34, 44, 70, 71, 73, 86, 87, 88, 113
Watkins–9, 11, 78
Watson–46, 79, 113
Watterman–31
Webb–74, 104
Weber–43
Weddington–69
Wellman–87
Wells–6, 8, 35, 49, 86, 87, 88, 104, 106, 118
Werrick–121
Wheatley–24
Wheeler–7
Whitaker–88, 102
White–11, 32, 47
Whitley–9
Whitt–116
Wicker–77, 88, 114
Wilcox–103, 107
Wiley–7, 92
Williams–6, 7, 33, 35, 47, 49, 57, 92, 117, 152
Williamson–27, 67, 114
Wills–19, 32, 43, 44, 52, 67, 73, 86, 88, 104
Wilson–9
Wingham–67
Wire–9
Wireman–72, 91, 97
Witcher–31
Witten–8
Wohlford–47, 88
Wolf–43
Wood–6
Woods–27, 33, 67, 79, 114
Woody–88
Wooten–6, 7
Workman–57
Wright–32, 33, 51, 56, 57, 63, 88, 94, 104, 118
Wysong–95

Y

Yerrace–53, 108
Youmans–13, 51
Younce–90
Young–6, 8, 106, 109

Z

Zack–89

www.ingramcontent.com/pod-product-compliance
Lightning Source LLC
Chambersburg PA
CBHW080638170426
43200CB00015B/2885